information
systems

Paige Baltzan
Daniels College of Business
University of Denver

Amy Phillips
Daniels College of Business
University of Denver

McGraw-Hill
Irwin

McGraw-Hill
Irwin

information
systems

VICE PRESIDENT AND EDITOR-IN-CHIEF **Brent Gordon**

PUBLISHER **Paul Ducham**

DIRECTOR OF DEVELOPMENT **Ann Torbert**

DEVELOPMENT EDITOR II **Trina Hauger**

VICE PRESIDENT AND DIRECTOR OF MARKETING **Robin J. Zwettler**

MARKETING MANAGER **Natalie Zook**

VICE PRESIDENT OF EDITING, DESIGN AND PRODUCTION **Sesha Bolisetty**

MANAGER OF PHOTO, DESIGN & PUBLISHING TOOLS **Mary Conzachi**

LEAD PRODUCTION SUPERVISOR **Michael R. McCormick**

SENIOR DESIGNER **Mary Kazak Sander**

SENIOR PHOTO RESEARCH COORDINATOR **Jeremy Cheshareck**

MEDIA PROJECT MANAGER **Joyce J. Chappetto**

COVER DESIGN **Cara Hawthorne, Cara David Design**

TYPEFACE **10/12 Minion Pro Regular**

COMPOSITOR **Laserwords Private Limited**

PRINTER **Quad/Graphics**

M: INFORMATION SYSTEMS

Published by McGraw-Hill/Irwin, a business unit of The McGraw-Hill Companies, Inc., 1221 Avenue of the Americas, New York, NY, 10020.

Some ancillaries, including electronic and print components, may not be available to customers outside the United States.

This book is printed on acid-free paper.

3 4 5 6 7 8 9 0 QDB/QDB 1 0 9 8 7 6 5 4 3 2 1 0

ISBN 978-0-07-337683-7
MHID 0-07-337683-3

Library of Congress Control Number: 2010920112

brief contents

contents

module two ESSENTIALS OF INFORMATION SYSTEMS 89

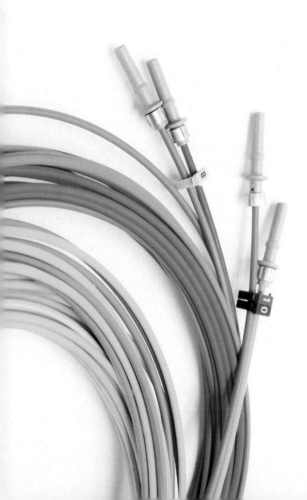

module three ENTERPRISE INFORMATION SYSTEMS 193

module four DEVELOPING INFORMATION SYSTEMS 275

information
systems

coming up

Most organizations today rely heavily on the use of information technologies to run various aspects of their businesses. Whether it is to order and ship goods, interact with customers, or conduct other business functions, information technology is often the underlying infrastructure used to perform such activities. Information technology enables companies to perform a variety of tasks both efficiently and effectively. Moreover, information technology allows an organization to remain competitive in today's fast-paced world. This is especially true when one considers the burgeoning popularity of conducting business over the Internet.

Organizations that fail to take advantage of information technology run the risk of falling behind others that adopt information technology solutions. Organizations must adapt to technological advances and innovations to keep pace with today's rapidly changing environment. Their competitors certainly will!

Though technology can be an exciting phenomenon on its own, as a business student you should understand that successful organizations do not utilize technology simply for the sake of technology itself. There must be a solid business reason for implementing technology. Using a technological solution just because it is available is not a good business strategy.

The purpose of Module One is to raise awareness of the vast opportunities that occur when you understand the tight correlation between business and technology. Business strategies and processes should always drive your technology choices. Although sometimes awareness of an emerging technology can lead to new strategic directions, the role of information technology, for the most part, is to support business strategies and process. Understanding business strategies and determining technology support structures is an important discussion and is covered thoroughly throughout this module. ■

BUSINESS DRIVEN INFORMATION SYSTEMS

module one
BUSINESS DRIVEN INFORMATION SYSTEMS
ch. 1 Information Systems in Business
ch. 2 Strategic Decision Making
ch. 3 Ebusiness

module two
ESSENTIALS OF INFORMATION SYSTEMS

module three
ENTERPRISE INFORMATION SYSTEMS

module four
DEVELOPING INFORMATION SYSTEMS

information systems in business

what's in IT for me?

This chapter sets the stage for the textbook. It starts from ground zero by providing a clear description of what information technology is and how it fits into business strategies and organizational activities. It then provides an overview of how organizations operate in competitive environments and must continually define and redefine their business strategies to create competitive advantages. Doing so allows organizations to survive and thrive. Importantly, information technology is shown as a key enabler to help organizations operate successfully in such competitive environments.

You, as a business student, must understand the tight correlation between business and technology. You must first understand information technology's role in daily business activities, and then understand information technology's role in supporting and implementing enterprisewide initiatives and global business strategies. After reading this chapter, you should have acquired a solid understanding of business driven information systems, technology fundamentals, and business strategy.

SECTION 1.1 >>
Information Systems in Business
- Information Technology's Role in Business
- Information Technology Basics
- Roles and Responsibilities in Information Technology
- Measuring Information Technology's Success

SECTION 1.2 >>
Business Strategy
- Identifying Competitive Advantages
- The Five Forces Model—Evaluating Business Segments
- The Three Generic Strategies—Creating a Business Focus
- Value Chain Analysis—Targeting Business Process

nformation is everywhere. Most organizations value information as a strategic asset. Consider Apple and its iPod, iPod accessories, and iTunes Music Store. Apple's success depends heavily on information about its customers, suppliers, markets, and operations for each of these product lines. For example, Apple must be able to predict the number of people who will purchase an iPod to help estimate iPod accessory and iTunes sales within the next year. Estimating too many buyers will lead Apple to produce an excess of inventory; estimating too few buyers will potentially mean lost sales due to lack of product (resulting in even more lost revenues from iTunes downloads).

Understanding the direct impact information has on an organization's bottom line is crucial to running a successful business. This text focuses on information, business, technology, and the integrated set of activities used to run most organizations. Many of these activities are the hallmarks of business today—supply chain management, customer relationship management, enterprise resource planning, outsourcing, integration, ebusiness, and others.

●● SECTION 1.1 Information Systems in Business

LEARNING OUTCOMES

LO1.1 Describe the functional areas of a business and why they must work together for the business to be successful.

LO1.2 Explain information technology's role in business and how you measure success.

LO1.3 Compare management information systems (MIS) and information technology (IT), and define the relationships among people, information technology, and information.

LO1.4 Compare the responsibilities of a chief information officer (CIO), chief technology officer (CTO), chief security officer (CSO), chief privacy officer (CPO), and chief knowledge officer (CKO).

LO1.5 Explain the gap between IT and the business, along with the primary reason this gap exists.

●● LO1.1

Describe the functional areas of a business and why they must work together for the business to be successful.

INFORMATION TECHNOLOGY'S ROLE IN BUSINESS

Students frequently ask, "Why do we need to study information technology?" The answer is simple: Information technology is everywhere in business. Understanding information technology provides great insight to anyone learning about business.

It is easy to demonstrate information technology's role in business by reviewing a copy of popular business magazines such as *BusinessWeek*, *Fortune*, or *Fast Company*. Placing a marker (such as a Post-it Note) on each page that contains a technology-related article or advertisement indicates that information technology is everywhere in business (see Figure 1.1). These are *business* magazines, not *technology* magazines, yet they are filled with technology. Students who understand technology have an advantage in business.

These magazine articles typically discuss such topics as databases, customer relationship management, web services, supply chain management, security, ethics, business intelligence, and so on. They also focus on companies such as Siebel,

FIGURE **1.1** Technology in *BusinessWeek and Fortune*

Oracle, Microsoft, and IBM. This text explores these topics in detail, along with reviewing the associated business opportunities and challenges.

Information Technology's Impact on Business Operations

Figure 1.2 highlights the business functions receiving the greatest benefit from information technology, along with the common business goals associated with information technology projects, according to *CIO* magazine.[1]

Achieving the results outlined in Figure 1.2, such as reducing costs, improving productivity, and generating growth, is not easy. Implementing a new accounting system or marketing plan is not likely to generate long-term growth or reduce costs across an entire organization. Businesses must undertake enterprisewide initiatives to achieve broad general business goals such as reducing costs. Information technology plays a critical role in deploying such initiatives by facilitating communication and increasing business intelligence. For example, instant messaging and WiMax allow people across an organization to communicate in new and innovative ways.[2]

FIGURE 1.2 Business Benefits and Information Technology Project Goals

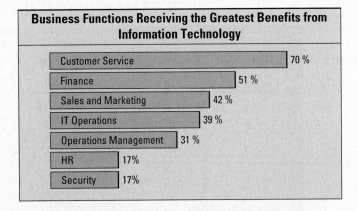

Business Functions Receiving the Greatest Benefits from Information Technology

- Customer Service — 70 %
- Finance — 51 %
- Sales and Marketing — 42 %
- IT Operations — 39 %
- Operations Management — 31 %
- HR — 17%
- Security — 17%

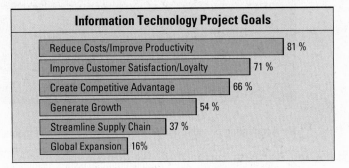

Information Technology Project Goals

- Reduce Costs/Improve Productivity — 81 %
- Improve Customer Satisfaction/Loyalty — 71 %
- Create Competitive Advantage — 66 %
- Generate Growth — 54 %
- Streamline Supply Chain — 37 %
- Global Expansion — 16%

Understanding information technology begins with gaining an understanding of how businesses function and IT's role in creating efficiencies and effectiveness across the organization. Typical businesses operate by functional areas (often called functional silos). Each area undertakes a specific core business function (see Figure 1.3).[3]

fyi

People in China and India Are Starving for Your Jobs

"When I was growing up in Minneapolis, my parents always said, 'Tom, finish your dinner. There are people starving in China and India.' Today I tell my girls, 'Finish your homework, because people in China and India are starving for your jobs.' And in a flat world, they can have them, because there's no such thing as an American job anymore." Thomas Friedman.

In his book, *The World Is Flat,* Thomas Friedman describes the unplanned cascade of technological and social shifts that effectively leveled the economic world and "accidentally made Beijing, Bangalore, and Bethesda next-door neighbors." The video of Thomas Friedman's lecture at MIT discussing the flat world is available at http://mitworld.mit.edu/video/266. If you want to be prepared to compete in a flat world, you must watch this video and answer the following questions:

- Do you agree or disagree with Friedman's assessment that the world is flat?
- What are the potential impacts of a flat world for a student performing a job search?
- What can students do to prepare themselves for competing in a flat world?

FIGURE 1.3 Departmental Structure of a Typical Organization

COMMON DEPARTMENTS IN AN ORGANIZATION

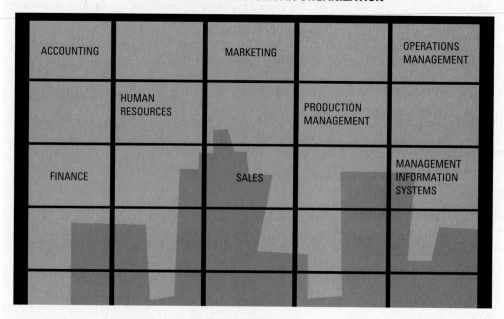

- **Accounting** provides quantitative information about the finances of the business including recording, measuring, and describing financial information.

- **Finance** deals with the strategic financial issues associated with increasing the value of the business, while observing applicable laws and social responsibilities.

- **Human resources (HR)** includes the policies, plans, and procedures for the effective management of employees (human resources).

- **Sales** is the function of selling a good or service and focuses on increasing customer sales, which increases company revenues.

- **Marketing** is the process associated with promoting the sale of goods or services. The marketing department supports the sales department by creating promotions that help sell the company's products.

- **Operations management (OM)** The management of systems or processes that convert or transform resources (including human resources) into goods and services.

- **Management information systems (MIS)** is a general name for the business function and academic discipline covering the application of people, technologies, and procedures—collectively called information systems—to solve business problems.

Functional areas are anything but independent in a business. In fact, functional areas are *interdependent* (see Figure 1.4). Sales must rely on information from operations to understand inventory, place orders, calculate transportation costs, and gain insight into product availability based on production schedules. For an organization to succeed, every department or functional area must work together sharing common information and not be a "silo." Information technology can enable departments to more efficiently and effectively perform their business operations.

Individuals anticipating a successful career in business, whether it is in accounting, finance, human resources, or operation management, must understand information technology including:

- Information technology basics.
- Roles and responsibilities in information technology.
- Measuring information technology's success.

●● LO1.2

Explain information technology's role in business and how you measure success.

●● LO1.3

Compare management information systems (MIS) and information technology (IT), and define the relationships among people, information technology, and information.

FIGURE 1.4 | Marketing Working with Other Organizational Departments

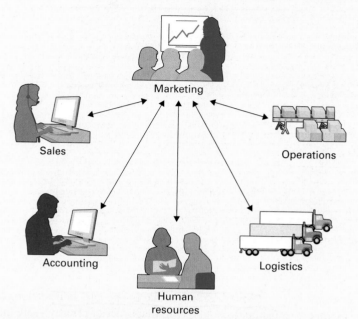

Functional organization—Each functional area has its own systems and communicates with every other functional area (diagram displays Marketing communicating with all other functional areas in the organization).

When beginning to learn about information technology it is important to understand:[4]

- Data, information, and business intelligence
- IT resources
- IT cultures

Data, Information, and Business Intelligence

It is important to distinguish between data and information. *Data* are raw facts that describe the characteristics of an event. Characteristics for a sales event could include the date, item number, item description, quantity ordered, customer name, and shipping details. *Information* is data converted into a meaningful and useful context. Information from sales events could include best-selling item, worst-selling item, best customer, and worst customer. *Business intelligence* refers to applications and technologies that are used to gather, provide access to, and analyze data and information to support

INFORMATION TECHNOLOGY BASICS

Information technology (IT) is a field concerned with the use of technology in managing and processing information. Information technology can be an important enabler of business success and innovation. This is not to say that IT *equals* business success and innovation or that IT *represents* business success and innovation. Information technology is most useful when it leverages the talents of people. Information technology in and of itself is not useful unless the right people know how to use and manage it effectively.

Management information systems is a business function just as marketing, finance, operations, and human resources management are business functions. Formally defined, *management information systems (MIS)* is a general name for the business function and academic discipline covering the application of people, technologies, and procedures—collectively called information systems—to solve business problems. To perform the MIS function effectively, almost all organizations today, particularly large and medium-sized ones, have an internal IT department, often called Information Technology (IT), Information Systems (IS), or Management Information Systems (MIS).

| FIGURE | 1.5 | Data in an Excel Spreadsheet |

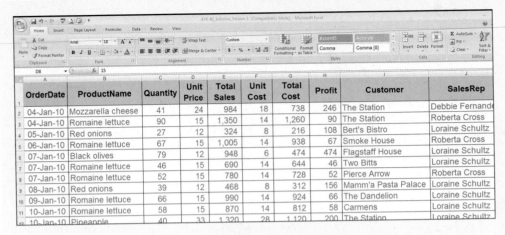

	OrderDate	ProductName	Quantity	Unit Price	Total Sales	Unit Cost	Total Cost	Profit	Customer	SalesRep
2	04-Jan-10	Mozzarella cheese	41	24	984	18	738	246	The Station	Debbie Fernande
3	04-Jan-10	Romaine lettuce	90	15	1,350	14	1,260	90	The Station	Roberta Cross
4	05-Jan-10	Red onions	27	12	324	8	216	108	Bert's Bistro	Loraine Schultz
5	06-Jan-10	Romaine lettuce	67	15	1,005	14	938	67	Smoke House	Roberta Cross
6	07-Jan-10	Black olives	79	12	948	6	474	474	Flagstaff House	Loraine Schultz
7	07-Jan-10	Romaine lettuce	46	15	690	14	644	46	Two Bitts	Loraine Schultz
8	07-Jan-10	Romaine lettuce	52	15	780	14	728	52	Pierce Arrow	Roberta Cross
9	08-Jan-10	Red onions	39	12	468	8	312	156	Mamm'a Pasta Palace	Loraine Schultz
10	09-Jan-10	Romaine lettuce	66	15	990	14	924	66	The Dandelion	Loraine Schultz
11	10-Jan-10	Romaine lettuce	58	15	870	14	812	58	Carmens	Loraine Schultz
12	10-Jan-10	Pineapple	40	33	1,320	28	1,120	200	The Station	Loraine Schultz

Rows of data in an Excel spreadsheet.

decision-making efforts. Business intelligence helps companies gain a more comprehensive knowledge of the factors affecting their business, such as metrics on sales, production, and internal operations that help companies make better business decisions (see Figures 1.5, 1.6, 1.7).

IT Resources

The plans and goals of the IT department must align with the plans and goals of the organization. Information technology can enable an organization to increase efficiency in manufacturing, retain key customers, seek out new sources of supply, and introduce effective financial management.

It is not always easy for managers to make the right choices when using IT to support (and often drive) business initiatives. Most managers understand their business initiatives well, but are often at a loss when it comes to knowing how to use and manage IT effectively in support of those initiatives. Managers who understand what IT is, and what IT can and cannot do, are in the best position for success. In essence,

- *People* use
- *information technology* to work with
- *information* (see Figure 1.8).

Those three key resources—people, information, and information technology (in that order of priority)—are inextricably linked. If one fails, they all fail. Most important, if one fails, then chances are the business will fail.

IT Cultures

An organization's culture plays a large role in determining how successfully it will share information. Culture will influence the way people use information (their information behavior) and will reflect the importance that company leaders attribute to the

| FIGURE | 1.6 | Data Turned into Information |

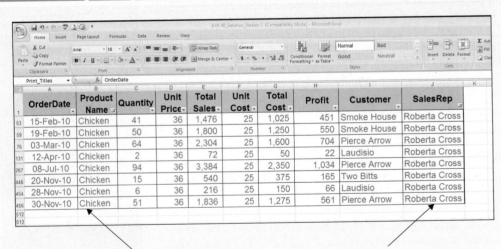

	OrderDate	Product Name	Quantity	Unit Price	Total Sales	Unit Cost	Total Cost	Profit	Customer	SalesRep
53	15-Feb-10	Chicken	41	36	1,476	25	1,025	451	Smoke House	Roberta Cross
59	19-Feb-10	Chicken	50	36	1,800	25	1,250	550	Smoke House	Roberta Cross
76	03-Mar-10	Chicken	64	36	2,304	25	1,600	704	Pierce Arrow	Roberta Cross
131	12-Apr-10	Chicken	2	36	72	25	50	22	Laudisio	Roberta Cross
267	08-Jul-10	Chicken	94	36	3,384	25	2,350	1,034	Pierce Arrow	Roberta Cross
446	20-Nov-10	Chicken	15	36	540	25	375	165	Two Bitts	Roberta Cross
454	28-Nov-10	Chicken	6	36	216	25	150	66	Laudisio	Roberta Cross
456	30-Nov-10	Chicken	51	36	1,836	25	1,275	561	Pierce Arrow	Roberta Cross

Data features, such as Autofilter, turn data into information. This view shows all of Roberta Cross's chicken sales.

FIGURE **1.7** Information Turned into Business Intelligence

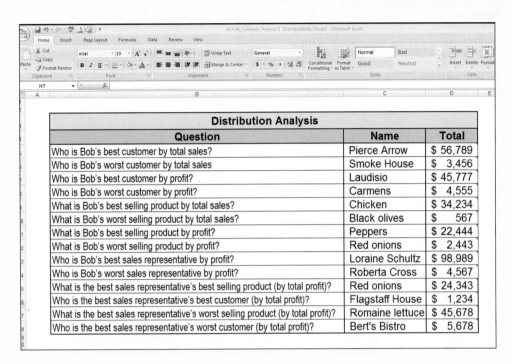

Distribution Analysis		
Question	**Name**	**Total**
Who is Bob's best customer by total sales?	Pierce Arrow	$ 56,789
Who is Bob's worst customer by total sales	Smoke House	$ 3,456
Who is Bob's best customer by profit?	Laudisio	$ 45,777
Who is Bob's worst customer by profit?	Carmens	$ 4,555
What is Bob's best selling product by total sales?	Chicken	$ 34,234
What is Bob's worst selling product by total sales?	Black olives	$ 567
What is Bob's best selling product by profit?	Peppers	$ 22,444
What is Bob's worst selling product by profit?	Red onions	$ 2,443
Who is Bob's best sales representative by profit?	Loraine Schultz	$ 98,989
Who is Bob's worst sales representative by profit?	Roberta Cross	$ 4,567
What is the best sales representative's best selling product (by total profit)?	Red onions	$ 24,343
Who is the best sales representative's best customer (by total profit)?	Flagstaff House	$ 1,234
What is the best sales representative's worst selling product (by total profit)?	Romaine lettuce	$ 45,678
Who is the best sales representative's worst customer (by total profit)?	Bert's Bistro	$ 5,678

Advanced analytical tools, such as Pivot Tables, uncover business intelligence in the data. For example, best customer, worst customer, and best sales representative's best-selling product.

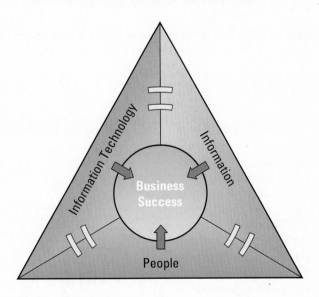

omg lol

Wikiblunders

According to *PC World* these false facts all appeared on Wikipedia:

1. Robbie Williams eats domestic pets in pubs for money.
2. David Beckham was a Chinese goalkeeper in the 18th century.
3. Paul Reiser's dead. (Reiser is an actor.)
4. Sinbad's dead. (Sinbad is an actor.)
5. Sergey Brin's sexy, dating Jimmy Wales, and dead. (Brin founded Google and Wales founded Wikipedia.)
6. Tony Blair worships Hitler. (Blair is the former Prime Minister of the United Kingdom.)
7. The Duchess of Cornwall's Christian name is Cow-miller.
8. The University of Cincinnati's former president is a whore.
9. Robert Byrd's dead. (Byrd is a U.S. Senator from West Virginia.)
10. Ted Kennedy died in January.
11. John Seigenthaler helped assassinate John and Robert Kennedy. (Seigenthaler is a journalist.)
12. A yacht killed British TV presenter Vernon Kay.
13. Conan O'Brien assaults sea turtles while canoeing.
14. British TV gardener Alan Titchmarsh published a new version of the Kama Sutra.
15. Sienna Miller has modeled nude. (Miller is an actress.)

We know that people use information technology to work with information. Knowing this, how could these types of errors occur? What could happen if you decided to use Wikipedia to collect business intelligence for a research paper? What could Wikipedia do to help prevent these types of errors?

FIGURE 1.9	Different Information Cultures Found in Organizations

Organizational Information Cultures	
Information-Functional Culture	Employees use information as a means of exercising influence or power over others. For example, a manager in sales refuses to share information with marketing. This causes marketing to need the sales manager's input each time a new sales strategy is developed.
Information-Sharing Culture	Employees across departments trust each other to use information (especially about problems and failures) to improve performance.
Information-Inquiring Culture	Employees across departments search for information to better understand the future and align themselves with current trends and new directions.
Information-Discovery Culture	Employees across departments are open to new insights about crisis and radical changes and seek ways to create competitive advantages.

use of information in achieving success or avoiding failure. Four common information-sharing cultures exist in organizations today: information-functional, information-sharing, information-inquiring, and information-discovery (see Figure 1.9).[5]

An organization's IT culture can directly affect its ability to compete in the global market. If an organization operates with an information-functional culture, it will have a great degree of difficulty operating. Getting products to market quickly and creating a view of its end-to-end (or entire) business from sales to billing will be a challenge. If an organization operates with an information-discovery culture it will be able to get products to market quickly and easily see a 360-degree view of its entire organization. Employees will be able to use this view to better understand the market and create new products that offer a competitive advantage.

 LO1.4

Compare the responsibilities of a chief information officer (CIO), chief technology officer (CTO), chief security officer (CSO), chief privacy officer (CPO), and chief knowledge officer (CKO).

LO1.5

Explain the gap between IT and the business, along with the primary reason this gap exists.

| FIGURE | 1.10 | Average CIO Compensation by Industry |

Industry	Average CIO Compensation
Wholesale/Retail/Distribution	$243,304
Finance	$210,547
Insurance	$197,697
Manufacturing	$190,250
Medical/Dental/Health Care	$171,032
Government	$118,359
Education	$ 93,750

The *chief information officer (CIO)* is responsible for (1) overseeing all uses of information technology and (2) ensuring the strategic alignment of IT with business goals and objectives. The CIO often reports directly to the CEO (see Figure 1.10 for average CIO compensation). CIOs must possess a solid understanding of every aspect of an organization coupled with tremendous insight into the capability of IT. Broad roles of a CIO include:

- *Manager*—ensure the delivery of all IT projects, on time and within budget.
- *Leader*—ensure the strategic vision of IT is in line with the strategic vision of the organization.
- *Communicator*—advocate and communicate the IT strategy by building and maintaining strong executive relationships.[7]

Although CIO is considered a position within IT, CIOs must be concerned with more than just IT. According to a recent survey (see Figure 1.11), most CIOs ranked "enhancing customer satisfaction" ahead of their concerns for any specific aspect of IT. We should applaud CIOs who possess the broad business view that customer satisfaction is more crucial and critical than specific aspects of IT.[8]

The *chief technology officer (CTO)* is responsible for ensuring the throughput, speed, accuracy, availability, and reliability

ROLES AND RESPONSIBILITIES IN INFORMATION TECHNOLOGY

Employees across the organization must work closely together to develop strategic initiatives that create competitive advantages. Understanding the basic structure of a typical IT department including titles, roles, and responsibilities will help an organization build a cohesive enterprisewide team. Information technology is a relatively new functional area, having been around formally in most organizations only for about 40 years. Job titles, roles, and responsibilities often differ from organization to organization. Nonetheless, clear trends are developing toward elevating some IT positions within an organization to the strategic level.

Most organizations maintain positions such as chief executive officer (CEO), chief financial officer (CFO), and chief operations officer (COO) at the strategic level. Recently there are more IT-related strategic positions such as chief information officer (CIO), chief technology officer (CTO), chief security officer (CSO), chief privacy officer (CPO), and chief knowledge officer (CKO).

J. Greg Hanson is proud to be the first CIO of the U.S. Senate. Contrary to some perceptions, the technology found in the Senate is quite good, according to Hanson. Hanson's responsibilities include creating the Senate's technology vision, leading the IT department, and deploying the IT infrastructure. Hanson must work with everyone from the 137 network administrators to the senators themselves to ensure that everything is operating smoothly.[6]

| FIGURE | 1.11 | What Concerns CIOs the Most? |

CIO's Concerns	Percentage
Enchancing customer satisfaction	94%
Security	92
Technology evaluation	89
Budgeting	87
Staffing	83
ROI analysis	66
Building new applications	64
Outsourcing hosting	45

of an organization's information technology. CTOs have direct responsibility for ensuring the efficiency of IT systems throughout the organization. Most CTOs possess well-rounded knowledge of all aspects of IT, including hardware, software, and telecommunications. CTOs typically report to the CIO. The role of CTO is similar to CIO, except that CIO must take on the additional responsibility of ensuring that IT aligns with the organization's strategic initiatives.

The *chief security officer (CSO)* is responsible for ensuring the security of IT systems and developing strategies and IT safeguards against attacks from hackers and viruses. The role of a CSO has been elevated in recent years because of the number of attacks from hackers and viruses. Most CSOs possess detailed knowledge of networks and telecommunications because hackers and viruses usually find their way into IT systems through networked computers.

The *chief privacy officer (CPO)* is responsible for ensuring the ethical and legal use of information within an organization. CPOs are the newest senior executive position in IT. Recently, 150 of the Fortune 500 companies added the CPO position to their list of senior executives. Many CPOs are lawyers by training, enabling them to understand the often complex legal issues surrounding the use of information.[9]

The *chief knowledge officer (CKO)* is responsible for collecting, maintaining, and distributing the organization's knowledge. The CKO designs programs and systems that make it easy for people to reuse knowledge. These systems create repositories of organizational documents, methodologies, tools, and practices, and they establish methods for filtering the information. The CKO must continuously encourage employee contributions to

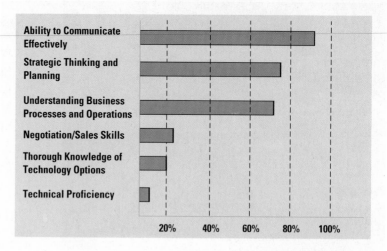

Figure 1.12 — Skills Pivotal for Success in Executive IT Roles

not have a different individual for each of these positions, they must have leaders taking responsibility for all these areas of concern. The individuals responsible for enterprisewide IT and IT-related issues must provide guidance and support to the organization's employees. Figure 1.12 displays the personal skills pivotal for success in an executive IT role.

The Gap Between Business Personnel and IT Personnel

One of the greatest challenges today is effective communication between business personnel and IT personnel. Figure 1.12 clearly demonstrates the importance of communication for IT

> "One of the greatest challenges today is effective communication between business personnel and IT personnel."

keep the systems up-to-date. The CKO can contribute directly to the organization's bottom line by reducing the learning curve for new employees or employees taking on new roles.

Danny Shaw was the first CKO at Children's Hospital in Boston. His initial task was to unite information from disparate systems to enable analysis of both the efficiency and effectiveness of the hospital's care. Shaw started by building a series of small, integrated information systems that quickly demonstrated value. He then gradually built on those successes, creating a knowledge-enabled organization one layer at a time. Shaw's information systems have enabled administrative and clinical operational analyses.[10]

All the above IT positions and responsibilities are critical to an organization's success. While many organizations may

executives. Business personnel possess expertise in functional areas such as marketing, accounting, sales, and so forth. IT personnel have the technological expertise. Unfortunately, a communications gap often exists between the two. Business personnel have their own vocabularies based on their experience and expertise. IT personnel have their own vocabularies consisting of acronyms and technical terms. Effective communication between business and IT personnel should be a two-way street with each side making the effort to understand each other (including written and oral communication).

Improving Communication Business personnel must seek to increase their understanding of IT. Although they do not need to know every technical detail, it is beneficial to understand what IT can and cannot accomplish. Business managers and leaders should read business-oriented IT magazines, such as *InformationWeek* and *CIO*, to increase their IT knowledge.

At the same time, an organization must develop strategies for integrating its IT personnel into the various business functions. Too often, IT personnel are left out of strategy meetings because of the belief they do not understand the business so they will not add any value. That is a dangerous position to take. IT personnel must understand the business if the organization is going to determine which technologies can benefit (or hurt) the business. With a little effort to communicate, IT personnel might provide information on the functionality available in an information system, which could add tremendous value to a meeting about how to improve customer service. Working together, business and IT personnel have the potential to create competitive advantages, reduce costs, and streamline business processes.

It is the CIO's responsibility to ensure effective communications between business and IT personnel. While the CIO assumes the responsibility on an enterprisewide level, it is each employee's responsibility to communicate effectively on a personal level.

●● LO1.2

Explain information technology's role in business and how you measure success.

MEASURING INFORMATION TECHNOLOGY'S SUCCESS

IT has become an important part of organizations' strategy, competitive advantage, and profitability. There is management pressure to build systems faster, better, and at minimum cost. The return on investment that an organization can achieve from the money it spends on IT has come under increased scrutiny from senior business executives and directors. Consequently, IT now has to operate like other parts of the organization, being aware of its performance and its contribution to the organization's success and opportunities for improvement. So what is it that managers need to know about measuring the success of information technology?

The first thing managers need to understand about IT success is that it is incredibly difficult to measure. Determining the return on investment (ROI) of new computer equipment is difficult. For example, what is the ROI of a fire extinguisher? If the fire extinguisher is never used, the return on the investment is low. If the extinguisher puts out a fire that could destroy the entire building, then its ROI is high. This is similar to IT systems. If a company implements a $5,000 firewall to prevent virus attacks on the computer systems and it never stops a virus, the company lost $5,000. If the firewall stops viruses that could have cost the company millions of dollars, then the ROI of that firewall is significantly greater than $5,000. A few questions executives recently raised regarding their IT systems include:

- Is the internal IT operation performing satisfactorily?
- Should I outsource some or all of the IT operations?
- How is my outsourcer performing?
- What are the risk factors to consider in an IT project?
- What questions should be asked to ensure an IT project proposal is realistic?
- What are the characteristics of a healthy project?
- Which factors are most critical to monitor to ensure the project remains on track?[11]

quantifiable measures to business processes, especially qualitative ones such as customer service? What kind of information best reflects progress, or the lack of it?

Key performance indicators (KPIs) are the measures that are tied to business drivers. Metrics are the detailed measures that feed those KPIs. Performance metrics fall into a nebulous area of business intelligence that is neither technology- nor business-centered, but this area requires input from both IT and business professionals to find success. Cisco Systems implemented a cross-departmental council to create metrics for improving business process operations. The council developed metrics to evaluate the efficiency of Cisco's online order processing and discovered that due to errors, more than 70 percent of online orders required manual input and were unable to be automatically routed to manufacturing. By changing the process and adding new information systems, within six months the company doubled the percentage of orders that went directly to manufacturing.[14]

Efficiency and Effectiveness Metrics

Organizations spend enormous sums of money on IT to compete in today's fast-paced business environment. Some organizations spend up to 50 percent of their total capital expenditures on IT. To justify these expenditures, an organization must measure the payoff of these investments, their impact on business performance, and the overall business value gained.

Efficiency and effectiveness metrics are two primary types of IT metrics. *Efficiency IT metrics* measure the performance

To offer detailed information to all layers of management, General Electric Co. (GE) invested $1.5 billion in employee time, hardware, software, and other technologies to implement a real-time operations monitoring system. GE's executives use the new system to monitor sales, inventory, and savings across the company's 13 global business operations every 15 minutes. This allows GE to respond to changes, reduce cycle times, and

> "Managers need to ask themselves how they are going to manage IT projects when it is so incredibly difficult to measure IT projects."

improve risk management on an hourly basis instead of waiting for monthly or quarterly reports. GE estimates the $1.5 billion investment will provide a 33 percent return over five years.[12]

IT professionals know how to install and maintain information systems. Business professionals know how to run a successful business. But how does a company decide if an information system helps make a business successful? Peter Drucker, a famous management guru, once stated that if you cannot measure it, you cannot manage it. Managers need to ask themselves how they are going to manage IT projects when it is so incredibly difficult to measure IT projects.[13]

The answer lies in the metrics. Designing metrics requires an expertise that neither IT nor business professionals usually possess. Metrics are about neither technology nor business strategy. The questions that arise in metrics design are almost philosophical: How do you define success? How do you apply

of the IT system itself such as throughput, speed, and availability. *Effectiveness IT metrics* measure the impact IT has on business processes and activities including customer satisfaction, conversion rates, and sell-through increases. Peter Drucker offers a helpful distinction between efficiency and effectiveness. Drucker states that managers "Do things right" and/or "Do the right things." Doing things right addresses efficiency—getting the most from each resource. Doing the right things addresses effectiveness—setting the right goals and objectives and ensuring they are accomplished.[15]

Efficiency focuses on the extent to which an organization is using its resources in an optimal way, while effectiveness focuses on how well an organization is achieving its goals and objectives. The two—efficiency and effectiveness—are definitely interrelated. However, success in one area does not necessarily imply success in the other.

Benchmarking—Baseline Metrics

Regardless of what is measured, how it is measured, and whether it is for the sake of efficiency or effectiveness, there must be **benchmarks,** or baseline values the system seeks to attain. **Benchmarking** is a process of continuously measuring system results, comparing those results to optimal system performance (benchmark values), and identifying steps and procedures to improve system performance.

Consider online government services (egovernment) as an illustration of benchmarking efficiency IT metrics and effectiveness IT metrics (see survey results in Figure 1.13). From an effectiveness point of view, Canada ranks number one in terms of egovernment satisfaction of its citizens. (The United States ranks third.) The survey, sponsored by Accenture, also included such attributes as customer-service vision, initiatives for identifying services for individual citizen segments, and approaches to offering egovernment services through multiple-service delivery channels. These are all benchmarks at which Canada's government excels.[16]

In contrast, the *United Nations Division for Public Economics and Public Administration* ranks Canada sixth in terms of efficiency IT metrics. (The United States ranked first.) This particular ranking, based purely on efficiency IT metrics, includes benchmarks such as the number of computers per 100 citizens, the number of Internet hosts per 10,000 citizens, and the percentage of the citizen online population. Therefore, while Canada lags in IT efficiency, it is the premier egovernment provider in terms of effectiveness.[17]

Governments hoping to increase their egovernment presence would benchmark themselves against these sorts of efficiency and effectiveness metrics. There is a high degree of correlation between egovernment efficiency and effectiveness, although it is not absolute.

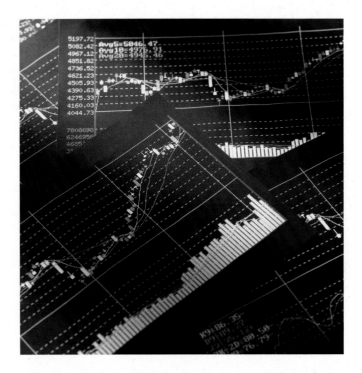

The Interrelationship Between Efficiency and Effectiveness IT Metrics

Efficiency IT metrics focus on the technology itself. Figure 1.14 highlights the most common types of efficiency IT metrics.

While these efficiency metrics are important to monitor, they do not always guarantee effectiveness. Effectiveness IT metrics are determined according to an organization's goals, strategies, and objectives. Here, it becomes important to consider the strategy an organization is using, such as a broad cost leadership strategy (Walmart, for example), as well as specific goals and objectives such as increasing new customers by 10 percent or reducing new-product development cycle times to six months. Figure 1.15 displays the broad, general effectiveness IT metrics.

In the private sector, eBay constantly benchmarks its information technology efficiency and effectiveness. Maintaining constant website availability and optimal throughput performance is critical to eBay's success.[18]

Jupiter Media Metrix ranked eBay as the website with the highest visitor volume (efficiency) for the fourth year in a row, with an 80 percent growth from the previous year. The auction website averaged 8 million unique visitors during each week of the holiday season with daily peaks exceeding 12 million visitors. To ensure constant availability and reliability of its systems, eBay implemented ProactiveNet, a performance measurement and management-tracking tool. The

FIGURE	1.13	Egovernment Ranking for Efficiency and Effectiveness

Efficiency	Effectiveness
1. United States (3.11)	1. Canada
2. Australia (2.60)	2. Singapore
3. New Zealand (2.59)	3. United States
4. Singapore (2.58)	4. Denmark
5. Norway (2.55)	5. Australia
6. Canada (2.52)	6. Finland
7. United Kingdom (2.52)	7. Hong Kong
8. Netherlands (2.51)	8. United Kingdom
9. Denmark (2.47)	9. Germany
10. Germany (2.46)	10. Ireland

FIGURE 1.14 | Common Types of Efficiency IT Metrics

Efficiency IT Metrics	
Throughput	The amount of information that can travel through a system at any point in time.
Transaction speed	The amount of time a system takes to perform a transaction.
System availability	The number of hours a system is available for users.
Information accuracy	The extent to which a system generates the correct results when executing the same transaction numerous times.
Web traffic	Includes a host of benchmarks such as the number of page views, the number of unique visitors, and the average time spent viewing a web page.
Response time	The time it takes to respond to user interactions such as a mouse click.

tool allows eBay to monitor its environment against baseline benchmarks, which helps the eBay team keep tight control of its systems. The new system has resulted in improved system availability with a 150 percent increase in productivity as measured by system uptime.[19]

Be sure to consider the issue of security while determining efficiency and effectiveness IT metrics. When an organization offers its customers the ability to purchase products over the Internet, it must implement the appropriate security. It is actually inefficient for an organization to implement security measures for Internet-based transactions as compared to processing nonsecure transactions. However, an organization will probably have a difficult time attracting new customers and increasing web-based revenue if it does not implement the necessary security measures. Purely from an efficiency IT metric point of view, security generates some inefficiency. From an organization's business strategy point of view, however, security should lead to increases in effectiveness metrics.

Figure 1.16 depicts the interrelationships between efficiency and effectiveness. Ideally, an organization should operate in the upper right-hand corner of the graph, realizing both significant increases in efficiency and effectiveness. However, operating in the upper left-hand corner (minimal effectiveness with increased efficiency) or the lower right-hand corner (significant effectiveness with minimal efficiency) may be in line with an organization's particular strategies. In general, operating in the lower left-hand corner (minimal efficiency and minimal effectiveness) is not ideal for the operation of any organization.

●● SECTION 1.2 Business Strategy

LEARNING OUTCOMES

LO1.6 Explain why competitive advantages are typically temporary.

LO1.7 List and describe each of the five forces in Porter's Five Forces Model.

LO1.8 Compare Porter's three generic strategies.

FIGURE 1.15 | Common Types of Effectiveness IT Metrics

Effectiveness IT Metrics	
Usability	The ease with which people perform transactions and/or find information. A popular usability metric on the Internet is degrees of freedom, which measures the number of clicks required to find desired information.
Customer satisfaction	Measured by such benchmarks as satisfaction surveys, percentage of existing customers retained, and increases in revenue dollars per customer.
Conversion rates	The number of customers an organization "touches" for the first time and persuades to purchase its products or services. This is a popular metric for evaluating the effectiveness of banner, pop-up, and pop-under ads on the Internet.
Financial	Such as return on investment (the earning power of an organization's assets), cost-benefit analysis (the comparison of projected revenues and costs including development, maintenance, fixed, and variable), and break-even analysis (the point at which constant revenues equal ongoing costs).

L01.9 Describe the relationship between business processes and value chain analysis.

●● L01.6

Explain why competitive advantages are typically temporary.

IDENTIFYING COMPETITIVE ADVANTAGES

To survive and thrive, an organization must create a competitive advantage. A *competitive advantage* is a product or service that an organization's customers place a greater value on than similar offerings from a competitor. Unfortunately, competitive advantages are typically temporary because competitors often seek ways to duplicate the competitive advantage. In turn, organizations must develop a strategy based on a new competitive advantage.

When an organization is the first to market with a competitive advantage, it gains a first-mover advantage. The *first-mover advantage* occurs when an organization can significantly impact its market share by being first to market with a competitive advantage. FedEx created a first-mover advantage by creating its customer self-service software, which allows people and organizations to request parcel pickups, print mailing slips, and

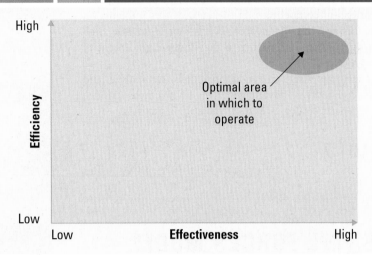

FIGURE **1.16** The Interrelationships Between Efficiency and Effectiveness

track parcels online. Other parcel delivery companies quickly began creating their own online services. Today, customer self-service on the Internet is a standard for doing business in the parcel delivery business.

As organizations develop their competitive advantages, they must pay close attention to their competition through environmental scanning. *Environmental scanning* is the acquisition and analysis of events and trends in the environment external to an organization. Information technology has the opportunity to play an important role in environmental scanning.

Frito-Lay, a premier provider of snack foods such as Cracker Jacks and Cheetos, does not just send its representatives into

---

What happens on youtube stays on youtube— FOREVER

Are you looking for great career advice? Here it is: **Never** post anything on publicly accessible websites that you would not feel comfortable showing a recruiter or hiring manager. This includes inappropriate photos; negative comments about jobs, professors, or people; and binge drinking at a holiday party. Future employers will Google you!

The bad news: You have to continue to keep your cyber profile squeaky clean for the rest of your life. Companies can and will fire you for inappropriate website postings. One interesting story occurred

when two employees created a private, password-protected group on MySpace where they would complain about their jobs, post derogatory comments about their managers, and highlight new top-secret product information. The managers, being computer savvy, obtained the password and immediately fired the two individuals after reviewing the site. Now one of the individuals is suing the former managers for invasion of privacy.

Do you agree that if you post something online it is open for the world to see? What do you consider is inappropriate material that you should never post to the web? What can you do to remove inappropriate material posted to the web by a friend that identifies you? How do efficiency and effectiveness enter into this scenario? Was MySpace the most efficient and effective way for the two employees to communicate? What is the potential argument each of these sides might use in order to win the lawsuit?

grocery stores to stock shelves; they carry handheld computers and record the product offerings, inventory, and even product locations of competitors. Frito-Lay uses this information to gain business intelligence on everything from how well competing products are selling to the strategic placement of its own products.

Organizations use three common tools to analyze and develop competitive advantages: (1) Five Forces Model, (2) three generic strategies, and (3) value chain analysis.

●● LO1.7

List and describe each of the five forces in Porter's Five Forces Model.

THE FIVE FORCES MODEL— EVALUATING BUSINESS SEGMENTS

Michael Porter's Five Forces Model is a useful tool to aid organizations facing the challenging decision of entering a new industry or industry segment. The *Five Forces Model* helps determine the relative attractiveness of an industry and includes:

1. Buyer power.
2. Supplier power.
3. Threat of substitute products or services.
4. Threat of new entrants.
5. Rivalry among existing competitors (see Figure 1.17).

Buyer Power

Buyer power in the Five Forces Model is high when buyers have many choices of whom to buy from and low when their choices are few. To reduce buyer power (and create a competitive advantage), an organization must make it more attractive for customers to buy from it instead of its competition. One of the best IT-based examples is the loyalty programs that many organizations offer.

| FIGURE | 1.17 | Porter's Five Forces Model |

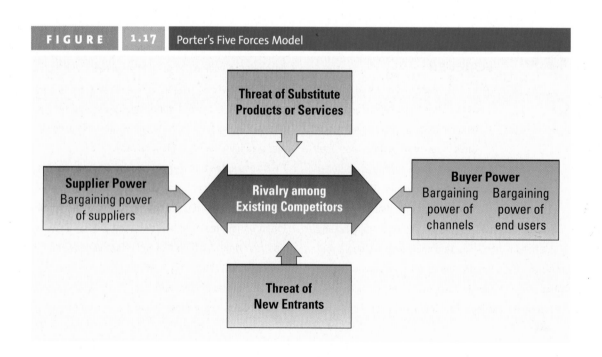

Loyalty programs reward customers based on the amount of business they do with a particular organization. The travel industry is famous for its loyalty programs such as frequent-flyer programs for airlines and frequent-guest programs for hotels. Keeping track of the activities and accounts of many thousands or millions of customers covered by loyalty programs is not practical without large-scale IT systems. Loyalty programs are a good example of using IT to reduce buyer power; because of the rewards (e.g., free airline tickets, upgrades, or hotel stays) travelers receive, they are more likely to be loyal to or give most of their business to a single organization.

Supplier Power

Supplier power in the Five Forces Model is high when buyers have few choices of whom to buy from and low when their choices are many. Supplier power is the converse of buyer power: A supplier organization in a market will want buyer power to be low. A *supply chain* consists of all parties involved, directly or indirectly, in the procurement of a product or raw material. In a typical supply chain, an organization will probably be both a supplier (to customers) and a customer (of other supplier organizations) (see Figure 1.18).

As a buyer, the organization can create a competitive advantage by locating alternative supply sources. IT-enabled business-to-business (B2B) marketplaces can help. A *business-to-business (B2B) marketplace* is an Internet-based service that brings together many buyers and sellers (discussed in detail in Chapter 3). One important variation of the B2B marketplace is a private exchange. A *private exchange* is a B2B marketplace in which a single buyer posts its needs and then opens the bidding to any supplier who would care to bid. Bidding is typically carried out through a reverse auction. A *reverse auction* is an auction format in which increasingly lower bids are solicited from organizations willing to supply the desired product or service at an increasingly lower price. As the bids get lower and lower, more and more suppliers drop out of the auction. Ultimately, the organization with the lowest bid wins. Internet-based reverse auctions are an excellent example of the way that information technology can reduce supplier power for an organization and create a competitive advantage.

Threat of Substitute Products or Services

The *threat of substitute products or services* in the Five Forces Model is high when there are many alternatives to a product or service and low when there are few alternatives from which to choose. Ideally, an organization would like to be in a market in which there are few substitutes for the products or services it offers. Of course, that is seldom possible today, but an organization can still create a competitive advantage by using switching costs.

Switching costs are costs that can make customers reluctant to switch to another product or service. A switching cost need not have an associated *monetary* cost. Amazon.com offers an example. As customers purchase products at Amazon.com over time, Amazon develops a profile of their shopping and purchasing habits, enabling Amazon to offer products tailored to a particular customer based on the customer's profile. If the customer decides to shop elsewhere, there is an associated switching cost because the new site will not have the profile of the customer's past purchases. In this way, Amazon.com has reduced the threat of substitute products or services by creating a "cost" to the consumer to switch to another online retailer.

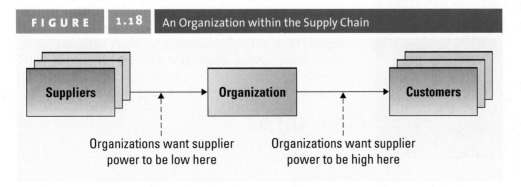

| FIGURE | 1.18 | An Organization within the Supply Chain |

Suppliers → Organization → Customers

Organizations want supplier power to be low here

Organizations want supplier power to be high here

The cell phone industry offers another good example of switching costs. Cell phone providers want to keep their customers as long as possible. Many cell phone providers offer their customers free phones or unlimited minutes if they will sign a one- or two-year contract. This creates a switching cost for the customers if they decide to change providers because they will be required to pay a penalty for breaking their contract. Another switching cost for the cell phone customer was losing the actual cell phone number; however, this switching cost has been removed with the implementation of *local number portability (LNP)* or the ability to "port" cell phone numbers to new providers. Within the context of Porter's Five Forces Model, eliminating this switching cost creates a greater threat of substitute products or services for the supplier. That is, customers can now expect to see more new cell phone providers cropping up over the next several years. They will compete on price, quality, and services with the big-name cell phone providers such as AT&T and Verizon because cell phone numbers can be moved from one provider to another. When businesses reduce or eliminate switching costs, the consumer gains more power.

Threat of New Entrants

The *threat of new entrants* in the Five Forces Model is high when it is easy for new competitors to enter a market and low when there are significant entry barriers to entering a market. An entry barrier is a product or service feature that customers have come to expect from organizations in a particular industry and must be offered by an entering organization to compete and survive. For example, a new bank must offer its customers an array of IT-enabled services, including ATM use, online bill paying, and account monitoring. These are significant barriers to entering the banking market. At one time, the first bank to offer such services gained a valuable first-mover advantage, but only temporarily, as other banking competitors developed their own IT systems.

Rivalry Among Existing Competitors

Rivalry among existing competitors in the Five Forces Model is high when competition is fierce in a market and low when competition is more complacent. Although competition is always more intense in some industries than in others, the overall trend is toward increased competition in almost every industry.

The retail grocery industry is intensively competitive. While Kroger, Safeway, and Albertsons in the United States compete in many different ways, essentially they try to beat or match the competition on price. Most of them have loyalty programs that give shoppers special discounts. Customers get lower prices while the store gathers valuable information on buying habits to create pricing strategies. In the future, expect to see grocery stores using wireless technologies to track customer movement throughout the store and match it to products purchased to determine product placement and pricing strategies. Such a system will be IT-based and a huge competitive advantage to the first store to implement it.

Since margins are low in the retail grocery market, grocers build efficiencies into their supply chains, connecting with their suppliers in IT-enabled information partnerships such as the one between Wal-Mart and its suppliers. Communicating with suppliers over telecommunications networks rather than using paper-based systems makes the procurement process faster, cheaper, and more accurate. That equates to lower prices for customers and increased rivalry among existing competitors.

●● **LO1.8**

Compare Porter's three generic strategies.

THE THREE GENERIC STRATEGIES—CREATING A BUSINESS FOCUS

Once the relative attractiveness of an industry is determined and an organization decides to enter that market, it must formulate a strategy for entering the new market. An organization can follow Porter's three generic strategies when entering a new market: (1) broad cost leadership, (2) broad differentiation, or (3) focused strategy. Broad strategies reach a large market segment, while focused strategies target a niche market. A focused strategy concentrates on either cost leadership or differentiation. Trying to be all things to all people, however, is a recipe for disaster, since it is difficult to project a consistent image to the entire marketplace. Porter suggests that an organization is wise to adopt only one of the three generic strategies illustrated in Figure 1.19.

To illustrate the use of the three generic strategies, consider Figure 1.20. The matrix shown demonstrates the relationships among strategies (cost leadership versus differentiation) and market segmentation (broad versus focused).

- **Hyundai** is following a broad cost leadership strategy. Hyundai offers low-cost vehicles, in each particular model stratification, that appeal to a large audience.

- **Audi** is pursuing a broad differentiation strategy with its Quattro models available at several price points. Audi's differentiation is safety, and it prices its various Quattro models (higher than Hyundai) to reach a large, stratified audience.

- **Kia** has a more focused cost leadership strategy. Kia mainly offers low-cost vehicles in the lower levels of model stratification.

- **Hummer** offers the most focused differentiation strategy of any in the industry (including Mercedes-Benz).

●● LO1.9

Describe the relationship between business processes and value chain analysis.

VALUE CHAIN ANALYSIS—TARGETING BUSINESS PROCESSES

Once an organization enters a new market using one of Porter's three generic strategies, it must understand, accept, and successfully execute its business strategy. Every aspect of the organization contributes to the success (or failure) of the chosen strategy. The business processes of the organization and the value chain they create play an integral role in strategy execution. Figure 1.21 combines Porter's Five Forces and his three generic strategies creating business strategies for each segment.[20]

| FIGURE | 1.19 | Porter's Three Generic Strategies |

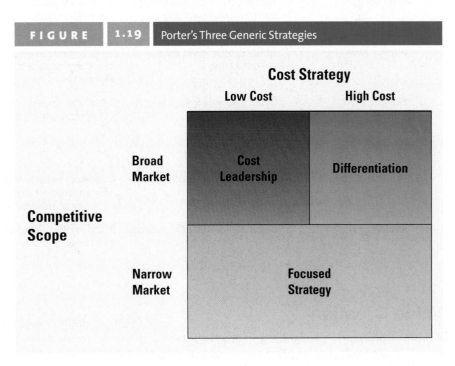

FIGURE   1.20   Porter's Three Generic Strategies in the Auto Industry

Cost Leadership strategy   Differentiation strategy

Broad market — Hyundai / Audi

Focused market — Kia / Hummer

FIGURE   1.21   Generic Strategies and Industry Forces

Generic Strategies			
Industry Force	**Cost Leadership**	**Differentiation**	**Focused**
Entry Barriers	Ability to cut price in retaliation deters potential entrants.	Customer loyalty can discourage potential entrants.	Focusing develops core competencies that can act as an entry barrier.
Buyer Power	Ability to offer lower price to powerful buyers.	Large buyers have less power to negotiate because of few close alternatives.	Large buyers have less power to negotiate because of few alternatives.
Supplier Power	Better insulated from powerful suppliers.	Better able to pass on supplier price increases to customers.	Suppliers have power because of low volumes, but a differentiation-focused firm is better able to pass on supplier price increases.
Threat of Substitutes	Can use low price to defend against substitutes.	Customers become attached to differentiating attributes, reducing threat of substitutes.	Specialized products and core competency protect against substitutes.
Rivalry	Better able to compete on price.	Brand loyalty to keep customers from rivals.	Rivals cannot meet differentiation-focused customer needs.

Value Creation

A ***business process*** is a standardized set of activities that accomplish a specific task, such as processing a customer's order. To evaluate the effectiveness of its business processes, an organization can use Michael Porter's value chain approach. An organization creates value by performing a series of activities that Porter identified as the value chain. The ***value chain*** approach views an organization as a series of processes, each of which adds value to the product or service for each customer. To create a competitive advantage, the value chain must enable the organization to provide unique value to its customers. In addition to the firm's own value-creating activities, the firm operates in a value system of vertical activities including those of upstream suppliers and downstream channel members. To achieve a competitive advantage, the firm must perform one or more value-creating activities in a way that creates more overall value than do competitors. Added value is created through lower costs or superior benefits to the consumer (differentiation).

Organizations can add value by offering lower prices or by competing in a distinctive way. Examining the organization as a value chain (actually numerous distinct but inseparable value chains) leads to identifying the important activities that add value for customers and then finding IT systems that sup-

or service. This generates a quantifiable metric, displayed in percentages in Figure 1.22, for how each activity adds value (or reduces value). The competitive advantage decision then is to (1) target high value-adding activities to further enhance their value, (2) target low value-adding activities to increase their value, or (3) perform some combination of the two.

Organizations should attempt to use information technology to add value to both primary and support value activities. One example of a primary value activity facilitated by IT is the development of a marketing campaign management system that could target marketing campaigns more efficiently, thereby reducing marketing costs. The system would also help the organization better pinpoint target market needs, thereby increasing sales. One example of a support value activity facilitated by IT is the development of a human resources system that could

> ## Organizations should attempt to use information technology to add value to both primary and support value activities.

port those activities. Figure 1.22 depicts a value chain. Primary value activities, shown at the bottom of the graph, acquire raw materials and manufacture, deliver, market, sell, and provide after-sales services. Support value activities, along the top of the graph, such as firm infrastructure, human resource management, technology development, and procurement, support the primary value activities.

The goal is to survey the customers and ask them the extent to which they believe each activity adds value to the product

more efficiently reward employees based on performance. The system could also identify employees who are at risk of leaving their jobs, allowing the organization to find additional challenges or opportunities that would help retain these employees and thus reduce turnover costs.

Value chain analysis, a highly useful tool, provides hard and fast numbers for evaluating the activities that add value to products and services. An organization can find additional value by analyzing and constructing its value chain in terms of Porter's

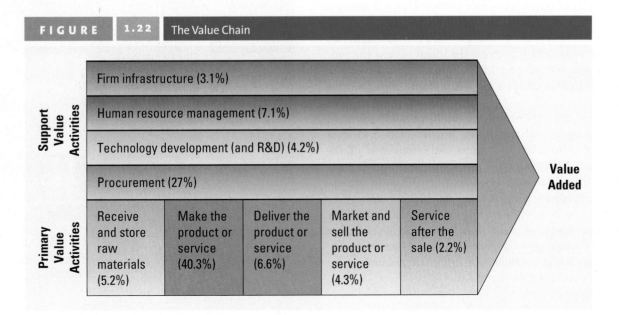

FIGURE 1.22 The Value Chain

FIGURE **1.23** The Value Chain and Porter's Five Forces

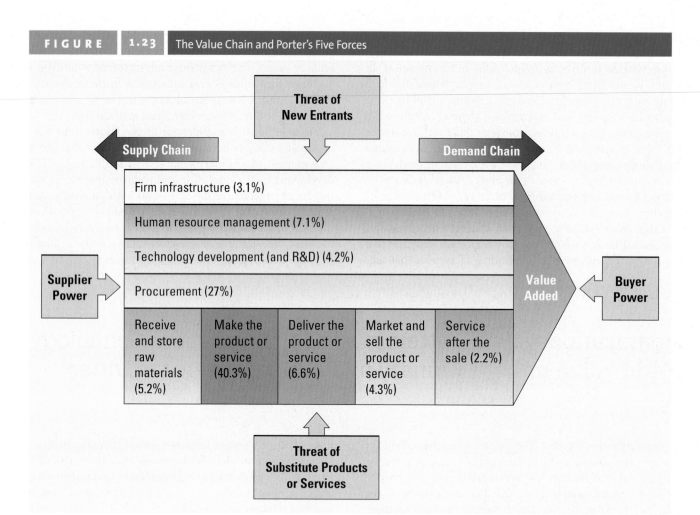

A company can implement its selected strategy by means of programs, budgets, and procedures. Implementation involves organization of the firm's resources and motivation of the employees to achieve objectives. How the company implements its chosen strategy can have a significant impact on its success. In a large company, the personnel implementing the strategy are usually different from those formulating the strategy. For this reason, proper communication of the strategy is critical. Failure can result if the strategy is misunderstood or if lower-level managers resist its implementation because they do not understand the process for selecting the particular strategy.

Five Forces (see Figure 1.23). For example, if an organization wants to decrease its buyer's or customer's power, it can construct its value chain activity of "service after the sale" by offering high levels of quality customer service. This will increase the switching costs for its customers, thereby decreasing their power. Analyzing and constructing its support value activities can help an organization decrease the threat of new entrants. Analyzing and constructing its primary value activities can help an organization decrease the threat of substitute products or services.

BUSTED

Listen to Spider-Man; He Knows What He's Talking About!

Spider-Man's infamous advice—"With great power comes great responsibility"—should be applied to every type of technology you encounter in business. Technology provides countless opportunities for businesses, but it can also lead to countless pitfalls and traps. A great example is how many companies profited from online trading; and how many people lost their life savings in online trading scams. For example, Bernard Madoff, the owner of a high-profile New York investment company, was able to forge investment statements and allegedly spent almost $50 billion of his client's money.

Texting is a great asset for any company that requires instant communication, but it also digitizes conversations that can be tracked and retrieved. David Colby, the CFO of Wellpoint, was busted carrying on multiple affairs, even once texting "ABORT!!" to one of his many girlfriends after discovering she was pregnant. Colby carried on relationships with more than 30 women and proposed to at least 12 of them.

AOL brings the power of the Internet to millions of people, and Craigslist allows anyone to become a provider of goods and services. Unfortunately, Craigslist does not describe exactly what types of goods and services are allowed. Adam Vitale was sentenced to two years in prison after he found a way to bypass AOL's spam filters and spammed 1.2 million AOL users. Vitale also had 22 prior convictions, including running an online prostitution ring through Craigslist.

When competing in business, you must analyze the good and the bad associated with every technology you encounter. Choose a company that primarily operates online—such as eBay, Netflix, or Amazon—and analyze all of the business opportunities along with the potential pitfalls you might encounter if you were the owner of the company.

An organization must continually adapt to its competitive environment, which can cause its business strategy to change. To remain successful, an organization should use Porter's Five Forces, the three generic strategies, and value chain analysis to adopt new business strategies. ■

CHECK OUT www.mhhe.com/baltzanm

for additional study materials including quizzes and PowerPoint presentations.

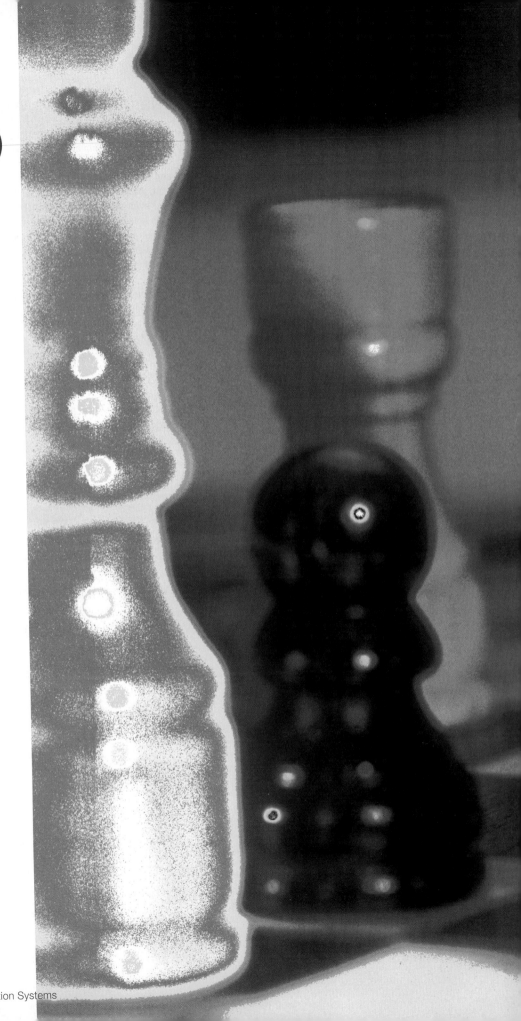

chapter two

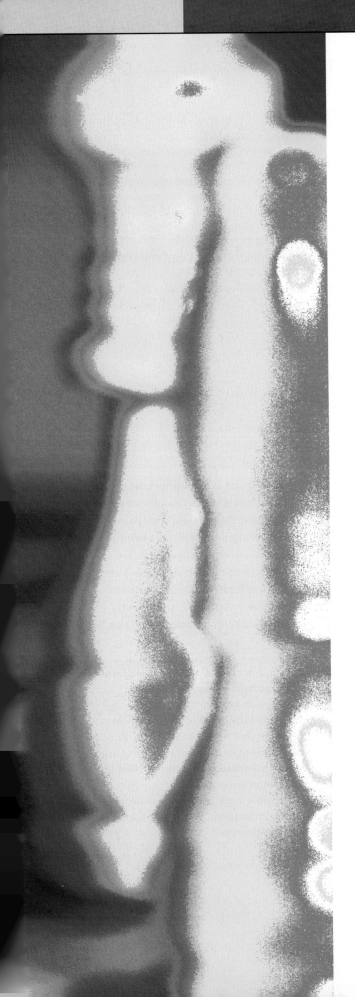

strategic
decision making

what's in IT for me?

This chapter describes various types of decision-making information systems used to run basic business processes and facilitate sound and proper decision making. Using decision-making information systems to improve and reengineer businesses processes can significantly help organizations by improving efficiency and effectiveness, and even by redefining industry standards.

You, as a business student, can gain valuable insight into an organization by understanding the types of information systems that exist in and across enterprises. When you understand how to utilize these systems to improve decision making and problem solving you can vastly improve organizational performance. After reading this chapter, you should have gained an appreciation of the various kinds of information systems employed by organizations and how you can use them to help make strategically informed decisions.

Decision-making and problem-solving abilities are now the most sought-after traits in up-and-coming executives, according to a recent survey of 1,000 executives by Caliper Associates, as reported in *The Wall Street Journal.* To put it mildly, decision makers and problem solvers have limitless career potential.[1]

Decision making and problem solving in today's electronic world encompass large-scale, opportunity-oriented, strategically focused solutions. The traditional "cookbook" approach to decision making simply will not work. This chapter focuses on technology to help make decisions, solve problems, and find new innovative opportunities. The chapter also highlights how to bring people together with the best IT processes and tools in complete, flexible solutions that can seize business opportunities and combat business challenges (see Figure 2.1).

LEARNING OUTCOMES

LO2.1 Explain the difference between transactional information and analytical information. Be sure to provide an example of each.

LO2.2 Define TPS, DSS, and EIS and explain how an organization can use these systems to make decisions and gain competitive advantages.

LO2.3 Describe the three quantitative models typically used by decision support systems.

LO2.4 Describe the relationship between digital dashboards and executive information systems.

LO2.5 Identify the four types of artificial intelligence systems.

omg lol

Driving While Breast Feeding—For Real?

How do people make decisions? Almost daily you can read about someone who makes a decision the majority of the population finds completely unbelievable and the law finds absolutely unacceptable. Listed here are a few of the recent news headlines that simply defy rational thinking and boggle the decision-making psyche.

- **Mother Caught Driving While Breast-Feeding and Talking on a Cell Phone:** A woman in Ohio was charged with child endangerment after police said she admitted to breastfeeding her child and talking on a cell phone while she was driving her other children to school. We have all heard of multitasking, but this is taking it to the extreme.

- **Souper Drive:** A woman in South Florida was caught driving, talking on a cell phone that she placed on her left shoulder, and eating from a cup of soup placed in her left hand. The woman would take her hands off the

wheel and use her right hand to spoon soup, while she continued to talk on the phone. It is common knowledge that it is inappropriate to talk with your mouth full. Perhaps she didn't understand that it was also inappropriate to drive!

- **Driving and Swimming:** A man in California was cited for driving while carrying a swimming pool. Yes, this man decided that it was a good decision to drive with one hand, while he used the other hand to hold onto his new swimming pool that was placed on the roof of his car. Not only was this a bad decision, but he also decided to enlist the help of his three children who were leaning out of the car windows, not wearing seat belts, and also helping to hold onto the swimming pool. Perhaps this man should invest in some rope or bungee cords?

- **Diaper Duty:** A woman in Baltimore was charged with diapering while

driving. Yes, this woman decided that the best time to change her child's diaper was while she was driving 65 mph down the highway. If you have ever changed a diaper, you know that it definitely requires two hands, and the fact that her child was not in a car seat and located in the front of the car just makes you wonder why anyone would make such a dreadful decision.

If people make such terrible decisions about something as highly policed as driving, just imagine the problems that are going to occur when they start making decisions about a business. What can you do to ensure your employees are making solid business decisions? Find an example of a company that found itself in a terrible mess because its employees made bad decisions. What could the company do to protect itself from employee blunders?

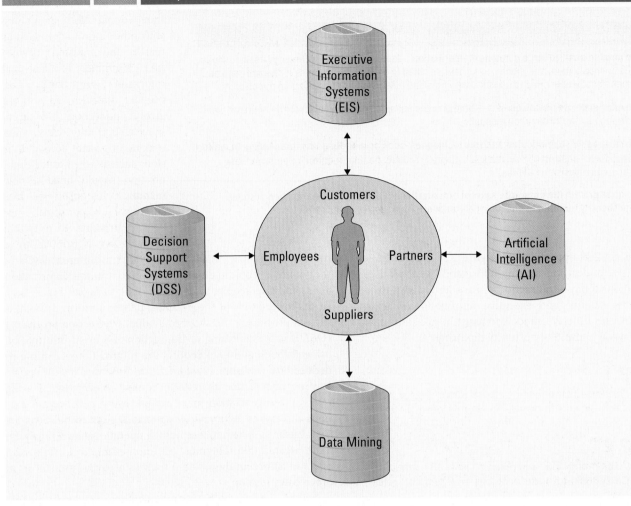

DECISION MAKING

What is the value of information? The answer to this important question varies. Karsten Solheim would say the value of information is its ability to lower a company's handicap. Solheim, an avid golfer, invented a putter, one with a "ping," that led to a successful golf equipment company and the Ping golf clubs. Ping Inc., a privately held corporation, was the first to offer customizable golf clubs. The company prides itself on being a just-in-time manufacturer that depends on flexible information systems to make informed production decisions. Ping's production systems scan large amounts of information and pull orders that meet certain criteria such as order date (this week), order priority (high), and customer type (Gold). Ping then manufactures the appropriate products, allowing it to carry less than 5 percent of inventory in its warehouse. PING depends on its flexible information systems for production decision support and thanks information technology for the explosion of its business over the past decade.[2]

Business is accelerating at a breakneck pace. The more information a business acquires, the more difficult it becomes to make decisions. The amount of information people must understand to make good decisions is growing exponentially. In the past, people could rely on manual processes to make decisions because they had limited amounts of information to process. Today, with massive volumes of available information it is almost impossible for people to make decisions without the aid of information systems. Highly complex decisions—involving far more information than the human brain can comprehend—must be made in increasingly shorter time frames. Figure 2.2 highlights the primary reasons dependence on information systems to make decisions is growing and will continue to grow.

A ***model*** is a simplified representation or abstraction of reality. Models can be used to calculate risks, understand uncertainty, change variables, and manipulate time. Decision-making information systems work by building models out of organizational information to lend insight into important

Reasons for Growth of Decision-Making Information Systems

1. **People need to analyze large amounts of information**—Improvements in technology itself, innovations in communication, and globalization have resulted in a dramatic increase in the alternatives and dimensions people need to consider when making a decision or appraising an opportunity.

2. **People must make decisions quickly**—Time is of the essence and people simply do not have time to sift through all the information manually.

3. **People must apply sophisticated analysis techniques, such as modeling and forecasting, to make good decisions**—Information systems substantially reduce the time required to perform these sophisticated analysis techniques.

4. **People must protect the corporate asset of organizational information**—Information systems offer the security required to ensure organizational information remains safe.

business issues and opportunities. Figure 2.3 displays three common types of decision-making information systems used in organizations today—transaction processing systems, decision support systems, and executive information systems. Each system uses different models to assist in decision making, problem solving, and opportunity capturing.

●● LO2.1

Explain the difference between transactional information and analytical information. Be sure to provide an example of each.

●● LO2.2

Define TPS, DSS, and EIS and explain how an organization can use these systems to make decisions and gain competitive advantages.

TRANSACTION PROCESSING SYSTEMS

Transactional information encompasses all of the information contained within a single business process or unit of work, and its primary purpose is to support the performing of daily operational tasks. Examples of transactional information include purchasing stocks, making an airline reservation, or withdrawing cash from an ATM. Organizations use transactional information when performing operational tasks and repetitive decisions such as analyzing daily sales reports to determine how much inventory to carry. *Analytical information* encompasses all organizational information, and its primary purpose is to support the performing

of managerial analysis tasks. Analytical information includes transactional information along with other information such as market and industry information. Examples of analytical information are trends, sales, product statistics, and future growth projections. Managers use analytical information when making important ad hoc decisions such as whether the organization should build a new manufacturing plant or hire additional sales personnel.

The structure of a typical organization is similar to a pyramid. Organizational activities occur at different levels of the pyramid. People in the organization have unique information needs and thus require various sets of IT tools (see Figure 2.4). At the lower levels of the pyramid, people perform daily tasks such as processing transactions. *Online transaction processing (OLTP)* is the capturing of transaction and event information using technology to (1) process the information according to defined business rules, (2) store the information, and (3) update existing information to reflect the new information. During OLTP, the organization must capture every detail of transactions and events. A *transaction processing system (TPS)* is the basic business system that serves the operational level (analysts) in an organization. The most common example of a TPS is an operational accounting system such as a payroll system or an order-entry system.

Moving up through the organizational pyramid, people (typically managers) deal less with the details ("finer" information) and more with meaningful aggregations of information

FIGURE   2.3   IT Systems in an Enterprise

Executives	Executive Information Systems (EIS)
Managers	Decision Support Systems (DSS)
Analysts	Transaction Processing Systems (TPS)

Organizational Levels

("coarser" information) that help them make broader decisions for the organization. (Granularity means fine and detailed or "coarse" and abstract information.) *Online analytical processing (OLAP)* is the manipulation of information to create business intelligence in support of strategic decision making. *Business intelligence* is a broad, general term describing information that people use to support their decision-making efforts.

●● L02.2

Define TPS, DSS, and EIS and explain how an organization can use these systems to make decisions and gain competitive advantages.

●● L02.3

Describe the three quantitative models typically used by decision support systems.

FIGURE **2.4**   Enterprise View of Information and Information Technology

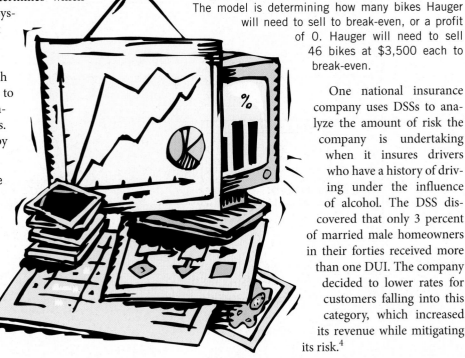

DECISION SUPPORT SYSTEMS

At limousine and transportation company BostonCoach, managers must dispatch fleets of hundreds of vehicles as efficiently as possible. BostonCoach requires a real-time dispatching system that considers inventory, customer needs, and soft dimensions such as weather and traffic. Researchers at IBM's Thomas J. Watson Research Center built BostonCoach a mathematical algorithm for a custom dispatch system that combines information about weather, traffic conditions, driver locations, and customer pickup requests and determines which cars to assign to which customers. The system is so efficient that, after launching it in Atlanta, BostonCoach experienced a 20 percent increase in revenues.[3]

A *decision support system (DSS)*, such as BostonCoach's, models information to support managers and business professionals during the decision-making process. Three quantitative models often used by DSS include:

1. *Sensitivity analysis* is the study of the impact that changes in one (or more) parts of the model have on other parts of the model. Users change the value of one variable repeatedly and observe the resulting changes in other variables.

2. *What-if analysis* checks the impact of a change in an assumption on the proposed solution. For example, "What will happen to the supply chain if a hurricane in South Carolina reduces holding inventory from 30 percent to 10 percent?" Users repeat this analysis until they understand all the effects of various situations. Figure 2.5 displays an example of what-if analysis using Microsoft Excel. The tool is calculating the net effect of a 35 percent increase in sales on the company's bottom line.

3. *Goal-seeking analysis* finds the inputs necessary to achieve a goal such as a desired level of output. Instead of observing how changes in a variable affect other variables as in what-if analysis, goal-seeking analysis sets a target value (a goal) for a variable and then repeatedly changes other variables until the target value is achieved. For example, "How many customers are required to purchase a new product to increase gross profits to $5 million?" Figure 2.6 displays a goal-seeking scenario using Microsoft Excel. The model is determining how many bikes Hauger will need to sell to break-even, or a profit of 0. Hauger will need to sell 46 bikes at $3,500 each to break-even.

One national insurance company uses DSSs to analyze the amount of risk the company is undertaking when it insures drivers who have a history of driving under the influence of alcohol. The DSS discovered that only 3 percent of married male homeowners in their forties received more than one DUI. The company decided to lower rates for customers falling into this category, which increased its revenue while mitigating its risk.[4]

FIGURE 2.5 Example of What-If Analysis in Microsoft Excel

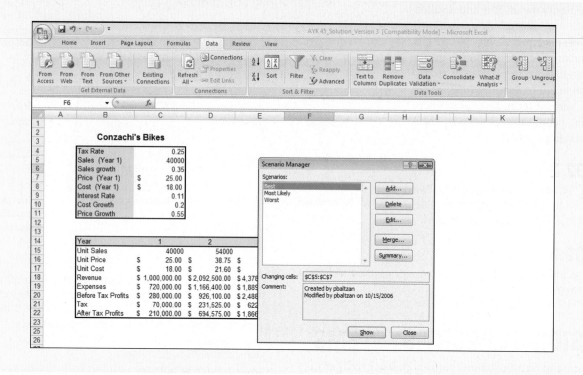

FIGURE 2.6 Example of Goal-Seeking Analysis in Microsoft Excel

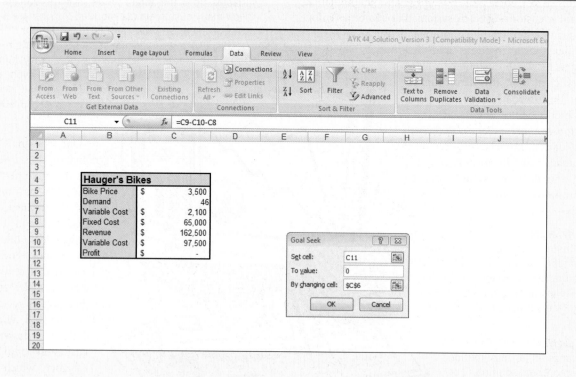

BUSTED The Criminal in the Cube Next Door

What if the person sitting in the cube next to you was running a scam that cost your company $7 billion? An employee at a French bank allegedly used his inside knowledge of business processes to bypass the systems and make roughly $73 billion in bogus trades that cost the bank more than $7 billion to unwind.

Findings from the U.S. Secret Service and its examination of 23 incidents conducted by 26 insiders determined that 70 percent of the time, insiders took advantage of failures in business process rules

and authorization mechanisms to steal from the company. Seventy-eight percent of the time, insiders were authorized and active computer users, and a surprising 43 percent used their own username and passwords to commit their crime.

This is a daunting reminder that every employee has the potential to become a knowledgeable insider, and if they ever turned bad in a fraudulent, criminal, even destructive way, they could do tremendous damage to your company. You need to protect your company's assets, and many

of your DSS and EIS systems contain the business intelligence your company needs to operate effectively. What types of sensitive information is housed in a company's TPS, DSS, and EIS? What issues could you encounter if one of your employees decided to steal the information housed in your DSS? How could you protect your EIS from unethical users? What would you do if you thought the person sharing your cube was a rogue insider?

Figure 2.7 displays how a TPS is used within a DSS. The TPS supplies transaction-based data to the DSS. The DSS summarizes and aggregates the information from the many different TPS systems, which assists managers in making informed decisions. Burlington Northern and Santa Fe Railroad (BNSF) regularly tests its railroad tracks. Each year hundreds of train derailments result from defective tracks. Using a DSS to schedule train track replacements helped BNSF decrease its rail-caused derailments by 33 percent.[5]

●● LO2.2
Define TPS, DSS, and EIS and explain how an organization can use these systems to make decisions and gain competitive advantages.

●● LO2.4
Describe the relationship between digital dashboards and executive information systems.

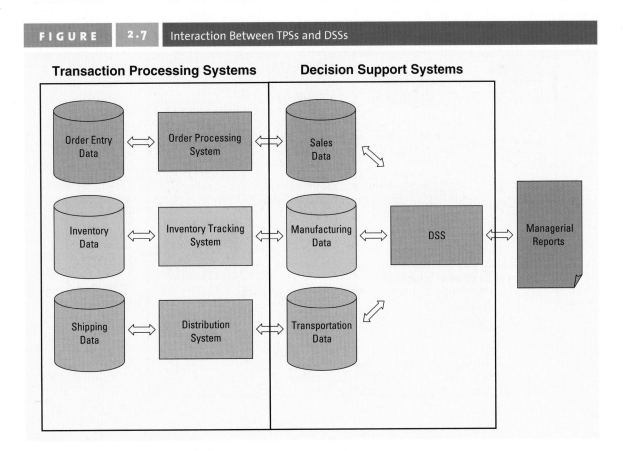

FIGURE 2.7 Interaction Between TPSs and DSSs

EXECUTIVE INFORMATION SYSTEMS

An *executive information system (EIS)* is a specialized DSS that supports senior-level executives within the organization. An EIS differs from a DSS because an EIS typically contains data from external sources as well as data from internal sources (see Figure 2.8).

Consolidation, drill-down, and slice-and-dice are a few of the capabilities offered in most EISs.

- **Consolidation** involves the aggregation of information and features simple roll-ups to complex groupings of interrelated information. Many organizations track financial information at a regional level and then consolidate the information at a single global level.

- **Drill-down** enables users to view details, and details of details, of information. Viewing monthly, weekly, daily, or even hourly information represents drill-down capability.

- **Slice-and-dice** is the ability to look at information from different perspectives. One slice of information could display all product sales during a given promotion. Another slice could display a single product's sales for all promotions.[6]

Digital Dashboards

A common feature of an EIS is a digital dashboard. *Digital dashboards* integrate information from multiple components and tailor the information to individual preferences. Digital dashboards commonly use indicators to help executives quickly identify the status of key information or critical success factors. Following is a list of features included in a dashboard designed for a senior executive of an oil refinery:

- A hot list of key performance indicators, refreshed every 15 minutes.
- A running line graph of planned versus actual production for the past 24 hours.
- A table showing actual versus forecasted product prices and inventories.
- A list of outstanding alerts and their resolution status.
- A graph of crude-oil stock market prices.
- A scroll of headline news from Petroleum Company news, an industry news service.

Digital dashboards, whether basic or comprehensive, deliver results quickly. As digital dashboards become easier to use, more executives can perform their own analysis without inundating

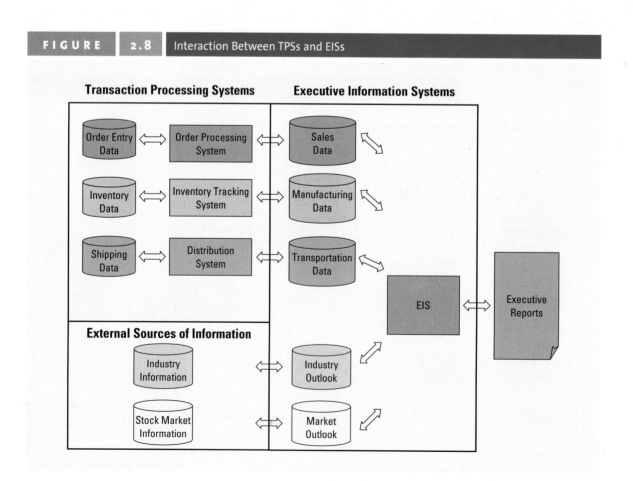

FIGURE 2.8 Interaction Between TPSs and EISs

Got Junk?
Get a Hunk!

Do you enjoy kidnapping your rival's team mascot or toilet-papering their frat houses? If so, you might find your ideal career at College Hunks Hauling Junk. The company launched in 2005 and hires college students and recent college grads to pick up junk. The founder, Nick Friedman, had a goal of capturing that friendly rivalry so often associated with college life and turn it into profits. When the company first launched, the haulers from Virginia found that their truck had been lathered in shaving cream and draped with a University of Maryland

flag. The Virginia haulers retaliated and, soon after, dead fish were found coating the seats of the Maryland's truck. Friedman decided to use this energy as incentive instead of reprimanding the rather unorthodox behavior. "We wanted to harness that competitive, prankster enthusiasm and channel it for good," states Friedman.

Freidman made a bold move and decided that instead of tracking typical key performance metrics such as revenue, average job size, customer loyalty, etc., he would track volume of junk collected and amount of junk donated or recycled. The winning team gains such things as bragging rights and banners, modest monetary prizes, and 'first table to

eat' at the annual company meeting. Most employees check the dashboard daily to view their own and rivals' latest standings.

Why do you think competition is helping College Hunks Hauling Junk exceed its revenue goals? If you were to build a team competition dashboard for your school or your work, what types of metrics would it track? What types of motivators would you use to ensure your team is always in the green? What types of external information would you want tracked in your dashboard? Could an unethical person use the information from your dashboard to hurt your team or your organization? What can you do to mitigate these risks?

IT personnel with questions and requests for reports. According to an independent study by Nucleus Research, there is a direct correlation between use of digital dashboards and companies' return on investment (ROI). Figure 2.9 and Figure 2.10 display two different digital dashboards from Visual Mining.[7]

3. **Cost driver**—examples include number of repair trucks in the field, repair jobs completed per day, and call center productivity.

Kheradpir has memorized the screens and can tell at a glance when the lines on the charts are not trending as expected. The

---

> # "Executive information systems are starting to take advantage of artificial intelligence to help executives make strategic decisions."

EIS systems, such as digital dashboards, allow executives to move beyond reporting to using information to directly impact business performance. Digital dashboards help executives react to information as it becomes available and make decisions, solve problems, and change strategies daily instead of monthly.

Verizon Communications CIO Shaygan Kheradpir tracks 100-plus major IT systems on a single screen called "The Wall of Shaygan." Every 15 seconds, a new set of charts communicating Verizon's performance flashes onto a giant LCD screen in Kheradpir's office. The 44 screen shots cycle continuously, all day long, every day. The dashboard includes more than 300 measures of business performance that fall into one of three categories:

1. **Market pulse**—examples include daily sales numbers, market share, and subscriber turnover.

2. **Customer service**—examples include problems resolved on the first call, call center wait times, and on-time repair calls.

system informs him of events such as the percentage of customer calls resolved by voice systems, number of repair trucks in the field, and amount of time to resolve an IT system issue. The dashboard works the same way for 400 managers at every level of Verizon.[8]

 LO2.5

Identify the four types of artificial intelligence systems.

ARTIFICIAL INTELLIGENCE

Executive information systems are starting to take advantage of artificial intelligence to help executives make strategic decisions. RivalWatch, based in Santa Clara, California, offers a strategic business information service using artificial intelligence that enables organizations to track the product offerings, pricing policies, and promotions of online competitors.

FIGURE 2.9 Visual Mining NetCharts Corporate Financial Dashboard

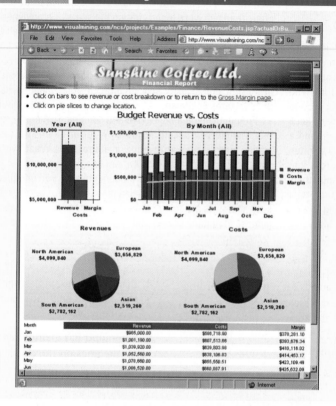

FIGURE 2.10 Visual Mining NetCharts Marketing Communications Dashboard

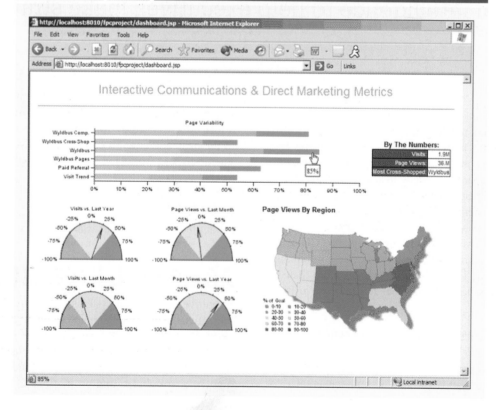

Clients can determine the competitors they want to watch and the specific information they wish to gather, ranging from products added, removed, or out of stock to price changes, coupons offered, and special shipping terms. Clients can check each competitor, category, and product either daily, weekly, monthly, or quarterly.

"Competing in the Internet arena is a whole different ballgame than doing business in the traditional brick-and-mortar world because you're competing with the whole world rather than the store down the block or a few miles away," said Phil Lumish, vice president of sales and marketing at RivalWatch .com. "With new products and campaigns being introduced at a breakneck pace, ebusinesses need new tools to monitor the competitive environment, and our service is designed specifically to meet that need."[9]

Intelligent systems are various commercial applications of artificial intelligence. *Artificial intelligence (AI)* simulates human intelligence such as the ability to reason and learn. AI systems can learn or understand from experience, make sense of ambiguous or contradictory information, and even use reasoning to solve problems and make decisions effectively. AI systems can perform such tasks as boosting productivity in factories by monitoring equipment and signaling when preventive maintenance is required. The ultimate goal of AI is the ability to build a system that can mimic human intelligence. AI systems are beginning to show up everywhere:

- At Manchester Airport in England, the Hefner AI Robot Cleaner alerts passengers to security and nonsmoking rules while it scrubs up to 65,600 square feet of floor per day. Laser scanners and ultrasonic detectors keep it from colliding with passengers.

- Shell Oil's SmartPump keeps drivers in their cars on cold, wet winter days. It can service any automobile built after 1987 that has been fitted with a special gas cap and a windshield-mounted transponder that tells the robot where to insert the pump.

- Matsushita's courier robot navigates hospital hallways, delivering patient files, X-ray films, and medical supplies.

- The FireFighter AI Robot can extinguish flames at chemical plants and nuclear reactors with water, foam, powder, or inert gas. The robot puts distance between the human operator and the fire.[10]

AI systems dramatically increase the speed and consistency of decision making, solve problems with incomplete information, and resolve complicated issues that cannot be solved by conventional computing. There are many categories of AI systems; four of the most familiar are: (1) expert systems, (2) neural networks, (3) genetic algorithms, and (4) intelligent agents.

Expert Systems

Expert systems are computerized advisory programs that imitate the reasoning processes of experts in solving difficult problems. Human expertise is transferred to the expert system, and users can access the expert system for specific advice. Most expert systems reflect expertise from many humans and can therefore perform better analysis than any single expert. Typically, the system includes a knowledge base containing various accumulated experience and a set of rules for applying the knowledge base to each particular situation. The best-known expert systems play chess and assist in medical diagnosis. Expert systems are the most commonly used form of AI in the business arena because they fill the gap when human experts are difficult to find or retain, or are too expensive.

Neural Networks

A *neural network,* also called an *artificial neural network,* is a category of AI that attempts to emulate the way the human brain works. The types of decisions for which neural networks are most useful are those that involve pattern or image recognition because a neural network can learn from the information it processes. Neural networks analyze large quantities of

information to establish patterns and characteristics in situations where the logic or rules are unknown.

The finance industry is a veteran in neural network technology and has been relying on various forms of it for over two decades. The industry uses neural networks to review loan applications and create patterns or profiles of applications that fall into two categories: approved or denied. One neural network has become the standard for detecting credit card fraud. Since 1992, this technology has slashed fraud by 70 percent for U.S. Bancorp. Now, even small credit unions are required to use the software in order to qualify for debit-card insurance from Credit Union National Association.[11]

Additional examples of neural networks include:

- Citibank uses neural networks to find opportunities in financial markets. By carefully examining historical stock market data with neural network software, Citibank financial managers learn of interesting coincidences or small anomalies (called market inefficiencies). For example, it could be that whenever IBM stock goes up, so does Unisys stock. Or it might be that a U.S. Treasury note is selling for 1 cent less in Japan than it is in the United States. These snippets of information can make a big difference to Citibank's bottom line in a very competitive financial market.

- In Westminster, California, a community of 87,000 people, police use neural network software to fight crime. With crime reports as input, the system detects and maps local crime patterns. Police say that with this system they can better predict crime trends, improve patrol assignments, and develop better crime prevention programs.

- Fingerhut, the mail-order company based in Minnesota, has 6 million people on its customer list. To determine which customers were and were not likely to order from its catalog, Fingerhut recently switched to neural network software. The company finds that the new software is more effective and expects to generate millions of dollars by fine-tuning its mailing lists.

- Fraud detection widely uses neural networks. Visa, Master-Card, and many other credit card companies use a neural network to spot peculiarities in individual accounts. MasterCard estimates neural networks save it $50 million annually.

- Many insurance companies (Cigna, AIG, Travelers, Liberty Mutual, Hartford) along with state compensation funds and other carriers use neural network software to identify fraud. The system searches for patterns in billing charges, laboratory tests, and frequency of office visits. A claim for which the diagnosis was a sprained ankle but included an electrocardiogram would be flagged for the account manager.

- FleetBoston Financial Corporation uses a neural network to watch transactions with customers. The neural network can detect patterns that may indicate a customer's growing dissatisfaction with the company. The neural network looks for signs such as decreases in the number of transactions or in the account balance of one of FleetBoston's high-value customers.

Neural networks' many features include:

- Learning and adjusting to new circumstances on their own.
- Lending themselves to massive parallel processing.
- Functioning without complete or well-structured information.
- Coping with huge volumes of information with many dependent variables.
- Analyzing nonlinear relationships in information (they have been called fancy regression analysis systems).

The biggest problem with neural networks to date has been that the hidden layers are hidden. It is difficult to see how the neural network is learning and how the neurons are interacting. Newer neural networks no longer hide the middle layers. With these systems, users can manually adjust the weights or connections, giving them more flexibility and control.

Fuzzy logic is a mathematical method of handling imprecise or subjective information. The basic approach is to assign values between 0 and 1 to vague or ambiguous information. The higher the value, the closer it is to 1. The value zero is used to represent nonmembership, and the value one is used to represent membership. For example, fuzzy logic is used in washing machines that determine by themselves how much water to use or how long to wash (they continue washing until the water is clean). In accounting and finance, fuzzy logic allows people to analyze information with subjective financial values (intangibles such as goodwill) that are very important considerations in economic analysis. Fuzzy logic and neural networks are often combined to express complicated and subjective concepts in a form that makes it possible to simplify the problem and apply rules that are executed with a level of certainty.[12]

Genetic Algorithms

A **genetic algorithm** is an artificial intelligence system that mimics the evolutionary, survival-of-the-fittest process to generate increasingly better solutions to a problem. A genetic algorithm is essentially an optimizing system: It finds the combination of inputs that gives the best outputs.

> "Fuzzy logic is a mathematical method of handling imprecise or subjective information."

Genetic algorithms are best suited to decision-making environments in which thousands, or perhaps millions, of solutions are possible. Genetic algorithms can find and evaluate solutions with many more possibilities, faster and more thoroughly than a human. Organizations face decision-making environments for all types of problems that require optimization techniques such as the following:

- Business executives use genetic algorithms to help them decide which combination of projects a firm should invest in, taking complicated tax considerations into account.

- Investment companies use genetic algorithms to help in trading decisions.

- Telecommunication companies use genetic algorithms to determine the optimal configuration of fiber-optic cable in a network that may include as many as 100,000 connection points. The genetic algorithm evaluates millions of cable configurations and selects the one that uses the least amount of cable.[13]

Intelligent Agents

An *intelligent agent* is a special-purpose knowledge-based information system that accomplishes specific tasks on behalf of its users. Intelligent agents use their knowledge base to make decisions and accomplish tasks in a way that fulfills the intentions of a user. Intelligent agents usually have a graphical representation such as "Sherlock Holmes" for an information search agent.

Nations and the International Federation of Robotics, more than half the AI robots will be toys and the other half will perform services. Bots will deactivate bombs, clean skyscraper windows, and vacuum homes.[14]

Multi-Agent Systems and Agent-Based Modeling

What do cargo transport systems, book distribution centers, the video game market, a flu epidemic, and an ant colony have in common? They are all complex adaptive systems and thus share some characteristics. By observing parts of the ecosystem, like ant or bee colonies, artificial intelligence scientists can use hardware and software models that incorporate insect characteristics and behavior to (1) learn how people-based systems behave; (2) predict how they will behave under a given set of circumstances; and (3) improve human systems to make them more efficient and effective. This concept of learning from ecosystems and adapting their characteristics to human and organizational situations is called biomimicry.

In the last few years, AI research has made much progress in modeling complex organizations as a whole with the help of multi-agent systems. In a multi-agent system, groups of

> "In the last few years, AI research has made much progress in modeling complex organizations as a whole with the help of multi-agent systems."

One of the simplest examples of an intelligent agent is a shopping bot. A *shopping bot* is software that will search several retailer websites and provide a comparison of each retailer's offerings including price and availability. Increasingly, intelligent agents handle the majority of a company's Internet buying and selling and handle such processes as finding products, bargaining over prices, and executing transactions. Intelligent agents also have the capability to handle all supply chain buying and selling.

Another application for intelligent agents is in environmental scanning and competitive intelligence. For instance, an intelligent agent can learn the types of competitor information users want to track, continuously scan the web for it, and alert users when a significant event occurs.

By 2010, some 4 million AI robots are expected to populate homes and businesses, performing everything from pumping gas to delivering mail. According to a new report by the United

intelligent agents have the ability to work independently and to interact with each other. The simulation of a human organization using a multi-agent system is called agent-based modeling. Agent-based modeling is a way of simulating human organizations using multiple intelligent agents, each of which follows a set of simple rules and can adapt to changing conditions.

Agent-based modeling systems are being used to model stock market fluctuations, predict the escape routes that people seek in a burning building, estimate the effects of interest rates on consumers with different types of debt, and anticipate how changes in conditions will affect the supply chain, to name just a few. Examples of companies that have used agent-based modeling to their advantage include:

- Southwest Airlines—to optimize cargo routing.

- Procter & Gamble—to overhaul its handling of what the company calls its "supply network" of 5 billion consumers in 140 countries.

- Air Liquide America—to reduce production and distribution costs of liquefied industrial gases.
- Merck & Co.—to find more efficient ways of distributing anti-AIDS drugs in Africa.
- Ford Motor Co.—to build a model of consumer preferences and find the best balance between production costs and customers' demands.
- Edison Chouest Offshore LLC—to find the best way to deploy its service and supply vessels in the Gulf of Mexico.[15]

Data Mining

Walmart consolidates point-of-sale details from its 3,000 stores and uses AI to transform the information into business intelligence. Data-mining systems sift instantly through the information to uncover patterns and relationships that would elude an army of human researchers. The results enable Walmart to predict sales of every product at each store with uncanny accuracy, translating into huge savings in inventories and maximum payoff from promotional spending.[16]

Data-mining software typically includes many forms of AI such as neural networks and expert systems. Data-mining tools apply algorithms to information sets to uncover inherent trends and patterns in the information, which analysts use to develop new business strategies. Analysts use the output from data-mining tools to build models that, when exposed to new information sets, perform a variety of data analysis functions. The analysts provide business solutions by putting together the analytical techniques and the business problem at hand, which often reveals important new correlations, patterns, and trends in information. A few of the more common forms of data-mining analysis capabilities include cluster analysis, association detection, and statistical analysis. Data mining is covered in detail in Chapter 9.

●● SECTION 2.2 Business Processes

LEARNING OUTCOMES

LO2.6 Describe business processes and their importance to an organization.

LO2.7 Differentiate between customer facing processes and business facing processes.

LO2.8 Compare business process improvement and business process reengineering.

LO2.9 Describe the importance of business process modeling (or mapping) and business process models.

LO2.10 Explain business process management along with the reason for its importance to an organization.

●● LO2.6

Describe business processes and their importance to an organization.

●● LO2.7

Differentiate between customer facing processes and business facing processes.

Living the DREAM

Virtual Nonprofits Helping Sustainability—What Are You Talking About?

SecondLife is an online 3D virtual world where its millions of residents create the content. Virtual worlds are exciting for any innovative businessperson who wants to find new ways to collaborate, train employees, and market products. A few business possibilities in a virtual world include:

- Holding a virtual meeting with sales managers located in Europe and Asia, which saves money and reduces carbon emissions.
- Presenting new sales initiatives and product ideas and discussing them with a virtual focus group, which reduces the amount of mail required for promotional materials.
- Selling products and services in Second Life by creating an event to promote the product: a concert, a class, a famous speaker, a party, a contest.

Innovative individuals are pursing ways to use SecondLife to help nonprofits such as Global Kids. Global Kids is a nonprofit group working to prepare urban youth to become global citizens and community leaders. With help from Main Grid content creators and consultants like The Magicians and the Electric Sheep Company, Global Kids created a program in which students in New York City collaborate with Teen Grid Residents from around the world. The teens had to finish the interactive adventure to participate in a real-world essay contest. Winners of the contest received cash prizes (in U.S. dollars) and were part of an awards ceremony co-broadcast into the Teen Grid and on stage in New York City.

The benefits for social entrepreneurship and sustainability in a virtual world are endless. Identify a way you could use SecondLife to help tackle an environmental issue, sustainable business idea, or social entrepreneurship endeavor. What types of roadblocks do you expect to encounter as you deploy your SecondLife project? What types of security and ethical issues do you anticipate encountering in a virtual world?

UNDERSTANDING THE IMPORTANCE OF BUSINESS PROCESSES

Businesses gain a competitive edge when they minimize costs and streamline their business processes. Columbia Sportswear Company is a global leader in the design, production, marketing, and distribution of outdoor apparel and footwear. The company is always looking to make the members of its highly mobile workforce more responsive and efficient while also helping them enjoy better work–life balance. Columbia Sportswear wanted new ways to streamline its operations to get up-to-the-minute information to employees working across multiple time zones. The company deployed innovative Microsoft messaging software to give its workers flexible, safeguarded access to messages from anywhere in the world. This helps the company speed every aspect of its business, and gives employees more freedom to enjoy an active lifestyle.[17]

Most organizations pride themselves on providing breakthrough products and services for customers. Unfortunately, if customers do not receive what they want quickly, accurately, and hassle-free even fantastic offerings will not save an organization from annoying its customers and ultimately eroding the firm's financial performance.

mail-order companies, requesting new telephone service from a telephone company, and administering Social Security payments. Making the checkout procedure quick and easy is a great way for grocery stores to increase profits. How long will a customer wait in line to pay for groceries? Automatic checkout systems at grocery stores are an excellent example of business process improvement.

Examining business processes helps an organization determine bottlenecks, eliminate duplicate activities, combine related activities, and identify smooth-running processes. To stay competitive, organizations must optimize and automate their business processes. Organizations are only as effective as their business processes. Developing logical business

> **The best way an organization can satisfy customers and spur profits is by completely understanding all of its business processes.**

The best way an organization can satisfy customers and spur profits is by completely understanding all of its business processes. Waiting in line at a grocery store is a great example of the need for an organization to understand and improve its business processes. In this case, the "process" is called checkout, and the purpose is to pay for and bag groceries. The process begins when a customer steps into line and ends when the customer receives the receipt and leaves the store. The *process* steps are the activities the customer and store personnel do to complete the transaction. A *business process* is a standardized set of activities that accomplish a specific task, such as processing a customer's order.[18]

Business processes transform a set of inputs into a set of outputs (goods or services) for another person or process by using people and tools. This simple example describes a customer checkout process. Imagine other business processes: developing new products, building a new home, ordering clothes from

processes can help an organization achieve its goals. For example, an automobile manufacturer might have a goal to reduce the time it takes to deliver a car to a customer. The automobile manufacturer cannot hope to meet this goal with an inefficient ordering process or a convoluted distribution process. Sales representatives might be making mistakes when completing order forms, data-entry clerks might not accurately code order information, and dock crews might be inefficiently loading cars onto trucks. All of these errors increase the time it will take to get the car to the customer. Improving any one of these business processes can have a significant effect on the total distribution process, made up of the order entry, production scheduling, and transportation processes. Figure 2.11 displays several sample business processes.[19]

Some processes (such as a programming process) may be contained wholly within a single department. However, most processes (such as ordering a product) are cross-departmental,

FIGURE **2.11** Sample Business Processes

ACCOUNTING/FINANCE BUSINESS PROCESSES

Accounts payable
Accounts receivable
Bank account reconciliation
Depreciation, Invoicing
Month-end closing procedures

ENVIRONMENTAL BUSINESS PROCESSES

Environmental protection
Hazardous waste management
Air/water/soil resource management

HUMAN RESOURCES BUSINESS PROCESSES

Disabilities employment policies
Employee hiring policies
Health care benefits
Resignations and terminations
Workplace safety rules and guidelines

MANAGEMENT INFORMATION SYSTEMS BUSINESS PROCESSES

Disaster recovery procedures
Backup/Recovery procedures
Service agreements
Emergency services
Internet use policy
Email policy

Customer Facing Processes	Industry-Specific Customer Facing Processes	Business Facing Processes
Order processing	Banking—Loan processing	Strategic planning
Customer service	Insurance—Claims processing	Tactical planning
Sales process	Government—Grant allocation	Budget forecasting
Customer billing	Hotel—Reservation handling	Training
Order shipping	Airline—Baggage handling	Purchasing raw materials

spanning the entire organization. Figure 2.12 displays the different categories of cross-departmental business processes. *Customer facing processes* result in a product or service that is received by an organization's external customer. *Business facing processes* are invisible to the external customer but essential to the effective management of the business and include goal setting, day-to-day planning, performance feedback, rewards, and resource allocation.[20]

●● LO2.8

Compare business process improvement and business process reengineering.

BUSINESS PROCESS IMPROVEMENT

Improving business processes is paramount to stay competitive in today's electronic marketplace. Organizations must improve their business processes because customers are demanding better products and services; if customers do not receive what they want from one supplier, they can simply click a mouse and have many other choices. *Business process improvement* attempts

to understand and measure the current process and make performance improvements accordingly.

Figure 2.13 illustrates the basic steps for business process improvement. Organizations begin by documenting what they currently do, and then they establish a way to measure the process, follow the process, measure the performance, and finally identify improvement opportunities based on the collected information. The next step is to implement process improvements and measure the performance of the new improved process. The loop repeats over and over again as it is continuously improved.[21]

Business processes should drive technology choices. Not the other way around. Businesses that choose technology and then attempt to implement business processes based on the technology typically fail. All business processes should be based on business strategies and goals. After determining the most efficient and effective business process, an organization can find the technology that can be used to support the business process. Of course, this does not always happen and often individuals find themselves in the difficult position of changing a business process because the technology cannot support the ideal solution.

This method for improving business processes is effective to obtain gradual, incremental improvement. However, several factors have accelerated the need to radically improve business processes. The most obvious is technology. New technologies (like the Internet and wireless) rapidly bring new capabilities to businesses, thereby raising the competitive bar and the need to improve business processes dramatically. For example, Amazon.com reinvented the supply chain of selling books by using the Internet. Amazon is a book-selling business, yet it fundamentally changed the way customers purchase books.

Another apparent trend is the flattening of the global world through technology bringing more companies and more customers into the marketplace and greatly increasing competition. A customer today can just as easily order a bottle of wine from a winery in France as a wholesaler in the United States. In today's marketplace, major technological and business changes are required just to stay in the game. As a result, companies have requested methods for faster business process improvement. Also, companies want breakthrough performance changes, not just incremental changes, and they want it now. Because the rate of change has increased for everyone, few businesses can afford a slow change process. One approach for rapid change and dramatic improvement is business process reengineering.

●● LO2.8

Compare business process improvement and business process reengineering.

BUSINESS PROCESS REENGINEERING

Business process reengineering (BPR) is the analysis and redesign of workflow within and between enterprises. BPR relies on a different school of thought than business process improvement. *In the extreme,* BPR assumes the current process is irrelevant, does not work, or is broken and must be overhauled from scratch. Such a clean slate enables business process designers to disassociate themselves from today's process and focus on a new process. It is like the designers projecting themselves into the future and asking: What should the process look like? What do customers want it to look like? What do other employees want it to look like? How do best-in-class companies do it? How can new technology facilitate the process?[22]

Figure 2.14 displays the basic steps in a business process reengineering effort. It begins with defining the scope and objectives of the reengineering project, and then goes through a learning process (with customers, employees, competitors, noncompetitors, and new technology). Given this knowledge base, the designers can create a vision for the future and design new business processes by creating a plan of action based on the gap between current processes, technologies, structures, and process vision. It is then a matter of implementing the chosen solution.[23]

Finding Opportunity Using BPR

Companies frequently strive to improve their business processes by performing tasks faster, cheaper, and better. Figure 2.15 displays different ways to travel the same road. A company could improve the way that it travels the road by moving from foot to horse and then from horse to car. However, true BPR would look at taking a different path. A company could forget about traveling on the same old road and use an airplane to get to its final destination. Companies often follow the same indirect path for doing business,

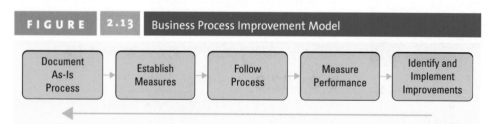

| FIGURE | 2.13 | Business Process Improvement Model |

| Document As-Is Process | → | Establish Measures | → | Follow Process | → | Measure Performance | → | Identify and Implement Improvements |

not realizing there might be a different, faster, and more direct way of doing business.[24]

Creating value for the customer is the leading factor for instituting BPR, and information technology often plays an important enabling role. Radical and fundamentally new business processes enabled Progressive Insurance to slash the claims settlement from 31 days to four hours. Typically, car insurance companies follow this standard claims resolution process: The customer gets into an accident, has the car towed, and finds a ride home. The customer then calls the insurance company to begin the claims process, which usually takes over a month (see Figure 2.16).

Progressive Insurance improved service to its customers by offering a mobile claims process. When a customer has a car accident, he or she calls in the claim on the spot. The Progressive claims adjustor comes to the accident and performs a mobile claims process, surveying the scene and taking digital

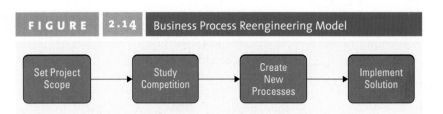

FIGURE | 2.14 | Business Process Reengineering Model

Set Project Scope → Study Competition → Create New Processes → Implement Solution

Selecting a Process for Reengineering

An organization can reengineer its cross-departmental business processes or an individual department's business processes according to its needs. When selecting a business process to reengineer, wise organizations will focus on those core processes that are critical to their performance, rather than marginal processes that have little impact. Reengineering practitioners can use several criteria to determine the importance of the process:

> "Business process reengineering (BPR) is the analysis and redesign of workflow within and between enterprises."

photographs. The adjustor then offers the customer on-site payment, towing services, and a ride home. (see Figure 2.16).[25]

A true BPR effort does more for a company than simply improve it by performing a process better, faster, and cheaper. Progressive Insurance's BPR effort redefined best practices for its entire industry. Figure 2.17 displays the different types of change an organization can achieve, along with the magnitude of change and the potential business benefit.[26]

- Is the process broken?
- Is it feasible that reengineering of this process will succeed?
- Does it have a high impact on the agency's strategic direction?
- Does it significantly impact customer satisfaction?
- Is it antiquated?
- Does it fall far below best-in-class?
- Is it crucial for productivity improvement?
- Will savings from automation be clearly visible?
- Is the return on investment from implementation high and preferably immediate?

Pitfalls of BPR

One hazard of BPR is that the company becomes so wrapped up in fighting its own demons that it fails to keep up with its competitors in offering new products or services. While American Express tackled a comprehensive reengineering of its credit card business, MasterCard and Visa introduced a new product—the corporate procurement card. American Express lagged a full year behind before offering its customers the same service.

 LO2.9

Describe the importance of business process modeling (or mapping) and business process models.

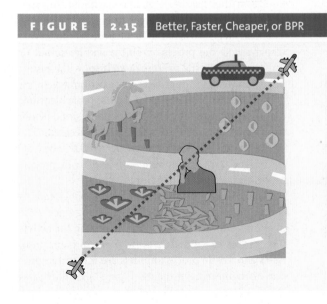

FIGURE | 2.15 | Better, Faster, Cheaper, or BPR

FIGURE　2.16　Auto Insurance Claims Processes

Company A: Claims Resolution Process　　　Progressive Insurance: Claims Resolution Process

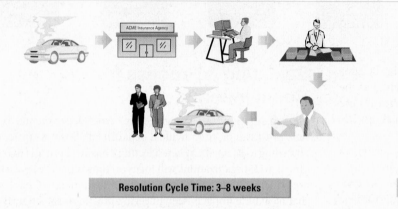

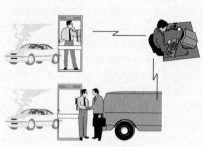

Resolution Cycle Time: 3–8 weeks　　　　　Resolution Cycle Time: 30 min–3 hours

BUSINESS PROCESS MODELING

After choosing the processes to reengineer, the organization must determine the most efficient way to begin revamping the processes. To determine whether each process is appropriately structured, organizations should create a cross-functional team to build process models that display input–output relationships among process-dependent operations and departments. They should create business process models documenting a step-by-step process sequence for the activities that are required to convert inputs to outputs for the specific process.

Business process modeling (or **mapping**) is the activity of creating a detailed flowchart or process map of a work process showing its inputs, tasks, and activities, in a structured sequence. A **business process model** is a graphic description of a process,

showing the sequence of process tasks, which is developed for a specific purpose and from a selected viewpoint. A set of one or more process models details the many functions of a system or subject area with graphics and text, and its purpose is to:

- Expose process detail gradually and in a controlled manner.
- Encourage conciseness and accuracy in describing the process model.
- Focus attention on the process model interfaces.
- Provide a powerful process analysis and consistent design vocabulary.[27]

A business process model typically displays activities as boxes and uses arrows to represent data and interfaces. Business process modeling usually begins with a functional process representation of *what* the process problem is or an As-Is process model. **As-Is process models** represent the current state of the operation that has been mapped, without any specific improvements or changes to existing processes. The next step is to build a To-Be process model that displays *how* the process problem will be solved or implemented. **To-Be process models** show the results of applying change improvement opportunities to the current (As-Is) process model. This approach ensures that the process is fully and clearly understood before the details of a process solution are decided. The To-Be process model shows *how* the *what* is to be realized. Figure 2.18 displays the As-Is and To-Be process models for ordering a hamburger.[28]

Analyzing As-Is business process models leads to success in business process reengineering since these diagrams are very powerful in visualizing the activities, processes, and data flow of an organization. As-Is and To-Be process models are integral in process reengineering projects. Figure 2.19 illustrates

FIGURE　2.17　Process Change Spectrum

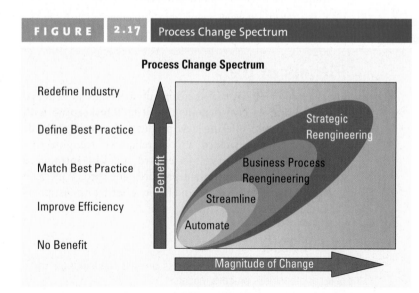

Process Change Spectrum

Redefine Industry

Define Best Practice

Match Best Practice

Improve Efficiency

No Benefit

Benefit

Strategic Reengineering

Business Process Reengineering

Streamline

Automate

Magnitude of Change

FIGURE 2.18 As-Is and To-Be Process Model for Ordering a Hamburger

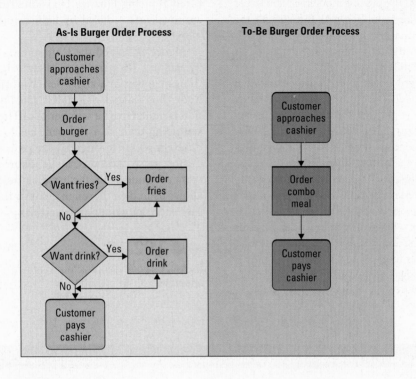

FIGURE 2.19 As-Is Process Model for Order Fulfillment

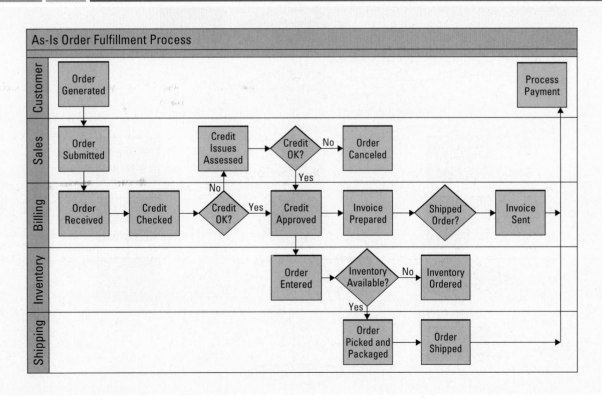

an As-Is process model of an order-fulfillment process developed by a process modeling team representing all departments that contribute to the process. The process modeling team traces the process of converting the input (orders) through all the intervening steps until the final required output (payment) is produced. The map displays the cross-functional departments involved in a typical order-fulfillment process.[29]

It is easy to become bogged down in excessive detail when creating an As-Is process model. The objective is to aggressively eliminate, simplify, or improve the To-Be processes. Successful process improvement efforts result in positive answers to the key process design or improvement question: Is this the most efficient and effective process for accomplishing the process goals? This process modeling structure allows the team to identify all the critical interfaces, overlay the time to complete various processes, start to define the opportunities for process simulation, and identify disconnects (illogical, missing, or extraneous steps) in the processes. Figure 2.20 displays a sample customer service business process As-Is model.[30]

The consulting firm KPMG Peat Marwick uses process modeling as part of its business reengineering practice.

Recently the firm helped a large financial services company slash costs and improve productivity in its Manufactured Housing Finance Division. Turnaround time for loan approval was reduced by half, using 40 percent fewer staff members.

Modeling helped the team analyze the complex aspects of the project. "In parts of the loan origination process, a lot of things happen in a short period of time," according to team leader Bob Karrick of KPMG. "During data capture, information is pulled from a number of different sources, and the person doing the risk assessment has to make judgment calls at different points throughout the process. There is often a need to stop, raise questions, make follow-up calls, and so on and then continue with the process modeling effort. Modeling allows us to do a thorough analysis that takes into account all these decision points and variables."[31]

●● LO2.10

Explain business process management along with the reason for its importance to an organization.

FIGURE 2.20 Customer Service As-Is Process Model

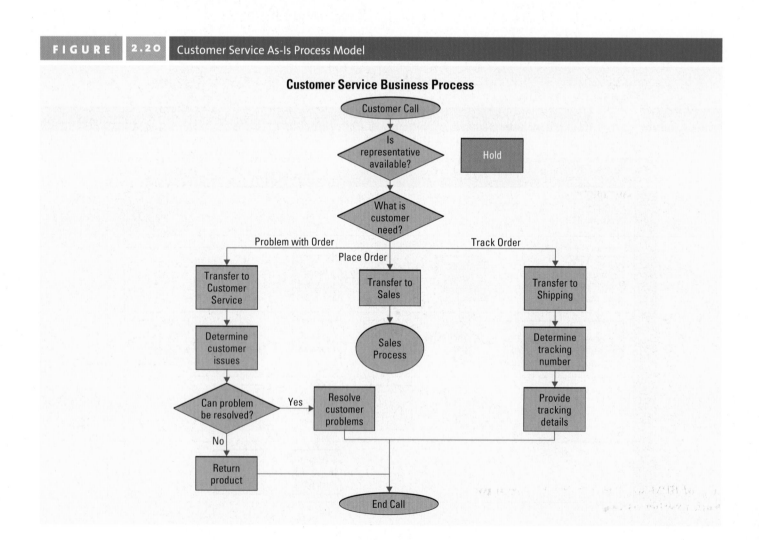

Customer Service Business Process

BUSINESS PROCESS MANAGEMENT

A key advantage of technology is its ability to improve business processes. Working faster and smarter has become a necessity for companies. Initial emphasis was given to areas such as production, accounting, procurement, and logistics. The next big areas to discover technology's value in business process were sales and marketing automation, customer relationship management, and supplier relationship management. Some of these processes involve several departments of the company and some are the result of real-time interaction of the company with its suppliers, customers, and other business partners. The latest area to discover the power of technology in automating and reengineering business process is business process management. *Business process management (BPM)* integrates all of an organization's business process to make individual processes more efficient. BPM can be used to solve a single glitch or to create one unifying system to consolidate a myriad of processes.

Many organizations are unhappy with their current mix of software applications and dealing with business processes that are subject to constant change. These organizations are turning to BPM systems that can flexibly automate their processes and glue their enterprise applications together. Figure 2.21 outlines a few key reasons organizations are embracing BPM technologies.

BPM technologies effectively track and orchestrate the business process. BPM can automate tasks involving information from multiple systems, with rules to define the sequence in which the tasks are performed as well as responsibilities, conditions, and other aspects of the process. BPM can benefit an organization by updating processes in real-time, reducing expenses, automating key decisions, and improving productivity. BPM not only allows a business process to be executed more efficiently, but it also provides the tools to measure performance and identify opportunities for improvement—as well as to easily make changes in processes to act upon those opportunities such as:

- Bringing processes, people, and information together.
- Breaking down the barriers between business areas and finding owners for the processes.
- Managing business processes within the enterprise and outside the enterprise with suppliers, business partners, and customers.
- Looking at automation horizontally instead of vertically.[32]

Is BPM for Business or Information Technology?

A good BPM solution requires two great parts to work together as one. Since BPM solutions cross application and system boundaries, they often

need to be sanctioned and implemented by the IT organization, while at the same time BPM products are business tools that business managers need to own. Therefore, confusion often arises as to whether business or IT managers should be responsible for driving the selection of a new BPM solution.

The key requirement for BPM's success in an organization is the understanding that it is a collaboration of business and IT, and thus both parties need to be involved in evaluating, selecting, and implementing a BPM solution. IT managers

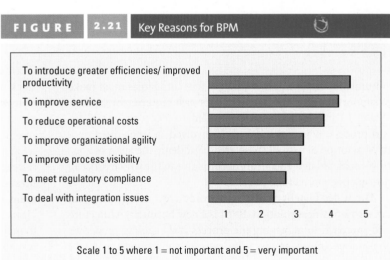

FIGURE 2.21 Key Reasons for BPM

Scale 1 to 5 where 1 = not important and 5 = very important

need to understand the business drivers behind the processes, and business managers need to understand the impact the BPM solution may have on the infrastructure. Generally, companies that have successfully deployed BPM solutions are those whose business and IT groups have worked together as a cohesive team.

All companies can benefit from a better understanding of their key business processes, analyzing them for areas of improvement and implementing improvements. BPM applications have been successfully developed to improve complex business issues of some medium-to large-sized companies. Like many large-scale implementation projects, BPM solutions are most successful in companies with a good understanding of their technology landscape and management willing to approach business in a new way. BPM solutions are truly driven by the business process and the company's owners.[33]

Effective BPM solutions allow business owners to manage many aspects of the technology through business rules they develop and maintain. Companies that cannot support or manage cultural and organizational changes may lack positive BPM results.

BPM Risks and Rewards

If an organization is considering BPM, it must be aware of the risks involved in implementing these systems. One factor that commonly derails a BPM project has nothing to do with technology and everything to do with people. BPM projects involve

show me *the* MONEY

If It Ain't Broke, Don't Fix It

Do you hate waiting in line at the grocery store? Do you find it frustrating when you go to the video store and cannot find the movie you wanted to rent? Do you get annoyed when the pizza delivery person brings you the wrong order? This is your chance to reengineer the annoying process that drives you crazy. Choose a problem you are currently experiencing, and reengineer the process to make it more efficient and effective. Be sure to provide an As-Is and To-Be business process model.

and roles created to support BPM help maximize the continuous benefits to ensure success.

An IT director from a large financial services company gave this feedback when asked about his experience in using a BPM solution to improve the company's application help desk process. "Before BPM, the company's application help desk was a manual process, filled with inefficiencies, human error, and no personal accountability. In addition, the old process provided no visibility into the process. There was absolutely no way to

> ## One factor that commonly derails a BPM project has nothing to do with technology and everything to do with people.

cultural and organizational changes that companies must make to support the new management approach required for success. Where 10 area leaders once controlled 10 pieces of an end-to-end process, now a new group is involved in implementing a BPM solution across all these areas. Suddenly the span of control is consolidated and all are accountable to the whole process, not just one piece of the puzzle.

The added benefit of BPM is not only a technology solution, but also a business solution. BPM is a new business architecture and approach to managing the process and enabling proactive, continuous improvement. The new organizational structure

track requests, since it was all manual. Business user satisfaction with the process was extremely low. A BPM solution provided a way for the company to automate, execute, manage, and monitor the process in real time. The biggest technical challenge in implementation was ensuring that the user group was self-sufficient. While the company recognized that the IT organization is needed, it wanted to be able to maintain and implement any necessary process changes with little reliance on IT. It views process management as empowering the business users to maintain, control, and monitor the process. BPM goes a long way to enable this process."[34]

Business Process Modeling Examples

A picture is worth a thousand words. Just ask Wayne Kendrick, a system analyst for Mobil Oil Corporation in Dallas, Texas. Kendrick, whose work involves planning and designing complex processes, was scheduled to make a presentation to familiarize top management with a number of projects his group was working on. "I was given 10 minutes for my presentation, and I had 20 to 30 pages of detailed documentation to present. Obviously, I could not get through it all in the time allocated." Kendrick turned to business process models to help communicate his projects. "I think people can relate to pictures better than words," Kendrick said. He applied his thinking to his presentation by using Microsoft's Visio to create business process models and graphs to represent the original 30 pages of text. "It was an effective way to get people interested in my projects and to quickly see the importance of each project," he stated. The process models worked and Kendrick received immediate approval to proceed with all of his projects. Figures 2.22 through 2.27 offer examples of business process models.[35] ■

| FIGURE | 2.22 | Ebusiness Process Model |

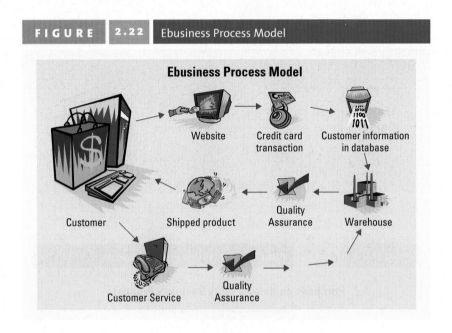

Ebusiness Process Model

| FIGURE | 2.23 | Online Banking Process Model |

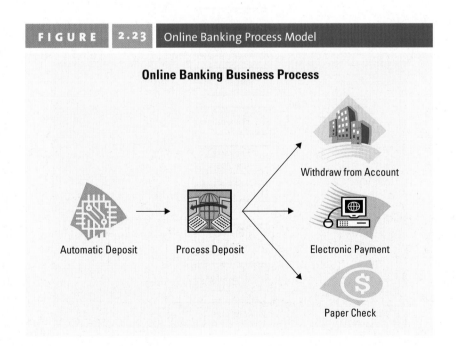

Online Banking Business Process

FIGURE 2.24 Customer Order Business Process Model

Order Business Process

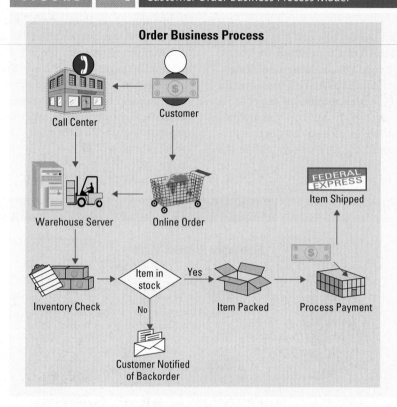

FIGURE 2.25 eBay Buyer Business Process Model

Purchase an Item on eBay Business Process

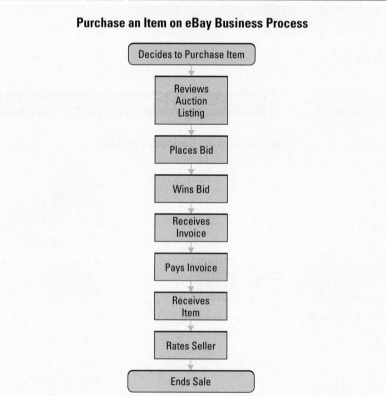

FIGURE 2.26 eBay Seller Business Process Model

FIGURE 2.27 Business Process Improvement Model

Sell an Item on eBay Business Process

Process Improvement Model

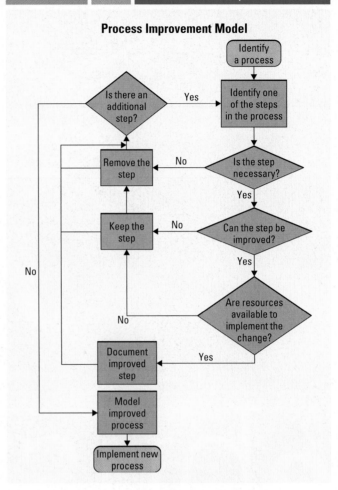

CHECK OUT www.mhhe.com/baltzanm

for additional study materials including quizzes
and PowerPoint presentations.

02222

ebusiness

chapter

what's in IT for me?

Managers must understand the importance of doing business on the Internet and how it has revolutionized the way business is performed. Ebusiness offers new opportunities for growth and new ways of performing business activities that were simply not possible before the Internet. More than just giving organizations a means of conducting transactions, ebusiness provides companies with the ability to develop and maintain customer relationships, supplier relationships, and even employee relationships between and within enterprises.

You, as a business student, should understand the fundamental impact of the Internet on business. As future managers and organizational knowledge workers, you need to understand what benefits ebusiness can offer an organization and your career. In addition, you need to understand the challenges that come along with adoption of web technologies and how web 2.0 is impacting communication. You need to be aware of the various strategies organizations can use to deploy ebusiness, as well as recent trends and methods of measuring ebusiness success. This chapter will give you this knowledge and help prepare you for success in today's electronic global marketplace.

One of the biggest forces changing business is the Internet. By age 21, California vocalist Colbie Caillat swiftly evolved from an aspiring R&B/folk singer to an American pop sensation with the marketing assistance of a little networking tool called MySpace. Caillat recorded a handful of songs, posted them on her MySpace page, and generated virtually no response for the first few months. To her astonishment, when she added the single "Bubbly" to the site, people noticed, and as word of mouth spread her page pulled in a few thousand hits a day. After she had accumulated 6,240 friends, *Rolling Stone* highlighted her as one of the top female artists on MySpace. For four months, she was the number one unsigned artist and garnered over 14 million plays. With such an appealing statistic on her résumé, record labels began courting her and she signed to Universal Republic, as her number of online friends surpassed the 100,000 mark.[1]

Ebusiness is the conducting of business on the Internet, not only buying and selling, but also serving customers and collaborating with business partners. Organizations realize that putting up simple websites for customers, employees, and partners does not create an ebusiness. Ebusiness websites must

Ebusiness is the conducting of business on the Internet, not only buying and selling, but also serving customers and collaborating with business partners.

create a buzz, much as Amazon has done in the bookselling industry. Ebusiness websites must be innovative, add value, and provide useful information. In short, the site must build a sense of community and collaboration, eventually becoming the port of entry for business. Understanding ebusiness begins with understanding:

- Disruptive technology.
- Evolution of the Internet.
- Accessing Internet information.
- Providing Internet information.

●● SECTION 3.1 Business and the Internet

LEARNING OUTCOMES

LO3.1 Compare disruptive and sustaining technologies.

LO3.2 Explain how the Internet caused disruption among businesses.

LO3.3 Define the relationship between the Internet and the World Wide Web.

LO3.4 Describe the different methods an organization can use to access information.

LO3.5 Compare the three different types of service providers.

●● **LO3.1**

Compare disruptive and sustaining technologies.

●● **LO3.2**

Explain how the Internet caused disruption among businesses.

DISRUPTIVE TECHNOLOGY

Polaroid, founded in 1937, produced the first instant camera in the late 1940s. The Polaroid camera was one of the most exciting technological advances the photography industry had ever seen. By using a Polaroid camera, customers no longer had to depend on others to develop their pictures. The technology was innovative and the product was high-end. The company eventually went public, becoming one of Wall Street's most prominent enterprises, with its stock trading above $60 in 1997. In 2002, the stock was down to 8 cents and the company declared bankruptcy.[2]

How could a company like Polaroid, which had innovative technology and a captive customer base, go bankrupt? Perhaps company executives failed to use Porter's Five Forces to analyze the threat of substitute products or services. If they had, would they have noticed the two threats, one-hour film processing and digital cameras, that eventually stole Polaroid's market share? Would they have understood that their customers, people who want instant access to their pictures without having a third party involved, would be the first to use one-hour film processing and the first to purchase digital cameras? Could the company have found a way to compete with one-hour film processing and the digital camera to save Polaroid?

Most organizations face the same dilemma as Polaroid—the criteria an organization uses to make business decisions for its present business could possibly create issues for its future business. Essentially, what is best for the current business could ruin it in the long term. Some observers of our business environment have an ominous vision of the future—digital Darwinism. *Digital Darwinism* implies that organizations which cannot adapt to the new demands placed on them for surviving in the information age are doomed to extinction.[3]

FIGURE 3.1 Disruptive and Sustaining Technologies

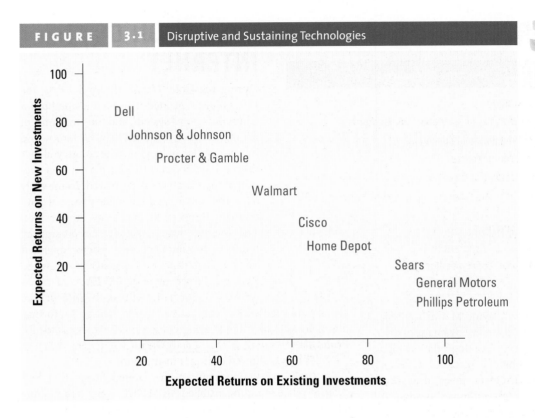

better, faster, and cheaper products in established markets. Incumbent companies most often lead sustaining technology to market, but virtually never lead in markets opened by disruptive technologies. Figure 3.1 displays companies that are expecting future growth to occur from new investments (disruptive technology) and companies that are expecting future growth to occur from existing investments (sustaining technology).

Disruptive technologies typically cut into the low end of the marketplace and eventually evolve to displace high-end competitors and their reigning technologies. Sony is a perfect example of a company that entered the low end of the marketplace and eventually evolved to displace its high-end competitors. Sony started as a tiny company that built portable, battery-powered transistor radios people could carry around with them. The sound quality of Sony's transistor radios was poor because the transistor amplifiers were of lower quality than traditional vacuum tubes, which produce a better sound. But, customers were willing to overlook sound quality for the convenience of portability. With the experience and revenue stream from the portables, Sony improved its technology to produce cheap, low-end transistor amplifiers that were suitable for home use and invested those revenues to improve the technology further, which produced better radios.[4]

Disruptive versus Sustaining Technology

A *disruptive technology* is a new way of doing things that initially does not meet the needs of existing customers. Disruptive technologies tend to open new markets and destroy old ones. A *sustaining technology,* on the other hand, produces an improved product customers are eager to buy, such as a faster car or larger hard drive. Sustaining technologies tend to provide us with

BUSTED Excuse Me, But You Are Sitting on My Domain Name

Did you know that you can make a living naming things? Eli Altman has been naming things since he was six years old and has named more than 400 companies and brands while working for A Hundred Monkeys, a branding consulting company. Altman, a veteran in the naming business, recently started to notice an unfamiliar trend in the industry: nonsensical names. English grammar rules are very precise and dictate that an *e* or an *o* usually precedes an *r*. How were these new companies' names such as Flickr, Socializr, Zoomr, Rowdii, Yuuguu, and Oooooc even possible? The answer: the Internet!

With the rise of the Internet, traditional names made of words such as Apple, Harley, and The Gap are gone with the wind. If you are thinking they are not cool enough for business today, you are wrong. The real reason for the crazy business names has to do with "domain squatting" or "cyber squatting," the practice of buying up a domain in order to profit from a trademarked name. For example, if you wanted to start a business called Drink, chances are a domain squatter has already purchased drink.com and is just waiting for you to pay big bucks to buy the domain name. Recently the domain sex.com was bought for $8 and sold for $3 million. Domain squatting is big business. Too bad it is illegal and prohibited under the 1999 Anticybersquatting Consumer

Protection Act, as well as a set of international guidelines called the Uniform Domain-Name Dispute-Resolution Policy. Disputes are usually mediated by the National Arbitration Forum or the U.N.'s World Intellectual Property Organization.

The Internet is a disruptive technology. When the Internet started taking the business world by storm, there were many unforeseen pitfalls, such as domain squatting. Do you agree or disagree that domain squatting should be illegal? Would you consider the individual who purchased sex.com to be an entrepreneur or a crook? If you were starting a business and someone was squatting on your domain, what course of action would you take?

| FIGURE | 3.2 | Companies That Capitalized on Disruptive Technology |

Company	Disruptive Technology
Charles Schwab	Online brokerage
Hewlett-Packard	Microprocessor-based computers; ink-jet printers
IBM	Minicomputers; personal computers
Intel	Low-end microprocessors
Intuit	QuickBooks software; TurboTax software; Quicken software
Microsoft	Internet-based computing; operating system software; SQL and Access database software
Oracle	Database software
Quantum	3.5-inch disks
Sony	Transistor-based consumer electronics

EVOLUTION OF THE INTERNET

During the Cold War in the mid-1960s, the U.S. military decided it needed a bombproof communications system, and thus the concept for the Internet was born. The system would link computers throughout the country, allowing messages to get through even if a large section of the country was destroyed. In the early days, the only linked computers were at government think tanks and a few universities. The Internet was essentially an emergency military communications system operated by the Department of Defense's Advanced Research Project Agency (ARPA) and called ARPANET. Formally defined, the *Internet* is a global public network of computer networks that pass information from one to another using common computer protocols. *Protocols* are standards that specify the format of data as well as the rules to be followed during transmission.

In time, every university in the United States that had defense-related funding installed ARPANET computers. Gradually, the Internet moved from a military pipeline to a communications tool for scientists. As more scholars came online, system administration transferred from ARPA to the National Science Foundation. Years later, businesses began using the Internet, and the administrative responsibilities were once again transferred. Today, no one party operates the Internet; however, several entities oversee the Internet and set standards including:

The *Innovator's Dilemma*, a book by Clayton M. Christensen, discusses how established companies can take advantage of disruptive technologies without hindering existing relationships with customers, partners, and stakeholders. Xerox, IBM, Sears, and DEC all listened to existing customers, invested aggressively in technology, had their competitive antennae up, and still lost their market-dominant positions. Christensen states that these companies may have placed too much emphasis on satisfying customers' current needs, while neglecting to adopt new disruptive technology that will meet customers' future needs, thus causing the companies to eventually lose market share. Figure 3.2 highlights several companies that launched new businesses by capitalizing on disruptive technologies.[5]

The Internet—Business Disruption

When the Internet was in its early days, no one had any idea how massive it would become. Computer companies did not think it would be a big deal; neither did the phone companies or cable companies. Difficult to access and operate, it seemed likely to remain an arcane tool of the Defense Department and academia. However, the Internet grew, and grew, and grew. It began with a handful of users in the mid-1960s and reached 1 billion by 2005 (see Figure 3.3 and Figure 3.4). Estimates predict there will be more than 3 billion Internet users by 2010. Already, villages in Indonesia and India have Internet access before they have electricity.[6] Figure 3.5 displays several ways the Internet is changing business.

- **Internet Engineering Task Force (IETF):** The protocol engineering and development arm of the Internet.

| FIGURE | 3.3 | Internet Penetration by World Region |

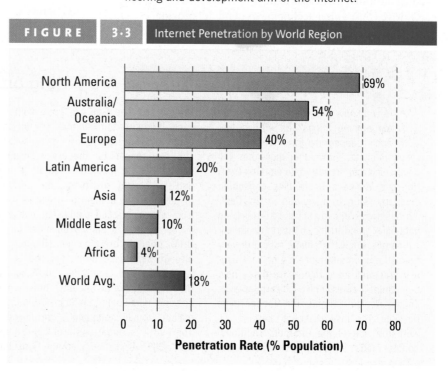

●● L03.3

Define the relationship between the Internet and the World Wide Web.

FIGURE 3.4 World Internet Users

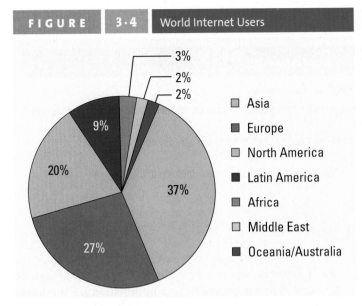

FIGURE 3.4 World Internet Users

Pie chart legend:
- Asia — 37%
- Europe — 27%
- North America — 20%
- Latin America — 9%
- Africa — 3%
- Middle East — 2%
- Oceania/Australia — 2%

- Internet Architecture Board (IAB): Responsible for defining the overall architecture of the Internet, providing guidance and broad direction to the IETF.

- Internet Engineering Steering Group (IESG): Responsible for technical management of IETF activities and the Internet standards process.

Evolution of the World Wide Web

People often interchange the terms *Internet* and the *World Wide Web,* but these terms are not synonymous. Throughout the 1960s, 1970s, and 1980s, the Internet was primarily used by the Department of Defense to support activities such as email and transferring files. The Internet was restricted to noncommercial activities, and its users included government employees, researchers, university professors, and students. The World Wide Web changed the purpose and use of the Internet.

Some hobbies change the world. In 1994, Stanford Ph.D. students Jerry Yang and David Filo posted a list of their favorite sites on the web. The exact date they posted the links is lost to history, but we do know the list's original name: "Jerry and David's Guide to the World Wide Web." By April 1994, it had a new tongue-in-cheek name: "Yet Another Hierarchical Officious Oracle," or *Yahoo!* for short. Yahoo! represented the first attempt to catalog the web, offering directory-style listings of

FIGURE 3.5 The Internet's Impact on Business

Industry	Business Changes Due to Technology
Travel	Travel site Expedia.com is now the biggest leisure-travel agency, with higher profit margins than even American Express. Thirteen percent of traditional travel agencies closed in 2002 because of their inability to compete with online travel.
Entertainment	The music industry has kept Napster and others from operating, but $35 billion annual online downloads are wrecking the traditional music business. U.S. music unit sales are down 20 percent since 2000. The next big entertainment industry to feel the effects of ebusiness will be the $67 billion movie business.
Electronics	Using the Internet to link suppliers and customers, Dell dictates industry profits. Its operating margins rose from 7.3 percent in 2002 to 8 percent in 2003, even as it took prices to levels where rivals cannot make money.
Financial services	Nearly every public efinance company makes money, with online mortgage service Lending Tree growing 70 percent a year. Processing online mortgage applications is now 40 percent cheaper for customers.
Retail	Less than 5 percent of retail sales occur online. EBay is on track this year to become one of the nation's top 15 retailers, and Amazon.com will join the top 40. WalMart ebusiness strategy is forcing rivals to make heavy investments in technology.
Automobiles	The cost of producing vehicles is down because of SCM and web-based purchasing. EBay has become the leading U.S. used-car dealer, and most major car sites are profitable.
Education and training	Cisco saved $133 million in one year by moving training sessions to the Internet.

FIGURE 3.6 Reasons for World Wide Web Growth

Reasons for Growth of the World Wide Web
■ The microcomputer revolution made it possible for an average person to own a computer.
■ Advancements in networking hardware, software, and media made it possible for business PCs to be inexpensively connected to larger networks.
■ Browser software such as Microsoft's Internet Explorer and Netscape Navigator gave computer users an easy-to-use graphical interface to find, download, and display web pages.
■ The speed, convenience, and low cost of email have made it an incredibly popular tool for business and personal communications.
■ Basic web pages are easy to create and extremely flexible.

every site that mattered—with tiny sunglasses marking sites deemed truly cool. When providing exhaustive coverage became impossible, Yahoo! was reborn as a web portal, combining the directory with search, news headlines, instant messaging, email, photo hosting, job listings, and assorted other services. As other major portals such as Lycos and Excite died off or were consumed by bigger fish, Yahoo! continued to expand. Though surpassed by the Google search juggernaut, Yahoo! remains a true Internet icon.

The *World Wide Web (WWW)* is a global hypertext system that uses the Internet as its transport mechanism. *Hypertext transport protocol (HTTP)* is the Internet standard that supports the exchange of information on the WWW. By defining universal resource locators (URLs) and how they can be used to retrieve resources anywhere on the Internet, HTTP enables web authors to embed hyperlinks in web documents. HTTP defines the process by which a web client, called a browser, originates a request for information and sends it to a web server, a program designed to respond to HTTP requests and provide the desired information. In a hypertext system, users navigate by clicking a hyperlink embedded in the current

document. The action displays a second document in the same or a separate browser window. The web has quickly become the ideal medium for publishing information on the Internet and serves as the platform for the electronic economy. Figure 3.6 displays the reasons for the popularity and growth in the WWW.

The WWW remained primarily text-based until 1991 when two events occurred that would forever change the web and the amount and quality of information available (see Figure 3.7). First, Tim Berners-Lee built the first website on August 6, 1991 (http://info.cern.ch/—the site has been archived). The site provided details about the World Wide Web including how to build a browser and set up a web server. It also housed the world's first web directory, since Berners-Lee later maintained a list of other websites apart from his own.[7]

Second, Marc Andreesen developed a new computer program called the NCSA Mosaic (National Center for Supercomputing Applications at the University of Illinois) and gave it away! The browser made it easier to access the websites that had started to appear. Soon websites contained more than just text; they also had sound and video files (see Figure 3.8). These

FIGURE 3.7 The Internet's Impact on Information

Internet's Impact on Information	
Easy to compile	Searching for information on products, prices, customers, suppliers, and partners is faster and easier when using the Internet.
Increased richness	*Information richness* refers to the depth and breadth of information transferred between customers and businesses. Businesses and customers can collect and track more detailed information when using the Internet.
Increased reach	*Information reach* refers to the number of people a business can communicate with, on a global basis. Businesses can share information with numerous customers all over the world.
Improved content	A key element of the Internet is its ability to provide dynamic relevant content. Buyers need good content descriptions to make informed purchases, and sellers use content to properly market and differentiate themselves from the competition. Content and product description establish the common understanding between both parties to the transaction. As a result, the reach and richness of that content directly affects the transaction.

FIGURE 3.8 File Formats Offered over the WWW

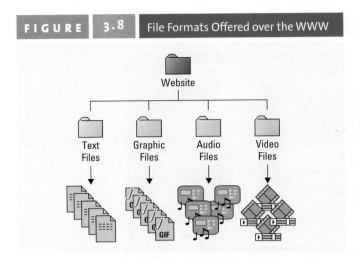

Website

Text Files | Graphic Files | Audio Files | Video Files

GIF

pages, written in the hypertext markup language (HTML), have links that allow the user to quickly move from one document to another, even when the documents are stored in different computers. Web browsers read the HTML text and convert it into a web page.[8]

By eliminating time and distance, the Internet makes it possible to perform business in ways not previously imaginable. The *digital divide* is when those with access to technology

India, the digital divide was a way of life, until recently. Media Lab Asia sells telephony and email services via a mobile Internet kiosk mounted on a bicycle, which is known as an "info-thelas." The kiosk has an onboard computer equipped with an antenna for Internet service and a specially designed all-day battery. Over 2,000 villages have purchased the kiosk for $1,200, and another 600,000 villages are interested.[9]

WEB 2.0

Web 2.0's vast disruptive impact is just beginning. *Web 2.0* is a set of economic, social, and technology trends that collectively form the basis for the next generation of the Internet—a more mature, distinctive medium characterized by user participation, openness, and network effects. Although the term suggests a new version of the World Wide Web, it does not refer to an update to web technical specifications; instead, it refers to changes in the ways software developers and end users use the web as a platform. According to Tim O'Reilly, "Web 2.0 is the business revolution in the computer industry caused by the move to the Internet as platform, and an attempt to understand the rules for success on that new platform." Figure 3.9 displays the move from web 1.0 to web 2.0, and Figure 3.10 displays the timeline of web 1.0 and web 2.0.[10]

> "By eliminating time and distance, the Internet makes it possible to perform business in ways not previously imaginable."

have great advantages over those without access to technology. People living in the village of Siroha, India, must bike five miles to find a telephone. For over 700 million rural people living in

More than just the latest technology buzzword, web 2.0 is a transformative force that is propelling companies across all industries toward a new way of doing business. Those who act

FIGURE 3.9 The Move from Web 1.0 to Web 2.0

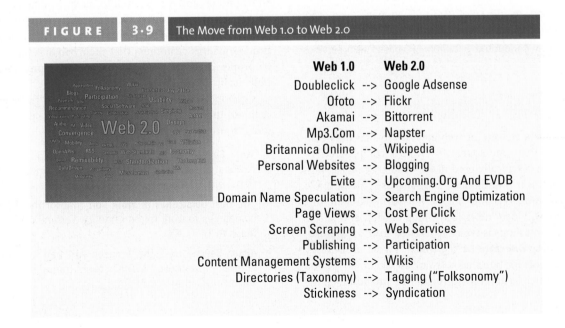

Web 1.0		Web 2.0
Doubleclick	-->	Google Adsense
Ofoto	-->	Flickr
Akamai	-->	Bittorrent
Mp3.Com	-->	Napster
Britannica Online	-->	Wikipedia
Personal Websites	-->	Blogging
Evite	-->	Upcoming.Org And EVDB
Domain Name Speculation	-->	Search Engine Optimization
Page Views	-->	Cost Per Click
Screen Scraping	-->	Web Services
Publishing	-->	Participation
Content Management Systems	-->	Wikis
Directories (Taxonomy)	-->	Tagging ("Folksonomy")
Stickiness	-->	Syndication

FIGURE 3.10 Timeline of Web 1.0

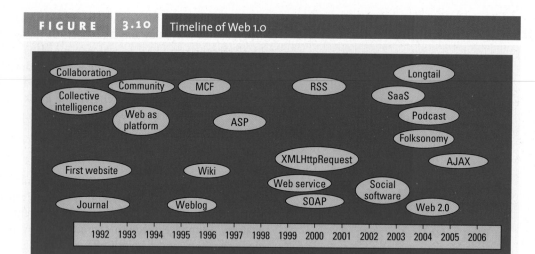

on the web 2.0 opportunity stand to gain an early-mover advantage in their markets. What is causing this change? Consider the following raw demographic and technological drivers:

- One billion people around the globe now have access to the Internet.

- Mobile devices outnumber desktop computers by a factor of two.

- Nearly 50 percent of all U.S. Internet access is now via always-on broadband connections.[11]

Combine these drivers with the fundamental laws of social networks and lessons from the web's first decade, and you get web 2.0, the next-generation, user-driven, intelligent web:

- In the first quarter of 2006, MySpace.com signed up 280,000 new users each day and had the second most Internet traffic of any website.

- By the second quarter of 2006, 50 million blogs were created—new ones were added at a rate of two per second.

- In 2005, eBay conducted 8 billion API-based web services transactions.[12]

Mashups

A *web mashup* is a website or web application that uses content from more than one source to create a completely new service. The term is typically used in the context of music; putting Jay-Z lyrics over a Radiohead song makes something old become new. The web version of a mashup allows users to mix map data, photos, video, news feeds, blog entries, and so on. Content used in mashups is typically sourced from an *application programming interface (API),* which is a set of routines, protocols, and tools for building software applications. A good API makes it easier to develop a program by providing all the

building blocks. A programmer puts the blocks together. Most operating environments, such as Microsoft Windows, provide an API so that programmers can write applications consistent with the operating environment. Many people experimenting with mashups are using Microsoft, Google, eBay, Amazon, Flickr, and Yahoo APIs, which has led to the creation of mashup editors. *Mashup editors* are WYSIWYGs (What You See Is What You Get) for mashups. They provide a visual interface to build a mashup, often allowing the user to drag and drop data points into a web application.

Whoever thought technology could help sell bananas? Dole Organic now places three-digit farm codes on each banana and creates a mashup using Google Earth and its banana database. Socially and environmentally conscious buyers can plug the numbers into Dole's website and look at a bio of the farm where the bananas were raised. The site tells the story of the farm and its surrounding community, lists its organic certifications, posts some photos, and offers a link to satellite images of the farm in Google Earth. Customers can personally monitor the production and treatment of their fruit from the tree to the grocer. The process assures customers that their bananas have been raised to proper organic standards on an environmentally friendly, holistically minded plantation.

Corporations from IBM to Google to E*Trade are jumping onboard the trend of mixing and matching software from different sources.[13] Here are a few examples:

- **1001 Secret Fishing Holes:** over a thousand fishing spots in national parks, wildlife refuges, lakes, campgrounds, historic trails, etc. (Google Maps API).

- **100 Best Companies to Work For:** map of the 100 best U.S. companies to work for as rated by *Fortune* magazine (Google Maps API).

- **Album Covers:** uses the Amazon API and an Ajax-style user interface to retrieve CD/DVD covers from the Amazon catalog (Amazon eCommerce API).

- **Gawker:** a handy mashup for keeping up with celebrity sightings in New York City. Readers are encouraged to email as soon as the celeb is spotted (Google Maps API).

- **Gigul8tor:** provides a data entry page where bands can enter information about upcoming gigs and venues. Gigul8tor displays a list of possible locations depending on the venue engine and enters event information right into Eventful in an interface designed just for bands. It shows how different user interfaces could be built in front of Eventful with mashup techniques.

- **GBlinker:** a Google pin wired to a serial port so it flashes when email arrives.

- **OpenKapow:** offers a platform for creating web-based APIs, feeds, and HTML snippets from any website, taking mashup possibilities way beyond the more than 300 APIs offered on ProgrammableWeb.

- **The Hype Machine:** combines blog posts from a set of curated music blogs with Amazon sales data and upcoming events. The Hype Machine tracks songs and discussion posted on the best blogs about music. It integrates with iTunes to take customers right from the web page to the track they are interested in. If the customer prefers buying through Amazon, The Hype Machine figures out what CD page to display.

- **Zillow:** sophisticated home valuation tools with 65 million listings and extensive data on comparables (Microsoft Virtual Earth API).

- **ProgrammableWeb:** the favorite community website of mashup developers; provides comprehensive listings of APIs available on the web and includes forums where developers can discuss how to best use them.[14]

THE FUTURE—WEB 3.0

Web 3.0 is a term that has been coined with different meanings to describe the evolution of web usage and interaction among several separate paths. These include transforming the web into a database, a move toward making content accessible by multiple nonbrowser applications, the leveraging of artificial intelligence technologies, or the semantic web. The **semantic web** is an evolving extension of the World Wide Web in which web content can be expressed not only in natural language, but also in a format that can be read and used by software agents, thus permitting them to find, share, and integrate information more easily. It derives from W3C director Sir Tim Berners-Lee's vision of the web as a universal medium for data, information, and knowledge exchange. There is considerable debate as to what the term *web 3.0* means, but many agree it encompasses one or more of the following:

1. Transforming the web into a database.

2. An evolutionary path to artificial intelligence.

3. The realization of semantic web and service-oriented architecture.

4. Evolution toward 3D.[15]

COMPANIES HAVE LONGED TO INTEGRATE EXISTING SYSTEMS IN ORDER TO IMPLEMENT INFORMATION TECHNOLOGY SUPPORT FOR BUSINESS PROCESSES THAT COVER THE ENTIRE BUSINESS VALUE CHAIN.

Transforming the Web into a Database

The first step toward a web 3.0 is the emergence of the data-driven web as structured data records are published to the web in formats that are reusable and able to be queried remotely. Because of the recent growth of standardized query language for searching across distributed databases on the web, the data-driven web enables a new level of data integration and application interoperability, making data as openly accessible and linkable as web pages. The data-driven web is the first step on the path toward the full semantic web. In the data-driven web phase, the focus is on making structured data available using databases. The full semantic web stage will widen the scope such that both structured data and even what is traditionally thought of as unstructured or semistructured content (such as web pages, documents, email, etc.) will be widely available in common formats.

An Evolutionary Path to Artificial Intelligence

Web 3.0 has also been used to describe an evolutionary path for the web that leads to artificial intelligence that can reason about the web in a quasi-human fashion. Some skeptics regard this as an unobtainable vision. However, companies such as IBM and Google are implementing new technologies that are yielding surprising information, such as predicting hit songs by mining information on college music websites. There is also debate over whether the driving force behind web 3.0 will be intelligent systems, or whether intelligence will emerge in a more organic fashion, from systems of intelligent people, such as via collaborative filtering services like del.icio.us, Flickr, and Digg that extract meaning and order from the existing web and how people interact with it.[16]

The Realization of the Semantic Web and SOA

Related to the artificial intelligence direction, web 3.0 could be the realization of a possible convergence of the semantic web and service-oriented architecture (SOA). A *service-oriented architecture (SOA)* is a business-driven IT architectural approach that supports integrating a business as linked, repeatable tasks or services. SOA is basically a collection of services that communicate with each other, for example, passing data from one service to another or coordinating an activity between one or more services. Companies have longed to integrate existing systems in order to implement information technology support for business processes that cover the entire business value chain. The main drivers for SOA adoption are that it links computational resources and promotes their reuse. SOA is covered in detail in Chapter 5.

Enterprise architects believe that SOA can help businesses respond more quickly and cost-effectively to changing market conditions. This style of architecture can simplify interconnection to—and usage of—existing IT (legacy) assets.[17]

Evolution Toward 3D

Another possible path for web 3.0 is toward the three-dimensional vision championed by the Web3D Consortium. This would involve the web transforming into a series of 3D spaces, taking the concept realized by Second Life further. This could open up new ways to connect and collaborate using 3D shared spaces.

 **L03.4**

Describe the different methods an organization can use to access information.

ACCESSING INTERNET INFORMATION

Many restaurant and franchise experts believe that Cold Stone Creamery's franchisee intranet is what keeps the company on the fast track. Franchisee owners communicate with other owners through Creamery Talk, the company's intranet-based chat room. Since it launched, Creamery Talk has turned into a franchisee's black book, with tips on everything from storefront design to equipment repair. When one owner's freezer broke recently, a post to the chat room turned up an easy fix involving a $21 motor fan.[18]

Four common tools for accessing Internet information include:

- Intranet
- Extranet
- Portal
- Kiosk

Intranet

An *intranet* is an internalized portion of the Internet, protected from outside access, that allows an organization to provide access to information and application software to only its employees. An intranet is an invaluable tool for presenting organizational information as it provides a central location for employees. It can host all kinds of company-related information such as benefits, schedules, strategic directions, and employee directories. At many companies, each department has its own web page on the intranet for departmental information sharing. An intranet is not necessarily open to the external Internet and enables organizations to make internal resources available using familiar Internet clients, such as web browsers, newsreaders, and email.

Intranet publishing is the ultimate in electronic publishing. Companies realize significant returns on investment (ROI) simply by publishing information, such as employee manuals or telephone directories, on intranets rather than printed media.

Citigroup's Global Corporate and Investment Banking division uses an intranet to provide its entire IT department with access to all IT projects including information on project owners, delivery dates, key resources, budget information, and project metrics. Providing this information via an intranet, or one convenient location, has enabled Citigroup to gain a 15 percent improvement in IT project delivery.[19]

Extranet

An *extranet* is an intranet that is available to strategic allies (such as customers, suppliers, and partners). Many companies are building extranets as they begin to realize the benefit of offering individuals outside the organization access to intranet-based information and application software such as order processing. Having a common area where employees, partners, vendors, and customers access information can be a major competitive advantage for an organization.

Walmart created an extranet for its suppliers, which can view detailed product information at all Walmart locations. Suppliers log on to Walmart's extranet and view metrics on products such as current inventory, orders, forecasts, and marketing campaigns. This helps Walmart's suppliers maintain their supply chains and ensure Walmart never runs out of products.[20]

Portal

Portal is a very generic term for what is in essence a technology that provides access to information. A *portal* is a website that offers a broad array of resources and services, such as email, online discussion groups, search engines, and online shopping malls.

Not so long ago, the only way to get any return on the junk in your garage was to hold a yard sale. EBay changed all that. Now tens of thousands of small and medium-size businesses use eBay as their primary storefront, bringing ecommerce to the people. According to eBay lore, the first item auctioned was a broken laser pointer that sold for $14.83, proving that someone somewhere will buy just about anything. Several billion dollars' worth of transactions later, the proof is on firmer ground than ever.

There are general portals and specialized or niche portals. Leading general portals include Yahoo!, Netscape, Microsoft, and America Online. Examples of niche portals include Garden.com (for gardeners), Fool.com (for investors), and SearchNetworking.com (for network administrators).

Pratt & Whitney, one of the largest aircraft-engine manufacturers in the world, has saved millions of dollars with its field service portal initiative. Pratt & Whitney's sales and service field offices are geographically scattered around the globe and were connected via expensive dedicated lines. The company saved $2.6 million annually by replacing the dedicated lines with high-speed Internet access to its field service portal. Field staff can find information they need in a fraction of the time it took before. The company estimates this change will save another $8 million per year in "process and opportunity" savings.[21]

Kiosk

A *kiosk* is a publicly accessible computer system that has been set up to allow interactive information browsing. In a kiosk, the computer's operating system has been hidden from view, and the program runs in a full-screen mode, which provides a few simple tools for navigation.

Jason Suker walked into the Mazda showroom in Bountiful, Utah, and quickly found what he was looking for in a car dealership—a web kiosk, one of six stationed around the showroom. Using the kiosk, he could track down the latest pricing information from sites like Kelley Blue Book and Edmunds.com. Suker, eyeing a four-year-old limited-edition Miata in mint condition, quickly pulled up the average retail price on Kelley Blue Book. At $16,000, it was $500 more than the dealer's price. Then, on eBay, Suker checked bids for similar models and found they were going for far less. With a sales representative looking over his shoulder to confirm his findings, the skeptical Suker made a lowball offer and expected the worst: endless haggling over price. However, the sales representative, after commending Suker for his research talent, eventually compromised and offered up the Miata for $13,300.

It was an even better deal for Bountiful Mazda. By using a kiosk to help Suker find the bargain price he wanted, the dealership moved a used car (with a higher profit margin than a new model) and opened the door to the unexpected up-sell with a $1,300, 36,000-mile service warranty.[22]

 L03.5

Compare the three different types of service providers.

PROVIDING INTERNET INFORMATION

British Airways, the $11.9 billion airline, outsourced the automation of its FAQ (frequently asked questions) web pages. The airline needed to automatically develop, manage, and post different sets of FAQs for British Airway's loyalty program customers, allowing the company to offer special promotions based on the customer's loyalty program status (gold, silver, bronze). The company outsourced the project to application service provider RightNow Technologies. The new system is helping British Airways create the right marketing programs for the appropriate customer tier.[23]

The three common forms of service providers are:

1. Internet service provider (ISP).
2. Online service provider (OSP).
3. Application service provider (ASP).

Internet Service Provider

An *Internet service provider (ISP)* is a company that provides individuals and other companies access to the Internet along with additional related services, such as website building. An ISP has the equipment and the telecommunication line access required to have a point of presence on the Internet for different geographic areas. Larger ISPs have their own high-speed

Who Knew Sugar Cane Was a Deadly Weapon?

You might have read the section on Internet access and thought, "No big deal." Well think again. Internet access is a very big deal. A 15-year-old teenager in Palm Bay, Florida, recently discovered that the access privileges to his computer had been changed by his older brother. Most of us would think that this type of "punked" scheme should be anticipated from an older sibling. Unfortunately, this teenager did not find any humor in his brother's punk, and he became uncontrollably violent and started throwing things. He then grabbed a knife and a piece of sugar cane and reportedly beat his brother with the sugar cane and threatened his mother with the knife while pushing her abusively. I've never actually seen a piece of sugar cane, but I can only imagine that it must have hurt.

The mother, unable to control the situation, called the police, and the teenager was arrested and charged with aggravated assault and battery. This case could go all the way to court, and, if it does, they will try this teenager as an adult because threatening someone with a deadly weapon is serious business. We are referring to the knife he held to his mother, not the sugar cane!

When you are considering Internet services for your business, you need to take access seriously. What might happen if one of your employees is about to close a huge multi-million-dollar deal and the Internet access goes down and the deal is lost? What might happen if an employee working on a month-long report catches a virus and the report is inaccessible? What might happen if you run a hospital and your scheduling software crashes and you have no idea which patients are scheduled to which operating rooms and with which doctors? These are far worse scenarios than a teenage boy not gaining access to his email or Facebook page. What can you do to prevent unnecessary, computer-related violence in your workplace?

leased lines so they are less dependent on telecommunication providers and can deliver better service to their customers. Among the largest national and regional ISPs are AT&T WorldNet, IBM Global Network, MCI, Netcom, UUNet, and PSINet.

FIGURE 3.11 Common ISP Services

Common ISP Services

- **Web hosting.** Housing, serving, and maintaining files for one or more websites is a widespread offering.

- **Hard-disk storage space.** Smaller sites may need only 300 to 500 MB (megabytes) of website storage space, whereas other ebusiness sites may need at least 10 GB (gigabytes) of space or their own dedicated web server.

- **Availability.** To run an ebusiness, a site must be accessible to customers 24 × 7. ISPs maximize the availability of the sites they host using techniques such as load balancing and clustering many servers to reach 100 percent availability.

- **Support.** A big part of turning to an ISP is that there is limited worry about keeping the web server running. Most ISPs offer 24 × 7 customer service.

Navigating the different options for an ISP can be daunting and confusing. There are more than 7,000 ISPs in the United States; some are large with household names, and others are literally one-person operations. Although Internet access is viewed as a commodity service, in reality features and performance can differ tremendously among ISPs. Figure 3.11 highlights common ISP features.

Another member of the ISP family is the *wireless Internet service provider (WISP),* an ISP that allows subscribers to connect to a server at designated hotspots or access points using a wireless connection. This type of ISP offers access to the Internet and the web from anywhere within the zone of coverage provided by an antenna. This is usually a region with a radius of one mile. Figure 3.12 displays a brief overview of how this technology works.

One example of a WISP is T-Mobile International, a company that provides access to wireless laptop users in more than 2,000 locations including airports, airline clubs, Starbucks coffeehouses, and Borders Books. A wireless service called T-Mobile HotSpot allows customers to access the Internet and T-Mobile's corporate intranet via a wireless network from convenient locations away from their home or office. T-Mobile International is the first mobile communications company to extend service on both sides of the Atlantic, offering customers the advantage of using their wireless services when traveling worldwide.[24]

FIGURE 3.12 Wireless Access Diagram

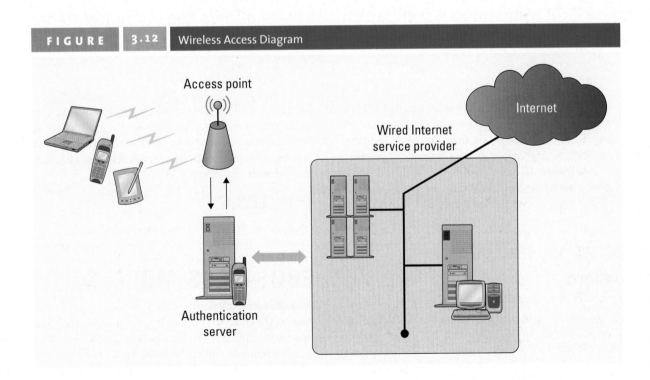

Online Service Provider

An *online service provider (OSP)* offers an extensive array of unique services such as its own version of a web browser. The term *online service provider* helps to distinguish ISPs that offer Internet access and their own online content, such as America Online (AOL), from ISPs that simply connect users directly with the Internet, such as EarthLink. Connecting to the Internet through an OSP is an alternative to connecting through one of the national ISPs, such as AT&T or MCI, or a regional or local ISP.

Application Service Provider

An *application service provider (ASP)* is a company that offers an organization access over the Internet to systems and related services that would otherwise have to be located in personal or organizational computers. Employing the services of an ASP is essentially outsourcing part of a company's business logic. Hiring an ASP to manage a company's software allows the company to hand over the operation, maintenance, and upgrade responsibilities for a system to the ASP.

One of the most important agreements between the customer and the ASP is the service level agreement. *Service level agreements (SLAs)* define the specific responsibilities of the service provider and set the customer expectations. SLAs include such items as availability, accessibility, performance, maintenance, backup/recovery, upgrades, equipment ownership, software ownership, security, and confidentiality. For example, an SLA might state that the ASP must have the software available and

L03.9 Describe ebusiness along with its benefits and challenges.

L03.10 Define mcommerce and explain how an egovernment could use it to increase its efficiency and effectiveness.

EBUSINESS BASICS

In 2003, Tom Anderson and Chris DeWolf started MySpace, a social networking website that offers its members information about the independent music scene around the country representing both Internet culture and teenage culture. Musicians sign up for free MySpace home pages where they can post tour dates, songs, and lyrics. Fans sign up for their own web pages to link to favorite bands and friends. MySpace is now the world's fifth most popular English-language website with over 100 million users.[26]

One of the biggest benefits of the Internet is its ability to allow organizations to perform business with anyone, anywhere, anytime. *Ecommerce* is the buying and selling of goods and services over the Internet. Ecommerce refers only to online transactions. *Ebusiness,* derived from the term ecommerce, is the conducting of business on the Internet, not only buying and selling, but also serving customers and collaborating with business partners. The primary difference between ecommerce and ebusiness is that ebusiness also refers to online exchanges of information, such as a manufacturer allowing its suppliers to monitor production schedules or a financial institution allowing its customers to review their banking, credit card, and mortgage accounts.

In the past few years, ebusiness seems to have permeated every aspect of daily life. Both individuals and organizations

> "Hiring an ASP to manage a company's software allows the company to hand over the operation, maintenance, and upgrade responsibilities for a system"

accessible from 7:00 A.M. to 7:00 P.M. Monday through Friday. It might also state that if the system is down for more than 60 minutes, there will be no charge for that day. Most industry analysts agree that the ASP market is growing rapidly. International Data Corporation (IDC) expected the worldwide ASP market to grow from around $13 billion in 2005 to $23 billion by 2008.[25] Figure 3.13 displays the top ISPs, OSPs, and ASPs.

 SECTION 3.2 Ebusiness

LEARNING OUTCOMES

L03.6 Compare the four types of ebusiness models.

L03.7 Describe how an organization's marketing, sales, accounting, and customer service departments can use ebusiness to increase revenues or reduce costs.

L03.8 Explain why an organization would use metrics to determine a website's success.

have embraced Internet technologies to enhance productivity, maximize convenience, and improve communications globally. From banking to shopping to entertainment, the Internet has become integral to daily life. Figure 3.14 provides examples of a few industries using ebusiness.

 L03.6

Compare the four types of ebusiness models.

EBUSINESS MODELS

A *ebusiness model* is an approach to conducting electronic business on the Internet. Ebusiness transactions take place between two major entities—businesses and consumers. All ebusiness activities happen within the framework of two types of business relationships: (1) the exchange of products and services between businesses (business-to-business, or B2B) and (2) the exchange

FIGURE | **3.13** | Top ISPs, OSPs, and ASPs

Company	Description	Specialty
Appshop www.appshop.com	Application service provider	Oracle 11i ebusiness suite applications
BlueStar Solutions www.bluestarsolutions.com	Application service provider	Managing ERP solutions with a focus on SAP
Concur www.concur.com	Internet service provider	Integrates B2B procurement
Corio www.corio.com	Application service provider	Specializes in Oracle applications
Employease www.employease.com	Online service provider	Human resource applications services
Intacct www.intacct.com	Online service provider	Online general ledger service
LivePerson www.liveperson.com	Online service provider	Real-time chat provider
NetLedger www.netledger.com	Online service provider	Web-based accounting platform
Outtask www.outtask.com	Application service provider	Integration of budgeting, customer service, sales management, and human resources applications
RightNow www.rightnow.com	Online service provider, Internet service provider	Suite of customer service applications
Salesforce.com www.salesforce.com	Online service provider	Suite of customer service applications
Salesnet www.salesnet.com	Online service provider	Suite of sales force automation products and services
Surebridge www.surebridge.com	Application service provider	High-tech manufacturing, distribution, health care applications
UpShot www.upshot.com	Online service provider	Sales force automation products and services
USi www.usinternetworking.com	Application service provider	Ariba, Siebel, Microsoft, and Oracle customer base

of products and services with consumers (business-to-consumer, or B2C) (see Figure 3.15).

The primary difference between B2B and B2C are the customers; B2B customers are other businesses while B2C markets to consumers. Overall, B2B relations are more complex and have higher security needs; plus B2B is the dominant ebusiness force, representing 80 percent of all online business.[27] Figure 3.16 illustrates all the ebusiness models: Business-to-business, business-to-consumer, consumer-to-consumer, and consumer-to-business.

Business-to-Business (B2B)

Business-to-business (B2B) applies to businesses buying from and selling to each other over the Internet. Online access to data, including expected shipping date, delivery date, and shipping status, provided either by

FIGURE | **3.14** | Overview of Several Industries Using Ebusiness

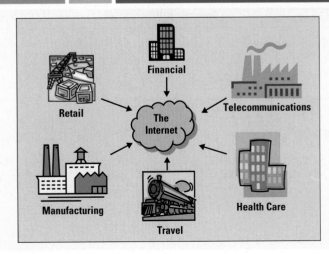

FIGURE **3.15** Basic Ebusiness Models

Ebusiness Term	Definition
Business-to-business (B2B)	Applies to businesses buying from and selling to each other over the Internet.
Business-to-consumer (B2C)	Applies to any business that sells its products or services to consumers over the Internet.
Consumer-to-business (C2B)	Applies to any consumer that sells a product or service to a business over the Internet.
Consumer-to-consumer (C2C)	Applies to sites primarily offering goods and services to assist consumers interacting with each other over the Internet.

	Business	Consumer
Business	B2B	B2C
Consumer	C2B	C2C

FIGURE **3.16** Ebusiness Models

Business-to-Business (B2B)

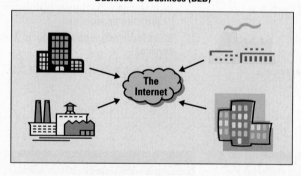

Business-to-Consumer (B2C)

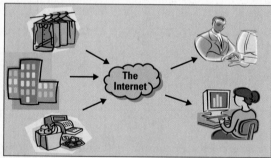

Consumer-to-Business (C2B)

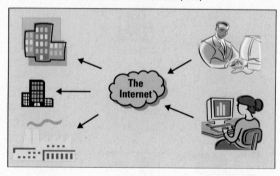

Consumer-to-Consumer (C2C)

the seller or a third-party provider is widely supported by B2B models. Electronic marketplaces represent a new wave in B2B ebusiness models. **Electronic marketplaces,** or **emarketplaces,** are interactive business communities providing a central market where multiple buyers and sellers can engage in ebusiness activities (see Figure 3.17). They present structures for conducting commercial exchange, consolidating supply chains, and creating new sales channels. Their primary goal is to increase market efficiency by tightening and automating the relationship between buyers and sellers. Existing emarketplaces allow access to various mechanisms in which to buy and sell almost anything, from services to direct materials.

FIGURE 3.17   Business-to-Business Emarketplace Overview

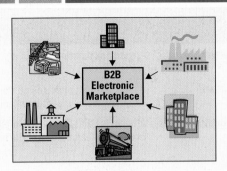

Business-to-Consumer (B2C)

Business-to-consumer (B2C) applies to any business that sells its products or services to consumers over the Internet. Carfax has been in the vehicle history report business for 20 years with an original customer base of used-car dealers. "The Internet was just a new way for us to reach the consumer market," Carfax President Dick Raines said. Carfax spent $20 million on print and TV ads to attract customers to its website. Customers can purchase a Carfax report for $14.95 or six days of reports for $19.95. Carfax has now launched a part-nership program for small auto dealers' websites and a cash-back program offer-ing customers 20 percent of revenues received for their referrals. "We continue to look for more and more ways to add value," Raines said.[28] Common B2C ebusi-ness models include eshops and emalls.

Eshop An **eshop,** sometimes referred to as an **estore** or **etailer,** is a version of a retail store where customers can shop at any hour of the day without leaving their home or office. These online stores sell and support a variety of prod-ucts and services. The online businesses channeling their goods and services via the Internet only, such as Amazon.com, are called pure plays. The others are an extension of traditional retail outlets that sell online as well as through a traditional physical store. They are generally known as "bricks and clicks" or "click and mortar" organizations, such as the Gap (www.gap.com) and Best Buy (www.bestbuy.com) (see Figure 3.18).

Emall An **emall** consists of a number of eshops; it serves as a gateway through which a visitor can access other eshops. An emall may be generalized or specialized depending on the prod-ucts offered by the eshops it hosts. Revenues for emall operators include membership fees from participating eshops, advertis-ing, and possibly a fee on each transaction if the emall operator also processes payments. Eshops in emalls benefit from brand reinforcement and increased traffic as visiting one shop on the emall often leads to browsing "neighboring" shops. An example of an emall is the Arizona emall www.1az1.com/shopping.

Consumer-to-Business (C2B)

Consumer-to-business (C2B) applies to any consumer that sells a product or service to a business over the Internet. One example of this ebusiness model is Priceline.com where bid-ders (or customers) set their prices for items such as airline tickets or hotel rooms, and a seller decides whether to supply them. The demand for C2B ebusiness will increase over the next few years due to customers' desire for greater convenience and lower prices.

Consumer-to-Consumer (C2C)

Consumer-to-consumer (C2C) applies to sites primarily offering goods and services to assist consumers interacting with each other over the Internet. EBay, the Internet's most successful C2C online auction website, links like-minded buyers and sellers for a small commission. Figure 3.19 displays the different types of online auctions.

C2C online communities, or virtual com-munities, interact via email groups, web-based discussion forums, or chat rooms. C2C business models are consumer-driven and opportunities are available to satisfy most consumers' needs, ranging from finding a mortgage to job hunting. They are global swap shops based on customer-centered communication. One C2C community, KazaA, allows users to download MP3 music files, enabling users to exchange files. Figure 3.20 highlights the different types of C2C commu-nities that are thriving on the Internet.

Like many seminal web events, Craigslist started as a quirky side project seemingly devoid of commercial possibilites. In March 1995, Craig Newmark quit his job as a software archi-tect for Charles Schwab in San Francisco and started a mailing

FIGURE 3.18 Types of Businesses

Business Types

Brick-and-mortar business	A business that operates in a physical store without an Internet presence.
Pure-play (virtual) business	A business that operates on the Internet only without a physical store. Examples include Amazon.com and Expedia.com.
Click-and-mortar business	A business that operates in a physical store and on the Internet. Examples include REI and Barnes and Noble.

list where subscribers could share information about interesting cultural events in the Bay Area. "I was reflecting on how much people helped each other out on the Net, in those days, on the WELL and usenet news groups," he says via email. As the list grew, people began posting messages looking for apartments, jobs, and other topics. In October 1995, Craig turned his private list into a public website at Cnewmark.com. In September 1997, Craig's list became Craigslist.org. In early 1998, the site began charging a nominal fee for job listings (though the vast majority of ads remain free), and in 1999 Craigslist.org incorporated and began paying its employees. Today, there are 450 local versions of Craigslist in 50 countries, and more than 25 million people visit them each month. The service has been credited with (or blamed for, depending on your point of view) taking the classified ad market away from established newspapers. But Craigslist's greatest contribution may be in proving that, like politics, the greatest global movements are always local.

●● LO3.7

Describe how an organization's marketing, sales, accounting, and customer service departments can use ebusiness to increase revenues or reduce costs.

ORGANIZATIONAL STRATEGIES FOR EBUSINESS

To be successful in ebusiness, an organization must master the art of electronic relationships. Traditional means of customer acquisition such as advertising, promotions, and public relations are just as important with a website. Primary business areas taking advantage of ebusiness include:

- Marketing/sales
- Financial services
- Procurement
- Customer service
- Intermediaries

Marketing/Sales

Direct selling was the earliest type of ebusiness and has proven to be a stepping-stone to more complex commerce operations. Successes such as eBay, Barnes and Noble, Dell Inc., and Travelocity have sparked the growth of this segment, proving customer acceptance of ebusiness direct selling. Marketing and sales departments are initiating some of the most exciting ebusiness innovations (see Figure 3.21).

Cincinnati's WCPO-TV was a ratings blip in 2002 and is now the number three ABC affiliate in the nation. WCPO-TV credits its success largely to digital billboards that promote different programming depending on the time of day. The billboards are updated directly from a website. The station quickly noticed that when current events for the early-evening news were plugged during the afternoon, ratings spiked.

The digital billboards let several companies share one space and can change messages directly from the company's computer. In the morning, a department store can advertise a sale, and in the afternoon, a restaurant can advertise its specials. Eventually customers will be able to buy billboard sign time in hour or minute increments. Current costs to share a digital billboard are $40,000 a month, compared with $10,000 for one standard billboard.[29]

Ebusiness provides an easy way to penetrate a new geographic territory and extend global reach. Large, small, or specialized businesses can use their online sales sites to sell on a worldwide basis with little extra cost. This ability to tap into expanded domestic or even international markets can be an immediate revenue boost to artists, jewelry makers, wineries, and the like, for initial orders and especially for reorders.

The Hotel Gatti (www.hotel-gatti.com) is a small hotel in northern Italy catering primarily to Italian travelers. By introducing its own website with English-language options, it significantly extended its geographic reach. Now, at very little cost, the hotel communicates with and takes reservations from potential customers in the United States and other English-speaking countries. The bottom line is that ebusiness now allows any company to market and sell products globally, regardless of its size.[30]

FIGURE 3.19 Online Auctions

Online Auctions

Electronic Auction (e-auction)	Sellers and buyers solicit consecutive bids from each other and prices are determined dynamically.
Forward Auction	An auction that sellers use as a selling channel to many buyers and the highest bid wins.
Reverse Auction	An auction that buyers use to purchase a product or service, selecting the seller with the lowest bid.

FIGURE 3.20 C2C Communities

C2C Communities

- **Communities of interest**—People interact with each other on specific topics, such as golfing and stamp collecting.

- **Communities of relations**—People come together to share certain life experiences, such as cancer patients, senior citizens, and car enthusiasts.

- **Communities of fantasy**—People participate in imaginary environments, such as fantasy football teams and playing one-on-one with Michael Jordan.

FIGURE 3.21 Generating Revenue on the Internet through Marketing and Sales Departments

Marketing and Sales Ebusiness Innovations

- An *online ad* is a box running across a web page that is often used to contain advertisements. The banner generally contains a link to the advertiser's website. Web-based advertising services can track the number of times users click the banner, generating statistics that enable advertisers to judge whether the advertising fees are worth paying. Banner ads are like living, breathing classified ads.

- A *pop-up ad* is a small web page containing an advertisement that appears on the web page outside of the current website loaded in the browser. A *pop-under ad* is a form of a pop-up ad that users do not see until they close the current web browser screen.

- *Associate programs (affiliate programs)* allow businesses to generate commissions or royalties from an Internet site. For example, a business can sign up as an associate of a major commercial site such as Amazon. The business then sends potential buyers to the Amazon site using a code or banner ad. The business receives a commission when the referred customer makes a purchase on Amazon.

- *Viral marketing* is a technique that induces websites or users to pass on a marketing message to other websites or users, creating exponential growth in the message's visibility and effect. One example of successful viral marketing is Hotmail, which promotes its service and its own advertisers' messages in every user's email notes. Viral marketing encourages users of a product or service supplied by an ebusiness to encourage friends to join. Viral marketing is a word-of-mouth type advertising program.

- *Mass customization* is the ability of an organization to give its customers the opportunity to tailor its products or services to the customers' specifications. For example, customers can order M&M's with customized sayings such as "Marry Me."

- *Personalization* occurs when a website can know enough about a person's likes and dislikes that it can fashion offers that are more likely to appeal to that person. Personalization involves tailoring a presentation of an ebusiness website to individuals or groups of customers based on profile information, demographics, or prior transactions. Amazon uses personalization to create a unique portal for each of its customers.

- A *blog* (the contraction of the phrase "web log") is a website in which items are posted on a regular basis and displayed in reverse chronological order. Like other media, blogs often focus on a particular subject, such as food, politics, or local news. Some blogs function as online diaries. A typical blog combines text, images, and links to other blogs, web pages, and other media related to its topic. Since its appearance in 1995, blogging has emerged as a popular means of communication, affecting public opinion and mass media around the world.

- *Real simple syndications (RSS)* is a family of web feed formats used for web syndication of programs and content. RSS is used by (among other things) news websites, blogs, and podcasting, which allows consumers and journalists to have news constantly fed to them instead of searching for it. In addition to facilitating syndication, RSS allows a website's frequent readers to track updates on the site.

- *Podcasting* is the distribution of audio or video files, such as radio programs or music videos, over the Internet to play on mobile devices and personal computers. Podcasting's essence is about creating content (audio or video) for an audience that wants to listen when they want, where they want, and how they want. Podcasters' websites also may offer direct download of their files, but the subscription feed of automatically delivered new content is what distinguishes a podcast from a simple download or real-time streaming. Usually, the podcast features one type of show with new episodes either sporadically or at planned intervals such as daily, weekly, etc.

- *Search engine optimization (SEO)* is a set of methods aimed at improving the ranking of a website in search engine listings. Search engines display different kinds of listings in the search engine results pages (SERPs), including: pay-per-click advertisements, paid inclusion listings, and organic search results. SEO is primarily concerned with advancing the goals of websites by improving the number and position of organic search results for a wide variety of relevant keywords. SEO strategies can increase the number of visitors and the quality of visitors, where quality means visitors who complete the action the site intends (e.g., purchase, sign up, learn something).

  SEO, or "white hat SEO," is distinguished from "black hat SEO," or spamdexing, by methods and objectives. *Spamdexing* uses a variety of deceptive techniques in an attempt to manipulate search engine rankings, whereas legitimate SEO focuses on building better sites and using honest methods of promotion. What constitutes an honest, or ethical, method is an issue that has been the subject of numerous debates.

Financial Services

Financial services websites are enjoying rapid growth as they help consumers, businesses, and financial institutions distribute information with greater convenience and richness than is available in other channels. Consumers in ebusiness markets pay for products and services using a credit card or one of the methods outlined in Figure 3.22. Online business payments differ from online consumer payments because businesses tend to make large purchases (from thousands to millions of dollars) and typically do not pay with a credit card. Businesses make online payments using electronic data interchange (EDI) (see Figure 3.23). Transactions between businesses are complex and typically require a level of system integration between the businesses.

Many organizations are now turning to providers of electronic trading networks for enhanced Internet-based network and messaging services. Electronic trading networks are service providers that manage network services. They support business-to-business integration information exchanges,

improved security, guaranteed service levels, and command center support (see Figure 3.24). As electronic trading networks expand their reach and the number of Internet businesses continues to grow, so will the need for managed trading services. Using these services allows organizations to reduce time to market and the overall development, deployment, and maintenance costs associated with their integration infrastructures.

Traders at Vanguard Petroleum Corporation spent most days on the phone, patrolling the market for pricing and volume information in order to strike the best possible deal. The process was slow and tied up traders on one negotiation at a time, making it inherently difficult to stay on top of quickly changing prices. One winter, for example, the weather got cold and stayed cold, causing propane prices to increase dramatically. The price was moving so fast that Vanguard was missing opportunities to buy, sell, and execute deals since it was able to complete only one deal at a time.

To bridge these shortcomings and speed the process, Vanguard became one of the first users of Chalkboard, a

FIGURE 3.22	Types of Online Consumer Payments

Online Consumer Payments	
Financial cybermediary	A *financial cybermediary* is an Internet-based company that facilitates payments over the Internet. PayPal is the best-known example of a financial cybermediary.
Electronic check	An *electronic check* is a mechanism for sending a payment from a checking or savings account. There are many implementations of electronic checks, with the most prominent being online banking.
Electronic bill presentment and payment (EBPP)	An *electronic bill presentment and payment (EBPP)* is a system that sends bills over the Internet and provides an easy-to-use mechanism (such as clicking on a button) to pay the bill. EBPP systems are available through local banks or online services such as Checkfree and Quicken.
Digital wallet	A *digital wallet* is both software and information—the software provides security for the transaction and the information includes payment and delivery information (for example, the credit card number and expiration date).

FIGURE 3·23 Types of Online Business Payments

Online Business Payments

Electronic data interchange (EDI) is a standard format for exchanging business data. One way an organization can use EDI is through a value-added network. A *value-added network (VAN)* is a private network, provided by a third party, for exchanging information through a high-capacity connection. VANs support electronic catalogs (from which orders are placed), EDI-based transactions (the actual orders), security measures such as encryption, and EDI mailboxes.

Financial EDI (financial electronic data interchange) is a standard electronic process for B2B market purchase payments. National Cash Management System is an automated clearinghouse that supports the reconciliation of the payments.

commodity markets electronic trading network that is now part of ChemConnect, a B2B emarketplace. Vanguard uses Chalk-board to put bids and offers in front of hundreds of traders and complete various trades at multiple delivery points simultaneously. Vanguard now completes deals in real-time and is able to access a broader audience of buyers and sellers.[31]

Procurement

Web-based procurement of maintenance, repair, and operations (MRO) supplies was expected to reach more than $200 billion worldwide by the year 2009. *Maintenance, repair, and operations (MRO) materials* (also called *indirect materials*) are necessary for running an organization but do not relate to the company's primary business activities. Typical MRO goods include office supplies (such as pens and paper), equipment, furniture, computers, and replacement parts. In the traditional

approach to MRO purchasing, a purchasing manager would receive a paper-based request for materials. The purchasing manager would need to search a variety of paper catalogs to find the right product at the right price. Not surprisingly, the administrative cost for purchasing indirect supplies often exceeded the unit value of the product itself. According to the Organization for Economic Cooperation and Development (OECD), companies with more than $500 million in revenue spend an estimated $75 to $150 to process a single purchase order for MRO supplies.[32]

Eprocurement *Eprocurement* is the B2B purchase and sale of supplies and services over the Internet. The goal of many eprocurement applications is to link organizations directly to preapproved suppliers' catalogs and to process the entire purchasing transaction online. Linking to electronic catalogs significantly reduces the need to check the timeliness and accuracy of supplier information.

An *electronic catalog* presents customers with information about goods and services offered for sale, bid, or auction on the Internet. Some electronic catalogs manage large numbers of individual items, and search capabilities help buyers navigate quickly to the items they want to purchase. Other electronic catalogs emphasize merchandise presentation and special offers, much as a retail store is laid out to encourage impulse or

FIGURE 3·24 Diagram of an Electronic Trading Network

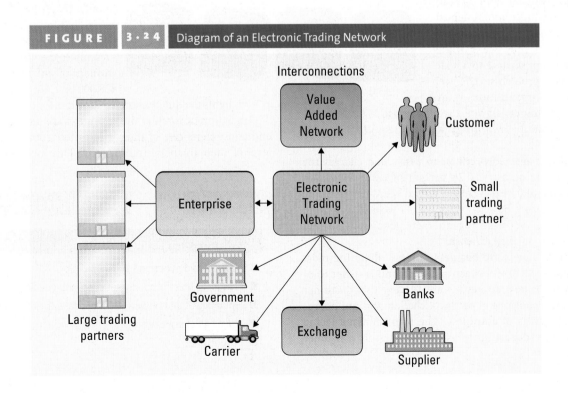

omg lol

Welcome to the Anti-Social Networking Revolution

Have you ever received a friend application on Facebook and thought you are not a friend but an enemyface? Well one smart individual has created an application that allows you to tell your enemies as well as your friends what you really think about them: introducing the Enemybook. The Enemybook allows users to add enemies as well as friends on Facebook, and you can describe in detail exactly how you know the person and why you truly hate them. Another great feature, instead of poking them, you can flip them the bird.

Have you noticed that individuals have a great deal of power when it comes to the Internet? That wimpy kid who used to be picked on in high school can now Enemybook those bullies all over Facebook. The same power has been given to the consumer. Prior to the Internet, if a customer was angry, they could write a letter or make a phone call, but their individual power was relative weak. Now, they can create a website or upload a video to YouTube bashing a product or service, and their efforts can be viewed by millions and millions of people.

The power has shifted to the hands of the consumer.

What issues can your company anticipate from consumers? What power does one unhappy consumer have and what methods could they use to communicate their issues? What role does viral marketing play in the unhappy consumer scenario? What can a company do to protect itself from the wrath of an unhappy blogger or tweeter?

---

add-on buying. As with other aspects of ebusiness, it is important to match electronic catalog design and functionality to a company's business goals.

Customer Service

Ebusiness enables customers to help themselves by combining the communications capability of a traditional customer response system with the content richness only the web can provide—all available and operating 24 × 7. As a result, conducting business via the web offers customers the convenience they want while freeing key support staff to tackle more complex problems. The web also allows an organization to provide better customer service through email, special messages, and private password-web access to special areas for top customers.

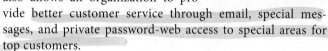

Vanguard manages $690 billion in assets and charges the lowest fees in the industry: 0.26 percent of assets versus an industry average of 0.81 percent. Vanguard keeps fees down by teaching its investors how to better use its website. For good reason: A web log-on costs Vanguard mere pennies, while each call to a service rep is a $9 expense.[33]

Customer service is the business process where the most human contact occurs between a buyer and a seller. Not surprisingly, ebusiness strategists are finding that customer service via the web is one of the most challenging and potentially lucrative areas of ebusiness. The primary issue facing customer service departments using ebusiness is consumer protection.

Consumer Protection An organization that wants to dominate by using superior customer service as a competitive advantage must not only consider how to service its customers, but also how to protect its customers. Organizations must recognize that many consumers are unfamiliar with their digital choices, and some ebusinesses are well aware of these vulnerabilities. For example, 17-year-old Miami high school senior Francis Cornworth offered his "Young Man's Virginity" for sale on eBay. The offer attracted a $10 million phony bid. Diana Duyser of Hollywood, Florida, sold half of a grilled cheese sandwich that resembles the Virgin Mary to the owners of an online casino for $28,000 on eBay. Figure 3.25 highlights the different protection areas for consumers.[34]

Regardless of whether the customers are other businesses or end consumers, one of their greatest concerns is the security level of their financial transactions. This includes all aspects

FIGURE	3.25	Consumer Protection

Issues for Consumer Protection
■ Unsolicited goods and communication
■ Illegal or harmful goods, services, and content
■ Insufficient information about goods or their suppliers
■ Invasion of privacy
■ Cyberfraud

of electronic information, but focuses mainly on the information associated with payments (e.g., a credit card number) and the payments themselves, that is, the "electronic money." An organization must consider such issues as encryption, secure socket layers (SSL), and secure electronic transactions (SET), as explained in Figure 3.26.

Intermediaries

Intermediaries are agents, software, or businesses that bring buyers and sellers together that provide a trading infrastructure to enhance ebusiness. With the introduction of ecommerce there was much discussion about disintermediation of middle people/organizations; however, recent developments in ebusiness have seen more reintermediation. *Reintermediation* refers to using the Internet to reassemble buyers, sellers, and other partners in a traditional supply chain in new ways. Examples include New York-based e-Steel Corp. and Philadelphia-based PetroChem-Net Inc. bringing together producers, traders, distributors, and buyers of steel and chemicals, respectively, in web-based marketplaces. Figure 3.27 lists intermediaries and their functions.

 L03.8

Explain why an organization would use metrics to determine a website's success.

FIGURE **3.26** Ebusiness Security

Ebusiness Security

Encryption scrambles information into an alternative form that requires a key or password to decrypt the information. Encryption is achieved by scrambling letters, replacing letters, replacing letters with numbers, and other ways.

A *secure socket layer (SSL)* (1) creates a secure and private connection between a client and server computer, (2) encrypts the information, and (3) sends the information over the Internet. SSL is identified by a website address that includes an "s" at the end—http**s**.

A *secure electronic transaction (SET)* is a transmission security method that ensures transactions are secure and legitimate. Similar to SSL, SET encrypts information before sending it over the Internet. However, SET also enables customer authentication for credit card transactions. SETs are endorsed by major ecommerce players including MasterCard, American Express, Visa, Netscape, and Microsoft.

MEASURING EBUSINESS SUCCESS

Traffic on the Internet retail site for Walmart grew 66 percent in one year. The site receives over 500,000 visitors daily (6.5 million per week), downloads 2 million web pages daily, and averages 60,000 users logged on simultaneously. Walmart's primary concern is maintaining optimal performance for online transactions. A disruption to the website directly affects the company's bottom line and customer loyalty. The company monitors and tracks the hardware, software, and network running the company's website to ensure high quality of service.[35]

The Yankee Group reports that 66 percent of companies determine website success solely by measuring the amount of

FIGURE **3.27** Types of Intermediaries

Type of Intermediary	Description	Example
Internet service providers	Make money selling a service, not a product	Earthlink.com, Comcast.com, AOL.com
Portals	Central hubs for online content	Yahoo.com, MSN.com, Google.com
Content providers	Use the Internet to distribute copyrighted content	wsj.com, cnn.com, espn.com
Online brokers	Intermediaries between buyers and sellers of goods and services	charlesschwab.com, fidelity.com, datek.com
Market makers	Aggregate three services for market participants: a place, rules, and infrastructure	amazon.com, ebay.com, priceline.com
Online service providers	Extensive online array of services	xdrive.com, lawinfo.com
Intelligent agents	Software applications that follow instructions and learn independently	Sidestep.com, WebSeeker.com, iSpyNOW.com
Application service providers	Sell access to Internet-based software applications to other companies	ariba.com, commerceone.com, ibm.com
Infomediaries	Provide specialized information on behalf of producers of goods and services and their potential customers	autobytel.com, BizRate.com

FIGURE   3.28   Website Effectiveness Metrics

Effectiveness Website Metrics

Cookie—a small file deposited on a hard drive by a website containing information about customers and their web activities. Cookies allow websites to record the comings and goings of customers, usually without their knowledge or consent.

Click-through—a count of the number of people who visit one site and click on an advertisement that takes them to the site of the advertiser. Tracking effectiveness based on click-throughs guarantees exposure to target ads; however, it does not guarantee that the visitor liked the ad, spent any substantial time viewing the ad, or was satisfied with the information contained in the ad.

Banner ad—advertises the products and services of another business, usually another dot-com business. Advertisers can track how often customers click on banner ads resulting in a click-through to their website. Often the cost of the banner ad depends on the number of customers who click on the banner ad. Tracking the number of banner ad clicks is one way to understand the effectiveness of the ad on its target audience.

traffic. Unfortunately, large amounts of website traffic does not necessarily indicate large sales. Many websites with lots of traffic have minimal sales. The best way to measure a site's success is to measure such things as the revenue generated by web traffic, the number of new customers acquired by web traffic, and any reductions in customer service calls resulting from web traffic.[36]

Ashley Qualls is not your average high school student; the 17-year-old is the CEO of a million-dollar business. Ashley is the head of whateverlife.com, a website she started when she was just 14—with $8 borrowed from her mother. Now, just three years later, the website grosses more than $1 million a year, providing Ashley and her working-class family a sense of security they had never really known. This teenage CEO bought her family a four-bedroom house and built herself an office in the basement. It all started with capitalism 101, the law of supply and demand. Ashley became interested in graphic design just as the online social networking craze began to catch fire. When she saw her friends personalizing their MySpace pages, she began creating MySpace background designs through Whateverlife. The designs are cheery, colorful, and whimsical, with lots of hearts, Ashley's favorites.

Website Metrics

Figure 3.28 displays a few metrics an organization can use to measure website effectiveness.

To help understand advertising effectiveness, interactivity measures are tracked and monitored. ***Interactivity*** measures

> Tying purchase amounts to website visits makes it easy to communicate the business value of the website.

the visitor interactions with the target ad. Such interaction measures include the duration of time the visitor spends viewing the ad, the number of pages viewed, and even the number of repeat visits to the target ad. Interactivity measures are a giant step forward for advertisers, since traditional advertising methods—newspapers, magazines, radio, and television—provide few ways to track effectiveness metrics. Interactivity metrics measure actual consumer activities, something that was impossible to do in the past, and provide advertisers with tremendous amounts of business intelligence.

The ultimate outcome of any advertisement is a purchase. Tying purchase amounts to website visits makes it easy to communicate the business value of the website. Organizations use metrics to tie revenue amounts and new customer creation numbers directly back to the websites or banner ads. Organizations can observe through ***clickstream data*** the exact pattern of a consumer's navigation through a site. Clickstream data can reveal a number of basic data points on how consumers interact with websites. Figure 3.29 displays different types of clickstream metrics.

Marc Barach is the co-inventor and chief marketing officer of Ingenio, a start-up company that specializes in connecting people in real-time. When the Internet first emerged, banner ads were the prevalent marketing tools. Next came pay-per-click where the company pays the search engine each time its website is accessed from a search. Today 35 percent of online spending occurs through pay-per-clicks. Unfortunately,

> ## A GROWING NUMBER OF COMPANIES ARE ALREADY USING THE INTERNET TO STREAMLINE THEIR BUSINESS PROCESSES, PROCURE MATERIALS, SELL PRODUCTS, AUTOMATE CUSTOMER SERVICE, AND CREATE NEW REVENUE STREAMS.

pay-per-clicks are not suitable for all businesses. Roofers, plumbers, auto repair people, and cosmetic surgeons rarely have websites and do not generate business via pay-per-clicks. Barach believes that the next line of Internet advertising will be pay-per-call, and Ingenio has invested five years and $50 million in building the platform to run the business. Here is how pay-per-call works:

- The user types a keyword into a search engine.
- The search engine passes the keyword to Ingenio.
- Ingenio determines the category and sends back the appropriate merchant's unique, traceable 800 telephone number.
- The 800 number routes through Ingenio's switches, and Ingenio charges the merchant when a customer calls.

A Jupiter Research study discovered that businesses were willing to pay between $2 and $35 for each call lead.[37]

Figure 3.30 provides definitions of common metrics based on clickstream data. To interpret such data properly, managers try to benchmark against other companies. For instance, consumers seem to visit their preferred websites regularly, even checking back to the website multiple times during a given session. Consumers tend to become loyal to a small number of sites, and they tend to revisit those sites a number of times during a particular session.

 L03.9

Describe ebusiness along with its benefits and challenges.

EBUSINESS BENEFITS AND CHALLENGES

According to an NUA Internet Survey, the Internet links more than 1 billion people worldwide. Experts expected global Internet usage to nearly triple between 2006 and 2010, making ebusiness a more significant factor in the global economy. As ebusiness improves, organizations will experience benefits and challenges alike. Figure 3.31 details ebusiness benefits for an organization.

The Internet is forcing organizations to refocus their information systems from the inside out. A growing number of companies are already using the Internet to streamline their business processes, procure materials, sell products, automate

FIGURE 3.29 Clickstream Data Metrics

Clickstream Data Metrics
■ The number of page views (i.e., the number of times a particular page has been presented to a visitor).
■ The pattern of websites visited, including most frequent exit page and most frequent prior website.
■ Length of stay on the website.
■ Dates and times of visits.
■ Number of registrations filled out per 100 visitors.
■ Number of abandoned registrations.
■ Demographics of registered visitors.
■ Number of customers with shopping carts.
■ Number of abandoned shopping carts.

FIGURE 3.30 Definitions of Website Metrics

Visitor	Visitor Metrics
Unidentified visitor	A visitor is an individual who visits a website. An "unidentified visitor" means that no information about that visitor is available.
Unique visitor	A unique visitor is one who can be recognized and counted only once within a given period of time. An accurate count of unique visitors is not possible without some form of identification, registration, or authentication.
Session visitor	A session ID is available (e.g., cookie) or inferred by incoming address plus browser type, which allows a visitor's responses to be tracked within a given visit to a website.
Tracked visitor	An ID (e.g., cookie) is available that allows a user to be tracked across multiple visits to a website. No information, other than a unique identifier, is available for a tracked visitor.
Identified visitor	An ID is available (e.g., cookie or voluntary registration) that allows a user to be tracked across multiple visits to a website. Other information (name, demographics, possibly supplied voluntarily by the visitor) can be linked to this ID.
Exposure	Exposure Metrics
Page exposures (page-views)	The number of times a particular web page has been viewed by visitors in a given time period, without regard to duplication.
Site exposures	The number of visitor sessions at a website in a given time period, without regard to visitor duplication.
Visit	Visit Metrics
Stickiness (visit duration time)	The length of time a visitor spends on a website. Can be reported as an average in a given time period, without regard to visitor duplication.
Raw visit depth (total web pages exposure per session)	The total number of pages a visitor is exposed to during a single visit to a website. Can be reported as an average or distribution in a given time period, without regard to visitor duplication.
Visit depth (total unique web pages exposure per session)	The total number of unique pages a visitor is exposed to during a single visit to a website. Can be reported as an average or distribution in a given time period, without regard to visitor duplication.
Hit	Hit Metrics
Hits	When visitors reach a website, their computer sends a request to the site's computer server to begin displaying pages. Each element of a requested page (including graphics, text, interactive items) is recorded by the website's server log file as a "hit."
Qualified hits	Exclude less important information recorded in a log file (such as error messages, etc.).

FIGURE 3.31 Ebusiness Benefits

Ebusiness Benefits	
Highly Accessible	Businesses can operate 24 hours a day, 7 days a week, 365 days a year.
Increased Customer Loyalty	Additional channels to contact, respond to, and access customers helps contribute to customer loyalty.
Improved Information Content	In the past, customers had to order catalogs or travel to a physical facility before they could compare price and product attributes. Electronic catalogs and web pages present customers with updated information in real-time about goods, services, and prices.
Increased Convenience	Ebusiness automates and improves many of the activities that make up a buying experience.
Increased Global Reach	Business, both small and large, can reach new markets.
Decreased Cost	The cost of conducting business on the Internet is substantially smaller than traditional forms of business communication.

customer service, and create new revenue streams. Although the benefits of ebusiness systems are enticing, developing, deploying, and managing these systems is not always easy. Unfortunately, ebusiness is not something a business can just go out and buy. Figure 3.32 details the challenges facing ebusiness.

A key element of emarketplaces is their ability to provide not only transaction capabilities but also dynamic, relevant content to trading partners. The original ebusiness websites provided shopping cart capabilities built around product catalogs. As a result of the complex emarketplace that must support existing business processes and systems, content is becoming even more critical for emarketplaces. Buyers need good content description to make informed purchases, and sellers use content to properly market and differentiate themselves from the competition. Content and product description establish the common understanding between both parties to the transaction. As a result, the accessibility, usability, accuracy, and richness of that content directly affect the transaction. Figure 3.33 displays the different benefits and challenges of various emarketplace revenue models.

FIGURE 3·3² Ebusiness Challenges

Ebusiness Challenges	
Protecting Consumers	Consumers must be protected against unsolicited goods and communication, illegal or harmful goods, insufficient information about goods or their suppliers, invasion of privacy, and cyberfraud.
Leveraging Existing Systems	Most companies already use information technology to conduct business in non-Internet environments, such as marketing, order management, billing, inventory, distribution, and customer service. The Internet represents an alternative and complementary way to do business, but it is imperative that ebusiness systems integrate existing systems in a manner that avoids duplicating functionality and maintains usability, performance, and reliability.
Increasing Liability	Ebusiness exposes suppliers to unknown liabilities because Internet commerce law is vaguely defined and differs from country to country. The Internet and its use in ebusiness have raised many ethical, social, and political issues, such as identity theft and information manipulation.
Providing Security	The Internet provides universal access, but companies must protect their assets against accidental or malicious misuse. System security, however, must not create prohibitive complexity or reduce flexibility. Customer information also needs to be protected from internal and external misuse. Privacy systems should safeguard the personal information critical to building sites that satisfy customer and business needs. A serious deficiency arises from the use of the Internet as a marketing means. Sixty percent of Internet users do not trust the Internet as a payment channel. Making purchases via the Internet is considered unsafe by many. This issue affects both the business and the consumer. However, with encryption and the development of secure websites, security is becoming less of a constraint for ebusinesses.
Adhering to Taxation Rules	The Internet is not yet subject to the same level of taxation as traditional businesses. While taxation should not discourage consumers from using electronic purchasing channels, it should not favor Internet purchases over store purchases either. Instead, a tax policy should provide a level playing field for traditional retail businesses, mail-order companies, and Internet-based merchants. The Internet marketplace is rapidly expanding, yet it remains mostly free from traditional forms of taxation. In one recent study, uncollected state and local sales taxes from ebusiness were projected to exceed $60 billion in 2008.

Revenue Models	Advantages	Limitation
Transaction fees	■ Can be directly tied to savings (both process and price savings) ■ Important revenue source when high level of liquidity (transaction volume) is reached	■ If process savings are not completely visible, use of the system is discouraged (incentive to move transactions offline) ■ Transaction fees likely to decrease with time
License fees	■ Creates incentives to do many transactions ■ Customization and back-end integration leads to lock-in of participants	■ Up-front fee is a barrier to entry for participants ■ Price differentiation is complicated
Subscription fees	■ Creates incentives to do transactions ■ Price can be differentiated ■ Possibility to build additional revenue from new user groups	■ Fixed fee is a barrier to entry for participants
Fees for value-added services	■ Service offering can be differentiated ■ Price can be differentiated ■ Possibility to build additional revenue from established and new user groups (third parties)	■ Cumbersome process for customers to continually evaluate new services
Advertising fees	■ Well-targeted advertisements can be perceived as value-added content by trading participants ■ Easy to implement	■ Limited revenue potential ■ Overdone or poorly targeted advertisements can be disturbing elements on the website

FIGURE 3·34 Extended Ebusiness Models

	Business	Consumer	Government
Business	B2B conisint.com	B2C dell.com	B2G lockheedmartin.com
Consumer	C2B priceline.com	C2C ebay.com	C2G eGov.com
Government	G2B export.gov	G2C medicare.gov	G2G disasterhelp.gov

LO3.10

Define mcommerce and explain how an egovernment could use it to increase its efficiency and effectiveness.

NEW TRENDS IN EBUSINESS: EGOVERNMENT AND MCOMMERCE

Recent business models that have arisen to enable organizations to take advantage of the Internet and create value are within egovernment. *Egovernment* involves the use of strategies and technologies to transform government(s) by improving the delivery of services and enhancing the quality of interaction between the citizen-consumer within all branches of government (refer to Figure 3.34).

One example of an egovernment portal, FirstGov.gov, the official U.S. gateway to all government information, is the catalyst for a growing electronic government. Its powerful search engine and ever-growing collection of topical and customer-focused links connect users to millions of web pages, from the federal government, to local and tribal governments, to foreign nations around the world. Figure 3.35 highlights specific egovernment models.

FIGURE 3·35 Egovernment Models

Egovernment Models	
Consumer-to-government (C2G)	C2G will mainly constitute the areas where a consumer (or citizen) interacts with the government. It will include areas like elections, when citizens vote for government officials; census, where the consumer provides demographic information to the government; taxation, where the consumer is paying taxes to the government.
Government-to-business (G2B)	This model includes all government interaction with business enterprises whether it is procurement of goods and services from suppliers or information regarding legal and business issues that is transmitted electronically.
Government-to-consumer (G2C)	Governments around the world are now dealing with consumers (or citizens) electronically, providing them with updated information. Governments are also processing applications for visas, renewal of passports and driver's licenses, advertising of tender notices, and other services online.
Government-to-government (G2G)	Governments around the world are now dealing with other governments electronically. Still at an inception stage, this ebusiness model will enhance international trade and information retrieval, for example, on criminal records of new migrants. At the state level, information exchange and processing of transactions online will enable enhanced efficiencies.

FIGURE | 3.36 | Mcommerce Technology Overview

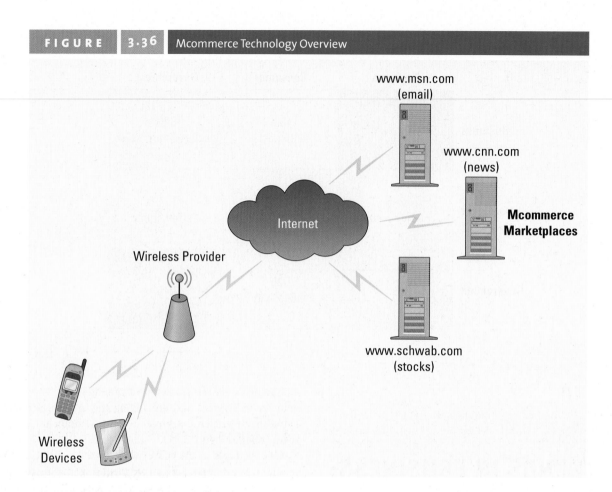

Mobile commerce, or mcommerce, is the ability to purchase goods and services through a wireless Internet-enabled device.

Mcommerce

In a few years, Internet-enabled mobile devices will outnumber PCs. *Mobile commerce, or mcommerce,* is the ability to purchase goods and services through a wireless Internet-enabled device. The emerging technology behind mcommerce is a mobile device equipped with a web-ready micro-browser. To take advantage of the mcommerce market potential, handset manufacturers Nokia, Ericsson, Motorola, and Qualcomm are working with tele-communication carriers AT&T Wireless and Sprint to develop smartphones. Using new forms of technology, smartphones offer fax, email, and phone capabilities all in one, paving the way for mcommerce to be accepted by an increasingly mobile workforce. Figure 3.36 gives a visual overview of mcommerce.

Amazon.com has collaborated with Nokia to pioneer a new territory. With the launch of its Amazon.com Anywhere service, it has become one of the first major online retailers to recognize and do something about the potential of Internet-enabled wireless devices. As content delivery over wireless devices becomes faster, more secure, and scalable, mcommerce will surpass landline ebusiness (traditional telephony) as the method of choice for digital commerce transactions. According to the research firm Strategy Analytics, the global mcommerce market was expected to be worth more than $200 billion by 2005, with some 350 million customers generating almost 14 billion transactions annually. Additionally, information activities like email, news, and stock quotes will progress to personalized transactions, "one-click" travel reservations, online auctions, and video-conferencing.[38]

Organizations face changes more extensive and far reaching in their implications than anything since the modern industrial revolution occurred in the early 1900s. Technology is a primary force driving these changes. Organizations that want to survive must recognize the immense power of technology, carry out required organizational changes in the face of it, and learn to operate in an entirely different way. ∎

What Is Email Shouting?

When you start working, chances are you will use email to communicate with your boss, colleagues, and customers. Glaring errors, such as misspellings and poor grammar, are simply unacceptable in corporate email. The following is basic email etiquette all students should use:

- **Email name:** lil_cutie_baby_79@email.com will not be taken seriously by potential employers. Drop your high school and college emails and create a professional email account using Google Gmail or Hotmail and FirstnameLastname@email.com.

- **Spelling and grammar:** All emails must display good spelling and grammar, and you must always run spell check prior to sending your email. In fact, you can set this as an automatic task in most email systems. Please be aware that spell check cannot distinguish between alternative spellings of the same word such as there, their, and they're or to, two, and too, so check your grammar, also.

- **Be brief:** Emails should be brief—end of story. Provide your reader with the email purpose as quickly as you can, and be sure to include the necessary detail. Using bullets is a great idea if you have many points to make as it is easier for the reader to quickly comprehend your email.

- **No abbreviations plz:** Do not use text messaging abbreviations in emails. You would not walk around the office talking in code, so do not use it in your email.

- **DO NOT YELL:** Be careful when using ALL CAPS as it can appear that you are yelling. It is inappropriate to yell in the work environment.

- **Never hit "Reply All":** From this day forward, pretend that that feature is disconnected. There is nothing more embarrassing than hitting reply all and telling everyone on the email list your confidential information. Make it a rule to never hit "reply all." Hit "reply" and add each name individually. I know this sounds painful, but it is not nearly as painful as the embarrassment of telling everyone in your organization your height, weight, birth date, and Social Security number when replying to an HR survey.

Email etiquette sounds more like common sense than anything else, so why is it important to follow at work? What might happen to your job if you sent out an emarketing campaign containing spelling and grammatical errors? There is a saying that the Internet can make mistakes happen faster. What do you think that means? What can you do to ensure you avoid email blunders?

CHECK OUT www.mhhe.com/baltzanm

for additional study materials including quizzes and PowerPoint presentations.

coming up

Module Two concentrates on the essential components of information systems. Most people view IT strictly from a technological paradigm, but in fact, IT's power and influence is not so much a factor of its technical nature, but rather of what that technical infrastructure carries, houses, and supports: information. And information is power to an organization. This Module highlights this point and raises awareness of the significance of information to organizational success. Understanding how enterprise architectures support information, how employees access and analyze information to make business decisions, and how wireless and mobile technologies can enable information access 24x7 are the primary learning goals of Module Two. Properly managing information is a key organizational resource and can give a company a definite competitive advantage over competitors. The bottom line is that managers who treat information as a corporate asset yield success in the marketplace.

The module begins by covering information ethics and information security. With the many new governance and compliance regulations, all managers must understand the ethical issues surrounding information. As a key organizational resource, information must be protected from misuse and harm. This involves addressing ethical concerns around the collection, storage, and usage of information; protecting information privacy; and ensuring that information is secure against unauthorized access and attack. ■

Essentials of Information Systems

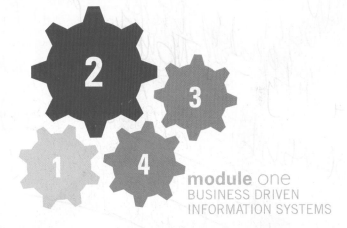

module one
BUSINESS DRIVEN
INFORMATION SYSTEMS

module two
ESSENTIALS OF INFORMATION
SYSTEMS
ch. 4 Ethics and Information Security
ch. 5 Enterprise Architectures
ch. 6 Databases and Data Warehouses
ch. 7 Networks, Telecommunications,
and Mobile Technology

module three
ENTERPRISE
INFORMATION SYSTEMS

module four
DEVELOPING
INFORMATION SYSTEMS

ethics
+ information
security

chapter four

This chapter concerns itself with protecting information from potential misuse. Organizations must ensure they collect, capture, store, and use information in an ethical manner. This could be any type of information they collect and utilize, including information about customers, partners, and employees. Companies must ensure that personal information collected about someone remains private. This is not just a nice thing to do. The law requires it. Perhaps more importantly, information must be physically kept secure to prevent access and possible dissemination and use by unauthorized sources.

You, the business student, must understand ethics and security because they are the top concerns voiced by customers today. These concerns directly influence a customer's likelihood to embrace electronic technologies and conduct business over the web. In this sense, these concerns affect a company's bottom line. You can find evidence in recent news reports about how the stock price of organizations dramatically falls when information privacy and security breaches are made known. Further, organizations face potential litigation if they fail to meet their ethical, privacy, and security obligations concerning the handling of information in their companies.

Ethics and security are two fundamental building blocks for all organizations. In recent years, such events as the Enron and Martha Stewart scandals along with 9/11 have shed new light on the meaning of ethics and security. When the behavior of a few individuals can destroy billion-dollar organizations, the value of ethics and security should be evident.

●● SECTION 4.1 Ethics

LEARNING OUTCOMES

LO4.1 Explain the ethical issues surrounding information technology.

LO4.2 Identify the differences between an ethical computer use policy and an acceptable use policy.

LO4.3 Describe the relationship between an email privacy policy and an Internet use policy.

LO4.4 Explain the effects of spam on an organization.

LO4.5 Summarize the different monitoring technologies and explain the importance of an employee monitoring policy.

ETHICS

Ian Clarke, the inventor of a file-swapping service called Freenet, decided to leave the United States for the United Kingdom, where copyright laws are more lenient. Wayne Rosso, the inventor of a file-sharing service called Grokster, left the United States for Spain, again saying goodbye to tough U.S. copyright protections. The U.S. copyright laws, designed decades before the invention of the Internet, make file sharing and many other Internet technologies illegal. Although some individuals use file sharing in unethical manners, such as downloading music and movies illegally, file sharing has many positive benefits, such as improving drug research, software development, and the flow of information.[1]

The ethical issues surrounding copyright infringement and intellectual property rights are consuming the ebusiness world. Advances in technology make it easier for people to copy everything from music to pictures. Technology poses new challenges for our **ethics**—the principles and standards that guide our behavior toward other people. Review Figure 4.1 for an overview of concepts, terms, and ethical issues stemming from advances in technology.

The Securities Exchange Commission (SEC) began inquiries into Enron's accounting practices on October 22, 2001. David Duncan, the Arthur Andersen partner in charge of Enron, instructed his team to begin destroying paper and electronic Enron-related records on October 23, 2001. Kimberly Latham, a subordinate to Duncan, sent instructions on October 24, 2001, to her entire team to follow Duncan's orders and even compiled a list of computer files to delete. Arthur Andersen blames Duncan for destroying thousands of Enron-related documents. Duncan blames the Arthur Andersen attorney, Nancy Temple, for sending him a memo instructing him to destroy files. Temple blames Arthur Andersen's document deletion policies.[2]

Regardless of who is to blame, the bigger issue is that the destruction of files after a federal investigation has begun is both unethical and illegal. A direct corporate order to destroy information currently under federal investigation poses a dilemma for any professional. Comply, and you participate in potentially criminal activities; refuse, and you might find yourself looking for a new job.

Privacy is one of the largest ethical issues facing organizations. **Privacy** is the right to be left alone when you want to be, to have control over your own personal possessions, and not to be observed without your consent. Privacy is related to **confidentiality**, which is the assurance that messages and information are available only to those who are authorized to view them. Some of the most problematic decisions facing organizations lie in the murky and turbulent waters of privacy. The burden comes from the knowledge that each time employees make a decision regarding issues of privacy, the outcome could potentially sink the company.

Trust between companies, customers, partners, and suppliers is the support structure of ebusiness. One of the main ingredients in

FIGURE 4.1	Technology-Related Ethical Issues
Intellectual property	Intangible creative work that is embodied in physical form.
Copyright	The legal protection afforded an expression of an idea, such as a song, video game, and some types of proprietary documents.
Fair use doctrine	In certain situations, it is legal to use copyrighted material.
Pirated software	The unauthorized use, duplication, distribution, or sale of copyrighted software.
Counterfeit software	Software that is manufactured to look like the real thing and sold as such.

trust is privacy. Privacy continues to be one of the primary barriers to the growth of ebusiness. People are concerned their privacy will be violated because of interactions on the web. Unless an organization can effectively address this issue of privacy, its customers, partners, and suppliers might lose trust in the organization, which would hurt its business. In keeping with its mandate to gather intelligence, the CIA is watching YouTube. U.S. spies, now under the Director of National Intelligence (DNI), are looking increasingly online for intelligence; they have become major consumers of social media. "We're looking at YouTube, which carries some unique and honest-to-goodness intelligence," said Doug Naquin, director of the DNI Open Source Center. "We're looking at chat rooms and things that didn't exist five years ago, and trying to stay ahead. We have groups looking at what they call 'Citizens Media': people taking pictures with their cell phones and posting them on the Internet." Figure 4.2 displays the results from a *CIO* survey as to how privacy issues reduce trust for ebusinesses.

●● LO4.1

Explain the ethical issues surrounding information technology.

FIGURE **4.2** Trust and Ebusiness

Primary Reasons Privacy Issues Reduce Trust for Ebusiness

1. Loss of personal privacy
2. Thirty-seven percent of Internet users are "a lot" more inclined to purchase a product on a website that has a privacy policy
3. Effective privacy and security would convert more Internet users to Internet buyers

INFORMATION ETHICS

Information ethics concerns the ethical and moral issues arising from the development and use of information technologies, as well as the creation, collection, duplication, distribution, and processing of information itself (with or without the aid of computer technologies). Individuals determine how to use information and how information affects them. How individuals behave toward each other, how they handle information and technology, are largely influenced by their ethics. Ethical dilemmas usually arise not in simple, clear-cut situations but out of a clash between competing goals, responsibilities, and loyalties. Inevitably, the decision process has more than one socially acceptable "correct" decision. Figure 4.3 contains examples of ethically questionable or unacceptable uses of information technology.

My **Not** To-Do List

Do You Really Want to Risk it?

Ethics. It's just one tiny word, but it has monumental impact on every area of business. From the magazines, blogs, and newspapers you read to the courses you take, you will encounter ethics because it is a hot topic in today's electronic world. Technology has provided so many incredible opportunities, but it has also provided those same opportunities to unethical people. Discuss the ethical issues surrounding each of the following situations (yes, these are true stories):

- A girl raises her hand in class and states "I can legally copy any DVD I get from Netflix because Netflix purchased the DVD and the copyright only applies to the company who purchased the product."
- A student stands up the first day of class before the professor arrives and announces that his fraternity scans textbooks and

that he has the textbook for this course on his thumb drive, which he will gladly sell for $20. Several students pay on the spot and upload the scanned textbook to their PCs. One student takes down the student information and contacts the publisher about the incident.

- A senior manager is asked to monitor his employee's email because there is a rumor that the employee is looking for another job.
- A vice president of sales asks her employee to burn all of the customer data onto an external hard drive because she made a deal to provide customer information to a strategic partner.
- A senior manager is asked to monitor his employee's email to discover if she is sexually harassing another employee.
- An employee is looking at the shared network drive and discovers his boss's entire hard drive, including his email backup, has been copied to the network and is visible to all.
- An employee is accidently copied on an email that lists the targets for the next round of layoffs.

Examples of Questionable Information Technology Use

Individuals copy, use, and distribute software.

Employees search organizational databases for sensitive corporate and personal information.

Organizations collect, buy, and use information without checking the validity or accuracy of the information.

Individuals create and spread viruses that cause trouble for those using and maintaining IT systems.

Individuals hack into computer systems to steal proprietary information.

Employees destroy or steal proprietary organization information such as schematics, sketches, customer lists, and reports.

People make arguments for or against—justify or condemn—the behaviors in Figure 4.3. Unfortunately, there are few hard and fast rules for always determining what is and is not ethical. Knowing the law will not always help because what is legal might not always be ethical, and what might be ethical is not always legal. For example, Joe Reidenberg received an offer for cell phone service from AT&T Wireless. The offer revealed that AT&T Wireless had used Equifax, a credit reporting agency, to identify Joe Reidenberg as a potential customer. Overall, this strategy seemed like good business. Equifax could generate additional revenue by selling information it already owned and AT&T Wireless could identify target markets, thereby increasing response rates to its marketing campaigns.

Unfortunately, the Fair Credit Reporting Act (FCRA) forbids repurposing credit information except when the information is used for "a firm offer of credit or insurance." In other words, the only product that can be sold based on credit information is credit. A representative for Equifax stated, "As long as AT&T Wireless (or any company for that matter) is offering the cell phone service on a credit basis, such as allowing the use of the service before the consumer has to pay, it is in compliance with the FCRA." However, the question remains—is it ethical?[3]

This is a good example of the ethical dilemmas facing organizations. Because technology is so new and pervasive in unexpected ways, the ethics surrounding information are still being defined. Figure 4.4 displays the four quadrants of ethical and legal behavior. The ideal goal for organizations is to make decisions within quadrant I that are both legal and ethical.

Information Has No Ethics

Jerry Rode, CIO of Saab Cars USA, realized he had a public relations fiasco on his hands when he received an email from an irate customer. Saab had hired four Internet marketing companies to distribute electronic information about Saab's new models

to its customers. Saab specified that the marketing campaign be opt-in, implying that it would contact only the people who had agreed to receive promotions and marketing material via email. Unfortunately, one of the marketing companies apparently had a different definition of opt-in and was emailing all customers regardless of their opt-in decision.

Rode fired the errant marketing company and immediately developed a formal policy for the use of customer information. "The customer doesn't see ad agencies and contracted marketing firms. They see Saab USA spamming them," Rode said. "Finger-pointing after the fact won't make your customers feel better."[4]

Information has no ethics. Information does not care how it is used. It will not stop itself from spamming customers, sharing itself if it is sensitive or personal, or revealing details to third parties. Information cannot delete or preserve itself. Therefore, it falls on the shoulders of those who own the information to develop ethical guidelines on how to manage the information. Figure 4.5 provides an overview of some of the important laws that individuals must follow when they are attempting to manage and protect information.

FIGURE 4·4 Acting Ethically and Legally Are Not Always the Same

	Legal	Illegal
Ethical	I	II
Unethical	III	IV

●● LO4.2

Identify the differences between an ethical computer use policy and an acceptable use policy.

●● LO4.3

Describe the relationship between an email privacy policy and an Internet use policy.

●● LO4.4

Explain the effects of spam on an organization.

FIGURE 4.5 Established Information-Related Laws

Established Information-Related Laws

Privacy Act—1974	Restricts what information the federal government can collect; allows people to access and correct information on themselves; requires procedures to protect the security of personal information; and forbids the disclosure of name-linked information without permission.
Family Education Rights and Privacy Act—1974	Regulates access to personal education records by government agencies and other third parties and ensures the right of students to see their own records.
Cable Communications Act—1984	Requires written or electronic consent from viewers before cable TV providers can release viewing choices or other personally identifiable information.
Electronic Communications Privacy Act—1986	Allows the reading of communications by a firm and says that employees have no right to privacy when using their companies' computers.
Computer Fraud and Abuse Act—1986	Prohibits unauthorized access to computers used for financial institutions, the U.S. government, or interstate and international trade.
The Bork Bill (officially known as the Video Privacy Protection Act, 1988)	Prohibits the use of video rental information on customers for any purpose other than that of marketing goods and services directly to the customer.
Communications Assistance for Law Enforcement Act—1994	Requires that telecommunications equipment be designed so that authorized government agents are able to intercept all wired and wireless communications being sent or received by any subscriber. The act also requires that subscriber call-identifying information be transmitted to a government when and if required.
Freedom of Information Act—1967, 1975, 1994, and 1998	Allows any person to examine government records unless it would cause an invasion of privacy. It was amended in 1974 to apply to the FBI, and again in 1994 to allow citizens to monitor government activities and information gathering, and once again in 1998 to access government information on the Internet.
Health Insurance Portability and Accountability Act (HIPAA)—1996	Requires that the health care industry formulate and implement regulations to keep patient information confidential.
Identity Theft and Assumption Deterrence Act—1998	Strengthened the criminal laws governing identity theft making it a federal crime to use or transfer identification belonging to another. It also established a central federal service for victims.
USA Patriot Act—2001 and 2003	Allows law enforcement to get access to almost any information, including library records, video rentals, bookstore purchases, and business records when investigating any act of terrorist or clandestine intelligence activities. In 2003, Patriot II broadened the original law.
Homeland Security Act—2002	Provided new authority to government agencies to mine data on individuals and groups including emails and website visits; put limits on the information available under the Freedom of Information Act; and gave new powers to government agencies to declare national heath emergencies.
Sarbanes-Oxley Act—2002	Sought to protect investors by improving the accuracy and reliability of corporate disclosures and requires companies to (1) implement extensive and detailed policies to prevent illegal activity within the company, and (2) to respond in a timely manner to investigate illegal activity.
Fair and Accurate Credit Transactions Act—2003	Included provisions for the prevention of identity theft including consumers' right to get a credit report free each year, requiring merchants to leave all but the last five digits of a credit card number off a receipt, and requiring lenders and credit agencies to take action even before a victim knows a crime has occurred when they notice any circumstances that might indicate identity theft.
CAN-Spam Act—2003	Sought to regulate interstate commerce by imposing limitations and penalties on businesses sending unsolicited email to consumers. The law forbids deceptive subject lines, headers, return addresses, etc., as well as the harvesting of email addresses from websites. It requires businesses that send spam to maintain a do-not-spam list and to include a postal mailing address in the message.

> **"ORGANIZATIONS SHOULD DEVELOP WRITTEN POLICIES ESTABLISHING EMPLOYEE GUIDELINES, PERSONNEL PROCEDURES, AND ORGANIZATIONAL RULES FOR INFORMATION."**

DEVELOPING INFORMATION MANAGEMENT POLICIES

Treating sensitive corporate information as a valuable resource is good management. Building a corporate culture based on ethical principles that employees can understand and implement is responsible management. In an effort to provide guidelines for ethical information management, *CIO* magazine (along with over 100 CIOs) developed six principles for ethical information management displayed in Figure 4.6.

Organizations should develop written policies establishing employee guidelines, personnel procedures, and organizational rules for information. These policies set employee expectations about the organization's practices and standards and protect the organization from misuse of computer systems and IT resources. If an organization's employees use computers at work, the organization should, at a minimum, implement epolicies. ***Epolicies*** are policies and procedures that address the ethical use of computers and Internet usage in the business environment. These policies typically embody the following:

- Ethical computer use policy.
- Information privacy policy.
- Acceptable use policy.
- Email privacy policy.
- Internet use policy.
- Anti-spam policy.

FIGURE 4.6 *CIO* Magazine's Six Principles for Ethical Information Management

Six Principles for Ethical Information Management

1. Information is a valuable corporate asset and should be managed as such, like cash, facilities, or any other corporate asset.
2. The CIO is steward of corporate information and is responsible for managing it over its life cycle—from its generation to its appropriate destruction.
3. The CIO is responsible for controlling access to and use of information, as determined by governmental regulation and corporate policy.
4. The CIO is responsible for preventing the inappropriate destruction of information.
5. The CIO is responsible for bringing technological knowledge to the development of information management practices and policies.
6. The CIO should partner with executive peers to develop and execute the organization's information management policies.

Ethical Computer Use Policy

In a case that illustrates the perils of online betting, a leading Internet poker site reported that a hacker exploited a security flaw to gain an insurmountable edge in high-stakes, no-limit Texas hold-'em tournaments—the ability to see his opponents' hole cards. The cheater, whose illegitimate winnings were estimated at between $400,000 and $700,000 by one victim, was an employee of AbsolutePoker.com, who hacked the system to show that it could be done. Regardless of what business a company operates—even one that many view as unethical—the company must protect itself from unethical employee behavior.

One of the essential steps in creating an ethical corporate culture is establishing an ethical computer use policy. An ***ethical computer use policy*** contains general principles to guide computer user behavior. For example, the ethical computer use policy might explicitly state that users should refrain from playing computer games during working hours. This policy ensures the users know how to behave at work and the organization has a published standard by which to deal with user infractions. For example, after appropriate warnings, the company may terminate an employee who spends significant amounts of time playing computer games at work.

There are variations in how organizations expect their employees to use computers, but in any approach, the overriding principle when seeking appropriate computer use should be informed consent. The users should be *informed* of the rules and, by agreeing to use the system on that basis, *consent* to abide by the rules.

An organization should make a conscientious effort to ensure all users are aware of the policy through formal training and other means. If an organization were to have only one epolicy, it should be an ethical computer use policy since it is the starting point and the umbrella for any other policies the organization might establish.

Information Privacy Policy

Scott Thompson is the executive vice president of Inovant, the company Visa set up to handle its technology. Thompson errs on the side of caution in regard to Visa's information: He bans the use of Visa's customer information for anything outside its intended purpose—billing.

Visa's customer information details how people are spending their money, in which stores, on which days, and even at what time of day. Sales and marketing departments around the country no doubt are salivating at any prospect of gaining access to Visa's databases. "They would love to refine the information into loyalty programs, target markets, or even partnerships with Visa. There are lots of creative people coming up with these ideas. This whole area of information sharing is enormous and growing. For the marketers, the sky's the limit," Thompson said. Privacy specialists along with Thompson developed a strict credit card information policy, which the company follows.

The question now is can Thompson guarantee that unethical use of his information will not occur? Many experts do not believe that he can. In a large majority of cases, the unethical use of information happens not through the malicious scheming of a rogue marketer, but rather unintentionally. For instance, information is collected and stored for some purpose, such as record keeping or billing. Then, a sales or marketing professional figures out another way to use it internally, share it with partners, or sell it to a trusted third party. The information is "unintentionally" used for new purposes. The classic example of this type of unintentional information reuse is the Social Security number, which started simply as a way to identify government retirement benefits and is now used as a sort of universal personal ID, found on everything from drivers' licenses to savings accounts.

An organization that wants to protect its information should develop an information privacy policy. An **information privacy policy** contains general principles regarding information privacy. Figure 4.7 highlights a few guidelines an organization can follow when creating an information privacy policy.

FIGURE	4.7	Organizational Guidelines for Creating an Information Privacy Policy

Creating an Information Privacy Policy

1. **Adoption and implementation of a privacy policy.** An organization engaged in online activities or ebusiness has a responsibility to adopt and implement a policy for protecting the privacy of personal information. Organizations should also take steps that foster the adoption and implementation of effective online privacy policies by the organizations with which they interact, for instance, by sharing best practices with business partners.

2. **Notice and disclosure.** An organization's privacy policy must be easy to find, read, and understand. The policy must clearly state:
   - What information is being collected?
   - The use of information being collected.
   - Possible third-party distribution of that information.
   - The choices available to an individual regarding collection, use, and distribution of the collected information.
   - A statement of the organization's commitment to information security.
   - What steps the organization takes to ensure information quality and access.

3. **Choice and consent.** Individuals must be given the opportunity to exercise choice regarding how personal information collected from them online may be used when such use is unrelated to the purpose for which the information was collected. At a minimum, individuals should be given the opportunity to opt out of such use.

4. **Information security.** Organizations creating, maintaining, using, or disseminating personal information should take appropriate measures to assure its reliability and should take reasonable precautions to protect it from loss, misuse, or alteration.

5. **Information quality and access.** Organizations should establish appropriate processes or mechanisms so that inaccuracies in material personal information, such as account or contact information, may be corrected. Other procedures to assure information quality may include use of reliable sources, collection methods, appropriate consumer access, and protection against accidental or unauthorized alteration.

FIGURE 4.8 Acceptable Use Policy Stipulations

Acceptable Use Policy Stipulations

1. Not using the service as part of violating any law.

2. Not attempting to break the security of any computer network or user.

3. Not posting commercial messages to groups without prior permission.

4. Not performing any nonrepudiation.

5. Not attempting to send junk email or spam to anyone who does not want to receive it.

6. Not attempting to mail bomb a site. A *mail bomb* is sending a massive amount of email to a specific person or system resulting in filling up the recipient's disk space, which, in some cases, may be too much for the server to handle and may cause the server to stop functioning.

Acceptable Use Policy

An *acceptable use policy (AUP)* is a policy that a user must agree to follow in order to be provided access to a network or to the Internet. *Nonrepudiation* is a contractual stipulation to ensure that ebusiness participants do not deny (repudiate) their online actions. A nonrepudiation clause is typically contained in an AUP.

Many businesses and educational facilities require employees or students to sign an acceptable use policy before gaining network access. When signing up with an Internet service provider (ISP), each customer is typically presented with an AUP, which states that they agree to adhere to certain stipulations (see Figure 4.8).

Email Privacy Policy

Email is so pervasive in organizations that it requires its own specific policy. In a recent survey, 80 percent of professional workers identified email as their preferred means of corporate communications. Trends also show a dramatic increase in the adoption rate of instant messaging (IM) in the workplace. While email and IM are common business communication tools, there are risks associated with using them. For instance, a sent email is stored on at least three or four different computers (see Figure 4.9). Simply deleting an email from one computer does not delete it off the other computers. Companies can mitigate many of the risks of using electronic messaging systems

by implementing and adhering to an email privacy policy.[5]

One of the major problems with email is the user's expectations of privacy. To a large extent, this exception is based on the false assumption that email privacy protection exists somehow analogous to that of U.S. first-class mail. This is simply not true. Take the example of London lawyer Richard Phillips. After his secretary spilled a little ketchup on his pants, Phillips demanded restitution from her—via email—in the amount of a measly £4. The subject line of that email: "Ketchup Trousers." The secretary failed to pay immediately, owing to her mother's sudden death, but quickly made the David versus Goliath matter public, humiliating Phillips. His firm later said Phillips had resigned, but it was careful to note that the departure had nothing to do with the trousers incident.

Generally, the organization that owns the email system can operate the system as openly or as privately as it wishes. That means that if the organization wants to read everyone's email, it can do so. If it chooses not to read any, that is allowable too. Hence, it is up to the organization to decide how much, if any, email it is going to read. Then, when it decides, it must inform the users, so that they can consent to this level of intrusion. In other words, an *email privacy policy* details the extent to which email messages may be read by others.

FIGURE 4.9 Email Is Stored on Multiple Computers

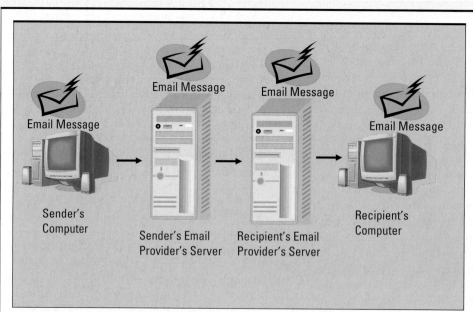

Email Message   Email Message   Email Message   Email Message

Sender's Computer   Sender's Email Provider's Server   Recipient's Email Provider's Server   Recipient's Computer

Deleting an email from the recipient's computer does not delete it from the sender's computer or the provider's computers.

Email privacy

FIGURE 4.10   Email Privacy Policy Stipulations

Email Privacy Policy Stipulations

1. The policy should be complementary to the ethical computer use policy.

2. It defines who legitimate email users are.

3. It explains the backup procedure so users will know that at some point, even if a message is deleted from their computer, it will still be on the backup tapes.

4. It describes the legitimate grounds for reading someone's email and the process required before such action can be taken.

5. It informs that the organization has no control of email once it is transmitted outside the organization.

6. It explains what will happen if the user severs his or her connection with the organization.

7. It asks employees to be careful when making organizational files and documents available to others.

Organizations must create an email privacy policy. Figure 4.10 displays a few of the key stipulations generally contained in an email privacy policy.

Internet Use Policy

Similar to email, the Internet has some unique aspects that make it a good candidate for its own policy. These include the large amounts of computing resources that Internet users can expend, thus making it essential that such use be legitimate. In addition, the Internet contains numerous materials that some believe are offensive and, hence, some regulation is required. An **Internet use policy** contains general principles to guide the proper use of the Internet. Figure 4.11 lists a few important stipulations that might be included in an Internet use policy.

Anti-Spam Policy

Chief technology officer (CTO) of the law firm Fenwick and West, Matt Kesner reduced incoming spam by 99 percent and found himself a corporate hero. Before the spam reduction, the law firm's partners (whose time is worth $350 to $600 an hour)

found themselves spending hours each day sifting through 300 to 500 spam messages. The spam blocking engineered by Kesner traps between 5,000 and 7,000 messages a day.[6]

Spam is unsolicited email. An **anti-spam policy** simply states that email users will not send unsolicited emails (or spam). Spam plagues all levels of employees within an organization from receptionists to CEOs. Estimates indicate that spam accounts for 40 percent to 60 percent of most organizations' email traffic. Ferris Research says spam cost U.S. businesses over $10 billion in 2005, and Nucleus Research stated that companies forfeit $874 per employee annually in lost productivity from spam alone. Spam clogs email systems and siphons IT resources away from legitimate business projects.[7]

It is difficult to write anti-spam policies, laws, or software because there is no such thing as a universal litmus test for spam. One person's spam is another person's newsletter. End users have to be involved in deciding what spam is because what is unwanted can vary widely not just from one company to the next, but from one person to the next. What looks like spam to the rest of the world could be essential business communications for certain employees.

John Zarb, CIO of Libbey, a manufacturer of glassware, china, and flatware, tested Guenivere (a virus and subject-line filter) and SpamAssassin (an open source spam filter). He had to shut them off after 10 days because they were rejecting important legitimate emails. As Zarb quickly discovered, once an organization starts filtering email, it runs the risk of blocking legitimate emails that look like spam. Avoiding an unacceptable level of "false positives" requires a delicate balancing act. The IT team tweaked the spam filters and today, the filters block about 70 percent of Libbey's spam, and Zarb said the "false positive"

fyi

Spam: It's Not Just for Dinner

Spam is a promise of wealth. Spam is an email or newsletter that you didn't ask for but has been sent in bulk by someone you don't even know. The purpose of spam is to make money, and it works because people buy products advertised in junk email. Spammers distribute their emails through spam-friendly ISPs or by turning an unsuspecting individual's computer into a spam-machine (commonly referred to as hijacking). Of course CAN-SPAM, the Controlling the

Assault of Non-Solicited Pornography and Marketing Act of 2003, made spamming illegal, but is has yet to stop spammers. One of the world's most famous spammers, Robert Soloway, was sentenced to 47 months in prison and a $700,000 fine after being convicted of sending spam through hijacked computers with false headers containing Microsoft's MSN and Hotmail addresses, which he used to make the emails appear legitimate. He was also hit by a $7 million lawsuit from Microsoft. Ouch!

The latest spam craze, m-spam or mobile phone spamming, is a form of spam that sends

unsolicited text messages to mobile phones. A new issue associated with m-spam is the cost for the end user. That's right. The end user might have to pay to receive the spam because many wireless carriers charge fees for receiving text messages.

You can bet that someday you are going to be faced with spammers attacking your company and harassing your employees. What can you do to ensure your employees are not inundated with spam? What can you do to ensure none of your employees ever send spam? What are the potential business ramifications if your work computers are hijacked by spammers?

Internet use policy

FIGURE 4.11 Internet Use Policy Stipulations

Internet Use Policy Stipulations

1. The policy should describe available Internet services because not all Internet sites allow users to access all services.

2. The policy should define the organization's position on the purpose of Internet access and what restrictions, if any, are placed on that access.

3. The policy should complement the ethical computer use policy.

4. The policy should describe user responsibility for citing sources, properly handling offensive material, and protecting the organization's good name.

5. The policy should clearly state the ramifications if the policy is violated.

FIGURE 4.12 Spam Prevention Tips

Spam Prevention Tips

- **Disguise email addresses posted in a public electronic place.** When posting an email address in a public place, disguise the address through simple means such as replacing "jsmith@domain.com" with "jsmith at domain dot com." This prevents spam from recognizing the email address.

- **Opt out of member directories that may place an email address online.** Choose not to participate in any activities that place email addresses online. If an email address is placed online be sure it is disguised in some way.

- **Use a filter.** Many ISPs and free email services now provide spam filtering. While filters are not perfect, they can cut down tremendously on the amount of spam a user receives.

rate is far lower, but still not zero. Figure 4.12 highlights a few methods an organization can follow to prevent spam.

L04.5

Summarize the different monitoring technologies and explain the importance of an employee monitoring policy.

ETHICS IN THE WORKPLACE

Concern is growing among employees that infractions of corporate policies—even accidental ones—will be a cause for disciplinary action. The Whitehouse.gov Internet site displays the U.S. president's official website and updates on bill signings and new policies. Whitehouse.com, however, leads to a trashy site that capitalizes on its famous name. A simple mistype from .gov to .com could potentially cost someone her or his job if the company has a termination policy for viewing illicit websites. Monitoring employees is one of the largest issues facing CIOs when they are developing information management policies.

Legal precedents that hold businesses financially responsible for their employees' actions drives the decision of whether to monitor what employees do on company time with corporate resources. Increasingly, employee monitoring is not a choice; it is a risk-management obligation. Michael Soden, CEO of the

Bank of Ireland, issued a mandate stating that company employees could not surf illicit websites with company equipment. Next, he hired Hewlett-Packard to run the IT department. A Hewlett-Packard employee soon discovered illicit websites on Soden's computer. Soden resigned.[8]

A survey of workplace monitoring and surveillance practices by the American Management Association (AMA) and the ePolicy Institute showed the degree to which companies are turning to monitoring:

- 82 percent of the study's 1,627 respondents acknowledged conducting some form of electronic monitoring or physical surveillance.

- 63 percent of the companies stated that they monitor Internet connections.

- 47 percent acknowledged storing and reviewing employee email messages.[9]

Monitoring Technologies

Many employees use their company's high-speed Internet access to shop, browse, and surf the web. Fifty-nine percent of all 2004 web purchases in the United States were made from the workplace, according to ComScore Networks. Vault.com determined that 47 percent of employees spend at least half an hour a day surfing the web.[10]

This research indicates that managers should monitor what their employees are doing with their web access. Most managers do not want their employees conducting personal business during working hours. For these reasons many organizations have increasingly taken the Big Brother approach to web monitoring with software that tracks Internet usage and even allows the boss to read employees' email. Figure 4.13 highlights a few reasons the effects of employee monitoring are worse than the lost productivity from employee web surfing.

This is the thinking at SAS Institute, a private software company consistently ranked in the top 10 on many "Best Places to Work" surveys. SAS does not monitor its employees' web usage. The company asks its employees to use company resources responsibly, but does not mind if they occasionally check sports scores or use the web for shopping.

Many management gurus advocate that organizations whose corporate cultures are based on trust are more successful than those whose corporate cultures are based on distrust.

Before an organization implements monitoring technology it should ask itself, "What does this say about how the organization feels about its employees?" If the organization really does not trust its employees, then perhaps it should find new ones. If an organization does trust its employees, then it might want to treat them accordingly. An organization that follows its employees' every keystroke is unwittingly undermining the relationships with its employees.[11]

Information technology monitoring is tracking people's activities by such measures as number of keystrokes, error rate, and number of transactions processed. Figure 4.14 displays different types of monitoring technologies currently available.

Monitoring employee behavior should not just extend to the employee, but to how employees monitor each other. In 2002 a 14-year-old Canadian boy named Ghyslain Raza innocently swung a golf-ball retriever around in a quiet corner of his high school, pretending he was *The Phantom Menace*'s Darth Maul. He videotaped it, and he left the tape at school, where it was found several months later. Not long after, Raza became an Internet sensation, known today as the "Star Wars kid," with fans adding light-saber effects and music, and creating video revisions that number over a hundred. The embarrassing footage has since become one of the Internet's most popular, hav-

FIGURE   4·13   Employee Monitoring Effects

Employee Monitoring Effects

1. Employee absenteeism is on the rise, hitting 21 percent in 2004. The lesson here might be that more employees are missing work to take care of personal business. Perhaps losing a few minutes here or there—or even a couple of hours—is cheaper than losing entire days.

2. Studies indicate that electronic monitoring results in lower job satisfaction, in part because people begin to believe the quantity of their work is more important than the quality.

3. Electronic monitoring also induces what psychologists call "psychological reactance": the tendency to rebel against constraints. If you tell your employees they cannot shop, they cannot use corporate networks for personal business, and they cannot make personal phone calls, then their desire to do all these things will likely increase.

ing been spoofed on TV shows ranging from *American Dad* to *The Colbert Report* to *Arrested Development*. In 2003, Raza sued the individuals who posted the video online, and the case was settled.

Employee Monitoring Policies

Women are known to engage in a little private chitchat in the ladies' room, but how would they feel if the conversation was broadcast on CNN during a presidential speech? When newsreader Kyra Phillips made a pit stop, she unfortunately left her microphone on, broadcasting the news that her sister-in-law was a "control freak," among numerous other pronouncements. Phillips later laughed it off and even provided a *Late Show* "Top 10" list of excuses for why it happened. Sample: "How was I supposed to know we had a reporter embedded in the bathroom?"

Although this reporter was able to laugh off the incident, an organization must ensure its employees are comfortable with any monitoring it is undertaking, including monitoring the restroom.

The best path for an organization planning to engage in employee monitoring is open communication surrounding the issue. A recent survey discovered that communication about monitoring issues is weak for most organizations. One in five companies did not even have an acceptable use policy and one in four companies did not have an Internet use policy. Companies that did have policies usually tucked them into the rarely probed recesses of the employee handbook, and then the policies tended to be of

FIGURE   4·14   Monitoring Technologies

Common Monitoring Technologies

Key logger, or key trapper, software	A program that, when installed on a computer, records every keystroke and mouse click.
Hardware key logger	A hardware device that captures keystrokes on their journey from the keyboard to the motherboard.
Cookie	A small file deposited on a hard drive by a website containing information about customers and their web activities. Cookies allow websites to record the comings and goings of customers, usually without their knowledge or consent.
Adware	Software that generates ads that install themselves on a computer when a person downloads some other program from the Internet.
Spyware (sneakware or stealthware)	Software that comes hidden in free downloadable software and tracks online movements, mines the information stored on a computer, or uses a computer's CPU and storage for some task the user knows nothing about.
Web log	Consists of one line of information for every visitor to a website and is usually stored on a web server.
Clickstream	Records information about a customer during a web surfing session such as what websites were visited, how long the visit was, what ads were viewed, and what was purchased.

the vague and legal jargon variety: "XYZ company reserves the right to monitor or review any information stored or transmitted on its equipment." Reserving the right to monitor is materially different from clearly stating that the company does monitor, listing what is tracked, describing what is looked for, and detailing the consequences for violations.

An organization must formulate the right monitoring policies and put them into practice. Employee monitoring policies explicitly state how, when, and where the company monitors its employees. CSOs that are explicit about what the company does in the way of monitoring and the reasons for it, along with actively educating their employees about what unacceptable behavior looks like, will find that employees not only acclimate quickly to a policy, but also reduce the CSO's burden by policing themselves. Figure 4.15 displays several common stipulations an organization can follow when creating an employee monitoring policy.

FIGURE 4.15 Employee Monitoring Policy Stipulations

Employee Monitoring Policy Stipulations

1. Be as specific as possible.
2. Always enforce the policy.
3. Enforce the policy in the same way for everyone.
4. Expressly communicate that the company reserves the right to monitor all employees.
5. Specifically state when monitoring will be performed.
6. Specifically state what will be monitored (email, IM, Internet, network activity, etc.).
7. Describe the types of information that will be collected.
8. State the consequences for violating the policy.
9. State all provisions that allow for updates to the policy.
10. Specify the scope and manner of monitoring for any information system.
11. When appropriate, obtain a written receipt acknowledging that each party has received, read, and understood the monitoring policies.

●● SECTION 4.2 Information Security

LEARNING OUTCOMES

L04.6 Describe the relationship between information security policies and an information security plan.

L04.7 Summarize the five steps to creating an information security plan.

L04.8 Provide an example of each of the three primary information security areas: (1) authentication and authorization, (2) prevention and resistance, and (3) detection and response.

L04.9 Describe the relationships and differences between hackers and viruses.

HOW MUCH WILL DOWNTIME COST YOUR BUSINESS?

The old business axiom "time is money" needs to be updated to more accurately reflect the crucial interdependence between IT and business processes. To reflect the times, the phrase should state "uptime is money." The leading cause of downtime is a software failure followed by human error, according to Infonetics research. Unplanned downtime can strike at any time from

BUSTED I'm Being Fired for Smoking, but I Was at Home and It Was Saturday

If on the weekend you like to smoke and eat fast food, you need to be careful, not because it is bad for you but because it just might get you fired. Corporations are starting to implement policies against smoking and obesity and are testing their employees for tobacco use and high-blood pressure. If the tests are positive, the employee can face fines or even dismissal. At Weyco Inc., four employees were fired for refusing to take a test to determine whether they smoke cigarettes. Weyco

Inc. adopted a policy that mandates that employees who smoke will be fired, even if the smoking happens after business hours or at home. Howard Weyers, Weyco founder, believes the anti-smoking policies were designed to protect the firm from high health care costs. "I don't want to pay for the results of smoking," states Weyers.

Minority and pregnant woman are protected by law from discrimination in the workplace. Unfortunately, if you have a

few bad habits, you are on your own. How would you feel if you were fired because you were smoking on the weekend? Do you agree that unhealthy habits warrant disciplinary actions? If companies are allowed to implement policies against smoking and obesity, what unhealthy habit might be next? To date, there have not been any policies on the consumption of alcohol outside of work. Do you agree that overeating and smoking are worse than a drinking habit?

> ## THE OLD BUSINESS AXIOM "TIME IS MONEY" NEEDS TO BE UPDATED TO MORE ACCURATELY REFLECT THE CRUCIAL INTERDEPENDENCE BETWEEN IT AND BUSINESS PROCESSES. TO REFLECT THE TIMES, THE PHRASE SHOULD STATE "UPTIME IS MONEY."

any number of causes, ranging from tornadoes to sink overflows to network failures to power outages. Although natural disasters may appear to be the most devastating causes of IT outages, they are hardly the most frequent or biggest threats to uptime. Figure 4.16 highlights sources of unplanned downtime.

According to Gartner Group, on average, enterprises lose $108,000 of revenue every hour their IT infrastructure is down. Figure 4.17 displays the four categories associated with downtime, according to the Gartner Group. A few questions companies should ask when determining the cost of downtime include:

- How many transactions can the company afford to lose without significantly impacting business?
- Does the company depend upon one or more mission-critical applications to conduct business?
- How much revenue will the company lose for every hour a critical application is unavailable?
- What is the productivity cost associated with each hour of downtime?

- How will collaborative business processes with partners, suppliers, and customers be affected by an unexpected IT outage?
- What is the total cost of lost productivity and lost revenue during unplanned downtime?

The reliability and resilience of IT systems have never been more essential for success as businesses cope with the forces of globalization, 24 × 7 operations, government and trade regulations, and overextended IT budgets and resources. Any unexpected IT downtime in today's business environment has the potential to cause both short- and long-term costs with far-reaching consequences. Section 4.2 explains how you can use security to combat the threat of downtime. Understanding how to secure a business network is critical to keeping downtime to a minimum and uptime to a maximum.

PROTECTING INTELLECTUAL ASSETS

Smoking is not just bad for a person's health; it seems that it is also bad for company security. With companies banning smoking inside their offices, smokers are forced outside—usually to specific smoking areas in the back of the building. The doors leading out to them are a major security hole, according to a study undertaken by NTA Monitor Ltd., a U.K.-based Internet security tester.

NTA's tester was able to easily get inside a corporate building through a back door that was left open so smokers could easily and quickly get out and then back in, according to the company. Once inside, the tester asked an employee to take him to a meeting room, claiming the IT department had sent him. Even without a pass, he reportedly gained access unchallenged and was then able to connect his laptop to the company's network.

Organizational information is intellectual capital. Just as organizations protect their assets—keeping their money in an insured bank or providing a safe working environment for employees—they must also protect their intellectual capital. An organization's intellectual capital includes everything from its patents

FIGURE	4.16	Sources of Unplanned Downtime

Sources of Unplanned Downtime		
Bomb threat	Hacker	Snowstorm
Burst pipe	Hail	Sprinkler malfunction
Chemical spill	Hurricane	Static electricity
Construction	Ice storm	Strike
Corrupted data	Insects	Terrorism
Earthquake	Lightning	Theft
Electrical short	Network failure	Tornado
Epidemic	Plane crash	Train derailment
Equipment failure	Frozen pipe	Smoke damage
Evacuation	Power outage	Vandalism
Explosion	Power surge	Vehicle crash
Fire	Rodents	Virus
Flood	Sabotage	Water damage (various)
Fraud	Shredded data	Wind

FIGURE | **4·17** | The Cost of Downtime

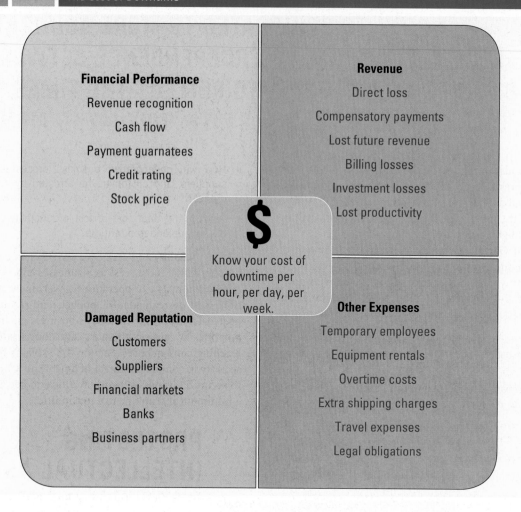

Financial Performance

Revenue recognition

Cash flow

Payment guarnatees

Credit rating

Stock price

Revenue

Direct loss

Compensatory payments

Lost future revenue

Billing losses

Investment losses

Lost productivity

$

Know your cost of downtime per hour, per day, per week.

Damaged Reputation

Customers

Suppliers

Financial markets

Banks

Business partners

Other Expenses

Temporary employees

Equipment rentals

Overtime costs

Extra shipping charges

Travel expenses

Legal obligations

to its transactional and analytical information. With security breaches on the rise and computer hackers everywhere, an organization must put in place strong security measures to survive.

The Health Insurance Portability and Accountability Act (HIPAA) protects the privacy and security of personal health records and has the potential to impact every business in the United States. HIPAA affects all companies that use electronic data interchange (EDI) to communicate personal health records. HIPAA requires health care organizations to develop, implement, and maintain appropriate security measures when sending electronic health information. Most important, these organizations must document and keep current records detailing how they are performing security measures for all transmissions of health information. On April 21, 2005, security rules for HIPAA became enforceable by law.

The Health Information Management Society estimated that 70 percent of all health care providers failed to meet the April 2005 deadline for privacy rule compliance. Health care organizations need to take HIPAA regulations seriously since noncompliance can result in substantial fines and even imprisonment.[12]

Beyond the health care industry, all businesses must understand the importance of information security, even if it is not enforceable by law. *Information security* is a broad term encompassing the protection of information from accidental or intentional misuse by persons inside or outside an organization. Figure 4.18 displays the typical size of an organization's information security budget relative to the organization's overall IT budget from the CSI/FBI Computer Crime and Security Survey. Forty-six percent of respondents indicated that their organization spent between 1 and 5 percent of the total IT budget on security. Only 16 percent indicated that their organization spent less than 1 percent of the IT budget on security.

Figure 4.19 displays the spending per employee on computer security broken down by both public and private industries. The highest average computer security investment per employee was found in the transportation industry.[13]

Security is perhaps the most fundamental and critical of all the technologies/disciplines an organization must have squarely

FIGURE 4.18 Organization's Security Budget

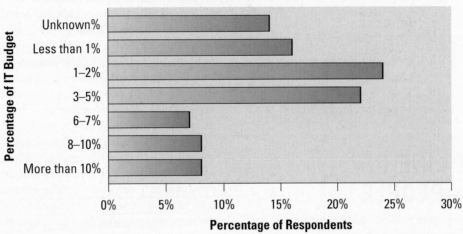

Percentage of IT Budget Spent on Information Security

FIGURE 4.19 Security Spending per Employee

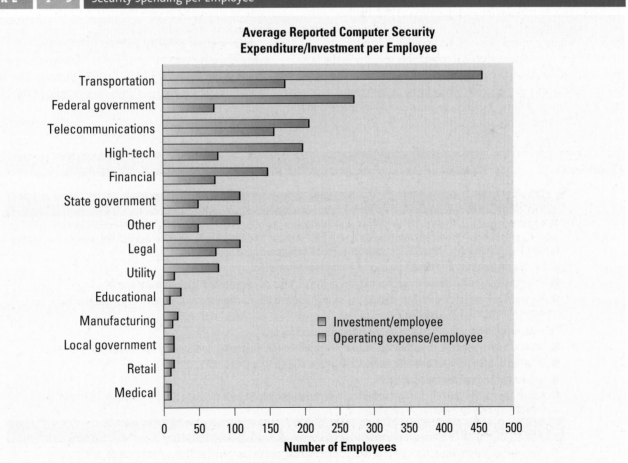

Average Reported Computer Security
Expenditure/Investment per Employee

in place to execute its business strategy. Without solid security processes and procedures, none of the other technologies can develop business advantages.

L04.6

Describe the relationship between information security policies and an information security plan.

L04.7

Summarize the five steps to creating an information security plan.

THE FIRST LINE OF DEFENSE—PEOPLE

With current advances in technologies and business strategies, organizations are able to determine valuable information such as who are the top 20 percent of the customers that produce 80 percent of all revenues. Most organizations view this type of information as valuable intellectual capital, and they are implementing security measures to prevent the information from walking out the door or falling into the wrong hands. Enterprises can implement information security lines of defense through people first and through technology second.

Adding to the complexity of information security is the fact that organizations must enable employees, customers, and partners to access information electronically to be successful in this electronic world. Doing business electronically automatically creates tremendous information security risks for organizations. Surprisingly, the biggest issue surrounding information security is not a technical issue, but a people issue.

The CSI/FBI Computer Crime and Security Survey reported that 38 percent of respondents indicated security incidents originated within the enterprise. **Insiders** are legitimate users who purposely or accidentally misuse their access to the environment and cause some kind of business-affecting incident. Most information security breaches result from people misusing an organization's information either advertently or inadvertently. For example, many individuals freely give up their passwords or write them on sticky notes next to their computers, leaving the door wide open to intruders.[14]

The director of information security at a large health care company discovered how easy it was to create an information security breach when she hired outside auditors to test her company's security awareness. In one instance, auditors found that staff members testing a new system had accidentally exposed the network to outside hackers. In another, auditors were able to obtain the passwords of 16 employees when the auditors posed as support staff; hackers frequently use such "social engineering" to obtain passwords. **Social engineering** is using one's social skills to trick people into revealing access credentials or other information valuable to the attacker. Dumpster diving, or looking through people's trash, is another way social engineering hackers obtain information.[15]

Information security policies identify the rules required to maintain information security. An **information security plan** details how an organization will implement the information security policies. Figure 4.20 is an example of the University of Denver's Information Security Plan.

FIGURE	4.20	Sample Information Security Plan

Interim Information Security Plan

This Information Security Plan ("Plan") describes the University of Denver's safeguards to protect information and data in compliance ("Protected Information") with the Financial Services Modernization Act of 1999, also known as the Gramm Leach Bliley Act, 15 U.S.C. Section 6801. These safeguards are provided to:

- Ensure the security and confidentiality of Protected Information;
- Protect against anticipated threats or hazards to the security or integrity of such information; and
- Protect against unauthorized access to or use of Protected Information that could result in substantial harm or inconvenience to any customer.

This Information Security Plan also provides for mechanisms to:

- Identify and assess the risks that may threaten Protected Information maintained by the University of Denver;
- Develop written policies and procedures to manage and control these risks;
- Implement and review the plan; and
- Adjust the plan to reflect changes in technology, the sensitivity of covered data and information and internal or external threats to information security.

Identification and Assessment of Risks to Customer Information

The University of Denver recognizes that it has both internal and external risks. These risks include, but are not limited to:

- Unauthorized access of Protected Information by someone other than the owner of the covered data and information

- Compromised system security as a result of system access by an unauthorized person
- Interception of data during transmission
- Loss of data integrity
- Physical loss of data in a disaster
- Errors introduced into the system
- Corruption of data or systems
- Unauthorized access of covered data and information by employees
- Unauthorized requests for covered data and information
- Unauthorized access through hardcopy files or reports
- Unauthorized transfer of covered data and information through third parties

The University of Denver recognizes that this may not be a complete list of the risks associated with the protection of Protected Information. Since technology growth is not static, new risks are created regularly. Accordingly, the Information Technology Department and the Office of Student Affairs will actively participate with and seek advice from an advisory committee made up of university representatives for identification of new risks. The University of Denver believes current safeguards used by the Information Technology Department are reasonable and, in light of current risk assessments, are sufficient to provide security and confidentiality to Protected Information maintained by the University.

Information Security Plan Coordinators

The University CIO and the Vice President for Student Affairs, in consultation with an advisory committee, have been appointed as the coordinators of this Plan. They are responsible for assessing the risks associated with unauthorized transfers of covered data and information and implementing procedures to minimize those risks to the University of Denver.

Design and Implementation of Safeguards Program

Employee Management and Training

During employee orientation, each new employee in departments that handle Protected Information will receive proper training on the importance of confidentiality of Protected Information.

Physical Security

- The University of Denver has addressed the physical security of Protected Information by limiting access to only those employees who have a business reason to know such information.

Information Systems

The University of Denver has policies governing the use of electronic resources and firewall and wireless policies. The University of Denver will take reasonable and appropriate steps consistent with current technological developments to make sure that all Protected Information is secure and to safeguard the integrity of records in storage and transmission. The University of Denver will develop a plan to ensure that all electronic Protected Information is encrypted in transit.

Selection of Appropriate Service Providers

Due to the specialized expertise needed to design, implement, and service new technologies, vendors may be needed to provide resources that the University of Denver determines not to provide on its own. In the process of choosing a service provider that will maintain or regularly access Protected Information, the evaluation process shall include the ability of the service provider to safeguard Protected Information. Contracts with service providers may include the following provisions:

- A stipulation that the Protected Information will be held in strict confidence and accessed only for the explicit business purpose of the contract;
- An assurance from the contract partner that the partner will protect the Protected Information it receives.

Continuing Evaluation and Adjustment

This Information Security Plan will be subject to periodic review and adjustment, especially when due to the constantly changing technology and evolving risks. The Coordinators, in consultation with the Office of General Counsel, will review the standards set forth in this policy and recommend updates and revisions as necessary. It may be necessary to adjust the plan to reflect changes in technology, the sensitivity of student/customer data and internal or external threats to information security.

FIGURE 4.21 Creating an Information Security Plan

Five Steps for Creating an Information Security Plan

1. Develop the information security policies	Identify who is responsible and accountable for designing and implementing the organization's information security policies. Simple, yet highly effective types of information security policies include requiring users to log off of their systems before leaving for lunches or meetings, never sharing passwords with anyone, and changing personal passwords every 60 days. The chief security officer (CSO) will typically be responsible for designing these information security policies.
2. Communicate the information security policies	Train all employees on the policies and establish clear expectations for following the policies. For example, let all employees know that they will receive a formal reprimand for leaving a computer unsecured.
3. Identify critical information assets and risks	Require the use of user IDs, passwords, and antivirus software on all systems. Ensure any systems that contain links to external networks have the appropriate technical protections such as firewalls or intrusion detection software. A ***firewall*** is hardware and/or software that guards a private network by analyzing the information leaving and entering the network. ***Intrusion detection software (IDS)*** searches out patterns in information and network traffic to indicate attacks and quickly responds to prevent any harm.
4. Test and reevaluate risks	Continually perform security reviews, audits, background checks, and security assessments.
5. Obtain stakeholder support	Gain the approval and support of the information security polices from the board of directors and all stakeholders.

The first line of defense an organization should follow is to create an information security plan detailing the various information security policies. A detailed information security plan can alleviate people-based information security issues. Figure 4.21 displays the five steps for creating an information security plan.

Top 10 Questions Managers Should Ask Regarding Information Security

1. Does our Board of Directors recognize information security is a board-level issue that cannot be left to the IT department alone?

2. Is there clear accountability for information security in our organization?

3. Do our Board members articulate an agreed-upon set of threats and critical assets? How often do we review and update these?

4. How much is spent on information security and what is it being spent on?

5. What is the impact on the organization of a serious security incident?

6. Does our organization view information security as an enabler? (For example, by implementing effective security, could we enable our organization to increase business over the Internet?)

7. What is the risk to our business of getting a reputation for low information security?

8. What steps have we taken to ensure that third parties will not compromise the security of our organization?

9. How do we obtain independent assurance that information security is managed effectively in our organization?

10. How do we measure the effectiveness of our information security activities?

Businesses consider desktop users to be the biggest security risk to their networks, despite increased concern over outsourced labor and remote users. Figures from a recent Sophos network security survey indicated that businesses still see office-bound employees as those most likely to expose their networks to IT threats. Such users were considered the greatest threat to security by 44 percent of respondents. Mobile employees, are considered to be a greater security threat by 31 percent of respondents. Other users considered to be a threat to network security include contractors and outsourced labor, at 14 percent, and guests, at 11 percent. Sophos's head of technology, Paul Ducklin, said, "This is a representation of how common telecommuting and remote working has become," to the extent that half of those in the office are also remote workers. "The obvious thing we can draw from the results is that administrators haven't become complacent about desktop security," Ducklin said. He also pointed out that while some organizations employ a "stricter regimen for outside than inside," the physical risks to equipment associated with mobile users—such as the loss of or damage to a laptop—are unavoidable.

Figure 4.22 provides the top 10 questions from Ernst & Young that managers should ask to ensure their information is secure.

● ● **LO4.8**

Provide an example of each of the three primary information security areas: (1) authentication and authorization, (2) prevention and resistance, and (3) detection and response.

● ● **LO4.9**

Describe the relationships and differences between hackers and viruses.

THE SECOND LINE OF DEFENSE—TECHNOLOGY

Arkansas State University (ASU) recently completed a major network upgrade that brought gigabit-speed network capacity to every dorm room and office on its campus. The university was concerned that the new network would be a tempting playground for hackers. To reduce its fear, the university installed intrusion detection software (IDS) from Cisco Systems to stay on top of security and potential network abuses. Whenever the IDS spots a potential security threat, such as a virus or a hacker, it alerts the central management system. The system automatically pages the IT staff, who deal with the attack by shutting off access to the system, identifying the hacker's location, and calling campus security.[16]

Once an organization has protected its intellectual capital by arming its people with a detailed information security plan, it can begin to focus its efforts on deploying the right types of information security technologies such as the IDS installed at Arkansas State.

Organizations can deploy numerous technologies to prevent information security breaches. When determining which types of technologies to invest in, it helps to understand the three primary information security areas:

1. Authentication and authorization.
2. Prevention and resistance.
3. Detection and response.[17]

Authentication and Authorization

Authentication is a method for confirming users' identities. Once a system determines the authentication of a user, it can then determine the access privileges (or authorization) for that

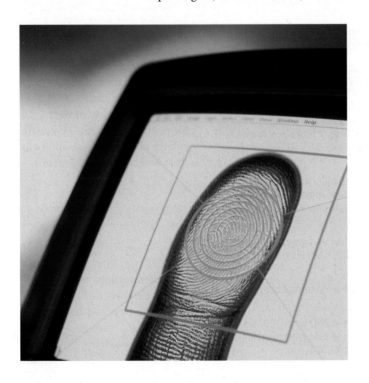

user. **Authorization** is the process of giving someone permission to do or have something. In multiple-user computer systems, user access or authorization determines such things as file access, hours of access, and amount of allocated storage space. Authentication and authorization techniques are broken down into three categories, and the most secure type involves a combination of all three:

1. Something the user knows such as a user ID and password.
2. Something the user has such as a smart card or token.
3. Something that is part of the user such as a fingerprint or voice signature.

Something the User Knows Such as a User ID and Password
The first type of authentication, using something the user knows, is the most common way to identify individual users and typically consists of a unique user ID and password. However, this is actually one of the most *ineffective* ways for determining authentication because passwords are not secure. All it typically takes to crack a password is enough time. More than 50 percent of help-desk calls are password related, which can cost an organization significant money, and passwords are vulnerable to being coaxed out of somebody by a social engineer.

Identity theft is the forging of someone's identity for the purpose of fraud. The fraud is often financial fraud, to apply for and use credit cards in the victim's name or to apply for a loan. By 2003, online banking was not yet ubiquitous but everyone could see that, eventually, it would be. Everyone includes Internet criminals, who by then had already built software capable of surreptitiously grabbing personal information from online forms, like the ones used for online banking. The first of these so-called form-grabbing viruses was called Berbew and was wildly effective. Lance James, a researcher with Secure Science Corp., believes it operated undetected for as long as nine months and grabbed as much as 113GB of data—millions of personal credentials. Like all exploits, Berbew was eventually detected and contained, but, as is customary with viruses, strands of Berbew's form-grabbing code were stitched into new viruses that had adapted to defenses. The process is not unlike horticulturalists' grafting pieces of one plant onto another in order to create hardier mums. Figure 4.23 displays several examples of identity theft.

Phishing is a common way to steal identities online. **Phishing** is a technique to gain personal information for the purpose of identity theft, usually by means of fraudulent email. One way to accomplish phishing is to send out email messages that look as though they came from legitimate businesses such as AOL, MSN, or Amazon. The messages appear to be genuine with official-looking formats and logos. These emails typically ask for verification of important information like passwords and account numbers. The reason given is often that this personal information is required for accounting or auditing purposes. Since the emails look authentic, up to one in five recipients respond with the information, and subsequently becomes a victim of identity theft and other fraud.

Something the User Has Such as a Smart Card or Token
The second type of authentication, using something that the user has, offers a much more effective way to identify individuals than a user ID and password. Tokens and smart cards are two of the primary forms of this type of authentication. **Tokens** are small electronic devices that change user passwords automatically. The user enters his or her user ID and token-displayed password to gain access to the network. A **smart card** is a device that is around the same size as a credit card, containing embedded technologies that can store information and small amounts of software to perform some limited processing. Smart cards can act as identification instruments, a form of digital cash, or a data storage device with the ability to store an entire medical record.

Something That Is Part of the User Such as a Fingerprint or Voice Signature
The third kind of authentication, using something that is part of the user, is by far the best and most effective way to manage authentication. **Biometrics** (narrowly defined) is the identification

FIGURE 4.23 Examples of Identity Theft

Identity Theft Examples

An 82-year-old woman in Fort Worth, Texas, discovered that her identity had been stolen when the woman using her name was involved in a four-car collision. For 18 months, she kept getting notices of lawsuits and overdue medical bills that were really meant for someone else. It took seven years for her to get her financial good name restored after the identity thief charged over $100,000 on her 12 fraudulently acquired credit cards.

A 42-year-old retired Army captain in Rocky Hill, Connecticut, found that an identity thief had spent $260,000 buying goods and services that included two trucks, a Harley-Davidson motorcycle, and a time-share vacation home in South Carolina. The victim discovered his problem only when his retirement pay was garnished to pay the outstanding bills.

In New York, members of a pickpocket ring forged the driver's licenses of their victims within hours of snatching the women's purses. Stealing a purse typically nets around $200, if not less. But stealing the person's identity can net on average between $4,000 and $10,000.

A crime gang took out $8 million worth of second mortgages on victims' homes. It turned out the source of all the instances of identity theft came from a car dealership.

The largest identity-theft scam to date in U.S. history was broken up by police in 2002 when they discovered that three men had downloaded credit reports using stolen passwords and sold them to criminals on the street for $60 each. Many millions of dollars were stolen from people in all 50 states.

Prevention and Resistance

Prevention and resistance technologies stop intruders from accessing intellectual capital. A division of Sony Inc., Sony Pictures Entertainment (SPE), defends itself from attacks by using an intrusion detection system to detect new attacks as they occur. SPE develops and distributes a wide variety of products including movies, television, videos, and DVDs. A compromise to SPE security could cost the company valuable intellectual capital as well as millions of dollars and months of time. The company needed an advanced threat management solution that would take fewer resources to maintain and require limited resources to track and respond to suspicious network activity. The company installed an advanced intrusion detection system allowing it to monitor all of its network activity including any potential security breaches.[18]

The cost of downtime or network operation failures can be devastating to any business. For example, eBay experienced a 22-hour outage in June 2000 that caused the company's market cap to plunge an incredible $5.7 billion. Downtime costs for businesses can vary from $100 to $1 million per hour. An organization must prepare for and anticipate these types of outages resulting most commonly from hackers and viruses. Technologies available to help prevent and build resistance to attacks include content filtering, encryption, and firewalls.[19]

Content Filtering

Content filtering occurs when organizations use software that filters content to prevent the transmission of unauthorized information. Organizations can use content filtering technologies to filter email and prevent emails containing sensitive information from transmitting, whether the transmission was malicious or accidental. It can also filter emails and prevent any suspicious files from transmitting such as potential virus-infected files. Email content filtering can also filter for spam, a form of unsolicited email. Organizational losses from spam were expected to be about $198 billion in 2007 (see Figure 4.24).[20]

Sean Lane's purchase was supposed to be a surprise for his wife. Then it appeared as a news headline, "Sean Lane bought 14k

of a user based on a physical characteristic, such as a fingerprint, iris, face, voice, or handwriting. Unfortunately, biometric authentication can be costly and intrusive. For example, iris scans are expensive and considered intrusive by most people. Fingerprint authentication is less intrusive and inexpensive but is also not 100 percent accurate. Biometrics are being used to help clear airport security in about four minutes. The Clear Card is a preregistered form of ID that lets travelers bypass airport security lines. The card works by storing biometrics of iris and fingerprint inside a microchip on the card. At the airport, the user swipes the card at a security kiosk and the computer matches the biometrics on the card with the fingerprint or iris. If it matches, the user is ready for takeoff. The card is available for $100 along with a $28 fee for a Transportation Security Administration background check.

> ❝ Prevention and resistance technologies stop intruders from accessing intellectual capital. ❞

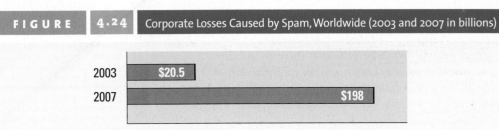

| FIGURE | 4.24 | Corporate Losses Caused by Spam, Worldwide (2003 and 2007 in billions) |

2003 — $20.5
2007 — $198

White Gold 1/5 ct Diamond Eternity Flower Ring from over-stock.com," on the social networking website Facebook. Without Lane's knowledge, the headline was visible to everyone in his online network, including 500 classmates from Columbia University and 220 other friends, co-workers, and acquaintances. And his wife. The wraps came off his Christmas gift thanks to an advertising feature called Beacon, which shares news of Facebook members' online purchases with their friends. The idea, according to the company, is to allow merchants to effectively turn millions of Facebook users into a word-of-mouth promotion service. Lane called it "Christmas ruined," and more than 50,000 other users signed a petition calling on Facebook to stop broadcasting people's transactions without their consent.

Encryption

Encryption scrambles information into an alternative form that requires a key or password to decrypt the information. If there is an information security breach and the information was encrypted, the person stealing the information will be unable to read it. Encryption can switch the order of characters, replace

FIGURE **4.25** Public Key Encryption (PKE) System

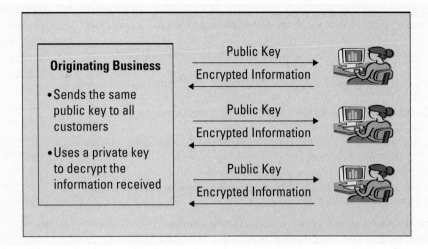

characters with other characters, insert or remove characters, or use a mathematical formula to convert the information into some sort of code. Companies that transmit sensitive customer information over the Internet, such as credit card numbers, frequently use encryption.

Some encryption technologies use multiple keys like public key encryption. *Public key encryption (PKE)* is an encryption system that uses two keys: a public key that everyone can have and a private key for only the recipient (see Figure 4.25). When implementing security using multiple keys, the organization provides the public key to all of its customers (end consumers and other businesses). The customers use the public key to encrypt their information and send it along the Internet. When it arrives at its destination, the organiza-

tion would use the private key to unscramble the encrypted information.

Firewalls

One of the most common defenses for preventing a security breach is a firewall. A *firewall* is hardware and/or software that guards a private network by analyzing the information leaving and entering the network. Firewalls examine each message that wants entrance to the network. Unless the message has the correct markings, the firewall prevents it from entering the network. Firewalls can even detect computers communicating with the Internet without approval. As Figure 4.26 illustrates, organizations typically place a firewall between a server and the Internet.

FIGURE **4.26** Sample Firewall Architecture Connecting Systems Located in Chicago, New York, and Boston

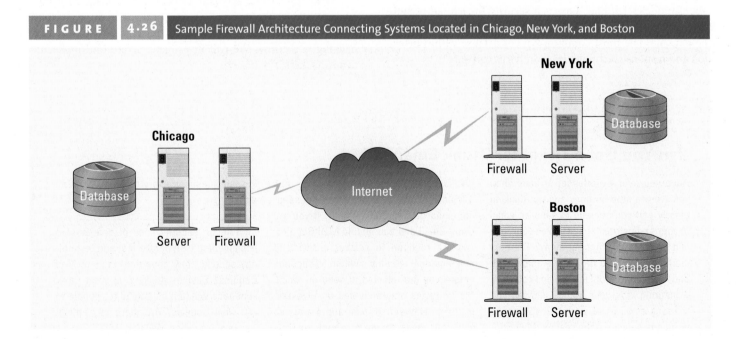

FIGURE   4.27   Hackers and Viruses

Hackers—people very knowledgeable about computers who use their knowledge to invade other people's computers.

- *White-hat hackers*—work at the request of the system owners to find system vulnerabilities and plug the holes.
- *Black-hat hackers*—break into other people's computer systems and may just look around or may steal and destroy information.
- *Hactivists*—have philosophical and political reasons for breaking into systems and will often deface the website as a protest.
- *Script kiddies* or *script bunnies*—find hacking code on the Internet and click-and-point their way into systems to cause damage or spread viruses.
- *Cracker*—a hacker with criminal intent.
- *Cyberterrorists*—seek to cause harm to people or to destroy critical systems or information and use the Internet as a weapon of mass destruction.

Viruses—software written with malicious intent to cause annoyance or damage.

- *Worm*—a type of virus that spreads itself, not only from file to file, but also from computer to computer. The primary difference between a virus and a worm is that a virus must attach to something, such as an executable file, in order to spread. Worms do not need to attach to anything to spread and can tunnel themselves into computers.
- *Denial-of-service attack (DoS)*—floods a website with so many requests for service that it slows down or crashes the site.
- *Distributed denial-of-service attack (DDoS)*—attacks from multiple computers that flood a website with so many requests for service that it slows down or crashes. A common type is the Ping of Death, in which thousands of computers try to access a website at the same time, overloading it and shutting it down.
- *Trojan-horse virus*—hides inside other software, usually as an attachment or a downloadable file.
- *Backdoor programs*—viruses that open a way into the network for future attacks.
- *Polymorphic viruses and worms*—change their form as they propagate.

Detection and Response

The final area where organizations can allocate resources is in detection and response technologies. If prevention and resistance strategies fail and there is a security breach, an organization can use detection and response technologies to mitigate the damage. The most common type of defense within detection and response technologies is antivirus software.

A single worm can cause massive damage. In August 2003, the "Blaster worm" infected over 50,000 computers worldwide and was one of the worst outbreaks of the year. Jeffrey Lee Parson, 18, was arrested by U.S. cyber investigators for unleashing the damaging worm on the Internet. The worm replicated itself repeatedly, eating up computer capacity, but did not damage information or programs. The worm generated so much traffic that it brought entire networks down.

The FBI used the latest technologies and code analysis to find the source of the worm. Prosecutors said that Microsoft suffered financial losses that significantly exceeded $5,000, the statutory threshold in most hacker cases. Parson, charged with intentionally causing or attempting to cause damage to a computer, was sentenced to 18 months in prison, three years of supervised release, and 100 hours of community service. "What you've done is a terrible thing. Aside from injuring people and their computers, you shook the foundation of technology," U.S. District Judge Marsha Pechman told Parson.

"With this arrest, we want to deliver a message to cyber-hackers here and around the world," said U.S. Attorney John McKay in Seattle. "Let there be no mistake about it, cyber-hacking is a crime. We will investigate, arrest, and prosecute cyber-hackers."[21]

omg lol

Can You Get a Ticket for Drunk Emailing?

Have you ever experienced a time when you were a little bit tipsy and not thinking clearly and you decided to send an email to your ex-boyfriend to tell him you still love him or to the girl that got away? The next morning, you were probably embarrassed and humiliated by the emails, and you were wondering why your friends allowed you to drunk email. Well, no more worries, as Google is coming to the rescue. Mail Goggles is one of Google's latest features, and it is designed to prevent users from sending embarrassing drunk emails. If you are using Gmail and you enable Mail Goggles, you are required to answer a series of mathematical equations within 60 seconds before you are allowed to send an email. Mail Goggles only activates on weekend evenings between 10 p.m. and 4 a.m., so you don't have to worry about answering the questions every time you send an email.

Information security lines of defense are implemented with people first and technology second. How does that apply to Mail Goggles? Besides drinking, in what other instances would it be helpful for people to use Mail Goggles? Are there any ethical issues surrounding Mail Goggles?

Typically, people equate viruses (the malicious software) with hackers (the people). While not all types of hackers create viruses, many do. Figure 4.27 provides an overview of the most common types of hackers and viruses.

Some of the most damaging forms of security threats to ebusiness sites include malicious code, hoaxes, spoofing, and sniffers (see Figure 4.28).

Implementing information security lines of defense through people first and through technology second is the best way for an organization to protect its vital intellectual capital. The first line of defense is securing intellectual capital by creating an information security plan detailing the various information security policies. The second line of defense is investing in technology to help secure information through authentication and authorization, prevention and resistance, and detection and response. ■

FIGURE **4.28** Security Threats to Ebusiness

Security Threats to Ebusiness

Elevation of privilege is a process by which a user misleads a system into granting unauthorized rights, usually for the purpose of compromising or destroying the system. For example, an attacker might log onto a network by using a guest account, and then exploit a weakness in the software that lets the attacker change the guest privileges to administrative privileges.

Hoaxes attack computer systems by transmitting a virus hoax, with a real virus attached. By masking the attack in a seemingly legitimate message, unsuspecting users more readily distribute the message and send the attack on to their co-workers and friends, infecting many users along the way.

Malicious code includes a variety of threats such as viruses, worms, and Trojan horses.

Spoofing is the forging of the return address on an email so that the message appears to come from someone other than the actual sender. This is not a virus but rather a way by which virus authors conceal their identities as they send out viruses.

Spyware is software that comes hidden in free downloadable software and tracks online movements, mines the information stored on a computer, or uses a computer's CPU and storage for some task the user knows nothing about. According to the National Cyber Security Alliance, 91 percent of the study had spyware on their computers that can cause extremely slow performance, excessive pop-up ads, or hijacked home pages.

A *sniffer* is a program or device that can monitor data traveling over a network. Sniffers can show all the data being transmitted over a network, including passwords and sensitive information. Sniffers tend to be a favorite weapon in the hacker's arsenal.

Packet tampering consists of altering the contents of packets as they travel over the Internet or altering data on computer disks after penetrating a network. For example, an attacker might place a tap on a network line to intercept packets as they leave the computer. The attacker could eavesdrop or alter the information as it leaves the network.

CHECK OUT www.mhhe.com/baltzanm

for additional study materials including quizzes
and PowerPoint presentations.

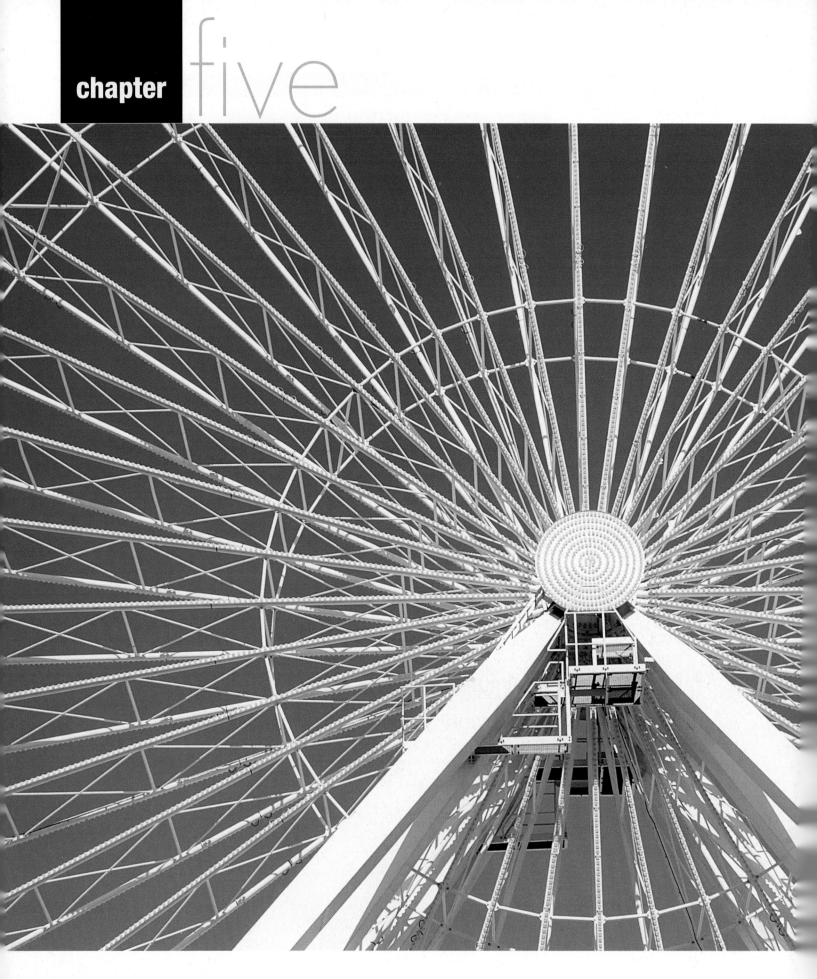

chapter five

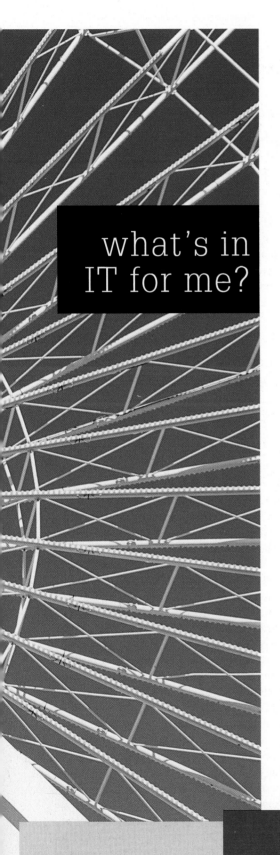

enterprise
architectures

Why do you, as a business student, need to understand the underlying technology of any business? Isn't this technical stuff something that businesses hire nerds and geeks for? Every manager in the 21st century must have a base-level appreciation of what technology can and cannot do for the business. The information presented in this chapter attempts to create a more level playing field between managers and IT staff, who are already ingrained in technology terms and acronyms.

If you understand the concepts of planning and development of information systems, you can think about how information technology can be used to support business decisions. This is a critical skill for any businessperson, no matter if they are just starting out or a seasoned Fortune 500 employee. Learning about information architectures will give you a competitive advantage because understanding how information systems work can provide you with feedback on overall business performance.

After reading this chapter, you should have many of the skills needed to become directly involved in analyzing current business systems, in recommending needed changes in business processes, in evaluating alternative hardware and software options, and in judging the technical feasibility of a project.

SECTION 5.1 >>
Managing Enterprise Architectures
- Enterprise Architectures
- Information Architecture
- Infrastructure Architecture
- Application Architecture

SECTION 5.2 >>
Architecture Trends
- Service Oriented Architecture
- Virtualization
- Grid Computing

nterprise architecture lies at the heart of most companies' operating capabilities. Changes in IT lead therefore to fundamental changes in how businesses operate. Since many companies depend on these technologies, no longer is IT simply nice to have; no longer is IT just value-adding. It has become vital.

Recent advances have led to major changes in how IT services are delivered. Low-cost computing power has driven a shift toward more distributed processing. Internetworking technologies, which provide a low-cost way to connect virtually everyone on the same network, present new possibilities for addressing business computing needs. The operational mechanisms at the heart of many businesses continue to evolve. New technologies add to, improve, and interconnect older systems to yield architectures with complex operational characteristics.

More importantly, new approaches to system design and development now enable large, complex applications to be built from reusable modules linked through shared services and common interfaces. This approach dramatically increases

 LO5.1

Explain the three components of an enterprise architecture.

ENTERPRISE ARCHITECTURES

A 66-hour failure of an FBI database that performed background checks on gun buyers was long enough to allow criminals to buy guns. The database failed at 1:00 p.m. on a Thursday and was not restored until 7:30 a.m. Sunday. The FBI must complete a gun check within three days; if it fails to do so, a merchant is free to make the sale. During this outage, any gun checks that were in progress were not finished, allowing merchants to complete those gun sales at their own discretion.[1]

> To support the volume and complexity of today's user and application requirements, information technology needs to take a fresh approach to enterprise architectures by constructing smarter, more flexible environments that protect from system failures and crashes.

the ability to reuse data, information, and applications and to share a common infrastructure, which further increases the flexibility and speed with which new value-creating IT-enabled business initiatives can be launched and globally deployed.

While enterprise architecture alone cannot convey sustainable proprietary advantage, businesses that remain chained to a legacy of incompatible and inflexible proprietary architectures find themselves at a significant strategic disadvantage as they attempt to keep pace with increasingly shorter cycles of innovation, productivity, and return on investments. This chapter covers the basics of enterprise architecture including terminology, characteristics, and associated managerial responsibilities for building a solid enterprise architecture.

 SECTION 5.1 Managing Enterprise Architectures

LEARNING OUTCOMES

LO5.1 Explain the three components of an enterprise architecture.

LO5.2 Describe how an organization can implement a solid information architecture.

To support the volume and complexity of today's user and application requirements, information technology needs to take a fresh approach to enterprise architectures by constructing smarter, more flexible environments that protect from system failures and crashes. *Enterprise architectures (EA)* include the plans for how an organization will build, deploy, use, and share its data, processes, and IT assets. A unified enterprise architecture will standardize enterprisewide hardware and software systems, with tighter links to the business strategy. A solid enterprise architecture can decrease costs, increase standardization, promote reuse of IT assets, and speed development of new systems. The right enterprise architecture can make IT cheaper, strategic, and more responsive. The primary business goals of enterprise architectures are displayed in Figure 5.1.

Experts liken an EA plan to a blueprint. Just like you would never build a house without a blueprint, enterprise architecture gives a company a look into its processes, down to its data and technology, and how they are supporting the goals of the company, to make the processes more efficient and more effective, and to reduce costs. To be successful, however, an EA program must address more than just technology. With enterprise architecture, the subject is the business, and must be looked at with up to four different lenses: business, data, applications, and technology architecture. Trying to line those up is

My Not To-Do List

Honestly, My Dog Ate My Homework

Here are a few real-life examples of the most unusual excuses employees gave for missing work.

- I woke up in Canada.
- I got caught selling an alligator.
- My buddies locked me in the trunk of an abandoned car.
- My mom said I was not allowed to go to work today.
- I'm just not into it today.
- I accidentally hit a nun with my motorcycle.
- A random person threw poison ivy in my face, and now I have a rash.
- I'm convinced my spouse is having an affair, and I'm staying home to catch them.
- I was injured chasing a seagull.
- I have a headache from eating hot peppers.

This chapter focuses on enterprise architectures, which are the main building blocks that function together to control the entire organization's systems. If your architecture is down, nothing in your organization can work, similar to how your health controls your ability to work. There is nothing more frustrating than attempting to do business with an organization when its systems have crashed, Internet access is down, or wireless network is malfunctioning. When these types of issues occur, you will seldom hear the truth about what is really happening. Companies don't want to broadcast that they are experiencing technical difficulties because of hackers, an unpaid electric bill, or squirrels that broke into the data center and ate through all of the wires (yes, that has really happened).

How many times have you called a company and the customer service representative has stated that the system is down or that the system is really slow? How many times have you missed submitting an assignment because your Internet service was down? Why is it important for an organization to have its systems available 24 hours a day, 7 days a week, 365 days a year? Why would a company hide the real reason that its systems are malfunctioning? What could happen if customers were informed that the systems were down due to hackers? How can an organization safeguard its systems?

FIGURE 5.1 Primary Business Goals of Enterprise Architectures

Reduce costs/improve productivity 81%
Improve customer satisfaction 71%
Create competitive advantages 66%
Generate growth 54%
Generate new revenue streams 43%
Optimize the supply chain 37%

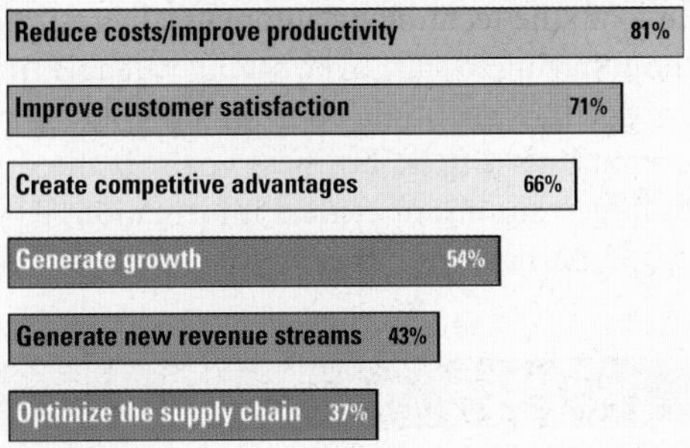

what enterprise architecture is all about. Therefore, enterprise architectures are never static; they continually change. Organizations use enterprise architects to help manage change. An ***enterprise architect*** is a person grounded in technology, fluent in business, and provides the important bridge between IT and the business. T-Mobile International's enterprise architects review projects to ensure they are soundly designed, meet the business objectives, and fit with the overall enterprise architecture. One T-Mobile project was to create software that would let subscribers customize the ring sounds on their cell phones. The project group assumed it would have to create most of the software from scratch. However, T-Mobile's EAs found software already written elsewhere at T-Mobile that could be reused to create the new application. The reuse reduced the development cycle time by eight months, and the new application was available in less than six weeks.[2]

Companies that have created solid enterprise architectures, such as Vingin Mobile and T-Mobile, are reaping huge rewards in savings, flexibility, and business alignment. Basic enterprise architectures contain three components (see Figure 5.2).

1. ***Information architecture*** identifies where and how important information, such as customer records, is maintained and secured.
2. ***Infrastructure architecture*** includes the hardware, software, and telecommunications equipment that, when combined, provides the underlying foundation to support the organization's goals.
3. ***Application architecture*** determines how applications integrate and relate to each other.

LO5.2

Describe how an organization can implement a solid information architecture.

INFORMATION ARCHITECTURE

Information architecture identifies where and how important information, such as customer records, is maintained and secured. A single backup or restore failure can cost an organization more than time and money; some data cannot be re-created, and the business intelligence lost from that data can be tremendous. Chief information officers (CIO) should have enough confidence in their backup and recovery systems that they could walk around and randomly pull out cables to prove that the systems are safe. The CIO should also be secure enough to perform this test during peak business hours. If the thought of this test makes the CIO cringe, then the organization's customers should be cringing also. Figure 5.3 shows the three primary areas an enterprise information architecture should focus on:

1. Backup and recovery
2. Disaster recovery
3. Information security

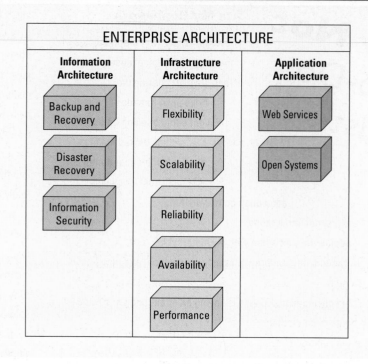

FIGURE 5.2 Three Components of Enterprise Architecture

Backup and Recovery

Each year businesses lose time and money because of system crashes and failures. One way to minimize the damage of a system crash is to have a backup and recovery strategy in place. A *backup* is an exact copy of a system's information. *Recovery* is the ability to get a system up and running in the event of a system crash or failure and includes restoring the information backup. Many different types of backup and recovery media are available, including redundant storage servers, tapes, disks, and even CDs and DVDs. All the different types of backup and recovery media are reliable; their primary differences are the speed and associated costs.

A chain of more than 4,000 franchise locations, 7-Eleven Taiwan uploads backup and recovery information from its central location to all its chain locations daily. The company implemented a new technology solution that could quickly and reliably download and upload backup and recovery information. In addition, when a connection fails during the download or upload, the technology automatically resumes the download without having to start over, saving valuable time.[3]

Organizations should choose a backup and recovery strategy that is in line with its business goals. If the organization deals with large volumes of critical information, it will require daily backups, perhaps even hourly backups, to storage servers. If the

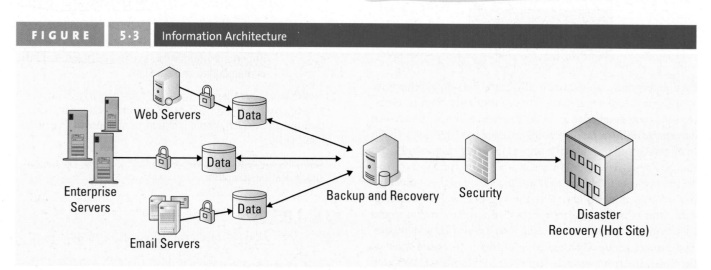

FIGURE 5.3 Information Architecture

organization deals with small amounts of noncritical information, then it might require only weekly backups to external hard drives, tapes, CDs, or DVDs. Deciding how often to back up information and what media to use is a critical business decision. If an organization decides to back up on a weekly basis, then it is taking the risk that, if a total system crash occurs, it could lose a week's worth of work. If this risk is acceptable, then a weekly backup strategy will work. If this risk is unacceptable, then the organization needs to move to a daily backup strategy. Some organizations find the risk of losing a day's worth of work too high and move to an hourly backup strategy.

Two techniques used to help in case of system failure are fault tolerance and failover. **Fault tolerance** is a computer system designed that in the event a component fails, a backup component or procedure can immediately take its place with no loss of service. Fault tolerance can be provided via software, embedded in hardware, or provided by some combination. **Failover** is a backup in which the functions of a computer component (such as a processor, server, network, or database) are assumed by secondary system components when the primary component becomes unavailable through either failure or scheduled downtime. A failover procedure involves automatically offloading tasks to a standby system component so that the procedure is as seamless as possible to the end user. Used to make systems more fault tolerant, failover is typically an integral part of mission-critical systems that must be constantly available, such as systems used in the financial industry.[4]

Disaster Recovery

A northern Ohio power company, FirstEnergy, missed signs that there were potential problems in its portion of North America's electrical grid. The events that followed left an estimated 50 million people in the Northeast and Canada in the dark. The failings are laid out in the widely reported findings of a joint U.S./Canadian task force that investigated the causes of the blackout and recommended what to do to avoid big-scale outages in the future. The report detailed many procedures and best practices including:

- Mind the enterprise architectures.
- Monitor the quality of computer networks that provide data on power suppliers and demand.
- Make sure the networks can be restored quickly in the case of downtime.
- Set up disaster recovery plans.
- Provide adequate staff training, including verbal communication protocols so that operators are aware of any IT-related problems that may be affecting their situational awareness of the power grid.

Disasters such as power outages, floods, and even harmful hacking strike businesses every day. Organizations must develop a disaster recovery plan to prepare for such occurrences. A **disaster recovery plan** is a detailed process for recovering information or an IT system in the event of a catastrophic

Zombies Attack the University of Florida

Backup and recovery are essential for any computer system. Hopefully, most of you have a backup of your data. If you have not, let me ask you a question: How painful would it be if someone stole your laptop right now? How much critical information would you lose? How many hours would it take you to recreate your data? Perhaps that will motivate you to implement a backup procedure. Now, how many of you have a disaster recovery plan? I'd be surprised if any of you have disaster recovery plans for your personal computers. Disaster recovery occurs when your best friend decides to dump a grande latte on your computer or your roommate accidently washes your thumb drive.

Disaster recovery plans are crucial for any business, and you should ensure that your company has everything it needs to continue operations if there is ever a disaster, such as 9/11. Now, you need to decide which disasters are worth worrying about and which ones are probably never going to occur. For example, if you live in Colorado, chances are good you don't have to worry about hurricanes, but avalanches are another story. There are a few companies who take disaster recovery too far, such as the University of Florida that lists the disaster recovery plans for a zombie apocalypse on its disaster recovery website. Yes, you read that correctly. The zombie apocalypse disaster recovery exercise details how the school could respond to an outbreak of the undead, along with plans for dealing with hurricanes and pandemics. I guess you can never be too prepared to deal with the unexpected!

How often does a company need to back up its data? Where should the backup be stored? What types of disasters should companies in your state prepare for in case of an emergency? Why is it important to test the backup? What could happen to a company if it failed to back up its data and applications?

disaster such as a fire or flood. Spending on disaster recovery is rising worldwide among financial institutions (see Figure 5.4).

A comprehensive disaster recovery plan considers the location of the backup information. Many organizations store backup information in an off-site facility. StorageTek, a worldwide technology company that delivers a broad range of data storage offerings, specializes in providing off-site information

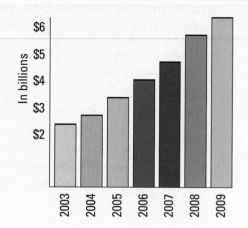

storage and disaster recovery solutions. A comprehensive disaster recovery plan also foresees the possibility that not only the computer equipment but also the building where employees work may be destroyed. A *hot site* is a separate and fully equipped facility where the company can move immediately after a disaster and resume business. A *cold site* is a separate facility that does not have any computer equipment, but is a place where employees can move after a disaster.

A *disaster recovery cost curve* charts (1) the cost to the organization of the unavailability of information and technology and (2) the cost to the organization of recovering from a disaster over time. Figure 5.5 displays a disaster recovery cost curve and shows that where the two lines intersect is the best recovery plan in terms of cost and time. Creating an organization's disaster recovery cost curve is no small task. It must consider the cost of losing information and technology within each department or functional area, and the cost of losing information and technology across the whole enterprise. During the first few hours of a disaster, those costs will be low but become increasingly higher over time. With those costs in hand, an organization must then determine the costs of recovery. Cost of recovery during the first few hours of a disaster is exceedingly high and diminishes over time.

On April 18, 1906, San Francisco was rocked by an earthquake that destroyed large swathes of the city and claimed the lives of more than 3,000 inhabitants of the Bay area. More than a century later, a bigger, bolder, rebuilt, and more resilient San Francisco is more important than ever. Now it serves as the heart of the global IT industry and a major world financial center. However, San Francisco remains well aware of the terrible potential that exists along the San Andreas fault.

The vast skyscrapers downtown may now be built to withstand huge pressures, but what about the infrastructure and the systems that keep modern business ticking—and the people who must be able to access them? *Business continuity planning (BCP)* is a plan for how an organization will recover and restore partially or completely interrupted critical function(s) within a predetermined time after a disaster or extended disruption. Business continuity and disaster recovery are serious issues for all organizations in the Bay area, including the Union Bank of California, which is based in the heart of downtown San Francisco.[5]

Barry Cardoza, head of business continuity planning and disaster recovery at Union Bank of California, said, "You have disasters that you can see coming and you've got disasters that you can't see coming and an earthquake is an example of [the latter]. And you don't know how bad it's going to be until it hits."[6]

As such, the bank must have processes in place ahead of such an event to mitigate the threat. Simply reacting is not a strategy. The continuity department must also understand every aspect of the business and weigh downtime for each in terms of financial and reputational damage. Union Bank of California has created a disaster recovery plan that includes multiple data centers in diverse locations, mirrored sites that can take over at the flick of a switch, hot sites where staff can walk in and start working exactly as they would if they were in their normal location, and a vast amount of redundancy. In addition, the bank has created real-time mirroring between data centers. It is now a matter of minutes not hours for Union Bank of California to be up and running in the event of a disaster.

Information Security

Security professionals are under increasing pressure to do the job right and cost-effectively as networks extend beyond organizations to remote users, partners, and customers, and to cell

Aftermath of 1906 San Francisco earthquake.

phones, PDAs, and other mobile devices. Regulatory requirements to safeguard data have increased. Concerns about identity theft are at an all-time high. Hacking and other unauthorized access contribute to the approximately 10 million instances of identity theft each year, according to the Federal Trade Commission. Good information architectures include a strong information security plan, along with managing user access and up-to-date antivirus software and patches.[7]

Managing User Access

Managing user access to information is a critical piece of the information architecture. Passwords may still be the weakest link in the security chain. At Vitas Healthcare Corporation, with a workforce of 6,000 and operations across 15 states, authorized employees enter as many as a half-dozen passwords a day to access multiple systems. While it is important to maintain password discipline to

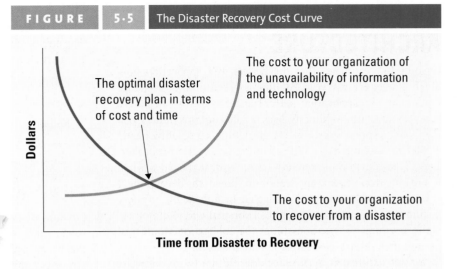

FIGURE 5·5 The Disaster Recovery Cost Curve

The optimal disaster recovery plan in terms of cost and time

The cost to your organization of the unavailability of information and technology

Dollars

The cost to your organization to recover from a disaster

Time from Disaster to Recovery

The main focus for most managers is preventing hackers, spammers, and other malcontents from entering their networks, and nearly two-thirds are looking to enhance their

> "Security professionals are under increasing pressure to do the job right and cost-effectively as networks extend beyond organizations to remote users, partners, and customers, and to cell phones, PDAs, and other mobile devices."

secure customers' health care data, maintaining and managing the situation creates a drag on the IT department. "Our help desk spends 30 percent of their time on password management and provisioning," said John Sandbrook, senior IT director.

The company began using Fischer International Corporation's Identity Management Suite to manage passwords and comply with data-access regulations such as the Sarbanes-Oxley Act. The ID-management product includes automated audit, reporting, and compliance capabilities, plus a common platform for password management, provisioning, and self-service. With the software, the company can enforce stronger passwords with seven, eight, or nine characters, numbers, and capital letters that frequently change. The company anticipates curbing help-desk password time by 50 percent.[8]

Up-to-Date Antivirus Software and Patches

Security is a top priority for business managers, regardless of the size of their company. Among Fortune 500 companies, more than 80 percent of those surveyed described updating security procedures, tools, and services as a key business priority. That desire holds true for small, midsize, or large companies and for IT managers and corporate managers.

network-security-management, intrusion-detection, content-filtering, and anti-spam software. More than half also plan to upgrade their encryption software.

Microsoft issues patches for its software on the second Tuesday of every month. These patches must be downloaded and installed on all systems across the entire enterprise if the company wants to keep its systems protected. At OMD, a media buying and planning subsidiary of Omnicom Group Inc., the network administrator had to manually install critical patches on all 100 servers, taking more than a week to deploy the patch across the company. Now, OMD uses automated installation software for patches and upgrades. The company purchased software that lets it move ahead with applying patches without taking down entire systems and balancing patch-deployment timing among servers so that all departments were not down at once during a patch install. Given everything else that security professionals need to think about, automated installation software is a welcome relief.[9]

●● L05.3

List and describe the five-ilities in an infrastructure architecture.

INFRASTRUCTURE ARCHITECTURE

Gartner Inc. estimates that the typical web application goes down 170 hours per year. At Illinois-based online brokerage OptionsXpress, application performance problems can have a serious impact on livelihoods. Nearly 7,000 options traders visit the OptionsXpress website at any given time, completing nearly 20,000 transactions a day. With all this online traffic, the brokerage's IT administrators were always up against the clock when re-creating troublesome applications offline in the development environment. The company struggled to unlock the mystery behind a problematic trading application that was forcing traders to resubmit orders. Sometimes the application would just die and then restart itself for no apparent reason.[10]

Infrastructure architecture includes the hardware, software, and telecommunications equipment that, when combined, provides the underlying foundation to support the organization's goals (see Figure 5.6). As an organization changes, its systems must be able to change to support its operations. If an organization grows by 50 percent in a single year, its systems must be able to handle a 50 percent growth rate. Systems that cannot adapt to organizational changes can severely hinder the organization's ability to operate. The future of an organization depends on its ability to meet its partners and customers on their terms, at their pace, any time of the day, in any geographic location. The following are the five primary characteristics of a solid infrastructure architecture:

1. Flexibility
2. Scalability
3. Reliability
4. Availability
5. Performance

Flexibility

Organizations must watch today's business, as well as tomorrow's, when designing and building systems. Systems must be flexible enough to meet all types of business changes. For example, a system might be designed to include the ability to handle multiple currencies and languages, even though the company is not currently performing business in other countries. When the company starts growing and performing business in new countries, the system will already have the flexibility to handle multiple currencies and languages. If the company failed to recognize that its business would someday be global, it would need to redesign all its systems to handle multiple currencies and languages, not easy once systems are up and running.

| FIGURE | 5.6 | Infrastructure Architecture Characteristics |

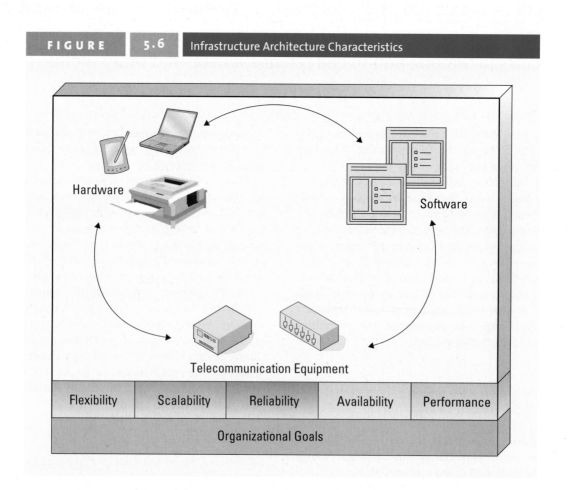

Scalability

Estimating organizational growth is a challenging task. Growth can occur in a number of different forms including more customers and product lines and expansion into new markets. *Scalability* refers to how well a system can adapt to increased demands. A number of factors can create organizational growth including market, industry, and economy factors. If an organization grows faster than anticipated, it might experience all types of performance degradations, ranging from running out of disk space to a slowdown in transaction speeds. Anticipating expected—and unexpected—growth is key to building scalable systems that can support that growth.

MSNBC's website typically received moderate traffic. On September 11, 2001, the site was inundated with more than 91 million page views as its customers were trying to find out information about the terrorist attacks. Fortunately, MSNBC had anticipated this type of surging demand and built scalable systems accordingly, allowing it to handle the increased page view requests.[11]

Capacity planning determines the future IT infrastructure requirements for new equipment and additional network capacity. Performing a capacity plan is one way to ensure the IT infrastructure is scalable. It is cheaper for an organization to implement an IT infrastructure that considers capacity growth at the beginning of a system launch than to try to upgrade equipment and networks after the system has been implemented. Not having enough capacity leads to performance issues and hinders the ability of employees to perform their jobs. If 100 workers are using the Internet to perform their jobs and the company purchases bandwidth that is too small and the network capacity is too small, the employees will spend a great deal of time just waiting to get information from the Internet. Waiting for an Internet site to return information is not very productive.

Web 2.0 is driving demand for capacity planning. Delivering entertainment-grade video over the Internet poses significant challenges as service providers scale solutions to manage millions of users, withstand periods of peak demand, and deliver a superior quality of experience while balancing network capacity and efficient capital investment. Given the success of YouTube and the likelihood of similar video experiences, the bandwidth required to transport video services will continue to increase and the possibility of video degradation will become more challenging. Since video cannot tolerate packet loss (e.g., blocks of data lost), congestion due to overuse is not acceptable—admitting just one more stream to a network near peak capacity could degrade the video and broadcast quality for all users.

Reliability

Reliability ensures all systems are functioning correctly and providing accurate information. Reliability is another term for accuracy when discussing the correctness of systems within the context of efficiency IT metrics. Inaccurate information processing occurs for many reasons, from the incorrect entry of data to information corruption. Unreliable information puts the organization at risk when making decisions based on the information.

Availability

Availability (an efficiency IT metric) addresses when systems can be accessed by users. *High availability* refers to a system or component that is continuously operational for a desirably long length of time. Availability is typically measured relative to "100 percent operational" or "never failing." A widely held but difficult-to-achieve standard of availability for a system or product is known as "five 9s" (99.999 percent) availability. Some companies have systems available 24 × 7 to support business operations and global customer and employee needs. With the emergence of the web, companies expect systems to operate around the clock. A customer who finds that a website closes at 9:00 p.m. is not going to be a customer long.

Systems, however, must come down for maintenance, upgrades, and fixes. One challenge organizations face is determining when to schedule system downtime if the system is expected to operate continually. Exacerbating the negative impact of scheduled system downtime is the global nature of business. Scheduling maintenance during the evening might seem like a great idea, but the evening in one city is the morning somewhere else in the world, and global employees may not be able to perform their jobs if the system is down. Many organizations overcome this problem by having redundant systems, allowing the organization to take one system down by switching over to a redundant, or duplicate, system.

Performance

Performance measures how quickly a system performs a certain process or transaction (in terms of efficiency IT metrics of both speed and throughput). Not having enough performance capacity can have a devastating, negative impact on a business.

A customer will wait only a few seconds for a website to return a request before giving up and moving on to another website. To ensure adaptable systems performance, capacity planning helps an organization determine future IT infrastructure requirements for new equipment and additional network capacity. It is cheaper for an organization to design and implement an IT infrastructure that envisions performance capacity growth than to update all the equipment after the system is already operational.

Abercrombie & Fitch (A&F) uses the Internet to market its distinctive image of being a fashion trendsetter to one of its largest customer segments, college students. The company designed its enterprise architecture with the help of IBM, which ensured www.abercrombie.com paralleled the same sleek but simple design of *A&F Quarterly,* the company's flagship magazine. Abercrombie & Fitch knew that its website had to be accessible, available, reliable, and scalable to meet the demands of its young customers. Young customers tend to be Internet savvy, and their purchasing habits vary from customers who only shop for sale items at midnight to customers who know exactly what they want immediately. The highly successful website gives customers not only an opportunity to shop online, but also a taste of the Abercrombie & Fitch lifestyle through downloadable MP3s, calendars, and desktop accessories.[12]

 LO5.4

Compare web services and open systems.

APPLICATION ARCHITECTURE

Gartner Inc. research indicates that application problems are the single largest source of downtime, causing 40 percent of annual downtime hours and 32 percent of average downtime costs. *Application architecture* determines how applications integrate and relate to each other. Advances in integration technology— primarily web services and open systems—are providing new ways for designing more agile, more responsive enterprise architectures that provide the kind of value businesses need. With these new architectures, IT can build new business capabilities faster, cheaper, and in a vocabulary the business can understand.[13]

Web Services

Web services are quickly becoming the next major frontier in computing. *Web services* contain a repertoire of web-based data and procedural resources that use shared protocols and standards permitting different applications to share data and services. The major application of web services is the integration among different applications (refer to Figure 5.7). Before web services, organizations had trouble with interoperability. *Interoperability* is the capability of two or more computer

systems to share data and resources, even though they are made by different manufacturers. If a manufacturing system can talk to (share information with) a shipping system, interoperability exists between the two systems. The traditional way that organizations achieved interoperability was to build integrations. Now, an organization can use web services to perform the same task.

Verizon's massive enterprise architecture includes three different companies—GTE, Bell Atlantic, and NYNEX—each with its own complex systems. To find a customer record in any of the three companies' systems, Verizon turns to its search

FIGURE   5·7   Web Service Architecture

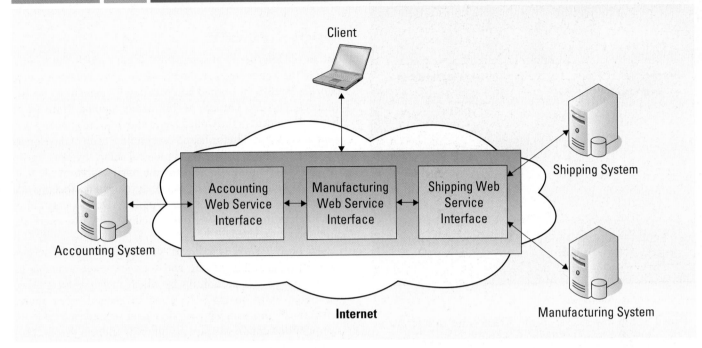

engine, called Spider. Spider is Verizon's version of Google, and it is helping Verizon's business to thrive.

Spider contains a vital customer information web service that encapsulates Verizon's business rules, which help it to access the correct data repository when looking for customer information. Whenever a new system is built that needs to link to customer information, all the system developer has to do is reuse the web service that will link to the customer records. Because Verizon has the web service in place as part of its enterprise architecture, development teams can build new applications within a month, as opposed to six months.

Web services encompass all the technologies that are used to transmit and process information on and across a network, most specifically the Internet. It is easiest to think of an individual web service as software that performs a specific task,

with that task being made available to any user who needs its service. For example, a "Deposit" web service for a banking system might allow customers to perform the task of depositing money to their accounts. The web service could be used by a bank teller, by the customer at an ATM, and/or by the customer performing an online transaction through a web browser.

The "Deposit" web service demonstrates one of the great advantages of using the web service model to develop applications. Developers do not have to reinvent the wheel every time they need to incorporate new functionality. A web service is really a piece of reusable software code. A software developer can quickly build a new application by using many of these pieces of reusable code. The two primary parts of web services are events and services.

Events Events are the eyes and ears of the business expressed in technology—they detect threats and opportunities and alert those who can act on the information. Pioneered by telecommunication and financial services companies, this involves using IT systems to monitor a business process for events that matter—a stock-out in the warehouse or an especially large charge on a consumer's credit card—and automatically alert the people best equipped to handle the issue. For example, a credit monitoring system automatically alerts a credit supervisor and shuts down an account when the system processes a $7,000 charge on a credit card with a $6,000 limit.

Services Services are more like software products than they are coding projects. They must appeal to a broad audience, and they need to be reusable if they are going to have an impact on productivity. Early forms of services were

defined at too low a level in the architecture to interest the business, such as simple "Print" and "Save" services. The new services are being defined at a higher level; they describe such things as "Credit Check," "Customer Information," and "Process Payment." These services describe a valuable business process. For example, "Credit Check" has value not just for programmers who want to use that code in another application, but also for businesspeople who want to use it across multiple products, such as auto loans and mortgages, or across multiple business.

The trick to building services is finding the right level of granularity. T-Mobile builds services starting at the highest level and then works its way down to lower levels, helping to ensure it does not build services that no one uses. The company first built a "Send Message" web service and then built a "Send SMS Message" web service that sends messages in special formats to different devices such as cell phones and pagers.

Lydian Trust's enterprise architects designed a web service called "Get Credit" that is used by several different business units for loan applications. "Get Credit" seeks out credit ratings over the Internet from the major credit bureaus. One day, one of the credit bureau's web servers crashed, and Lydian Trust's "Get Credit" web service could not make a connection. Since the connection to the server was loosely linked, the system did not know what to do. "Get Credit" was not built to make more than one call. So, while it waited for a response, hundreds of loan applications sat idle.

Lydian Trust's loan officers had to work overnight to ensure that all of the applications were completed within 24 hours as promised by the company. Fortunately, Lydian Trust's customers never felt the pain; however, its employees did. Systems must be designed to deal with the existence of certain events, or the lack of an event, in a way that does not interrupt the overall business. The "Get Credit" web service has been modified to include an automatic email alert to a supervisor whenever the web service encounters a delay.[14]

Open Systems

Microsoft Internet Explorer (MSIE) is very much the incumbent in the web browser arena. Before the arrival of open source Mozilla Firefox, MSIE had an estimated 97 percent of market share. Firefox has cut into MSIE's niche, dipping MSIE usage below 90 percent in the United States and down to about 60 percent in Germany. Firefox has an open source team of developers and testers. The Mozilla Firefox project's launch by Netscape in 1998 was a defining moment for the open source movement. Firefox is a leader in the open source developments that provide low cost and a lot of options for technology. Developers of Firefox interact through newsgroups, mailing lists, IRC channels, and various websites.[15]

An *open system* is a broad, general term that describes nonproprietary IT hardware and software made available by the standards and procedures by which their products work, making it easier to integrate them. In general, *open source* refers to any program whose source code is made available for use or modification as users or other developers see fit. Historically, the makers of proprietary software have generally not made source code available. Open source software is usually developed as a public collaboration and made freely available. Amazon.com embraced open source technology, converting from Sun's proprietary operating system to Linux. The switch to an open source operating system, such as Linux, is simplifying the process by which Amazon.com associates can build links to Amazon.com applications into their websites.

The designs of open systems allow for information sharing. In the past, different systems were independent of each other and operated as individual islands of control. The sharing of information was accomplished through software drivers and devices that routed data allowing information to be translated and shared between systems. Although this method is still widely used, its limited capability and added cost are not an effective solution for most organizations. Another drawback to the stand-alone system is it can communicate only with components developed by a single manufacturer. The proprietary nature of these systems usually results in costly repair, maintenance, and expansion because of a lack of competitive forces. On the other hand, open system integration is designed to:

- Allow systems to seamlessly share information. The sharing of information reduces the total number of devices, resulting in an overall decrease in cost.

- Capitalize on enterprise architectures. This avoids installing several independent systems, which creates duplication of devices.

- Eliminate proprietary systems and promote competitive pricing. Often a sole-source vendor can demand its price and may even provide the customer with less than satisfactory service. Utilization of open systems allows users to purchase systems competitively.[16]

LO5.5 Describe the business value in deploying a service oriented architecture.

LO5.6 Explain the need for interoperability and loose coupling in building today's IT systems.

LO5.7 Identify the logical functions used in a virtualized environment.

LO5.8 Explain the business benefits of grid computing.

ARCHIECTURE TRENDS

To keep business systems up-and-running 24 × 7 × 365 while continuing to be flexible, scalable, reliable, and available is no easy task. Organizations today must continually watch new architecture trends to ensure they can keep up with new and

business needs. It helps businesses increase the flexibility of their processes, strengthen their underlying IT architecture, and reuse their existing IT investments by creating connections among disparate applications and information sources.

SOA is not a concrete architecture: It is something that leads to a concrete architecture (as illustrated in Figure 5.8). It might be described as a style, paradigm, concept, perspective, philosophy, or representation. That is, SOA is not a concrete tool or framework to be purchased. It is an approach, a way of thinking, a value system that leads to certain concrete decisions when designing a concrete architecture.

Crutchfield, in Charlottesville, Virginia, sells electronics through three channels: the web, a call center, and two retail shops. With a service oriented architecture, a single application now handles the initial order processing from all three sales channels, with fraud checking and the workflow encapsulated using a series of messages. Although simple to build, Crutchfield's SOA is rigorous, averaging 3,800 daily orders that book on average $1.1 million daily in revenues.[17]

"Organizations today must continually watch new architecture trends to ensure they can keep up with new and disruptive technologies."

disruptive technologies. This section discusses three architecture trends that are quickly becoming requirements for all businesses including:

- Service Oriented Architectures
- Virtualization
- Grid Computing

●● LO5.5

Describe the business value in deploying a service oriented architecture.

●● LO5.6

Explain the need for interoperability and loose coupling in building today's IT systems.

SERVICE ORIENTED ARCHITECTURE

Service oriented architecture (SOA) is a business-driven IT architectural approach that supports integrating a business as linked, repeatable tasks or services. SOA helps today's businesses innovate by ensuring that IT systems can adapt quickly, easily, and economically to support rapidly changing

SOA Business Benefits

The reality in IT enterprises is that architectures are heterogeneous across operating systems, applications, system software, and application infrastructure. Some existing applications are used to run current business processes, so starting from scratch to build a new architecture is not an option. Enterprises should quickly respond to business changes with agility; leverage existing investments in applications and application infrastructure to address newer business requirements; and support new channels of interactions with customers, partners, and suppliers. SOA with its loosely coupled nature allows enterprises to plug in new services or upgrade existing services in a granular fashion. This enables businesses to address the new business requirements, provides the option to make the services consumable across different channels, and exposes the existing enterprise and legacy applications as services, thereby safeguarding existing IT infrastructure investments (see Figure 5.9). The key technical concepts of SOA are:

- *Services*—a business task
- *Interoperability*—the capability of two or more computer systems to share data and resources, even though they are made by different manufacturers
- *Loose coupling*—the capability of services to be joined together on demand to create composite services, or disassembled just as easily into their functional components[18]

FIGURE 5.8 The Service Oriented Architecture

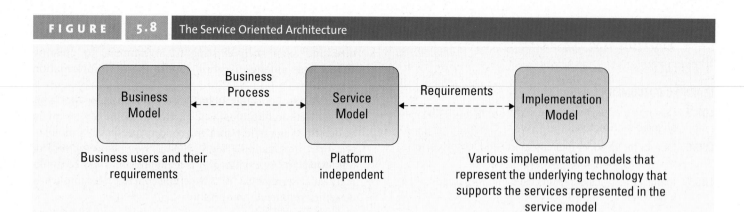

FIGURE 5.9 SOA Integration

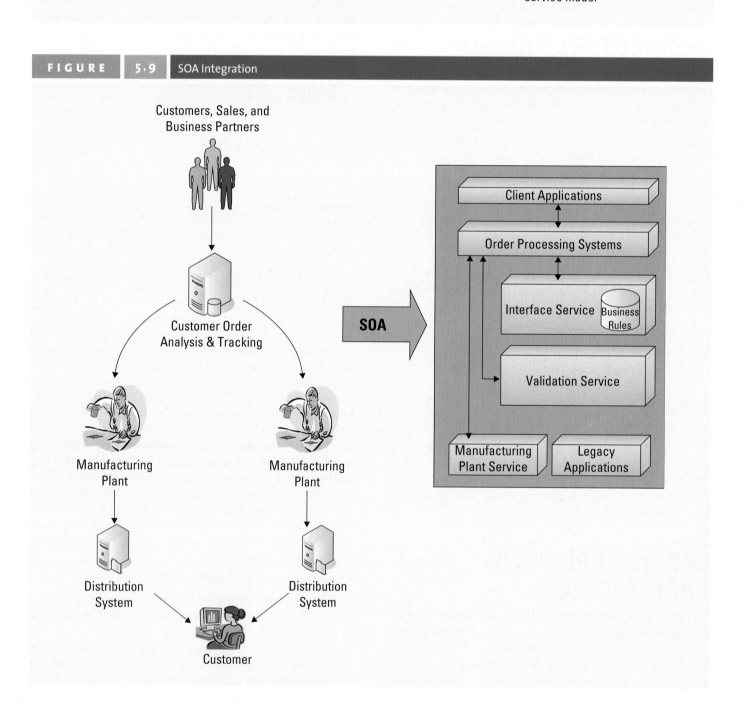

Service

Service oriented architecture begins with a service—an SOA *service* being simply a business task, such as checking a potential customer's credit rating when opening a new account. It is important to stress that this is part of a business process. As mentioned in the previous section, services are "like" software products, however, when describing SOA, do not think about software or IT. Think about what a company does on a day-to-day basis, and break up those business processes into repeatable business tasks or components.

SOA provides the technology underpinnings for working with services that are not just software or hardware, but rather business tasks. It is a pattern for developing a more flexible kind of software application that can promote loose coupling among software components while reusing existing investments in technology in new, more valuable ways across the organization. SOA is based on standards that enable interoperability, business agility, and innovation to generate more business value for those who use these principles.

SOA helps companies become more agile by aligning business needs and the IT capabilities that support these needs. Business drives requirements for IT; SOA enables the IT environment to effectively and efficiently respond to these requirements. SOA is about helping companies apply reusability and flexibility that can lower cost (of development, integration, maintenance), increase revenue, and obtain sustainable competitive advantage through technology.

It is very important to note that SOA is an evolution. Although its results are revolutionary, it builds on many technologies used in the marketplace, such as web services, transactional technologies, information-driven principles, loose coupling, components, and object-oriented design. The beauty of SOA is that these technologies exist together in SOA through standards, well-defined interfaces, and organizational commitments to reuse key services instead of reinventing the wheel. SOA is not just about technology, but about how technology and business link themselves for a common goal of business flexibility.

Businesses have become increasingly complex over the past couple of decades. Factors such as mergers, regulations, global competition, outsourcing, and partnering have resulted in a massive increase in the number of applications any given company might use. These applications were implemented with little knowledge of the other applications with which they would be required to share information in the future. As a result, many companies are trying to maintain IT systems that coexist but are not integrated.

SOA can help provide solutions to companies that face a variety of business issues; Figure 5.10 lists some of those.[19]

Interoperability

As defined in the previous section, interoperability is the capability of two or more computer systems to share data and resources, even though they are made by different manufacturers. Businesses today use a variety of systems that have resulted

---

omg lol

I Don't Have a Temperature, but I'm Positive I Have a Virus

There is nothing worse than finishing your paper at 4 a.m. and finding out that your computer has a virus and you just lost your entire document. Well, there might be one thing that is worse. You submit your final paper, which is worth 50 percent of your grade, and then you head off to Florida for spring break. You return to find that you failed the course and you frantically check email to find out what happened. In your email is a message from your professor informing you that your paper was corrupt and couldn't be opened and that you had 24 hours to resend the file, which, of course, you missed because you were lying on the beach.

There is an entrepreneur in every bunch, and good business-people can take lemons

and make lemonade. One such savvy individual saw lemonade in the corrupted file issue and launched Corrupted-Files.com, which sells students (for only $3.95) intentionally corrupted files. Why would anyone want to purchase a corrupted file? According to the website the reasons are obvious.

"Step 1: After purchasing a file, rename the file e.g. Mike_Final-Paper. Step 2: Email the file to your professor along with your 'here's my assignment' e-mail. Step 3: It will take your professor several hours if not days to notice your file is 'unfortunately' corrupted. Use the time this website just bought you wisely and finish that paper!!! This download includes a 2, 5, 10, 20, 30 and 40 page corrupted Word file. Use the appropriate file size to match each assignment.

Who's to say your 10 page paper didn't get corrupted? Exactly! No one can! It's the perfect excuse to buy yourself extra time and not hand in a garbage paper. Cheating is not the answer to procrastination!— Corrupted-Files.com is! Keep this site a secret!"

When discussing service oriented architectures, there are three primary components, services, interoperability, and loose coupling. What is the service in Corrupted-Files.com? Does it matter if a student is using a Mac or a PC when submitting the corrupted file, and how does this relate to interoperability? Analyze Corrupted-Files .com in terms of loose coupling.

FIGURE 5.10 Business Issues and SOA Solutions

Business Issues	SOA Solutions
■ Agents unable to see policy coverage information remotely ■ Calls/faxes used to get information from other divisions ■ Clinical patient information stored on paper ■ Complex access to supplier design drawings	Integrate information to make it more accessible to employees.
■ High cost of handling customer calls ■ Reconciliation of invoice deductions and rebates ■ Hours on hold to determine patient insurance eligibility ■ High turnover leading to excessive hiring and training costs	Understand how business processes interact to better manage administrative costs.
■ Decreasing customer loyalty due to incorrect invoices ■ Customers placed on hold to check order status ■ Inability to quickly update policy endorsements ■ Poor service levels	Improve customer retention and deliver new products and services through reuse of current investments.
■ Time wasted reconciling separate databases ■ Manual processes such as handling trade allocations ■ Inability to detect quality flaws early in cycle ■ High percentage of scrap and rework	Improve people productivity with better business integration and connectivity.

in a heterogeneous environment. This heterogeneity has inundated businesses with the lack of interoperability. However, since SOA is based on open standards, businesses can create solutions that draw upon functionality from these existing, previously isolated systems that are portable and/or interoperable, regardless of the environment in which they exist.

A web service was defined earlier as an open standards way of supporting interoperability. Web services are frequently application programming interfaces (API) that can be accessed over a network, such as the Internet, and executed on a remote system hosting the requested services. SOA is a style of architecture that enables the creation of applications that are built by combining loosely coupled and interoperable services. These services interoperate based on a formal definition that is independent of the underlying platform and programming language. In SOA, since the basic unit of communication is a message rather than an operation, web services are usually loosely coupled. Although SOA can exist without web services, the best-practice implementation of SOA for flexibility always involves web services.

Technically, web services are based on *Extensible Markup Language (XML),* a markup language for documents containing structured information. The technical specifics of XML's capabilities go beyond the scope of this book, but for our purposes, they support things such as ebusiness transactions, mathematical equations, and a thousand other kinds of structured information. XML is a common data representation that can be used as the medium of exchange between programs that are written in different programming languages and execute different kinds of machine instructions. In simple terms, think about XML as the official translator for structured information. Structured information is both the content (word, picture, and so on) and the role it plays. XML is the basis for all web service technologies and the key to interoperability; every web service specification is based on XML.

Loose Coupling

Part of the value of SOA is that it is built on the premise of loose coupling of services. *Loose coupling* is the capability of services to be joined on demand to create composite services or disassembled just as easily into their functional components.

Loose coupling is a way of ensuring that the technical details such as language, platform, and so on are decoupled from the service. For example, look at currency conversion. Today all banks have multiple currency converters, all with different rate refreshes at different times. By creating a common service "conversion of currency" that is loosely coupled to all banking functions that require conversion, the rates, times, and samplings can be averaged to ensure floating the treasury in the most effective manner possible. Another example is common customer identification. Most businesses lack a common customer ID and, therefore, have no way to determine who the customers are and what they buy for what reason. Creating a common customer ID that is independent of applications and databases allows loosely coupling the service "Customer ID" to data, and applications without the application or database ever knowing who it is or where it is.

The difference between traditional, tightly bound interactions and loosely coupled services is that, before the transaction occurs, the functional pieces (services) operating within the SOA are dormant and disconnected. When the business process initiates, these services momentarily interact with each other. They do so for just long enough to execute their piece of the overall process, and then they go back to their dormant state, with no long-standing connection to the other services with which they just interacted. The next time the same service is called, it could be as part of a different business process with different calling and destination services.

A great way to understand this is through the analogy of the telephone system. At the dawn of widespread phone usage, operators had to physically plug in a wire to create a semipermanent connection between two parties. Callers were "tightly bound" to each other. Today you pick up your cell phone and put it to your ear, and there's no dial tone—it's disconnected. You enter a number, push "Talk," and only then does the process initiate, establishing a loosely coupled connection just long enough for your conversation. Then when the conversation is over, your cell phone goes back to dormant mode until a new connection is made with another party. As a result, supporting a million cell phone subscribers does not require that the cell phone service provider support a million live connections; it requires supporting only the number of simultaneous conversations at any given time. It allows for a much more flexible and dynamic exchange.[20]

●● LO5.7

Identify the logical functions used in a virtualized environment.

VIRTUALIZATION

Virtualization is a framework of dividing the resources of a computer into multiple execution environments. It is a way of increasing physical resources to maximize the investment in hardware. Generally, this process is done with virtualization software, running on the one physical unit that emulates multiple pieces of hardware.

In a virtualized environment, the logical functions of computing, storage, and network elements are separated from their physical functions. Functions from these resources can then be manually or automatically allocated to meet the changing needs and priorities of a business. These concepts can be applied broadly across the enterprise, from data-center resources to PCs and printers.

Through virtualization, people, processes, and technology work together more efficiently to meet increased service levels. Since capacity can be allocated dynamically, chronic over-provisioning is eliminated and an entire IT architecture is simplified (see Figure 5.11).

Even something as simple as partitioning a hard drive is considered virtualization because you take one drive and partition it to create two separate hard drives. Devices, applications, and users are able to interact with the virtual machines as if it were a real single logical resource.

What Are Virtual Machines?

System virtualization (often referred to as "server virtualization" or "desktop virtualization," depending on the role of the virtualized system) is the ability to present the resources of a single computer as if it is a collection of separate computers ("virtual machines"), each with its own virtual CPUs, network interfaces, storage, and operating system.

Virtual machine technology was first implemented on mainframes in the 1960s to allow the expensive systems to be partitioned into separate domains and used more efficiently by more users and applications. As standard PC servers became more powerful in the past decade, virtualization has been brought to the desktop and notebook processors to provide the same benefits.[21]

Virtual machines appear both to the user within the system and the world outside as separate computers, each with its own network identity, user authorization and authentication capabilities, operating system version and configuration, applications,

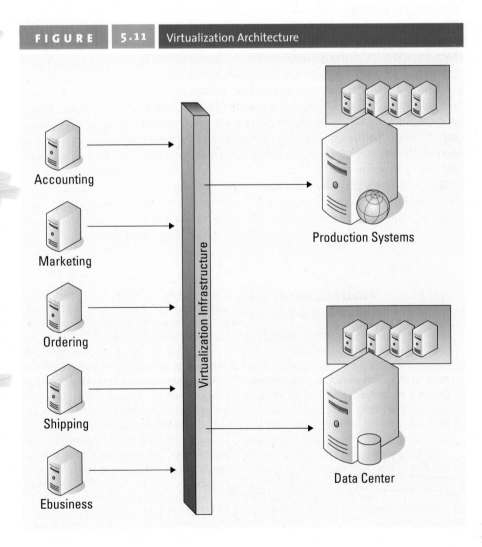

FIGURE 5.11 Virtualization Architecture

Accounting
Marketing
Ordering
Shipping
Ebusiness

Virtualization Infrastructure

Production Systems

Data Center

and data. The hardware is consistent across all virtual machines: While the number or size of them may differ, devices are used that allow virtual machines to be portable, independent of the actual hardware type on the underlying systems.

Figure 5.12 shows an overview of what a system virtualization framework looks like.

Virtualization Business Benefits

Virtualization is by no means a new technology. As previously mentioned, mainframe computers have offered the ability to host multiple operating systems for over 30 years. However, several trends have moved virtualization into the spotlight, such as hardware being underutilized, data centers running out of space, energy costs increasing, and system administration costs mounting. The U.S. Environmental Protection Agency recently proclaimed that data centers consumed 61 billion kilowatt-hours of electricity. That is roughly 1.6 percent of total U.S. electricity consumption and is worth about $4.5 billion. Assuming current trends continue, by 2011 the national energy consumption by data centers is expected to nearly double, making energy efficiency a top priority.[22]

The first major virtualization trend highlights hardware being underutilized. In the April 1965 issue of *Electronics* magazine, Gordon Moore first offered his observation about processor computing power, which has come to be known as Moore's law. In describing the increasing power of computing power, Moore stated: "The complexity for minimum component costs has increased at a rate of roughly a factor of two per year." What he means is that each year (actually, most people estimate the time frame at around 18 months), for a given size processor, twice as many individual components can be squeezed onto a similarly sized piece of silicon. Put another way, every new generation of chip delivers twice as much processing power as the previous generation—at the same price.

Moore's law demonstrates increasing returns—the amount of improvement itself grows over time because there's an exponential increase in capacity for every generation of processor improvement. That exponential increase is responsible for the mind-boggling improvements in computing—and the increasing need for virtualization.[23]

Today, many data centers have machines running at only 10 to 15 percent of total processing capacity, which translates to 85 to 90 percent of the machine's power being unused. In a way, Moore's law is no longer relevant to most companies because they are not able to take advantage of the increased power available to them.

Moore's law not only enables virtualization, but also effectively makes it mandatory. Otherwise, increasing amounts of computing power will go to waste each year.

fyi

Virtualization for Your Cell Phone

Virtualization is a difficult concept to understand. The formal definition is a framework dividing the resources of a computer into multiple execution environments. OK, let's try that again in English. Imagine you have three cell phones, one for the company you work for, one for a company you are starting on the side, and one for personal calls. For the most part, the phones are idle and they seldom ever ring at the same time. Because the phones are idle the majority of the time, you notice that it's a waste of time and resources to support idle time, especially when you are paying for cell service on each phone. You decide to use virtualization to help your situation.

What this would do is essentially put three virtual cell phones on one device. The individual services and application for each phone would be independently stored on the one device. From the device's perspective, it sees three separate virtual phones. This saves time and money in expenses and maintenance. You could even use virtualization to turn your cell phone into a scanner. Just visit ScanR.com; for just $5 a month you can use the camera on your phone to scan documents. Take a photo of any document, business card, or whiteboard and upload it to ScanR's website, and in minutes it is returned to you in a digital file. Could be helpful if your friend has to miss class and you want to save your professor's notes.

Virtualization is a hot topic these days as more and more businesses focus on social responsibility and attempt to find ways to reduce their carbon footprints. What are the potential environmental impacts of virtualization? What are the business advantages of virtualization? What risks are associated with virtualization?

FIGURE 5.12 System Virtualization

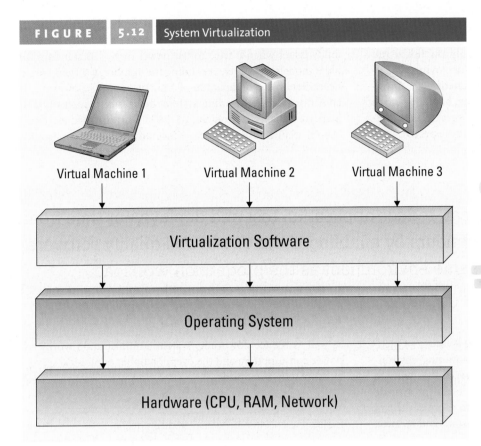

Virtual Machine 1   Virtual Machine 2   Virtual Machine 3

Virtualization Software

Operating System

Hardware (CPU, RAM, Network)

A second virtualization trend concentrates on data centers running out of space. The business world has undergone an enormous transformation over the past 20 years. In 1985, the vast majority of business processes were paper based. Computerized systems were confined to so-called backroom automation: payroll, accounting, and the like. That has all changed, thanks to the steady march of Moore's law. Business process after business process has been captured in software and automated, moving from paper to computers.[24]

The rise of the Internet has exponentially increased this transformation. Companies want to communicate with customers and partners in real time, using the worldwide connectivity of the Internet. Naturally, this has accelerated the move to computerized business processes.

Boeing's latest airliner, the 787 Dreamliner, is being designed and built in a radically new way. Boeing and each of its suppliers use computer-aided design (CAD) software to design their respective parts of the plane. All communication about the project uses the CAD designs as the basis for discussion. Use of CAD software enables testing to be done in computer models rather than the traditional method of building physical prototypes, thereby speeding completion of the plane by a year or more.

The Dreamliner project generates enormous amounts of data. Just one piece of the project—a data warehouse containing project plans—runs to 19 terabytes of data. The net effect of all this and similar projects at other companies is that huge numbers of servers have been put into use over the past decade, which is causing a real-estate problem—companies are running out of space in their data centers.[25]

Virtualization, by offering the ability to host multiple guest systems on a single physical server, helps organizations to reclaim data center territory, thereby avoiding the expense of building out more data center space. This is an enormous benefit of virtualization because data centers cost in the tens of millions of dollars to construct.

Rapidly escalating energy costs are also furthering the trend toward virtualization. The cost of running computers, coupled with the fact that many of the machines filling up data centers are running at low utilization rates, means that virtualization's ability to reduce the total number of physical servers can significantly reduce the overall cost of energy for companies. Data center power is such an issue that energy companies are putting virtualization programs into place to address it.

These trends reveal why virtualization is a technology whose time has come. The exponential power growth of computers, the substitution of automated processes for manual work, the increasing cost to power the multitude of computers, and the high personnel cost to manage that multitude all cry out for a less expensive way to run data centers. In fact, a newer, more efficient method of running data centers is critical because, given the trends mentioned above, the traditional methods of delivering computing are becoming cost prohibitive.

Virtualization enables data center managers to make far better use of computer resources than in nonvirtualized environments, and it enables an enterprise to maximize its investment in hardware. Underutilized hardware platforms and server sprawl—today's norm—can become things of the past. By virtualizing a large deployment of older systems on a few highly scalable, highly reliable, enterprise-class servers, businesses can substantially reduce costs related to hardware purchases, provisioning, and maintenance.

Additional Virtualization Benefits

Virtualization offers more than server consolidation benefits as described in the previous section. Rapid application deployment, dynamic load balancing, and streamlined disaster recovery top the list of additional benefits. Virtualization technologies can reduce application test and deployment time from days or weeks to a matter of hours by enabling users to test and qualify software in isolation but also in the same environment as the production workload.

Virtualization, in all its forms, is a highly disruptive yet clearly beneficial technology. Enterprises are deploying virtualization for a number of real and significant benefits. The strongest driver—business continuity—is surprising, but many of the other drivers, such as flexibility and agility, server consolidation, and reduced administration costs, are fully expected.

The facility suffered from several problems. Some of its applications had reliability issues, but the IT staff faced compatibility issues when it tried to use newer servers as standbys for older models. However, expanding the number of servers would necessitate a major upgrade of the data center's power needs and the associated cooling system. To reduce complexity and increase capacity and reliability, the IT staff installed a virtualization architecture to increase flexibility and system reliability,

> **Virtualization technologies can reduce application test and deployment time from days or weeks to a matter of hours by enabling users to test and qualify software in isolation but also in the same environment as the production workload.**

Other advantages of virtualization include a variety of security benefits (stemming from centralized computing environments); improved service-level management (i.e., the ability to manage resource allocation against service levels for specific applications and business users); the ability to more easily run legacy systems; greater flexibility in locating staff; and reduced hardware and software costs.

In its 620-acre facility in Lafayette, Indiana, Subaru of Indiana produces cars and SUVs for its parent company, Fuji Heavy Industries, and Camry vehicles for Toyota. It has the capacity to produce 21,800 vehicles a month, using the just-in-time method of manufacturing. This method requires a streamlined production line, with highly accurate and reliable inventory controls. A lack of any one component can stop the assembly line and trigger problems up and down the supply chain.

as well as reduce downtime, system administration workload, power consumption, and the overall number of physical servers by more than two-thirds.[26]

 LO5.8

Explain the business benefits of grid computing.

GRID COMPUTING

When you turn on the light, the power grid delivers exactly what you need, instantly. Computers and networks can now work that way using grid computing. *Grid computing* is an aggregation of geographically dispersed computing, storage, and network resources, coordinated to deliver improved performance, higher quality of service, better utilization, and easier access to data.

Living the DREAM

Recycle Your Phone

I know that you are all excited to get the new iPhone with its numerous applications and cool games, but what are you going to do with your old cell phone? You can help the environment and recycle your phone, PDA, charger, and batteries. More than 14 million Americans recycled their cell phones in 2007, helping to save energy and keep usable materials out of landfills. Cell phones are made of precious metals, copper, and plastics, each of which requires energy to mine and manufacture. Recycling conserves these materials so they can be turned into new products, thereby saving energy. Remember these three things prior to recycling your cell phone:

1. Terminate your phone service.
2. Clear the phones memory of contacts and other stored information.
3. Remove the SIM card.

If your old cell phone is still working, you might also want to consider donating it to charity. There are many programs that will accept working cell phones that they donate to people in need (such as survivors of domestic violence) because old cell phones can still dial 911 even after the service is disconnected. To find local agencies where you can donate your cell phone, just visit ncadv.org.

Cell phones are only a small percentage of the total computer equipment organizations replace each year. What happens to all of those old laptops, notebooks, BlackBerrys, servers, and monitors? What is the environmental impact of throwing a computer system into a landfill? What can companies do to recycle their computer equipment? What can the government do to help motivate companies and individuals to recycle?

Grid computing enables the virtualization of distributed computing and data resources such as processing, network bandwidth, and storage capacity to create a single system image, granting users and applications seamless access to vast IT capabilities. Virtualizing these resources yields a scalable, flexible pool of processing and data storage that the enterprise can use to improve efficiency. Moreover, it will help create a sustainable competitive advantage by streamlining product development and allowing focus to be placed on the core business. Over time, grid environments will enable the creation of virtual organizations and advanced web services as partnerships and collaborations become more critical in strengthening each link in the value chain (see Figure 5.13).

FIGURE 5.13 Virtual Organizations Using Grid Computing

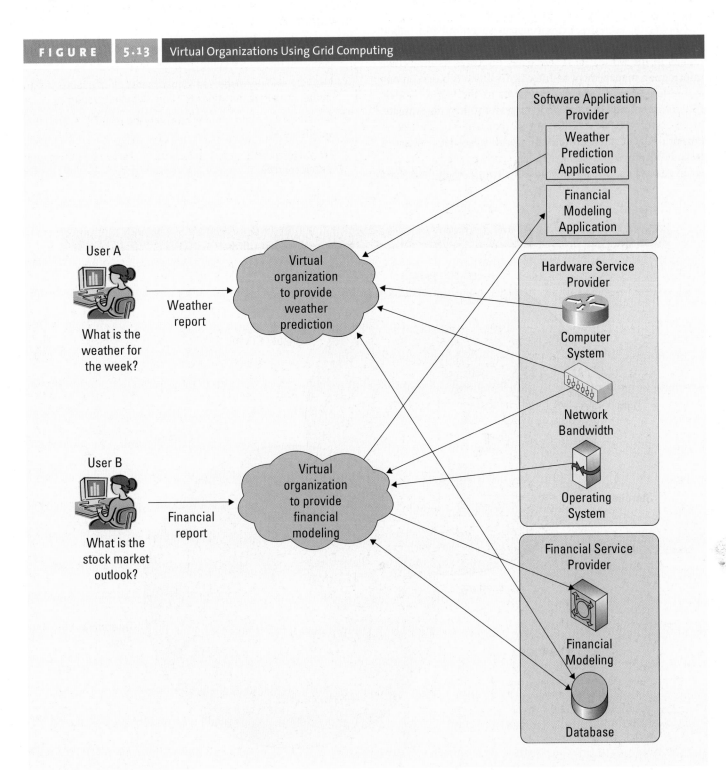

Grid Computing Business Benefits

At its core, grid computing is based on an open set of standards and protocols (e.g., Open Grid Services Architecture) that enable communication across heterogeneous, geographically dispersed environments, as shown in Figure 5.14. With grid computing, organizations can optimize computing and data resources, pool them for large-capacity workloads, share them across networks, and enable collaboration.

Google, the secretive, extraordinarily successful $6.1 billion global search engine company, is one of the most recognized brands in the world. Yet it selectively discusses its innovative information management architecture—which is based on one of the largest grid computing systems in the world. Google runs on hundreds of thousands of servers—by one estimate, in excess of 450,000—racked up in thousands of clusters in dozens of data centers around the world. It has data centers in Ireland, Virginia, and California. It recently opened a new center in Atlanta and is currently building two football-field-sized centers in The Dalles, Oregon. By having its servers and data centers distributed geographically, Google delivers faster performance to its worldwide audience.[27]

Grid computing goes far beyond sheer computing power. Today's operating environments must be resilient, flexible, and integrated as never before. Organizations around the world are experiencing substantial benefits by implementing grids in critical business processes to achieve both business and technology benefits. These business benefits include:

- Improving productivity and collaboration of virtual organizations and respective computing and data resources.

- Allowing widely dispersed departments and businesses to create virtual organizations to share data and resources.

- Building robust and infinitely flexible and resilient operational architectures.

- Providing instantaneous access to massive computing and data resources.

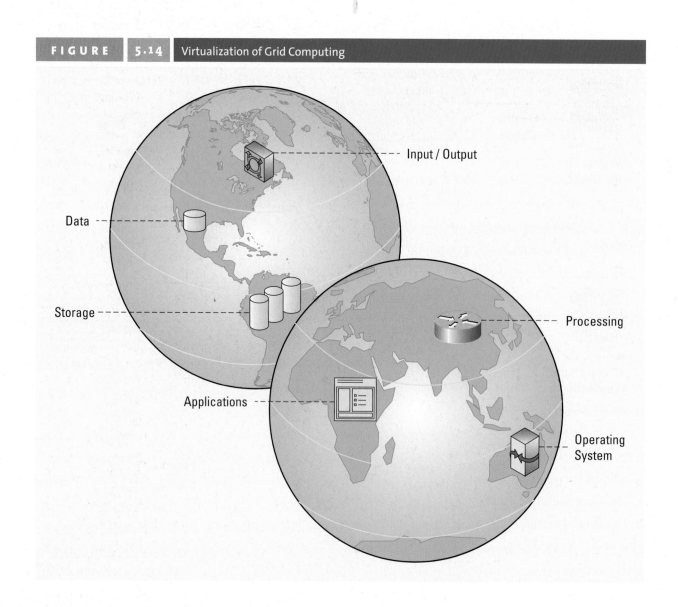

FIGURE 5.14 Virtualization of Grid Computing

- Leveraging existing capital investments, which in turn help to ensure optimal utilization and costs of computing capabilities.[28]

Many organizations have started identifying the major business areas for grid computing business applications. Some examples of major business areas include:

- Life sciences, for analyzing and decoding strings of biological and chemical information.

- Financial services, for running long, complex financial models and arriving at more accurate decisions.

- Higher education for enabling advanced, data- and computation-intensive research.

- Engineering services, including automotive and aerospace, for collaborative design and data-intensive testing.

- Government, for enabling seamless collaboration and agility in both civil and military departments and other agencies.

- Collaborative games for replacing the existing single-server online games with more highly parallel, massively multiplayer online games.

In this pervasive need of information anytime and anywhere, the explosive grid computing environments have now proven to be so significant that they are often referred to as being the world's single and most powerful computer solutions. ■

CHECK OUT www.mhhe.com/baltzanm

for additional study materials including quizzes and PowerPoint presentations.

databases
+ data warehouses

what's in IT for me?

This chapter introduces the concept of information and its relative importance to organizations. It distinguishes between data stored in transactional databases and information housed in enterprisewide data warehouse systems. The chapter also provides an overview of database fundamentals and the steps required to integrate various bits of data stored across multiple, operational data stores into a comprehensive and centralized repository of summarized information, which can be turned into powerful business intelligence.

You, as a business student, must understand the difference between transactional data and summarized information and the different types of questions you would use a transactional database or enterprise data warehouse to answer. You need to be aware of the complexity of storing data in databases and the level of effort required to transform operational data into meaningful, summarized information. You need to realize the power of information and the competitive advantage a data warehouse brings an organization in terms of facilitating business intelligence. Understanding the power of information will help you prepare to compete in a global marketplace. Armed with the power of information you will make smart, informed, and data-supported managerial decisions.

chapter

Six

SECTION 6.1 >>

Database Fundamentals

- Organizational Information
- Storing Organizational Information
- Relational Database Fundamentals
- Relational Database Advantages
- Database Management Systems
- Integrating Information Among Multiple Databases

SECTION 6.2 >>

Data Warehouse Fundamentals

- Accessing Organizational Information
- History of Data Warehousing
- Data Warehouse Fundamentals
- Data Mining and Business Intelligence

nformation is powerful. Information is useful in telling an organization how its current operations are performing and estimating and strategizing how future operations might perform. New perspectives open up when people have the right information and know how to use it. The ability to understand, digest, analyze, and filter information is key to success for any professional in any industry. This chapter demonstrates the value an organization can uncover and create by learning how to manage, access, and analyze organizational information.

It is important to distinguish between data and information. *Data* are raw facts that describe the characteristics of an event. Characteristics for a sales event could include the date, item number, item description, quantity ordered, customer name, and shipping details. *Information* is data converted into a meaningful and useful context. Information from sales events could include best-selling item, worst-selling item, best customer, and worst customer.

●● SECTION 6.1 Database Fundamentals

LEARNING OUTCOMES

LO6.1 List, describe, and provide an example of each of the five characteristics of high quality information.

LO6.2 Define the relationship between a database and a database management system.

LO6.3 Describe the advantages an organization can gain by using a database.

LO6.4 Define the fundamental concepts of the relational database model.

LO6.5 Describe the two primary methods for integrating information across multiple databases.

LO6.6 Compare relational integrity constraints and business-critical integrity constraints.

LO6.7 Describe the benefits of a data-driven website.

●● LO6.1

List, describe, and provide an example of each of the five characteristics of high quality information.

ORGANIZATIONAL INFORMATION

Google recently reported a 200 percent increase in sales of its new Enterprise Search Appliance tool. Companies use the tool within an enterprise information portal (EIP) to search corporate information for answers to customer questions and to fulfill sales orders. Hundreds of Google's customers are already using the tool—Xerox, Hitachi Data Systems, Nextel Communications, Procter & Gamble, Discovery Communications, Cisco Systems, and Boeing. The ability to search, analyze, and comprehend information is vital for any organization's success. The incredible 200 percent growth in sales of Google's Search Appliance tool is a strong indicator that organizations are coveting technologies that help organize and provide access to information.[1]

Information is everywhere in an organization. When addressing a significant business issue, employees must be able to obtain and analyze all the relevant information so they can make the best decision possible. Organizational information comes at different levels and in different formats and "granularities." *Information granularity* refers to the extent of detail within the information (fine and detailed or coarse and abstract). Employees must be able to correlate the different levels, formats, and granularities of information when making decisions. For example, if employees are using a supply

┌ omg lol

That's Not My Mother in the Casket!

Information—you simply can't put a value on having the right (or the cost of having the wrong) information. Just look at the mistake made at the Crib Point cemetery in Victoria, Australia, when they were burying Mrs. Ryan, an 85-year-old woman with almost 70 children, grandchildren, and great grandchildren attending her funeral. The bereaved family of Mrs. Ryan was shocked to lift the lid of her coffin during the funeral to discover another woman lying in her clothes and jewelry. Where was the body of Mrs. Ryan? Mrs. Ryan had been buried earlier that day in the other woman's clothes, jewelry, and plot.

What type of information blunder could possibly occur to allow someone to be buried in the wrong clothes, coffin, and plot?

What could the cemetery do to ensure its customers are buried in the correct places? Why is the quality of information important to any business? What issues can occur when a business uses low quality information to make decisions?

chain management system to make decisions, they might find that their suppliers send information in different formats and granularity at different levels. One supplier might send detailed information in a spreadsheet, another supplier might send summary information in a Word document, and still another might send aggregate information from a database. Employees will need to compare these different types of information for what they commonly reveal to make strategic decisions. Figure 6.1 displays types of information found in organizations.

Successfully collecting, compiling, sorting, and finally analyzing information from multiple levels, in varied formats, exhibiting different granularity can provide tremendous insight into how an organization is performing. Taking a hard look at organizational information can yield exciting and unexpected results such as potential new markets, new ways of reaching customers, and even new ways of doing business.

Samsung Electronics took a detailed look at over 10,000 reports from its resellers to identify "lost deals" or orders lost to competitors. The analysis yielded the enlightening result that 80 percent of lost sales occurred in a single business unit, the health care industry. Furthermore, Samsung was able to identify that 40 percent of its lost sales in the health care industry were going to one particular competitor. Before performing the analysis, Samsung was heading into its market blind. Armed with this valuable information, Samsung is changing its selling strategy in the health care industry by implementing a new strategy to work more closely with hardware vendors to win back lost sales.[2]

Not all companies are successful at managing information. Staples, the office-supplies superstore, opened its first store in 1986 with state-of-the-art technology. The company experienced rapid growth and soon found itself overwhelmed with the resulting volumes of information. The state-of-the-art technology quickly became obsolete, and the company was unable to obtain any insight into its massive volumes of information. A simple query such as identifying the customers who purchased a computer, but not software or peripherals, took hours. Some queries required several days to complete and by the time the managers received answers to their queries it was too late for action.[3]

FIGURE 6.1 Levels, Formats, and Granularities of Organizational Information

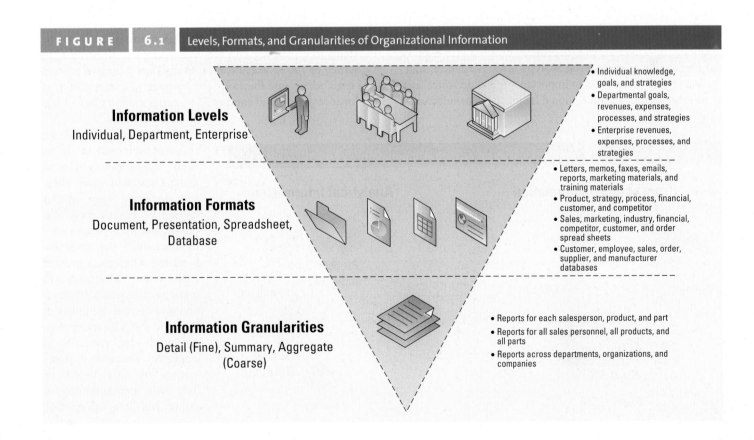

Information Levels
Individual, Department, Enterprise

- Individual knowledge, goals, and strategies
- Departmental goals, revenues, expenses, processes, and strategies
- Enterprise revenues, expenses, processes, and strategies

Information Formats
Document, Presentation, Spreadsheet, Database

- Letters, memos, faxes, emails, reports, marketing materials, and training materials
- Product, strategy, process, financial, customer, and competitor
- Sales, marketing, industry, financial, competitor, customer, and order spread sheets
- Customer, employee, sales, order, supplier, and manufacturer databases

Information Granularities
Detail (Fine), Summary, Aggregate (Coarse)

- Reports for each salesperson, product, and part
- Reports for all sales personnel, all products, and all parts
- Reports across departments, organizations, and companies

After understanding the different levels, formats, and granularities of information, it is important to look at a few additional characteristics that help determine the value of information. These characteristics are type (transactional and analytical), timeliness, and quality.

The Value of Transactional and Analytical Information

As discussed previously in the text, there are two primary types of information, transactional and analytical. Recall that *transactional information* encompasses all of the information contained within a single business process or unit of work, and its primary purpose is to support the performing of daily operational tasks. Organizations capture and store transactional information in databases, and they use it when performing operational tasks and repetitive decisions such as analyzing daily sales reports and production schedules to determine how much inventory to carry.

plant or hire additional sales personnel. Figure 6.2 displays different types of transactional and analytical information.

The Value of Timely Information

The need for timely information can change for each business decision. Some decisions require weekly or monthly information while other decisions require daily information. Timeliness is an aspect of information that depends on the situation. In some industries, information that is a few days or weeks old can be relevant while in other industries information that is a few minutes old can be almost worthless. Some organizations, such as 911 centers, stock traders, and banks, require consolidated, up-to-the-second information, 24 hours a day, seven days a week. Other organizations, such as insurance and construction companies, require only daily or even weekly information.

Real-time information means immediate, up-to-date information. *Real-time systems* provide real-time information in

> The growing demand for real-time information stems from organizations' need to make faster and more effective decisions, keep smaller inventories, operate more efficiently, and track performance more carefully.

Recall that *analytical information* encompasses all organizational information, and its primary purpose is to support the performing of managerial analysis tasks. Analytical information is used when making important ad hoc decisions such as whether the organization should build a new manufacturing

response to query requests. Many organizations use real-time systems to exploit key corporate transactional information. In a survey of 700 IT executives by Evans Data Corp., 48 percent of respondents said they were already analyzing information in or near real-time, and another 25 percent reported plans to add real-time systems.[4]

The growing demand for real-time information stems from organizations' need to make faster and more effective decisions, keep smaller inventories, operate more efficiently, and track performance more carefully. But timeliness is relative. Organizations need fresh, timely information to make good decisions. Information also needs to be timely in the sense that it meets employees' needs—but no more. If employees can absorb information only on an hourly or daily basis, there is no need to gather real-time information

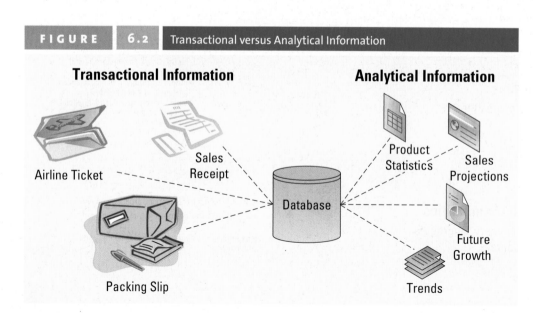

| FIGURE | 6.2 | Transactional versus Analytical Information |

Transactional Information — Airline Ticket, Sales Receipt, Packing Slip → Database

Analytical Information — Database → Product Statistics, Sales Projections, Future Growth, Trends

FIGURE **6.3** Five Common Characteristics of High Quality Information

Accuracy	Are all the values correct? For example, is the name spelled correctly? Is the dollar amount recorded properly?
Completeness	Are any of the values missing? For example, is the address complete including street, city, state, and zip code?
Consistency	Is aggregate or summary information in agreement with detailed information? For example, do all total fields equal the true total of the individual fields?
Uniqueness	Is each transaction, entity, and event represented only once in the information? For example, are there any duplicate customers?
Timeliness	Is the information current with respect to the business requirements? For example, is information updated weekly, daily, or hourly?

in smaller increments. For example, MBIA Insurance Corp. uses overnight updates to feed its real-time systems. Employees use this information to make daily risk decisions for mortgages, insurance policies, and other services. The company found that overnight updates were sufficient, as long as users could gain immediate access to the information they needed to make business decisions during the day.[5]

Most people request real-time information without understanding one of the biggest pitfalls associated with real-time information—continual change. Imagine the following scenario: Three managers meet at the end of the day to discuss a business problem. Each manager has gathered information at different times during the day to create a picture of the situation. Each manager's picture may be different because of this time discrepancy. Their views on the business problem may not match since the information they are basing their analysis on is continually changing. This approach may not speed up decision making, and may actually slow it down.

The timeliness of the information required must be evaluated for each business decision. Organizations do not want to find themselves using real-time information to make a bad decision faster.

The Value of Quality Information

Westpac Financial Services (WFS), one of the four major banks in Australia, serves millions of customers from its many core systems, each with its own database. The databases maintain information and provide users with easy access to the stored information. Unfortunately, the company failed to develop information-capturing standards, which led to inconsistent organizational information. For example, one system had a field to capture email addresses while another system did not. Duplicate customer information among the different

systems was another major issue, and the company continually found itself sending conflicting or competing messages to customers from different operations of the bank. A customer could also have multiple accounts within the company, one representing a life insurance policy and one representing a credit card. WFS had no way to identify that the two different customer accounts were for the same customer.

WFS had to solve its information quality problems immediately if it was to remain competitive. The company purchased NADIS (Name & Address Data Integrity Software), a software solution that filters customer information, highlighting missing, inaccurate, and redundant information. Customer service ratings are on the rise for WFS now that the company can operate its business with a single and comprehensive view of each one of its customers.[6]

Business decisions are only as good as the quality of the information used to make the decisions. Figure 6.3 reviews five characteristics common to high quality information: accuracy, completeness, consistency, uniqueness, and timeliness. Figure 6.4 highlights several issues with low quality information including:

1. The first issue is *missing* information. The customer's first name is missing. (See #1 in Figure 6.4.)

2. The second issue is *incomplete* information since the street address contains only a number and not a street name.

3. The third issue is a probable *duplication* of information since the only slight difference between the two customers is the spelling of the last name. Similar street addresses and phone numbers make this likely.

4. The fourth issue is potential *wrong* information because the customer's phone and fax numbers are the same. Some customers might have the same number for phone and fax line, but the fact that the customer also has this number in the email address field is suspicious.

5. The fifth issue is definitely an example of *inaccurate* information since a phone number is located in the email address field.

6. The sixth issue is *incomplete* information since there is not a valid area code for the phone and fax numbers.

FIGURE 6.4 Low Quality Information Example

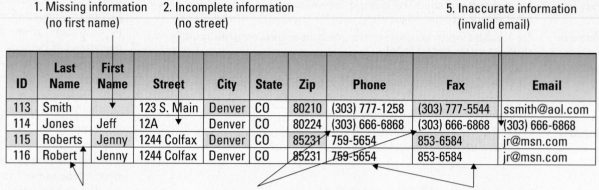

1. Missing information (no first name) 2. Incomplete information (no street) 5. Inaccurate information (invalid email)

ID	Last Name	First Name	Street	City	State	Zip	Phone	Fax	Email
113	Smith		123 S. Main	Denver	CO	80210	(303) 777-1258	(303) 777-5544	ssmith@aol.com
114	Jones	Jeff	12A	Denver	CO	80224	(303) 666-6868	(303) 666-6868	(303) 666-6868
115	Roberts	Jenny	1244 Colfax	Denver	CO	85231	759-5654	853-6584	jr@msn.com
116	Robert	Jenny	1244 Colfax	Denver	CO	85231	759-5654	853-6584	jr@msn.com

3. Probable duplicate information (similar names, same address, phone number) 4. Potential wrong information (are the phone and fax numbers the same or is this an error?) 6. Incomplete information (missing area codes)

Recognizing how low quality information issues occur will allow organizations to begin to correct them. The four primary sources of low quality information are:

1. Online customers intentionally enter inaccurate information to protect their privacy.
2. Different systems have different information entry standards and formats.
3. Call center operators enter abbreviated or erroneous information by accident or to save time.
4. Third-party and external information contains inconsistencies, inaccuracies, and errors.[7]

Addressing the above sources of information inaccuracies will significantly improve the quality of organizational information and the value that can be extracted from the information.

Understanding the Costs of Poor Information
Using the wrong information can lead to making the wrong decision. Making the wrong decision can cost time, money, and even reputations. Every business decision is only as good as the information used to make the decision. Bad information can cause serious business ramifications such as:

- Inability to accurately track customers, which directly affects strategic initiatives.
- Difficulty identifying the organization's most valuable customers.
- Inability to identify selling opportunities and wasted revenue from marketing to nonexisting customers and nondeliverable mail.
- Difficulty tracking revenue because of inaccurate invoices.
- Inability to build strong relationships with customers—which increases buyer power.

Understanding the Benefits of Good Information
High quality information can significantly improve the chances of making a good decision and directly increase an organization's bottom line. Lillian Vernon Corp., a catalog company, used web analytics to discover that men preferred to shop at Lillian Vernon's website instead of looking through its paper catalog. Based on this information, the company began placing male products more prominently on its website and soon realized a 15 percent growth in sales to men.[8]

Another company discovered that Phoenix, Arizona, is not a good place to sell golf clubs, even with its high number of golf courses. An analysis revealed that typical golfers in Phoenix are either tourists or conventioneers. These golfers usually bring their clubs with them while visiting Phoenix. The analysis further revealed that two of the best places to sell golf clubs in the United States are Rochester, New York, and Detroit, Michigan.[9]

There are numerous examples of companies that have used their high quality information to make solid strategic business decisions. High quality information does not automatically guarantee that every decision made is going to be a good one, since people ultimately make decisions. But such information ensures that the basis of the decisions is accurate. The success of the organization depends on appreciating and leveraging the true value of timely and high quality information.

STORING ORGANIZATIONAL INFORMATION

Organizational information is stored in a database. Applications and programs, such as supply chain management systems, and customer relationship management systems, access the data in the database so the program can consult it to answer queries. The records retrieved in answer to questions become information that can be used to make decisions. The computer program used to manage and query a database is known as a database management system (DBMS). The properties and design of database systems are included in the study of information science.

The central concept of a database is that of a collection of records, or pieces of information. Typically, a given database has a structural description of the type of facts held in that database: This description is known as a schema. The schema describes the objects that are represented in the database and the relationships among them. There are a number of different ways of organizing a schema, that is, of modeling the database structure. These are known as database models (or data models). The most commonly used model today is the relational model, which represents all information in the form of multiple related tables each consisting of rows and columns. This model represents relationships by the use of values common to more than one table. Other models, such as the hierarchical model, and the network model, use a more explicit representation of relationships.

Many professionals consider a collection of data to constitute a database only if it has certain properties; for example, if the data are managed to ensure integrity and quality, if it allows

> The central concept of a database is that of a collection of records, or pieces of information.

shared access by a community of users, if it has a schema, or if it supports a query language. However, there is no definition of these properties that is universally agreed upon.[10]

RELATIONAL DATABASE FUNDAMENTALS

There are many different models for organizing information in a database, including the hierarchical database, network database, and the most prevalent—the relational database model. Broadly defined, a **database** maintains information about various types of objects (inventory), events (transactions), people (employees), and places (warehouses). In a **hierarchical database model**, information is organized into a tree-like structure that allows repeating information using parent/child relationships in such a way that it cannot have too many relationships. Hierarchical structures were widely used in the first mainframe database management systems. However, owing to their restrictions, hierarchical structures often cannot be used to relate to structures that exist in the real world. The **network database model** is a flexible way of representing objects and their relationships. Where the hierarchical model structures data as a tree of records, with each record having one parent record and many children, the network model allows each record to have multiple parent and child records, forming a lattice structure. The **relational database model** is a type of database that stores information in the form of logically related two-dimensional tables. This text focuses on the relational database model.

Consider how the Coca-Cola Bottling Company of Egypt (TCCBCE) implemented an inventory-tracking database to improve order accuracy by 27 percent, decrease order response time by 66 percent, and increase sales by 20 percent. With over 7,400 employees, TCCBCE owns and operates 11 bottling plants and 29 sales and distribution centers, making it one of the largest companies in Egypt.

Traditionally, the company sent distribution trucks to each customer's premises to take orders and deliver stock. Many problems were associated with this process including numerous information entry errors, which caused order-fulfillment time to take an average of three days. To remedy the situation, Coca-Cola decided to create presales teams equipped with handheld devices to visit customers and take orders electronically. On returning to the office, the teams synchronized orders with the company's inventory-tracking database to ensure automated processing and rapid dispatch of accurate orders to customers.[11]

Entities and Attributes

Figure 6.5 illustrates the primary concepts of the relational database model—entities, entity classes, attributes, keys, and relationships. An *entity* in the relational database model is a person, place, thing, transaction, or event about which information is stored. A table in the relational database model is a collection of similar entities. The tables of interest in Figure 6.5 are *CUSTOMER, ORDER, ORDER LINE, PRODUCT,* and *DISTRIBUTOR.* Notice that each entity class (the collection of similar entities) is stored in a different two-dimensional table. *Attributes,* also called fields or columns, are characteristics or properties of an entity class. In Figure 6.5 the attributes for *CUSTOMER* include *Customer ID, Customer Name, Contact Name,* and *Phone.* Attributes for *PRODUCT* include *Product ID, Product Description,* and *Price.* Each specific entity in an entity class (e.g., Dave's Sub Shop in the *CUSTOMER* table) occupies one row in its respective table. The columns in the table contain the attributes.

Keys and Relationships

To manage and organize various entity classes within the relational database model, developers must identify primary keys and foreign keys and use them to create logical relationships. A *primary key* is a field (or group of fields) that uniquely identifies a given entity in a table. In *CUSTOMER,* the *Customer ID* uniquely identifies each entity (customer) in the table and is the primary key. Primary keys are important because they provide a way of distinguishing each entity in a table.

A *foreign key* in the relational database model is a primary key of one table that appears as an attribute in another table and acts to provide a logical relationship between the two tables. Consider Hawkins Shipping, one of the distributors appearing in the *DISTRIBUTOR* table. Its primary key, *Distributor ID,* is DEN8001. Notice that *Distributor ID* also appears as an attribute in the ORDER table. This establishes the fact that Hawkins Shipping (*Distributor ID* DEN8001) was responsible for delivering orders 34561 and 34562 to the appropriate customer(s). Therefore, *Distributor ID* in the *ORDER* table creates a logical relationship (who shipped what order) between *ORDER* and *DISTRIBUTOR.*

●● LO6.3

Describe the advantages an organization can gain by using a database.

●● LO6.6

Compare relational integrity constraints and business-critical integrity constraints.

Determining Information Quality Issues

Real People is a magazine geared toward working individuals that provides articles and advice on everything from car maintenance to family planning. *Real People* is currently experiencing problems with its magazine distribution list. More than 30 percent of the magazines mailed are returned because of incorrect address information, and each month it receives numerous calls from angry customers complaining that they have not yet received their magazines. Here is a sample of *Real People*'s customer information. Create a report detailing all of the issues with the information, potential causes of the information issues, and solutions the company can follow to correct the situation.

ID	First Name	Middle Initial	Last Name	Street	City	State	Zip Code
433	M	J	Jones	13 Denver	Denver	CO	87654
434	Margaret	J	Jones	13 First Ave.	Denver	CO	87654
434	Brian	F	Hoover	Lake Ave.	Columbus	OH	87654
435	Nick	H	Schweitzer	65 Apple Lane	San Francisco	OH	65664
436	Richard	A		567 55th St.	New York	CA	98763
437	Alana	B	Smith	121 Tenny Dr.	Buffalo	NY	142234
438	Trevor	D	Darrian	90 Fresrdestil	Dallas	TX	74532

RELATIONAL DATABASE ADVANTAGES

From a business perspective, database information offers many advantages, including:

- Increased flexibility.
- Increased scalability and performance.
- Reduced information redundancy.
- Increased information integrity (quality).
- Increased information security.

Increased Flexibility

Databases tend to mirror business structures, and a good database can handle changes quickly and easily, just as any good business needs to be able to handle changes quickly

Order Number: 34562

Coca-Cola Bottling Company of Egypt
Sample Sales Order

| Customer: | Dave's Sub Shop | Date: | 8/6/2008 |

Quantity	Product	Price	Amount
100	Vanilla Coke	$0.55	$55

Distributor Fee $12.95
Order Total $67.95

CUSTOMER

Customer ID	Customer Name	Contact Name	Phone
23	Dave's Sub Shop	David Logan	(555)333-4545
43	Pizza Palace	Debbie Fernandez	(555)345-5432
765	T's Fun Zone	Tom Repicci	(555)565-6655

ORDER

Order ID	Order Date	Customer ID	Distributor ID	Distributor Fee	Total Due
34561	7/4/2008	23	DEN8001	$22.00	$145.75
34562	8/6/2008	23	DEN8001	$12.95	$67.95
34563	6/5/2008	765	NY9001	$29.50	$249.50

ORDER LINE

Order ID	Line Item	Product ID	Quantity
34561	1	12345AA	75
34561	2	12346BB	50
34561	3	12347CC	100
34562	1	12349EE	300
34563	1	12345AA	100
34563	2	12346BB	100
34563	3	12347CC	50
34563	4	12348DD	50
34563	5	12349EE	100

DISTRIBUTOR

Distributor ID	Distributor Name
DEN8001	Hawkins Shipping
CHI3001	ABC Trucking
NY9001	Van Distributors

PRODUCT

Product ID	Product Description	Price
12345AA	Coca-Cola	$0.55
12346BB	Diet Coke	$0.55
12347CC	Sprite	$0.55
12348DD	Diet Sprite	$0.55
12349EE	Vanilla Coke	$0.55

and easily. Equally important, databases provide flexibility in allowing each user to access the information in whatever way best suits his or her needs. The distinction between logical and physical views is important in understanding flexible database user views. The **physical view** of information deals with the physical storage of information on a storage device such as a hard disk. The **logical view** of information focuses on how users logically access information to meet their particular business needs. This separation of logical and physical views is what allows each user to access database information differently. That is, while a database has only one physical view, it can easily support multiple logical views. In the previous database illustration, for example, users could perform a query to determine which distributors delivered shipments to Pizza Palace last week. At the same time, another person could perform some sort of statistical analysis to determine the frequency at which Sprite and Diet Coke appear on the same order. These represent two very different logical views, but both views use the same physical view.

Consider another example—a mail-order business. One user might want a report presented in alphabetical format, in which case last name should appear before first name. Another user, working with a catalog mailing system, would want customer names appearing as first name and then last name. Both are easily achievable, but different logical views of the same physical information.

Increased Scalability and Performance

The official website of The American Family Immigration History Center, www.ellisisland.org, generated over 2.5 billion hits in its first year of operation. The site offers easy access to immigration information about people who entered America through the Port of New York and Ellis Island between 1892 and 1924. The database contains over 25 million passenger names correlated to 3.5 million images of ships' manifests.[12]

Only a database could "scale" to handle the massive volumes of information and the large numbers of users required for the successful launch of the Ellis Island website. **Scalability** refers to how well a system can adapt to increased demands. **Performance** measures how quickly a system performs a certain process or transaction. Some organizations must be able to support hundreds or thousands of online users including employees, partners, customers, and suppliers, who all want to access and share information. Databases today scale to exceptional levels, allowing all types of users and programs to perform information-processing and information-searching tasks.

Reduced Information Redundancy

Redundancy is the duplication of information, or storing the same information in multiple places. Redundant information occurs because organizations frequently capture and store the same information in multiple locations. The primary problem with redundant information is that it is often inconsistent, which makes it difficult to determine which values are the most current or most accurate. Not having correct information is confusing and frustrating for employees and disruptive to an organization. One primary goal of a database is to eliminate information redundancy by recording each piece of information in only one place in the database. Eliminating information redundancy saves space, makes performing information updates easier, and improves information quality.

Increased Information Integrity (Quality)

Information integrity is a measure of the quality of information. Within a database environment, *integrity constraints* are rules that help ensure the quality of information. Integrity constraints can be defined and built into the database design. The database (more appropriately, the database management system, which is discussed below) ensures that users can never violate these constraints. There are two types of integrity constraints: (1) relational integrity constraints and (2) business-critical integrity constraints.

Relational integrity constraints are rules that enforce basic and fundamental information-based constraints. For example, an operational integrity constraint would not allow someone to create an order for a nonexistent customer, provide a markup percentage that was negative, or order zero pounds of raw materials from a supplier. *Business-critical integrity constraints* enforce business rules vital to an organization's success and often require more insight and knowledge than relational integrity constraints. Consider a supplier of fresh produce to large grocery chains such as Kroger. The supplier might implement a business-critical integrity constraint stating that no product returns are accepted after 15 days past delivery. That would make sense because of the chance of spoilage of the produce. These types of integrity constraints tend to mirror the very rules by which an organization achieves success.

The specification and enforcement of integrity constraints produce higher quality information that will provide better support for business decisions. Organizations that establish specific procedures for developing integrity constraints typically see a decline in information error rates and an increase in the use of organizational information.

Increased Information Security

Information is an organizational asset. Like any asset, the organization must protect its information from unauthorized users or misuse. As systems become increasingly complex and more available over the Internet, security becomes an even bigger issue. Databases offer many security features including passwords, access levels, and access controls. Passwords provide authentication of the user who is gaining access to the system. Access levels determine who has access to the different types of information, and access controls determine what type of access they have to the information. For example, customer service representatives might need read-only access to customer order information so they can answer customer order inquiries; they might not have or need the authority to change or delete order information. Managers might require access to employee files, but they should have access only to their own employees' files, not the employee files for the entire company. Various security features of databases can ensure that individuals have only certain types of access to certain types of information.

Databases can increase personal security as well as information security. The Chicago Police Department (CPD) has relied on a crime-fighting system called Citizen and Law Enforcement Analysis and Reporting (CLEAR). CLEAR electronically streamlines the way detectives enter and access critical information to help them solve crimes, analyze crime patterns, and ultimately promote security in a proactive manner. The CPD enters 650,000 new criminal cases and 500,000 new arrests into CLEAR each year.[13]

●● L06.2
Define the relationship between a database and a database management system.

●● L06.7
Describe the benefits of a data-driven website.

DATABASE MANAGEMENT SYSTEMS

Ford's European plant manufactures more than 5,000 vehicles a day and sells them in over 100 countries worldwide. Every component of every model must conform to complex European standards, including passenger safety standards and pedestrian and environmental protection standards. These standards govern each stage of Ford's manufacturing process from design to final production. The company needs

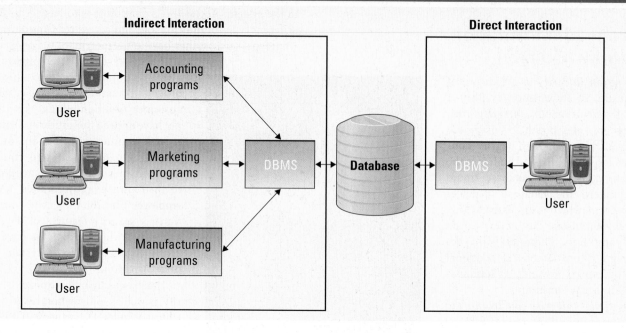

to obtain many thousands of different approvals each year to comply with the standards. Overlooking just one means the company cannot sell the finished vehicle, which brings the production line to a standstill and could potentially cost Ford up to 1 million euros per day. Ford built the Homologation Timing System (HTS), based on a relational database, to help it track and analyze these standards. The reliability and high performance of the HTS have helped Ford substantially reduce its compliance risk.[14]

A database management system is used to access information from a database. A *database management system (DBMS)* is software through which users and application programs interact with a database. The user sends requests to the DBMS and the DBMS performs the actual manipulation of the information in the database. There are two primary ways that users can interact with a DBMS: (1) directly and (2) indirectly, as displayed in Figure 6.6. In either case, users access the DBMS and the DBMS accesses the database.

Data-Driven Websites

The pages on a website must change according to what a site visitor is interested in browsing. Consider for example, a company selling sports cars. A database is created with information on each of the currently available cars (e.g., make, model, engine details, year, a photograph, etc.). A visitor to the website clicks on Porsche, for example, enters the price range he or she is interested in, and hits "Go." The visitor is presented with information on available cars within the price range and an invitation to purchase or request more information from the company. Via a secure administration area on the website, the company has the ability to modify, add, or remove cars to the database.[15]

A *data-driven website* is an interactive website kept constantly updated and relevant to the needs of its customers through the use of a database. Data-driven websites are especially useful when the site offers a great deal of information, products, or services. Website visitors are frequently angered if they are buried under an avalanche of information when searching a site. A data-driven website invites visitors to select and view what they are interested in by inserting a query. The website analyzes the query and then custom builds a web page in real-time that satisfies the query. Figure 6.7 displays a Wikipedia user querying business intelligence and the database sending back the appropriate web page that satisfies the user's request.[16]

Data-Driven Website Business Advantages

When building a website, ask two primary questions to determine if the site needs a database:

1. How often will the content change?
2. Who will be making the content changes?

FIGURE 6.7   Wikipedia—Data-Driven Website

① Search Query

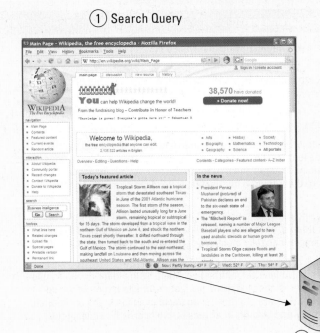

③ Results

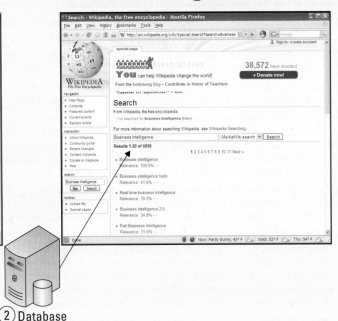

② Database

For a general informational website with static information, it is best to build a "static" website—one that a developer can update on an as-needed basis, perhaps a few times a year. A static website is less expensive to produce and typically meets business needs.

For a website with continually changing information—press releases, new product information, updated pricing, etc.—it is best to build a data-driven website. Figure 6.8 displays the many advantages associated with a data-driven website.[17]

Data-Driven Business Intelligence

Companies can gain business intelligence by viewing the data accessed and analyzed from their website. Figure 6.9 displays how running queries or using analytical tools, such as a Pivot Table, on the database that is attached to the website can offer insight into the business, such as items browsed, frequent requests, items bought together, etc.

 LO6.5

Describe the two primary methods for integrating information across multiple databases.

INTEGRATING INFORMATION AMONG MULTIPLE DATABASES

Until the 1990s, each department in the United Kingdom's Ministry of Defense (MOD) and Army headquarters had its own systems, each system had its own database, and sharing information among the departments was difficult. Manually inputting the same information multiple times into the different systems was also time consuming and inefficient. In many cases, management could not even compile the information it required to answer questions and make decisions.

The Army solved the problem by integrating its systems, or building connections between its many databases. These integrations allow the Army's multiple systems to automatically communicate by passing information between the databases, eliminating the need for manual information entry into multiple systems because after entering the information once, the integrations send the information immediately to all other databases. The integrations not only enable the different departments to share information, but have also dramatically increased the quality of the information. The army can now

FIGURE 6.8 Data-Driven Website Advantages

Data-Driven Website Advantages

- **Development:** Allows the website owner to make changes any time—all without having to rely on a developer or knowing HTML programming. A well-structured, data-driven website enables updating with little or no training.

- **Content management:** A static website requires a programmer to make updates. This adds an unnecessary layer between the business and its web content, which can lead to misunderstandings and slow turnarounds for desired changes.

- **Future expandability:** Having a data-driven website enables the site to grow faster than would be possible with a static site. Changing the layout, displays, and functionality of the site (adding more features and sections) is easier with a data-driven solution.

- **Minimizing human error:** Even the most competent programmer charged with the task of maintaining many pages will overlook things and make mistakes. This will lead to bugs and inconsistencies that can be time consuming and expensive to track down and fix. Unfortunately, users who come across these bugs will likely become irritated and may leave the site. A well-designed, data-driven website will have "error trapping" mechanisms to ensure that required information is filled out correctly and that content is entered and displayed in its correct format.

- **Cutting production and update costs:** A data-driven website can be updated and "published" by any competent data-entry or administrative person. In addition to being convenient and more affordable, changes and updates will take a fraction of the time that they would with a static site. While training a competent programmer can take months or even years, training a data-entry person can be done in 30 to 60 minutes.

- **More efficient:** By their very nature, computers are excellent at keeping volumes of information intact. With a data-driven solution, the system keeps track of the templates, so users do not have to. Global changes to layout, navigation, or site structure would need to be programmed only once, in one place, and the site itself will take care of propagating those changes to the appropriate pages and areas. A data-driven infrastructure will improve the reliability and stability of a website, while greatly reducing the chance of "breaking" some part of the site when adding new areas.

- **Improved stability:** Any programmer who has to update a website from "static" templates must be very organized to keep track of all the source files. If a programmer leaves unexpectedly, it could involve re-creating existing work if those source files cannot be found. Plus, if there were any changes to the templates, the new programmer must be careful to use only the latest version. With a data-driven website, there is peace of mind, knowing the content is never lost—even if your programmer is.

FIGURE 6.9 BI in a Data-Driven Website

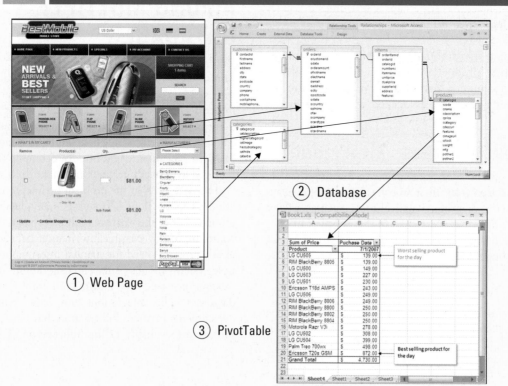

① Web Page

② Database

③ PivotTable

generate reports detailing its state of readiness and other vital issues, nearly impossible tasks before building the integrations among the separate systems.[18]

An *integration* allows separate systems to communicate directly with each other. Similar to the UK's army, an organization will maintain multiple systems, with each system having its own database. Without integrations, an organization will (1) spend considerable time entering the same information in multiple systems and (2) suffer from the low quality and inconsistency typically embedded in redundant information. While most integrations do not eliminate all redundant information, they can ensure the consistency of it across multiple systems.

An organization can choose from two integration methods. The first is to create forward and backward integrations that link processes (and their underlying databases) in the value chain. A *forward integration* takes information entered into a given system and sends it automatically to all downstream systems and processes. A *backward integration* takes information entered into a given system and sends it automatically to all upstream systems and processes.

Figure 6.10 demonstrates how this method works across the systems or processes of sales, order entry, order fulfillment, and billing. In the order entry system, for example, an employee can update the information for a customer. That information, via the integrations, would be sent upstream to the sales system and downstream to the order fulfillment and billing systems.

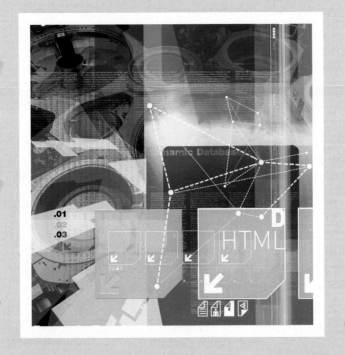

Ideally, an organization wants to build both forward and backward integrations, which provide the flexibility to create, update, and delete information in any of the systems. However, integrations are expensive and difficult to build and maintain and most organizations build only forward integrations (sales through billing in Figure 6.10). Building only forward integrations implies that a change in the initial system (sales) will result in changes occurring in all the other systems. Integration of information is not possible for any changes occurring outside the initial system, which again can result in inconsistent organizational information. To address this issue, organizations can enforce business rules that all systems, other than the initial system, have read-only access to the integrated information. This will require users to change information in the initial system only, which will always trigger the integration and ensure that organizational information does not get out of sync.

The second integration method builds a central repository for a particular type of information. Figure 6.11 provides an example of customer information integrated using this method across four different systems in an organization. Users can create, update, and delete customer information only in the central customer database. As users perform these tasks on the central customer database, integrations automatically send the new and/or updated customer information to the other systems. The other systems limit users to read-only access of the customer information stored in them. Again, this method does not eliminate redundancy—but it does ensure consistency of the information among multiple systems.

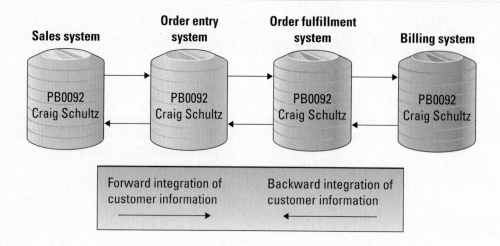

FIGURE 6.11 Integrating Customer Information among Databases

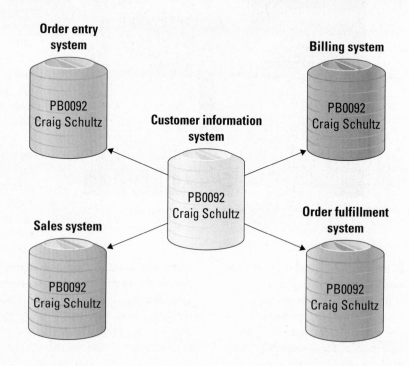

SECTION 6.2 Data Warehouse Fundamentals

LEARNING OUTCOMES

LO6.8 Describe the roles and purposes of data warehouses and data marts in an organization.

LO6.9 Compare the multidimensional nature of data warehouses (and data marts) with two-dimensional nature of databases.

LO6.10 Identify the importance of ensuring cleanliness of information throughout an organization.

LO6.11 Explain the relationship between business intelligence and a data warehouse.

ACCESSING ORGANIZATIONAL INFORMATION

Applebee's Neighborhood Grill & Bar posts annual sales in excess of $3.2 billion and is actively using information from its data warehouse to increase sales and cut costs. The company gathers daily information for the previous day's sales into its data warehouse from 1,500 restaurants located in 49 states and seven countries.

Understanding regional preferences, such as patrons in Texas preferring steaks more than patrons in New England, allows the company to meet its corporate strategy of being a neighborhood grill appealing to local tastes. The company has found tremendous value in its data warehouse by being able to make business decisions about customers' regional needs. The company also uses data warehouse information to perform the following:

- Base its labor budgets on actual number of guests served per hour.

- Develop promotional sale item analysis to help avoid losses from overstocking or understocking inventory.

- Determine theoretical and actual costs of food and the use of ingredients.[19]

HISTORY OF DATA WAREHOUSING

In the 1990s as organizations began to need more timely information about their business, they found that traditional operational information systems were too cumbersome to provide relevant information efficiently and quickly. Operational systems typically include accounting, order entry, customer

Sorry, I Didn't Mean to Post Your Social Security Number on the Internet

Programming 101 teaches all students that security is the crucial part of any system. You must secure your data! It appears that some people working for the state of Oklahoma forgot this important lesson when tens of thousands of Oklahoma residents had their sensitive data—including numbers—posted on the Internet for the general public to access. You have probably heard this type of report before, but have you heard that the error went unnoticed for three years? A programmer reported the problem, explaining how he could easily change the page his browser was pointing to and grab the entire database for the state of Oklahoma. Also, because of the programming, malicious users could easily tamper with the database by changing data or adding fictitious data. If you are still thinking that isn't such a big deal, it gets worse. The website also posted the Sexual and Violent Offender Registry. Yes, the Department of Corrections employee data were also available for the general public to review.

Why is it important to secure data? What can happen if someone accesses your customer database? What could happen if someone changes the information in your customer database and adds fictitious data? Who should be held responsible for the state of Oklahoma data breech? What are the business risks associated with data security?

service, and sales and are not appropriate for business analysis for the following reasons:

- Information from other operational applications is not included.

- Operational systems are not integrated, or not available in one place.

- Operational information is mainly current—does not include the history that is required to make good decisions.

- Operational information frequently has quality issues (errors)—the information needs to be cleansed.

- Without information history, it is difficult to tell how and why things change over time.

- Operational systems are not designed for analysis and decision support.

Follow the Data

There is a classic line in the movie *All the President's Men,* which covers the Watergate investigation, where Deep Throat meets with Bob Woodward and coolly advises him to "follow the money." Woodward follows the money, and the Watergate investigation ends with President Nixon's resignation.

If you want to find out what is happening in today's data-filled world, you could probably change those words to "follow the data." IDC reports that the amount of information stored in the digital universe is projected to hit nearly 1.8 zettabytes by 2011, representing a tenfold increase in five years. One of the newest forms of legal requirements emerging from the data explosion is ediscovery, the legal requirements mandating that an organization must archive all forms of software communications, including email, text messages, and multimedia. Yes, the text message you sent four years ago could come back to haunt you.

Organizations today have more data than they know what to do with and are frequently overwhelmed with data management. Getting at such data and presenting them in a useful manner for cogent analysis is a tremendous task that haunts managers. What do you think is involved in data management? What is contained in the zettabytes of data stored by organizations? Why would an organization store data? How long should an organization store its data? What are the risks associated with failing to store organizational data?

During the latter half of the 20th century, the numbers and types of databases increased. Many large businesses found themselves with information scattered across multiple platforms and variations of technology, making it almost impossible for any one individual to use information from multiple sources. Completing reporting requests across operational systems could take days or weeks using antiquated reporting tools that were designed more or less to execute the business rather than run the business. From this idea, the data warehouse was born as a place where relevant information could be held for completing strategic reports for management. The key here is the word *strategic* as most executives were less concerned with the day-to-day operations than they were with a more overall look at the model and business functions.

A key idea within data warehousing is to take information from multiple platforms/technologies (as varied as spreadsheets, databases, and word files) and place them in a common location that uses a common querying tool. In this way operational databases could be held on whatever system was most efficient for the operational business, while the reporting/strategic information could be held in a common location using a common language. Data warehouses take this a step further by giving the information itself commonality by defining what each term means and keeping it standard. An example of this would be gender, which can be referred to in many ways (Male, Female, M/F, 1/0), but should be standardized on a data warehouse with one common way of referring to each sex (M/F).

This design makes decision support more readily available without affecting day-to-day operations. One aspect of a data warehouse that should be stressed is that it is *not* a location for *all* a business's information, but rather a location for information that is interesting, or information that will assist decision makers in making strategic decisions relative to the organization's overall mission.

Data warehousing is about extending the transformation of data into information. Data warehouses offer strategic level, external, integrated, and historical information so businesses can make projections, identify trends, and decide key business issues. The data warehouse collects and stores integrated sets of historical information from multiple operational systems and feeds them to one or more data marts. It may also provide end-user access to support enterprisewide views of information.

⬤⬤ LO6.8

Describe the roles and purposes of data warehouses and data marts in an organization.

⬤⬤ LO6.9

Compare the multidimensional nature of data warehouses (and data marts) with two-dimensional nature of databases.

⬤⬤ LO6.10

Identify the importance of ensuring cleanliness of information throughout an organization.

DATA WAREHOUSE FUNDAMENTALS

A *data warehouse* is a logical collection of information—gathered from many different operational databases—that supports business analysis activities and decision-making tasks. The primary purpose of a data warehouse is to aggregate information throughout an organization into a single repository in such a way that employees can make decisions and undertake business analysis activities. Therefore, while databases store the details of all transactions (for instance, the sale of a product) and events (hiring a new employee), data warehouses store that

FIGURE 6.12 Model of a Typical Data Warehouse

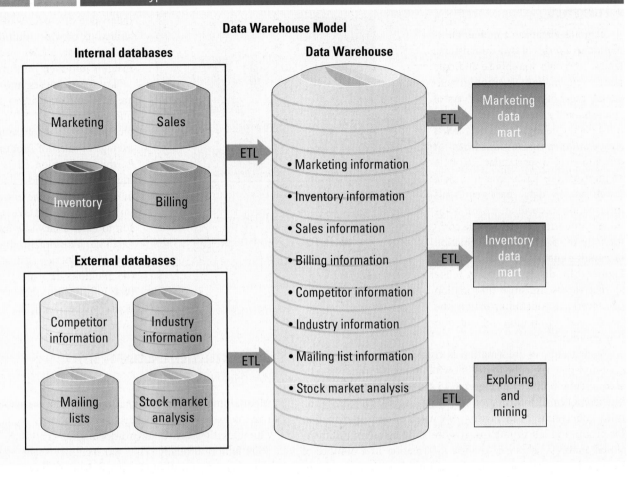

Data Warehouse Model

same information but in an aggregated form more suited to supporting decision-making tasks. Aggregation, in this instance, can include totals, counts, averages, and the like.

The data warehouse modeled in Figure 6.12 compiles information from internal databases or transactional/operational databases and external databases through *extraction, trans-*

ing focused information subsets particular to the needs of a given business unit such as finance or production and operations.

Lands' End created an organizationwide data warehouse so all its employees could access organizational information. Lands' End soon discovered that there could be "too much of a good thing." Many of its employees would not use the data

> "The primary purpose of a data warehouse is to aggregate information throughout an organization into a single repository in such a way that employees can make decisions and undertake business analysis activities."

formation, and loading (ETL), which is a process that extracts information from internal and external databases, transforms the information using a common set of enterprise definitions, and loads the information into a data warehouse. The data warehouse then sends subsets of the information to data marts. A *data mart* contains a subset of data warehouse information. To distinguish between data warehouses and data marts, think of data warehouses as having a more organizational focus and data marts hav-

warehouse because it was simply too big, too complicated, and had too much irrelevant information. Lands' End knew there was valuable information in its data warehouse, and it had to find a way for its employees to easily access the information. Data marts were the perfect solution to the company's information overload problem. Once the employees began using the data marts, they were ecstatic at the wealth of information. Data marts were a huge success for Lands' End.[20]

Multidimensional Analysis

A relational database contains information in a series of two-dimensional tables. In a data warehouse and data mart, information is multidimensional, meaning it contains layers of columns and rows. For this reason, most data warehouses and data marts are *multidimensional databases*. A *dimension* is a particular attribute of information. Each layer in a data warehouse or data mart represents information according to an additional dimension. A **cube** is the common term for the representation of multidimensional information. Figure 6.13 displays a cube (cube a) that represents store information (the layers), product information (the rows), and promotion information (the columns).

Once a cube of information is created, users can begin to slice-and-dice the cube to drill down into the information. The second cube (cube b) in Figure 6.13 displays a slice representing promotion II information for all products at all stores. The third cube (cube c) in Figure 6.13 displays only information for promotion III, product B, at store 2. By using multidimensional analysis, users can analyze information in a number of ways and with any number of dimensions. Users might want to add dimensions of information to a current analysis including

product category, region, and even forecasted versus actual weather. The true value of a data warehouse is its ability to provide multidimensional analysis that allows users to gain insights into their information.

Data warehouses and data marts are ideal for off-loading some of the querying against a database. For example, querying a database to obtain an average of sales for product B at store 2 while promotion III is under way might create a considerable processing burden for a database, essentially slowing down the time it takes another person to enter a new sale into the same database. If an organization performs numerous queries against a database (or multiple databases), aggregating that information into a data warehouse will be beneficial.

Information Cleansing or Scrubbing

Maintaining quality information in a data warehouse or data mart is extremely important. The Data Warehousing Institute estimates that low-quality information costs U.S. businesses $600 billion annually. That number may seem high, but it is not. If an organization is using a data warehouse or data mart to allocate dollars across advertising strategies, low-quality

---

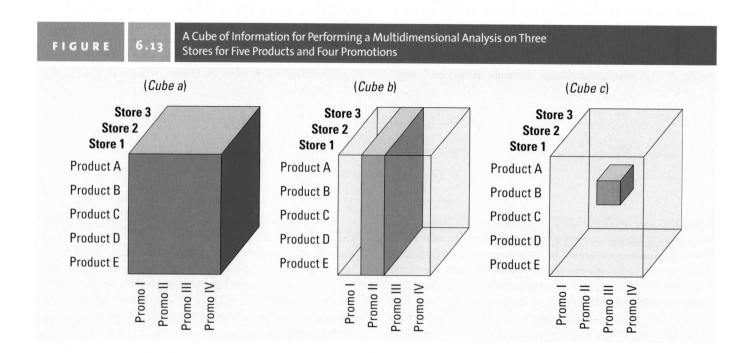

| FIGURE | 6.13 | A Cube of Information for Performing a Multidimensional Analysis on Three Stores for Five Products and Four Promotions |

information will definitely have a negative impact on its ability to make the right decision.[21]

To increase the quality of organizational information and thus the effectiveness of decision making, businesses must formulate a strategy to keep information clean. This is the concept of *information cleansing or scrubbing*, a process that weeds out and fixes or discards inconsistent, incorrect, or incomplete information.

Specialized software tools exist that use sophisticated algorithms to parse, standardize, correct, match, and consolidate data warehouse information. This is vitally important because data warehouses often contain information from several different databases, some of which can be external to the organization. In a data warehouse, information cleansing occurs first during the ETL process and second on the information once it is in the data warehouse. Companies can choose information cleansing software from several different vendors including Oracle, SAS, Ascential Software, and Group 1 Software. Ideally, scrubbed information is error-free and consistent.

Dr Pepper/Seven Up, Inc., was able to integrate its myriad databases in a data warehouse (and subsequently data marts) in less than two months, giving the company access to consolidated, clean information. Approximately 600 people in the company regularly use the data marts to analyze and track beverage sales across multiple dimensions, including various distribution routes such as bottle/can sales, fountain food-service sales, premier distributor sales, and chain and national accounts. The company is now performing in-depth analysis of up-to-date sales information that is clean and error-free.[22]

FIGURE 6.14 Contact Information in Operational Systems

Billing
Contact: Hans Hultgren 555-1211

The billing system has "accounts payable" customer contact information

Customer Service
Contact: Anne Logan 555-1288
Contact: Deborah Bridge 555-6543

The customer service system has the "product user" customer contact information

Marketing
Contact: Paul Bauer 555-2211
Contact: Don McCubbrey 555-3434

Sales
Contact: Paul Bauer 555-2211
Contact: Don McCubbrey 555-3434

The marketing and sales system has "decision maker" customer contact information.

Looking at customer information highlights why information cleansing is necessary. Customer information exists in several operational systems. In each system all details of this customer information could change from the customer ID to contact information (see Figure 6.14). Determining which contact information is accurate and correct for this customer depends on the business process that is being executed.

Figure 6.15 displays a customer name entered differently in multiple operational systems. Information cleansing allows an organization to fix these types of inconsistencies and cleans the information in the data warehouse. Figure 6.16 displays the typical events that occur during information cleansing.

fyi

Want Free Books? Just Ask Google

Google is scanning all or parts of the book collections of the University of Michigan, Harvard University, Stanford University, the New York Public Library, and Oxford University as part of its Google Print Library Project. It intends to make those texts searchable on Google.

The Authors Guild filed a lawsuit against Google, alleging that its scanning and digitizing of library books constitutes a "massive" copyright infringement. "This is a plain and brazen violation of copyright law," Nick Taylor, president of the New York-based Authors Guild, said in a statement about the lawsuit, which is seeking class action status. "It's not up to Google or anyone other than the authors, the rightful owners of these copyrights, to decide whether and how their works will be copied."

A new settlement in the lawsuit is allowing Google to move forward with its Print Library Project (books.google.com). According to Google, the new agreement will allow:

- **Access to books:** Provide access to out-of-print books that were recently only available in a few libraries.
- **Online access:** Customers will be able to purchase full online access to millions of books. Customers will be able to read an entire book from any Internet-connected device.
- **Library and university access:** Libraries, universities, and other organizations will be able to purchase institutional subscriptions, providing their users with access to the complete text of millions of titles while compensating authors and publishers for the service. The institutions can also offer terminals where users can access the full text of millions of out-of-print books for free.
- **Buying or borrowing actual books:** Customers can find print book resources directly from the site.

Do you view Google's Print Library Project as a violation of copyright laws? If you were a publisher, how would you feel about Google's project? If you were an author, how would you feel about having your book posted for free on Google Books? What do you think the future of the book publishing industry will look like based on Google's radical new Google Book's website?

FIGURE 6.15 Standardizing Customer Name from Operational Systems

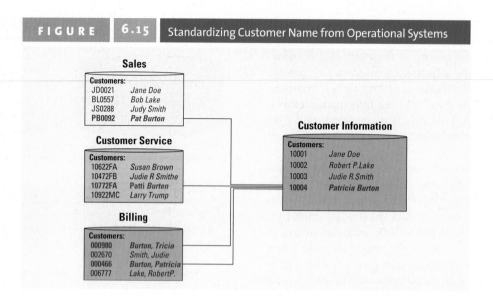

Achieving perfect information is almost impossible. The more complete and accurate an organization wants its information to be, the more it costs. The trade-off for perfect information lies in accuracy versus completeness. Accurate information means it is correct, while complete information means there are no blanks. A birth date of 2/31/10 is an example of complete but inaccurate information (February 31 does not exist). An address containing Denver, Colorado, without a zip code is an example of incomplete information that is accurate. For their information, most organizations determine a percentage high enough to make good decisions at a reasonable cost, such as 85 percent accurate and 65 percent complete.

●● LO6.11

Explain the relationship between business intelligence and a data warehouse.

DATA MINING AND BUSINESS INTELLIGENCE

Data mining is the process of analyzing data to extract information not offered by the raw data alone. Data mining can also begin at a summary information level (coarse granularity) and progress through increasing levels of detail (drilling down), or the reverse (drilling up).

To perform data mining, users need data-mining tools. **Data-mining tools** use a variety of techniques to find patterns and relationships in large volumes of information and infer rules from them that predict future behavior and guide decision making. Data-mining tools for data warehouses help users uncover business intelligence in their data. Data mining and business intelligence are covered in detail in Chapter 9. ■

FIGURE 6.16 Information Cleansing Activities

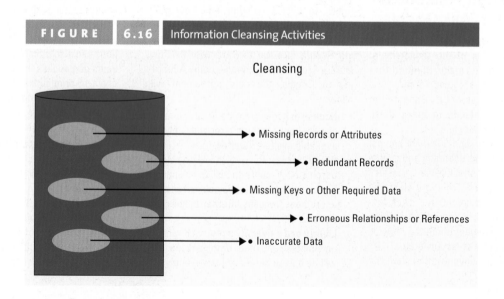

Living the
DREAM

Ice Cream Social Takes on a Whole New Meaning

When we all scream for ice cream, Ben & Jerry's screams for business intelligence and the ability to track the ingredients and life of every single pint. When a consumer calls in with a complaint, Ben & Jerry's staff matches the specific pint with its suppliers for milk, eggs, cherries, or whatever to determine where the quality issue occurred. The business intelligence (BI) tools let Ben & Jerry's officials access, analyze, and act on customer information collected by the sales, finance, purchasing, and quality assurance departments. The technology allowed Ben & Jerry's to track more than 12,500 consumer contacts, and information ranged from comments about the ingredients used in ice cream to queries about social causes supported by the company.

One of Ben & Jerry's most interesting social causes is its PartnerShop Program, a form of social enterprise in which nonprofit organizations leverage the power of business for community benefit. According to Ben & Jerry's website, PartnerShops are Ben & Jerry's scoop shops that are independently owned and operated by community-based nonprofit organizations. Ben & Jerry's waives the standard franchise fees and provides additional support to help nonprofits operate strong businesses. PartnerShops offer job and entrepreneurial training to youth and young adults that may face barriers to employment. As PartnerShop operators, nonprofits retain their business proceeds to support their programs.

Why is it important for an organization to participate in social enterprise programs? How can Ben & Jerry's use its BI systems to help its new PartnerShops owners succeed? What types of BI would a Ben & Jerry's want to track to help run the PartnerShops? What are the ethical issues surrounding barriers to employment, and how is Ben & Jerry's helping overcome this problem?

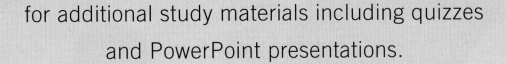

CHECK OUT www.mhhe.com/baltzanm

for additional study materials including quizzes and PowerPoint presentations.

chapter seven

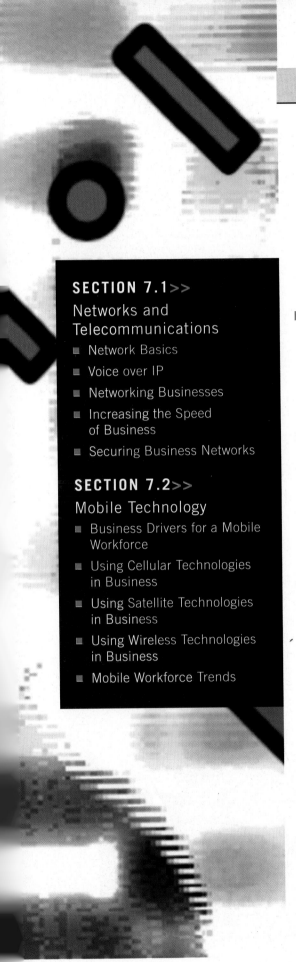

networks,
+ telecommunications,
mobile technology

what's in IT for me?

The pace of technological change never ceases to amaze. What only a few years ago would have been considered *Star Trek* technology is becoming normal. What used to take hours to download over a dial-up modem connection can now transfer in a matter of seconds through an invisible, wireless network connection from a computer thousands of miles away. We are living in an increasingly wireless present and hurtling ever faster toward a wireless future. The tipping point of ubiquitous, wireless, handheld, mobile computing is not far away.

As a business student, you must understand the concepts of network architecture and mobile technology to be able to understand how information technology can be used to support your business decisions. This is a critical skill for business executives, regardless if you are a novice or a seasoned Fortune 500 employee. By learning about the various concepts discussed in this chapter, you will develop a better understanding of how business can leverage technologies to compete in today's mobile world.

In addition, after reading this chapter, you should have many of the skills needed to become directly involved in analyzing current networking architectures, in recommending needed changes in mobile business processes, and in evaluating alternative networking options.

Change is everywhere in the information technology domain, but nowhere is change more evident and more dramatic than in the realm of telecommunications and networking. Most information systems today rely on digital networks to communicate information in the form of data, graphics, video, and voice. Companies large and small from all over the world use networked systems and the Internet to locate suppliers and buyers, to negotiate contracts with them, and to provide bigger, better, and faster services than ever before.

Telecommunication systems enable the transmission of data over public or private networks. A *network* is a communications, data exchange, and resource-sharing system created by linking two or more computers and establishing standards, or protocols, so that they can work together. Telecommunication systems and networks are traditionally complicated and historically inefficient. However, businesses can benefit from

●● SECTION 7.1 Networks and Telecommunications

LEARNING OUTCOMES

LO7.1 Compare LANs, WANs, and MANs.

LO7.2 Describe the business benefits associated with VoIP.

LO7.3 Explain the difference between a VPN and a VAN.

LO7.4 Identify the advantages and disadvantages of broadband technology.

LO7.5 List and describe many of the network security problems.

●● LO7.1

Compare LANs, WANs, and MANs.

> ## Change is everywhere in the information technology domain, but nowhere is change more evident and more dramatic than in the realm of telecommunications and networking.

today's modern network infrastructures that provide reliable global reach to employees and customers. Businesses around the world are moving to network infrastructure solutions that allow greater choice in how they go to market—solutions with global reach. These alternatives include wireless, voice over Internet protocol (VoIP), and radio frequency identification (RFID). This chapter takes a detailed look at key telecommunication, network, and wireless technologies being integrated into businesses around the world.

NETWORK BASICS

Networks range from small two-computer networks to the biggest network of all, the Internet. A network provides two principle benefits: the ability to communicate and the ability to share. Music is the hot product line at coffee retailer Starbucks. In Starbucks stores, customers can shop for music wirelessly through iTunes free, thanks to the company's own increasingly sophisticated in-store network.

Today's corporate digital networks include a combination of local area networks and the Internet. A *local area network (LAN)* is designed to connect a group of computers in close proximity to each other such as in an office building, a school, or a home. A LAN is useful for sharing resources like files, printers, games, or other applications. A LAN in turn often connects to other LANs, and to the Internet or wide area networks. A *wide area network (WAN)* spans a large geographic area, such as a state, province, or country. WANs often connect multiple smaller networks, such as local area networks or metropolitan area networks (MANs). A *metropolitan area network (MAN)* is a large computer network usually spanning a city.

Direct data communication links between a company and its suppliers or customers, or both, have been successfully used to give the company a strategic advantage. The Sabre airline reservation system is a classic example of a strategic information system that depends upon communication provided through a network. Sabre Airline Solutions pioneered technological advances for the industry in areas such as revenue management, pricing, flight scheduling, cargo, flight operations, and crew scheduling. In addition, not only did Sabre help invent ecommerce (now referred to as ebusiness) for the travel industry, but the company also holds claim to progressive solutions that defined—and continue to revolutionize—the travel and transportation marketplace.[1]

The remainder of this chapter assumes a basic understanding of the fundamentals of networks and telecommunications.

Using Networks and Telecommunications for Business Advantages

After gaining an understanding of networking and telecommunication fundamentals, it is easy to apply these to competitive advantages for any business including:

- Voice over IP.
- Networking businesses.
- Increasing the speed of business.
- Securing business networks.

 LO7.2
Describe the business benefits associated with VoIP.

VOICE OVER IP

Originally, phone calls made over the Internet had a reputation of offering poor call quality, lame user interfaces, and low call-completion rates. With new and improved technology and IT infrastructures, Internet phone calls now offer similar quality to traditional landline and cellular telephone calls. Today, many consumers are making phone calls over the Internet by using voice over Internet protocol (VoIP). *Voice over IP (VoIP)* uses TCP/IP technology to transmit voice calls over long-distance telephone lines. VoIP transmits over 10 percent of all phone calls in the United States and this number is growing exponentially.

The telecom industry is experiencing great benefits from combining VoIP with emerging standards that allow for easier development, interoperability among systems, and application integration. This is a big change for an industry that had relied on proprietary systems to keep customers paying for upgrades and new features. The VoIP and open standards combination has produced more choices, lower prices, and new applications.

Many VoIP companies, including Vonage, 8 × 8, and AT&T (CallVantage), typically offer calling within the United States for a fixed fee and a low per-minute charge for international calls. Broadband Internet access (broadband is described in detail later in this chapter) is required, and regular house phones plug in to an analog telephone adapter provided by the company or purchased from a third party (such as DLink or Linksys) as displayed in Figure 7.1.

Since VoIP uses existing network and Internet infrastructure to route telephone calls more efficiently and inexpensively than traditional telephone service, VoIP offers businesses significant cost savings, productivity gains, and service enhancements.

Unfortunately, VoIP routes calls through the same paths used by network and Internet traffic, therefore it has the same vulnerabilities and is subject to the same Internet threats. Much like data, VoIP traffic can be intercepted, captured, or modified. Any threat that slows or degrades service even slightly will disrupt business. As a result, VoIP traffic must be secured.

Skype has long been one of the most popular VoIP options for consumers—largely because of its low cost (free for calls between Skype users and only a few dollars per month to call landlines). Now, it is gaining popularity in the business world as well.

The company has been adding features that make it more business-friendly. Two examples are the Windows Installer/

FIGURE 7.1 Diagram of VoIP Connection

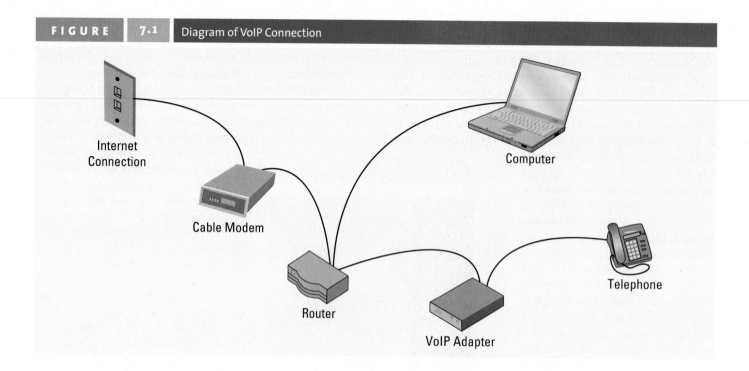

Internet Connection

Cable Modem

Computer

Router

VoIP Adapter

Telephone

MSI package that makes it easy to roll out the application to multiple machines and the Skype for Business Control Panel that allows administrators to manage all of a company's Skype accounts from a centralized interface. The small-business market is especially amenable to Skype's budget-friendly and feature-rich service.

Rip Curl is one of the greatest surf and snow brands in the world. With more than 1,200 staff members and a retail presence in more than 60 countries, the company faces communications challenges in keeping abreast of global industry trends, sharing global marketing plans, coordinating events, and collaborating on design initiatives across many regions.

Rip Curl's finance and marketing divisions have been using Skype's free instant messaging and video calls for more than two years to track communications with international colleagues.

Recently, Rip Curl's head of IT directed all staff to use Skype as their preferred method of communication.[2]

Skype already includes many features that make it attractive to business users, including call forwarding and the ability to filter and block unwanted calls. In addition, Skype's conference calling feature lets users have conversations with multiple people (up to 10 participants), mixing participants who are using Skype, regular landline phones, and mobile phones.

Skype allows users to do more than just place voice calls. For instance, users with computers equipped with web cams can make video calls to get "face time" with coworkers or clients—without the hassle or expense of traveling. In addition to features built into the Skype software, many useful add-in programs are available to download that add functionality and enhance productivity (see Figure 7.2).[3]

BUSTED Never Run with Your iPod

Jennifer Goebel, a 27-year-old female, was disqualified from her first place spot in the Lakefront Marathon in Milwaukee after race officials spotted her using an iPod. Officials nullified Goebel's first place time of 3:02:50 because of a controversial 2007 rule put into place banning headphones or portable music devices by U.S. Track and Field (USTAF), the governing body for running events. Race officials only decided to take action after viewing online photos of Goebel using her iPod during the last part of the race. The interesting part of this story—Goeble posted the photos herself on her website. USTAF claims the ban is required because music could give some runners a competitive advantage, as well as safety concerns when runners can't hear race announcements.

Do you agree with the USTAF's decision to disqualify Jennifer Goebel? How could an iPod give a runner a competitive advantage?

With so many wireless devices entering the market, it is almost impossible to keep up with the surrounding laws. Do you think Goebel was aware of the headphone ban? In your state, what are the rules for using wireless devices while driving? Do you agree with these rules? How does a business keep up with the numerous, ever-changing rules surrounding wireless devices? What could happen to a company that fails to understand the laws surrounding wireless devices?

FIGURE	7.2	Skype Add-In Programs

Add-in	Function
Skype Office Toolbar	This add-on makes calls to names or phone numbers in a Word document, Excel spreadsheet, or PowerPoint presentation. After installing the add-in, users can use it to turn phone numbers in the document into links, which can be clicked to make a voice call or send an SMS message. Users can send the file they are working on in the Office application to a Skype contact.
Skylook	This add-on is an extension to Outlook that records calls and voice-mail to MP3 files and accesses them from Outlook. Users can call Outlook contacts over Skype and have emails read over the phone.
HotRecorder for VoIP	This add-on records Skype calls automatically using a third-party program, such as HotRecorder for VoIP (HR4VoIP). It works with Skype 3.0, as well as other VoIP applications such as Net2Phone, Google Talk, and Yahoo Messenger.
Universal Chat Translator	Today's business world is increasingly international in nature. If a user needs to communicate with people who speak another language, install the Universal Chat Translator to translate Skype chat conversations and read them. The add-on translator supports Arabic, Chinese (simplified and traditional), Dutch, French, German, Greek, Japanese, Italian, Korean, Portuguese, Russian, and Spanish. It translates the messages sent to the other language and translates the received messages to English. The translation takes place in real time for active chats or conversations can be stored in a chat history.
uSeeToo	This add-on shares photos, drawings, maps, and other graphical images. Users can add text captions and other content. It includes a drawing board, and it allows users to create, show, and save multiple boards.
PresenterNet	This add-in conducts interactive web meetings, sales presentations, "webinars," and more, using PowerPoint and Skype teleconferencing. It works with Windows, Windows Mobile, Linux, and Macintosh, and with Internet Explorer, Firefox, and Safari browsers.
Unyte	This add-in shares desktop applications with Skype contacts and others, and will share with multiple users.
TalkandWrite Extra for Skype 3.0	This add-on is a document collaboration program that allows two users to remotely work on the same document and annotate it, add text, and more, with the changes made by either party immediately made available to both.
RemoteCall	This add-in connects to remote desktops during a Skype call by clicking an icon added to the Skype Contacts and Tools menus.

Skype also uses a file transfer feature that makes it easier to collaborate with colleagues over the phone; users can send copies of reports, pictures, or other files they need to share—with no limits on file size. This feature can be disabled if an administrator does not want users to be able to transfer files due to security or privacy issues.

Some features available using VoIP solutions include:

- Business application integration (for instance, tying IP telephony to a customer database).
- Calendar integration.
- Call waiting.
- Caller ID.
- Click-of-a-mouse simplicity—employees make or transfer calls right on their computer.
- Conference call capabilities with on-screen document sharing.
- Comprehensive information about each caller.
- Desktop application (i.e., Microsoft Outlook) integration.
- Dial-by-name capability.
- Easy navigation.

- Four or five-digit dialing to anyone, regardless of location.
- Mobility—users can work from anywhere.
- Three-way calling.[4]

 L07.3

Explain the difference between a VPN and a VAN.

NETWORKING BUSINESSES

Retailer REI reports that one-third of all customers who buy online and pick up at the store make another purchase while there, spending an average of $90. From a technology perspective, in-store pick up needs to have some level of inventory integration to work effectively. The integration of data is critical in being able to display to the consumer the availability of products at the closest geographic store.[5]

To set up an ebusiness even a decade ago would have required an individual organization to assume the burden of developing the entire network infrastructure. Today, industry-leading companies have developed Internet-based products and services to handle many aspects of customer and supplier interactions.

FIGURE   7·3   Business Network Characteristics

- Provide for the transparent exchange of information with suppliers, trading partners, and customers.

- Reliably and securely exchange information internally and externally via the Internet or other networks.

- Allow end-to-end integration and provide message delivery across multiple systems, in particular, databases, clients, and servers.

- Respond to high demands with scalable processing power and networking capacity.

- Serve as the integrator and transaction framework for both digital businesses and traditional brick-and-mortar businesses that want to leverage the Internet for any type of business.

"In today's retail market, you cannot be a credible national retailer without having a robust website," says Dennis Bowman, senior vice president and CIO of Circuit City, who adds that customers now expect seamless retailing between online and in-store just as they expect stores that are clean and well stocked. For this reason, retailers are working furiously to integrate their ebusiness sites with their inventory and point-of-sale (POS) systems so that they can accept in-store returns of merchandise bought online and allow customers to buy on the web and pick up in the store.

Some companies, such as Best Buy, Office Depot, and Sears, already have their physical and online stores integrated. These companies have been the fast movers because they already had an area in their stores for merchandise pickup (usually for big, bulky items such as TVs and appliances), and because long before the web they had systems and processes in place that facilitated the transfer of a sale from one store to another. To take on the challenge of business integration, an organization needs a secure and reliable network for mission-critical systems (see Figure 7.3).

A *virtual private network (VPN)* is a way to use the public telecommunication infrastructure (e.g., Internet) to provide secure access to an organization's network (see Figure 7.4).

A *valued-added network (VAN)* is a private network, provided by a third party, for exchanging information through a high-capacity connection.

Organizations engaging in ebusiness have relied largely on VPNs, VANs, and other dedicated links handling electronic data interchange transactions. These traditional solutions are still deployed in the market, and for many companies will likely hold a strategic role for years to come. However, these conventional technologies present significant challenges:

- By handling only limited kinds of business information, these contribute little to a reporting structure intended to provide a comprehensive view of business operations.

- They offer little support for the real-time business process integration that will be essential in the digital marketplace.

- Relatively expensive and complex to implement, conventional technologies make it difficult to expand or change networks in response to market shifts.

●● LO7.4

Identify the advantages and disadvantages of broadband technology.

INCREASING THE SPEED OF BUSINESS

Transmission can occur at different speeds. By speed we do not mean how fast the signal travels in terms such as miles per hour, but rather the volume of data that can be transmitted per unit of time. Terms such as bandwidth, hertz (Hz), and baud are used to describe transmission speeds, whereas a measure such as bits transmitted per second (bits per second, or bps) would be more understandable. *Bandwidth* is the difference between the highest and the lowest frequencies that can be transmitted on a single medium, and it is a measure of the medium's capacity. *Hertz* is cycles per second, and *baud* is the number of signals sent per second. If each cycle sends one signal that transmits exactly one bit of data, which is often the case, then all these terms are identical.

In information technology publications, baud was formerly used for relatively slow speeds such as 2,400 baud (2,400 bits per second) or 14,400 baud (14,400 bps), while hertz (with an appropriate prefix) was used for

FIGURE   7·4   Virtual Private Network Overview

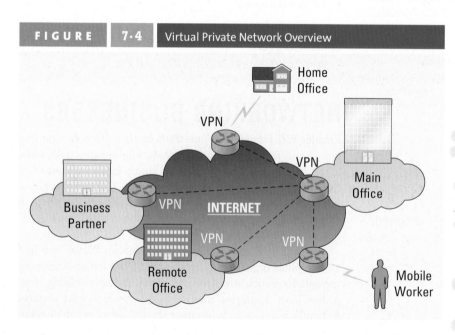

Home Office

VPN

VPN

Main Office

Business Partner

VPN   INTERNET

VPN   VPN

Remote Office

Mobile Worker

higher speeds such as 500 megahertz (500 million bps) or 2 gigahertz (2 billion bps). More recently, the term *baud* has fallen into disfavor, but hertz is still widely used. For clarity, we will stick with bps in this chapter.

The notion of bandwidth, or capacity, is important for telecommunications. For example, approximately 50,000 bits (Os and 1s) are required to represent one page of data. To transmit this page over a 128,000 bps (128 Kbps) digital subscriber line (DSL) would take only four-tenths of a second. Graphics require approximately 1 million bits for one page. This would require about 8 seconds over a 128 Kbps DSL. Full-motion video transmission requires the enormous bandwidth of 12 million bps, and thus data compression techniques must be employed to be able to send video over the existing telephone network. The bandwidth determines what types of communication— voice, data, graphics, full-motion video—can reasonably be transmitted over a particular medium. Figure 7.5 outlines the typical transmission speeds found in business today (a few of the technologies mentioned in Figure 7.5 will be discussed in detail in the next section). Figure 7.6 gives an overview of the average time required to download specific Internet functions.[6]

High-speed Internet, once an exotic and expensive service used only by larger companies, is now an inexpensive mainstream offering. The term **broadband** generally refers to high-speed Internet connections transmitting data at speeds greater than 200 kilobytes per second (Kbps), compared to the 56 Kbps maximum speed offered by traditional dial-up connections. While traditional dial-up access (using normal voice telephone

FIGURE	7·5	Telecommunications Transmission Speeds

Transmission Medium	Typical Speeds
Twisted pair—voice telephone	14.4 Kbps–56 Kbps
Twisted pair—digital telephone	128 Kbps–1.544 Mbps
Twisted pair—LAN	10 Mbps–100 Mbps
Coaxial cable—LAN	10 Mbps–1 Gbps
Wireless—LAN	6 Mbps–54 Mbps
Microwave—WAN	50 Kbps–100 Mbps
Satellite—WAN	50 Kbps–100 Mbps
Fiber-optic cable—WAN	100 Mbps–100 Gbps

KEY: bps = bits per second
Kbps = thousand bits per second
Mbps = million bits per second
Gbps = billion bits per second

line technology) suffices for some consumers, many need or want the much faster connections that technological advances now allow. The right option for Internet access will depend on a company's needs and which services are available. Figure 7.7 lists some of the advantages and disadvantages of current conventional broadband technology available.[7]

 LO7.5

List and describe many of the network security problems.

⌐ omg lol

Call 911, McNugget Outage

Cellular technologies have changed the way we do business, and it is hard to imagine life without them. Just think of email. How did anyone survive without email? And let's not even talk about life before cell phones. There are so many wonderful advantages of using wireless technologies in business, but there are also some serious disadvantages, like the ability to make a bad decision faster.

A woman in Florida called 911 three times after a McDonald's employee told her they were out of Chicken McNuggets. A police report states that Latreasa Goodman, a 27-year-old female, told authorities she paid for a 10-piece McNugget meal

and was later informed that the restaurant had sold out of McNuggets. Goodman says she was refused a refund and told all sales were final by the cashier. The cashier told police she offered Goodman a larger portion of different food for the same price, but Goodman became irate and called 911. "This is an emergency. If I would have known they didn't have McNuggets, I wouldn't have given my money, and now she wants to give me a McDouble, but I don't want one," Goodman told police and continued to state, "This is an emergency." Goodman was cited on a misuse of 911 charge. A McDonald's spokesman says Goodman should have been given a refund

and that she is being issued a gift card for a free meal.

It is so easy to pick up the phone, from anywhere, at anytime, and make a bad call. How many times do you see people making calls on their cell phones from inappropriate locations? If this woman had to wait in line to use a pay phone, do you think it would have given her the time to calm down and rethink her decision? With technology and the ability to communicate at our fingertips, do you agree that it is easier than ever to make a bad decision? What can you do to ensure you think before you communicate?

FIGURE   7·6   Internet Function Average Download Time

Internet Function	Dial-up (56K)	Satellite (512K)	DSL (1M)	Cable (1M)	Wireless (5M)
An email	1 sec.		<1 sec.		
A basic web page (25K)	10 sec.		<1 sec.		
One five-minute song (5M)	15 min.	2 min.	1 min.		40 sec.
One two-hour movie (500M)	20 hrs.	4 hrs.	2 hrs.		70 min.

SECURING BUSINESS NETWORKS

Networks are a tempting target for mischief and fraud. An organization has to be concerned about proper identification of users and authorization of network access, the control of access, and the protection of data integrity. A firm must identify users before they are granted access to a corporate network, and that access should be appropriate for the given user. For example, an organization may allow outside suppliers access to its internal network to learn about production plans, but the firm must prevent them from accessing other information such as financial records. In addition, the organization should preserve the integrity of its data; users should be allowed to change and update only well-specified data. These problems are exacerbated on the Internet where individuals must be very concerned about fraud, invalid purchases, and misappropriation of credit card information.

Providing network security is a difficult challenge. Almost all networks require some kind of log-on, including user name and password. Many people are casual with their passwords, making them easy to guess. A good password has both letters and numbers along with a few punctuation marks for added security. Most corporate security goes far beyond passwords, however. One common approach is a firewall, a computer that sits between an internal network and the Internet. The firewall allows access to internal data from specified incoming sites but tries to detect unauthorized access attempts and prevent them from occurring.

FIGURE   7·7   Advantages and Disadvantages of Broadband Technology

Technology	Typical Download Speed (Mbps)	Typical Uplink Speed (Mbps)	Advantages	Disadvantages
Digital subscriber line (DSL)	.5–3	1.0	– Good upload rates – Uses existing telephone lines	– Speeds vary depending on distance from telephone company's central office – Slower downloads than less expensive alternatives
Cable	.5–4	.5–1	– Uses existing cable infrastructure – Low-cost equipment	– Shared connections can overload system, slowing upload times
TI/T3 dedicated line	1.5–3	1.5–3	– Uses existing phone wiring	– Performance drops significantly with range – Susceptible to cross talk
Fiber-to-the-home	4.5	10.2	– Fast data speeds – Infrastructure has long life expectancy – Low maintenance – Low power costs	– Not widely available – Significant deployment cost (for company)
Fixed wireless	.5–12	.5	– Typically inexpensive to install, no underground digging	– Weather, topography, buildings, and electronics can cause interference
Satellite	.5–2	.05	– Nearly universal coverage – Available in otherwise inaccessible areas	– Expensive service/equipment – Upload/download delays

For highly secure communications, a sender can encrypt data, that is, encode the data so that someone without the "key" to decode them cannot read the message. There are a number of encryption approaches, and controversy exists over how strong the encryption should be. The most secure approaches use longer keys, making it much more difficult for an intruder to compute the key. The U. S. government is concerned about terrorists and criminals who might have access to strong encryption that is beyond the capabilities of law enforcement authorities to decrypt. There are export restrictions on encryption programs.

For Internet commerce, various schemes have been proposed for sending credit card or other payments over the network in a secure manner. Some involve encryption and others various forms of digital certificates or digital cash. Many firms worry that customers will not want to complete transactions on the Internet because of the fear their credit card numbers might be stolen. However, a law limits individual liability for credit card misuse to $50.

Data Sharing

Even more important than the sharing of technology resources is the sharing of data. Either a LAN or a WAN permits users on the network to get data (if they are authorized to do so) from other points on the network. It is very important, for example, for managers to be able to retrieve overall corporate sales forecasts from corporate databases to use in developing spreadsheets (or any other program used for business analysis) to project future activity. To satisfy customers, automobile dealers need to be able to locate particular vehicle models and colors with specific equipment installed. Managers at various points in a supply chain need to have accurate, up-to-date data on inventory levels and locations. Accountants at corporate headquarters need to be able to retrieve summary data on sales and expenses from each of the company's divisional computer centers. The chief executive officer, using an executive information system, needs to be able to access up-to-the-minute data on business trends from the corporate network.

●● SECTION 7.2 Mobile Technology

LEARNING OUTCOMES

LO7.6 Explain the business benefits of using wireless technology.

LO7.7 Identify the advantages and disadvantage of deploying cellular technology.

LO7.8 Describe how satellite technology works.

RAPID AND WIDESPREAD GROWTH OF MOBILE TECHNOLOGY IN THE 21ST CENTURY HAS SHAPED ONE OF THE LARGEST TECHNOLOGY MARKETS AFTER THE PC REVOLUTION IN THE 1980S AND 1990S. "

L07.9 Explain how LBS, GPS, and GIS help to create business value.

L07.10 Describe RFID and how it can be used to help make a supply chain more effective.

L07.11 List and discuss the wireless trends that consumers and businesses can benefit from.

⬤⬤ **L07.6**

Explain the business benefits of using wireless technology.

BUSINESS DRIVERS FOR A MOBILE WORKFORCE

Dr Pepper/Seven Up Inc., of Plano, Texas, monitors the operation of its vending machines via wireless technology. Dr Pepper/Seven Up Inc. has installed specialized hardware and software along with wireless technology in vending machines. The software collects inventory, sales, and "machine-health" data at each vending machine, and then, on a daily basis, the Dr Pepper/Seven Up Inc. network operations center polls each machine. A dome antenna atop the vending machine allows broadcast and reception via a wireless network. The data are aggregated and stored at a separate facility. With client software installed on their PCs, managers and sales personnel at Dr Pepper/Seven Up Inc. can access the data via a secure website. Management at Dr Pepper/Seven Up Inc. is excited about the business value of the data being collected, both for daily operations and in the potential for data mining (see Chapter 6). Information like this is helpful when considering new placements of vending machines or locations

where multivendor machines might be warranted, such as in front of a Target store or high-traffic supermarket. Dr Pepper/Seven Up Inc. can use the data to plan loading of trucks and truck routes.[8]

Rapid and widespread growth of mobile technology in the 21st century has shaped one of the largest technology markets after the PC revolution in the 1980s and 1990s. Untethered connectivity, anytime, anywhere, has fueled a major market and technology disruption, which has permeated almost every consumer market worldwide. The domino effect of the success of mobile technology has resulted in opportunities for innovation and creativity in technology, marketing, and business strategy.

Companies worldwide are going mobile to increase productivity, speed delivery to market, and reduce operating costs. Retail, distribution, and manufacturing businesses are no exception. Wireless transmissions rely on radio waves (e.g., cellular technology), microwaves, and satellites to send data across high-frequency radio ranges that later connect to wired media.

United Parcel Service and FedEx have been using mobile technologies for years, making it possible for information about dispatching and deliveries to travel between couriers and central stations. FedEx's famous tracking system, which can find a package's location from its tracking number, uses a wireless courier-management system.

The terms *mobile* and *wireless* are often used synonymously, but actually denote two different technologies. *Mobile* means the technology can travel with the user, but it is not necessarily in real-time; users can download software, email messages, and web pages onto their personal digital assistant (PDA), laptop, or other mobile device for portable reading or reference. Information collected while on the road can be synchronized with a PC or corporate server.

Wireless, on the other hand, refers to any type of electrical or electronic operation that is accomplished without the use of a "hard wired" connection. International Data Corporation expected nearly two-thirds of handheld devices to include integrated wireless networking by 2010. Figure 7.8 displays the factors inspiring the growth of wireless technologies.

State government agencies, such as transportation departments, use wireless devices to collect field information—tracking inventory, reporting times, monitoring logistics, and completing forms—all from a mobile environment. The transportation industry is using mobile devices to help determine current locations and alternate driving routes.

Mobile technologies are transforming how we live, work, and play. Handheld devices continue to offer additional functionality, and cellular networks are advancing rapidly in their increased speed and throughput abilities (cellular networks will be described in detail in the next section). These enabling technologies fuel widespread adoption and creation of new and innovative ways to perform business. The big changes that will re-create workplaces, industries, and organizations are coming from mobile and wireless technologies. Figure 7.9 displays a few common examples of mobile technologies that are changing our world.

The retail industry is fiercely competitive. With the advent of the World Wide Web, nontraditional companies such as Amazon.com have emerged and have made brick-and-mortar companies like Barnes & Noble rethink their strategy. Competition is also driving profit margins down. The success of a retailer depends on inventory management, cost control, and proactive customer service. To gain the competitive advantage, more and more retailers are turning to mobile applications to enhance worker productivity, operational efficiencies, and anytime, anywhere customer service. On the sales floor and in the warehouse, mobile solutions can help track materials and shipments from supplier and distributors to the customers, manage inventory, and support point-of-sales activities. Since vast amounts of data can be collected in an automated fashion, analysis can be done much faster and the results can be used continuously to improve operations and customer service. Figure 7.10 briefly describes several important steps companies should take to formulate an effective mobile strategy.[9]

A relatively small number of enterprises (less than 25 percent) have a specific mobile strategy in place. Most struggle with individual mobile projects or try to link mobility to a broader IT strategy. Companies must focus on building a mobile strategy that addresses the peculiarities inherent in mobile computing. The strategy should leverage a number of uses across a variety of lines of businesses within the company to maximize the ROI (return on investment), standardize on architectures and platforms, and provide the most secure infrastructure available to eliminate (as much as possible) extremely costly data loss and security breaches inherent in mobile business. Understanding the different types of mobile technologies available will help executives determine how to best equip

FIGURE	7.8	Wireless Drivers

Drivers of Wireless Technology Growth	
Universal access to information and applications	People are mobile and have more access to information than ever before, but they still need to get to the point where they can access all information anytime, anywhere, anyplace.
The automation of business processes	Wireless technologies have the ability to centralize critical information and eliminate redundant processes.
User convenience, timeliness, and ability to conduct business 24x7x365	People delayed in airports no longer have to feel cut off from the world or their office. Through wireless tools and wireless solutions such as a BlackBerry RIM device, they can access their information anytime, anywhere, anyplace.

FIGURE	7.9	Mobile Devices Changing Business

Mobile Devices Changing Business

- **Wireless local area network (wLAN):** uses radio waves rather than wires to transmit information across a local area network.

- **Cellular phones and pagers:** provide connectivity for portable and mobile applications, both personal and business.

- **Cordless computer peripherals:** connect wirelessly to a computer, such as a cordless mouse, keyboard, and printer.

- **Satellite television:** allows viewers in almost any location to select from hundreds of channels.

- **WiMAX wireless broadband:** enables wireless networks to extend as far as 30 miles and transfer information, voice, and video at faster speeds than cable. It is perfect for Internet service providers (ISPs) that want to expand into sparsely populated areas, where the cost of bringing in cable wiring or DSL is too high.

- **Security sensor:** alerts customers to break-ins and errant pop flies. Its dual sensors record vibration and acoustic disturbances—a shattered window—to help avoid false alarms.

| FIGURE 7.10 | Steps to Take for Deploying Mobile Strategies |

Steps	Description
Defining risks	Before a realistic assessment of any mobile strategy can be put in place, companies must define evaluation criteria. Many companies look at technology and applications in isolation, without defining any potential risks to the organization: risks both if the project is undertaken and if it is not.
Knowing the limits of technology	It is imperative that companies not only examine the abilities of any technology to provide needed functionality, but also to explore any limits of the chosen technology. Setting realistic expectations for any mobile technology, both to IT resources deploying the solution and to the ultimate users, is a necessary component of any successful mobile strategy.
Protecting data from loss	Companies must take concrete and immediate steps to assure protection of mobile corporate information assets. Security must be a multi-faceted approach and encompass a variety of techniques covering all areas of exposure.
Compliance in the mobile enterprise	The move to mobility, with far more devices "free to roam wild," will cause a major upsurge in occurrences of data breaches, some of which may not even be discovered, or not discovered for a significant period. Companies must formulate a mobile security strategy before the problem becomes overwhelming.
Staying flexible and embracing change	Companies should not assume that once created, a mobile strategy is a fixed and/or finished product. With the high rate of change in the marketplace (e.g., devices, connection types, applications), it is incumbent upon the organization to monitor and modify the policy on a regular basis.

their workforce. These mobile technologies are discussed in the remainder of this section and include:

- Using cellular technologies in business.
- Using satellite technologies in business.
- Using wireless technologies in business.
- Mobile business trends.

LO7.7

Identify the advantages and disadvantage of deploying cellular technology.

USING CELLULAR TECHNOLOGIES IN BUSINESS

Continental Airlines passengers in Houston will be able to board flights using just a cell phone or personal-digital assistant instead of a regular boarding pass at Bush Intercontinental Airport. The program could expand to airlines and airports nationwide. Instead of a paper pass, Continental Airlines and the Transportation Security Administration will let passengers show a code the airline has sent to their cell phone or PDA. The two-dimensional bar code, a jumble of squares and rectangles, stores the passenger's name and flight information. A TSA screener will confirm the bar code's authenticity with a handheld scanner. Passengers still need to show photo identification. The electronic boarding pass also works at airport gates. If a passenger's cell phone or mobile device loses power, the passenger can get a paper boarding pass from a kiosk or a Continental agent. Houston-based Continental, the nation's number four airline, has been working on the new feature for years to increase efficiency, eliminate paperwork, and make travel easier.[10]

In less than 20 years, the mobile telephone has gone from being rare, expensive equipment of the business elite to a pervasive, low-cost personal item. Several countries, including the United Kingdom, now have more mobile phones than people. There are over 500 million active mobile phone accounts in China. Luxembourg has the highest mobile phone penetration rate in the world, at 164 percent. The total number of mobile phone subscribers in the world was estimated at 3.3 billion at the end of 2007, thus reaching an equivalent of over half the planet's population. At present, Africa has the largest growth rate of cellular subscribers in the world, its markets expanding nearly twice as fast as Asian markets. The availability of prepaid or pay-as-you-go services, where the subscriber is not committed to a long-term contract, has helped fuel this growth in Africa as well as in other continents.[11]

Cellular telephones (cell phones) work by using radio waves to communicate with radio antennas (or towers) placed within adjacent geographic areas called cells. A telephone message is transmitted to the local cell by the cellular telephone and then is passed from antenna to antenna, or cell to cell, until it reaches the cell of its destination, where it is transmitted to the receiving telephone. As a cellular signal travels from one cell into another, a computer that monitors signals from the cells switches the conversation to a radio channel assigned to the next cell. In a typical analog cell phone system in the United States, the cell phone carrier receives about 800 frequencies to use across the city. The carrier chops up the city into cells. Each cell is typically 10 square miles. Cells are normally thought of as hexagons on a big hexagonal grid, such as what Figure 7.11 illustrates. Each cell has a base station that consists of a tower and a small building containing the radio equipment.[12]

Older cellular systems are analog, and newer cellular systems are digital. Personal communication services (PCS) are one popular type of digital cellular service. PCS are entirely digital. They can transmit both voice and data and operate in a higher frequency range (1,900 MHz) than analog cellular telephones (analog cellular service operates in the 800 and 900 MHz bands). These digital cellular systems are capable of sending and receiving short text messages.

PCS are second-generation (2G) mobile communications technology, and analog cellular systems are first generation (1G). Second-generation cellular networks are, circuit-switched digital networks that can transmit data at about 10 kilobits per second (Kbps), which is extremely slow. Third-generation (3G) networks use a newer packet-switched technology that is much more efficient (and hence faster) than dedicated circuit-switched networks. Third-generation networks have speeds ranging from 120 to 144 Kbps for mobile users in, for example, a car, and up to 2 gigabits per second (Gbps) for stationary users. These 3G networks are designed for high-speed transmission of multimedia data and voice. The major network operators are providing 3G services, and some groups and companies have already started working on fourth-generation (4G) mobile phone system. The 4G technology will take mobile communication another step up to integrate radio and television transmissions, and to consolidate the world's phone standards into one high-speed technology. Figure 7.12 displays many of the cellular technologies along with their advantages and disadvantages.

The Finnish government decided that the fastest way to warn citizens of disasters was the mobile phone network. In Japan, mobile phone companies provide immediate notification of

earthquakes and other natural disasters to their customers free of charge. In the event of an emergency, disaster response crews can locate trapped or injured people using the signals from their mobile phones. An interactive menu accessible through the phone's Internet browser notifies the company if the user is safe or in distress. In Finland, rescue services suggest hikers carry mobile phones in case of emergency even when deep in the forests beyond cellular coverage, as the radio signal of a cell phone attempting to connect to a base station can be detected by overflying rescue aircraft with special detection gear. In addition, users in the United States can sign up through their provider for free text messages when an Amber Alert goes out for a missing person in their area.[13]

FIGURE 7.11 | Cellular Technology Overview

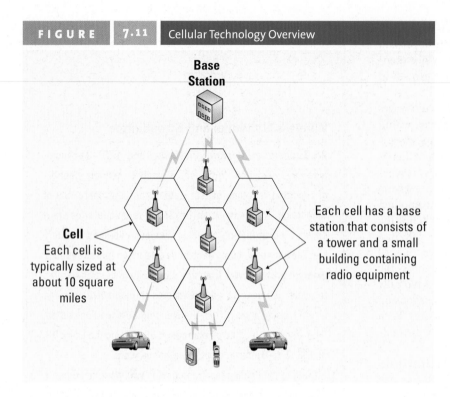

Base Station

Cell
Each cell is typically sized at about 10 square miles

Each cell has a base station that consists of a tower and a small building containing radio equipment

Personal Digital Assistants

Personal digital assistants (PDA) are small, handheld computers capable of entirely digital communications transmission. They have built-in wireless telecommunications capabilities as well as work-organization software. PDAs can display, compose, send, and receive email messages, and some models can provide wireless access to the Internet. Unlike mobile phones, PDAs do not require subscription-based network services. They are stand-alone mini-computers, much like PCs before the Internet.

The first generation of successful PDAs were Palm Pilots. They primarily functioned as electronic organizers with support for address books, calendars, email, notes, and so on. The PDA only occasionally needs to connect to a companion PC for synchronization. For instance, a PDA can be synchronized with a PC address book, calendar, and email inbox via a USB cable. Newer PDA models can also connect to PCs wirelessly via Bluetooth (described in the next section), or connect to the Internet via wireless.

A *smartphone* combines the functions of a cellular phone and a PDA in a single device. It differs from a normal cell phone in that it has an operating system and local storage, so users can add and store information, send and receive email, and install programs to the phone as they could with a PDA. A smartphone gives users the best of both worlds—it has much the same capabilities as a PDA and the communications ability of a mobile phone.

As the old saying goes, "timing is everything." Nowhere is that more true than in the real estate business in Hawaii. Real estate agents continue to look for tools that will give them an edge. Real-time access to their area's multiple listing service (MLS)

The latest trends in cell phones reflect a convergence of voice, video, and data communications. By blending information with entertainment, cell phones are center-stage in the evolving trend of mobile infotainment. As an example, the Apple iPhone is a revolutionary mobile phone that allows users to make calls, surf the web (Google and Yahoo! are built right in) over a wi-fi connection, email a photo, use a widescreen iPod with touch controls to various content—including music, audiobooks, videos, TV shows, and movies. Technically speaking, the iPhone is a smartphone, discussed in the next section.

FIGURE 7.12 | Cellular Technology Advantages and Disadvantages

Generation	Technology	Advantages and Disadvantages
1G	AMPS (Advanced Mobile Phone Service)	– Analog voice service only
2G	CDMA (Code Division Multiple Access)	– Digital voice service
	TDMA (Time Division Multiple Access)	– 9.6 Kbps to 14.4 Kbps data service
	GSM (Global Systems for Mobile Communications	– Enhanced calling features (such as caller ID)
	PDC (Personal Digital Cellular)	– No always-on data connection
3G	W-CDMA (Wideband Code Division Multiple Access)	– Superior voice quality
		– Always-on data connection up to 2 Mbps
		– Broadband data services (such as streaming audio and video)
4G	W-CDMA (Wideband Code Division Multiple Access)	– Wi-fi access networks
		– Always-on data connection 20–100 Mbps
	MC-CDMA (Multi Carrier CDMA)	– Converged data and voice over IP

provides one way for agents to take advantage of timing. MLS offers a database of local properties for sale, with the ability to sort them by a variety of criteria. An agent who accesses a home's listing as soon as it hits the MLS gains a key advantage against the competition because the agent can immediately request a viewing or, at a minimum, simply drive by the location with a client.

Real estate agents are rarely in their offices, so they require technology that not only provides real-time access to their local MLS but also enables them to manage contact information,

devices. These devices communicate with each other using a variety of wires, cables, radio signals, and infrared light beams, and an even greater variety of connectors, plugs, and protocols. Bluetooth technology eliminates the need for wires that tangle everyday lives. **Bluetooth** is a telecommunications industry specification that describes how mobile phones, computers, and personal digital assistants (PDAs) can be easily interconnected using a short-range wireless connection. Bluetooth headsets allow users to cut the cord and make calls even while their cell phones are tucked away in a briefcase. Wireless Bluetooth print-

> "The latest trends in cell phones reflect a convergence of voice, video, and data communications."

keep their calendars current, send and receive emails, view documents, calculate basic mortgage numbers and more. The lighter the solution, the better, so that they can leave the laptop behind when necessary. In addition, if they can combine that with cell phone functionality, they need only one device to conduct business.

Many real estate agents in Hawaii are using smartphones as a solution to their needs. Easy to carry and dependable, smartphones give them real-time access to their local MLS, enabling them to learn about properties as soon as they are listed for sale.

Bluetooth

Electronic devices can connect to one another in many different ways. The various pieces and parts of computers, entertainment systems, and telephones, make up a community of electronic

ing allows users of a Bluetooth-enabled PDA or laptop to attach to a printer via a Bluetooth adapter connected to the printer's communication port.

Since Bluetooth's development in 1994 by the Swedish telecommunications company Ericsson, more than 1,800 companies worldwide have signed on to build products to the wireless specification and promote the new technology in the marketplace. The engineers at Ericsson code-named the new wireless technology Bluetooth to honor a 10th century Viking king, Harald Bluetooth, who is credited with uniting Denmark and bringing order to the country.

Bluetooth capability is enabled in a device by means of an embedded Bluetooth chip and supporting software. Although Bluetooth is slower than competing wireless LAN technologies, the Bluetooth chip enables Bluetooth networking to be built into a wide range of devices—even small devices such as cellular phones and PDAs. Bluetooth's maximum range is 30 feet, limiting it to gadget-to-gadget communication.

One challenge to wireless devices is their size. Everyone wants their mobile devices to be small, but many people also curse the tiny, cryptic keyboards that manufacturers squeeze into smart phones and PDAs. The laws of physics have proved a significant barrier to solving this problem, but VKB Inc.'s Bluetooth Virtual Keyboard offers a possible solution (see Figure 7.13). VKB's technology uses a red laser to illuminate a virtual keyboard outline on any surface. Despite its futuristic look, the laser is really just a visual guide to where users put their fingers. A separate illumination and sensor module invisibly tracks when and where each finger touches the surface, translating that into keystrokes or other commands.

| FIGURE | 7.13 | Bluetooth Virtual Keyboard |

Beams of light, which detect the user's movements, make up this virtual keyboard.

●● **L07.8**

Describe how satellite technology works.

●● **L07.9**

Explain how LBS, GPS, and GIS help to create business value.

USING SATELLITE TECHNOLOGIES IN BUSINESS

A special variation of wireless transmission employs satellite communication to relay signals over very long distances. A communications *satellite* is a big microwave repeater in the sky; it contains one or more transponders that listen to a particular portion of the electromagnetic spectrum, amplifying incoming signals, and retransmitting them back to Earth. A *microwave transmitter* uses the atmosphere (or outer space) as the transmission medium to send the signal to a microwave receiver. The microwave receiver then either relays the signal

This problem can be solved by bouncing microwave signals off communication satellites, enabling them to serve as relay stations for microwave signals transmitted from terrestrial stations (as illustrated in Figure 7.14). Communication satellites are cost effective for transmitting large quantities of data over very long distances. Satellites are typically used for communication in large, geographically dispersed organizations that would be difficult to tie together through cabling media or terrestrial microwave. Originally, this microwave technology was used almost exclusively for satellite and long-range communication. Recently, however, developments in cellular technology allow complete wireless access to networks, intranets, and the Internet via microwave transmission.

> A special variation of wireless transmission employs satellite communication to relay signals over very long distances.

to another microwave transmitter or translates the signal to some other form, such as digital impulses. Microwave signals follow a straight line and do not bend with the curvature of the Earth; therefore, long-distance terrestrial transmission systems require that microwave transmission stations be positioned about 37 miles apart, making this form of transmission expensive.

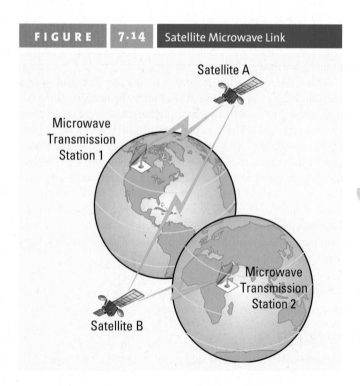

| FIGURE | 7.14 | Satellite Microwave Link |

Conventional communication satellites move in stationary orbits approximately 22,000 miles above the Earth. A newer satellite medium, the low-orbit satellite, travels much closer to the Earth and is able to pick up signals from weak transmitters. Low-orbit satellites also consume less power and cost less to launch than conventional satellites. With such wireless networks, businesspeople almost anywhere in the world will have access to full communication capabilities, including voice communication via satellite phones, videoconferencing, and multimedia-rich Internet access.

General Motors is serious about satellite radio. Previously, GM made XM satellite radio standard on all Cadillacs, and now the subscription radio service will also be available for all new Buick, Hummer, and Saab models as well. The move enlarges XM's customer base while also giving drivers a chance to test the technology for three months free of charge.

The devices used for satellite communication range from handheld units to mobile base stations to fixed satellite dish receivers. The peak data transmission speeds range from 2.4 Kbps to 2 Mbps, depending on the solution being sought. For the everyday mobile professional, satellite communication does not provide a compelling benefit, but for people requiring voice and data access from remote locations or guaranteed coverage in non-remote locations, satellite technology may be worth while. Also, some satellite service providers offer roaming between existing cellular systems and satellite systems.[14]

Satellite-based location will shape the future, creating new applications. Besides emergency call location and navigation in cars and on mobile phones, a range of new services will appear: personal assistance and medical care, localized

Ding-a-Ling Took My $400!

Does it get any better than satellite television and radio with their endless options for entertainment choices? For some customers, these endless options just end up giving them a headache and endless frustration. One customer, Mary Cox, decided that her satellite television had terrible reception and she wanted to disconnect her service and find an alternative. This was the single decision that began her nightmare. Soon after disconnecting her service, Mary noticed a direct withdrawal on her bank account for a $430 early termination fee from her satellite provider. This unplanned expense soon cost Mary hundreds of dollars in overdraft charges from her other bills because she never anticipated this expense. To top it all off, Mary received a phone call from a satellite customer service representative asking if she was satisfied with the company and would she consider reconnecting her service, and the person said his name was Ding-a-Ling.

The number one rule you should all remember is that you never give any company your checking account number or direct access to your bank account. If you want to establish a good relationship with a company, it is best to give them your credit card number. When a relationship with a supplier turns sour, the last thing you want is for them to have direct access to your checking account.

Do you think what the satellite provider did was ethical? What could Mary do when disconnecting her service to avoid this type issue? Can credit card companies enter your bank account and take out as much money as you owe at any time they want? Why is it important to never give a supplier direct access to your business checking account?

presence services, finding friends, gaming, localized blogs, and so on. To enable the wide commercial success of each service, several key technological challenges need to be met: accuracy; ubiquity of service, including in dense urban areas and inside buildings; and delivery of information instantaneously.

Location-based services (LBS) are wireless mobile content services that provide location-specific information to mobile users moving from location to location. The market for location-based services is tremendous, with a variety of available and future services in a number of market segments: mobile telephony, enterprise, vertical markets, automotive and consumer devices. Figure 7.15 highlights many of the location-based services market segments that are currently pushing this technology.

Have you ever needed an ATM and not known where to find one? For tourists and businesspeople traveling far from home, that is an all-too-familiar predicament. Each year, 2 million cardholders contact MasterCard via telephone or the website looking for the location of nearby ATMs; some 70 percent of inquiries are received from international travelers venturing outside their home countries.

MasterCard now provides cardholders with a mobile, location-based search and directory service, so they can request the location of the nearest ATM be sent to their mobile phone via SMS (Short Message Service, or text message). The service, which works with all major mobile operators in the United States, is provided by MasterCard to cardholders free of charge (although operator text message rates may apply).

A user that employs location-based services on a regular basis faces a potential privacy problem. Many users consider location information to be highly sensitive and are concerned about a number of privacy issues, including:

- Target marketing: Mobile users' locations can be used to classify customers for focused marketing efforts.
- Embarrassment: One customer's knowledge of another's location may lead to embarrassing situations.
- Harassment: Location information can be used to harass or attack a user.
- Service denial: A health insurance firm might deny a claim if it learned that a user visited a high-risk area.
- Legal restrictions: Some countries regulate the use of personal data.

Unlike other information in cyberspace, location information has the potential to allow an adversary to physically locate a person, and therefore most wireless subscribers have legitimate concerns about their personal safety if such information should fall into the wrong hands. Laws and rules of varying clarity, offering different degrees of protection, have been or are being enacted in the United States, the European Union, and Japan.

FIGURE 7.15 Location-Based Services Market Segments

Mass Market	
Emergency Services	■ Locate emergency call ■ Roadside assistance
Navigation Services	■ Navigation to point of interest (directions, maps) ■ Etourism ■ Avoidance of traffic jams
Tracking Services	■ Find-a-friend ■ Tracking of children ■ Elderly
Location Advertising	■ Located video push
Gaming	■ N-Gage (allows multiple gamers to play against each other over Bluetooth or wireless phone network connections)
Professional Market	
Workforce Organization	■ Field force management ■ Optimization of routes ■ Logistics ■ Enterprise resource planning
Security	■ Field tracking ■ Worker protection

Global Positioning System (GPS)

The most popular location-based service used today is Global Positioning System. The **Global Positioning System (GPS)** is a constellation of 24 well-spaced satellites that orbit the Earth and make it possible for people with ground receivers to pinpoint

seen revenue climb 60 percent to $117 million with net profits of $30.7 million. With new federal regulation forcing wireless operators to include GPS in their phones and networking equipment, chip demand is exploding. Recently Sirf Technology has developed a golf GPS that helps golfers calculate the distance from the tee to the pin, or to know exactly where they are with relation to features such as hidden bunkers, water hazards, or greens. The United States Golf Association now permits distance-measuring devices for use in tournaments at the discretion of the organizers.[15]

The market for GPS services has grown to more than $5 billion with expectations for demand to double over the next few years. Tracking, navigation, and hardware promise to be multibillion-dollar markets by 2010. UPS has outfitted 75,000 drivers with GPS-enabled handhelds to help them reach destinations more efficiently. The handhelds will also trigger email alerts if a company vehicle speeds or ventures into unauthorized areas. Steve Wozniak, Apple co-founder, started a company in 2002 named Wheels of Zeus that combines GPS data with local

> The Global Positioning System (GPS) is a constellation of 24 well-spaced satellites that orbit the Earth and make it possible for people with ground receivers to pinpoint their geographic location.

their geographic location. The location accuracy is anywhere from 10 to 100 meters for most equipment. Accuracy can be pinpointed to within one meter with special military-approved equipment. Figure 7.16 illustrates the GPS architecture.

The GPS is owned and operated by the U.S. Department of Defense but is available for general use around the world. In 1993, the Defense Department made this global positioning technology available for commercial use to anyone who has a GPS device. GPS devices have special microprocessors that analyze satellite signals. Sirf Technology specializes in building GPS microprocessors for phones, electronics, and car navigation systems. Since going public in 2004, Sirf Technology has

wireless networking. The technology helps parents keep tabs on their children or can alert IT managers when company-owned computers leave the premises. Zingo, in the United Kingdom, uses GPS-enabled cars and text messaging to help subscribers hail cabs.

A **geographic information system (GIS)** is designed to work with information that can be shown on a map. Companies that deal in transportation use GISs combined with database and GPS technology. Airlines and shipping companies can plot routes with up-to-the-second information on the location of all their transport vehicles. Hospitals can keep track of where personnel are located by using a GIS and sensors that pick up the transmission of badges worn by hospital staff.

Automobiles have GPSs linked to maps that display, in a screen on the dashboard, driving directions and exact location of the vehicle. GM offers the OnStar system, which sends a continuous stream of information to the OnStar center about the car's exact location. The OnStar Vehicle Diagnostics automatically performs hundreds of diagnostic checks on four key operating systems—the engine/transmission, antilock brakes, air bags, and OnStar systems—in GM vehicles. The vehicle is programmed to send the results via email to the owner each month. The unique email report also provides maintenance reminders based on the current odometer reading, remaining engine oil life, and other relevant ownership information.[16]

Some cell phone providers equip their phones with GPS chips that enable users to be located to within a geographical location about the size of a tennis court. This allows emergency services such as 911 to find a cell phone user. Marketers are monitoring cell phone GPS development, hoping to be able to call potential customers when they are walking past their store to let them know of a special sale.

American farmers on the leading edge use GPS satellite navigation to map and analyze fields, telling them where to apply the proper amounts of seeds, fertilizer, and herbicides. In the past farmers managed their business on a per-field basis; now they can micromanage. One Illinois farmer found that parts of his fields did not need any fertilizer after monitoring the soil. Less fertilizer lowers costs and reduces pollution from the runoff of water from the fields. One GPS application is to use geographic fixes from the GPS and a computerized counter to record how much grain is being harvested each second from each meter of the field. Then the farmer downloads this information into a personal computer, which produces a contour map that shows variations of, say, more than 60 bushels an acre. Cross-referencing this information to other variables, such as characteristics of the soil, allows the farmer to analyze why some land is less productive. The farmer combines these data with GPS navigational fixes to precisely apply herbicides or fertilizer only where it is really needed.[17]

A GIS is useful for mobile applications, but it offers benefits that go well beyond what is required in a mobile environment. For example, using a GIS, users can decide what information is and is not relevant to them, and formulate their queries based on their personal criteria. Unlike a paper map, a GIS allows for in-depth analysis and problem solving that can make marketing, sales, and planning much more successful. The following are some common GIS uses:

FIGURE 7.16 Global Positioning System Architecture

GPS Enabled Device

GPS Enabled Base Station

- **Finding what is nearby.** This is the most common use for mobile users. Given a specific location, the GIS finds sources within a defined radius. This may include entertainment venues, medical facilities, restaurants, or gas stations. Users might also use the GIS to locate vendors that sell a specific item they want. This promotes m-commerce by matching buyers with sellers. The results can be provided using a map of the surrounding area or the destination addresses.

- **Routing information.** This is another common use for mobile users. Once users have an idea of where they want to go, a GIS can provide directions on how to get there. Once again, this can be provided graphically using a map or with step-by-step instructions. For mobile applications, it is often helpful to provide routing information in conjunction with search services.

- **Information alerts.** Users may want to be notified when information that is relevant to them becomes available based on their location. For example, a commuter might want to know if he or she is entering a section of the highway that has traffic congestion, or a shopper might want to be notified if his or her favorite store is having a sale on a certain item.

- **Mapping densities.** For business analysis, knowing population densities can be extremely useful. This allows users to find out where high concentrations of a certain population may be. Densities are typically mapped based on a standard area unit, such as hectares or square miles making it easy to see distributions. Examples of density mapping may include the location of crime incidents for police to determine where additional patrolling is required, or of customers to help determine ideal field delivery routes.

- **Mapping quantities.** People map quantities to find out where the most or least of a feature may be. This information could, for example, be used to determine where to locate a new business or service. For example, if someone is interested in opening a Laundromat, it would be prudent to determine how many others are in the area and what the population base is. This type of mapping can be useful for urban planning and environmental studies; for example, for city planners who are trying to determine where to build more parks.[18]

A GIS can provide information and insight to both mobile users and people at fixed locations. This information uses the location coordinates provided by one of the positioning technologies to give details that are relevant to the user at that specific moment. Many of the location-based services discussed earlier in this section would benefit from the information provided from a GIS.

●● LO7.10

Describe RFID and how it can be used to help make a supply chain more effective.

USING WIRELESS TECHNOLOGIES IN BUSINESS

Denver International Airport (DIA) is betting that travelers will like getting something free, and so far, it looks like a good bet. The airport, one of the busiest in the Unites States, switched its public wi-fi offering from paid to advertising-supported. Within a week, and with no public notice of the change, wi-fi use grew tenfold. About 50 million passengers pass through DIA every year, with as many as 165,000 per day during busy times of the year. Now that wi-fi is free, there are 7,000 to 8,000 connections to the network per day. To link all those free users with the Internet, the airport had to increase its bandwidth and network infrastructure to allow 10 Mbps connections just for the wi-fi users.

Wireless fidelity (wi-fi) is a means of linking computers using infrared or radio signals. Wi-fi, or what is sometimes referred to as wireless LANs, represent only a small proportion of LANs in operation today, but a rapidly growing proportion. Wi-fi technology has obvious advantages for people on the move who need access to the Internet in airports, restaurants, and hotels. Wi-fi is also gaining acceptance as a home or neighborhood network, permitting an assortment of laptop and desktop computers to share a single broadband access point to the Internet. Wireless LANs are also moving into the corporate and commercial world, especially in older buildings and confined spaces where it would be difficult or impossible to establish a wired LAN or where mobility is paramount. Even in newer buildings, wireless LANs are often being employed as overlay networks. In such cases, wi-fi is installed in addition to wired LANs so that employees can easily move their laptops from office to office and can connect to the network in places such as lunchrooms and patios.

After years of discussion and delay, U.S. airlines will start offering in-flight Internet connections, instant messaging, and wireless email, thus turning the airplane cabin into a wi-fi hotspot. Helping lead many of the airlines into the new era is AirCell, which in June 2006 won exclusive air-to-ground wi-fi rights by plunking down $31.3 million for 3 MHz of terrestrial digital wireless spectrum at a Federal Communications Commission auction. The company has already inked deals with American Airlines and Virgin America to install its air-to-ground system equipment, which company founder Jimmy Ray has been fine-tuning for the past decade and a half. The system will take to the air as soon as American Airlines retrofits a few of its transcontinental 767-200s. Virgin America will do the same for its 10-plane fleet, in addition to 31 planes on order from Airbus. Figure 7.17 illustrates how this "wi-fi in the sky" will work.[19]

Recently, McDonald's has promised to outfit 14,000 of its locations with upscale coffee bars accompanied by expanded wi-fi service as the fast-food chain inches closer to offering the wireless technology free of charge. Currently, McDonald's provides wi-fi service to 15,000 of its 30,000 U.S. and international locations. The service is available most often through a credit card purchase or through Internet service provider Wayport.[20]

While wi-fi is hot, security is not. With a laptop in the passenger seat of his SUV and a special antenna on the roof, Mike Outmesguine ventured off to sniff out wireless networks between Los Angeles and San Francisco. While en route, he got a big whiff of insecurity.

While his 800-mile drive confirmed that the number of wireless networks is growing explosively, he also found that only a

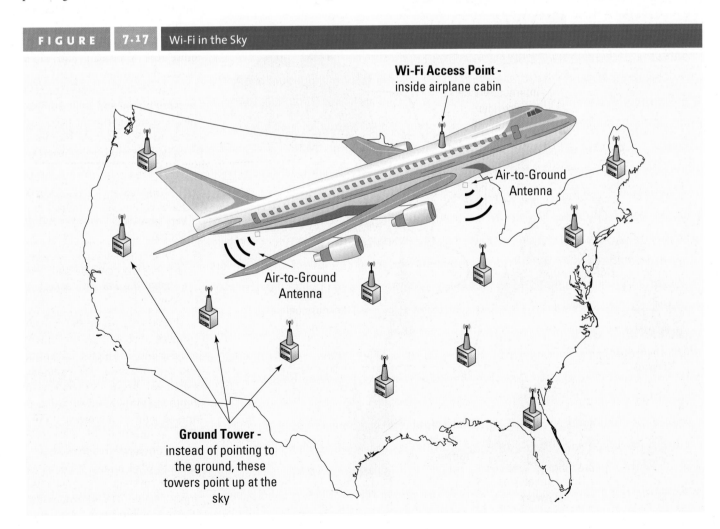

FIGURE 7.17 Wi-Fi in the Sky

Wi-Fi Access Point - inside airplane cabin

Air-to-Ground Antenna

Air-to-Ground Antenna

Ground Tower - instead of pointing to the ground, these towers point up at the sky

third used basic encryption, a key security measure. In nearly 40 percent of the networks not a single change had been made to the gear's wide-open default settings.

"They took it out of the box, powered it up, and it worked. And they left it alone," said Outmesguine, who owns a technical services company. He frequently goes out on such drives in search of insecure networks. While Outmesguine says he doesn't try to break in, others aren't so benign. If criminals were to target unsecured wireless routers, they could create an attack that could piggyback across thousands of wi-fi networks in urban areas such as Chicago or New York City. A wi-fi attack could take over 20,000 wireless routers in New York City within a two-week period, with most of the infections occurring within the first day.[21]

WiMAX

The main problems with broadband access are that it is expensive and it does not reach all areas. The main problem with wi-fi access is that hotspots are very small, so coverage is sparse. An evolving technology that can solve all of these problems is called WiMAX. *WiMAX,* or Worldwide Interoperability for Microwave Access, is a telecommunications technology aimed at providing wireless data over long distances in a variety of ways, from point-to-point links to full mobile cellular type access. WiMAX can cover a stretch of as much as 3,000 square miles depending on the number of users. In New York City, for example, many base stations will be required around the city to meet the heavy demand, while a sparsely populated region will need fewer.

Sprint Nextel along with Google is developing a new mobile Internet portal using WiMAX wireless technology to offer web search and social networking. Sprint's WiMAX for high-speed wireless and its services for detecting location will be combined with Google tools including email, chat, and other applications. Sprint aims to use the emerging WiMAX technology to better compete with rival wireless and wired broadband networks. Sprint planned to test the WiMAX service in Chicago, Baltimore, and Washington by the end of 2008 with a goal of attaining coverage for 100 million people.[22]

WiMAX offers web access speeds that are five times faster than typical wireless networks, though they are still slower than wired broadband. Higher-end notebook computers will have WiMAX technology built starting in late in 2008, though WiMAX cards that plug into a slot in the computer will also be available. Companies such as Nokia, Motorola, and Samsung Electronics are also making mobile devices and infrastructure with WiMAX technology.

WiMAX could potentially erase the suburban and rural blackout areas that currently have no broadband Internet access because phone and cable companies have not yet run the necessary wires to those remote locations.

A WiMAX system consists of two parts:

- A WiMAX tower. A single WiMAX tower can provide coverage to a very large area—as big as 3,000 square miles.

- A WiMAX receiver. The receiver and antenna could be built into a laptop the way wi-fi access is today.[23]

A WiMAX tower station can connect directly to the Internet using a high-bandwidth, wired connection (for example, a T3 line). It can also connect to another WiMAX tower using a line-of-sight, microwave link. This connection to a second tower (often referred to as a backhaul) is what allows WiMAX to provide coverage to remote rural areas. Figure 7.18 illustrates the WiMAX architecture.

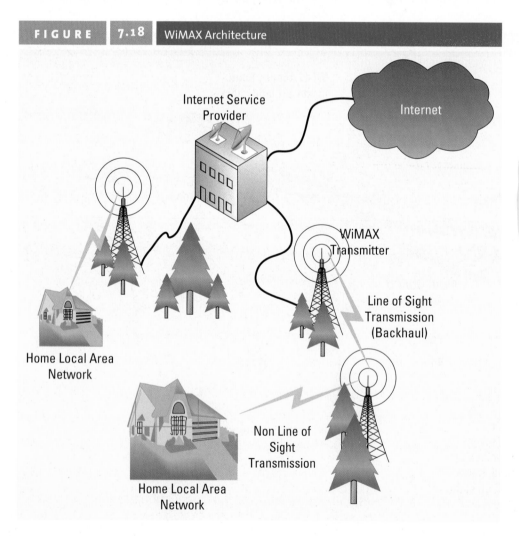

FIGURE 7.18 WiMAX Architecture

Internet Service Provider

Internet

WiMAX Transmitter

Line of Sight Transmission (Backhaul)

Home Local Area Network

Non Line of Sight Transmission

Home Local Area Network

FIGURE 7.19 WiMAX Benefits

Benefit	Description
Long Range	The most significant benefit of WiMAX compared to existing wireless technologies is the range. WiMAX has a communication range of up to 30 miles, enough to blanket an entire city.
Low Cost	Base stations will cost less than $20,000 but will still provide customers with T1-class connections.
Wireless	By using a WiMAX system, companies/residents no longer have to rip up buildings or streets or lay down expensive cables.
High Bandwidth	WiMAX can provide shared data rates of up to 70 Mbps. This is enough bandwidth to support more than 60 businesses at once with T1-type connectivity. It can also support over a thousand homes at 1 Mbps DSL-level connectivity.
Service	WiMAX can provide users with two forms of wireless service: 1. Non line of sight operates at 2 to 11 GHz, which at a lower level frequency has the ability to bend around obstacles more easily. A small antenna on a computer connects to the tower and is backward compatible with existing wi-fi technologies. 2. Line of sight can go as high as 66 GHz since the signal is stronger and more stable, which leads to greater bandwidth. A fixed dish antenna points straight at the tower or for communication between tower to tower.

Wi-fi-style access will be limited to a four-to-six mile radius (25 square miles of coverage, which is similar in range to a cell-phone zone). Through the stronger line-of-sight antennas, the WiMAX transmitting station would send data to WiMAX-enabled computers or routers set up within the transmitter's 30-mile radius. This is what allows WiMAX to achieve its maximum range. Figure 7.19 displays many of the benefits of the WiMAX technology.[24]

Radio Frequency Identification (RFID)

Radio frequency identification (RFID) technologies use active or passive tags in the form of chips or smart labels that can store unique identifiers and relay this information to electronic readers. RFID tags, often smaller than a grain of sand, combine tiny chips with an antenna. When a tag is placed on an item, it automatically radios its location to RFID readers on store shelves, checkout counters, loading bay doors, and shopping carts. With RFID tags, inventory is taken automatically and continuously. RFID tags can cut costs by requiring fewer workers for scanning items; they also can provide more current and more accurate information to the entire supply chain. Walmart saves on average $8.4 billion a year by installing RFID in many of its operations. Figure 7.20 illustrates one example of an RFID architecture.

The advent of RFID has allowed everyone from shipping companies to hospitals to reduce costs and overhead by creating visibility into inefficient business processes. Aberdeen's research shows that 38 percent of enterprises using RFID are

FIGURE 7.20 RFID Architecture

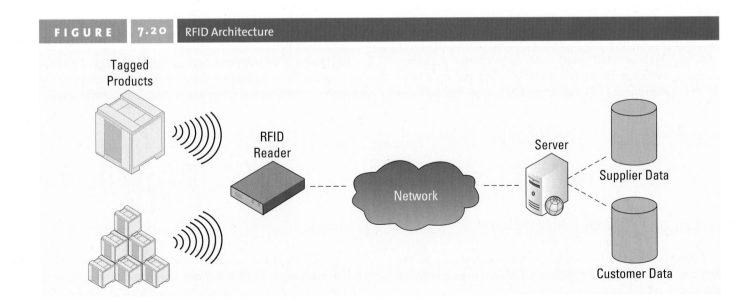

doing so to improve the cost, safety, and reliability of managing business processes. Organizations are leveraging RFID to improve the productivity of their workforce all while simplifying the implementation and ongoing management costs of their networks.[25]

When Walmart announced its RFID strategy in 2003, it was just one of many retailers that had become enamored of the technology. By placing RFID tags on cases and pallets shipped from manufacturers to Walmart distribution centers, companies would be able to keep close tabs on their shipments. In turn, that would allow Walmart and its suppliers to streamline their supply chains and ultimately ensure shelves were always fully stocked.

RFID tags represented the next big step forward from bar codes, the ubiquitous stripes on the sides of packages that provide basic product and pricing information. The simplest tags, passive RFID tags, require no internal power supply. Incoming radio frequency signals from RFID readers can transmit a minute electrical current, enough to power the integrated circuit in the tag and transmit a response. The key benefit is that the bar code on a case or pallet no longer needs to be swiped to identify the contents; the tag just needs to come within range of a reader—anywhere from a few feet up to 600 feet. In addition, RFID tags can transmit far more information about a product, including price, serial number, and even when and where it was made.

Much of the recent interest surrounding RFID has arisen from mandates and recommendations by government agencies such as the U.S. Department of Defense (DoD) and the Food and Drug Administration (FDA), and from a few private-sector megacorporations.

RFID technologies offer practical benefits to almost anyone who needs to keep track of physical assets. Manufacturers improve supply chain planning and execution by incorporating RFID technologies. Retailers use RFID to control theft, increase efficiency in their supply chains, and improve demand planning. Pharmaceutical manufacturers use RFID systems to combat the counterfeit drug trade and reduce errors in filling prescriptions. Machine shops track their tools with RFID to avoid misplacing tools and to track which tools touched a piece of work. RFID-enabled smart cards help control perimeter access to buildings. In the last couple of years, owing in large part to Walmart and DoD mandates, many major retail chains

seriously!

WeatherBots

Warren Jackson, an engineering graduate student at the University of Pennsylvania, was not interested in the weather until he started investigating how the National Weather Service collected weather data. The weather service has collected most of its information using weather balloons that carry a device to measure items like pressure, wind, and humidity. When the balloon reaches about 100,000 feet and pressure causes it to pop, the device falls and lands a substantial distance from its launch point. The National Weather Service and researchers sometimes look for the $200 device, but of the 80,000 sent up annually, they write many off as lost.

Convinced there had to be a better way, Jackson began designing a GPS-equipped robot that launches a parachute after the balloon pops, and brings the device back down to Earth, landing it at a predetermined location set by the researchers. The idea is so inventive that the university's Weiss Tech House—an organization that encourages students to innovate and bring their ideas to market— awarded Jackson and some fellow graduate engineering student's first prize in its third annual PennVention Contest. Jackson won $5,000 and access to expert advice on prototyping, legal matters, and branding.

GPS and GIS can be used in all sorts of devices, in many different industries, for multiple purposes. You want to compete and win first prize in the PennVention next year. Create a product, using a GPS or GIS, that is not currently in the market today that you will present at the fourth annual PennVention.

RFID tags differ from conventional bar code tags in a number of ways. These differences create the benefit of adopting the technology, while simultaneously creating the greatest concern

> ["RFID technologies offer practical benefits to almost anyone who needs to keep track of physical assets."]

and consumer goods manufacturers have begun testing pallet- and case-level merchandise tagging to improve management of shipments to customers.[26]

over the privacy issues involved. For example, under today's bar code technology, a pack of Wrigley's gum sold in Houston has the same bar code as a pack sold in New York City. With RFID, however, each pack would have a unique ID code that could be tied to the purchaser of that gum when the buyer uses an "item registration system" such as a frequent shopper card or a credit card.

The purchaser could then be tracked if he or she entered that same store again, or perhaps more frightening, entered any other store with RFID reading capability. Unlike a bar code, RFID tags can be read from much greater distances and the reading of such devices is nondirectional. This means that if someone enters a store with a pack of gum in a pocket or purse, the RFID reader can identify that pack of gum, the time and date it was purchased, where it was purchased, and how frequently the consumer comes into the store. If a credit card or a frequent shopper card was used to purchase the gum, the manufacturer and store could also tie that information to the consumer's name, address, and email and then direct targeted advertisements by gum companies as the shopper walks down the aisles, or send mailings through email or regular mail about other products.

As the technology behind RFID advances, the potential for privacy infringement does as well. RFID already has the capability to determine the distance of a tag from the reader location. With such technology already available, it is not difficult to imagine a situation in which retailers could determine the location of individuals within the store, and thus target specific advertisements to that customer based upon past purchases (as in the gum example used above). In effect, that store would be creating a personal log of past purchases, shopping patterns, and ultimately behavioral patterns. While such information gathering would be considered intrusive enough by many consumers' standards, the danger that such information could be sold to other retailers (similar to the way such profiles are currently sold regarding Internet commerce) could create potentially devastating information vulnerabilities. While some RFID critics have pointed out that the technology could lead to some sort of corporate "Big Brother," concern more widespread that allowing RFID to develop without legal restrictions will eliminate the possibility for consumers to refuse to give such information to retailers.[27]

Some steps are being taken to mitigate these privacy issues. For example, a recent proposal would require that all RFID-tagged products be clearly labeled. This would give consumers the choice to select products without RFID, or at a minimum to recognize that the items they select are being tracked. For those unsatisfied with disclosure, a growing number of products are designed to limit exposure to RFID tagged products. One such product is "Kill Codes," a command that turns off all RFID tags immediately as the consumer comes into contact with them, thus eliminating the effectiveness of the technology. Another countermeasure against RFID privacy invasion is "RSA Blocker Tags," which try to address privacy concerns while maintaining the integrity of the product. Under this technology, the item can be tracked only by that store's authorized reader, meaning customers cannot be tracked outside of the store in which they purchased the item.[28]

With RFID becoming both smarter and smaller, the possibilities for its uses are endless (see Figure 7.21). While RFID poses certain ethical dilemmas for government and commercial operations, it also simplifies life for the common person. As medical benefits are explored further, RFID tags will not only be used for convenience and profit, but also for saving lives.[29]

●● LO7.11

List and discuss the wireless trends that consumers and businesses can benefit from.

MOBILE WORKFORCE TRENDS

Airplane seats. Car dashboards. Digital cameras. Kiosks at shopping malls, school campuses, and hotels. Stadium bleachers. Handheld calculators. Kitchen appliances. These are just a few of the mobile devices and locations that are being wired for wireless. The visionary images of yesterday are giving way to a reality in which connectivity is nearly ubiquitous. Real-time information is now the currency of business and the enabler of groundbreaking innovations in education, entertainment, and media. The predictions help identify emerging mobile trends

FIGURE 7.21 Unusual Users of RFID

RFID Use	Description
Preventing toilets from overflowing	You can purchase a "smart" toilet, one that shuts itself off when it is close to overflowing. According to Aqua-One, its RFID-enhanced toilets are not only convenient, but they also prevent health risks in public places such as hospitals and nursing homes.
Identifying human remains	Hurricane Katrina left behind many unclaimed casualties, despite the tireless searches by countless people. Thanks to the VeriChip, RFID tags are now being used to locate bodies in an effort to reunite loved ones. This helps to identify cadavers during transport, and coroners are now able to collect body parts for burial in their rightful places.
Getting into nightclubs	Barcelona's Baja Beach Club is now grafting RFID tags into the arms of patrons who want instant access to the exclusive hangout. The tag also functions as a debit card.
Cooking with robots	Robotic pots and pans with RFID chips in the handles make it almost impossible to botch a meal. With these RFID chips, the cookware can be coordinated with a recipe card that has a similar chip. Then, the cookware will set its temperature and duration to the exact specifications the food calls for.
Timing athletic events	RFID transponders are being used as timing systems in major sporting events all over the world, including the Boston Marathon and Ironman championships. With a chip attached to an athlete's shoe, bicycle, etc., timing can begin and end with the utmost accuracy; the timer stops when the person crosses the finishing mat, which contains an antenna that will be signaled by the RFID chip. The technology is especially handy in very close finishes between competitors.
Tracking wheels of cheese	To track cheese through each process and handler until it is sold, RFID tags are being placed just under the edges of the food products. The industry is having problems with theft, loss, and even counterfeit cheese. While the idea of black market cheese may sound ridiculous, consider this—just one wheel of Parmesan cheese can be worth several hundred dollars.
Monitoring casinos	Casinos are already heavily monitored, but the unique betting habits of each player can now be logged, thanks to RFID tags inside betting chips. The chips keep track of high rollers and their spending patterns, and they make it even harder for thieves to counterfeit chips or steal them from other players. All of this technology is used to stack more odds in the house's favor.
Tracking razor blades	Thanks to low-cost RFID tags, Gillette can now afford to place small transponders in each package of its popular razor products. This is done in an attempt to salvage more razors as they make their way through a very convoluted supply chain. Many of the small products are lost or stolen. While it might sound trivial for the company to worry about losing a razor here and there, the problem is really far worse than that. Gillette's Mach 3 razor, retailing at more than $10 each, is one of the most commonly stolen items in a store.
Issuing passports	The U.S. State Department has approved of passports with microchips inside, and the technology is already being tested in trials. While the government maintains that its purpose is to improve communication between law enforcement agencies, others feel there will be more sinister repercussions.

and indicate ways that consumers and businesses will benefit. These trends include widespread use of mobile social networks, greater choice in multifunction devices, and more wireless home entertainment options.

- **Social networking gets mobilized.** Mobility is added to existing Internet business models, services, and behaviors, driving traffic for wireless operators. Those in their teens and twenties accustomed to constant connectivity and habit-forming websites, such as MySpace and Facebook, lead a wave of membership in mobile social networks. Location social networking including friend and event finder services are gaining popularity, even in the professional and over-50 segments. Google, Yahoo!, and Skype are more compelling for users than wireless brands, which are hard-pressed to compete. Social networking applications initially are pre-loaded on many mobile devices sold and later become downloadable.

- **Mobile TV.** In the short term, wireless users are unlikely to plunk down $5.99 to $9.99 per month for mobile TV service. Instead, look for per-view or per-minute pricing for "sneaking," a consumer tendency to watch key minutes of a sports event or drama while engaged in another activity. Sneaking leads to more regular viewing, and within three to five years, mobile TV will become an indispensable service. Broadcast TV is the primary driver of revenues and consumer adoption, but peer-to-peer video is gaining interest, too. Operators are squaring off with content providers over control of the subscriber relationship and user experience.

- **Multifunction devices become cheaper and more versatile.** Intense competition and margin pressure will continue in the handset market, forcing prices of third-generation (3G) handsets below $90 and making them affordable for a wide range of users. Seeking to replicate the success of camera phones, device manufacturers will produce more multifunction units with music-playing, location, video and other capabilities. Twenty percent of all handsets sold in North America are application specific—built for a usage proposition, such as music or video consumption or business productivity.

- **Location-based services.** GPS is the location technology of choice for the wireless industry. Handset manufacturers will continue to push GPS-enabled handsets as the technology evolves from popular in-car satellite navigation systems like TomTom to a broadly accepted feature in wireless phones. With Nokia having launched its first GPS-enabled handsets in early 2007 and bandwidth available to support new multimedia services, location-based service providers are building critical mass. Since there are 10 to 20 times more mobile phones sold than any other consumer electronics device, wireless is a huge driver for GPS adoption.

- **Mobile advertising.** Major brands are shifting from basic SMS marketing to more sophisticated multimedia advertising. RBC Capital Markets expects mobile marketing revenues to balloon from $45 million in 2005 to $1.5 billion by 2010. With the technological ability to target and measure the effectiveness of mobile advertising, brands are more strategic in their approach. Rich 3G content and video services and accuracy advancements in GPS-based location services deliver further value to brands targeting existing and potential customers in innovative ways.

- **Wireless providers move into home entertainment.** Mobile makes headway against fixed broadband operators, which have dominated Internet and cheaper voice service provision in the home. Wi-fi will remain the primary wireless access technology. The fixed operators may be strengthened by wi-fi capabilities in consumer electronics devices (set-top boxes, game consoles, and MP3 players) that enable cost-effective content downloads.

- **Wireless security moves to the forefront.** There is a monumental need to put strong security measures in place. This could be the year that hackers really start paying attention to millions of wireless devices, the growth in mobile data usage, and vulnerable points between mobile and fixed networks. CIOs consistently cite security as their number one concern in extending network access to wireless devices. Attacks, viruses, and data security now exceed device loss or theft as concerns. Emerging services, such as VoIP and mobile payments, provide additional challenges. Vulnerabilities directly affect the bottom line, corporate image, regulatory compliance, and competitive advantage.

- **Enterprise mobility.** Enterprises can't resist the convenient, reliable, attractively priced, bundled mobile solutions entering the market. Corporations switch from phones to mobile computers for transactions, data collection, and messaging for a wide variety of employees. Many voice communications processes, such as order placement and delivery notifications, dispatch operations, and remote asset monitoring, continue to shift to wireless data to increase information access and field transaction volume across organizations. Many corporations will completely replace their cellular handsets with a combined voice/data device or a data-only device.[30] ∎

CHECK OUT www.mhhe.com/baltzanm

for additional study materials including quizzes and PowerPoint presentations.

coming up

Organizations utilize various types of information systems to help run their daily operations. These are primarily transactional systems that concentrate on the management and flow of low-level data items pertaining to basic business processes such as purchasing and order delivery. The data are often rolled up and summarized into higher-level decision support systems to help firms understand what is happening in their organizations and how best to respond. To achieve seamless handling of the data, organizations must ensure that their enterprise information systems are tightly integrated. Doing so allows organizations to manage and process basic business processes as efficiently and effectively as possible and to make better informed decisions.

This module highlights the various types of enterprise information systems found in organizations and collaborative tools employees can use to facilitate communication and knowledge sharing. The chapters speak to various types of enterprise information systems and their role in helping firms reach their strategic goals. Though each chapter is devoted to specific types of enterprise systems, these systems must work in tandem with each other, giving enterprisewide views or 360-degree views of the business. Organizations that can correlate and summarize enterprisewide information are prepared to meet their strategic business goals and outperform their competitors. ◼

ENTERPRISE INFORMATION SYSTEMS

operations management + supply chain management

what's in IT for me?

nformation technology can be used to revolutionize and transform operations and supply chain management processes. Information systems enable companies to better manage the flow of information, materials, and financial payments that occurs between and among stages in a supply chain to maximize total supply chain effectiveness and profitability.

You, as a business student, need to know the significance of a supply chain to organizational success and the critical role information technology plays in ensuring smooth operations of a supply chain. A supply chain consists of all direct and indirect parties involved in the procurement of a product or raw material. These parties can be internal groups or departments within an organization or external partner companies and end customers.

This chapter emphasizes the important role information technology plays in providing an underlying infrastructure and coordination mechanisms needed for operations management and supply chains to function as effectively and efficiently as possible. Knowing this you will appreciate and understand the capabilities and limitations of operations management, the benefits and challenges of supply chain management, as well as future trends where information systems will play a critical part.

SECTION 8.1 >>

Operations Management

- Operations Management Fundamentals
- OM in Business
- IT's Role in OM
- Competitive OM Strategy
- OM and the Supply Chain

SECTION 8.2 >>

Supply Chain Management

- Supply Chain Fundamentals
- IT's Role in the Supply Chain
- Supply Chain Management Success Factors
- Supply Chain Management Success Stories
- Future Supply Chain Trends

roduction is the creation of goods and services using the factors of production: land, labor, capital, entrepreneurship, and knowledge. Production has historically been associated with manufacturing, but the nature of business has changed significantly in the last 20 years. The service sector, especially Internet services, has grown dramatically. The United States now has what is called a service economy—that is, one dominated by the service sector.

Organizations that excel in operations management, specifically supply chain management, perform better in almost every financial measure of success, according to a report from Boston-based AMR Research Inc. When supply chain excellence improves operations, companies experience a 5 percent higher profit margin, 15 percent less inventory, 17 percent stronger "perfect order" ratings, and 35 percent shorter cycle times than their competitors. "The basis of competition for winning companies in today's economy is supply chain superiority," said Kevin O'Marah, vice president of research at AMR Research. "These companies understand that value chain performance translates to productivity and market-share leadership. They also understand that supply chain leadership means more than just low costs and efficiency: It requires a superior ability to shape and respond to shifts in demand with innovative products and services."[1]

Collecting, analyzing, and distributing transactional information to all relevant parties, supply chain management (SCM) systems help all the different entities in the supply chain work together more effectively. SCM systems provide dynamic holistic views of organizations. Users can "drill down" into detailed analyses of supply chain activities to find valuable information on the organizational operations. This chapter explores the details of operations management and supply chain management.

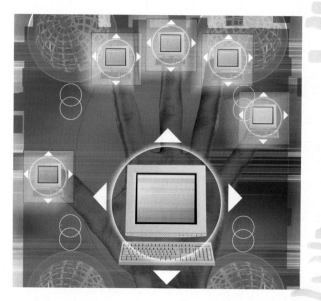

● ● **SECTION 8.1** Operations Management

LEARNING OUTCOMES

L08.1 Define the term operations management.

L08.2 Explain operations management's role in business.

L08.3 Describe the correlation between operations management and information technology.

L08.4 Describe the five characteristics of competitive priorities.

L08.5 Explain supply chain management and its role in a business.

● ● **L08.1**

Define the term operations management.

OPERATIONS MANAGEMENT FUNDAMENTALS

Books, DVDs, downloaded MP3s, and dental and medical procedures are all examples of goods and services. *Production management* describes all the activities managers do to help companies create goods. To reflect the change in importance from manufacturing to services, the term production often has been replaced by operations to reflect the manufacturing of both goods and services. *Operations management (OM)* is the management of systems or processes that convert or transform resources (including human resources) into goods and services. Operations management is responsible for managing the core processes used to manufacture goods and produce services.

Essentially, the creation of goods or services involves transforming or converting inputs into outputs. Various inputs such as capital, labor, and information are used to create goods or services using one or more transformation processes (e.g., storing, transporting, and cutting). A *transformation process* is often referred to as the technical core, especially in manufacturing organizations, and is the actual conversion of inputs to outputs.

To ensure that the desired outputs are obtained, an organization takes measurements at various points in the transformation process (feedback) and then compares them with previously established standards to determine whether corrective action is needed (control). Figure 8.1 depicts the conversion system.[2]

Figure 8.2 displays examples of inputs, transformation processes, and outputs. Although goods and services are listed separately in Figure 8.1 it is important to note that goods and services often occur jointly. For example, having the oil changed in a car is a service, but the oil that is delivered is a good. Similarly, house painting is a service, but the paint is a good. The goods–service combination is a continuum. It ranges from primarily goods with little service to primarily service with few

FIGURE 8.1 | Operations Involves the Conversion of Inputs into Outputs

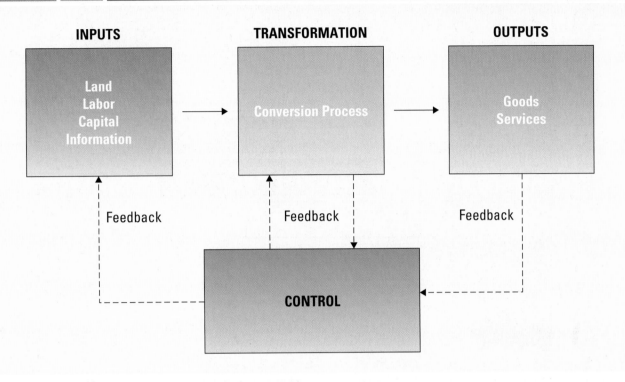

FIGURE 8.2 | Examples of Inputs, Transformation, and Outputs

Inputs	Transformation	Outputs
Restaurant inputs include hungry customers, food, wait staff	Well-prepared food, well served: agreeable environment	Satisfied customers
Hospital inputs include patients, medical supplies, doctors, nurses	Health care	Healthy individuals
Automobile inputs include sheet steel, engine parts, tires	Fabrication and assembly of cars	High-quality cars
College inputs include high school graduates, books, professors, classrooms	Imparting knowledge and skills	Educated individuals
Distribution center inputs include stock keeping units, storage bins, workers	Storage and redistribution	Fast delivery of available products

goods (see Figure 8.3). There are relatively few pure goods or pure services; therefore, organizations typically sell product packages, which are a combination of goods and services. This makes managing operations more interesting, and also more challenging.[3]

Value-added is the term used to describe the difference between the cost of inputs and the value of price of outputs. OM is critical to an organization because of its ability to increase value-added during the transformation process. In nonprofit organizations, the value of outputs (highway construction, police, and fire protection) is their value to society; the greater the value-added, the greater the effectiveness of the operations. In for-profit organizations, the value of outputs is measured by the prices that customers are willing to pay for those goods or services. Firms use the money generated by value-added for research and development, investment in new facilities and

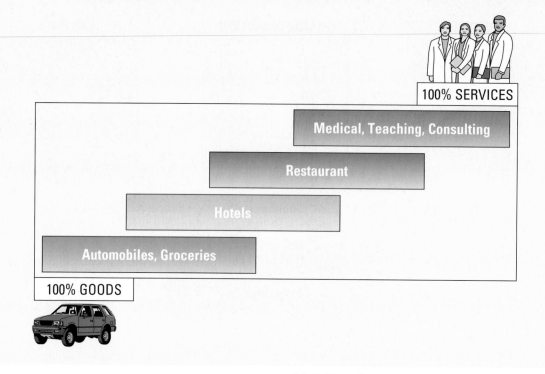

equipment, worker salaries, and profits. Consequently, the greater the value-added, the greater the amount of funds available for these important activities.

⬤⬤ L08.2

Explain operations management's role in business.

OM IN BUSINESS

The scope of OM ranges across the organization and includes many interrelated activities, such as forecasting, capacity planning, scheduling, managing inventories, assuring quality, motivating employees, deciding where to locate facilities, and more.

Reviewing the activities performed in an airline company makes it easy to understand how a service organization's OM team adds value. The company consists of the airplanes, airport facilities, and maintenance facilities, and typical OM activities include:

- **Forecasting:** Estimating seat demand for flights, weather and landing conditions, and estimates for growth or reduction in air travel are all included in forecasting.

- **Capacity planning:** This is the key essential metric for the airline to maintain cash flow and increase revenues. Underestimating or overestimating flights will hurt profits.

- **Scheduling:** The airline operates on tight schedules that must be maintained including flights, pilots, flight attendants, ground crews, baggage handlers, and routine maintenance.

- **Managing inventory:** Inventory of such items as foods, beverages, first-aid equipment, in-flight magazines, pillows, blankets, and life jackets is essential for the airline.

- **Assuring quality:** Quality is indispensable in an airline where safety is the highest priority. Today's travelers expect high-quality customer service during ticketing, check-in, curb service, and unexpected issues where the emphasis is on efficiency and courtesy.

- **Motivating and training employees:** Airline employees must be highly trained and continually motivated, especially when dealing with frustrated airline travelers.

- **Locating facilities:** Key questions facing airlines include which cities to offer services, where to host maintenance facilities, and where to locate major and minor hubs.[4]

Opposite from an airline is a bike factory, which is typically an assembly operation: buying components such as frames, tires, wheels, gears, and other items from suppliers, and then assembling bicycles. A bike factory also does some of the fabrication work itself, forming frames and making the gears and chains. Obviously, an airline company and a bike factory are completely different types of operations. One is primarily a service operation, the other a producer of goods. Nonetheless, these two operations have much in common. The same as the

airline, the bike factory must schedule production, deal with components, order parts and materials, schedule and train employees, ensure quality standards are met, and above all satisfy customers. In both organizations, the success of the business depends on short- and long-term planning and the ability of its executives and managers to make informed decisions.[5]

●● L08.3

Describe the correlation between operations management and information technology.

IT'S ROLE IN OM

Managers can use IT to heavily influence OM decisions including productivity, costs, flexibility, quality, and customer satisfaction. One of the greatest benefits of IT on OM is in making operational decisions because operations management exerts considerable influence over the degree to which the goals and objectives of the organization are realized. Most OM decisions involve many possible alternatives that can have varying impacts on revenues and expenses. OM information systems are critical for managers to be able to make well-informed decisions.

Decision support systems and *executive information systems* can help an organization perform what-if analysis, sensitivity analysis, drill-down, and consolidation. Numerous managerial and strategic key decisions are based on OM information systems that affect the entire organization, including:

- **What:** What resources will be needed, and in what amounts?
- **When:** When will each resource be needed? When should the work be scheduled? When should materials and other supplies be ordered? When is corrective action needed?
- **Where:** Where will the work be performed?
- **How:** How will the product or service be designed? How will the work be done (organization, methods, equipment)? How will resources be allocated?
- **Who:** Who will perform the work?

OM Strategic Business Systems

UPS uses package flow information systems at each of its locations. The custom-built systems combine operations strategy and mapping technology to optimize the way boxes are loaded and delivered. The goal is to use the package flow software to cut the distance that delivery trucks travel by more than

> One of the greatest benefits of IT on OM is in making operational decisions because operations management exerts considerable influence over the degree to which the goals and objectives of the organization are realized.

Need Wedding Money—Just Auction Off Your Bridesmaids

We all realize that the Internet is transforming the way we do business, attend college, and even communicate with our loved ones. But when will all of this Internet transformation go a step too far? I think it has already happened. I bet you thought that marriage was one of those special events to be shared with friends and family. Well, not anymore. Now you can auction off your bridesmaid's positions if you want to raise a little extra money for your wedding. Kelly Gray decided that is was a great idea, and she opened up her bridesmaid's spot on an eBay auction—yes, it is true. You really

have to wonder why anyone would pay to be in a wedding, as it is typically expensive to be a bridesmaid because you are expected to purchase your own dress and shoes and pay for your own travel costs, and let's not forget about the bachelorette party you are expected to throw. The good news is Gray made an astonishing $5,700, and her beautiful bridesmaid was none other than the Dr. Pepper Snapple Group. Yes, the Dr. Pepper Snapple Group saw this as a great publicity stunt and even upped their bid by donating $10,000 and all the Snapple the wedding guests could drink.

My only question is, What did the wedding photos look like?

"Production management" describes all of the activities managers do to help companies create goods and services. "Operations management" is the management of systems or processes that convert or transform resources into goods and services. As mentioned above, the Internet is changing the way people live their lives, and traditional processes, such as choosing your bridesmaids, are being transformed. Identify other goods and services that are being transformed though the use of technology.

---

100 million miles each year. The project will also help UPS streamline the profitability of each of its facility locations.[6]

Operations strategy is concerned with the development of a long-term plan for determining how to best utilize the major resources of the firm so that there is a high degree of compatibility between these resources and the firm's long-term corporate strategy. Operations strategy addresses very broad questions about how these major resources should be configured to achieve the desired corporate objectives. Some of the major long-term issues addressed in operations strategy include:

- How big to make the facilities?
- Where to locate the facilities?
- When to build additional facilities?
- What type of process(es) to install to make the products?

Each of these issues can be addressed by OM decision support systems. In developing an operations strategy, management needs to consider many factors. These include (a) the level of technology that is or will be available, (b) the required skill levels of the workers, and (c) the degree of vertical integration, in terms of the extent to which outside suppliers are used.

Today, many organizations, especially larger conglomerates, operate in terms of *strategic business units (SBUs),* which consist of several stand-alone businesses. When companies become really large, they are best thought of as being composed of a number of businesses (or SBUs). As displayed in Figure 8.4, operations strategy supports the long-range strategy developed at the SBU level.[7]

Decisions at the SBU level focus on being effective, that is, "on doing the right things." These decisions are sometimes

referred to as *strategic planning,* which focuses on long range planning such as plant size, location, and type of process to be used. The primary system used for strategic planning is a materials requirement planning system. *Materials requirement planning (MRP) systems* use sales forecasts to make sure that needed parts and materials are available at the right time and place in a specific company. The latest version of MRP is enterprise resource planning, which is discussed in detail in Chapter 10.[8]

Strategic decisions impact intermediate-range decisions, often referred to as tactical planning, which focuses on being efficient, that is, "doing things right." *Tactical planning* focuses on producing goods and services as efficiently as possible within the strategic plan. Here the emphasis is on producing quality products, including when material should be delivered, when products should be made to best meet demand, and what size the workforce should be. One of the primary systems used in tactical planning includes global inventory management. *Global inventory management systems* provide the ability to locate, track, and predict the movement of every component or material anywhere upstream or downstream in the production process. This allows an organization to locate and analyze its inventory anywhere in its production process.[9]

Finally, *operational planning and control (OP&C)* deals with the day-to-day procedures for performing work, including scheduling, inventory, and process management. *Inventory management and control systems* provide control and visibility to the status of individual items maintained in inventory. The software maintains inventory record accuracy, generates material requirements for all purchased items, and analyzes

FIGURE 8.4 Hierarchy of Operational Planning

Type of Planning	Time Frame	Issues	Decisions	Systems
Strategic Planning	Long range	Plant size, location, type of processes	How will we make the products? Where do we locate the facility or facilities? How much capacity do we require? When should we add additional capacity?	Materials requirement planning (MRP) systems
Tactical Planning	Intermediate range	Workforce size, material requirements	How many workers do we need? When do we need them? Should we work overtime or put on a section shift? When should we have material delivered? Should we have a finished goods inventory?	Global inventory management systems
Operational Planning and Control (OP&C)	Short range	Daily scheduling of employees, jobs, and equipment, process management, inventory management	What jobs do we work on today or this week? To whom do we assign what tasks? What jobs have priority?	Inventory management and control systems, transportation planning systems, distribution management systems

inventory performance. Inventory management and control software provides organizations with the information from a variety of sources including:

- Current inventory and order status.
- Cost accounting.
- Sales forecasts and customer orders.
- Manufacturing capacity.
- New-product introductions.[10]

Two additional OP&C systems include transportation planning and distribution management. *Transportation planning systems* track and analyze the movement of materials and products to ensure the delivery of materials and finished goods at the right time, the right place, and the lowest cost. *Distribution management systems* coordinate the process of transporting materials from a manufacturer to distribution centers to the final customers. Transportation routes directly affect the speed and cost of delivery. An organization will use these systems to help it decide if it wants to use an effectiveness route and ship its products directly to its customers or use an efficiency route and ship its products to a distributor that ships the products to customers.

 LO8.4

Describe the five characteristics of competitive priorities.

COMPETITIVE OM STRATEGY

The key to developing a competitive OM strategy lies in understanding how to create value-added goods and services for customers. Specifically, value is added through the competitive priority or priorities that are selected to support a given strategy. Five key competitive priorities translate directly into characteristics that are used to describe various processes by which a company can add value to its OM decisions including:

1. Cost
2. Quality
3. Delivery
4. Flexibility
5. Service[11]

Cost

Every industry has low-cost providers. However, being the low-cost producer does not always guarantee profitability and success. Products sold strictly on the basis of cost are typically commodity-like products including such goods as flour, petroleum, and sugar. In other words, customers cannot distinguish the products made by one firm from those of another. As a result, customers use cost as the primary determinant in making a purchasing decision.

Low-cost market segments are frequently very large, and many companies are lured by the potential for significant profits, which are associated with large unit volumes of product. As a consequence, the competition in this segment is exceedingly fierce—and so is the failure rate. After all, there can be only one lowest-cost producer, and that firm usually establishes the selling price in the market.

Quality

Quality can be divided into two categories—product quality and process quality. Product quality levels vary as to the particular market that it aims to serve. For example, a generic bike is of significantly different quality than the bike of a world-class cyclist. Higher quality products command higher prices in the marketplace. Organizations must establish the "proper level" of product quality by focusing on the exact requirements of their customers. Overdesigned products with too much quality will be viewed as being prohibitively expensive. Underdesigned products, on the other hand, will lose customers to products that cost a little more but are perceived by the customers as offering greater value.

Process quality is critical in every market segment. Regardless of whether the product is a generic bike or a bike for an international cyclist, customers want products without defects. Thus, the primary goal of process quality is to produce error-free products. The investment in improving quality pays

services. ISO is a worldwide federation of national standards bodies from more than 140 countries. ISO 900 standards require a company to determine customer needs, including regulatory and legal requirements. The company must also make communication arrangements to handle issues such as complaints. Other standards involve process control, product testing, storage, and delivery.

- **ISO 14000:** This collection of the best practices for managing an organization's impact on the environment does not prescribe specific performance levels, but establishes environmental management systems. The requirements for certification include having an environmental policy, setting specific improvement targets, conducting audits of environmental programs, and maintaining top management review of processes. Certification in ISO 14000 displays that a firm has a world-class management system in both quality and environmental standards.[14]

- **CMMI:** Capability Maturity Model Integration is a framework of best practices. The current version, CMMI-DEV, describes best practices in managing, measuring, and monitoring software development processes. CMMI does not describe the processes themselves; it describes the characteristics of good processes, thus providing guidelines for companies developing or honing their own sets of processes.[15]

> "The ability of a firm to provide consistent and fast delivery allows it to charge a premium price for its products."

off in stronger customer relationships and higher revenues. Many organizations use modern quality control standards, including:

- **Six sigma quality:** The goal is to detect potential problems to prevent their occurrence and achieve no more than 3.4 defects per million opportunities. That is important to companies like Bank of America, which makes 4 million transactions a day.[12]

- **Malcolm Baldrige National Quality Awards:** In 1987 in the United States, a standard was set for overall company quality with the introduction of the Malcolm Baldrige National Quality Awards, named in honor of the late U.S. secretary of commerce. Companies can apply for these awards in each of the following areas: manufacturing, services, small businesses, education, and health care. To qualify, an organization has to show quality in seven key areas: leadership, strategic planning, customer and market focus, information and analysis, human resources focus, process management, and business results.[13]

- **ISO 900:** The common name given to quality management and assurance standards. Comes from the *International Organization for Standardization (ISO),* a nongovernmental organization established in 1947 to promote the development of world standards to facilitate the international exchange of goods and

Delivery

Another key factor in purchasing decisions is delivery speed. The ability of a firm to provide consistent and fast delivery allows it to charge a premium price for its products. George Stalk, Jr., of the Boston Consulting Group, has demonstrated

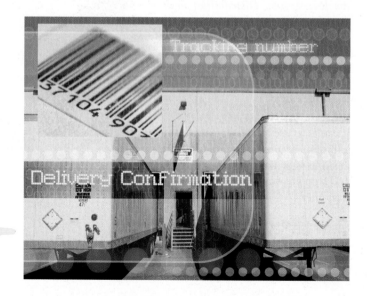

> # SUPPLY CHAIN MANAGEMENT (SCM) INVOLVES THE MANAGEMENT OF INFORMATION FLOWS BETWEEN AND AMONG STAGES IN A SUPPLY CHAIN TO MAXIMIZE TOTAL SUPPLY CHAIN EFFECTIVENESS AND PROFITABILITY.

that both profits and market share are directly linked to the speed with which a company can deliver its products relative to its competition. In addition to fast delivery, the reliability of the delivery is also important. In other words, products should be delivered to customers with minimum variance in delivery times.[16]

Flexibility

Flexibility, from a strategic perspective, refers to the ability of a company to offer a wide variety of products to its customers. Flexibility is also a measure of how fast a company can convert its process(es) from making an old line of products to producing a new product line. Product variety is often perceived by the customers to be a dimension of quality.

The flexibility of the manufacturing process at John Deere's Harvester Works in Moline, Illinois, allows the firm to respond to the unpredictability of the agricultural industry's equipment needs. By manufacturing such small-volume products as seed planters in "modules," or factories within a factory, Deere can offer farmers a choice of 84 different planter models with such a wide variety of options that farmers can have planters virtually customized to meet their individual needs. Its manufacturing process thus allows Deere to compete on both speed and flexibility.[17]

Currently, there appears to be a trend toward offering environmentally friendly products that are made through environmentally friendly processes. As consumers become more aware of the fragility of the environment, they are increasingly turning toward products that are safe for the environment. Several flexible manufacturers now advertise environmentally friendly products, energy-efficient products, and recycled products.

Service

With shortened product life cycles, products tend to migrate toward one common standard. As a consequence, these products are often viewed as commodities in which price is the primary differentiator. For example, the differences in laptops offered among PC manufactures are relatively insignificant so price is the prime selection criterion. For this reason, many companies attempt to place an emphasis on high-quality customer service as a primary differentiator. Customer service can add tremendous value to an ordinary product.

Businesses are always looking toward the future to find the next competitive advantage that will distinguish their products in the marketplace. To obtain an advantage in such a competitive environment, firms must provide "value-added" goods and services, and the primary area where they can capitalize on all five competitive priorities is in the supply chain.

●● L08.5

Explain supply chain management and its role in a business.

OM AND THE SUPPLY CHAIN

To understand a supply chain, consider a customer purchasing a Trek bike from a dealer. The supply chain begins when a customer places an order for a Trek bike with the dealer. The dealer purchases the bike from the manufacturer, Trek. Trek purchases the raw materials required to make the bike such as metal, packaging, and accessories from different suppliers. The supply chain for Trek encompasses every activity and party involved in the process of fulfilling the order from the customer for the new bike.

A *supply chain* consists of all parties involved, directly or indirectly, in the procurement of a product or raw material. *Supply chain management (SCM)* involves the management of information flows between and among stages in a supply chain to maximize total supply chain effectiveness and profitability. The four basic components of supply chain management are:

1. **Supply chain strategy**—the strategy for managing all the resources required to meet customer demand for all products and services.

2. **Supply chain partners**—the partners chosen to deliver finished products, raw materials, and services including pricing, delivery, and payment processes along with partner relationship monitoring metrics.

3. **Supply chain operation**—the schedule for production activities including testing, packaging, and preparation for delivery. Measurements for this component include productivity and quality.

4. **Supply chain logistics**—the product delivery processes and elements including orders, warehouses, carriers, defective product returns, and invoicing.[18]

Dozens of steps are required to achieve and carry out each of the above components. SCM software can enable an organization to generate efficiencies within these steps by automating and improving the information flows throughout and among the different supply chain components. Figures 8.5 and 8.6 display the typical supply chains for goods and services.

FIGURE 8.5 A Typical Manufacturing Supply Chain

FIGURE 8.5 — A Typical Manufacturing Supply Chain

Supplier

Supplier

Supplier

Storage (Raw Materials) → Manufacturing → Storage (Finished Goods) → Distribution → Retailer → Customer

FIGURE 8.6 A Typical Service Supply Chain

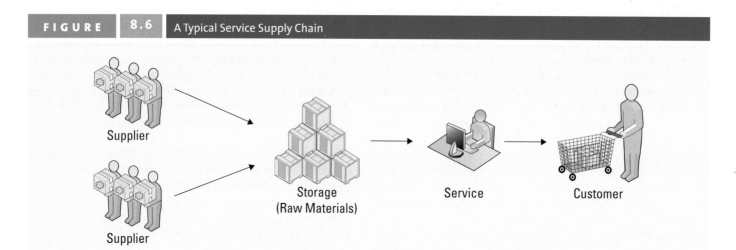

FIGURE 8.6 — A Typical Service Supply Chain

Supplier

Supplier

Storage (Raw Materials) → Service → Customer

fyi

Fixing the Post Office

Is there anything more frustrating than waiting in line at the Post Office? Well, not only are those lines frustrating, they are also becoming unprofitable. The United States Postal Service is looking at a $7 billion loss in 2009, one of the greatest catastrophes in its history.

What is killing the Post Office? Perhaps it is Stamps.com, a website that allows you to customize and print your own stamps 24 hours a day. Getting married? You can place a photo of the happy couple right on the stamp for the invitations. Starting a business? You can place your business logo on your stamps. Stamps.com even keeps track of all of a customer's postal spending using client codes, and it can recommend optimal

delivery methods. Plus, Stamps.com gives you postage discounts you can't even get at the Post Office or with a postage meter.

What new products are stealing business from the Post Office? How could the Post Office create new products and services to help grow its business? How could the Post Office use cost, quality, delivery, flexibility, and service to revamp its operations management processes?

Walmart and Procter & Gamble (P&G) implemented a successful SCM system that linked Walmart's distribution centers directly to P&G's manufacturing centers. Every time a Walmart customer purchases a P&G product, the system sends a message directly to the factory alerting P&G to restock the product. The system also sends an automatic alert to P&G whenever a product is running low at one of Walmart's distribution centers. This real-time information allows P&G to produce and deliver products to Walmart without having to maintain large inventories in its warehouses. The SCM system saves time, reduces inventory, and decreases order-processing costs for P&G, which P&G passes on to Walmart in the form of discounted prices.[19]

Figure 8.7 diagrams the stages of the SCM system for a customer purchasing a product from Walmart. The diagram demonstrates how the supply chain is dynamic and involves the constant flow of information between the different parties. For example, a customer purchases a product from Walmart and generates order information. Walmart supplies the order information to its warehouse or distributor. The warehouse or distributor transfers the order information to the manufacturer, who provides pricing and availability information to the store and replenishes the product. Partners transfer all payments electronically. Effective and efficient supply chain management systems can enable an organization to:

- Decrease the power of its buyers.
- Increase its own supplier power.
- Increase switching costs to reduce the threat of substitute products or services.
- Create entry barriers thereby reducing the threat of new entrants.
- Increase efficiencies while seeking a competitive advantage through cost leadership (see Figure 8.8).[20]

●● SECTION 8.2 Supply Chain Management

LEARNING OUTCOMES

LO8.6 List and describe the five components of a typical supply chain.

LO8.7 Define the relationship between information technology and the supply chain.

LO8.8 Identify the factors driving supply chain management.

LO8.9 Summarize the best practices for implementing a successful supply chain management system.

●● LO8.6

List and describe the five components of a typical supply chain.

FIGURE 8.7 Supply Chain for a Product Purchased from Walmart

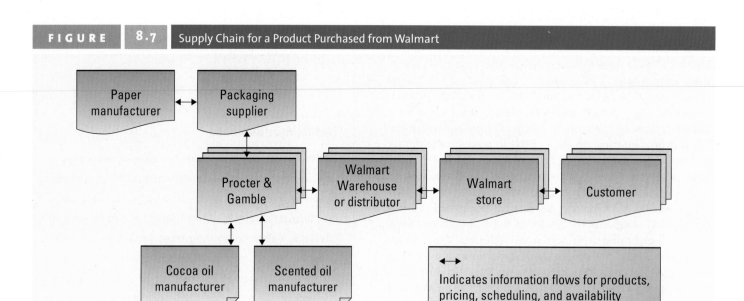

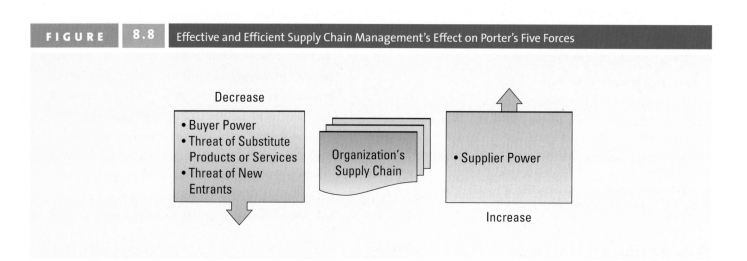

SUPPLY CHAIN FUNDAMENTALS

The average company spends nearly half of every dollar it earns on production needs—goods and services it needs from external suppliers to keep producing. In the past, companies focused primarily on manufacturing and quality improvements within their four walls; now their efforts extend beyond those walls to influence the entire supply chain including customers, customers' customers, suppliers, and suppliers' suppliers. Today's supply chain is a complex web of suppliers, assemblers, logistic firms, sales/marketing channels, and other business partners linked primarily through information networks and contractual relationships. SCM systems enhance and manage the relationships. The supply chain has three main links (see Figure 8.9):

1. Materials flow from suppliers and their upstream suppliers at all levels.

2. Transformation of materials into semifinished and finished products—the organization's own production processes.

3. Distribution of products to customers and their downstream customers at all levels.

Organizations must embrace technologies that can effectively manage and oversee their supply chains. SCM is becoming increasingly important in creating organizational efficiencies and competitive advantages. Best Buy checks inventory levels at each of its 750 stores in North America as often as every half hour with its SCM system, taking much of the guesswork out of inventory replenishment. Supply chain management improves ways for companies to find the raw components they need to make a product or service, manufacture that product or service,

FIGURE   8.9   A Typical Supply Chain

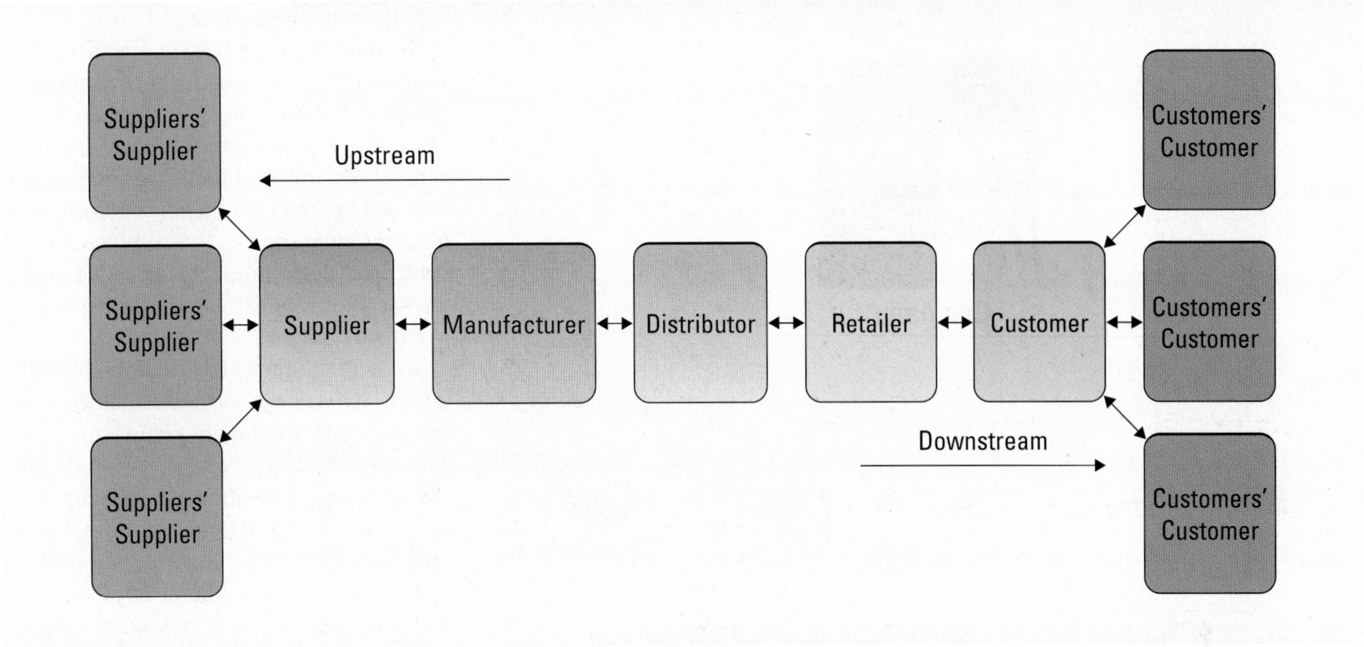

My Not To-Do List

Honestly, It Cost $7,500 for a Steak Dinner

The next time one of your employees submits an expense report, you might want to think twice: there are a number of websites offering all kinds of phony documentation that individuals can use to help cheat on their taxes, expense reports, or even spouses. Here are a few you should be aware of:

- **Customreceipts.com:** This site prints fake ATM receipts for those individuals who want to casually let other people see their massive bank balance.
- **Alibi Network:** Creates custom tailored excuses, such as a call claiming to be an "emergency" so that the employee can leave that boring meeting or dreadful company picnic. The site will even write and send false invitations for business events or

telephone an unfaithful partner "confirming" that their beloved will be caught up in a meeting.

- **CorruptedFiles.com:** Sells corrupted files guaranteed not to open on a Mac or PC, allowing employees to miss that deadline.
- **Restaurant Maloney & Porcelli's:** This innovative, yet perhaps unethical, restaurant started the "expense a steak" tool that works by entering the bill for the dinner and automatically creates a fake, work-related receipt ranging from cab rides to office supply stores. For example, enter a meal costing $149.37 and the program generates a $135.73 receipt from the "Office Supply Hut" and a $13.64 receipt from "The Panini Experience."

Does the existence of services like these affect how you will run your business? What would you do to an employee who was using one of these services? What would happen to a company's budget if it believed the fraudulent expenses were required to be paid by the business? How does the bullwhip effect enter into this scenario? How can a company fight back against these types of fraudulent activities without wasting enormous amounts of time and energy?

FIGURE 8.10 The Five Basic Supply Chain Management Components

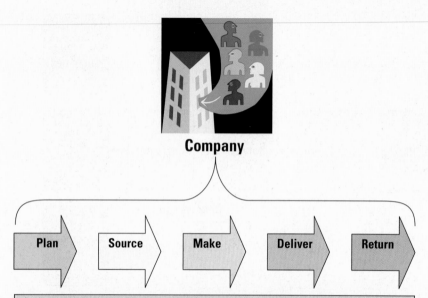

Company

THE FIVE BASIC SUPPLY CHAIN MANAGEMENT COMPONENTS
1. **Plan** – This is the strategic portion of supply chain management. A company must have a plan for managing all the resources that go toward meeting customer demand for products or services. A big piece of planning is developing a set of metrics to monitor the supply chain so that it is efficient, costs less, and delivers high quality and value to customers.
2. **Source** – Companies must carefully choose reliable suppliers that will deliver goods and services required for making products. Companies must also develop a set of pricing, delivery, and payment processes with suppliers and create metrics for monitoring and improving the relationships.
3. **Make** – This is the step where companies manufacture their products or services. This can include scheduling the activities necessary for production, testing, packaging, and preparing for delivery. This is by far the most metric-intensive portion of the supply chain, measuring quality levels, production output, and worker productivity.
4. **Deliver** – This step is commonly referred to as logistics. *Logistics* is the set of processes that plans for and controls the efficient and effective transportation and storage of supplies from suppliers to customers. During this step, companies must be able to receive orders from customers, fulfill the orders via a network of warehouses, pick transportation companies to deliver the products, and implement a billing and invoicing system to facilitate payments.
5. **Return** – This is typically the most problematic step in the supply chain. Companies must create a network for receiving defective and excess products and support customers who have problems with delivered products.

and deliver it to customers. Figure 8.10 highlights the five basic components of supply chain management.[21]

Technology advances in the five SCM components have significantly improved companies' forecasting and business operations. Businesses today have access to modeling and simulation tools, algorithms, and applications that can combine information from multiple sources to build forecasts for days, weeks, and months in advance. Better forecasts for tomorrow result in better preparedness today.

Mattel Inc. spent the past several years investing heavily in software and processes that simplify its supply chain, cut costs, and shorten cycle times. Using supply chain management strategies, the company cut weeks out of the time it takes to design, produce, and ship everything from Barbies to Hot Wheels. Mattel installed optimization software that measures, tweaks, and validates the operations of its seven distribution centers, seven manufacturing plants, and other facilities that make up its vast worldwide supply chain. Mattel improved forecasting from monthly to weekly. The company no longer produces more inventory than stores require and delivers inventory upon request. Mattel's supply chain moves quickly to make precise forecasts that help the company meet demand.[22]

●● L08.7

Define the relationship between information technology and the supply chain.

●● L08.8

Identify the factors driving supply chain management.

IT'S ROLE IN THE SUPPLY CHAIN

As companies evolve into extended organizations, the roles of supply chain participants are changing. It is now common for suppliers to be involved in product development and for distributors to act as consultants in brand marketing. The notion of virtually seamless information links within and between organizations is an essential element of integrated supply chains.

Information technology's primary role in SCM is creating the integrations or tight process and information linkages between functions within a firm—such as marketing, sales, finance, manufacturing, and distribution—and between firms, which allow the smooth, synchronized flow of both information and product between customers, suppliers, and transportation providers across the supply chain. Information technology integrates planning, decision-making processes, business operating processes, and information sharing for business performance management (see Figure 8.11). Considerable evidence shows that this type of supply chain integration results in superior supply chain capabilities and profits.[23]

Adaptec, Inc., of California manufactures semiconductors and markets them to the world's leading PC, server, and end-user markets through more than 115 distributors and thousands of value-added resellers worldwide. Adaptec designs and manufactures products at various third-party locations around the world. The company uses supply chain integration software over the Internet to synchronize planning. Adaptec personnel at the company's geographically dispersed locations communicate in real time and exchange designs, test results, and production and shipment information. Internet-based supply chain collaboration software helped the company reduce inventory levels and lead times.[24]

Although people have been talking about the integrated supply chain for a long time, it has only been recently that advances in information technology have made it possible to bring the idea to life and truly integrate the supply chain. Visibility, consumer behavior, competition, and speed are a few of the changes resulting from advances in information technology that are driving supply chains (see Figure 8.12).

Visibility

Supply chain visibility is the ability to view all areas up and down the supply chain. Making the change to supply chains requires a comprehensive strategy buoyed by information technology. Organizations can use technology tools that help them integrate upstream and downstream, with both customers and suppliers.

To make a supply chain work most effectively, organizations must create visibility in real time. Organizations must know about customer events triggered downstream, but so must their suppliers and their suppliers' suppliers. Without this information, partners throughout the supply chain can experience a bullwhip effect, in which disruptions intensify throughout the chain. The *bullwhip effect* occurs when distorted product demand information passes from one entity to the next throughout the supply chain. The misinformation regarding a slight rise in demand for a product could cause different members in the supply chain to stockpile inventory. These changes ripple throughout the supply chain, magnifying the issue and creating excess inventory and costs.[25]

Robots Took My Job

Kiva's little orange robots are becoming the latest craze and a truly fascinating innovation in warehouse management. Kiva's robots are replacing conveyor belts and carousels at the order fulfillment warehouses of retailers such as Zappos, Staples, and Diapers.com.

According to the Kiva site, the Kiva Mobile Fulfillment System (Kiva MFS) uses a breakthrough parallel processing approach to order fulfillment with a unique material handling system that simultaneously improves productivity, speed, accuracy, and flexibility. Every distribution center (DC) strives to attain flexible, efficient order fulfillment but struggles with the limitations of current tools. Traditional automation and sortation systems such as conveyors, tilt tray sorters, sliding shoe sorters, horizontal and vertical carousels, and other automated material handling systems simply tinker with Henry Ford's serial assembly line concept. Kiva Systems has created an innovative order fulfillment system that eliminates the constraints of existing warehouse automation and puts the supplier back in control.

In distribution centers, warehouses, and manufacturing plants equipped with the Kiva MFS, operators stand still while the products come to them. Pallets, cases, and orders are stored on inventory pods that are picked up and moved by a fleet of mobile robotic drive units. As a result, any product can go to any operator at any time to fill any order.

One of Kiva's biggest customers, Zappos, was recently acquired by Amazon. Why would this information be important to Kiva? What impact could Amazon have on Kiva's business? What impact could Kiva have on Amazon's business? What other types of businesses could use Kiva to improve distribution productivity? How would your warehouse employees react if you told them you were looking at implementing Kiva robots?

Today, information technology allows additional visibility in the supply chain. Electronic information flows allow managers to view their suppliers' and customers' supply chains. Some organizations have completely changed the dynamics of their industries because of the competitive advantage gained from high visibility in the supply chain. Dell is the obvious example.

FIGURE | 8.11 | The Integrated Supply Chain

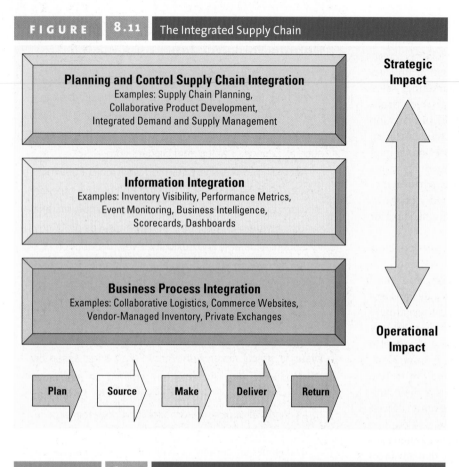

Planning and Control Supply Chain Integration
Examples: Supply Chain Planning,
Collaborative Product Development,
Integrated Demand and Supply Management

Information Integration
Examples: Inventory Visibility, Performance Metrics,
Event Monitoring, Business Intelligence,
Scorecards, Dashboards

Business Process Integration
Examples: Collaborative Logistics, Commerce Websites,
Vendor-Managed Inventory, Private Exchanges

Plan → Source → Make → Deliver → Return

Strategic Impact

Operational Impact

FIGURE | 8.12 | Factors Driving Supply Chain Management

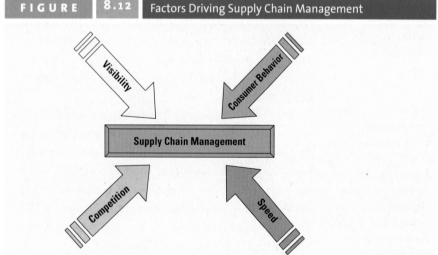

Visibility
Consumer Behavior
Supply Chain Management
Competition
Speed

The company's ability to get product to the customer and the impact of the economics have clearly changed the nature of competition and caused others to emulate this model.

Consumer Behavior

The behavior of customers has changed the way businesses compete. Customers will leave if a company does not continually meet their expectations. They are more demanding because

they have information readily available, they know exactly what they want, and they know when and how they want it.

Demand planning systems generate demand forecasts using statistical tools and forecasting techniques. Companies can respond faster and more effectively to consumer demands through supply chain enhancements such as demand planning software. Once an organization understands customer demand and its effect on the supply chain it can begin to estimate the impact that its supply chain will have on its customers and ultimately the organization's performance. The payoff for a successful demand planning strategy can be tremendous.

A study by Peter J. Metz, executive director of the MIT Center for ebusiness, found that companies have achieved impressive bottom-line results from managing demand in their supply chains, averaging a 50 percent reduction in inventory and a 40 percent increase in timely deliveries.[26]

Competition

Supply chain management software can be broken down into (1) supply chain planning software and (2) supply chain execution software. Both increase a company's ability to compete. ***Supply chain planning (SCP) systems*** use advanced mathematical algorithms to improve the flow and efficiency of the supply chain while reducing inventory. SCP depends entirely on information for its accuracy. An organization cannot expect the SCP output to be accurate unless correct and up-to-date information regarding customer orders, sales information, manufacturing capacity, and delivery capability is entered into the system.

An organization's supply chain encompasses the facilities where raw materials, intermediate products, and finished goods are acquired, transformed, stored, and sold. These facilities are connected by transportation links, where materials and products flow. Ideally, the supply chain consists of multiple organizations that function as efficiently and effectively as a single organization, with full information visibility. ***Supply chain execution (SCE) systems*** automate the different steps and stages of the supply chain. This could be as simple as electronically routing orders from a manufacturer to a supplier. Figure 8.13 details how SCP and SCE software correlate to the supply chain.

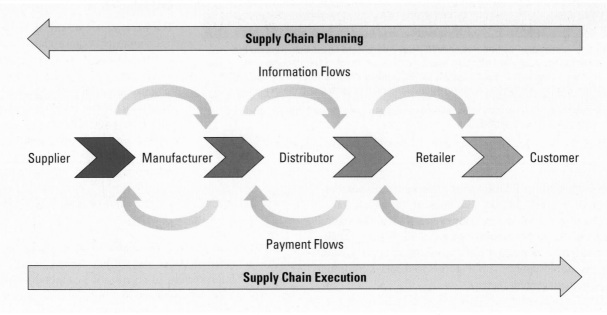

General Motors, Ford, and DaimlerChrysler made history when the three automotive giants began working together to create a unified supply chain planning/execution system that all three companies and their suppliers could leverage. Gary Lapidus, Goldman Sachs Group's senior analyst, estimated that Newco, the name of the joint venture, would have a potential market capitalization of between $30 billion and $40 billion, with annual revenues of about $3 billion.

The combined automotive giants' purchasing power is tremendous with GM spending $85 billion per year, Ford spending $80 billion, and DaimlerChrysler spending $73 billion. The ultimate goal of Newco was to process automotive production, from ordering materials and forecasting demand to making cars directly to consumer specifications through the web. The automotive giants understand the impact strategic supply chain planning and execution can have on their competition.[27]

Speed

During the past decade, competition has focused on speed. New forms of servers, telecommunications, wireless applications, and software are enabling companies to perform activities that were once never thought possible. These systems raise the accuracy, frequency, and speed of communication between suppliers and customers, as well as between internal users. Another aspect of speed is the company's ability to satisfy continually changing customer requirements efficiently, accurately, and quickly. Timely and accurate information

is more critical to businesses than ever before. Figure 8.14 displays the three factors fostering this change.

L08.9

Summarize the best practices for implementing a successful supply chain management system.

SUPPLY CHAIN MANAGEMENT SUCCESS FACTORS

To succeed in today's competitive markets, companies must align their supply chains with the demands of the markets they serve. Supply chain performance is now a distinct competitive advantage for companies proficient in the SCM area. Perdue Farms excels at decision making based on its supply chain management system. Perdue Farms moves roughly 1 million turkeys, each within 24 hours of processing, to reach holiday tables across the nation yearly. The task is no longer as complicated as it was before Perdue Farms invested $20 million in SCM technology. SCM makes Perdue more adept at delivering the right number of turkeys, to the right customers, at the right time.[28]

> To succeed in today's competitive markets, companies must align their supply chains with the demands of the markets they serve.

SCM Success Metrics

Supply chain management metrics can help an organization understand how it's operating over a given time period. Supply

FIGURE 8.14 Factors Fostering Speed

Three Factors Fostering Speed

1. Pleasing customers has become something of a corporate obsession. Serving the customer in the best, most efficient, and most effective manner has become critical, and information about issues such as order status, product availability, delivery schedules, and invoices has become a necessary part of the total customer service experience.

2. Information is crucial to managers' abilities to reduce inventory and human resource requirements to a competitive level.

3. Information flows are essential to strategic planning for and deployment of resources.

chain measurements can cover many areas including procurement, production, distribution, warehousing, inventory, transportation, and customer service. However, a good performance in one part of the supply chain is not sufficient. A supply chain is only as strong as its weakest link. The solution is to measure all key areas of the supply chain. Figure 8.15 displays common supply chain management metrics.[29]

To achieve success such as reducing operating costs, improving asset productivity, and compressing order cycle time, an organization should follow the seven principles of supply chain management outlined in Figure 8.16.

These seven principles run counter to previous built-in functional thinking of how companies organize, operate, and serve customers. Old concepts of supply chains are typified by discrete manufacturing, linear structure, and a focus on buy–sell transactions ("I buy from my suppliers, I sell to my customers"). Because the traditional supply chain is spread out linearly, some suppliers are removed from the end customer. Collaboration adds the value of visibility for these companies. They benefit by knowing immediately what is being transacted at the customer end of the supply chain (the end customer's activities are visible to them). Instead of waiting days or weeks (or months) for the information to flow upstream through the supply chain, with all the potential pitfalls of erroneous or missing information, suppliers can react in near real-time to fluctuations in end-customer demand.

Dell Inc. offers one of the best examples of an extremely successful SCM system. Dell's highly efficient build-to-order business model enables it to deliver customized computer systems quickly. As part of the company's continual effort to improve its supply chain processes, Dell deploys supply chain tools to provide global views of forecasted product demand and materials requirements, as well as improved factory scheduling and inventory management.[30]

Organizations should study industry best practices to improve their chances of successful implementation of SCM systems. The following are keys to SCM success.[31]

Make the Sale to Suppliers

The hardest part of any SCM system is its complexity because a large part of the system extends beyond the company's walls. Not only will the people in the organization need to change the way they work, but also the people from each supplier that is added to the network must change. Be sure suppliers are on board with the benefits that the SCM system will provide.

Wean Employees off Traditional Business Practices

Operations people typically deal with phone calls, faxes, and orders scrawled on paper and will most likely want to keep it that way. Unfortunately, an organization cannot disconnect the telephones and fax machines just because it is implementing a supply chain management system. If the organization cannot convince people that using the software will be worth their time, they will easily find ways to work around it, which will quickly decrease the chances of success for the SCM system.

Ensure the SCM System Supports the Organizational Goals

It is important to select SCM software that gives organizations an advantage in the areas most crucial to their business success. If the organizational goals support highly efficient strategies, be sure the supply chain design has the same goals.

Deploy in Incremental Phases and Measure and Communicate Success

Design the deployment of the SCM system in incremental phases. For instance, instead of installing a complete supply chain

FIGURE 8.15 Supply Chain Management Metrics

Supply Chain Management Metrics

- **Back order:** An unfilled customer order. A back order is demand (immediate or past due) against an item whose current stock level is insufficient to satisfy demand.

- **Customer order promised cycle time:** The anticipated or agreed upon cycle time of a purchase order. It is a gap between the purchase order creation date and the requested delivery date.

- **Customer order actual cycle time:** The average time it takes to actually fill a customer's purchase order. This measure can be viewed on an order or an order line level.

- **Inventory replenishment cycle time:** Measure of the manufacturing cycle time plus the time included to deploy the product to the appropriate distribution center.

- **Inventory turns (inventory turnover):** The number of times that a company's inventory cycles or turns over per year. It is one of the most commonly used supply chain metrics.

management system across the company and all suppliers at once, start by getting it working with a few key suppliers, and then move on to the other suppliers. Along the way, make sure each step is adding value through improvements in the supply chain's performance. While a big-picture perspective is vital to SCM success, the incremental approach means the SCM system should be implemented in digestible bites, and also measured for success one step at a time.

Be Future Oriented

The supply chain design must anticipate the future state of the business. Because the SCM system likely will last for many more years than originally planned, managers need to explore how flexible the systems will be when (not if) changes are required in the future. The key is to be certain that the software will meet future needs, not only current needs.[32]

SUPPLY CHAIN MANAGEMENT SUCCESS STORIES

Figure 8.17 depicts the top reasons more and more executives are turning to SCM to manage their extended enterprises. Figure 8.18 lists several companies using supply chain management to drive operations.

Apple Computer initially distributed its business operations over 16 legacy applications. Apple quickly realized that it needed a new business model centered on an integrated supply chain to drive performance efficiencies. Apple devised an implementation strategy that focused on specific SCM functions—finance, sales, distribution, and manufacturing—that would most significantly help its business. The company decided to deploy leading-edge functionality with a new business model that provided:

| FIGURE | 8.16 | Seven Principles of Supply Chain Management |

Seven Principles of Supply Chain Management

1. Segment customers by service needs, regardless of industry, and then tailor services to those particular segments.

2. Customize the logistics network and focus intensively on the service requirements and on the profitability of the preidentified customer segments.

3. Listen to signals of market demand and plan accordingly. Planning must span the entire chain to detect signals of changing demand.

4. Differentiate products closer to the customer, since companies can no longer afford to hold inventory to compensate for poor demand forecasting.

5. Strategically manage sources of supply, by working with key suppliers to reduce overall costs of owning materials and services.

6. Develop a supply chain information technology strategy that supports different levels of decision making and provides a clear view (visibility) of the flow of products, services, and information.

7. Adopt performance evaluation measures that apply to every link in the supply chain and measure true profitability at every stage.

- Build-to-order and configure-to-order manufacturing capabilities.
- Web-enabled configure-to-order order entry and order status for customers buying directly from Apple at Apple.com.
- Real-time credit card authorization.
- Available-to-promise and rules-based allocations.
- Integration to advanced planning systems.

Since its SCM system went live, Apple Computer has experienced substantial benefits in many areas including measurable improvements in its manufacturing processes, a decrease by 60 percent in its build-to-order and configure-to-order cycle times, and the ability to process more than 6,000 orders daily.[33]

| FIGURE | 8.17 | Top Reasons Executives Use SCM to Manage Extended Enterprises |

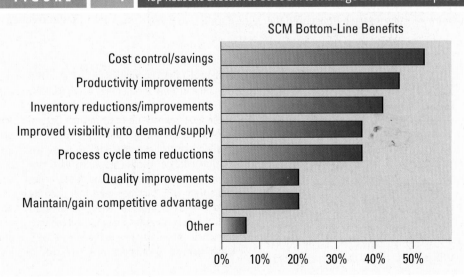

SCM Bottom-Line Benefits

Companies Using Supply Chain to Drive Operations	
Dell	Business grows 17 percent per year with a $40 billion revenue base.
Nokia	Supply chain best practices are turning ideas into profitable businesses.
Procter & Gamble	Consumer-driven supply chain is the defining architecture for large consumer companies. Best practices in product innovation and supply chain effectiveness are tops.
IBM	Hardware supply chain product-development processes overhauled to the tune of 70 percent better, faster, and cheaper.
Walmart Stores	Everyday low prices define the customer demand driving Walmart's partner integrated supply chain.
Toyota Motor	Lean is one of the top three best practices associated with benchmarked supply chain excellence.
The Home Depot	Cutting-edge supply chain management improved logistics and innovative services.
Best Buy	SCM has radically thinned inventories and delivered enviable business positions.
Marks & Spencer	A pioneer in the use of radio frequency identification (RFID) in stores, Marks & Spencer manages to grow and stay lean.

FUTURE SUPPLY CHAIN TRENDS

A television commercial shows a man in a uniform quietly moving through a family home. The man replaces the empty cereal box with a full one just before a hungry child opens the cabinet. He then opens a new sack of dog food as the hungry bulldog eyes him warily, and finally hands a full bottle of shampoo to the man in the shower who had just run out. The next wave in supply chain management will be home-based supply chain fulfillment.

Walgreens is differentiating itself from other national chains by marketing itself as the family's just-in-time supplier. Consumers today are becoming incredibly comfortable with the idea of going online to purchase products when they want, how they want, and at the price they want. Walgreens is developing custom websites for each household that allow families to order electronically and then at their convenience go to the store to pick up their goods at a special self-service counter or the drive-through window. Walgreens is making a promise that goes beyond low prices and customer service and extends right into the home.[34]

The functionality in supply chain management systems is becoming more and more sophisticated as supply chain management matures. Now and in the future, the next stages of SCM will incorporate more functions such as marketing, customer service, and product development. This will be achieved through more advanced communication networks, adoption of more user-friendly decision support systems, and availability of shared information to all participants in the supply chain. SCM is an ongoing development as technology makes it possible to acquire information ever more accurately and frequently from all over the world, and as it introduces new tools to aid in the analytical processes that deal with the supply chain's growing complexity.

According to Forrester Research, Inc., U.S. firms will spend $35 billion over five years to improve business processes that monitor, manage, and optimize their extended supply chains. Figure 8.19 displays the fastest growing SCM components that can have the greatest potential impact on an organization's bottom line.[35]

New technologies are also going to improve the supply chain. Radio frequency identification (RFID) technologies use

Living the DREAM

UPS Carbon Offsets Packages

UPS is betting that customers will pay the price of a small surcharge on UPS packages if it is cutting down on carbon emissions. UPS is the first small package carrier to offer carbon offsets to customers for $0.05 for UPS Ground and $0.20 for all other services. UPS will even match customer offset purchases in the next year for up to $1 million. Carbon offsets can easily be fabricated, but UPS has elected to have the Société Générale de Surveillance monitor its emissions, taking into account air and ground fleets, emissions from UPS facilities, and fuel used by third parties that provide delivery services to UPS. Carbon Neutral Company will monitor the whole offset process to make sure UPS stays honest. Customers are guaranteed that their packages will be environmentally friendly, while UPS gains green credits.

Why is it important to take into account environmental impacts of a company's supply chain? Would environmentally friendly shipping methods affect your choice of shipping vendor? What other companies have supply chains that are shipping-heavy and could use a model similar to that of UPS? What other companies have supply chains without any shipping components? What other areas of the supply chain could potentially affect carbon emissions?

FIGURE 8.19 Fast Growth SCM Components

Growing SCM Components	
Supply chain event management (SCEM)	Enables an organization to react more quickly to resolve supply chain issues. SCEM software increases real-time information sharing among supply chain partners and decreases their response time to unplanned events. SCEM demand will skyrocket as more and more organizations begin to discover the benefits of real-time supply chain monitoring.
Selling chain management	Applies technology to the activities in the order life cycle from inquiry to sale.
Collaborative engineering	Allows an organization to reduce the cost and time required during the design process of a product.
Collaborative demand planning	Helps organizations reduce their investment in inventory, while improving customer satisfaction through product availability.

active or passive tags in the form of chips or smart labels that can store unique identifiers and relay this information to electronic readers. RFID will become an effective tool for tracking and monitoring inventory movement in a real-time SCM environment. The real-time information will provide managers with an instant and accurate view of inventories within the supply chain.

Using current SCM systems, the RFID will check the inventory status and then trigger the replenishment process. Organizations using RFIDs will be able to quickly and accurately provide current inventory levels (in real-time) at any point in the supply chain. Reducing inventory levels to their reorder points allows electronic regeneration of replenishment orders. With quick and accurate information about inventories, the use of safety stock levels guarding against uncertainty can also be reduced. Hence, the potential benefits of RFIDs include a reduction of human intervention (or required labor) and holding fewer inventories, which nets a reduction in operating costs.

SCM applications have always been expensive, costing between $1 million and $10 million. As the industry matures and competition increases, vendors will continue adapting their pricing models to attract midsize and smaller companies.[36] ∎

BUSTED Political Supply Chains

The U.S. government crafted a deal with the United Arab Emirates (UAE) that would let a UAE-based firm, Dubai Ports World (DPW), run six major U.S. ports—New York, New Jersey, Baltimore, New Orleans, Miami, and Philadelphia. Currently, London-based Peninsular and Oriental Steam Navigation Co. (P&O), the fourth largest port operator in the world, runs the six ports. But the $6.8 billion sale of P&O to DPW would effectively turn over North American operations to the government-owned company in Dubai.

Some citizens are worried that the federal government may be outsourcing U.S. port operations to a company prone to terrorist infiltration by allowing a firm from the United Arab Emirates to run port operations within the United States. You have been called in on an investigation to determine the potential effects on U.S. businesses' supply chains if these ports were shut down due to terrorist activities. The United Arab Emirates has had people involved in terrorism. In fact, some of its financial institutions laundered the money for the 9/11 terrorists. Create an argument for or against outsourcing these ports to the UAE. Be sure to detail the effect on U.S. businesses' supply chains if these ports are subjected to terrorist acts.

CHECK OUT www.mhhe.com/baltzanm

for additional study materials including quizzes and PowerPoint presentations.

customer relationship
management+
business intelligence

This chapter discusses how information technology can be used to support firms in their interactions with customers. At the simplest level, organizations implement CRM to gain a better understanding of customer needs and behaviors, and information technology provides companies with a new channel to communicate with customers beyond those traditionally used by organizations such as face-to-face or paper-based methods.

Organizations recognize the importance of maintaining and fostering healthy relationships with customers. Doing so has a direct and positive effect on customer loyalty and retention. This greatly adds to a company's profitability and provides an edge over competitors who fail to foster customer relationships.

You, as a business student, must understand the critical relationship your business will have with its customers. You must also understand how to analyze your organizational data to ensure you are not just meeting, but exceeding your customer's expectations. Business intelligence (BI) is the best way to understand your customer's current—and more importantly—future needs. Like never before, enterprises are technologically empowered to reach their goals of integrating, analyzing, and making intelligent business decisions based on their data.

ustomer relationship management (CRM) involves managing all aspects of a customer's relationship with an organization to increase customer loyalty and retention and an organization's profitability. As organizations begin to migrate from the traditional product-focused organization toward customer-driven organizations, they are recognizing their customers as experts, not just revenue generators. Organizations are quickly realizing that without customers, they simply would not exist and it is critical they do everything they can to ensure their customers' satisfaction. In an age when product differentiation is difficult, CRM is one of the most valuable assets a company can acquire. The sooner a company embraces CRM the better off it will be and the harder it will be for competitors to steal loyal and devoted customers.

CUSTOMER RELATIONSHIP MANAGEMENT FUNDAMENTALS

When dealing with sick customers, flexibility is key. That is why Walgreens has made healthy investments in customer service over the past 30 years, originating the drive-through pharmacy and pioneering a network for refilling prescriptions at any location. Walgreens credits much of its growth to an increased investment in customer service. The company has developed new software that can print prescription labels in 14 languages and in large type for older patrons. Besides investing in customer-friendly technology, the 103-year-old chain is not forgetting the human touch. Walgreens spends more on payroll at stores where performance is below average, increasing the clerk-to-

> "Organizations are quickly realizing that without customers, they simply would not exist and it is critical they do everything they can to ensure their customers' satisfaction."

●● SECTION 9.1 Customer Relationship Management

LEARNING OUTCOMES

LO9.1 Compare operational and analytical customer relationship management.

LO9.2 Explain the formula an organization can use to find its most valuable customers.

LO9.3 Describe and differentiate the CRM technologies used by sales departments and customer service departments.

LO9.4 Describe and differentiate the CRM technologies used by marketing departments and sales departments.

LO9.5 Compare customer relationship management, supplier relationship management, partner relationship management, and employee relationship management.

●● LO9.1

Compare operational and analytical customer relationship management.

●● LO9.2

Explain the formula an organization can use to find its most valuable customers.

customer ratio; and it recently launched an online training program for all employees. With 19 straight quarters of double-digit earnings growth, the prescription appears to be working.

Today, most competitors are simply a mouse-click away. The intense competition in today's marketplace forces organizations to switch from sales-focused strategies to customer-focused strategies. Charles Schwab recouped the cost of a multimillion-dollar customer relationship management system in less than two years. The system, developed by Siebel, allows the brokerage firm to trace each interaction with a customer or prospective customer and then provide services (retirement planning, for instance) to each customer's needs and interests. The system provides Schwab with a complete view of its customers, which it uses to differentiate serious investors from nonserious investors. For example, automated deposits from paychecks are a sign of a serious investor, while stagnant balances signal a nonserious investor. Once Schwab is able to make this determination, the firm allocates its resources accordingly, saving money by not investing time or resources in subsidizing nonserious investors.[1]

Customer relationship management (CRM) involves managing all aspects of a customer's relationship with an organization to increase customer loyalty and retention and an organization's profitability. CRM allows an organization to gain insights into customers' shopping and buying behaviors. Kaiser Permanente undertook a CRM strategy to improve and prolong the lives of diabetics. After compiling CRM information on 84,000 diabetic patients, Kaiser found that only 20 percent were getting their eyes checked routinely. (Diabetes is the leading cause of blindness.) As a result, Kaiser is now enforcing rigorous eye-screening programs for diabetics, along with creating support groups for obesity and stress (two more factors that make diabetes even worse). This CRM-based "preventive medicine" approach is saving Kaiser money and, more importantly, improving the health of diabetic patients.[2]

Figure 9.1 provides an overview of a typical CRM system. Customers contact an organization through various means including call centers, web access, email, faxes, and direct sales. A single customer may access an organization multiple times through many different channels. The CRM system tracks every communication between the customer and the organization and provides access to CRM information across different systems from accounting to order fulfillment. Understanding all customer communications allows the organization to communicate effectively with each customer. It gives the organization a detailed understanding of each customer's products and services regardless of the customer's preferred communication channel. A customer service representative can easily view detailed account information and history through a CRM system when providing information to a customer such as expected delivery dates, complementary product information, and customer payment and billing information. Understanding the fundamentals of CRM includes the following:

- CRM as a business strategy.
- Business benefits of CRM.
- Evolution of CRM.
- Operational and analytical CRM.

CRM as a Business Strategy

Eddie Bauer ships 110 million catalogs a year, maintains two websites, and has more than 600 retail stores. The company collects information through customer transactions and analyzes the information to determine the best way to market to each individual customer. Eddie Bauer discovered that customers who shop across all three of its distribution channels—catalogs, websites, and stores—spend up to five times more than customers who shop through only one channel.

Michael Boyd, director of CRM at Eddie Bauer, stated, "Our experience tells us that CRM is in no way, shape, or form a software application. Fundamentally, it is a business strategy to try to optimize profitability, revenue, and satisfaction at an individual customer level. Everything in an organization, every single process, every single application, is a tool that can be used to serve the CRM goal."[3]

FIGURE **9.1** Customer Relationship Management Overview

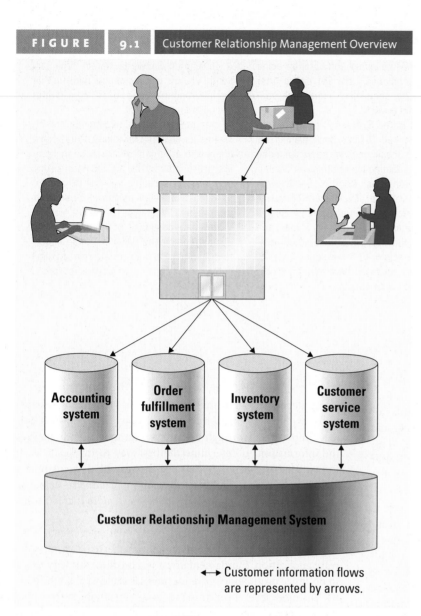

Customer Relationship Management System

◄—► Customer information flows
are represented by arrows.

It is important to realize that CRM is not just a technology, but also a strategy that an organization must embrace on an enterprise level. Although there are many technical components of CRM, it is actually a process and business goal simply enhanced by technology. Implementing a CRM system can help an organization identify customers and design specific marketing campaigns tailored to each customer, thereby increasing customer spending. A CRM system also allows an organization to treat customers as individuals, gaining important insights into their buying preferences and behaviors and leading to increased sales, greater profitability, and higher rates of customer loyalty.

When a "lucky ambassador" greets a Harrah's guest at a video-poker machine by name, wishes her a happy birthday, and offers free tickets to a show, luck has nothing to do with it. The moment customers insert their loyalty card into a slot machine, the casino giant's $30 million-plus CRM system reveals every move they have ever made at any of its 28 properties. "If you start to have a really unfortunate visit, you start to think, 'Man, that place is really just bad luck,'" said Gary Loveman, Harrah's president and CEO. "If we see that coming, we can intervene" with perks to soothe the pain of gambling losses. While many companies struggle to employ CRM successfully, gathering massive amounts of data without using it to benefit customers, Harrah's is building on its mastery. In the future, its slot machines will spout real-time monetary credits and dinner coupons using new customer-recognition software and hardware, leaving even its losing customers feeling a little luckier.[4]

Business Benefits of CRM

The company 1-800-Flowers.com achieved operational excellence by building customer intimacy to continue to improve profits and business growth. The company turned brand loyalty into brand relationships by using the vast amounts of information it collected to understand customers' needs and expectations. The floral delivery company adopted SAS Enterprise Miner to analyze the information in its CRM systems. Enterprise Miner sifts through information to reveal trends, explain outcomes, and predict results so that businesses can increase response rates and quickly identify their profitable customers. With the help of Enterprise Miner, 1-800-Flowers.com is continuing to thrive, averaging 17 percent annual increases in revenue.[5]

CRM is a business philosophy based on the premise that those organizations that understand the needs of individual customers are best positioned to achieve sustainable competitive advantage in the future. Many aspects of CRM are not new to organizations; CRM is simply performing current business better. Placing customers at the forefront of all thinking and decision making requires significant operational and technology changes.

A customer strategy starts with understanding who the company's customers are and how the company can meet strategic goals. *The New York Times* understands this and has spent the past decade researching core customers to find similarities among groups of readers in cities outside the New York metropolitan area. Its goal is to understand how to appeal to those groups and make *The New York Times* a national newspaper, expanding its circulation and the reach it offers to advertisers. *The New York Times* is growing in a relatively flat publishing market and has achieved a customer retention rate of 94 percent in an industry that averages roughly 60 percent.[6]

As the business world increasingly shifts from product focus to customer focus, most organizations recognize that treating existing customers well is the best source of profitable and sustainable revenue growth. In the age of ebusiness, however, an organization is challenged more than ever before to satisfy its customers. Figure 9.2 displays the benefits derived by an organization from a CRM strategy.

The National Basketball Association's New York Knicks are becoming better than ever at communicating with their fans. Thanks to a CRM solution, New York Knicks' management now knows which season-ticket holders like which players, what kind of merchandise they buy, and where they buy it. Management is finally able to send out fully integrated email campaigns that do not overlap with other marketing efforts.[7]

An organization can find its most valuable customers by using a formula that industry insiders call RFM—Recency, Frequency, and Monetary value. In other words, an organization must track:

- How recently a customer purchased items (recency).

- How frequently a customer purchases items (frequency).

- How much a customer spends on each purchase (monetary value).

Once a company has gathered this initial CRM information, it can compile it to identify patterns and create marketing campaigns, sales promotions, and services to increase business. For example, if Ms. Smith buys only at the height of the season, then the company should send her a special offer during the off-season. If Mr. Jones always buys software but never computers, then the company should offer him free software with the purchase of a new computer.

The CRM technologies discussed in this chapter can help organizations find answers to RFM and other tough questions, such as who are their best customers and which of their products are the most profitable.

Evolution of CRM

Knowing the customer, especially knowing the profitability of individual customers, is highly lucrative in the financial services industry. Its high transactional nature has always afforded the financial services industry more access to customer information than other industries have, but it has embraced CRM technologies only recently.

Barclays Bank is a leading financial services company operating in more than 70 countries. In the United Kingdom, Barclays has over 10 million personal customers and about 9.3 million credit cards in circulation, and it serves 500,000 small business customers. Barclays decided to invest in CRM technologies to help it gain valuable insights into its business and customers.

With the new CRM system, Barclays' managers are better able to predict the financial behavior of individual customers and assess whether a customer is likely to pay back a loan in full and within the agreed-upon time period. This helps Barclays manage its profitability with greater precision because it can charge its customers a more appropriate rate of interest based on the results of the customer's risk assessment. Barclays also uses a sophisticated customer segmentation system to identify groups of profitable customers, both on a corporate and personal level, which it can then target for new financial products. One of the most valuable pieces of information Barclays discovered was that about 50 percent of its customers are nonprofitable and that less than 30 percent of its customers provide 90 percent of its profits.[8]

There are three phases in the evolution of CRM: (1) reporting, (2) analyzing, and (3) predicting. **CRM reporting technologies** help organizations identify their customers across other applications. **CRM analysis technologies** help organizations segment their customers into categories such as best and worst customers. **CRM predicting technologies** help organizations make predictions regarding customer behavior such as which customers are at risk of leaving (see Figure 9.3).

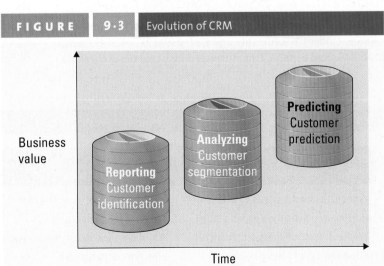

FIGURE **9.3** Evolution of CRM

Customer Power to the Rescue

Today, when one of your customers is unhappy, you don't have to worry about them telling a few friends and family; you have to worry about them telling everyone on the planet. Disgruntled employees and customers have many channels they can use to fight back against a faulty product or unethical company. Free or low-cost websites empower consumers to tell not only their friends, but also the world, about the way they have been treated. Here are a few examples:

- **Bad experience with Blue Marble Biking:** Tourist on biking tour is bitten by a dog and requires stitches. Company is barred from hotel because of incident; in turn, it bars the tourist from any further tours.
- **Best Buy receipt check:** Shopper declines to show register receipt for purchase to door guard at Lakewood Best Buy, which is voluntary. Employees attempt to seize cart, stand in shopper's path, and park a truck behind shopper's car to prevent departure.
- **Enterprise Rent-A-Car is a failing enterprise:** Enterprise Rent-A-Car did not honor reservations, did not have cars ready as stated, rented cars with nearly empty tanks, and charged higher prices to corporate account holders.

The Internet is raising the stakes for customer service. With the ability to create a website dedicated to a particular issue, a disgruntled customer can have nearly the same reach as a manufacturer. The Internet is making it more difficult for companies to ignore their customers' complaints. Search the web for the most outrageous story of a disgruntled customer. A few places to start include:

- **Complain Complain (complaincomplain .net):** provides professionally written, custom complaint letters to businesses.
- **The Complaint Department (www. thecomplaintdepartment.ca):** a for-fee consumer complaint resolution and letter writing service.
- **The Complaint Station (www.the complaintstation.com):** provides a central location to complain about issues related to companies' products, services, employment, and get rich quick scams.
- **Complaints.com Consumer Complaints (www.complaints.com):** database of consumer complaints and consumer advocacy.
- **Baddealings.com (www.baddealings .com):** forum and database on consumer complaints and scams on products and services.

Both operational and analytical CRM technologies can assist in customer reporting (identification), customer analysis (segmentation), and customer prediction. Figure 9.4 highlights a few of the important questions an organization can answer using CRM technologies.

Operational and Analytical CRM

Joe Guyaux knows the best way to win customers is to improve service. Under his leadership and with the help of Siebel CRM, the PNC retail banking team increased new consumer checking customers by 19 percent in one year. PNC retained 21 percent more of its consumer checking households as well as improved customer satisfaction by 9 percent.[9]

The two primary components of a CRM strategy are operational CRM and analytical CRM. **Operational CRM** supports traditional transactional processing for day-to-day front-office operations or systems that deal directly with the customers. **Analytical CRM** supports back-office operations and strategic analysis and includes all systems that do not deal directly with the customers. The primary difference between

FIGURE 9.4	Reporting, Analyzing, and Predicting Examples	
REPORTING "Asking What Happened"	**ANALYZING** "Asking Why It Happened"	**PREDICTING** "Asking What Will Happen"
What is the total revenue by customer?	Why did sales not meet forecasts?	What customers are at risk of leaving?
How many units did we manufacture?	Why was production so low?	What products will the customer buy?
Where did we sell the most products?	Why did we not sell as many units as last year?	Who are the best candidates for a mailing?
What were total sales by product?	Who are our customers?	What is the best way to reach the customer?
How many customers did we serve?	Why was customer revenue so high?	What is the lifetime profitability of a customer?
What are our inventory levels?	Why are inventory levels so low?	What transactions might be fraudulent?

operational CRM and analytical CRM is the direct interaction between the organization and its customers. Figure 9.5 provides an overview of operational CRM and analytical CRM.

●● L09.3

Describe and differentiate the CRM technologies used by sales departments and customer service departments.

●● L09.4

Describe and differentiate the CRM technologies used by marketing departments and sales departments.

USING IT TO DRIVE OPERATIONAL CRM

Figure 9.6 displays the different technologies marketing, sales, and customer service departments can use to perform operational CRM.

Marketing and Operational CRM

Companies are no longer trying to sell one product to as many customers as possible; instead, they are trying to sell one customer as many products as possible. Marketing departments are able to transform to this new way of doing business by using CRM technologies that allow them to gather and analyze customer information to deploy successful marketing campaigns. In fact, a marketing campaign's success is directly proportional to the organization's ability to gather and analyze the right information. The three primary operational CRM technologies a marketing department can implement to increase customer satisfaction are:

1. List generator.
2. Campaign management.
3. Cross-selling and up-selling.

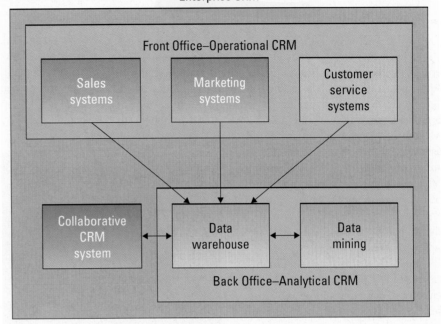

FIGURE 9.5 Operational CRM and Analytical CRM

List Generator *List generators* compile customer information from a variety of sources and segment the information for different marketing campaigns. Information sources include website visits, website questionnaires, online and offline surveys, flyers, toll-free numbers, current customer lists, and so on. After compiling the customer list, an organization can use criteria to filter and sort the list for potential customers. Filter and sort criteria can include such things as household income, education level, and age. List generators provide the marketing department with a solid understanding of the type of customer it needs to target for marketing campaigns.

Campaign Management *Campaign management systems* guide users through marketing campaigns performing such tasks as campaign definition, planning, scheduling, segmentation, and success analysis. These advanced systems can even calculate quantifiable results for return on investment (ROI) for each campaign and track the results in order to analyze and understand how the company can fine-tune future campaigns.

FIGURE 9.6 Operational CRM Technologies for Sales, Marketing, and Customer Service Departments

Operational CRM Technologies		
Marketing	**Sales**	**Customer Service**
1. List generator	1. Sales management	1. Contact center
2. Campaign management	2. Contact management	2. Web-based self-service
3. Cross-selling and up-selling	3. Opportunity management	3. Call scripting

Cross-Selling and Up-Selling

Two key sales strategies a marketing campaign can deploy are cross-selling and up-selling. **Cross-selling** is selling additional products or services to a customer. **Up-selling** is increasing the value of the sale. For example, McDonald's performs cross-selling by asking customers if they would like an apple pie with their meal. McDonald's performs up-selling by asking customers if they would like to super-size their meals. CRM systems offer marketing departments all kinds of information about their customers and their products, which can help them identify cross-selling and up-selling marketing campaigns.

The California State Automobile Association (CSAA) had to take advantage of its ability to promote and cross-sell CSAA automotive, insurance, and travel services to beat its competition. Accomplishing this task was easy once the company implemented E.piphany's CRM system. The system integrated information from all of CSAA's separate databases, making it immediately available to all employees through a web-based browser. Employees could quickly glance at a customer's profile and determine which services the customer currently had and which services the customer might want to purchase based on her or his needs as projected by the software.[10]

Sales and Operational CRM

Siebel, one of the largest providers of CRM software, had 33,000 subscribers in January 2005. Salesforce.com, provider of on-demand web-based customer relationship management software, added 40,000 subscribers during the first three months of 2005, more than all of Siebel's subscribers. Salesforce.com's total number of subscribers is over 500,000. Merrill Lynch, one of the biggest customers in the sales force market, signed on for 5,000 subscriptions for its global private client division, making the brokerage firm Salesforce.com's largest customer. Salesforce.com's new product, Customforce, includes tools for adding data analysis capabilities, spreadsheet-style mathematical formulas, business processes, and forecasting models.[11]

Sales departments were the first to begin developing CRM systems. Sales departments had two primary reasons to track customer sales information electronically. First, sales representatives were struggling with the overwhelming amount of customer account information they were required to maintain and track. Second, companies were struggling with the issue that much of their vital customer and sales information remained in the heads of their sales representatives. One of the first CRM components built to help address these issues was the sales force automation component. **Sales force automation (SFA)** is a system that automatically tracks all of the steps in the sales process. SFA products focus on increasing customer satisfaction, building customer relationships, and improving product sales by tracking all sales information.

Serving several million guests each year, Vail Resorts Inc. maintains dozens of systems across all seven of its properties. These systems perform numerous tasks including recording lift ticket, lodging, restaurant, conference, retail, and ski rental sales. Since a significant percentage of the company's revenue results from repeat guests, building stronger, more profitable relationships with its loyal customers is Vail Resorts first priority.

To improve its customer service and marketing campaign success, Vail deployed the Ascential CRM system, which integrated the customer information from its many disparate systems. The CRM system is providing Vail Resorts with a detailed level of customer insight, which helps the company personalize its guest offerings and promotions. By using a CRM system that integrates information from across all of its resorts and business lines, the company can determine what, where, and how its guests behave across all of its properties. For example, the company can now offer discounts on lift ticket and ski rentals for customers staying in its resorts. The three primary operational CRM technologies a sales department can implement to increase customer satisfaction are:

1. Sales management CRM systems.
2. Contact management CRM systems.
3. Opportunity management CRM systems.[12]

Sales Management CRM Systems

Figure 9.7 depicts the typical sales process, which begins with an opportunity and ends with billing the customer for the sale. Leads and potential customers are the lifeblood of all sales organizations, whether the products they are peddling are computers,

FIGURE 9·7 Overview of the Sales Process

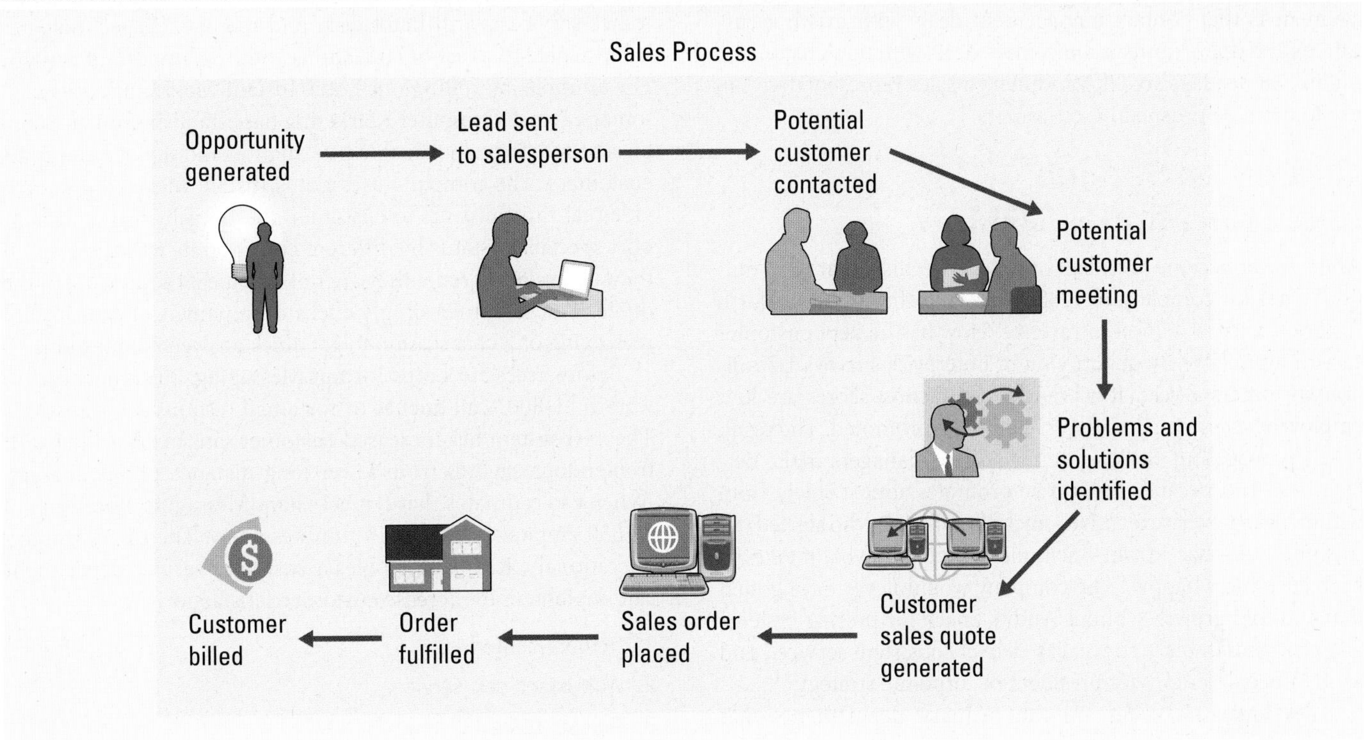

Sales Process

clothing, or cars. How the leads are handled can make the difference between revenue growth or decline. **Sales management CRM systems** automate each phase of the sales process, helping individual sales representatives coordinate and organize all of their accounts. Features include calendars to help plan customer meetings, alarm reminders signaling important tasks, customizable multimedia presentations, and document generation. These systems can even provide an analysis of the sales cycle and calculate how each individual sales representative is performing during the sales process.

Contact Management CRM Systems

A **contact management CRM system** maintains customer contact information and identifies prospective customers for future sales. Contact management systems include such features as maintaining organizational charts, detailed customer notes, and supplemental sales information. For example, a contact management system can take an incoming telephone number and display the caller's name along with notes detailing previous conversations. This allows the sales representative to answer the telephone and say, "Hi Sue, how is your new laptop working? How was your vacation to Florida?" without receiving any reminders of such details first from the customer. The customer feels valued since the sales associate knows her name and even remembers details of their last conversation!

A $16 billion technology company, 3M is a leader in health care, safety, electronics, telecommunications, office, and consumer markets. The company began to focus on streamlining

and unifying its sales processes with the primary goals of better customer segmentation and more reliable lead generation and qualification. To achieve these goals the company implemented a CRM system and soon found itself receiving the following benefits:

- Cutting the time it takes to familiarize sales professionals with new territories by 33 percent.
- Increasing management's visibility of the sales process.
- Decreasing the time it takes to qualify leads and assign sales opportunities by 40 percent.

One of the more successful campaigns driven by the CRM system allowed 3M to deliver direct mail to targeted government agencies and emergency services in response to the anthrax attacks in 2002. All inquiries to the mail campaign were automatically assigned to a sales representative who followed up with a quote. In little more than a week, the company had received orders for 35,000 respirator masks.[13]

Opportunity Management CRM Systems

Opportunity management CRM systems target sales opportunities by finding new customers or companies for future sales. Opportunity management systems determine potential customers and competitors and define selling efforts including budgets and schedules. Advanced opportunity management systems can even calculate the probability of a sale, which can save sales representatives significant time and money when attempting to find new customers. The primary difference between contact management and opportunity management is that contact management deals with existing customers and opportunity management deals with new customers. Figure 9.8 displays six CRM pointers a sales representative can use to increase prospective customers.

Customer Service and Operational CRM

Andy Taylor became president of Enterprise, his father's $76 million rental-car company, in 1980. Today, it is the largest in North America, with $7 billion in revenue. How has he kept customer service a priority? By quantifying it. Enterprise surveys 1.7 million customers a year. If a branch's satisfaction scores are low, employees, even vice presidents, cannot be promoted. The result is self-propagating. Seeking better scores, managers make better hires. And because Enterprise promotes almost solely from within, nearly every executive—including Taylor, who started out washing cars—has a front-line understanding of what it takes to keep customers happy. "The company would never have gotten that 100-fold growth without Andy's knack for putting systems and processes in place so you can deliver consistent service," said Sandy Rogers, senior vice president of corporate strategy.[14]

Sales and marketing are the primary departments that interact directly with customers before a sale. Most companies recognize the importance of building strong relationships during the marketing and sales efforts; however, many fail to realize the importance of continuing to build these relationships after the sale is complete. It is actually more important to build postsale relationships if the company wants to ensure customer loyalty and satisfaction. The best way to implement postsale CRM strategies is through the customer service department.

One of the primary reasons a company loses customers is bad customer service experiences. Providing outstanding customer service is a difficult task, and many CRM technologies are available to assist organizations with this important activity. For example, by rolling out Lotus Instant Messaging to its customers, Avnet Computer Marketing has established an efficient, direct route to push valuable information and updates out to its customers. The company uses Lotus Instant Messaging to provide real-time answers to customer questions by listing its support specialists' status by different colors on its website: green if they are available, red if they are not, or blue if they are out of the office. The customer simply clicks on a name to begin instant messaging or a chat session to get quick answers to questions.[15]

Before access to Lotus Instant Messaging, customers had to wait in "1-800" call queues or for email responses for answers. The new system has increased customer satisfaction along with tremendous savings from fewer long-distance phone charges. Avnet also estimates that Lotus Instant Messaging saves each of its 650 employees five to 10 minutes a day. The three primary operational CRM technologies a customer service department can implement to increase customer satisfaction are:

1. Contact center.
2. Web-based self-service.
3. Call scripting.[16]

Contact Center

Knowledge-management software, which helps call centers put consistent answers at customer-service representative's fingertips, is often long on promise and short on delivery. The problem? Representatives have to take time out from answering calls to input things they have learned—putting the "knowledge" in knowledge management.

FIGURE 9.8	CRM Pointers for Gaining Prospective Customers

CRM Pointers for Gaining Prospective Customers	
1. Get their attention	If you have a good prospect, chances are that he or she receives dozens of offers from similar companies. Be sure your first contact is professional and gets your customer's attention.
2. Value their time	When you ask for a meeting, you are asking for the most valuable thing a busy person has—time. Many companies have had great success by offering high-value gifts in exchange for a meeting with a representative. Just be careful because some organizations frown on expensive gifts. Instead, offer these prospective customers a report that can help them perform their jobs more effectively.
3. Overdeliver	If your letter offered a free DVD in exchange for a meeting, bring a box of microwave popcorn along with the movie. Little gestures like these tell customers that you not only keep your word, but also can be counted on to overdeliver.
4. Contact frequently	Find new and creative ways to contact your prospective customers frequently. Starting a newsletter and sending out a series of industry updates are excellent ways to keep in contact and provide value.
5. Generate a trustworthy mailing list	If you are buying a mailing list from a third party be sure that the contacts are genuine prospects, especially if you are offering an expensive gift. Be sure that the people you are meeting have the power to authorize a sale.
6. Follow up	One of the most powerful prospecting tools is a simple thank-you note. Letting people know that their time was appreciated may even lead to additional referrals.

FIGURE 9.9   Common Features Included in Contact Centers

Common Features Included in Contact Centers	
Automatic call distribution	A phone switch routes inbound calls to available agents.
Interactive voice response (IVR)	Directs customers to use touch-tone phones or keywords to navigate or provide information.
Predictive dialing	Automatically dials outbound calls and when someone answers, the call is forwarded to an available agent.

organization can have because maintaining a high level of customer support is critical to obtaining and retaining customers. Numerous systems are available to help an organization automate its contact centers. Figure 9.9 highlights a few of the features available in contact center systems.

Contact centers also track customer call history along with problem resolutions—information critical for providing a comprehensive customer view to the CSR. CSRs who can quickly comprehend and understand all of a customer's products and issues provide tremendous value to the customer and

Brad Cleveland, who heads the Incoming Calls Management Institute, said, "Software is just a tool. It doesn't do any good unless people across the organization are using it to its potential." Sharp Electronics is making it happen. Sharp's front-line representatives built the system from scratch. And as Sharp

> CSRs who can quickly comprehend and understand all of a customer's products and issues provide tremendous value to the customer and the organization.

rolled out its network over the past four years, representatives' compensation and promotions were tied directly to the system's use. As a result, the customer call experience at Sharp has improved dramatically: The proportion of problems resolved by a single call has soared from 76 percent to 94 percent.[17]

A *contact center* (or *call center*) is where customer service representatives (CSRs) answer customer inquiries and respond to problems through a number of different customer touchpoints. A contact center is one of the best assets a customer-driven

the organization. Nothing makes frustrated customers happier than not having to explain their problems to yet another CSR.

New emotion-detection software called Perform, created by Nice Systems, is designed to help companies improve customer service by identifying callers who are upset. When an elderly man distressed over high medical premiums hung up during his phone call to the Wisconsin Physician Services Insurance Corporation's call center, an IT system detected the customer's exasperation and automatically emailed a supervisor. The

Living the DREAM

Change.org

Change.org, a social activist website, is a resource for researching and organizing groups around social and political causes, called "Changes." Changes allow members with similar beliefs to post images, videos, blogs, and even donations to their nonprofit cause. Politicians need to find donors to

help them raise campaign funds so they can compete in elections. In fact, politicians in the last election raised upwards of $3 billion, with about $50 billion spent on finding the donors. Change.org wants to lower those fundraising costs, neutralize large donor's "special interest" money, and provide a place where the "average Joe" who can't afford a $2,500 fundraising dinner can be heard. Change.org's strategy is to create a database of politician profiles that align with each Change group. The Change groups are now empowered to pool together a pot of money to donate to relevant charities or

political candidates, as well as the power to lobby representatives.

Describe the differences between operational CRM and analytical CRM. What types of operational CRM would Change.org need to function? What types of analytical CRM would Change.org need to function? How could Change.org use marketing, sales, and customer service CRM technologies to help raise awareness and donations for nonprofit causes? Why is creating a social activist website a risky decision? Would you want to have your personal information stored on this website?

supervisor listened to a digital recording of the conversation, called the customer, and suggested ways to lower the premium. The system uses algorithms to determine a baseline of emotion during the first five to 10 seconds of a call, any deviation from the baseline triggers an alert.[18]

Web-Based Self-Service

Web-based self-service systems allow customers to use the web to find answers to their questions or solutions to their problems. FedEx uses web-based self-service systems to allow customers to track their own packages without having to talk to a CSR. FedEx customers can simply log on to FedEx's website and enter their tracking number. The website quickly displays the exact location of the package and the estimated delivery time.

Another great feature of web-based self-service is **click-to-talk** buttons. Click-to-talk buttons allow customers to click on a button and talk with a CSR via the Internet. Powerful customer-driven features like these add tremendous value to any organization by providing customers with real-time information without having to contact company representatives.[19]

Call Scripting

Being a CSR is not an easy task, especially when the CSR is dealing with detailed technical products or services. **Call scripting systems** access organizational databases that track similar issues or questions and automatically

with a comprehensive view of every customer, regardless of the pharmaceutical company. The company anticipated 20 percent annual growth primarily because of the successful implementation of its new system.[20]

Customer Relationship Management (CRM) Metrics

Brother International Corporation experienced skyrocketing growth in its sales of multifunction centers, fax machines, printers, and labeling systems in the late 1990s. Along with skyrocketing sales growth came a tremendous increase in customer service calls. When Brother failed to answer the phone fast enough, product returns started to increase. The company responded by increasing call center capacity, and the rate of returns began to drop. However, Dennis Upton, CIO of Brother International, observed that all the company was doing was answering the phone. He quickly realized that the company was losing a world of valuable market intelligence (business intelligence) about existing customers from all those telephone calls. The company decided to deploy SAP's CRM solution. The 1.8 million calls Brother handled dropped to 1.57 million, which reduced call center staff from 180 agents to 160 agents. Since customer demographic information is now stored and displayed on the agent's screen based on the incoming telephone

> "Call scripting systems access organizational databases that track similar issues or questions and automatically generate the details for the CSR who can then relay them to the customer."

generate the details for the CSR who can then relay them to the customer. The system can even provide a list of questions that the CSR can ask the customer to determine the potential problem and resolution. This feature helps CSRs answer difficult questions quickly while also presenting a uniform image so two different customers do not receive two different answers.

Documedics is a health care consulting company that provides reimbursement information about pharmaceutical products to patients and health care professionals. The company currently supports inquiries for 12 pharmaceutical companies and receives over 30,000 customer calls per month. Originally, the company had a data file for each patient and for each pharmaceutical company. This inefficient process resulted in the potential for a single patient to have up to 12 different information files if the patient was a client of all 12 pharmaceutical companies. To answer customer questions, a CSR had to download each customer file, causing tremendous inefficiencies and confusion. The company implemented a CRM system with a call scripting feature to alleviate the problem and provide its CSRs

number, the company has reduced call duration by an average of one minute, saving the company $600,000 per year. A company must continually monitor its efforts to ensure success.[21]

FIGURE 9.10 | CRM Metrics

Sales Metrics	Service Metrics	Marketing Metrics
Number of prospective customers	Cases closed same day	Number of marketing campaigns
Number of new customers	Number of cases handled by agent	New customer retention rates
Number of retained customers	Number of service calls	Number of responses by marketing campaign
Number of open leads	Average number of service requests by type	Number of purchases by marketing campaign
Number of sales calls	Average time to resolution	Revenue generated by marketing campaign
Number of sales calls per lead	Average number of service calls per day	Cost per interaction by marketing campaign
Amount of new revenue	Percentage compliance with service-level agreement	Number of new customers acquired by marketing campaign
Amount of recurring revenue	Percentage of service renewals	Customer retention rate
Number of proposals given	Customer satisfaction level	Number of new leads by product

Without understanding CRM's impact, a business will not be able to understand if its CRM practices are adding to its success. Using CRM metrics to track and monitor performance is a best practice for many companies. One rule for managers is to measure and monitor no more than seven (plus or minus two) key CRM metrics out of the hundreds of CRM metrics available. Figure 9.10 displays a few common CRM metrics tracked by organizations.[22]

> "Without understanding CRM's impact, a business will not be able to understand if its CRM practices are adding to its success."

USING IT TO DRIVE ANALYTICAL CRM

Maturing analytical CRM and behavioral modeling technologies are helping numerous organizations move beyond legacy benefits such as enhanced customer service and retention to systems that can truly improve business profitability. Unlike operational CRM that automates call centers and sales forces with the aim of enhancing customer transactions, analytical CRM solutions are designed to dig deep into a company's historical customer information and expose patterns of behavior on which a company can capitalize. Analytical CRM is primarily used to enhance and support decision making and works by identifying patterns in customer information collected from the various operational CRM systems.

For many organizations, the power of analytical CRM solutions provides tremendous managerial opportunities. Depending on the specific solution, analytical CRM tools can slice and dice customer information to create made-to-order views of customer value, spending, product affinities, percentile profiles, and segmentations. Modeling tools can identify opportunities for cross-selling, up-selling, and expanding customer relationships.

Personalization occurs when a website can know enough about a person's likes and dislikes to fashion offers that are more likely to appeal to that person. Many organizations are now utilizing CRM to create customer rules and templates that marketers can use to personalize customer messages.

The information produced by analytical CRM solutions can help companies make decisions about how to handle customers based on the value of each and every one. Analytical CRM can help reveal information about which customers are worth investing in, which should be serviced at an average level, and which should not be invested in at all.

Data gained from customers can also reveal information about employees. Wachovia Bank surveys customers—25,000 every month—for feedback on their service experience. It asks about individual employees and uses those answers in one-on-one staff coaching. A 20-minute coaching session at a Manhattan branch made clear how this feedback—each customer surveyed rates 33 employee behaviors—can improve service. The branch manager urged an employee to focus on sincerity rather than on mere friendliness, to "sharpen her antenna" so she would listen to customers more intuitively, and to slow down rather than hurry up. That focus on careful, sincere, intuitive service has paid off: Wachovia has held the top score among banks in the American Customer Satisfaction Index since 2001.[23]

Analytical CRM relies heavily on data warehousing technologies and business intelligence to glean insights into customer behavior (These are covered in detail in Section 9.2). These systems quickly aggregate, analyze, and disseminate customer information throughout an organization. Figure 9.11 displays a few examples of the kind of information insights analytical CRM can help an organization gain.[24]

UPS's data-intensive environment is supported by the largest IBM DB2 database in the world, consisting of 236 terabytes of data related to its analytical CRM tool. The shipping company's goal is to create one-to-one customer relationships, and it is using Quantum View tools that allow it to let customers tailor views of such things as shipment history and receive notices when a package arrives or is delayed. UPS has built more than 500 customer relationship management applications that run off of its data warehouse.[25]

Data warehouses are providing businesses with information about their customers and products that was previously impossible to locate, and the resulting payback can be tremendous. Organizations are now relying on business intelligence to provide them with hard facts that can determine everything from which type of marketing and sales campaign to launch, to which customers to target, at what time. Using CRM along with business intelligence allows organizations to make better, more informed decisions and to reap amazing unforeseen rewards.

FIGURE 9.11	Analytical CRM Information Examples

Analytical CRM Information Examples

1. Give customers more of what they want	Analytical CRM can help an organization go beyond the typical "Dear Mr. Smith" salutation. An organization can use its analytical CRM information to make its communications more personable. For example, if it knows a customer's shoe size and preferred brand it can notify the customer that there is a pair of size 12 shoes set aside to try on the next time the customer visits the store.
2. Find new customers similar to the best customers	Analytical CRM might determine that an organization does a lot of business with women 35 to 45 years old who drive SUVs and live within 30 miles of a certain location. The company can then find a mailing list that highlights this type of customer for potential new sales.
3. Find out what the organization does best	Analytical CRM can determine what an organization does better than its competitors. For example, if a restaurant caters more breakfasts to midsized companies than its competition does, it can purchase a specialized mailing list of midsized companies in the area and send them a mailing that features the breakfast catering specials.
4. Beat competitors to the punch	Analytical CRM can determine sales trends allowing an organization to offer the best customers deals before the competition has a chance to. For example, a clothing store might determine its best customers for outdoor apparel and send them an offer to attend a private sale right before the competition runs its outdoor apparel sale.
5. Reactivate inactive customers	Analytical CRM can highlight customers who have not done any business with the organization in a while. The organization can then send them a personalized letter along with a discount coupon. It will remind them of the company and may help spark a renewed relationship.
6. Let customers know they matter	Analytical CRM can determine what customers want and need, so an organization can contact them with this information. Anything from a private sale to a reminder that the car is due for a tune-up is excellent customer service.

Sears, Roebuck and Company is the third-largest U.S. retailer. Even though Sears does not know exactly "who" its customers are (by name and address) since many customers use cash or non-Sears credit cards, it can still benefit from analytical CRM technologies. Sears uses these technologies to determine what its generic customers prefer to buy and when they buy it, which enables the company to predict what they will buy. Using analytical CRM, Sears can view each day's sales by region, district, store, product line, and individual item. Sears can now monitor the precise impact of advertising, weather, and other factors on sales of specific items. For the first time, Sears can even group or "cluster," widely divergent types of items. For example, merchandisers can track sales of a store display marked "Gifts under $25" that might include sweatshirts, screwdrivers, and other unrelated items. The advertising department can then follow the sales of "Gifts under $25" to determine which products to place in its newspaper advertisements.[26]

●● LO9.5

Compare customer relationship management, supplier relationship management, partner relationship management, and employee relationship management.

CRM TRENDS: SRM, PRM, ERM

Organizations are discovering a wave of other key business areas where it is beneficial to take advantage of building strong relationships. These emerging areas include supplier relationship management (SRM), partner relationship management (PRM), and employee relationship management (ERM).

Supplier Relationship Management

Supplier relationship management (SRM) focuses on keeping suppliers satisfied by evaluating and categorizing suppliers for different projects, which optimizes supplier selection. SRM applications help companies analyze vendors based on a number of key variables including strategy, business goals, prices, and markets. The company can then determine the best supplier to collaborate with and can work on developing strong relationships with that supplier. The partners can then work together to streamline processes, outsource services, and provide products that they could not provide individually.

With the merger of the Bank of Halifax and Bank of Scotland, the new company, HBOS, implemented an SRM system to provide consistent information to its suppliers. The system integrates procurement information from the separate Bank of Halifax and Bank of Scotland operational systems, generating a single repository of management information for consistent reporting and analysis. Other benefits HBOS derived from the SRM solution include:

- A single consolidated view of all suppliers.
- Consistent, detailed management information allowing multiple views for every executive.
- Elimination of duplicate suppliers.[27]

Partner Relationship Management

Organizations have begun to realize the importance of building relationships with partners, dealers, and resellers. *Partner relationship management (PRM)* focuses on keeping vendors satisfied by managing alliance partner and reseller relationships that provide customers with the optimal sales channel. PRM's business strategy is to select and manage partners to optimize their long-term value to an organization. In effect, it means picking the right partners, working with them to help them be successful in dealing with mutual customers, and ensuring that partners and the ultimate end customers are satisfied and successful. Many of the features of a PRM application include real-time product information on availability, marketing materials, contracts, order details, and pricing, inventory, and shipping information.

PRM is one of the smaller segments of CRM that has superb potential. PRM grew from a $500 million business to a $1 billion business in less than four years. This is a direct reflection

---

fyi

YouTube Your Customers—It's Great for Business

JetBlue took an unusual and interesting CRM approach by using YouTube to apologize to its customers. JetBlue's founder and CEO, David Neeleman, apologized to customers via YouTube after a very, very bad week for the airline: 1,100 flights canceled due to snow storms and thousands of irate passengers. Neeleman's unpolished, earnest delivery made this apology worth accept- ing. But then again, we were not stuck on a tarmac for eight hours. With all of the new advances in technology and the many ways to reach customers, do you think using You- Tube was a smart approach? What else could JetBlue have done to help gain back its customers' trust?

Imagine you are the founder and CEO of GoodDog, a large pet food manufacturing company. Recently, at least 16 pet deaths have been tied to tainted pet food, fortu- nately not manufactured by your company. A recall of potentially deadly pet food has dog and cat owners studying their animals for even the slightest hint of illness and swamp- ing veterinarians nationwide with calls about symptoms both real and imagined. Create a strategy for using YouTube as a vehicle to communicate with your customers as they fear for their pets' lives. Be sure to highlight the pros and cons of using YouTube as a cus- tomer communication vehicle. Are there any other new technologies you could use as a customer communication vehicle that would be more effective than YouTube?

of the growing interdependency of organizations in the new economy. The primary benefits of PRM include:

- Expanded market coverage.
- Offerings of specialized products and services.
- Broadened range of offerings and a more complete solution.

Employee Relationship Management

Jim Sinegal runs Costco, one of the largest wholesale club chains, but there are two things he does not discount: employee benefits and customer service. Average hourly wages trounce those of rival Sam's Club, and 86 percent of workers have health insurance (versus a reported 47 percent at Sam's). Sinegal is not just being nice. Happy employees, he believes, make for happier customers. Low prices (he caps per-item profits at 14 percent) and a generous return policy certainly help. Although Wall Street has long been arguing for smaller benefits, a stingier return policy, and bigger profits, Sinegal sides with customers and staff. "We're trying to run Costco in a fashion that is not just going to satisfy our shareholders this year or this month," he said, "but next year and on into the future."[28]

Employee relationship management (ERM) provides employees with a subset of CRM applications available through a web browser. Many of the ERM applications assist the employee in dealing with customers by providing detailed information on company products, services, and customer orders.

At Rackspace, a San Antonio-based web-hosting company, customer focus borders on the obsessive. Joey Parsons, 24, won the Straightjacket Award, the most coveted employee distinction at Rackspace. The award recognizes the employee who best lives up to the Rackspace motto of delivering "fanatical support," a dedication to customers that is so intense it borders on the loony. Rackspace motivates its staff by treating each team as a separate business, which is responsible for its own profits and losses and has its own ERM website. Each month, employees can earn bonuses of up to 20 percent of their monthly base salaries depending on the performance of their units by both financial and customer-centric measurements such as customer turnover,

customer expansion, and customer referrals. Daily reports are available through the team's ERM website.[29]

THE UGLY SIDE OF CRM: WHY CRM MATTERS MORE NOW THAN EVER BEFORE

Business 2.0 ranked "You—the customer" as number one in the top 50 people who matter most in business and stated the following: "It has long been said that the customer is always right, but for a long time companies never really meant it. Now, companies have no choice as the power of the customer grows exponentially as the Internet grows. You—or rather, the collaborative intelligence of tens of millions of people, the networked you—continually create and filter new forms of content, anointing the useful, the relevant, and the amusing and rejecting the rest. You do it on websites like Amazon, Flickr, and YouTube, via podcasts and SMS polling, and on millions of self-published blogs.

"In every case, you have become an integral part of the action as a member of the aggregated, interactive, self-organizing, auto-entertaining audience. But the 'You Revolution' goes well beyond user-generated content. Companies as diverse as Delta Air Lines and T-Mobile are turning to you to create their ad slogans. Procter & Gamble and Lego are incorporating your ideas into new products. You constructed open source software and are its customer and its caretaker. None of this should be a surprise, since it was you—your crazy passions and hobbies and obsessions—that built out the web in the first place. And somewhere out there, you are building web 3.0. We do not yet know what that is, but one thing is for sure: It will matter."[30]

You have more power than ever before. A decade ago if you had a complaint against a company you could make a phone call or write a letter. Now you can literally contact hundreds or thousands of people to log your complaint. Figure 9.12 shows examples of you—the customer—taking your power to the people.

●● **SECTION 9.2** Business Intelligence

LEARNING OUTCOMES

LO9.6 Explain the problem associated with business intelligence. Describe the solution to this business problem.

LO9.7 Describe the three common forms of data-mining analysis.

LO9.8 Compare tactical, operational, and strategic BI.

LO9.9 Explain the organizationwide benefits of BI.

LO9.10 Describe the four categories of BI business benefits.

●● **LO9.6**

Explain the problem associated with business intelligence. Describe the solution to this business problem.

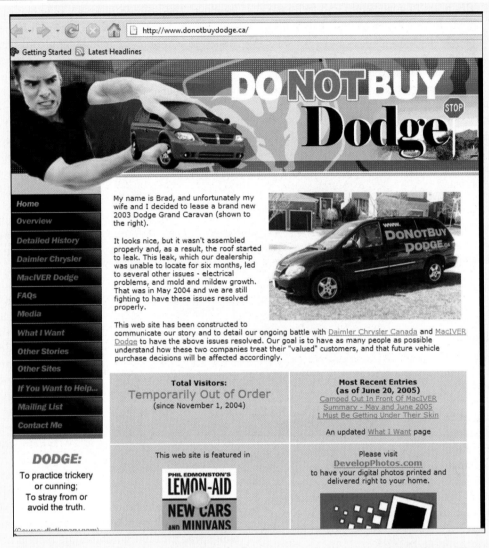

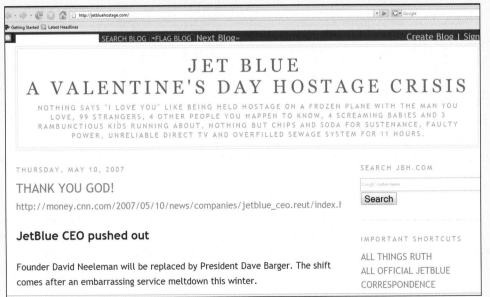

BUSINESS INTELLIGENCE

Business intelligence (BI) refers to applications and technologies that are used to gather, provide access to, and analyze data and information to support decision-making efforts. An early reference to business intelligence occurs in Sun Tzu's book *The Art of War*. Sun Tzu claims that to succeed in war, one should have full knowledge of one's own strengths and weaknesses and full knowledge of the enemy's strengths and weaknesses. Lack of either one might result in defeat. A certain school of thought draws parallels between the challenges in business and those of war, specifically:

- Collecting information.
- Discerning patterns and meaning in the information.
- Responding to the resultant information.[31]

Many organizations today find it next to impossible to understand their own strengths and weaknesses, let alone their enemies', because the enormous volume of organizational data is inaccessible to all but the IT department. Organization data include far more than simple fields in a database; it also includes voice mail, customer phone calls, text messages, video clips, along with numerous new forms of data.

The Problem: Data Rich, Information Poor

As businesses increase their reliance on enterprise systems such as CRM, they are rapidly accumulating vast amounts of data. Every interaction between departments or with the outside world, historical information on past transactions, as well as external market information, is entered into information systems for future use and access. Research from IDC expects businesses to face a data explosion over the next few years as the number of digital images, email in-boxes, and broadband connections doubles by 2010. The amount of data being generated is doubling every year, and some think it will soon begin to double every month. Data are a strategic asset for a business, and if the asset is not used, the business is wasting resources.[32]

An ideal business scenario would be as follows: An account manager, on her way to a client visit, looks up past proposals, as well as the client's ordering, payment, delivery, support, and marketing history. At a glance, she can tell that the client's ordering volumes have dropped lately. A few queries later she understands that the client has a support issue with a given product. The account manager calls her support department and learns that the defective part will be replaced within 24 hours. In addition, the marketing records show that the client recently attended a user conference and expressed interest in the new product line. With this information, the account manager is fully prepared for a constructive sales call. She understands all aspects of her client's relationship with her firm, understands the client's issues, and can confidently address new sales opportunities.

In most organizations, it would take the account manager, in the example above, hours or days to get answers to questions about her client. With all the data available, it is surprising how difficult it is for managers to get a clear picture of fundamental business information, such as inventory levels, orders in the pipeline, or client history. Many organizations contain disparate silos of information. Client orders and payment records are kept in the accounting system; installation and support information is stored in the customer service database; contact management software tracks the proposals and sales call history; and marketing contact history is kept by marketing. Rarely do these systems speak the same language, and there is no simple way for a nontechnical user to get answers quickly.

As a result, information has to be requested from different departments or IT, who must dedicate staff to pull together various reports. Responses can take weeks, by which time the information may be outdated. It has been said that organizations are data rich and information poor. The challenge is to transform data into useful information. With this information, employees gain knowledge that can be leveraged to increase company profitability.

The Solution: Business Intelligence

In every organization, employees make hundreds of decisions each day. They can range from whether to give a customer a discount, whether to start producing a part, whether to launch another direct-mail campaign, whether to order additional materials, and so on. These decisions are sometimes based on facts, but mostly based on experience, accumulated knowledge, and rule of thumb.

That poses a problem because experience, knowledge, and rule of thumb can take years to develop. Some employees never acquire them. Those who do may still fall prey to decision traps or biases in judgment. Improving the quality of business decisions has a direct impact on costs and revenue. For instance, giving a customer a discount may or may not help the bottom line, depending on the profitability of the client over the duration of

- **Government and defense:** Forecasting the cost of moving military equipment; testing strategies for potential military engagements; predicting resource consumption.
- **Airlines:** Capturing data on where customers are flying and the ultimate destination of passengers who change carriers in hub cities; thus, airlines can identify popular locations that they do not service and can check the feasibility of adding routes to capture lost business.

> "To improve the quality of business decisions, managers can provide existing staff with BI systems and tools that can assist them in making better, more informed decisions. The result creates an agile intelligent enterprise."

the relationship. To improve the quality of business decisions, managers can provide existing staff with BI systems and tools that can assist them in making better, more informed decisions. The result creates an agile intelligent enterprise. A few examples of using BI to make informed business decisions include:

- **Retail and sales:** Predicting sales; determining correct inventory levels and distribution schedules among outlets; and loss prevention.
- **Banking:** Forecasting levels of bad loans and fraudulent credit card use, credit card spending by new customers, and which kinds of customers will best respond to (and qualify for) new loan offers.
- **Operations management:** Predicting machinery failures; finding key factors that control optimization of manufacturing capacity.
- **Brokerage and securities trading:** Predicting when bond prices will change; forecasting the range of stock fluctuations for particular issues and the overall market; determining when to buy or sell stocks.
- **Insurance:** Forecasting claim amounts and medical coverage costs; classifying the most important elements that affect medical coverage; predicting which customers will buy new insurance policies.
- **Hardware and software:** Predicting disk-drive failures; forecasting how long it will take to create new chips; predicting potential security violations.
- **Law enforcement:** Tracking crime patterns, locations, and criminal behavior; identifying attributes to assist in solving criminal cases.

- **Health care:** Correlating demographics of patients with critical illnesses; developing better insights on symptoms and their causes and how to provide proper treatments.
- **Broadcasting:** Predicting what is best to air during prime time and how to maximize returns by interjecting advertisements.
- **Marketing:** Classifying customer demographics that can be used to predict which customers will respond to a mailing or buy a particular product.

The solution of implementing business intelligence systems and tools allows business users to receive data for analysis. (See Figure 9.13.)

Shell Services International's BI solution gave the company access to information about revenues between fuel and nonfuel business. Seeing that 20 percent of products were delivering 80 percent of sales, Shell significantly improved margin and turnover. It also negotiated better deals with suppliers and improved product master file management, which helped reduce working capital.[33]

Figure 9.14 displays how organizations using BI can find the root causes to problems and provide solutions simply by asking

FIGURE 9.13	BI Data Analysis	
Reliable		The data have been documented as the certified or approved data for the enterprise. The business users are confident that the data are the best possible and that they suit the decision-making purposes.
Consistent		The processes that deliver the data to the business community are well documented; there are no surprises such as missing or inaccurate data in the mix, analytics that will not run, response times that are unpredictable.
Understandable		The data have been defined in business terms; calculations and algorithms are easily accessed for comprehension. These are documented in a data dictionary or metadata repository that is easy to access and understand.
Easily manipulated		It is no longer required to have a PhD in statistics to get sophisticated analytics delivered to users' fingertips. And it is just as easy to change the question or set different parameters to twist and turn the data in ways unimaginable just a few years ago.[34]

"Why?" The process is initiated by analyzing a global report, say of sales per quarter. Every answer is followed by a new question, and users can drill deep down into a report to get to fundamental causes. Once they have a clear understanding of root causes, they can take highly effective action.

Finding the answers to tough business questions by using data that is reliable, consistent, understandable, and easily manipulated allows a business to gain valuable insight into such things as:

- **Where the business has been.** Historical perspective is always important in determining trends and patterns of behavior.

- **Where it is now.** Current situations are critical to either modify if not acceptable or encourage if they are trending in the right direction.

- **And where it will be in the near future.** Being able to predict with surety the direction of the company is critical to sound planning and to creating sound business strategies.[35]

●● LO9.7

Describe the three common forms of data-mining analysis.

●● LO9.8

Compare tactical, operational, and strategic BI.

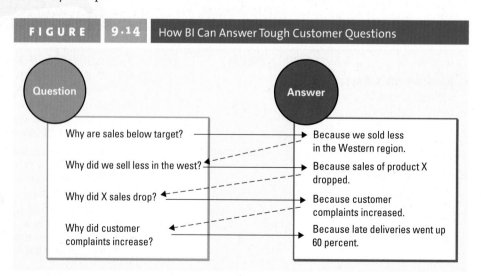

FIGURE 9.14 How BI Can Answer Tough Customer Questions

Question → Answer

Why are sales below target? → Because we sold less in the Western region.

Why did we sell less in the west? → Because sales of product X dropped.

Why did X sales drop? → Because customer complaints increased.

Why did customer complaints increase? → Because late deliveries went up 60 percent.

FIGURE   9.15   Operational, Tactical, Strategic BI

	Operational BI	Tactical BI	Strategic BI
Business focus	Manage daily operations, integrate BI with operational systems	Conduct short-term analysis to achieve strategic goals	Achieve long-term organizational goals
Primary users	Managers, analysts, operational users	Executives, managers	Executives, managers
Time frame	Intraday	Day(s) to weeks to months	Months to years
Data	Real-time metrics	Historical metrics	Historical metrics

OPERATIONAL, TACTICAL, AND STRATEGIC BI

Claudia Imhoff, president of Intelligent Solutions, believes it is useful to divide the spectrum of data mining analysis and business intelligence into three categories: operational, tactical, and strategic. Two trends are displayed when viewing the spectrum from operational through tactical to strategic. First, the analysis becomes increasingly complex and ad hoc. That is, it is less repetitive, less predictable, and it requires varying amounts and types of data. Second, both the risks and rewards of the analysis increase. That is, the often time-consuming, more strategic queries produce value less frequently but, when they do, the value can be extraordinary. Figure 9.15 illustrates the differences between strategic, tactical, and operational BI.[36]

These three forms are not performed in isolation from each other. It is important to understand that they must work with each other, feeding results from strategic to tactical to promote better operational decision making. Figure 9.16 demonstrates this synergy. In this example, strategic BI is used in the planning stages of a marketing campaign. The results of these analytics form the basis for the beginnings of a new campaign, targeting specific customers or demographics, for example. The daily analyses of the campaign are used by the more tactical form of BI to change the course of the campaign if its results are not tracking where expected.

For example, perhaps a different marketing message is needed, or the inventory levels are not sufficient to maintain the current sales pace so the scope of marketing might be changed. These results are then fed into the operational BI for immediate actions—offering a different product, optimizing the sale price of the product, or changing the daily message sent to selected customer segments.

For this synergy to work, the three forms of BI must be tightly integrated with each other. Minimal time should be lost transporting the results from one technological environment to another. Seamlessness in terms of data and process flow is a must. TruServ, the parent company of True Value Hardware has used BI software to improve efficiency of its distribution operations and reap a $50 million reduction in inventory costs. The marketing department uses BI to track sales promotion results such as which promotions were most popular by store or by region. Now that TruServ is building promotion histories in its databases, it can ensure all stores are fully stocked with adequate inventory. TruServ was able to achieve a positive return on investment in about five to six months.[37]

BI's Operational Value

A leading risk insurance company allows customers to access account information over the Internet. Previously, the company sent paper reports and diskettes to all of its customers. Any errors in the reports would take one to two months to correct because customers would first have to receive the report, catch the mistake, and then notify the company of the error. Now customers spot the errors in real time and notify the insurance company directly through the extranet, usually within a couple of days.[38]

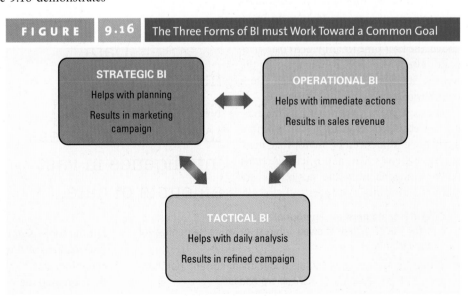

FIGURE   9.16   The Three Forms of BI must Work Toward a Common Goal

STRATEGIC BI
Helps with planning
Results in marketing campaign

OPERATIONAL BI
Helps with immediate actions
Results in sales revenue

TACTICAL BI
Helps with daily analysis
Results in refined campaign

Richard Hackathorn of Bolder Technologies developed an interesting graph to demonstrate the value of operational BI. Figure 9.17 shows the three latencies that impact the speed of decision making. These are data, analysis, and decision latencies.

- **Data latency** is the time duration to make data ready for analysis (i.e., the time for extracting, transforming, and cleansing the data), and loading the data into the database. All this can take time depending on the state of the operational data to begin with.

- **Analysis latency** is the time from which data are made available to the time when analysis is complete. Its length depends on the time it takes a business to do analysis. Usually, we think of this as the time it takes a human to do the analysis, but this can be decreased by the use of automated analytics that have thresholds. When the thresholds are exceeded, alerts or alarms can be issued to appropriate personnel, or they can cause exception processes to be initiated with no human intervention needed.

- **Decision latency** is the time it takes a human to comprehend the analytic result and determine an appropriate action. This form of latency is very difficult to reduce. The ability to remove the decision-making process from the human and automate it will greatly reduce the overall decision latency. Many forward-thinking companies are doing just that. For example, rather than send a high-value customer a letter informing him of a bounced check (which takes days to get to the customer), an automated system can simply send an immediate email or voice message informing the customer of the problem.

The key is to shorten these latencies so that the time frame for opportunistic influences on customers, suppliers, and others is faster, more interactive, and better positioned. As mentioned above, the best time to influence customers is not after they have left the store or the website. It is while they are still in the store or still wandering around the website.

For example, a customer who is searching a website for travel deals is far more likely to be influenced by appropriate messaging actions then and there. Actions taken immediately, while customers are still in the site, might include:

- Offering customers an appropriate coupon for the trip they showed interest in while searching for cheap airfares.

- Giving customers information about their current purchase such as the suggestion that visas are needed.

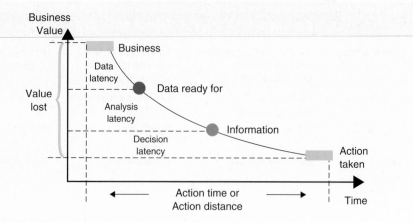

FIGURE 9.17 The Latency Between a Business Event and an Action Taken

- Congratulating them on reaching a certain frequent-buyer level and giving them 10 percent off an item.

A website represents another great opportunity to influence a customer, if the interactions are appropriate and timely. For example:

- A banner could announce the next best product to offer right after the customer puts an item in her basket.

- The customer could receive an offer for a product he just removed from his shopping basket.

- Appropriate instructions for the use of a product could come up on the customer's screen; perhaps warning a parent that the product should not be used by children under three.[39]

DATA MINING

At the center of any strategic, tactical, or operational BI effort is data mining. Ruf Strategic Solutions helps organizations employ statistical approaches within a large data warehouse to identify customer segments that display common traits. Marketers can then target these segments with specially designed products and promotions. **Data mining** is the process of analyzing data to extract information not offered by the raw data alone. Data mining can also begin at a summary information level (coarse granularity) and progress through increasing levels of detail (drilling down), or the reverse (drilling up). Data mining is the primary tool used to uncover business intelligence in vast amounts of data.[40]

To perform data mining, users need data-mining tools. **Data-mining tools** use a variety of techniques to find patterns and relationships in large volumes of information and infer rules from them that predict future behavior and guide decision making. Data mining uses specialized technologies

> **Data mining is the primary tool used to uncover business intelligence in vast amounts of data.**

and functionalities such as query tools, reporting tools, multidimensional analysis tools, statistical tools, and intelligent agents. Data mining approaches decision making with basically a few different activities in mind including:

- *Classification*—assign records to one of a predefined set of classes.
- *Estimation*—determine values for an unknown continuous variable behavior or estimated future value.
- *Affinity grouping*—determine which things go together.
- *Clustering*—segment a heterogeneous population of records into a number of more homogeneous subgroups.[41]

Sega of America, one of the largest publishers of video games, uses data mining and statistical tools to distribute its advertising budget of more than $50 million a year. Using data mining, product line specialists and marketing strategists "drill" into trends of each retail store chain. Their goal is to find buying trends that help them determine which advertising strategies are working best and how to reallocate advertising resources by media, territory, and time.[42]

Data-mining tools apply algorithms to information sets to uncover inherent trends and patterns in the information, which analysts use to develop new business strategies. Analysts use the output from data-mining tools to build models that, when exposed to new information sets, perform a variety of information analysis functions. The analysts provide business solutions by putting together the analytical techniques and the business problem at hand, which often reveals important new correlations, patterns, and trends. The more common forms of data-mining analysis capabilities include:

- Cluster analysis
- Association detection
- Statistical analysis.

Cluster Analysis

Cluster analysis is a technique used to divide an information set into mutually exclusive groups such that the members of each group are as close together as possible to one another and the different groups are as far apart as possible. Cluster analysis is frequently used to segment customer information for customer relationship management systems to help organizations identify customers with similar behavioral traits, such as clusters of best customers or onetime customers. Cluster analysis also has the ability to uncover naturally occurring patterns in information (see Figure 9.18).

Data-mining tools that "understand" human language are finding unexpected applications in medicine. IBM and the Mayo Clinic unearthed hidden patterns in medical records, discovering that infant leukemia has three distinct clusters, each of which probably benefits from tailored treatments. Caroline A. Kovac, general manager of IBM Life Sciences, expects that mining the records of cancer patients for clustering patterns

will turn up clues pointing the way to "tremendous strides in curing cancer."[43]

A great example of cluster analysis occurs when attempting to segment customers based on zip codes. Understanding the demographics, lifestyle behaviors, and buying patterns of the most profitable segments of the population at the zip code level is key to a successful target marketing strategy. Targeting only those who have a high propensity to purchase products and services will help a high-end business cut its sales and marketing costs tremendously. Understanding each customer segment by zip code allows a business to determine the importance of each segment.[44]

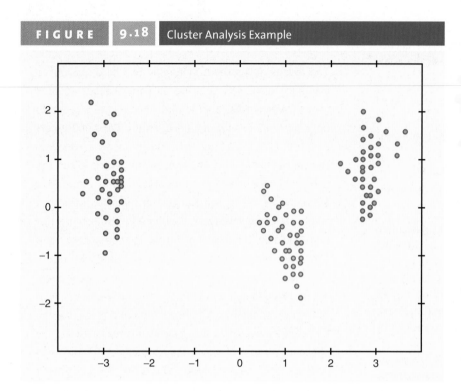

FIGURE 9.18 Cluster Analysis Example

One of the most common forms of association detection analysis is market basket analysis. ***Market basket analysis*** analyzes such items as websites and checkout scanner information to detect customers' buying behavior and predict future behavior by identifying affinities among customers' choices of products and services (see Figure 9.19). Market basket analysis is frequently used to develop marketing campaigns for cross-selling products and services (especially in banking, insurance, and finance) and for inventory control, shelf-product placement, and other retail and marketing applications.

Statistical Analysis

Statistical analysis performs such functions as information correlations, distributions, calculations, and variance analysis. Data-mining tools offer knowledge workers a wide range of powerful statistical capabilities so they can quickly build a variety of statistical models, examine the models' assumptions and validity, and compare and contrast the various models to determine the best one for a particular business issue.

Kraft is the producer of instantly recognizable food brands such as Oreo, Ritz, DiGiorno, and Kool-Aid. The company implemented two data-mining applications to assure consistent flavor, color, aroma, texture, and appearance for all of its food lines. One application analyzed product consistency and the other analyzed process variation reduction (PVR).

Association Detection

Whirlpool Corporation, a $4.3 billion home and commercial appliance manufacturer, employs hundreds of R&D engineers, data analysts, quality assurance specialists, and customer service personnel who all work together to ensure that each generation of appliances is better than the previous generation. Whirlpool is an example of an organization that is gaining business intelligence with association detection data-mining tools.[45]

Association detection reveals the degree to which variables are related and the nature and frequency of these relationships in the information. Whirlpool's warranty analysis tool, for instance, uses statistical analysis to automatically detect potential issues, provide quick and easy access to reports, and perform multidimensional analysis on all warranty information. This association detection data-mining tool enables Whirlpool's managers to take proactive measures to control product defects even before most of its customers are aware of the defect. The tool also allows Whirlpool personnel to devote more time to value-added tasks such as ensuring high quality on all products rather than waiting for or manually analyzing monthly reports.[46]

Many people refer to association detection algorithms as *association rule generators* because they create rules to determine the likelihood of events occurring together at a particular time or following each other in a logical progression. Percentages usually reflect the patterns of these events; for example, "55 percent of the time, events A and B occurred together," or "80 percent of the time that items A and B occurred together, they were followed by item C within three days."

FIGURE 9.19 Market Basket Analysis

The product consistency tool, SENECA (Sensory and Experimental Collection Application), gathers and analyzes information by assigning precise definitions and numerical scales to such qualities as chewy, sweet, crunchy, and creamy. SENECA then builds models, histories, forecasts, and trends based on consumer testing and evaluates potential product improvements and changes.

The PVR tool ensures consistent flavor, color, aroma, texture, and appearance for every Kraft product since even small changes in the baking process can result in huge disparities in taste. Evaluating every manufacturing procedure, from recipe instructions to cookie dough shapes and sizes, the PVR tool has the potential to generate significant cost savings for each product. Using these types of data-mining techniques for quality control and cluster analysis makes sure that the billions of Kraft products that reach consumers annually will continue to taste great with every bite.[47]

Forecasting is a common form of statistical analysis. Formally defined, *forecasts* are predictions made on the basis of time-series information. *Time-series information* is time-stamped information collected at a particular frequency. Examples of time-series information include web visits per hour, sales per month, and calls per day. Forecasting data-mining tools allow users to manipulate the time series for forecasting activities.

When discovering trends and seasonal variations in transactional information, use a time-series forecast to change the transactional information by units of time, such as transforming weekly information into monthly or seasonal information or hourly information into daily information. Companies base production, investment, and staffing decisions on a host of economic and market indicators in this manner. Forecasting models allow organizations to consider all sorts of variables when making decisions.

Nestlé Italiana is part of the multinational giant Nestlé Group and currently dominates Italy's food industry. The company improved sales forecasting by 25 percent with its data-mining forecasting solution that enables the company's managers to make objective decisions based on facts instead of subjective decisions based on intuition. Determining sales forecasts for seasonal confectionery products is a crucial and challenging task. During Easter, Nestlé Italiana has only four weeks to market, deliver, and sell its seasonal products. The Christmas time frame is a little longer, lasting from six to eight weeks, while other holidays such as Valentine's Day and Mother's Day have shorter time frames of about one week.

The company's data-mining solution gathers, organizes, and analyzes massive volumes of information to produce powerful models that identify trends and predict confectionery sales. The business intelligence created is based on five years of historical information and identifies what is important and what is not important. Nestlé Italiana's sophisticated data-mining tool predicted Mother's Day sales forecasts that were 90 percent accurate. The company has benefited from a 40 percent reduction in inventory and a 50 percent reduction in order changes, all due to its

forecasting tool. Determining sales forecasts for seasonal confectionery products is now an area in which Nestlé Italiana excels.[48]

Today, vendors such as Business Objects, Cognos, and SAS offer complete data-mining decision-making solutions. Moving forward, these companies plan to add more predictive analytical capabilities to their products. Their goal is to give companies more "what-if" scenario capabilities based on internal and external information.

●● L09.9
Explain the organizationwide benefits of BI.

●● L09.10
Describe the four categories of BI business benefits.

BUSINESS BENEFITS OF BI

Rapid innovations in systems and data-mining tools are putting operational, tactical, and strategic BI at the fingertips of executives, managers, and even customers. With the successful implementation of BI systems an organization can expect to receive the following:

Single Point of Access to Information for All Users With a BI solution, organizations can unlock information held within their databases by giving authorized users a single point of access to data. Wherever the data reside, whether stored in operational systems, data warehouses, data marts and/or enterprise applications, users can prepare reports and drill deep down into the information to understand what drives their business, without technical knowledge of the underlying data structures. The most successful BI applications allow users to do this with an easy-to-understand, nontechnical, graphical user interface.

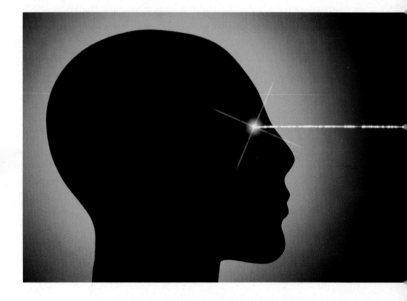

BI across Organizational Departments

There are many different uses for BI and one of its greatest benefits is that it can be used at every step in the value chain. All departments across an organization from sales to operations to customer service can benefit from the value of BI.

Volkswagen AG uses BI to track, understand, and manage data in every department—from finance, production, and development, to research, sales and marketing, and purchasing. Users at all levels of the organization access supplier and customer reports relating to online requests and negotiations, vehicle launches, and vehicle capacity management and tracking.[49]

Up-to-the-Minute Information for Everyone

The key to unlocking information is to give users the tools to quickly and easily find immediate answers to their questions. Some users will be satisfied with standard reports that are updated on a regular basis, such as current inventory reports, sales per channel, or customer status reports. However, the answers these reports yield can lead to new questions. Some users will want dynamic access to information. The information that a user finds in a report will trigger more questions, and these questions will not be answered in a prepackaged report.

While users may spend 80 percent of their time accessing standard or personalized reports, for 20 percent of their tasks, they need to obtain additional information not available in the original report. To address this need and to avoid frustration (and related report backlog for the IT team), a BI system should let users autonomously make ad hoc requests for information from corporate data sources.

For merchants of MasterCard International, access to BI offers the opportunity to monitor their businesses more closely on a day-to-day basis. Advertising agencies are able to use information from the extranet when developing campaigns for merchants. On the authorization side, a call center can pull up cardholder authorization transactions to cut down on fraud. MasterCard expects that in the long term and as business partners increasingly demand access to system data, the system will support more than 20,000 external users.[50]

Categories of BI Benefits

Management is no longer prepared to sink large sums of money into IT projects simply because they are the latest and greatest technology. Information technology has come of age, and it is expected to make a significant contribution to the bottom line.

When looking at how BI affects the bottom line, an organization should analyze not only the organizationwide business benefits, but also the various benefits it can expect to receive from a BI deployment. A practical way of breaking down these numerous benefits is to separate them into four main categories:

1. Quantifiable benefits.
2. Indirectly quantifiable benefits.

3. Unpredictable benefits.
4. Intangible benefits.

---

show me *the* MONEY

Virtual Girl, Living in a Virtual World

The virtual world of Second Life could become the first point of contact between companies and customers and could transform the whole customer experience. Since it began hosting the likes of Adidas, Dell, Reuters, and Toyota, Second Life has become technology's equivalent of India or China—everyone needs an office and a strategy involving it to keep their shareholders happy. But beyond opening a shiny new building in the virtual world, what can such companies do with their virtual real estate? Like many other big brands, PA Consulting has its own offices in Second Life and has learned that simply having an office to answer customer queries is not enough. Real people, albeit behind avatars, must be staffing the offices—in the same way that having a website is not enough if there is not a call center to back it up when a would-be customer wants to speak to a human being. The consultants believe call centers could one day ask customers to follow up a phone call with them by moving the query into a virtual world.

You are the executive director of a hospital and are overseeing the first virtual site being built in Second Life. Create a CRM strategy for doing business in a virtual world. Here are a few questions to get you started:

- How will customer relationships be different in a virtual world?
- What is your strategy for managing customer relationships in this new virtual environment?
- How will supporting Second Life customers differ from supporting traditional customers?
  - How will supporting Second Life customers differ from supporting website customers?
  - What customer security issues might you encounter in Second Life?
  - What customer ethical issues might you encounter in Second Life?

Quantifiable Benefits

Quantifiable benefits include working time saved in producing reports, selling information to suppliers, and so on. A few examples include:

- Moët et Chandon, the famous champagne producer, reduced its IT costs from approximately 30 cents per bottle to 15 cents per bottle.

- A leading risk insurance company provides customers with self-service access to their information in the insurance company's database and no longer sends paper reports. This one benefit alone saves the organization $400,000 a year in printing and shipping costs. The total three-year ROI for this BI deployment was 249 percent.

- Ingram Micro, a wholesale provider of high-tech goods and technology solutions providers, is working to create a new BI extranet to deliver advanced information to the company's suppliers and business partners. Says Ingram Micro CIO Guy Abramo, "Today it's incumbent on us to provide our partners with sell-through information so they can see what happened once their PCs hit distribution. That's critical for them to do inventory planning and manufacturing planning—helping them to understand what products are selling to what segments of the marketplace."[51]

Indirectly Quantifiable Benefits

Indirectly quantifiable benefits can be evaluated through indirect evidence—improved customer service means new business from the same customer, and differentiated service brings new customers. A few examples include:

- A customer of Owens & Minor cited extranet access to the data warehouse as the primary reason for giving the medical supplies distributor an additional $44 million in business.

- "When salespeople went out to visit TaylorMade's customers at golf pro shops and sporting goods retail chains, they didn't have up-to-date inventory reports. The sales reps would take orders for clubs, accessories, and clothing without confidence that the goods were available for delivery as promised," Tom Collard, information systems director with TaylorMade, said. "The technology has helped TaylorMade not only reduce costs by eliminating the reporting backlog . . . it has eliminated a lot of wasted effort that resulted from booking orders that it couldn't fill."[52]

Unpredictable Benefits

Unpredictable benefits are the result of discoveries made by creative users; a few examples include:

- Volkswagen's finance BI system allowed an interesting discovery that later resulted in significant new revenue. The customers of a particular model of the Audi product line had completely different behaviors than customers of other cars. Based on their socioeconomic profiles, they were thought to want long lease terms and fairly large upfront payments. Instead, the information revealed that Audi customers actually wanted shorter leases and to finance a large part of the purchase through the lease. Based on that insight, the company immediately introduced a new program combining shorter length of lease, larger upfront payments, and aggressive leasing rates, especially for that car model. The interest in the new program was immediate, resulting in over $2 million in new revenue.

- Peter Blundell, former knowledge strategy manager for British Airways, and various company executives had a suspicion that the carrier was suffering from a high degree of ticket fraud. To address this problem, Blundell and his team rolled out business intelligence. "Once we analyzed the data, we found that this ticket fraud was not an issue at all. What we had supposed was fraud was in fact either data quality issues or process problems," Blundell said. "What it did was give us so many unexpected opportunities in terms of understanding our business." Blundell estimated that the BI deployment has resulted in around $100 million in cost savings and new revenues for the airline.[53]

Intangible Benefits

Intangible benefits include improved communication throughout the enterprise, improved job satisfaction of empowered users, and improved knowledge sharing. A few examples include:

- The corporate human resources department at ABN AMRO Bank uses BI to gain insight into its workforce by analyzing information on such items as gender, age, tenure, and compensation. Thanks to this sharing of intellectual capital, the HR department is in a better position to demonstrate its performance and contribution to the business successes of the corporation as a whole.

- Ben & Jerry's uses BI to track, understand, and manage information on the thousands of consumer responses it receives on its products and promotional activities. Through daily customer feedback analysis, Ben & Jerry's is able to identify trends and modify its marketing campaigns and its products to suit consumer demand. ■

chapter ten

SECTION 10.1 >>
Enterprise Resource Planning

- Enterprise Resource Planning
- Core ERP Components
- Extended ERP Components
- Integrating SCM, CRM, and ERP
- Measuring ERP Success
- Choosing ERP Software

SECTION 10.2 >>
Collaboration Systems

- Teams, Partnerships, and Alliances
- Collaboration Systems
- Knowledge Management Systems
- Content Management Systems
- Workflow Management Systems
- Groupware Systems

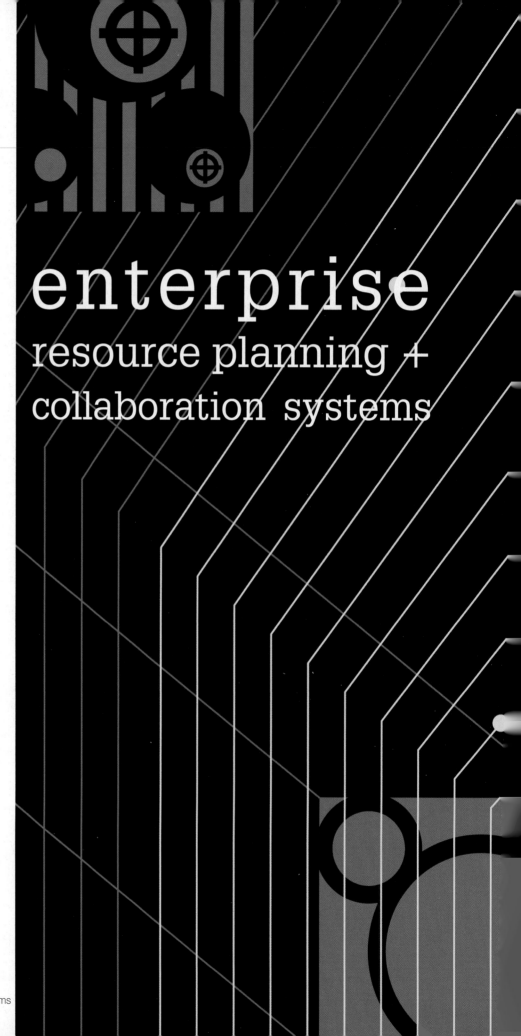

enterprise
resource planning +
collaboration systems

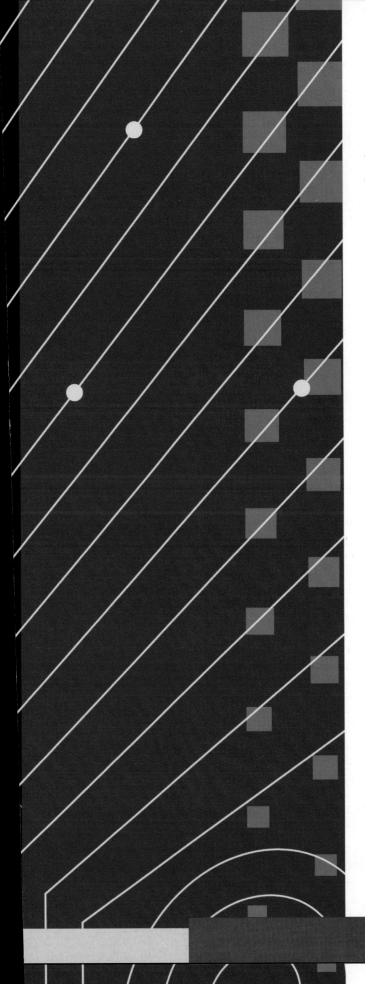

what's in IT for me?

nformation is a powerful asset. It is a key organizational asset that enables companies to carry out business initiatives and strategic plans. Companies that manage information are primed for competitive advantage and success. Information technology is the key tool allowing access and flow of information across enterprises.

As a business student, you must understand how to give employees, customers, and business partners access to information. This includes taking advantage of newer technologies such as knowledge management, enterprise portals, and collaboration tools. Doing so facilitates completion of tasks while encouraging the sharing and generation of new ideas that lead to the development of innovations, improved work habits, and best practices.

This chapter showcases how information technology can help you capitalize upon the power of information by providing mechanisms for improved information access, sharing, and application. This includes access and use of structured information found in transactional database and data warehouses, unstructured information found in textual documents and email messages, and information that organizational employees possess.

Enterprise resource planning (ERP) integrates all departments and functions throughout an organization into a single IT system (or integrated set of IT systems) so that employees can make decisions by viewing enterprisewide information on all business operations. Figure 10.1 highlights a few reasons ERP solutions have proven to be such a powerful force.

ERP as a business concept resounds as a powerful internal information management nirvana: Everyone involved in sourcing, producing, and delivering the company's product works with the same information, which eliminates redundancies, reduces wasted time, and removes misinformation.

●● SECTION 10.1
Enterprise Resource Planning

LEARNING OUTCOMES

LO10.1 Compare core enterprise resource planning components and extended enterprise resource planning components.

LO10.2 Describe the three primary components found in core enterprise resource planning systems.

LO10.3 Describe the four primary components found in extended enterprise resource planning systems.

LO10.4 Explain the business value of integrating supply chain management, customer relationship management, and enterprise resource planning systems.

LO10.5 Explain how an organization can use a balanced scorecard to measure ERP success.

ENTERPRISE RESOURCE PLANNING

Today's business leaders need significant amounts of information to be readily accessible with real-time views into their businesses so that decisions can be made when they need to be, without the added time of tracking data and generating reports. *Enterprise resource planning (ERP)* integrates all departments and functions throughout an organization into a single IT system (or integrated set of IT systems) so that employees can make decisions by viewing enterprisewide information on all business operations.

Many organizations fail to maintain consistency across business operations. If a single department, such as sales, decides to implement a new system without considering the other departments, inconsistencies can occur throughout the company. Not all systems are built to talk to each other and share data, and if sales suddenly implements a new system that marketing and accounting cannot use or is inconsistent in the way it handles information, the company's operations become siloed. Figure 10.2 displays sample data from a sales database, and Figure 10.3 displays samples from an accounting database. Notice the differences in data formats, numbers, and identifiers. Correlating this data would be difficult, and the inconsistencies would cause numerous reporting errors from an enterprisewide perspective.

Los Angeles is a city of 3.5 million, with 44,000 city employees, and a budget of $4 billion. Yet a few years ago each department conducted its own purchasing. That meant 2,000 people in 600 city buildings and 60 warehouses were ordering material. Some 120,000 purchase orders (POs) and 50,000 checks per year went to more than 7,000 vendors. Inefficiency was rampant.

"There was a lack of financial responsibility in the old system, and people could run up unauthorized expenditures," said Bob Jensen, the city's ERP project manager. Each department maintained its own inventories on different systems. Expense-item mismatches piled up. One department purchased one way, others preferred a different approach. Mainframe-based systems were isolated. The city chose an ERP system as part of a $22 million project to integrate purchasing and financial reporting across the entire city. The project resulted in cutting the check processing staff in half, processing POs faster than ever, reducing the number of workers in warehousing by 40 positions, decreasing inventories from $50 million to $15 million, and providing a single point of contact for each vendor. In addition, $5 million a year has been saved in contract consolidation.[1]

FIGURE	10.1	Reasons ERP Systems Are Powerful Organizational Tools

Reasons ERP Systems Are Powerful Organizational Tools
ERP is a logical solution to the mess of incompatible applications that had sprung up in most businesses.
ERP addresses the need for global information sharing and reporting.
ERP is used to avoid the pain and expense of fixing legacy systems.

Figure 10.4 shows how an ERP system takes data from across the enterprise, consolidates and correlates the data, and generates enterprisewide organizational reports. Original ERP implementations promised to capture all information onto one true "enterprise" system, with the ability to touch all the business processes within the organization. Unfortunately, ERP solutions have fallen short of these promises, and typical implementations have penetrated only 15 to 20 percent of the organization. The issue ERP intends to solve is that knowledge within a majority of organizations currently resides in silos that are maintained by a select few, without the ability to be shared across the organization, causing inconsistency across business operations.[2]

Turner Industries grew from $300 million in sales to $800 million in sales in less than 10 years thanks to the implementation of an ERP system. Ranked number 369 on the Forbes 500 list of privately held companies, Turner Industries is a leading industrial services firm. Turner Industries develops and deploys advanced software applications designed to maximize the productivity of its 25,000 employees and construction equipment valued at more than $100 million.

The company considers the biggest challenges in the industrial services industry to be completing projects on time, within budget, while fulfilling customers' expectations. To meet these challenges the company invested in an ERP system and named the project Interplan. Interplan won Constructech's Vision award for software innovation in the heavy construction industry. Interplan runs all of Turner's construction, turnaround, shutdown, and maintenance projects and is so adept at estimating and planning jobs that Turner Industries typically achieves higher profit margins on projects that use Interplan. As the ERP solution makes the company more profitable, the company can pass on the cost savings to its customers, giving the company an incredible competitive advantage.[3]

Enterprise resource planning systems provide organizations with consistency. An ERP system provides a method for the effective planning and controlling of

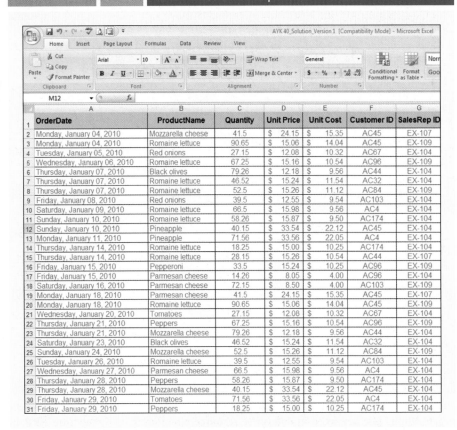

FIGURE 10.2 Sales Information Sample

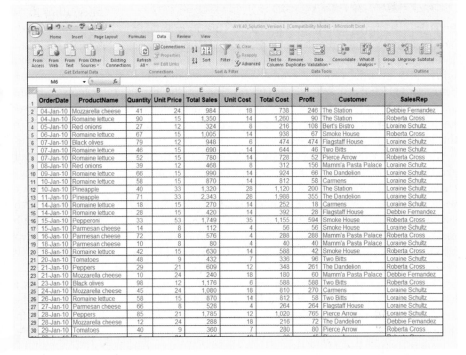

FIGURE 10.3 Accounting Information Sample

CHAPTER 10 | Enterprise Resource Planning and Collaboration Systems 247

FIGURE **10.4** Enterprise Resource Planning System

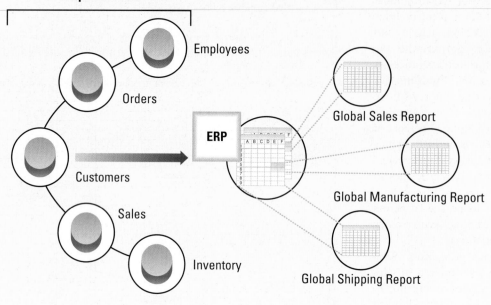

all the resources required to take, make, ship, and account for customer orders in a manufacturing, distribution, or service organization. The key word in enterprise resource planning is *enterprise* and there are two key components to ERP including:

- The heart of ERP
- The evolution of ERP

The Heart of ERP

Enterprise resource planning systems serve as the organization's backbone in providing fundamental decision-making support. In the past, departments made decisions independent of each other. ERP systems provide a foundation for collaboration between departments, enabling people in different business areas to communicate. ERP systems have been widely adopted in large organizations to store critical knowledge used to make the decisions that drive performance.

To be competitive, organizations must always strive for excellence in every business process enterprisewide, a daunting challenge if the organization has multisite operations worldwide. To obtain operational efficiencies, lower costs, improve supplier and customer relations, and increase revenues and market share, all units of the organization must work together harmoniously toward congruent goals. An ERP system will help an organization achieve this.

One company that has blazed a trail with ERP is Atlanta-based United Parcel Service of America, Inc. (UPS). UPS has developed a number of web-based applications that track information such as recipient signatures, addresses, time in

transit, and other shipping information. These services run on an ERP foundation that UPS customers can connect to using real-time ERP information obtained from the UPS website. Currently, 6.2 million tracking requests pass through the company's website each day. By automating the information delivery process, UPS has dramatically reduced the demand on its customer service representatives. Just as important, UPS has improved relationships with its business partners—in effect integrating its business with theirs—by making it easier for consumers to find delivery information without leaving the website of the merchant.[4]

The heart of an ERP system is a central database that collects information from and feeds information into all the ERP system's individual application components (called modules), supporting diverse business functions such as accounting, manufacturing, marketing, and human resources. When a user enters or updates information in one module, it is immediately and automatically updated throughout the entire system, as illustrated in Figure 10.5.

ERP automates business processes such as order fulfillment—taking an order from a customer, shipping the purchase, and then billing for it. With an ERP system, when a customer service representative takes an order from a customer, he or she has all the information necessary to complete the order (the customer's credit rating and order history, the company's inventory levels, and the delivery schedule). Everyone else in the company sees the same information and has access to the database that holds the customer's new order. When one department finishes with the order, it is automatically routed via the ERP system to the next department. To find out where the order is at any point, a user need only log in to the ERP system and track it down, as illustrated in Figure 10.6. The order process moves like a bolt of lightning through the organization, and customers get their orders faster and with fewer errors than ever before. ERP can apply that same magic to the other major business processes, such as employee benefits or financial reporting.[5]

ERP enables employees across the organization to share information across a single, centralized database. With extended portal capabilities, an organization can also involve its suppliers and customers in the workflow process, allowing ERP to penetrate the entire value chain, and help the organization achieve greater operational efficiency (see Figures 10.7 and 10.8).[6]

The Evolution of ERP

Originally, ERP solutions were developed to deliver automation across multiple units of an organization, to help facilitate the manufacturing process and address issues such as raw materials, inventory, order entry, and distribution. However, ERP was unable to extend to other functional areas of the company such as sales, marketing, and shipping. It could not tie in any CRM capabilities that would allow organizations to capture customer-specific information, nor did it work with websites or portals used for customer service or order fulfillment. Call center or

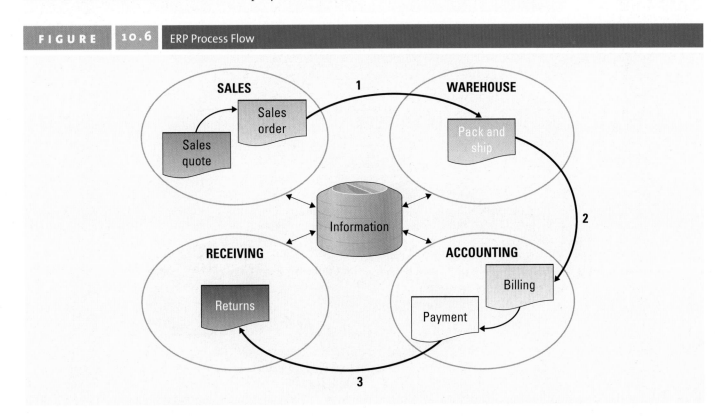

FIGURE 10.5 ERP Integration Data Flow

FIGURE 10.6 ERP Process Flow

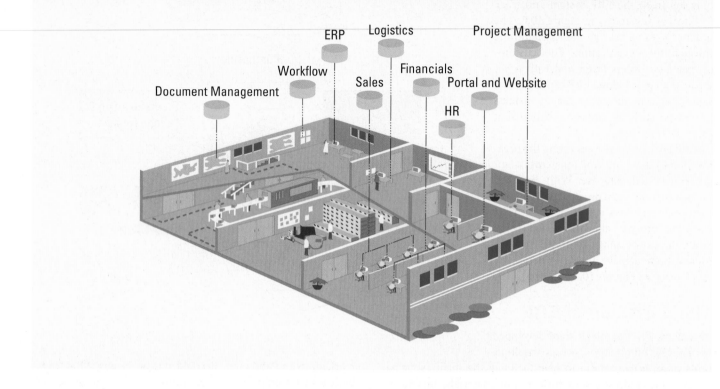

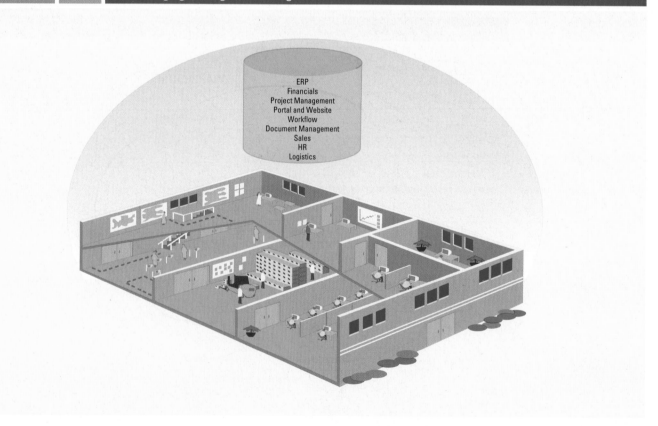

FIGURE 10.9 The Evolution of ERP

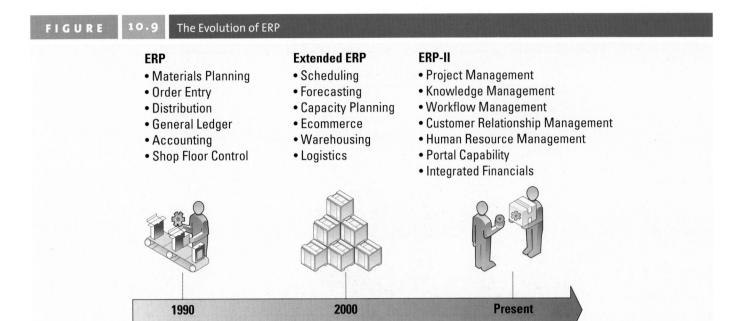

ERP
- Materials Planning
- Order Entry
- Distribution
- General Ledger
- Accounting
- Shop Floor Control

Extended ERP
- Scheduling
- Forecasting
- Capacity Planning
- Ecommerce
- Warehousing
- Logistics

ERP-II
- Project Management
- Knowledge Management
- Workflow Management
- Customer Relationship Management
- Human Resource Management
- Portal Capability
- Integrated Financials

1990   2000   Present

quality assurance staff could not tap into the ERP solution, nor could ERP handle document management, such as cataloging contracts and purchase orders.[7]

ERP has grown over the years to become part of the extended enterprise. From its beginning as a tool for materials planning, it has extended to warehousing, distribution, and order entry. With its next evolution, ERP expands to the front office including CRM. Now administrative, sales, marketing, and human resources staff can share a tool that is truly enterprisewide. To compete on a functional level today, companies must adopt an enterprisewide approach to ERP that utilizes the Internet and connects to every facet of the value chain. Figure 10.9 shows how ERP has grown since the 1990s to accommodate the needs of the entire organization.[8]

ERP II: Core and Extended Figure 10.10 provides an example of an ERP system with its core and extended components. *Core ERP components* are the traditional components included in most ERP systems and they primarily focus on internal operations. *Extended ERP components* are the extra components that meet the organizational needs not covered by the core components and primarily focus on external operations.

●● LO10.1

Compare core enterprise resource planning components and extended enterprise resource planning components.

●● LO10.2

Describe the three primary components found in core enterprise resource planning systems.

CORE ERP COMPONENTS

The three most common core ERP components focusing on internal operations are:

1. Accounting and finance.
2. Production and materials management.
3. Human resources.

Accounting and Finance ERP Components

Deeley Harley-Davidson Canada, the exclusive Canadian distributor of Harley-Davidson motorcycles, has improved inventory, turnaround time, margins, and customer satisfaction—all with the implementation of a financial ERP system. The system has opened up the power of information to the company and is helping it make strategic decisions when it still has the time to change things. The ERP system provides the company with ways to manage inventory, turnaround time, and utilize warehouse space more effectively.[9]

Accounting and finance ERP components manage accounting data and financial processes within the enterprise with functions such as general ledger, accounts payable, accounts receivable, budgeting, and asset management. One of the most useful features included in an ERP accounting/finance component is its credit-management feature. Most organizations manage their relationships with customers by setting credit limits, or a limit on how much a customer can owe at any one time. The company then monitors the credit limit whenever the customer places a new order or sends in a payment. ERP financial systems help to correlate customer orders with customer account balances determining credit

FIGURE **10.10** Core ERP Components and Extended ERP Components

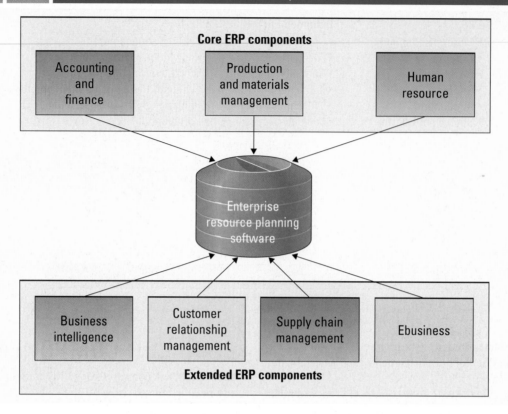

availability. Another great feature is the ability to perform product profitability analysis. ERP financial components are the backbone behind product profitability analysis and allow companies to perform all types of advanced profitability modeling techniques.

Production and Materials Management ERP Components

One of the main functions of an ERP system is streamlining the production planning process. *Production and materials management ERP components* handle the various aspects of production planning and execution such as demand forecasting, production scheduling, job cost accounting, and quality control. Companies typically produce multiple products, each of which has many different parts. Production lines, consisting of machines and employees, build the different types of products. The company must then define sales forecasting for each product to determine production schedules and materials purchasing. Figure 10.11 displays the typical ERP production planning process. The process begins with forecasting sales in order to plan operations. A detailed production schedule is developed if the product is produced, and a materials requirement plan is completed if the product is purchased.

Grupo Farmanova Intermed, located in Costa Rica, is a pharmaceutical marketing and distribution company that markets nearly 2,500 products to about 500 customers in Central and South America. The company identified a need for software that could unify product logistics management in a single country. It decided to deploy PeopleSoft financial and distribution ERP components allowing the company to improve customer data management, increase confidence among internal and external users, and coordinate the logistics of inventory. With the new software the company enhanced its capabilities for handling, distributing, and marketing its pharmaceuticals.[10]

Human Resources ERP Components

Human resources ERP components track employee information including payroll, benefits, compensation, and performance assessment, and assure compliance with the legal requirements of multiple jurisdictions and tax authorities. Human resources components even offer features that allow the organization to perform detailed analysis on its employees to determine such things as the identification of individuals who are likely to leave the company unless additional compensation or benefits are provided. These components can also identify which employees are using which resources, such as online training and long-distance telephone services. They can also help determine whether the most talented people are working for those

FIGURE 10.11 The Production Planning Process

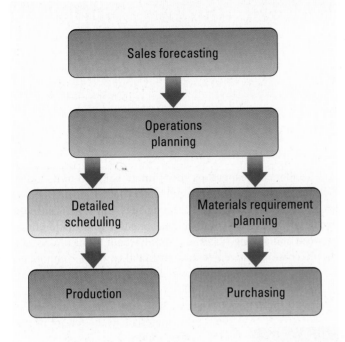

business units with the highest priority—or where they would have the greatest impact on profit.

●● LO10.1

Compare core enterprise resource planning components and extended enterprise resource planning components.

●● LO10.3

Describe the four primary components found in extended enterprise resource planning systems.

EXTENDED ERP COMPONENTS

Extended ERP components are the extra components that meet the organizational needs not covered by the core components and primarily focus on external operations. Many of the numerous extended ERP components are Internet-enabled and require interaction with customers, suppliers, and business partners outside the organization. The four most common extended ERP components are:

1. Business intelligence.
2. Customer relationship management.
3. Supply chain management.
4. Ebusiness.

show me the MONEY

Classic Cars

Classic Cars Inc. operates high-end automotive dealerships that offer luxury cars along with luxury service. The company is proud of its extensive inventory, top-of-the-line mechanics, and especially its exceptional service, which even includes a cappuccino bar at each dealership.

The company currently has 40 sales representatives at four locations. Each location maintains its own computer systems, and all sales representatives have their own contact management systems. This splintered approach to operations causes numerous problems, including customer communication issues, pricing strategy issues, and inventory control issues. A few examples include:

- A customer shopping at one dealership can go to another dealership and receive a different price quote for the same car.
- Sales representatives are frequently stealing each other's customers and commissions.
- Sales representatives frequently send their customers to other dealerships to see specific cars and when the customer arrives, the car is not on the lot.
- Marketing campaigns are not designed to target specific customers; they are typically generic, such as 10 percent off a new car.
- If a sales representative quits, all of his or her customer information is lost.

You are working for Customer One, a small consulting company that specializes in enterprisewide strategies. The owner of Classic Cars Inc., Tom Repicci, has hired you to help him formulate a strategy to put his company back on track. Develop a proposal for Tom, detailing how an ERP system can alleviate the company's issues and create new opportunities.

> EXTENDED ERP COMPONENTS ARE THE EXTRA COMPONENTS THAT MEET THE ORGANIZATIONAL NEEDS NOT COVERED BY THE CORE COMPONENTS AND PRIMARILY FOCUS ON EXTERNAL OPERATIONS.

Business Intelligence ERP Components

ERP systems offer powerful tools that measure and control organizational operations. Many organizations have found that these valuable tools can be enhanced to provide even greater value through the addition of powerful business intelligence systems. The business intelligence components of ERP systems typically collect information used throughout the organization (including data used in many other ERP components), organize it, and apply analytical tools to assist managers with decisions. Data warehouses are one of the most popular extensions to ERP systems, with over two-thirds of U.S. manufacturers adopting or planning such systems.[11]

Customer Relationship Management ERP Components

ERP vendors are expanding their functionality to provide services formerly supplied by customer relationship management (CRM) vendors such as Oracle and Siebel. *Customer relationship management* involves managing all aspects of a customer's relationship with an organization to increase customer loyalty and retention and an organization's profitability. CRM components provide an integrated view of customer data and interactions allowing organizations to work more effectively with customers and be more responsive to their needs. CRM components typically include contact centers, sales force automation, and marketing functions. These improve the customer experience while identifying a company's most (and least) valuable customers for better allocation of resources.

Supply Chain Management ERP Components

ERP vendors are expanding their functionality to provide services formerly supplied by supply chain management vendors such as i2 Technologies and Manugistics. *Supply chain management (SCM)* involves the management of information flows between and among stages in a supply chain to maximize total supply chain effectiveness and profitability. SCM components help an organization plan, schedule, control, and optimize the supply chain from its acquisition of raw materials to the receipt of finished goods by customers.

Ebusiness ERP Components

The original focus of ERP systems was the internal organization. In other words, ERP systems are not fundamentally ready for the external world of ebusiness. The newest and most exciting extended ERP components are the ebusiness components. *Ebusiness* means conducting business on the Internet, not only buying and selling, but also serving customers and collaborating with business partners. Two of the primary features of ebusiness components are elogistics and eprocurement. *Elogistics* manages the transportation and storage of goods. *Eprocurement* is the business-to-business (B2B) purchase and sale of supplies and services over the Internet.

Ebusiness and ERP complement each other by allowing companies to establish a web presence and fulfill orders expeditiously. A common mistake made by many businesses is deploying a web presence before the integration of back-office systems or an ERP system. For example, one large toy manufacturer announced less than a week before Christmas that it would be unable to fulfill any of its web orders. The company had all the

toys in the warehouse, but it could not organize the basic order processing function to get the toys delivered to the consumers on time.

Customers and suppliers are now demanding access to ERP information including order status, inventory levels, and invoice reconciliation. Plus, the customers and partners want all this information in a simplified format available through a website. This is a difficult task to accomplish because most ERP systems are full of technical jargon, which is why employee training is one of the hidden costs associated with ERP implementations. Removing the jargon to accommodate untrained customers and partners is one of the more difficult tasks when web-enabling an ERP system. To accommodate the growing needs of the ebusiness world, ERP vendors need to build two new channels of access into the ERP system information—one channel for customers (B2C) and one channel for businesses, suppliers, and partners (B2B).[12]

●● LO10.4

Explain the business value of integrating supply chain management, customer relationship management, and enterprise resource planning systems.

INTEGRATING SCM, CRM, AND ERP

Applications such as SCM, CRM, and ERP are the backbone of ebusiness. Integration of these applications is the key to success for many companies. Integration allows the unlocking of information to make it available to any user, anywhere, anytime. Originally, there were three top ERP vendors—PeopleSoft, Oracle, and SAP. In December 2004, Oracle purchased PeopleSoft for $10 billion, leaving two main competitors in the ERP market—Oracle and SAP.

Most organizations today have no choice but to piece their SCM, CRM, and ERP applications together since no one vendor can respond to every organizational need; hence, customers purchase applications from multiple vendors. Oracle and SAP both offer CRM and SCM components. However, these modules are not as functional or flexible as the modules offered by industry leaders of SCM and CRM such as Siebel and i2 Technologies, as depicted in Figures 10.12 and 10.13. As a result, organizations face the challenge of integrating their systems. For example, a single organization might choose its CRM components from Siebel, SCM components from i2, and financial components and HR management components from Oracle. Figure 10.14 displays the general audience and purpose for each of these applications that have to be integrated.

From its roots in the California Gold Rush era, San Francisco-based Del Monte Foods has grown to become the nation's largest producer and distributor of premium quality processed fruits, vegetables, and tomato products. With annual sales of over $3 billion, Del Monte is also one of the country's largest producers, distributors, and marketers of private-label food and pet products with a powerful portfolio of brands including Del Monte, StarKist, Nature's Goodness, 9Lives, and Kibbles 'n Bits.

Del Monte's acquisition of StarKist, Nature's Goodness, 9Lives, and Kibbles 'n Bits from the H. J. Heinz Company required an integration between Del Monte's and H. J. Heinz's business processes. Del Monte needed to overhaul its IT infrastructure, migrating from multiple platforms including UNIX and mainframe systems and consolidating applications centrally on a single system. The work required integration of business processes across manufacturing, financial, supply chain, decision support, and transactional reporting areas.

The revamp of Del Monte's architecture stemmed from a strategic decision. Del Monte decided to implement an ERP system to support its entire U.S. operations, with headquarters in San Francisco, operations in Pittsburgh, and distribution

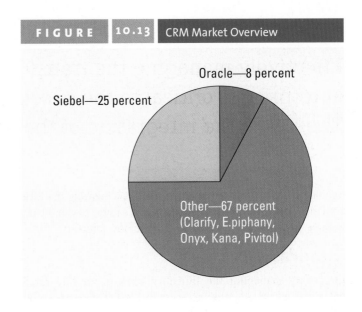

FIGURE 10.12 SCM Market Overview

Oracle—5 percent
Other—50 percent (Aspen Technology, Descartes, Retek)
i2—38 percent
Manugistics—7 percent

FIGURE 10.13 CRM Market Overview

Oracle—8 percent
Siebel—25 percent
Other—67 percent (Clarify, E.piphany, Onyx, Kana, Pivitol)

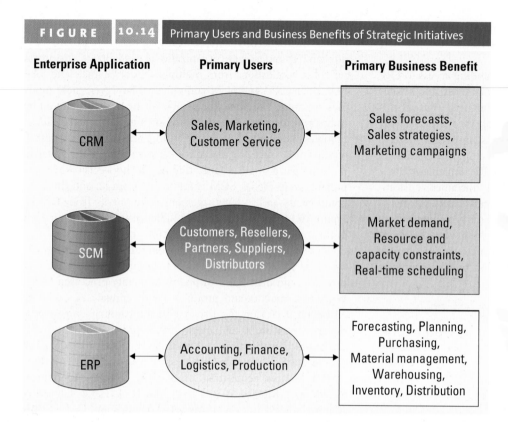

FIGURE 10.14 | Primary Users and Business Benefits of Strategic Initiatives

Enterprise Application	Primary Users	Primary Business Benefit
CRM	Sales, Marketing, Customer Service	Sales forecasts, Sales strategies, Marketing campaigns
SCM	Customers, Resellers, Partners, Suppliers, Distributors	Market demand, Resource and capacity constraints, Real-time scheduling
ERP	Accounting, Finance, Logistics, Production	Forecasting, Planning, Purchasing, Material management, Warehousing, Inventory, Distribution

An integrated enterprise infuses support areas, such as finance and human resources, with a strong customer orientation. Integrations are achieved using *middleware*—several different types of software that sit in the middle of and provide connectivity between two or more software applications. Middleware translates information between disparate systems. *Enterprise application integration (EAI) middleware* represents a new approach to middleware by packaging together commonly used functionality, such as providing prebuilt links to popular enterprise applications, which reduces the time necessary to develop solutions that integrate applications from multiple vendors. A few leading vendors of EAI middleware include Active Software, Vitria Technology, and Extricity. Figure 10.15 displays the data points where these applications integrate and illustrates the underlying premise of architecture infrastructure design.

Companies run on interdependent applications, such as SCM, CRM, and ERP. If one application performs poorly, the entire customer value delivery system is affected. For example, no matter how great a company is at CRM, if its SCM system does not work and the customer never receives the finished product, the company will lose that customer. The world-class enterprises of tomorrow must be built on the foundation of world-class applications implemented today.

centers and manufacturing facilities across the country. The company concluded that the only way it could unite its global operations and open its system to its customers, which are mainly large retailers, was through the use of an ERP system. Among other key factors was the need to embrace an ebusiness strategy. The challenge facing Del Monte was to select an ERP system to merge multiple systems quickly and cost effectively. If financial and customer service targets were to be achieved, Del Monte needed to integrate new businesses that more than

> ## "Effectively managing the transformation to an integrated enterprise is critical to the success of the 21st century organization. The key is the integration of the disparate IT applications."

doubled the size of the company. Since implementing the ERP system, customers and trading partners are now provided with a single, consistent, and integrated view of the company.[13]

Integration Tools

Effectively managing the transformation to an integrated enterprise is critical to the success of the 21st century organization. The key is the integration of the disparate IT applications.

Coca-Cola's business model is a common one among well-known franchisers. Coca-Cola gets the majority of its $18 billion in annual revenue from franchise fees it earns from bottlers all over the world. Bottlers, along with the franchise, license Coke's secret recipe and many others including recipes for Odwalla, Nestea, Minute Maid, and Sprite. Now Coca-Cola hopes that bottlers will also buy into adopting common business practices using a service-oriented architecture (SoA) ERP system.

FIGURE 10.15 Integrations between SCM, CRM, and ERP Applications

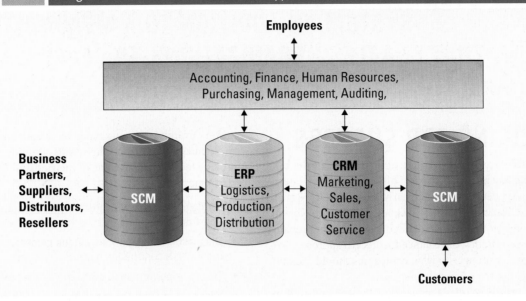

The target platform chosen by Coca-Cola is mySAP enterprise resource planning by SAP. If it works, Coca-Cola and its bottlers stand to make and save a lot of money, and SAP will be able to position itself as one of the dominant players in SoA-enabled ERP. Already, Coca-Cola and many of its bottlers use versions of SAP for finance, manufacturing, and a number of administrative functions. But Coca-Cola wants everyone to move to a "services" architecture environment.

Coca-Cola hopes that this services standardization will make its supply chain more efficient and reduce costs. In explaining why a services approach is so vitally important, Jean-Michel Ares, CIO of Coca-Cola, stated, "That will allow bottlers to converge one step at a time, one process area at a time, one module at a time, at a time that's right for the bottler. We can march across the bottling world incrementally."[14]

LO10.5

Explain how an organization can use a balanced scorecard to measure ERP success.

Living the

DREAM

Floating Homes and Brad Pitt

It is hard to imagine, but completely possible, that a Katrina-style hurricane will strike again. Hopefully, this time we will be prepared and able to handle the floods. If Brad Pitt has anything to say about it, we will be. Yes, I'm referring to Brad Pitt the actor. Pitt's Make it Right Foundation is building a Float House, a home that can break away from its moorings in the event of a flood and rise up to 12 feet on guideposts. The house, designed by Morphosis Architects, is covered with concrete and built with a polystyrene foam base. The Float House will break loose from any electrical lines and comes equipped with a battery backup that can last for three days. The price of the Float House has yet to be revealed, but a home that can save itself during a flood is like homeowner's insurance for its inhabitants.

Individuals and homes were not the only casualties associated with Hurricane Katrina. Businesses were wiped out, too. An ERP system houses all of the data associated with the business. What types of data would be lost if your ERP system was destroyed in a natural disaster? Could your company continue to operate if you lost your ERP data? What can an organization do to ensure its enterprisewide data are safe from natural disasters?

MEASURING ERP SUCCESS

Measuring ERP success is extremely difficult. One of the best methods is the balanced scorecard. This approach to strategic management was developed in the early 1990s by Drs. Robert Kaplan of the Harvard Business School and David Norton. Addressing some of the weaknesses and vagueness of previous measurement techniques, the balanced scorecard approach provides a clear prescription as to what companies should measure in order to balance the financial perspective.[15]

The *balanced scorecard* is a management system, in addition to a measurement system, that enables organizations to clarify their vision and strategy and translate them into action. It provides feedback around both the internal business processes and external outcomes in order to continuously improve strategic performance and results. When fully deployed, the balanced scorecard transforms strategic planning from an academic exercise into the nerve center of an enterprise. Kaplan and Norton describe the innovation of the balanced scorecard as follows: "The balanced scorecard retains traditional financial measures. But financial measures tell the story of past events, an adequate story for industrial age companies for which investments in long-term capabilities and customer relationships were not critical for success. These financial measures are inadequate, however, for guiding and evaluating the journey that information age companies must make to create future value through investment in customers, suppliers, employees, processes, technology, and innovation."[16]

The balanced scorecard views the organization from four perspectives, and users should develop metrics, collect data, and analyze their business relative to each of these perspectives:

- The learning and growth perspective.
- The internal business process perspective.
- The customer perspective.
- The financial perspective (see Figure 10.16).[17]

Companies cannot manage what they cannot measure. Therefore, metrics must be developed based on the priorities of the strategic plan, which provides the key business drivers and criteria for metrics that managers most desire to watch. Processes are then designed to collect information relevant to these metrics and reduce it to numerical form for storage, display, and analysis. Decision makers examine the outcomes of various measured processes and strategies and track the results to guide the company and provide feedback. The value of metrics is in their ability to provide a factual basis for defining:

- Strategic feedback to show the present status of the organization from many perspectives for decision makers.
- Diagnostic feedback into various processes to guide improvements on a continuous basis.
- Trends in performance over time as the metrics are tracked.
- Feedback around the measurement methods themselves and which metrics should be tracked.
- Quantitative inputs to forecasting methods and models for decision support systems.[18]

One warning regarding metrics—do not go crazy. The trick is to find a few key metrics to track that provide significant insight. Remember to tie metrics to other financial and business objectives in the firm. The key is to get good insight without becoming a slave to metrics. The rule of thumb is to develop seven key metrics, plus or minus two.[19]

CHOOSING ERP SOFTWARE

The many different ERP vendors on the market today each offer different ERP solutions. The core ERP functions for each vendor are the same and focus on financial, accounting, sales, marketing, human resource, operations, and logistics. ERP vendors differentiate themselves by offering unique functionality such as CRM and SCM systems.

Many customers find that their chosen ERP solution does not meet their expectations. Despite many improvements in the software, the industry itself is well aware that failed ERP implementations are still far too common. According to Gartner Research, the average failure rate for an ERP project is 66 percent. It is no wonder that some manufacturers view ERP as a necessary, strategic evil. The key word here though is *necessary*.[20]

Many companies strive to make good financial decisions by making smart investments. The best way to ensure a good investment in ERP is to understand why failure occurs and how to avoid it. The first challenge is that ERP is a product

FIGURE 10.16 The Four Primary Perspectives of the Balanced Scorecard

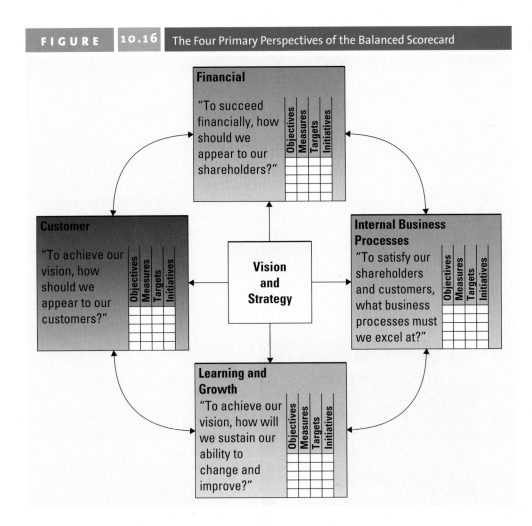

ERP has no major process gaps and very few minor ones. Think of a new ERP system as a suit. Typically, a customer buys a suit three ways:

1. Off the rack.
2. Off the rack and tailor it to fit.
3. Custom made.

The way the solution fits the business process will normally determine the satisfaction level of the client. Buying ERP off the rack is the equivalent of buying a canned software package. It fits some well, but some not at all. That is why a customer can tailor a suit so that it fits better. Modifications can be made to the software so that its processes line up better with the company processes. This is a good strategy, provided the chosen package supports this. The downside is that it can get very expensive. Finally, the custom system can provide a great fit, but the company must thoroughly understand what it is doing and be able to support the heavy financial burden associated with a custom-build.

that comes in many flavors. Its main purpose is to provide support and automation to a business process. The business world has many different business models, and there are just as many ERP products available that serve them.

Finding the Right ERP Solution

A good ERP system will be highly reflective of the business process in place at the company. This means the software must perform many different tasks and that makes it complex. Most companies do not carry a high degree of ERP software expertise on their staff and do not understand ERP to the degree they should, and this makes it easy to choose the wrong package. The key to making an effective purchase is to have solid business processes. Successful ERP projects share three basic attributes:

1. Overall fit.
2. Proper business analysis.
3. Solid implementation plans.[21]

Overall Fit
This refers to the degree of gaps that exist between the system and the business process. A well-fitting

Proper Business Analysis
The best way to determine which fit strategy is right is to conduct a thorough business analysis. Successful companies normally spend up to 10 percent of the project budget on a business analysis. A proper analysis must result in a documented list of the business processes at work within the company. This will provide a basic tool that can measure vendor capability.

Solid Implementation Plans
Like the installation of any successful process or piece of machinery, a plan is needed to monitor the quality objectives and timelines. It will also employ processes like workflow analysis and job combination to harvest savings.

A thorough implementation will transfer knowledge to the system users. When the project is complete the users of the new system must be capable of using the tools it provides. The users must also know what to do in cases when the process fluctuates. The majority of failed systems are the result of poor-quality implementation. It is important to remember that ERP is simply a tool. Tools that people do not know how to use can be as useless as having no tools at all.[22]

LEARNING OUTCOMES

LO10.6 Identify the different ways in which companies collaborate using technology.

LO10.7 Compare the different categories of collaboration technologies.

LO10.8 Define the fundamental concepts of a knowledge management system.

LO10.9 Provide an example of a content management system along with its business purpose.

10.10 Evaluate the advantages of using a workflow management system.

10.11 Explain how groupware can benefit a business.

TEAMS, PARTNERSHIPS, AND ALLIANCES

To be successful—and avoid being eliminated by the competition—an organization must constantly undertake new initiatives, address both minor and major problems, and capitalize on significant opportunities. To support these activities, an organization often will create and utilize teams, partnerships, and alliances because the expertise needed is beyond

fyi

Bean Integration

At Flavors, a premium coffee shop, customers receive more than just a great cup of coffee—they receive exposure to music, art, literature, and town events. Flavor's calendar for programs gives customers a quick view into this corner of the world—from live music and art displays to volunteering or a coffee tasting. Flavors offers the following:

- Music center: Information is available for all live music events occurring in the area. The store also hosts an open microphone two nights a week for local musicians.
- Art gallery: A space in the store is filled with great pieces from local artists.
- Book clubs: Customers can meet to discuss current and classic literature.
- Coffee sampler: Customers can sample coffees from around the world with the experts.
- Community events: Weekly meetings are held, where customers can find ways to become more involved in their community.
- Brewing courses: The finer details of the brewing, grinding, and blending equipment for sale in Flavor stores—from the traditional press to a digital espresso machine—are taught. There is also a trouble-shooting guide developed by brewing specialists.

Flavors' sales are great and profits are soaring; however, current operations need an overhaul. The owners of Flavors, J. P. Field and Marla Lily, built the business

piece by piece over the past 12 years. The following offers a quick look at current operations.

- Flavors does not receive any information on how many of its customers attend live music events. Musicians typically maintain a fan email listing and CD sales records for the event; however, this information is not always provided to the store.
- Book club events are booked and run through the local book store, Pages Up. Pages Up runs a tab during the book club and provides Flavors with a check at the end of each month for all book club events. Flavors has no access to

book club customer information or sales information.

- The artist gallery is run by several local artists who pay Flavors a small commission on each sale. Flavors has no input into the art contained in the store or information on customers who purchase art.
- Coffee sampler events are run through Flavors' primary operations.
- Community event information is open to all members of the community. Each event is run by a separate organization, which provides monthly event feedback to Flavors in a variety of formats from Word to Access files.
- Brewing and machine resource courses are run by the equipment manufacturer, and all customer and sales information is provided to Flavors in a Word document at the end of each year.

You have been hired as an integration expert by Flavors. The owners want to revamp the way the company operates so it can take advantage of marketing and sales opportunities across its many different lines of business, such as offering customers who attend book club events discounts on art and brewing and machine resource courses. They also want to gain a better understanding of how the different events affect sales. For example, should they have more open microphone nights or more book clubs? Currently, they have no way to tell which events result in higher sales. Create an integration strategy so Flavors can take advantage of CRM, SCM, and ERP across the company.

the scope of a single individual or organization. These teams, partnerships, and alliances can be formed internally among a company's employees or externally with other organizations (see Figure 10.17).

Businesses of all sizes and in all markets have witnessed the benefits of leveraging their IT assets to create competitive advantage. Whereas information technology efforts in the past

areas of their business to extend their technical and operational resources. In the outsourcing process, they save time and boost productivity by not having to develop their own systems from scratch. They are then free to concentrate on innovation and their core business.

Information technology makes such business partnerships and alliances easier to establish and manage. An *information*

> To be successful—and avoid being eliminated by the competition—an organization must constantly undertake new initiatives, address both minor and major problems, and capitalize on significant opportunities.

were aimed at increasing operational efficiency, the advent and proliferation of network-based computing (the Internet being the most visible, but not only, example) has enabled organizations to build systems with which all sorts of communities can interact. The ultimate result will allow organizations to do business with customers, business partners, suppliers, governments and regulatory agencies, and any other community relevant to their particular operation or activity.

In the same way that organizations use internal teams, they are increasingly forming alliances and partnerships with other organizations. The *core competency* of an organization is its key strength, a business function that it does better than any of its competitors. Apple Computer is highly regarded for its strength in product design, while Accenture's core competency is the design and installation of information systems. A *core competency strategy* is one in which an organization chooses to focus specifically on what it does best (its core competency) and forms partnerships and alliances with other specialist organizations to handle nonstrategic business processes. Strategic alliances enable businesses to gain competitive advantages through access to a partner's resources, including markets, technologies, and people. Teaming up with another business adds complementary resources and capabilities, enabling participants to grow and expand more quickly and efficiently, especially fast-growing companies that rely heavily on outsourcing many

partnership occurs when two or more organizations cooperate by integrating their IT systems, thereby providing customers with the best of what each can offer. The advent of the Internet has greatly increased the opportunity for IT-enabled business partnerships and alliances. Amazon developed a profitable business segment by providing ebusiness outsourcing services to other retailers that use Amazon's website software. Some well-known retailers partnering with Amazon include Office Depot and Target.[23]

●● LO10.6

Identify the different ways in which companies collaborate using technology.

●● LO10.7

Compare the different categories of collaboration technologies.

| FIGURE 10.17 | Teams, Partnerships, and Alliances Within and External to an Organization |

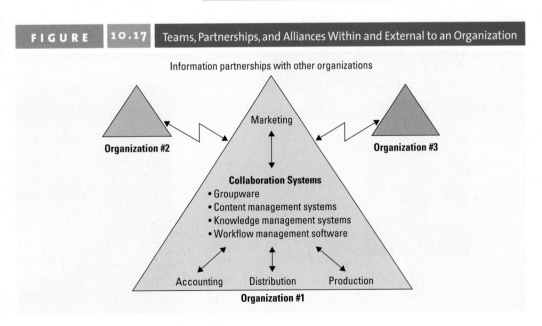

COLLABORATION SYSTEMS

Heineken USA has shortened its inventory cycle time for beer production and distribution from three months to four weeks. By using its collaborative system to forecast demand and expedite shipping, the company has dramatically cut inventory levels and shipping costs while increasing sales.

Over the past few years most business processes have changed on various dimensions (e.g., flexibility, interconnectivity, coordination style, autonomy) because of market conditions and organizational models. Frequently, information is located within physically separated systems as more and more organizations spread their reach globally. This creates a need for a software infrastructure that enables collaboration systems.

A *collaboration system* is an IT-based set of tools that supports the work of teams by facilitating the sharing and flow of information. Collaboration solves specific business tasks such as telecommuting, online meetings, deploying applications, and remote project and sales management (see Figure 10.18).

Collaboration systems allow people, teams, and organizations to leverage and build upon the ideas and talents of staff, suppliers, customers, and business partners. It involves a unique set of business challenges that:

- Include complex interactions between people who may be in different locations and desire to work across function and discipline areas.

- Require flexibility in work process and the ability to involve others quickly and easily.

- Call for creating and sharing information rapidly and effortlessly within a team.

Most organizations collaborate with other companies in some capacity. Consider the supplier-customer relationship, which can be thought of in terms of a continuous life cycle of engagement, transaction, fulfillment, and service activities. Rarely do companies excel in all four life cycle areas, either from a business process or from a technology-enabled aspect. Successful organizations identify and invest in their core competencies, and outsource or collaborate for those competencies that are not core to them. Collaboration systems fall into one of two categories:

1. *Unstructured collaboration* (sometimes referred to as *information collaboration*) includes document exchange, shared whiteboards, discussion forums, and email. These functions can improve personal productivity, reducing the time spent searching for information or chasing answers.

2. *Structured collaboration* (or *process collaboration*) involves shared participation in business processes, such as workflow, in which knowledge is hard-coded as rules. This is beneficial in terms of improving automation and the routing of information.

Regardless of location or format—be it unstructured or structured—relevant accurate information must be readily and

| FIGURE | 10.18 | Collaborative Business Areas |

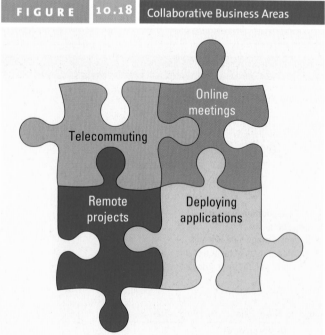

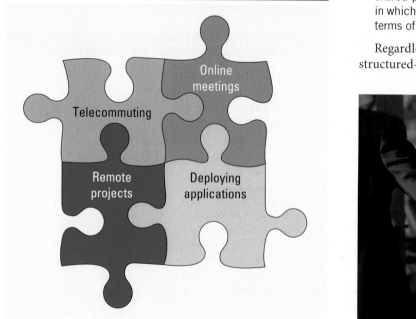

consistently available to those who need it anytime, anywhere, and on any device. The integration of IT systems enables an organization to provide employees, partners, customers, and suppliers with the ability to access, find, analyze, manage, and collaborate on content. The collaboration can be done across a wide variety of formats, languages, and platforms.

Lockheed Martin Aeronautics Company's ability to share complex project information across an extended supply chain in real time was key in its successful bid of a $19 billion Department of Defense (DoD) contract to build 21 supersonic stealth fighters. New government procurement rules require defense contractors to communicate effectively to ensure that deadlines are met, costs are controlled, and projects are managed throughout the life cycle of the contract.[24]

In anticipation of the contract, the Fort Worth, Texas, unit of Lockheed Martin developed a real-time collaboration system that can tie together its partners, suppliers, and DoD customers via the Internet. The platform lets participants collectively work on product design and engineering tasks as well as supply chain and life cycle management issues.

Lockheed will host all transactions and own the project information. The platform will let DoD and Lockheed project managers track the daily progress of the project in real time. This is the first major DoD project with such a requirement. The contract, awarded to the Lockheed unit and partners Northrop Grumman Corp. and BAE Systems, is the first installment in what could amount to a $200 billion program for 3,000 jet fighters over 40 years. The strengths of the collaboration process lie with the integration of many systems, namely:

- Knowledge management systems
- Content management systems
- Workflow management systems
- Groupware systems

 LO10.8

Define the fundamental concepts of a knowledge management system.

Social Not Working

There are a number of stories of new employees who spend so much time on social networking sites that they don't have time to perform their jobs, resulting in their termination. Here are a few tips on what you should *not* be doing with your social networking sites.

- Do not work on your personal social networking sites while at work.
- Be careful not to accidentally reply to multiple recipients on messages.
- Be sure to post a professional profile picture. Do not use shots of your children or your pets or your fraternity.
- Be careful to set up all of the security and privacy features in your profile.
- Do not ever address politics or religion.
- Never continually post something every 5 minutes or spam friends with messages. Every time you make a move on Facebook, other people know, and you don't want to become annoying.

Facebook, LinkedIn, Twitter, and MySpace seem to be everywhere, and it is not only new employees who are finding the sites difficult to use in a work environment. The question companies are asking is how to tap the social networking trend as a business opportunity, rather than simply a way to connect. Face-to-face networking enables employees to share ideas, information, and resources, but can social networking achieve the same goals? Sites such as LinkedIn are helpful in connecting with people you want to meet for professional purposes, and Twitter and Facebook can be helpful when trying to notify a group of people about a product promotion or event, but how can a business integrate social networking into its core processes and add real value to the bottom line?

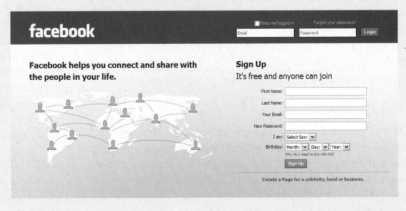

KNOWLEDGE MANAGEMENT SYSTEMS

Knowledge management (KM) involves capturing, classifying, evaluating, retrieving, and sharing information assets in a way that provides context for effective decisions and actions. It is best to think of KM in the broadest context. Succinctly put, KM is the process through which organizations generate value

entered into outsourcing agreements must address the thorny issue of transferring the knowledge of their full-time staff members, who are losing their jobs because of an outsourcing deal, to the outsourcer's employees.

Knowledge can be a real competitive advantage for an organization. Information technology can distribute an organization's knowledge base by interconnecting people and digitally gathering their expertise. The primary objective of knowledge management is to be sure that a company's knowledge of facts,

> "Knowledge management (KM) involves capturing, classifying, evaluating, retrieving, and sharing information assets in a way that provides context for effective decisions and actions."

from their intellectual and knowledge-based assets. Most often, generating value from such assets involves codifying what employees, partners, and customers know, and sharing that information among employees, departments, and even with other companies to devise best practices. It is important to note that the definition says nothing about technology; while KM is often facilitated by IT, technology by itself is not KM.

Think of a golf caddie as a simplified example of a knowledge worker. Good caddies do more than carry clubs and track down wayward balls. When asked, a good caddie will give advice to golfers, such as, "The wind makes the ninth hole play 15 yards longer." Accurate advice may lead to a bigger tip at the end of the day. The golfer, having derived a benefit from the caddie's advice, may be more likely to play that course again. If a good caddie is willing to share what he knows with other caddies, then they all may eventually earn bigger tips. How would KM work to make this happen? The caddie master may decide to reward caddies for sharing their knowledge by offering them credits for pro shop merchandise. Once the best advice is collected, the course manager would publish the information in notebooks (or make it available on PDAs) and distribute them to all the caddies. The end result of a well-designed KM program is that everyone wins. In this case, caddies get bigger tips and deals on merchandise, golfers play better because they benefit from the collective experience of caddies, and the course owners win because better scores lead to repeat business.

KM in Business

KM has assumed greater urgency in American business over the past few years as millions of baby boomers prepare to retire. When they punch out for the last time, the knowledge they gleaned about their jobs, companies, and industries during their long careers will walk out with them—unless companies take measures to retain their insights. In addition, CIOs who have

sources of information, and solutions are readily available to all employees whenever it is needed.

Such knowledge management requires that organizations go well beyond providing information contained in spreadsheets, databases, and documents. It must include expert information that typically resides in people's heads. A *knowledge management system (KMS)* supports the capturing, organization, and dissemination of knowledge (i.e., know-how) throughout an organization. It is up to the organization to determine what information qualifies as knowledge.

Explicit and Tacit Knowledge

Not all information is valuable. Individual companies must determine what information qualifies as intellectual and knowledge-based assets. In general, intellectual and knowledge-based assets fall into one of two categories: explicit or tacit. As a rule, *explicit knowledge* consists of anything that can be documented, archived, and codified, often with the help of IT. Examples of explicit knowledge are assets such as patents, trademarks, business plans, marketing research, and customer lists.

Tacit knowledge is the knowledge contained in people's heads. The challenge inherent in tacit knowledge is figuring out how to recognize, generate, share, and manage knowledge that resides in people's heads. While information technology in the form of email, instant messaging, and related technologies can help facilitate the dissemination of tacit knowledge, identifying it in the first place can be a major obstacle. Shadowing and joint problem solving are two best practices for transferring or re-creating tacit knowledge inside an organization.

Shadowing
With *shadowing*, less experienced staff observe more experienced staff to learn how their more experienced counterparts approach their work. Dorothy Leonard and Walter Swap, two knowledge management experts, stress the

importance of having the protégé discuss his or her observations with the expert to deepen the dialog and crystallize the knowledge transfer.

Joint Problem Solving

Another sound approach is *joint problem solving* by expert and novice. Because people are often unaware of how they approach problems or do their work and therefore cannot automatically generate step-by-step instructions for doing whatever they do, having a novice and expert work together on a project will bring the expert's approach to light. The difference between shadowing and joint problem solving is that shadowing is more passive. With joint problem solving, the expert and the novice work hand in hand on a task.[25]

Information is of little use unless it is analyzed and made available to the right people, at the right place, and at the right time. To get the most value from intellectual assets, knowledge must be shared. An effective KMS system should help do one or more of the following:

- Foster innovation by encouraging the free flow of ideas.
- Improve customer service by streamlining response time.
- Boost revenues by getting products and services to market faster.
- Enhance employee retention rates by recognizing the value of employees' knowledge.
- Streamline operations and reduce costs by eliminating redundant or unnecessary processes.

A creative approach to knowledge management can result in improved efficiency, higher productivity, and increased revenues in practically any business function. Figure 10.19 indicates the reasons organizations launch KMS.

Software is helping ChevronTexaco Corporation improve how it manages the assets in oil fields by enabling employees in multiple disciplines to easily access and share the information they need to make decisions. ChevronTexaco teams of 10 to 30 people are responsible for managing the assets, such as the drilling equipment, pipelines, and facilities, for a particular oil field. Within each team, earth scientists and various engineers with expertise in production, reservoir, and facilities work together to keep the oil field up and running. Each member of the asset team needs to communicate with other members to make decisions based on the collection and analysis of huge amounts of information from various departments. Individual team members can look at information from the perspective of their own department.

This has helped ChevronTexaco achieve a 30 percent productivity gain, a 50 percent improvement in safety performance, and more than $2 billion in operating cost reductions. Through KMSs, ChevronTexaco has restructured its gasoline retailing business and now drills oil and gas wells faster and cheaper.[26]

Not every organization matches ChevronTexaco's success with KM. Numerous KM projects have failed over the past few years, generating an unwillingness to undertake—or even

FIGURE 10.19 Key Reasons Organizations Launch Knowledge Management Systems

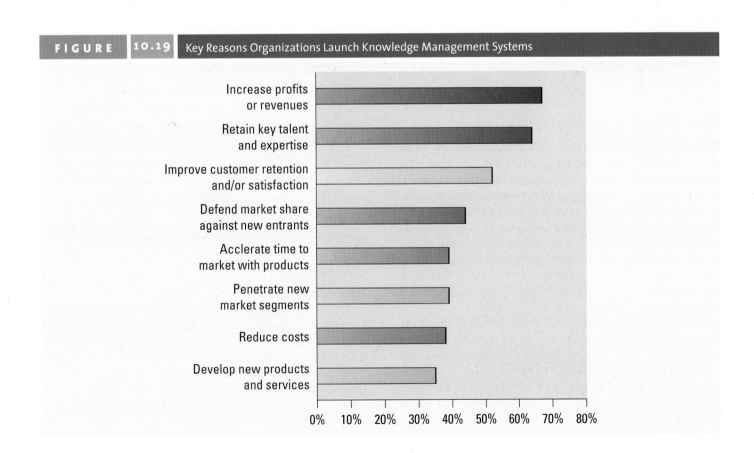

address—KM issues among many organizations. However, KM is an effective tool if it is tied directly to discrete business needs and opportunities. Beginning with targeted projects that deliver value quickly, companies can achieve the success that has proved elusive with many big-bang approaches. Successful KM projects typically focus on creating value in a specific process area, or even just for a certain type of transaction. Companies should start with one job at a time—preferably the most knowledge-oriented one—and build KM into a job function in a way that actually helps employees do their work better and faster, then expand to the next most knowledge-intensive job, and so on. Celebrating even small success with KM will help build a base of credibility and support for future KM projects.

KM Technologies

KM is not a purely technology-based concept. Organizations that implement a centralized database system, electronic message board, web portal, or any other collaborative tool in the hope that they have established a KMS are wasting both their time and money.

Although tools don't make a KMS, such a system does need tools, from standard, off-the-shelf email packages to sophisticated collaboration tools designed specifically to support community building and identity. Generally, KMS tools fall into one or more of the following categories:

- Knowledge repositories (databases).
- Expertise tools.
- Elearning applications.
- Discussion and chat technologies.
- Search and data mining tools.

KM and Social Networking

Companies that have been frustrated by traditional KM efforts are increasingly looking for ways to find out how knowledge flows through their organization, and social networking analysis can show them just that. *Social networking analysis (SNA)* is a process of mapping a group's contacts (whether personal or professional) to identify who knows whom and who works with whom. In enterprises, it provides a clear picture of how far-flung employees and divisions work together and can help identify key experts in the organization who possess the knowledge needed to, say, solve a complicated programming problem or launch a new product.

M&M maker Mars used SNA to identify how knowledge flows through its organizations, who holds influence, who gives the best advice, and how employees share information. The Canadian government's central IT unit used SNA to establish which skills it needed to retain and develop, and to determine who, among the 40 percent of the workforce that was due to

retire within five years, had the most important knowledge and experience to begin transferring to others.[27]

SNA is not a replacement for traditional KM tools such as knowledge databases or portals, but it can provide companies with a starting point for how best to proceed with KM initiatives. As a component to a larger KM strategy, SNA can help companies identify key leaders and then set up a mechanism, such as communities of practice, so that those leaders can pass on their knowledge to colleagues. To identify experts in their

FIGURE **10.20** Common Types of Content Management Systems

Common Types of Content Management Systems	
Document management system (DMS)	DMS—Supports the electronic capturing, storage, distribution, archiving, and accessing of documents. A DMS optimizes the use of documents within an organization independent of any publishing medium (for example, the web). A DMS provides a document repository with information about other information. The system tracks the editorial history of each document and its relationships with other documents. A variety of search and navigation methods are available to make document retrieval easy. A DMS manages highly structured and regulated content, such as pharmaceutical documentation.
Digital asset management system (DAM)	DAM—Though similar to document management, DAM generally works with binary rather than text files, such as multimedia file types. DAM places emphasis on allowing file manipulation and conversion, for example, converting GIF files to JPEG.
Web content management system (WCM)	WCM—Adds an additional layer to document and digital asset management that enables publishing content both to intranets and to public websites. In addition to maintaining the content itself, WCM systems often integrate content with online processes like ebusiness systems.

organizations, companies can use software programs that track email and other kinds of electronic communication.[28]

 **LO10.9**

Provide an example of a content management system along with its business purpose.

CONTENT MANAGEMENT SYSTEMS

A *content management system* provides tools to manage the creation, storage, editing, and publication of information in a collaborative environment. As a website grows in size and complexity, the business must establish procedures to ensure that things run

and web content management. Figure 10.20 highlights the three primary types of content management systems. Figure 10.21 lists the major content management system vendors.

Content management software is helping BMW Group Switzerland accelerate personalized, real-time information about products, services, prices, and events to its dealers countrywide. BMW uses a process that allows dealers to specify what information is seen by which employee, as well as to deliver marketing materials solely to members of the sales department, and technical specifications and support documents only to mechanics. That enhanced personalization eliminates the chance that information is sent to the wrong dealership or to the wrong individual, which provides higher quality customer service. The content management software also enables nontechnical employees to create pages using predefined layout templates, simplifying the web publishing

> "The content management system marketplace is complex, incorporating document management, digital asset management, and web content management."

smoothly. At a certain point, it makes sense to automate this process and use a content management system to manage this effectively. The content management system marketplace is complex, incorporating document management, digital asset management,

process. More than 500 people use the solution daily, and all employees are able to publish information without calling on IT specialists, while maintaining the look and feel of the BMW brand.[29]

FIGURE **10.21** Major Content Management Systems Vendors

Vendors	Strengths	Weaknesses	Costs
Documentum www.emc.com	Document and digital asset management	Personalization features not as strong as competitors	Major components start at less than $100,000
FatWire www.fatwire.com	Web content management	May not scale to support thousands of users	SPARK, $25,000; Update Engine, $70,000 and up
InterWoven www.interwoven.com	Collaboration, enterprise content management	Requires significant customization	InterWoven 5 Platform, $50,000; average cost for a new customer, $250,000
Percussion www.percussion.com	Web content management	May not scale to support thousands of users	Rhythmyx Content Manager, about $150,000
Stellent www.stellent.com	Document conversion to web-ready formats	Engineering for very large implementations with thousands of users	Content and Collaboration Servers, $50,000 to $250,000 each
Vignette www.vignette.com	Personalization	Document management and library services are not as robust as others	V6 Multisite Content Manager, $200,000 and up; V6 Content Suite, $450,000 and up

Working Wikis

Wikis are web-based tools that make it easy for users to add, remove, and change online content. **Business wikis** are collaborative web pages that allow users to edit documents, share ideas, or monitor the status of a project. Most people are familiar with Wikipedia, one of the largest online collaboration websites. Employees also use wikis to collaborate; for example, companies such as Intel, Motorola, IBM, and Sony use them for a host of tasks, from setting internal meeting agendas to posting documents related to new products. Many companies rely on wikis to engage customers in ongoing discussions about products. Wikis for Motorola and T-Mobile handsets serve as continually updated user guides. TV networks including ABC and CBS are creating fan wikis that let viewers interact with each other as they unravel mysteries from such shows as *Lost* and *CSI: Crime Scene Investigation*.[30]

A handful of tech-savvy employees at two very different European companies began dabbling in the use of wikis and witnessed a rapid spread of wikis at both companies—Finnish handset-maker Nokia and London- and Frankfurt-based investment bank Dresdner Kleinwort. Nokia estimates at least 20 percent of its 68,000 employees use wiki pages to update schedules and project status, trade ideas, edit files, and so on. "It's a reversal of the normal way things are done," says Stephen Johnston, senior manager for corporate strategy at Nokia, who helped pioneer the technology. Where Nokia once bought outside software to help foster collaboration, now "some of the most interesting stuff is emerging from within the company itself," says Johnston.

It is a similar tale at Dresdner Kleinwort. A few pioneers in the IT department at its London office sent a program called Socialtext to several groups to see how it might be used to facilitate different IT tasks. The wiki program spread so quickly that Dresdner Kleinwort decided to launch its own corporate wiki. By October 2006, the bank's 5,000 employees had created more than 6,000 individual pages and logged about 100,000 hits on the company's official wiki.

The experience of Nokia and Dresdner Kleinwort offer insight into how to nurture the use of a radically new technology to change the way organizations work. Clearly, not everyone recognizes the value of wikis right away. The initial efforts at Dresdner, for example, confused employees and had to be refined to make the technology easier to use. More important than tweaking the technology was a simple edict from one of the proponents: Do not send emails, use the wiki. Gradually, employees embraced the use of the wiki, seeing how it increased collaboration and reduced time-consuming email traffic.[31]

●● LO10.10

Evaluate the advantages of using a workflow management system.

WORKFLOW MANAGEMENT SYSTEMS

A *workflow* defines all the steps or business rules, from beginning to end, required for a business process. Therefore, *workflow management systems* facilitate the automation and management of business processes and control the movement of work through the business process. Work activities can be performed in series or in parallel and involve people and automated computer systems. In addition, many workflow management systems allow the opportunity to measure and analyze the execution of the process because workflow systems allow the flow of work between individuals and/or departments to be defined and tracked. Workflow software helps automate a range of business tasks and electronically route the right information to the right people at the right time. Users are notified of pending work, and managers can observe status and route approvals through the system quickly.

There are two primary types of workflow systems: messaging-based and database-based. *Messaging-based workflow systems* send work assignments through an email system. The workflow system automatically tracks the order for the work to be assigned and, each time a step is completed, the system automatically sends the work to the next individual in line. For example, each time a team member completes a piece of the project, the system would automatically send the document to the next team member.

Database-based workflow systems store documents in a central location and automatically ask the team members to access the document when it is their turn to edit the document. Project documentation is stored in a central location and team members are notified by the system when it is their turn to log in and work on their portion of the project.

Either type of workflow system helps to present information in a unified format, improves teamwork by providing automated process support, and allows team members to communicate and collaborate within a unified environment.

New York City was experiencing a record number of claims, ranging from injuries resulting from slips on sidewalks to medical malpractice at city hospitals. The city processes over 30,000 claims and incurs $250 million in claim costs annually.

omg lol

Twitter 101: Guide to Getting Fired

You can waste hours on Facebook trying to get fired, but that is not the most effective or efficient way these days because you can easily humiliate yourself out of job in 140 characters or less on Twitter. One infamous example was a post by "theconnor," who was offered a job by Cisco and decided that it was a great idea to Tweet the following:

> "Cisco just offered me a job! Now I have to weigh the utility of a fatty paycheck against the daily commute to San Jose and hating the work."

Almost immediately, Tim Levad, a "channel partner advocate" for Cisco Alert, shared this open response:

> "Who is the hiring manager. I'm sure they would love to know that you will hate the work. We here at Cisco are versed in the web."

"theconnor" instantly set his Twitter account to private and deleted all information from a home page, but it was too late, and the true identity of "theconnor" was revealed on cicsofatty.com by the end of the day. "Theconnor" was lampooned in a popular YouTube *meme* and, thanks to Google Cache, the deleted content of "theconnor's" homepage resurfaced on ciscofatty.com, a website erected to commemorate this cautionary tale.

What all students need to know: Never post anything you would not say to your mom, boss, or significant other anywhere on the Internet. And the part that you need to pay particular attention to: Twitter never forgets. *Never!* You can try to delete it, but it gets indexed by Google, re-Tweeted by others, and lives on–*forever.*

Claims are generally filed with the Comptroller's Office, which investigates them and offers to settle meritorious claims. The New York City Comptroller's Office, with the assistance of its consultants Xerox and Universal Systems Inc., utilized a workflow management system to enhance revenues and decrease operating costs. With the implementation of the Omnibus Automated Image Storage Information System (OAISIS) for processing contracts and claims, New York City will save over $20 million.

Numerous city organizations were involved in the workflow management system, including Bureau of Law and Adjustment, Office of Contracts/Administration, Management and Accounting Systems, and Bureau of Information Systems.

In supporting all these New York City organizations, the system performs many functions that were previously labor-intensive and detracted from the quality and efficiency of

investigation. Management can also see the entire claim process graphically and determine bottlenecks. Deployment of additional resources to needed areas occurs without a management analysis of a particular process problem.

●● LO10.11

Explain how groupware can benefit a business.

GROUPWARE SYSTEMS

Groupware is software that supports team interaction and dynamics including calendaring, scheduling, and video-conferencing. Organizations can use this technology to communicate, cooperate, coordinate, solve problems, compete, or negotiate. While traditional technologies like the

> "The groupware concept integrates various systems and functionalities into a common set of services or a single (client) application."

investigations. The workflow management system screens claims to determine accordance with statutory requirements. Acknowledgment letters are generated automatically, with little or no resource allocation involved in assignment of claims or routing of claims to specific work locations. Status letters are automatically generated by the system for certain claim types, thus allowing the Comptroller's Office to keep claimants informed two months, five months, and one year from the date of their filing. All this is done automatically by the workflow management system.

Workflow management systems allow management to schedule individual systematic claim reviews without disrupting the

telephone qualify as groupware, the term refers to a specific class of technologies relying on modern computer networks, such as email, newsgroups, videophones, and chat rooms. Groupware systems fall along two primary categories (see Figure 10.22):

1. Users of the groupware are working together at the same time (real-time or synchronous groupware) or different times (asynchronous groupware).

2. Users are working together in the same place (co-located or face-to-face) or in different places (non-co-located or distance).

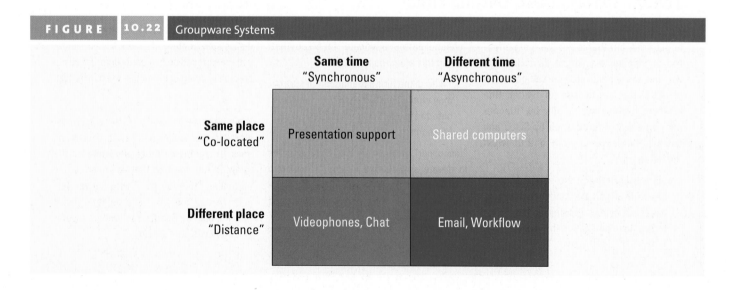

| FIGURE | 10.22 | Groupware Systems |

	Same time "Synchronous"	Different time "Asynchronous"
Same place "Co-located"	Presentation support	Shared computers
Different place "Distance"	Videophones, Chat	Email, Workflow

FIGURE 10.23 Groupware Advantages

Groupware System Advantages

Facilitating communication (faster, easier, clearer, more persuasive)

Enabling telecommuting

Reducing travel costs

Sharing expertise

Forming groups with common interests where it would not be possible to gather a sufficient number of people face-to-face

Saving time and cost in coordinating group work

Facilitating group problem solving

The groupware concept integrates various systems and functionalities into a common set of services or a single (client) application. In addition, groupware can represent a wide range of systems and methods of integration. Figure 10.23 displays the advantages groupware systems offer an organization over single-user systems.

Lotus Notes is one of the world's leading software solutions for collaboration that combines messaging, groupware, and the Internet. The structure of Notes allows it to track, route, and manage documents. Systems that lend themselves to Notes involve tracking, routing, approval, document management, and organization.

Toyota developed an intranet system to promote information sharing within the company and to raise productivity. Unfortunately, the company's conventional email system became overloaded, generating problems. Users did not receive incoming messages and were not able to send messages. Individual departments had introduced their own email systems, which were not always compatible. Messages to other mail systems, including those outside the company, experienced delays. To deal with these difficulties, Toyota's information systems department reviewed the email system and restructured it so that email, now recognized as an important communication tool, is utilized more effectively in business transactions.[32]

Videoconferencing

A *videoconference* is a set of interactive telecommunication technologies that allow two or more locations to interact via two-way video and audio transmissions simultaneously. It has also been called visual collaboration and is a type of groupware. Videoconferencing uses telecommunications of audio and video to bring people at different sites together for a meeting. This can be as simple as a conversation between two people in private offices (point-to-point) or involve several sites (multipoint) with more than one person in large rooms at different sites. Besides the audio and visual transmission of people, videoconferencing can be used to share documents, computer-displayed information, and whiteboards.[33]

FIGURE 10.24 Videoconferencing

Simple analog videoconferences could be established as early as the invention of the television. Such videoconferencing systems consisted of two closed-circuit television systems connected via cable. During the first manned space flights, NASA used two radio frequency (UHF or VHF) links, one in each direction. TV channels routinely use this kind of videoconferencing when reporting from distant locations, for instance. Then mobile links to satellites using special trucks became rather common (see Figure 10.24 for an example of videoconferencing).

Videoconferencing is now being introduced to online networking websites to help businesses form profitable relationships quickly and efficiently without leaving their place of work. Several factors support business use of videoconferencing, including:[34]

- Over 60 percent of face-to-face communication is nonverbal. Therefore, an enriched communications tool such as videoconferencing can promote an individual's or a team's identity, context, and emotional situation.

- Fifty-six percent of business professionals waste an estimated 30 minutes a day using inefficient communication methods, costing businesses an estimated $297 billion annually.

- The latest technology is available with reliable and easy-to-use conferencing, fostering collaboration at meetings.

- Enterprises that fail to use modern communications technologies run the very real risk of falling behind their competition.[35]

Web Conferencing

Web conferencing blends audio, video, and document-sharing technologies to create virtual meeting rooms where people "gather" at a password-protected website. There, they can chat in conference calls or use real-time text messages. They can mark up a shared document as if it were a blackboard, and even watch live software demos or video clips.

Perhaps the biggest surprise about web conferencing is its simplicity. Users only need to set up an account and download a few small software files. The best part about a web conference is that attendees do not have to have the same hardware or software. Every participant can see what is on anyone else's screen, regardless of the application being used (see Figure 10.25 for an example of web conferencing).[36]

Even with its video features, web conferencing is not quite like being there—or like being in a sophisticated (and pricey) videoconferencing facility. Still, professionals can accomplish more sitting at their desks than in an airport waiting to make travel connections. A growing number of companies are offering web conferencing. Leaders in this industry include WebEx, SameTime 2, and Elluminate Live.

Instant Messaging

Email is by far the dominant collaboration application, but real-time collaboration tools like instant messaging are creating a new communication dynamic within organizations. **Instant messaging** (sometimes called **IM** or **IMing**) is a type of communications service that enables someone to create a kind of private chat room with another individual in order to communicate in real-time over the Internet. In 1992, AOL deployed IM to the consumer market, allowing users to communicate with other IMers through a buddy list. Most of the popular instant messaging programs provide a variety of features, such as:

- Web links: Share links to favorite websites.
- Images: Look at an image stored on someone else's computer.
- Sounds: Play sounds.

FIGURE 10.25 Web Conferencing

- Files: Share files by sending them directly to another IMer.
- Talk: Use the Internet instead of a phone to talk.
- Streaming content: Receive real-time or near-real-time stock quotes and news.
- Instant messages: Receive immediate text messages.

Commercial vendors such as AOL and Microsoft offer free instant messaging tools. Real-time collaboration, such as instant messaging, live web conferencing, and screen or document sharing, creates an environment for decision making. AOL, Microsoft's MSN, and Yahoo! have begun to sell enterprise versions

BUSTED Steve Jobs Resurrected from the Afterlife

It's a pretty common, if not a little morbid, practice for news organizations to prepare obituaries well in advance of a celebrity's actual death to save time when the real event occurs. That's particularly the case with mammoth opuses like Steve Jobs's 17-page obituary (almost approaching the length of a biographic novel), which was accidently published on Bloomberg's financial website. The error occurred despite the news story bearing markers saying "Hold for Release" and "Do Not Use."

In addition to publishing the obituary, Bloomberg also accidentally published the list of people its reporters should contact when Steve Jobs does die. That list includes Microsoft founder Bill Gates, former Vice President Al Gore (a member of Apple's board of directors), and Google CEO Eric Schmidt. Bloomberg caught the mistake and pulled the obituary within minutes, but in today's instant information culture, the damage was already done. Now Jobs's obituary is all over the web, and, if he so desires, he has the unique opportunity to read his own obituary.

While Jobs is very much alive, a few stockholders may have gone into cardiac arrest after reading the obituary. What kind of financial impact could a story like this have on Apple? With so many different forms of collaboration, how does a company possibly monitor and track each one to ensure the content is error-free? Once erroneous content is posted to the Internet or written in a text message, what can a company do to rectify the situation?

FIGURE 10.26 Instant Messaging Application

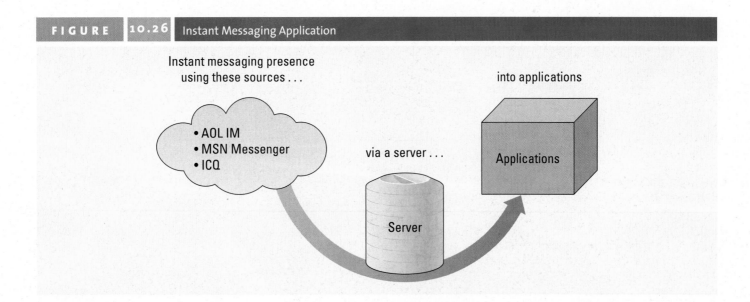

Instant messaging presence using these sources...

- AOL IM
- MSN Messenger
- ICQ

via a server...

Server

into applications

Applications

of their instant messaging services that match the capabilities of business-oriented products like IBM's Lotus Sametime. Figure 10.26 demonstrates the IM application presence within IT systems.

IBM Lotus software has released new versions of its real-time collaboration platform, IBM Lotus Instant Messaging and IBM Lotus Web Conferencing, plus its mobile counterpart, IBM Lotus Instant Messaging Everyplace. These built-for-business products let an organization offer presence awareness, secure instant messaging, and web conferencing. The products give employees instant access to colleagues and company information regardless of time, place, or device.

The bigger issue in collaboration for organizations is cultural. Collaboration brings teams of people together from different regions, departments, and even companies—people who bring different skills, perceptions, and capabilities. A formal collaboration strategy helps create the right environment as well as the right systems for team members. ■

CHECK OUT www.mhhe.com/baltzanm

for additional study materials including quizzes
and PowerPoint presentations.

coming up

This module describes the various ways information systems can be built to support 21st century global businesses, the challenges that come along with the process, and the beauty of how well things turn out if systems are built according to good design principles, sound management practices, and flexibility to support ever-changing business needs. This task not only requires extensive planning, but also incredible people skills to make it all happen. This is far easier said than done! Too often, information systems development projects are criticized for going over budget, being delayed, or lacking in desired functionality.

If a career in global business has crossed your mind, exploring global business and the impacts of competing in a global world is crucial. The United States is a market of about 290 million people, but there are over 6 billion potential customers in the 193 countries that make up the global market. Perhaps more interesting is that approximately 75 percent of the world's population lives in developing areas where technology, education, and per capita income still lag considerably behind those of developed (or industrialized) nations such as the United States.

You, the business student, should be familiarized with the potential of global business, including its many benefits and challenges. The demand for students with training in global business is almost certain to grow as the number of businesses competing in global markets increases.

This module comprises two chapters. Chapter 11 provides an overview of how enterprise applications are developed using the traditional systems development life cycle. Chapter 12 dives into innovation and entrepreneurship along with how to compete in the 21st century where globalization is key. ■

DEVELOPING INFORMATION SYSTEMS

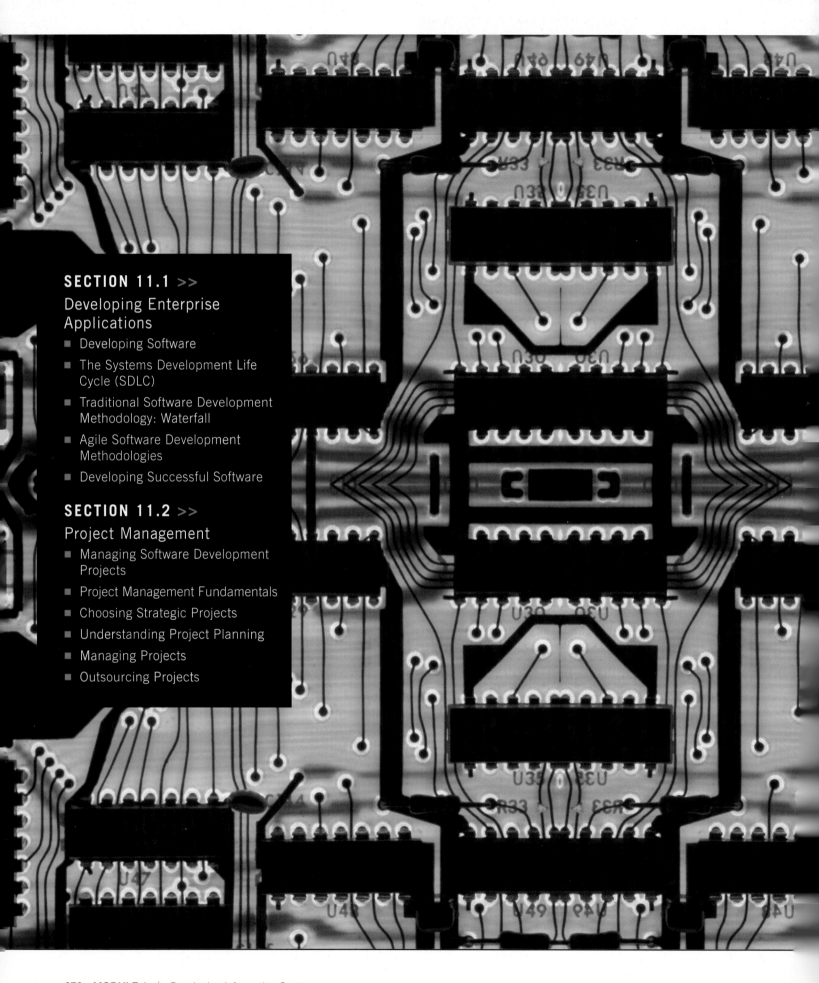

systems
development
+ project
management

eleven

This chapter provides an overview of how organizations build information systems. You as a business student, need to know this because information systems are the underlying foundation of how companies operate. A basic understanding of the principles of building information systems will make you a more valuable employee. You will be able to identify trouble spots early and make suggestions during the design process that will result in a better delivered information systems project—one that satisfies both you and your business.

Building an information system is analogous to constructing a house. You could sit back and let the developers do all the design work, construction, and testing with hopes that the house will satisfy your needs.

However, participating in the house building process helps to guarantee that your needs are not only being heard, but also being met. It is good business practice to have direct user input steering the development of the finished product.

The same is true for building information systems. Your knowledge of the systems development process will allow you to participate and ensur you are building flexible enterpris architectures that not only suppo current business needs, but also future business needs.

Every type of organization in business today, from farming to pharmaceutical to franchising, is affected by technology and the software developed to operate, improve, or innovate it. Companies are impacted by software solutions that enable them to improve their cost structure, manage people better, and develop and deliver new products to market. These organizational improvements help companies sustain their competitive advantage and position in the marketplace. They can solve complex problems, dislodge competitors, or create exciting opportunities to pursue. Organizations must learn and mature in their ability to identify, build, and implement systems to remain competitive.

Essentially, software built correctly can support nimble organizations and can transform as the organization and its business transforms. Software that effectively meets employee needs will help an organization become more productive and enhance decision making. Software that does not meet employee needs might have a damaging effect on productivity and can even cause a business to fail. Employee involvement along with using the right implementation methodology when developing software is critical to the success of an organization.

i2 Technologies' demand and supply planning module created serious inventory problems. The i2 deployment, part of a multimillion-dollar ebusiness upgrade, caused Nike CEO Philip Knight to famously say, "This is what we get for our $400 million?" The SCM vendor saw its stock plummet with the Nike disaster, along with its reputation. Katrina Roche, i2's chief marketing officer, asserted that Nike failed to use the vendor's implementation methodology and templates, which contributed to the problem.[1]

Software development problems often lead to high-profile disasters. Hershey's glitch in its ERP implementation made the front page of *The Wall Street Journal* and cost the company millions. Hershey said computer problems with its SAP software system created a backlog of orders, causing slower deliveries, and resulting in lower earnings. Statistics released in 2006 by the National Research Council show that U.S. companies spent $250 billion in 2005 to repair damage caused by software defects.[2]

If software does not work, the organization will not work. Traditional business risk models typically ignored software development, largely because most organizations considered the impact from software and software development on the business to be minor. In the digital age, however, software success, or failure, can lead directly to business success, or failure. Almost every large organization in the world relies on software, either to drive its business operations or to make its products work. As organizations' reliance on software grows, so do the business-related consequences of software successes and failures as displayed in Figure 11.1.[3]

The lucrative advantages of successful software implementations provide significant incentives to manage software development risks. However, according to the Chaos report from the Standish Group, a Massachusetts-based consultancy, more than half the software development projects undertaken in the United States come in late or over budget and the majority of successful projects maintain fewer features and functions than originally specified. Organizations also cancel around 33 percent of these projects during development. Understanding the basics of software development, or the systems development life cycle, will help organizations avoid potential software development pitfalls and ensure that software development efforts are successful.[4]

●● SECTION 11.1 Developing Enterprise Applications

LEARNING OUTCOMES

LO11.1 Identify the business benefits associated with successful software development.

LO11.2 Describe the seven phases of the systems development life cycle.

LO11.3 Summarize the different software development methodologies.

LO11.4 Define the relationship between the systems development life cycle and software development.

LO11.5 Compare the waterfall methodology and the agile methodology.

●● LO11.1

Identify the business benefits associated with successful software development.

DEVELOPING SOFTWARE

Nike's SCM system failure, which spun out of control to the tune of $400 million, is legendary. Nike blamed the system failure on its SCM vendor, i2 Technologies. Nike states that

●● LO11.2

Describe the seven phases of the systems development life cycle.

●● LO11.4

Define the relationship between the systems development life cycle and software development.

Business-Related Consequences of Software Success and Failure

Increase or decrease revenues—Organizations have the ability to directly increase profits by implementing successful IT systems. Organizations can also lose millions when software fails or key information is stolen or compromised.

Nike's poorly designed supply chain management software delayed orders, increased excess inventories, and caused earnings to fall 24 percent below expectations.

Repair or damage to brand reputation—Technologies such as CRM can directly enhance a company's brand reputation. Software can also severely damage a company's reputation if it fails to work as advertised or has security vulnerabilities that affect its customers' trust.

H&R Block customers were furious when the company accidentally placed its customers' passwords and Social Security numbers on its website.

Prevent or incur liabilities—Technology such as CAT scans, MRIs, and mammograms can save lives. Faulty technology used in airplanes, automobiles, pacemakers, or nuclear reactors can cause massive damage, injury, or death.

The parent company of bankrupt pharmaceutical distributor FoxMeyer sued SAP for $500 million over ERP software failure that allegedly crippled its operations.

Increase or decrease productivity—CRM and SCM software can directly increase a company's productivity. Large losses in productivity can also occur when software malfunctions or crashes.

The Standish Group estimates that defective software code accounted for 45 percent of computer-system downtime and cost U.S. companies $100 billion in lost productivity in 2003 alone.

THE SYSTEMS DEVELOPMENT LIFE CYCLE (SDLC)

The *systems development life cycle (SDLC)* is the overall process for developing information systems from planning and analysis through implementation and maintenance. The SDLC is the foundation for all systems development methodologies, and literally hundreds of different activities are associated with each phase in the SDLC. Typical activities include determining budgets, gathering system requirements, and writing detailed user documentation. The activities performed during each systems development project will vary.

The SDLC begins with a business need, followed by an assessment of the functions a system must have to satisfy the need, and ends when the benefits of the system no longer outweigh its maintenance costs. This is why it is referred to as a life cycle. The SDLC is comprised of seven distinct phases: planning, analysis, design, development, testing, implementation, and maintenance (see Figure 11.2).

1. **Planning:** The *planning phase* involves establishing a high-level plan of the intended project and determining project goals. Planning is the first and most critical phase of any systems development effort an organization undertakes, regardless of whether the effort is to develop a system that allows customers to order products over the Internet, determine the best logistical structure for warehouses around the world, or develop a strategic information alliance with another organization. Organizations must carefully plan the activities (and determine why they are necessary) to be successful.

2. **Analysis:** The *analysis phase* involves analyzing end-user business requirements and refining project goals into defined functions and operations of the intended system. *Business requirements* are the detailed set of business requests that the system must meet in order to be successful. The analysis phase is obviously critical. A good start is essential and the organization must spend as much time, energy, and resources as necessary to perform a detailed, accurate analysis.

3. **Design:** The *design phase* involves describing the desired features and operations of the system including screen layouts, business rules, process diagrams, pseudo code, and other documentation.

4. **Development:** The *development phase* involves taking all of the detailed design documents from the design phase and transforming them into the actual system. In this phase the project transitions from preliminary designs to the actual physical implementation.

FIGURE 11.2 The Systems Development Life Cycle

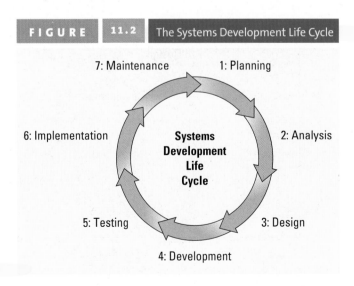

7: Maintenance   1: Planning
6: Implementation   **Systems Development Life Cycle**   2: Analysis
5: Testing   3: Design
4: Development

supporting the new system with frequent minor changes (for example, new reports or information capturing), and reviewing the system to be sure it is moving the organization toward its strategic goals.

●● LO11.3
Summarize the different software development methodologies.

●● LO11.5
Compare the waterfall methodology and the agile methodology.

TRADITIONAL SOFTWARE DEVELOPMENT METHODOLOGY: WATERFALL

Today, systems are so large and complex that teams of architects, analysts, developers, testers, and users must work together to create the millions of lines of custom-written code that drive enterprises. For this reason, developers have created a number of different systems development life cycle methodologies. A *methodology* is a set of policies, procedures, standards, processes, practices, tools, techniques, and tasks that people apply to technical and management challenges. It is used to manage the deployment of technology with work plans, requirements documents, and test plans. It is also used to deploy technology. A formal methodology could include coding standards, code libraries, development practices, and much more.

5. **Testing:** The *testing phase* involves bringing all the project pieces together into a special testing environment to test for errors, bugs, and interoperability and verify that the system meets all of the business requirements defined in the analysis phase.

6. **Implementation:** The *implementation phase* involves placing the system into production so users can begin to perform actual business operations with the system.

7. **Maintenance:** Maintaining the system is the final sequential phase of any systems development effort. The *maintenance phase* involves performing changes, corrections, additions, and upgrades to ensure the system continues to meet the business goals. This phase continues for the life of the system because the system must change as the business evolves and its needs change, demanding constant monitoring,

Waterfall Methodology

The oldest of these, and the best known, is the waterfall methodology: a sequence of phases in which the output of each phase becomes the input for the next (see Figure 11.3). The traditional *waterfall methodology* is an activity-based process in which each phase in the SDLC is performed sequentially from planning through implementation and maintenance. The traditional waterfall method no longer serves most of today's development efforts. The success rate for software development projects that follow this approach is about 1 in 10. Paul Magin, a senior executive with Part Miner, a leading supplier of technical components, states, "Waterfall is a punishing technology. It forces people to be accurate when they simply cannot. It is dangerous and least desirable in

| FIGURE | 11.3 | The Traditional Waterfall Methodology |

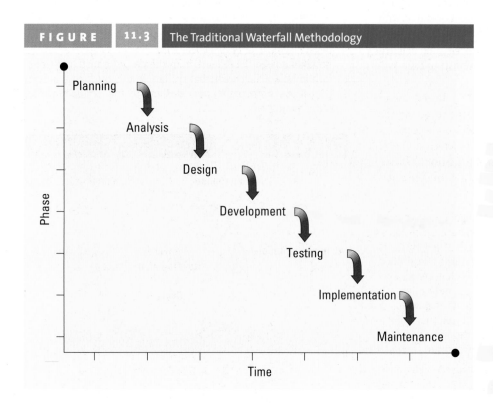

Reducing Ambiguity in Business Requirements

The number one reason projects fail is because of bad business requirements. Business requirements are considered "bad" because of ambiguity or insufficient involvement of end users during analysis and design. A requirement is unambiguous if it has the same interpretation for all parties. Different interpretations by different participants will usually result in unmet expectations. Here is an example of an ambiguous requirement and an example of an unambiguous requirement:

- **Ambiguous requirement:** The financial report must show profits in local and U.S. currencies.
- **Unambiguous requirement:** The financial report must show profits in local and U.S. currencies using the exchange rate printed in *The Wall Street Journal* for the last business day of the period being reported.

Ambiguity is impossible to prevent completely because it is introduced into requirements in natural ways. For example:

- Requirements can contain technical implications that are obvious to the IT developers but not to the customers.
- Requirements can contain business implications that are obvious to the customer but not to the IT developers.
- Requirements may contain everyday words whose meanings are "obvious" to everyone, yet different for everyone.
- Requirements are reflections of detailed explanations that may have included multiple events, multiple perspectives, verbal rephrasing, emotion, iterative refinement, selective emphasis, and body language—none of which are captured in the written statements.

You have been hired to build an employee payroll system for a new coffee shop. Review the following business requirements, and highlight any potential issues.

- All employees must have a unique employee ID.
- The system must track employee hours worked based on the employee's last name.
- Employees must be scheduled to work a minimum of eight hours per day.
- Employee payroll is calculated by multiplying the employee's hours worked by $7.25.
- Managers must be scheduled to work morning shifts.
- Employees cannot be scheduled to work more than eight hours per day.
- Servers cannot be scheduled to work morning, afternoon, or evening shifts.
- The system must allow managers to change and delete employees from the system.

today's development environment. It does not accommodate midcourse changes; it requires that you know exactly what you want to do on the project and a steady-state until the work is done; it requires guarantees that requirements will not change. We all know that it is nearly impossible to have all requirements up front. When you use a cascading method, you end up with cascading problems that are disastrous if not identified and corrected early in the process."[5]

Waterfall is inflexible, expensive, and requires rigid adherence to the sequentially based steps in the process. Figure 11.4 explains some issues related to the waterfall methodology.

Today's business environment is fierce. The desire and need to outsmart and outplay competitors remains intense. Given this drive for success, leaders push internal development teams and external vendors to deliver agreed upon systems faster and cheaper so they can realize benefits as early as possible. Even so, systems remain large and complex. The traditional waterfall methodology no longer serves as an adequate systems development methodology in most cases. Because this development environment is the norm and not the exception anymore, development teams use a new breed of alternative development methods to achieve their business objectives.

●● LO11.3
Summarize the different software development methodologies.

●● LO11.5
Compare the waterfall methodology and the agile methodology.

FIGURE 11.4	Issues Related to the Waterfall Methodology

Issues Related to the Waterfall Methodology	
The business problem	Any flaws in accurately defining and articulating the business problem in terms of what the business users actually require flow onward to the next phase.
The plan	Managing costs, resources, and time constraints is difficult in the waterfall sequence. What happens to the schedule if a programmer quits? How will a schedule delay in a specific phase impact the total cost of the project? Unexpected contingencies may sabotage the plan.
The solution	The waterfall methodology is problematic in that it assumes users can specify all business requirements in advance. Defining the appropriate IT infrastructure that is flexible, scalable, and reliable is a challenge. The final IT infrastructure solution must meet not only current but also future needs in terms of time, cost, feasibility, and flexibility. Vision is inevitably limited at the head of the waterfall.

AN AGILE METHODOLOGY AIMS FOR CUSTOMER SATISFACTION THROUGH EARLY AND CONTINUOUS DELIVERY OF USEFUL SOFTWARE COMPONENTS DEVELOPED BY AN ITERATIVE PROCESS WITH A DESIGN POINT THAT USES THE BARE MINIMUM REQUIREMENTS. "

AGILE SOFTWARE DEVELOPMENT METHODOLOGIES

Standish Group's CHAOS research clearly shows that the smaller the project, the greater the success rate. The iterative development style is the ultimate in small projects. Basically, *iterative development* consists of a series of tiny projects. Iterative has become the foundation of multiple agile types of methodologies. Figure 11.5 displays an iterative approach.[6]

An *agile methodology* aims for customer satisfaction through early and continuous delivery of useful software components developed by an iterative process with a design point that uses the bare minimum requirements. Agile is what it sounds like: fast and efficient, small and nimble, lower cost, fewer features, shorter projects. Using agile methods helps refine feasibility and

supports the process for getting rapid feedback as functionality is introduced. Developers can adjust as they move along and better clarify unclear requirements.

Magin also states that the key to delivering a successful product or system is to deliver value to users as soon as possible—give them something they want and like early to create buy-in, generate enthusiasm, and, ultimately, reduce scope. Using agile methodologies helps maintain accountability and helps to establish a barometer for the satisfaction of end users. It does no good to accomplish something on time and on budget if it does not satisfy the end user. The primary forms of agile methodologies include:

- Rapid prototyping or rapid application development methodology.
- Extreme programming methodology.
- Rational unified process (RUP) methodology.
- SCRUM methodology.[7]

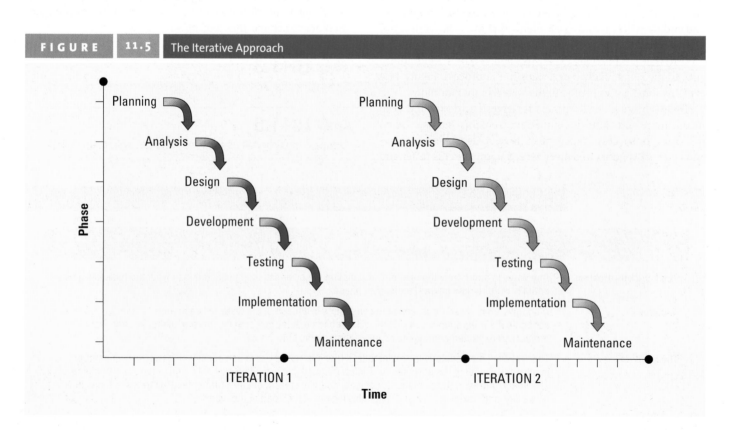

FIGURE 11.5 The Iterative Approach

It is important not to get hung up on the names of the methodologies—some are proprietary brand names, others are generally accepted names. It is more important to know how these alternative methodologies are used in today's business environment and the benefits they can deliver.

Rapid Application Development (RAD) Methodology

In response to the faster pace of business, rapid application development has become a popular route for accelerating systems development. *Rapid application development (RAD)* (also called *rapid prototyping*) *methodology* emphasizes extensive user involvement in the rapid and evolutionary construction of working prototypes of a system to accelerate the systems development process. Figure 11.6 displays the fundamentals of RAD.[8]

A *prototype* is a smaller-scale representation or working model of the users' requirements or a proposed design for an information system. The prototype is an essential part of the analysis phase when using the RAD methodology.

PHH Vehicle Management Services, a Baltimore fleet-management company with over 750,000 vehicles, wanted to build an enterprise application that opened the entire vehicle information database to customers over the Internet. To build the application quickly, the company abandoned the traditional waterfall approach. Instead, a team of 30 developers began prototyping the Internet application, and the company's customers evaluated each prototype for immediate feedback. The

| FIGURE | 11.6 | Fundamentals of RAD |

Fundamentals of RAD

Focus initially on creating a prototype that looks and acts like the desired system.

Actively involve system users in the analysis, design, and development phases.

Accelerate collecting the business requirements through an interactive and iterative construction approach.

development team released new prototypes that incorporated the customers' feedback every six weeks. The PHH Interactive Vehicle application went into production seven months after the initial work began. Over 20,000 customers, using a common browser, can now access the PHH Interactive site at any time from anywhere in the world to review their accounts, analyze billing information, and order vehicles.[9]

Extreme Programming Methodology

Extreme programming (XP) methodology, like other agile methods, breaks a project into tiny phases, and developers cannot continue on to the next phase until the first phase is complete. XP emphasizes the fact that the faster the communication or feedback the better the results. There are basically four parts: planning, designing, coding, and testing. Unlike other methodologies, these are not phases; they work in tandem with each other. Planning includes user stories, stand-up meetings, and small releases. The design segment also stresses to not add functionally until it is needed. In the coding part, the user is always available for feedback, developers work in pairs, and the code is written to an agreed standard. In testing, the tests are written before the code. Extreme programming users are embedded into the development process. This technique is powerful because of the narrow communication gap between developers and users—it is a direct link. This saves valuable time and, again, continues to clarify needed (and unneeded) requirements.

One reason for XP's success is its stress on customer satisfaction. XP empowers developers to respond to changing customer and business requirements, even late in the systems development life cycle, and XP emphasizes teamwork. Managers, customers, and developers are all part of a team dedicated to delivering quality software. XP implements a simple, yet effective way to enable groupware-style development. Kent Beck, the father of XP, proposes conversation as the paradigm and suggests using index cards as a means to create dialog between business and technology. XP is a lot like a jigsaw puzzle; there are many small pieces. Individually the pieces make no sense, but when they are combined (again and again) an organization can gain visibility into the entire new system.[10]

Rational Unified Process (RUP) Methodology

The *rational unified process (RUP) methodology,* owned by IBM, provides a framework for breaking down the development of software into four gates. Each gate consists of executable iterations of the software in development. A project stays in a gate until the stakeholders are satisfied, and then it either moves to the next gate or is cancelled. The gates include:

- **Gate One: Inception.** This phase includes inception of the business case. This phase ensures all stakeholders have a shared understanding of the system.

- **Gate Two: Elaboration.** This phase provides a rough order of magnitude. Primary questions answered in this phase deal with agreed-upon details of the system including the ability to provide an architecture to support and build the system.

- **Gate Three: Construction.** This phase includes building and developing the product.

- **Gate Four: Transition.** Primary questions answered in this phase address ownership of the system and training of key personnel.[11]

Because RUP is an iterative methodology, the user can reject the product and force the developers to go back to gate one. Approximately 500,000 developers have used RUP in software projects of varying sizes in the 20 years it has been available, according to IBM. RUP helps developers avoid reinventing the wheel and focuses on rapidly adding or removing reusable chunks of processes addressing common problems.

Scrum Methodology

Another agile methodology, **Scrum methodology** uses small teams to produce small pieces of deliverable software using sprints, or 30-day intervals, to achieve an appointed goal. In rugby, a scrum is a team pack and everyone in the pack works together to move the ball down the field. Under this methodology, each day ends or begins with a stand-up meeting to monitor and control the development effort.

Primavera Systems, Inc., a software solutions company was finding it increasingly difficult to use the traditional waterfall methodology for development so it moved to an agile methodology. Scrum's insistence on delivering complete increments of business value in 30-day learning cycles helped the teams learn rapidly. It forced teams to test and integrate experiments and encouraged them to release them into production. Primavera's shift resulted in highly satisfied customers and a highly motivated, energetic development environment. Dick Faris, CTO of Primavera, said, "Agile programming is very different and new. It is a different feel to the way programming happens. Instead of mindlessly cranking out code, the process is one of team dialogue, negotiation around priorities and time and talents. The entire company commits to a 30-day sprint and delivery of finished, tested software. Maybe it is just one specific piece of functionality but it's the real thing, including delivery and client review against needs and requirements. Those needs and requirements, by the way, change. That is the strength we saw in the Scrum process."[12]

Implementing Agile Methodologies

Amos Auringer, an executive adviser for the prestigious Gartner Group, said, "Concepts such as agile, RAD, and XP are all various approaches to the same model—idea, production, delivery. These models represent consolidated steps, skipped steps for project size, and compressed steps to achieve the same result—a delivered product. Emerging process engineering models tend to focus on eliminating or reducing steps. The SDLC phases do not change—we just learn how to do our jobs better and more efficiently."[13]

If organizations choose to adopt agile methodologies, it is important to educate those involved. For an agile process to work, it must be simple and quick. The Agile Alliance is a group of software developers whose mission is to improve software development processes; the group's manifesto is displayed in Figure 11.7. Decisions must be made quickly without

FIGURE	11.7	The Agile Alliance Manifesto

The Agile Alliance Manifesto

Early and continuous delivery of valuable software will satisfy the customer.

Changing requirements, even late in development, are welcome.

Business people and developers must work together daily throughout the project.

Projects should be built around motivated individuals. Give them the environment and support they need, and trust them to get the job done.

The best architectures, requirements, and designs emerge from self-organizing teams.

At regular intervals, the team should reflect on how to become more effective, then tune and adjust its behavior accordingly.

analysis paralysis. The best way to do this is to involve stakeholders, develop excellent communication processes, and implement strong project management skills. Understanding that communication is the most crucial aspect of a project is the core of collaborative development. Standish Group reports that projects in which users or user groups have a good understanding of their true needs have a better rate of return and lower risk. Strong project management is key to building successful enterprise applications and is covered in detail in the following section.

DEVELOPING SUCCESSFUL SOFTWARE

Gartner Research estimates that 65 percent of agile projects are successful. This success rate is extraordinary compared to the 10 percent success rate of waterfall projects. The following are the primary principles an organization should follow for successful agile software development.[14]

Slash the Budget

Small budgets force developers and users to focus on the essentials. Small budgets also make it easier to kill a failing project. For example, imagine that a project that has already cost $20 million is going down the tubes. With that much invested, it is tempting to invest another $5 million to rescue it rather than take a huge loss. All too often, the system fails and the company ends up with an even bigger loss.

Jim Johnson, chairman of the Standish Group, says he forced the CIO of one Fortune 500 company to set a $100,000 ceiling on all software development projects. There were no exceptions to this business rule without approval from the CIO and CEO. Johnson claims the company's project success rate went from 0 percent to 50 percent.[15]

If It Doesn't Work, Kill It

Bring all key stakeholders together at the beginning of a project and as it progresses bring them together again to evaluate the software. Is it doing what the business wants and, more important, requires? Eliminate any software that is not meeting business expectations. This is called triage, and it's "the perfect place to kill a software project," said Pat Morgan, senior program manager at Compaq's Enterprise Storage Group. He holds monthly triage sessions and says they can be brutal. "At one [meeting], engineering talked about a cool process they were working on to transfer information between GUIs. No one in the room needed it. We killed it right there. In our environment, you can burn a couple of million dollars in a month only to realize what you're doing isn't useful."[16]

> Strong project management is key to building successful enterprise applications

Keep Requirements to a Minimum

Start each project with what the software must absolutely do. Do not start with a list of everything the software should do. Every software project traditionally starts with a requirements document that will often have hundreds or thousands of business requirements. The Standish Group estimates that only 7 percent of the business requirements are needed for any given application. Keeping requirements to a minimum also means that scope creep and feature creep must be closely monitored. *Scope creep* occurs when the scope of the project increases. *Feature creep* occurs when developers add extra features that were not part of the initial requirements. Both scope creep and feature creep are major reasons software development fails.[17]

Test and Deliver Frequently

As often as once a week, and not less than once a month, complete a part of the project or a piece of software. The part must be working and it must be bug-free. Then have the customers test and approve it. This is the agile methodology's most radical departure from traditional development. In some traditional software projects, the customers did not see any working parts or pieces for years.

Assign Non-IT Executives to Software Projects

Non-IT executives should coordinate with the technical project manager, test iterations to make sure they are meeting user needs, and act as liaisons between executives and IT. Having the business side involved full-time will bring project ownership and a desire to succeed to all parties involved. SpreeRide, a Salt Lake City market research outfit, used the agile methodology to set up its company's website. The project required several business executives designated full-time. The company believes this is one of the primary reasons that the project was successfully deployed in less than three months.[18]

●● SECTION 11.2 Project Management

LEARNING OUTCOMES

LO11.6 Explain the triple constraint and its importance in project management.

LO11.7 Describe the project stakeholders' and executive sponsor's roles in choosing strategic projects.

LO11.8 Highlight the components of a project charter.

LO11.9 Describe the two primary diagrams most frequently used in project planning.

LO11.10 Identify the three primary areas a project manager must focus on managing to ensure success.

LO11.11 Explain the three different types of outsourcing.

No one would think of building an office complex by turning loose 100 different construction teams to build 100 different rooms with no single blueprint or agreed-upon vision of the completed structure. Yet this is precisely the situation in which many large organizations find themselves when managing information technology projects. Organizations routinely overschedule their resources (human and otherwise), develop redundant projects, and damage profitability by investing in nonstrategic efforts that do not contribute to the organization's bottom line. Project management offers a strategic framework for coordinating the numerous activities associated with organizational projects. Business leaders face a rapidly moving and unforgiving global marketplace that will force them to use every possible tool to sustain competitiveness—project management is one of those tools.

●● LO11.6
Explain the triple constraint and its importance in project management.

MANAGING SOFTWARE DEVELOPMENT PROJECTS

Analysts predict investment in IT projects worldwide through 2010 will be over $1 trillion. This is a staggering amount, and even more staggering is that nearly 70 percent of it will be merely washed down the drain as a result of failed projects! In addition to lost earnings, companies from Nestlé to Nike have experienced additional consequences of failed projects—a damaged brand, lost goodwill, the dissolution of partnerships, lost investment opportunities, and the effects of low morale.[19]

According to the Standish Group, just 29 percent of IT projects were completed on time, within budget, and with features and functions originally specified by the customer to deliver business value. The grim reality of failed projects faces many businesses today.[20]

With so many skilled and knowledgeable IT professionals at the helm of IT projects, how can this happen? Every day, organizations adopt projects that do not align with mission-critical initiatives; they overcommit financial and human capital; they sign off on low-value projects that consume valuable and scarce resources; and they agree to support projects that are poorly defined from requirements to planning.

IT projects typically fail because, in most instances, they are complex, made even more so by poor planning and unrealistic expectations; they are rushed due to increasingly demanding market pressure; and their scope becomes too unmanageable. Because this is today's reality, it is important to apply solid project management techniques and tools to increase the success rate of IT projects.

The Triple Constraint

A project's vision needs to be clear, concise, and comprehensible, but it also has to be the same to all stakeholders. It is imperative that everyone be on the same page. From a business perspective, everyone has to be aligned with the direction of the overall business and the project's overall objectives. It is key for members of an organization who desire to make meaningful contributions to understand the company's investment and selection strategy for projects and how it determines and prioritizes the project pipeline. Projects consume vast amounts of resources. It is imperative to understand how the organization allocates its scarce and valuable resources in order to get the big picture.

Figure 11.8 displays the relationships between the three primary variables in any project—time, cost, and scope. These three variables are interdependent. All projects are limited in some way by these three constraints. The Project Management Institute calls the framework for evaluating these competing demands the triple constraint.

The relationship between these variables is such that if any one of the three factors changes at least one other factor is likely to be affected. For example, moving up a project's finish date could result in either increasing costs to hire more staff or decreasing the scope to eliminate features or functions. Increasing a project's scope to include additional customer

FIGURE 11.8 Project Management Interdependent Variables

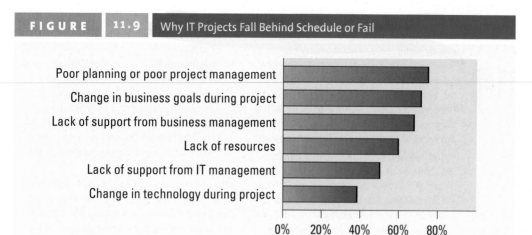

FIGURE 11.9 | Why IT Projects Fall Behind Schedule or Fail

Poor planning or poor project management

Change in business goals during project

Lack of support from business management

Lack of resources

Lack of support from IT management

Change in technology during project

0% 20% 40% 60% 80%

A successful project is typically on time, within budget, meets the business's requirements, and fulfills the customer's needs. The Hackett Group, an Atlanta-based consultancy, analyzed its client database, which includes 2,000 companies, including 81 Fortune 100 companies, and discovered:

- Three in 10 major IT projects fail.
- Twenty-one percent of the companies state that they cannot adjust rapidly to market changes.

requests could result in extending the project's time to completion or increasing the project's cost—or both—in order to accommodate the new scope changes. Project quality is affected by the project manager's ability to balance these competing demands. High quality projects deliver the agreed upon product or service on time and on budget.

Project management is the science of making intelligent trade-offs between time, cost, and scope. All three of the factors combined determine a project's quality. Benjamin Franklin's timeless advice—by failing to prepare, you prepare to fail—applies to many of today's software development projects. A recent survey concluded that the failure rate of IT projects is much higher in organizations that do not exercise disciplined project management. Figure 11.9 displays the top six reasons IT projects fail, according to *Information Week's* survey of 150 IT managers.

- One in four validates a business case for IT projects after completion.[21]

PROJECT MANAGEMENT FUNDAMENTALS

The Project Management Institute (PMI) defines a **project** as a temporary endeavor undertaken to create a unique product, service, or result. **Project management** is the application of knowledge, skills, tools, and techniques to project activities to meet project requirements. Projects are short-term efforts such as removing old servers, developing a custom ecommerce site, or merging databases. Figure 11.10 provides an overview of PMI and its fundamental project management terms all managers should know and understand.[22]

FIGURE 11.10 | Project Management Institute (PMI)

The **Project Management Institute (PMI)** develops procedures and concepts necessary to support the profession of project management (www.pmi.org). It has three areas of focus:
1. The distinguishing characteristics of a practicing professional (ethics).
2. The content and structure of the profession's body of knowledge (standards).
3. Recognition of professional attainment (accreditation).

Project deliverables are any measurable, tangible, verifiable outcome, result, or item that is produced to complete a project or part of a project. Examples of project deliverables include design documents, testing scripts, and requirements documents.

Project milestones represent key dates when a certain group of activities must be performed. For example, completing the planning phase might be a project milestone. If a project milestone is missed, then chances are the project is experiencing problems.

Project manager is an individual who is an expert in project planning and management, defines and develops the project plan, and tracks the plan to ensure the project is completed on time and on budget. The project manager is the person responsible for executing the entire project plan.

Project management office (PMO) is an internal department that oversees all organizational projects. This group must formalize and professionalize project management expertise and leadership. One of the primary initiatives of the PMO is to educate the organization on techniques and procedures necessary to run successful projects.

Before its merger with Hewlett-Packard, Compaq decided to analyze and prioritize its system development projects. Knowing that the CIO wanted to be able to view every project, project management leaders quickly identified and removed nonstrategic projects. At the end of the review process, the company cancelled 39 projects, saving the organization $15 million. Most Fortune 100 companies are receiving bottom-line benefits similar to Compaq's from implementing a project management solution.[23]

Most business managers are not project managers, however, it is inevitable that all managers will be part of a project team. Therefore, it is important to understand how a business manages its project and how the culture supports the effort. The art and science of project management must coordinate numerous activities as displayed in Figure 11.11. Project managers perform numerous activities. The remainder of this section focuses on four of these primary activities:

1. Choosing strategic projects.
2. Understanding project planning.
3. Managing projects.
4. Outsourcing projects.

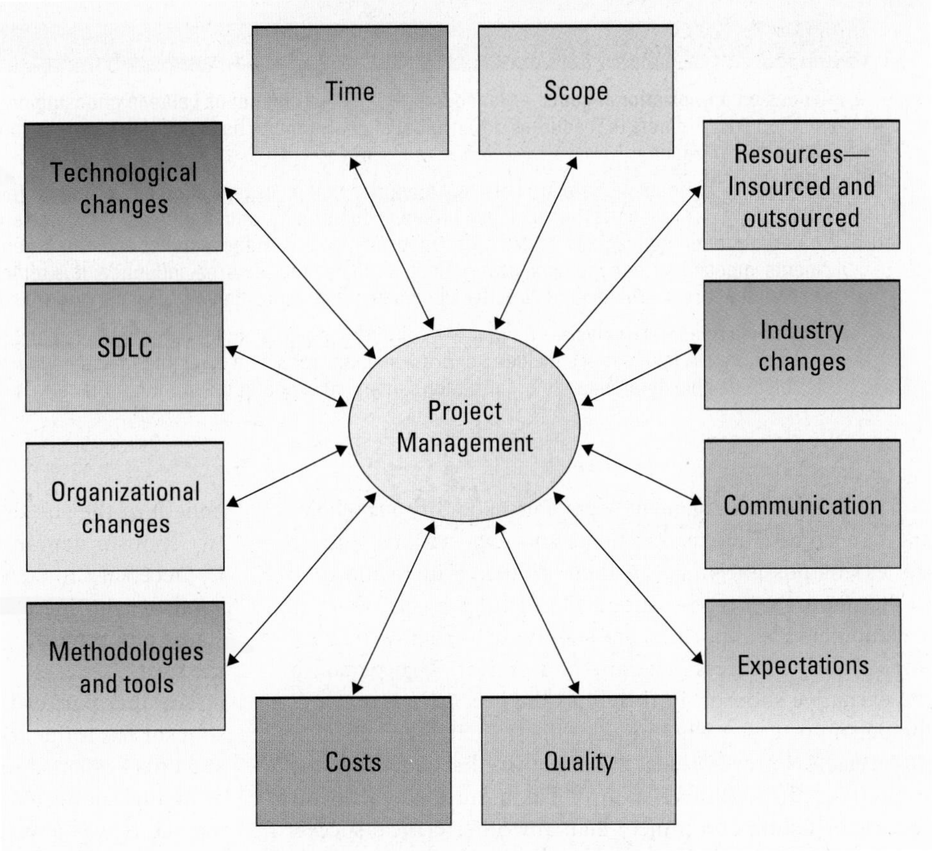

●● LO11.7

Describe the project stakeholders' and executive sponsor's roles in choosing strategic projects.

CHOOSING STRATEGIC PROJECTS

One of the most difficult decisions organizations make is determining the projects in which to invest time, energy, and resources. An organization must identify what it wants to do and how it is going to do it. The "what" part of this question focuses on issues such as justification for the project, definition of the project, and expected results of the project. The "how" part of the question deals with issues such as project approach, project schedule, and analysis of project risks. Determining which projects to focus corporate efforts on is as necessary to projects as each project is to an organization.

FIGURE 11.11 Project Management Roles

projects can take on a life of their own." Figure 11.12 displays the three common techniques an organization can use to select projects.[24]

Project stakeholders are individuals and organizations actively involved in the project or whose interests might be affected as a result of project execution or project completion. Stakeholders are not necessarily involved in the completion of project deliverables. For example, a chief financial officer (CFO)

["Determining which projects to focus corporate efforts on is as necessary to projects as each project is to an organization."]

Organizations also need to choose and prioritize projects in such a way that they can make responsible decisions as to which projects to eliminate. Jim Johnson, chairman of the Standish Group, has identified project management as the process that can make the difference in project success. According to Johnson, "Companies need a process for taking a regular look at their projects and deciding, again and again, if the investment is going to pay off. As it stands now, for most companies,

probably will not help test a new billing system, but she surely will be expecting the successful completion of the project.

Stakeholders, such as the CFO, also can exert influence over the project's objectives and outcomes. It is important for all stakeholders to understand the business objective of the project—once again, it is about getting the big picture. Stakeholders measure projects based on such factors as customer satisfaction, increased revenue, or decreased cost.

FIGURE **11.12** Techniques for Choosing Strategic Projects

Techniques for Choosing Strategic Projects

1. **Focus on organizational goals**—Managers are finding tremendous value in choosing projects that align with the organization's goals. Projects that address organizational goals tend to have a higher success rate since they are important to the entire organization.

2. **Categorize projects**—There are various categories that an organization can group projects into to determine a project's priority. One type of categorization includes problem, opportunity, and directives. Problems are undesirable situations that prevent an organization from achieving its goals. Opportunities are chances to improve the organization. Directives are new requirements imposed by management, government, or some other external influence. It is often easier to obtain approval for projects that address problems or directives because the organization must respond to these categories to avoid financial losses.

3. **Perform a financial analysis**—A number of different financial analysis techniques can be performed to help determine a project's priority. A few of these include net present value, return on investment, and payback analysis. These financial analysis techniques help determine the organization's financial expectations for the project.

The project management team must identify stakeholders, determine their requirements and expectations, and, to the extent possible, manage their influence in relationship to the requirements to ensure a successful project. While all stakeholders are important, one stands out as having the most impact on the success or failure of a project. That person is the executive sponsor. PMI defines the *executive sponsor* as the person or group who provides the financial resources for the project. However, research has shown that the leadership strength of the executive sponsor has more to do with the success or failure of a project than any other critical success factor. In fact, the executive sponsor should be accountable to the project team for much more than the financial backing. The executive sponsor communicates up the chain on behalf of the project; he or she supports the project manager by championing the project to others sharing the vision and benefit of the successfully completed project; and the executive sponsor demonstrates the commitment and accountability necessary to survive a project! If a team has a hands-off sponsor who merely reviews invoices and inquires as to the status of a project, then that project surely is in trouble from the start.[25]

Another part of the equation is influence. If the executive sponsor has influence, he or she can use that influence to gain and direct essential resources needed to accomplish the project. A highly connected executive sponsor could mean the difference between success and failure. The executive sponsor should be committed to use this influence to ensure the health of the project. Executive management support influences the process and progress of a project. No matter what the case, the lack of executive support and input can place a project at a severe disadvantage.

●● LO11.8

Highlight the components of a project charter.

●● LO11.9

Describe the two primary diagrams most frequently used in project planning.

UNDERSTANDING PROJECT PLANNING

Once an organization has selected strategic projects and identified its project manager it is time to build the critical component—the project plan. Building a project plan involves two key components:

- Project charter

- Project plan

Close Down

Death March

Edward Yourdon's book, *Death March,* describes the complete software developer's guide to surviving "mission impossible" projects. Today, IT projects are expected to achieve the impossible, overcome numerous constraints, and deal with elevated stress levels and imperfect working conditions. In *Death March,* legendary software developer Edward Yourdon comes to the rescue. Yourdan developed the Death March project style quadrant as displayed in the accompanying figure. If you have one goal, it should be to avoid all suicide projects!

Analyze your school and work projects, and find a project that would fit in each box. What could you have done differently on your suicide project to ensure its success? What can you do to avoid being placed on a suicide project? Given the choice, which type of project would you choose to work on and why?

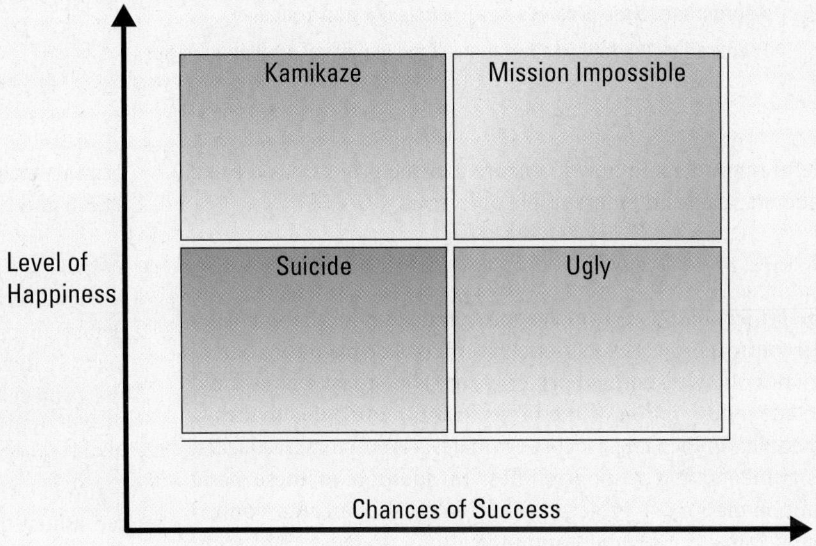

Project Charter

Many project professionals believe that a solid project is initiated with documentation that includes a project charter, a scope statement, and the project management plan. A **project charter** is a document issued by the project initiator or sponsor that formally authorizes the existence of a project and provides the project manager with the authority to apply organizational resources to project activities. In short, this means someone has stepped up to pay for and support the project. A project charter typically includes several elements.

- **Project scope** defines the work that must be completed to deliver a product with the specified features and functions. A project scope statement describes the business need, justification, requirements, and current boundaries for the project. The business need can be characterized by the problem the results of the project will satisfy. This is important in linking the project with the organization's overall business goals. The project scope statement includes constraints, assumptions, and requirements—all components necessary for developing accurate cost estimates.

- **Project objectives** are quantifiable criteria that must be met for the project to be considered a success.

- **Project constraints** are specific factors that can limit options. They include: budget, delivery

dates, available skilled resources, and organizational policies.

- **Project assumptions** are factors that are considered to be true, real, or certain without proof or demonstration. Examples include hours in a workweek or time of year the work will be performed.

The project objectives are one of the most important areas to define because they are essentially the major elements of the project. When an organization achieves the project objectives, it has accomplished the major goals of the project and the project scope is satisfied. Project objectives must include metrics so that the project's success can be measured. The metrics can include cost, schedule, and quality metrics along with a number of other metrics. Figure 11.13 displays the SMART criteria—

FIGURE 11.13 SMART Criteria for Successful Objective Creation

- Specific
- Measurable
- Agreed upon
- Realistic
- Time framed

FIGURE 11.14 Project Plan Characteristics

Characteristics of a Well-Defined Project Plan

Easy to understand

Easy to read

Communicated to all key participants (key stakeholders)

Appropriate to the project's size, complexity, and criticality

Prepared by the team, rather than by the individual project manager

useful reminders on how to ensure that the project has created understandable and measurable objectives.

Project Plan

The *project plan* is a formal, approved document that manages and controls project execution. Figure 11.14 displays the characteristics of a well-defined project plan. The project plan should include a description of the project scope, a list of activities, a schedule, time estimates, cost estimates, risk factors, resources, assignments, and responsibilities. In addition to these basic components, most project professionals also include contingency plans, review and communications strategies, and a *kill switch*—a trigger that enables a project manager to close the project prior to completion.

A good project plan should include estimates for revenue and strategic necessities. It also should include measurement and reporting methods and details as to how top leadership will engage in the project. A good plan informs stakeholders of the benefits of the project and justifies the investment, commitment, and risk of the project as it relates to the overall mission of the organization.[26]

An organization must build in continuous self-assessment, which allows earlier termination decisions on failing projects, with the associated cost savings. This frees capital and personnel for dedication to projects that are worth pursuing. The elimination of a project should be viewed as successful resource management, not as an admission of failure.

The most important part of the plan is communication. The project manager must communicate the plan to every member of the project team and to any key stakeholders and executives. The project plan must also include any project assumptions and be detailed enough to guide the execution of the project. A key to achieving project success is earning consensus and buy-in from all key stakeholders. By including key stakeholders in project plan development, the project manager allows them to have ownership of the plan. This often translates to greater commitment, which in turn results in enhanced motivation and productivity. The two primary diagrams most frequently used in project planning are PERT and Gantt charts.

PERT Chart A *PERT (Program Evaluation and Review Technique) chart* is a graphical network model that depicts a project's tasks and the relationships between those tasks. A *dependency* is a logical relationship that exists between the project tasks, or between a project task and a milestone. PERT charts define dependency between project tasks before those tasks are scheduled (see Figure 11.15). The boxes in Figure 11.15 represent project tasks, and the project manager can adjust the contents of the boxes to display various project attributes such as schedule and actual start and finish times.

FIGURE 11.15 PERT Chart Expert, a PERT Chart Example

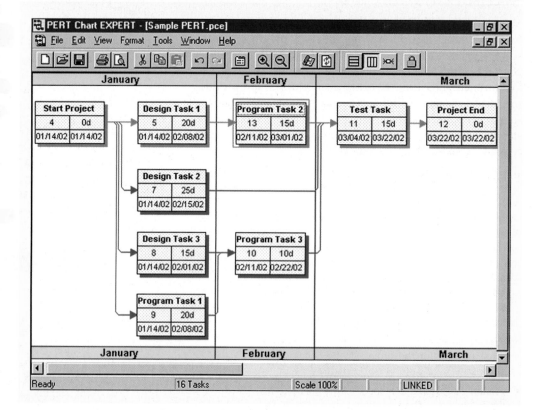

The arrows indicate that one task is dependent on the start or completion of another task. The **critical path** is a path from the start to the finish that passes through all the tasks that are critical to completing the project in the shortest amount of time. PERT charts frequently display a project's critical path.

Gantt Chart
A **Gantt chart** is a simple bar chart that depicts project tasks against a calendar. In a Gantt chart, tasks are listed vertically and the project's time frame is listed horizontally. A Gantt chart works well for representing the project schedule. It also shows actual progress of tasks against the planned duration. Figure 11.16 displays a software development project using a Gantt chart.

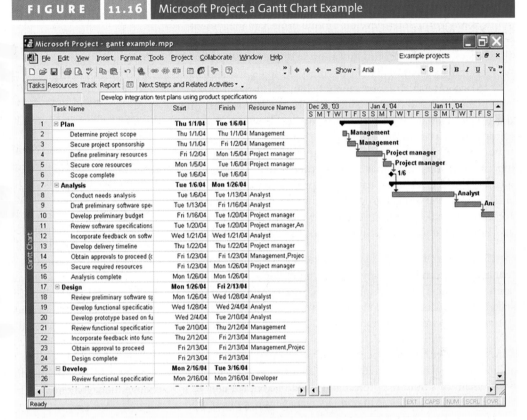

FIGURE 11.16 Microsoft Project, a Gantt Chart Example

●● LO11.10
Identify the three primary areas a project manager must focus on managing to ensure success.

MANAGING PROJECTS

Standish Group research clearly shows that projects are likely to be less challenged and more successful with a competent and skilled project manager on board. Again, a **project manager** is an individual who is an expert in project planning and management, defines and develops the project plan, and tracks the plan to ensure the project is completed on time and on budget. A project manager can, of course, bring enormous benefits to an organization such as reduced project expense, high company morale, and quicker time to market. A competent project manager sets the correct expectations early in the project with achievable milestones. Managing a project includes:

- Identifying requirements.
- Establishing clear and achievable objectives.
- Balancing the competing demands of quality, scope, time, and cost.
- Adapting the specifications, plans, and approach to the different concerns and expectations of the various stakeholders.[27]

In addition to managing these objectives, a successful project manager possesses a variety of hard and soft skills. Standish Group research also shows that successful project managers

have basic business operational knowledge and good business skills. When a project manager has a good grasp of the business operations, he or she can improve critical communication among the designers, developers, user community, and top leadership. An experienced project manager should be able to minimize scope and create a better estimate. He or she knows how to say no without creating controversy. And a good project manager should have learned that a happy stakeholder is one who is underpromised and overdelivered! A project manager must focus on managing three primary areas to ensure success:

1. People
2. Communications
3. Change.

Managing People

Managing people is one of the hardest and most critical efforts a project manager undertakes. Resolving conflicts within the team and balancing the needs of the project with the personal and professional needs of the team are two of the challenges facing project managers. More and more project managers are the main (and sometimes sole) interface with the client during the project. As such, communication, negotiation, marketing, and salesmanship are just as important to the project manager as financial and analytical acumen. Many times, the people management side of project management makes the difference in pulling off a successful project.

Managing Communications

While many companies develop unique project management frameworks based on familiar project management standards, all of them agree that communication is the key to excellent project management. This is quite easy to state, but not so easy to accomplish! It is extremely helpful if a project manager plans what and how to communicate as a formal part of the project management plan. Most often a document, it is referred to as a communications plan. A project manager distributes timely, accurate, and meaningful information regarding project objectives that involve time, cost, scope, and quality, and the status of each. The project manager shares small wins as the project progresses, informs others of needed corrections, makes requests known for additional resources, and keeps all stakeholders informed of the project schedule.

Receiving Feedback

Another aspect of a project management communications plan is to provide a method for continually obtaining and monitoring feedback from and for all stakeholders. This is not to say that a project manager needs to spend countless hours answering every email and responding to every question posed. Rather, the manager should develop a method for asking for specific feedback as part of the plan and responding to it in a timely, organized manner. Team members remain closest to the project and should be encouraged to share honest feedback. It is the project manager's responsibility to foster an environment of trust so that members feel safe to contribute their knowledge and ideas—even if it means relaying bad news or offering an opposing viewpoint.

Managing Change

Change, whether it comes in the form of a crisis, a market shift, or a technological development, is challenging for all organizations. Successful organizations and successful people learn to anticipate and react appropriately to change. Snap-on, a maker of tools and equipment for specialists such as car mechanics, is successful at managing change. The company recently increased profits by 12 percent while sales were down 6.7 percent. Dennis Leitner, vice president of IT, runs the IT group on a day-to-day basis and leads the implementation of all major software development initiatives. Each software development initiative is managed by both the business and IT. In fact, business resources are on the IT group's payroll, and they spend as much as 80 percent of their time learning what a business unit is doing and how IT can help make it happen. Leitner's role focuses primarily on strategic planning, change management, and setting up metrics to track performance.[28]

Dynamic organizational change is inevitable, and an organization must effectively manage change as it evolves. With the numerous challenges and complexities that organizations face in today's rapidly changing environment, effective change management thus becomes a critical core competency. *Change management* is a set of techniques that aid in evolution, composition, and policy management of the design and

---

show me *the* MONEY

Keeping Time

Time Keepers Inc. is a small firm that specializes in project management consulting. You are a senior project manager, and you have recently been assigned to the Tahiti Tanning Lotion account. The Tahiti Tanning Lotion company is currently experiencing a 10 percent success rate (90 percent failure rate) on all internal IT projects.

Your first assignment is to analyze one of the current project plans being used to develop a new CRM system (see the figure below). Review the project plan and create a document listing the numerous errors in the plan. Be sure to also provide suggestions on how to fix the errors.

	Task Name	Start	Finish	Resource Names
1	Project Plan	Mon 6/23/08	Fri 7/18/08	
2	Plan Project	Mon 6/23/08	Wed 6/25/08	Manager 1
3	Plan Resources	Mon 6/23/08	Wed 6/25/08	Manager 2
4	Plan Scope	Wed 6/25/08	Fri 6/27/08	Manager 3
5	Plan Deliverable	Wed 6/25/08	Fri 6/27/08	Manager 4
6	Requirements	Mon 6/30/08	Tue 7/1/08	
7	Product 1	Mon 6/30/08	Tue 7/1/08	Analyst 1,Analyst 2
8	Product 2	Mon 6/30/08	Tue 7/1/08	Analyst 1,Analyst 2
9	Product 3	Mon 6/30/08	Tue 7/1/08	Analyst 1,Analyst 2
10	Product 4	Mon 6/30/08	Tue 7/1/08	Analyst 1,Analyst 2
11	Design	Fri 7/4/08	Thu 7/10/08	
12	Product 1	Fri 7/4/08	Thu 7/10/08	Analyst 1,Analyst 2
13	Product 2	Fri 7/4/08	Thu 7/10/08	Analyst 1,Analyst 2
14	Product 3	Fri 7/4/08	Thu 7/10/08	Analyst 1,Analyst 2
15	Product 4	Fri 7/4/08	Thu 7/10/08	Analyst 1,Analyst 2
16	Test	Mon 7/14/08	Fri 7/18/08	
17	Product 1	Mon 7/14/08	Fri 7/18/08	Analyst 1,Analyst 2
18	Product 2	Mon 7/14/08	Fri 7/18/08	Analyst 1,Analyst 2
19	Product 3	Mon 7/14/08	Fri 7/18/08	Analyst 1,Analyst 2
20	Product 4	Mon 7/14/08	Fri 7/18/08	Analyst 1,Analyst 2
21	Implement	Mon 7/7/08	Fri 7/11/08	
22	Product 1	Mon 7/7/08	Fri 7/11/08	Analyst 1,Analyst 2
23	Product 2	Mon 7/7/08	Fri 7/11/08	Analyst 1,Analyst 2
24	Product 3	Mon 7/7/08	Fri 7/11/08	Analyst 1,Analyst 2
25	Product 4	Mon 7/7/08	Fri 7/11/08	Analyst 1,Analyst 2

FIGURE 11.17 Common Reasons Change Occurs

Common Reasons Change Occurs

1. An omission in defining initial scope
2. A misunderstanding of the initial scope
3. An external event such as government regulations that create new requirements
4. Organizational changes, such as mergers, acquisitions, and partnerships, that create new business problems and opportunities
5. Availability of better technology
6. Shifts in planned technology that force unexpected and significant changes to the business organization, culture, and/or processes
7. The users or management simply wanting the system to do more than they originally requested or agreed to
8. Management reducing the funding for the project or imposing an earlier deadline

implementation of a system. Figure 11.17 displays a few of the more common reasons change occurs.[29]

A *change management system* includes a collection of procedures to document a change request and define the steps necessary to consider the change based on the expected impact of the change. Most change management systems require that a change request form be initiated by one or more project stakeholders (systems owners, users, customers, analysts, developers). Ideally, these change requests are considered by a *change control board (CCB)* that is responsible for approving or rejecting all change requests. The CCB's composition typically includes a representative from each business area that has a stake in the project. The CCB's decision to accept or reject each change is based on an impact analysis of the change. For example, if one department wants to implement a change to the software that will increase both deployment time and cost, then the other business owners need to agree that the change is valid and that it warrants the extended time frame and increased budget.

Change is an opportunity, not a threat. Realizing that change is the norm rather than the exception will help an organization

> ## Change is an opportunity, not a threat.

stay ahead. Becoming a change leader and accepting the inevitability of change can help ensure that an organization can survive and even thrive in times of change. Figure 11.18 displays the three important guidelines change leaders can follow to make change effective both inside and outside their organizations.[30]

LO11.11

Explain the three different types of outsourcing.

OUTSOURCING PROJECTS

In the high-speed global business environment, an organization needs to maximize its profits, enlarge its market share, and restrain its ever-increasing costs. Businesses need to make every effort to rethink and adopt new processes, especially the prospective resources regarding insourcing and outsourcing. Two basic options are available to organizations wishing to develop and maintain their information systems—insourcing or outsourcing.

Insourcing (in-house development) is a common approach using the professional expertise within an organization to develop and maintain the organization's information technology systems. Insourcing has been instrumental in creating a viable supply of IT professionals and in creating a better quality workforce combining both technical and business skills.

FIGURE 11.18 Three Important Guidelines for Effective Change Management

Three Important Guidelines for Effectively Dealing with Change Management

1. **Institute change management polices**—Create clearly defined policies and procedures that must be followed each time a request for change is received.
2. **Anticipate change**—View change as an opportunity and embrace it.
3. **Seek change**—Every 6 to 12 months look for changes that may be windows of opportunity. Review successes and failures to determine if there are any opportunities for innovation.

Outsourcing is an arrangement by which one organization provides a service or services for another organization that chooses not to perform them in-house. In some cases, the entire information technology department is outsourced, including planning and business analysis as well as the installation, management, and servicing of the network and workstations. Outsourcing can range from a large contract under which an organization such as IBM manages IT services for a company such as Xerox to the practice of hiring contractors and temporary office workers on an individual basis. Figure 11.19 compares the functions companies have outsourced, and Figure 11.20 displays the primary reasons companies outsource.

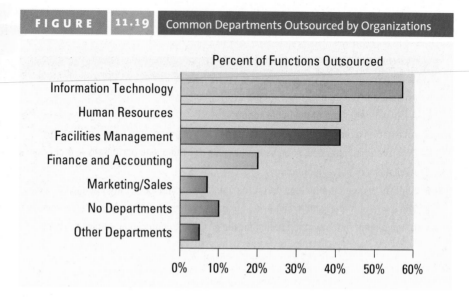

FIGURE 11.19 Common Departments Outsourced by Organizations

In the early 1990s, British Petroleum (BP) began looking at IT outsourcing as a way to radically reduce costs and gain more flexible and higher-quality IT resources that directly improve the overall business. Over the past decade, all companies within the global BP Group have incorporated outsourcing initiatives in their business plans. BP's information technology costs were reduced by 40 percent globally over the first three years of the outsourcing engagement and have continued at a 10 percent reduction year after year, leading to hundreds of millions of dollars in savings to BP.[31]

Information technology outsourcing enables organizations to keep up with market and technology advances—with less strain on human and financial resources and more assurance that the IT infrastructure will keep pace with evolving business priorities (see Figure 11.21). Planning, deploying, and managing IT environments is both a tactical and a strategic challenge that must take into account a company's organizational, industrial, and technological concerns. The three different forms of outsourcing options a project must consider are:

1. **Onshore outsourcing**—engaging another company within the same country for services.

2. **Nearshore outsourcing**—contracting an outsourcing arrangement with a company in a nearby country. Often this country will share a border with the native country.

3. **Offshore outsourcing**—using organizations from developing countries to write code and develop systems. In offshore outsourcing the country is geographically far away.

Since the mid-1990s, major U.S. companies have been sending significant portions of their software development work offshore—primarily to vendors in India, but also to vendors in China, Eastern Europe (including Russia), Ireland, Israel, and the Philippines. The big selling point for offshore outsourcing is inexpensive good work. A programmer who earns as much as $63,000 per year in the United States is paid as little as $5,000 per year

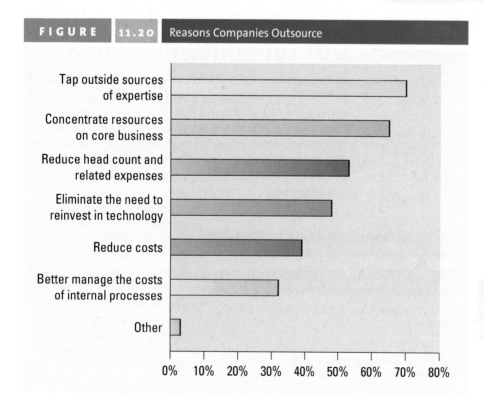

FIGURE 11.20 Reasons Companies Outsource

FIGURE 11.21 Outsourcing Models and Cost Savings

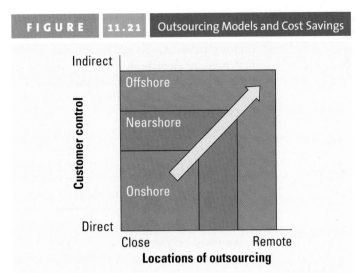

overseas (see Figure 11.22). Companies can easily realize cost savings of 30 to 50 percent through offshore outsourcing and still get the same, if not better, quality of service.[32]

Developed and developing countries throughout Europe and Asia offer some IT outsourcing services, but most are hampered to some degree by language, telecommunications infrastructure, or regulatory barriers. The first and largest offshore marketplace is India, whose English-speaking and technologically advanced population has built its IT services business into a $4 billion industry. Infosys, NIIT, Satyam, TCS, and Wipro are among the biggest Indian outsourcing service providers, each with a significant presence in the United States.[33]

Ever since Eastman Kodak announced it was outsourcing its information systems function in 1988 to IBM, DEC, and Businessland, large organizations have found it acceptable to transfer their IT assets, leases, and staff to outsourcers. In view of the changes in sourcing, the key question now is not "Should we outsource IT?" but rather "Where and how can we take advantage of the rapidly developing market of IT services providers?" Some of the influential drivers affecting the growth of the outsourcing market include:

- **Core competencies.** Many companies have recently begun to consider outsourcing as a means to fuel revenue growth rather than just a cost-cutting measure. Outsourcing enables an organization to maintain an up-to-date technology infrastructure while freeing it to focus on revenue growth goals by reinvesting cash and human capital in areas offering the greatest return on investment.

- **Financial savings.** It is typically cheaper to hire workers in China and India than similar workers in the United States. Technology is advancing at such an accelerated rate that companies often lack the resources, workforce, or expertise to keep up. It is close to impossible for an IT department to

omg lol

DUI in a Golf Cart

Swedish police stopped Bill Murray and charged him with drunk driving when he attempted to drive his golf cart from Café Opera, an upscale restaurant in the center of town, back to his hotel. A golf cart only goes about three miles per hour, and it seems odd that you can be issued a DUI for driving one. However, different countries have different laws. A few other cultural blunders you want to avoid include:

- Several managers of an American company realized the brand name of the cooking oil they were marketing in a Latin American country translated into Spanish as "Jackass Oil."
- American Motors was excited to market its new car, the Matador, which was based on the image of courage and strength. However, in Puerto Rico the name Matador equates to "killer," and

consumers were not willing to drive a Killer car on the country's hazardous roads.

- A new cologne advertisement pictured an idyllic scene with a man and his dog. It failed in Islamic countries because dogs are considered unclean.
- One popular Procter & Gamble European soap commercial featured a woman bathing and her husband entering the bathroom and smiling. P&G decided that the commercial did so well they would air it in Japan. The problem? The Japanese considered this ad an invasion of privacy, inappropriate behavior, and in very poor taste.
- One American refused to accept an offer of a cup of coffee from a Saudi businessman. Such a rejection is

considered very rude, and the entire deal was ended.

- A golf ball manufacturing company packaged golf balls in packs of four for convenient purchase in Japan. Unfortunately, pronunciation of the word "four" in Japanese sounds like the word "death," and items packaged in fours are unpopular.

Companies that are expanding globally are looking for opportunities, not problems. Yet local laws and procedures that come into play when setting up shop abroad—everything from hiring and firing to tax filings—can be a minefield. What types of culture, language, and legal issues should a company expect to encounter when dealing with an outsourcing company? What can a company do to mitigate these risks?

FIGURE 11.22 — Typical Salary Ranges for Computer Programmers

Country	Salary Range Per Year
China	$5,000–$9,000
India	6,000–10,000
Philippines	6,500–11,000
Russia	7,000–13,000
Ireland	21,000–28,000
Canada	25,000–50,000
United States	60,000–90,000

maintain a "best-of-breed" status, especially for small and medium-sized enterprises where cost is a critical factor.

- **Rapid growth.** A company's sustainability depends on both speed to market and ability to react quickly to changes in market conditions. By taking advantage of outsourcing, an organization is able to acquire best-practices process expertise. This facilitates the design, building, training, and deployment of business processes or functions.

- **Industry changes.** High levels of reorganization across industries have increased demand for outsourcing to better focus on core competencies. The significant increase in merger and acquisition activity created a sudden need to integrate multiple core and noncore business functions into one business, while the deregulation of the utilities and telecom industries created a need to ensure compliance with government rules and regulations. Companies in either situation turned to outsourcing so they could better focus on industry changes at hand.

- **The Internet.** The pervasive nature of the Internet as an effective sales channel has allowed clients to become more comfortable with outsourcing. Barriers to entry, such as lack of capital, are dramatically reduced in the world of ebusiness due to the Internet. New competitors enter the market daily.

- **Globalization.** As markets open worldwide, competition heats up. Companies may engage outsourcing service providers to deliver international services.[34]

Best Buy Co. Inc. is the number one U.S. specialty retailer for consumer electronics, personal computers, entertainment software, and appliances. Best Buy needed to find a strategic IT partner that could help the company leverage its IT functions to meet its business objectives. Best Buy also wanted to integrate its disparate enterprise systems and minimize its operating expenses. Best Buy outsourced these functions to Accenture, a global management consulting, technology services, and outsourcing company. The comprehensive outsourcing relationship that drove Best Buy's transformation produced spectacular results that were measurable in every key area of its business, such as a 20 percent increase in key category revenue that translated into a $25 million profit improvement.[35]

According to PricewaterhouseCoopers' survey of CEOs from 452 of the fastest growing U.S. companies, "Businesses that outsource are growing faster, larger, and more profitably than those that do not. In addition, most of those involved in outsourcing say they are saving money and are highly satisfied with their outsourcing service providers." Figure 11.23 lists common areas for outsourcing opportunities across industries.[36]

Outsourcing Benefits

The many benefits associated with outsourcing include:

- Increased quality and efficiency of a process, service, or function.
- Reduced operating expenses.
- Resources focused on core profit-generating competencies.
- Reduced exposure to risks involved with large capital investments.
- Access to outsourcing service provider's economies of scale.
- Access to outsourcing services provider's expertise and best-in-class practices.
- Access to advanced technologies.
- Increased flexibility with the ability to respond quickly to changing market demands.
- No costly outlay of capital funds.
- Reduced head count and associated overhead expense.
- Reduced frustration and expense related to hiring and retaining employees in an exceptionally tight job market.
- Reduced time to market for products or services.[37]

FIGURE 11.23 — Outsourcing Opportunities

Industry	Outsourcing Opportunities
Banking and finance	Check and electronic payment processing, credit report issuance, delinquency management, securities, and trades processing
Insurance	Claims reporting and investigation, policy administration, checkprocessing, risk assessment
Telecommunications	Invoice and bill production, transaction processing
Health care	Electronic data interchange, database management, accounting
Transportation	Ticket and order processing
Government	Loan processing, Medicaid processing
Retail	Electronic payment processing

Outsourcing Challenges

Outsourcing comes with several challenges. These arguments are valid and should be considered when a company is thinking about outsourcing. Many challenges can be avoided with proper research. The challenges include:

- **Contract length.** Most of the outsourced IT contracts are for a relatively long time period (several years). This is because of the high cost of transferring assets and employees as well as maintaining technological investment. The long contract causes three particular issues:

  1. Difficulties in getting out of a contract if the outsourcing service provider turns out to be unsuitable.

  2. Problems in foreseeing what the business will need over the next 5 or 10 years (typical contract lengths), hence creating difficulties in establishing an appropriate contract.

  3. Problems in reforming an internal IT department after the contract period is finished.

- **Competitive edge.** Effective and innovative use of IT can give an organization a competitive edge over its rivals. A competitive business advantage provided by an internal IT department that understands the organization and is committed to its goals can be lost in an outsourced arrangement. In an outsourced arrangement, IT staff are striving to achieve the goals and objectives of the outsourcing service provider, which may conflict with those of the organization.

- **Confidentiality.** In some organizations, the information stored in the computer systems is central to the enterprise's success or survival, such as information about pricing policies, product mixing formulas, or sales analysis. Some companies decide against outsourcing for fear of placing confidential information in the hands of the provider, particularly if the outsourcing service provider offers services to companies competing in the same marketplace. Although the organization usually dismisses this threat, claiming it is covered by confidentiality clauses in a contract, the organization must assess the potential risk and costs of a confidentiality breach in determining the net benefits of an outsourcing agreement.

- **Scope definition.** Most IT projects suffer from problems associated with defining the scope of the system. The same problem afflicts outsourcing arrangements. Many difficulties result from contractual misunderstandings between the organization and the outsourcing service provider. In such circumstances,

the organization believes that the service required is within the contract scope while the service provider is sure it is outside the scope and so is subject to extra fees.[38] ∎

CHECK OUT www.mhhe.com/baltzanm

for additional study materials including quizzes and PowerPoint presentations.

chapter twelve

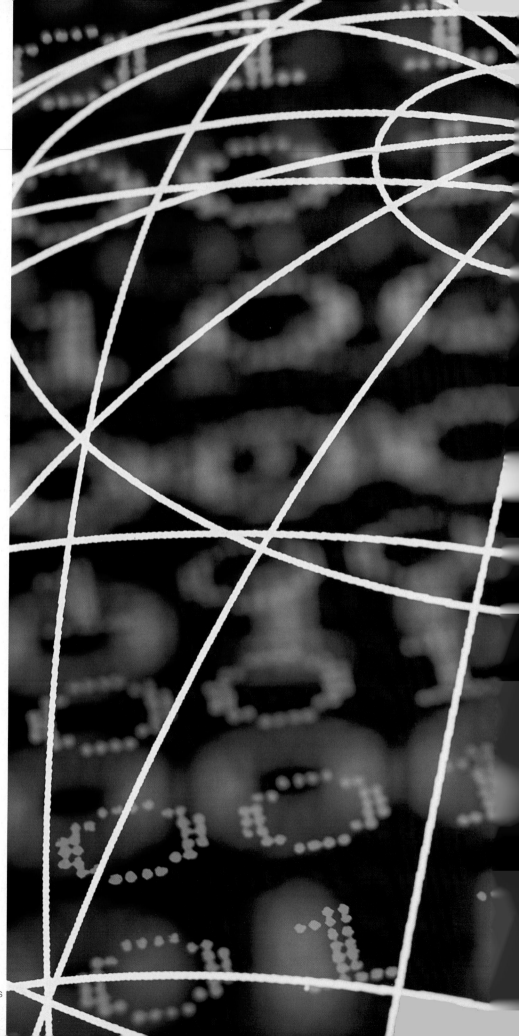

globalization, innovation,

+ 21st century organizational trends

what's in IT for me?

Have you ever dreamed of traveling to exotic cities like Paris, Tokyo, Rio de Janeiro, or Cairo? In the past, the closest many people ever got to working in such cities was in their dreams. Today, the situation has changed. Most major companies cite global expansion as a link to future growth. A recent study noted that 91 percent of the companies doing business globally believe it is important to send employees on assignments in other countries.

If a career in global business has crossed your mind, this chapter will help you understand the impacts of competing in a global world. The United States is a market of about 290 million people, but there are more than 6 billion potential customers in the 193 countries that make up the global market. Perhaps more interesting is that approximately 75 percent of the world's population lives in developing areas where technology, education, and per capita income still lag considerably behind those of developed (or industrialized) nations such as the United States.

You, the business student, should be familiar with the potential of global business, including its many benefits and challenges. The demand for students with training in global business is almost certain to grow as the number of businesses competing in global markets increases.

Whether they are in Berlin or Bombay, Kuala Lumpur or Kansas City, San Francisco or Seoul, organizations around the globe are developing new business models to operate competitively in a digital economy. These models are structured, yet agile; global, yet local; and they concentrate on maximizing the risk-adjusted return from both knowledge and technology assets.[1]

Globalization and working in an international global economy are integral parts of business today. Fortune 500 companies to mom-and-pop shops are now competing globally, and international developments affect all forms of business.

●● SECTION 12.1 Globalization

LEARNING OUTCOMES

LO12.1 Explain the cultural, political, and geoeconomic challenges facing global businesses.

LO12.2 Describe the four global IT business drivers that should be included in all IT strategies.

LO12.3 Describe governance and compliance and the associated frameworks an organization can implement.

LO12.4 Identify why an organization would need to understand global enterprise architectures when expanding operations abroad.

LO12.5 Explain the many different global information issues an organization might encounter as it conducts business abroad.

LO12.6 Identify global system development issues organizations should understand before building a global system.

●● LO12.1

Explain the cultural, political, and geoeconomic challenges facing global businesses.

●● LO12.2

Describe the four global IT business drivers that should be included in all IT strategies.

GLOBALIZATION

According to Thomas Friedman, the world is flat! Businesses are strategizing and operating on a global playing field. Traditional forms of business are simply not good enough in a global environment. Recall the way the Internet is changing business by reviewing Figure 12.1. To succeed in a global business environment, cultural, political, and geoeconomic (geographic and economic) business challenges must be confronted.

Cultural Business Challenges

Cultural business challenges include differences in languages, cultural interests, religions, customs, social attitudes, and political philosophies. Global businesses must be sensitive to such cultural differences. McDonald's, a truly global brand, has created several minority-specific websites in the United States: McEncanta for

FIGURE 12.1	Examples of How Technology Is Changing Business

Industry	Business Changes Due to Technology
Travel	Travel site Expedia.com is now the biggest leisure-travel agency, with higher profit margins than even American Express. Thirteen percent of traditional travel agencies closed in 2002 because of their inability to compete with online travel.
Entertainment	The music industry has kept Napster and others from operating, but $35 billion annual online downloads are wrecking the traditional music business. U.S. music unit sales are down 20 percent since 2000. The next big entertainment industry to feel the effects of ebusiness will be the $67 billion movie business.
Electronics	Using the Internet to link suppliers and customers, Dell dictates industry profits. Its operating margins rose from 7.3 percent in 2002 to 8 percent in 2003, even as it took prices to levels where rivals couldn't make money.
Financial services	Nearly every public efinance company remaining makes money, with online mortgage service Lending-Tree growing 70 percent a year. Processing online mortgage applications is now 40 percent cheaper for customers.
Retail	Less than 5 percent of retail sales occur online, but eBay was on track in 2003 to become one of the nation's top 15 retailers, and Amazon.com will join the top 40. Walmart's ebusiness strategy is forcing rivals to make heavy investments in technology.
Automobiles	The cost of producing vehicles is down because of SCM and web-based purchasing. Also, eBay has become the leading U.S. used-car dealer, and most major car sites are profitable.
Education and training	Cisco saved $133 million in 2002 by moving training sessions to the Internet, and the University of Phoenix online college classes please investors.

Hispanics, 365Black for African Americans, and i-am-asian for Asians. But these minority groups are not homogenous. Consider Asians: There are East Asian, Southeast Asian, Asian Indian, and, within each of these, divisions of national, regional, and linguistic nature. No company has the budget to create a separate website for every subsegment, but to assume that all Asian Americans fit into a single room—even a virtual room—risks a serious backlash. A company should ask a few key questions when creating a global website:

- Will the site require new navigational logic to accommodate cultural preferences?
- Will content be translated? If so, into how many languages?

- Will multilingual efforts be included in the main site or will it be a separate site, perhaps with a country-specific domain?
- Which country will the server be located in to support local user needs?
- What legal ramifications might occur by having the website targeted at a particular country, such as laws on competitive behaviors, treatment of children, or privacy?[2]

Political Business Challenges

Political business challenges include the numerous rules and regulations surrounding data transfers across national boundaries, especially personal information, tax implications, hardware and software importing and exporting, and trade agreements. The protection of personal information is a real concern for all countries. For example, evidence from a national survey about citizen satisfaction with the Canadian government online services speaks to the importance of paying attention to privacy concerns. This highly publicized survey, known as Citizens First, was administered by the Institute for Citizen-Centered Service (ICCS) and the Institute for Public Administration in Canada (IPCA). Results from the survey indicate that although other factors help promote citizen satisfaction with the Internet, such as outcome, ease of finding information, sufficient information, site navigation, and visual appeal, the key driver that directly impacts whether citizens will conduct online transactions is their concerns over information security and privacy.

For security, there are high levels of concerns over information storage, transmission, and access and identity

Where Have All the Good Workers Gone?

Sarah Schupp, the founder of University Parent.com, hired five new college graduates over the past year, which she quickly turned around and fired. One was fired on his first day for inappropriate sexual comments to a co-worker and another lasted a week before getting a pink slip.

"When you're hiring for sales, it's tricky to find a good fit, and selling advertising is not for everyone," says Schupp. "But you can't call in sick at 7:45 a.m. just because you don't want to come to work at 8 a.m."

Jeanne Achille, CEO of The Devon Group, was disenchanted with her recent hiring of a college graduate whose professors claimed was a "superstar." Achille fired the superstar within three weeks when it was discovered she spent hours online at work visiting a dating site, Tweeted about a night of partying, and then naively emailed in sick the next day. "Just who is supposed to be preparing these kids for the workplace?" questions Achille. "Is it home? Is it school? Or is there a layer we've missed?"

This question has reignited the debate about who is responsible for the quality of college graduates in the workplace. The tension has grown as young workers enter a labor force where employers are closely watching costs, including those for recruitment and training. Who do you think is responsible for preparing students for the working world? Why are new college graduates having a difficult time finding employment? What can you do to ensure you are not given the pink slip in your first month of work?

verification. For privacy and the protection of personal information, there are even stronger concerns about consolidation of information, unauthorized access, and sharing without permission.[3]

Global Geoeconomic Business Challenges

Geoeconomic refers to the effects of geography on the economic realities of international business activities. Even with the Internet, telecommunications, and air travel, the sheer physical distances covering the globe make it difficult to operate multinational business. Flying IT specialists into remote sites is costly, communicating in real-time across the globe's 24 time

Understanding the cultural, political, and geoeconomic business challenges is a good start to understanding global business, but the problems facing managers run far deeper. The remainder of this section focuses on business management issues that are central to all global business. Business managers must understand four primary areas—global IT business strategies, global enterprise architectures, global information issues, and global systems development—when running multinational companies (see Figure 12.2).

 **LO12.3**

Describe governance and compliance and the associated frameworks an organization can implement.

> As global operations expand and global competition heats up, pressure increases for companies to install global ebusiness applications for customers, suppliers, and employees.

zones is challenging, and finding quality telecommunication services in every country is difficult. Skilled labor supplies, cost of living, and labor costs also differ among the various countries. When developing global business strategies, all of these geoeconomic challenges must be addressed.

GLOBAL IT BUSINESS STRATEGIES

Global IT business strategies must include detailed information on the application of information technology across the organization. IT systems depend on global business drivers such as the nature of the industry, competitive factors, and environmental forces. For example, airlines and hotels have global customers who travel extensively and expect the same service regardless of location. Organizations require global IT systems that can provide fast, convenient service to all international employees who are servicing these customers. When a high-end hotel customer checks into a hotel in Asia she expects to receive the same high-end service as when she is checking into a hotel in Chicago or London. Figure 12.3 displays the global IT business drivers that should be included in all IT strategies.

Many global IT systems, such as finance, accounting, and operations management, have been in operation for years. Most multinational companies have global financial budgeting and cash management. As global operations expand and global competition heats up, pressure increases for companies to install global ebusiness applications for customers, suppliers, and employees. Examples include portals and websites geared toward customer service and supply chain management. In the past, such systems relied almost exclusively on privately constructed or government-owned telecommunications networks. But the explosive business use

FIGURE **12.2** Global IT Business Management Areas

Global IT Business Strategies

Global Systems Development

Global IT Business Management Areas

Global Enterprise Architectures

Global Information Issues

FIGURE 12.3 Global IT Business Drivers

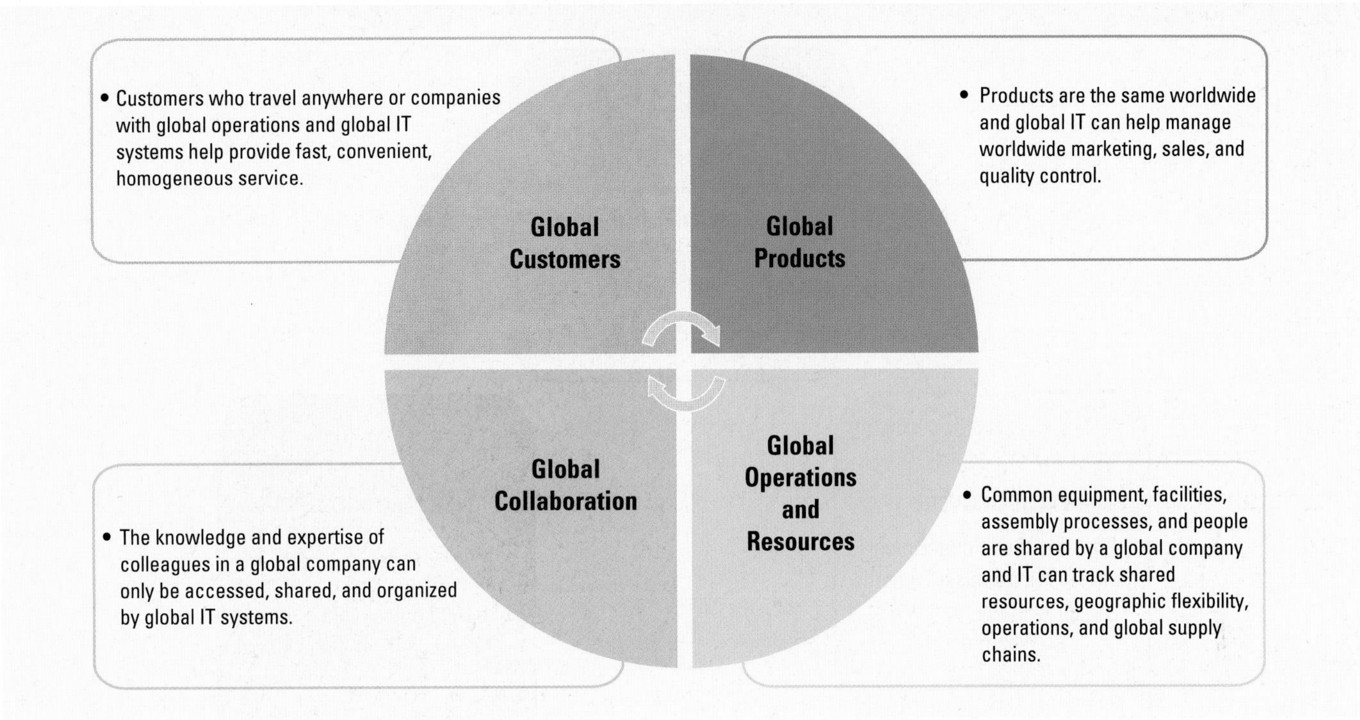

Global Customers

Global Products

Global Collaboration

Global Operations and Resources

- Customers who travel anywhere or companies with global operations and global IT systems help provide fast, convenient, homogeneous service.

- Products are the same worldwide and global IT can help manage worldwide marketing, sales, and quality control.

- The knowledge and expertise of colleagues in a global company can only be accessed, shared, and organized by global IT systems.

- Common equipment, facilities, assembly processes, and people are shared by a global company and IT can track shared resources, geographic flexibility, operations, and global supply chains.

of the Internet, intranets, and extranets for electronic commerce has made such applications more feasible for global companies.

Governance and Compliance

One fast-growing key area for all global business strategies includes governance and compliance. *Governance* is a method or system of government for management or control. *Compliance* is the act of conforming, acquiescing, or yielding. A few years ago the ideas of governance and compliance were relatively obscure. Today, the concept of formal IT governance and compliance is a must for virtually every company, both domestic and global. Key drivers for governance and compliance include financial and technological regulations as well as pressure from shareholders and customers.

Organizations today are subject to many regulations governing data retention, confidential information, financial accountability, and recovery from disasters. By implementing IT governance, organizations have the internal controls they need to meet the core guidelines of many of these regulations, such as the Sarbanes-Oxley Act of 2002.

IT governance essentially places structure around how organizations align IT strategy with business strategy, ensuring that companies stay on track to achieve their strategies and goals, and implementing good ways to measure IT's performance. Governance makes sure that all stakeholders' interests are considered and that processes provide measurable results. IT governance

should answer key questions including how the IT department is functioning overall, what key metrics management requires, and what return the business is getting from its IT investment. Figure 12.4 displays the five key areas of focus according to the IT Governance Institute.[4]

Organizations can follow a few different IT governance frameworks, including:

- **CoBIT:** *Information Systems Audit and Control Association (ISACA)* is a set of guidelines and supporting tools for IT governance that is accepted worldwide and generally used by auditors and companies as a way to integrate technology to implement controls and meet specific business objectives.

- **ITIL:** The *Information Technology Infrastructure Library (ITIL)* is a framework provided by the government of the United Kingdom and offers eight sets of management procedures: (1) service delivery, (2) service support, (3) service management, (4) Information and Communication Technology (ICT) infrastructure management, (5) software asset management, (6) business perspective, (7) security management, and (8) application management. ITIL is a good fit for organizations concerned about operations.

- **COSO:** Developed by the *Committee of Sponsoring Organizations (COSO)* is key for evaluating internal controls such as human resources, logistics, information technology, risk, legal, marketing and sales, operations, financial functions, procurement, and reporting. This is a more business-general framework that is less IT-specific.

FIGURE 12.4 IT Governance Institute Five Focus Areas

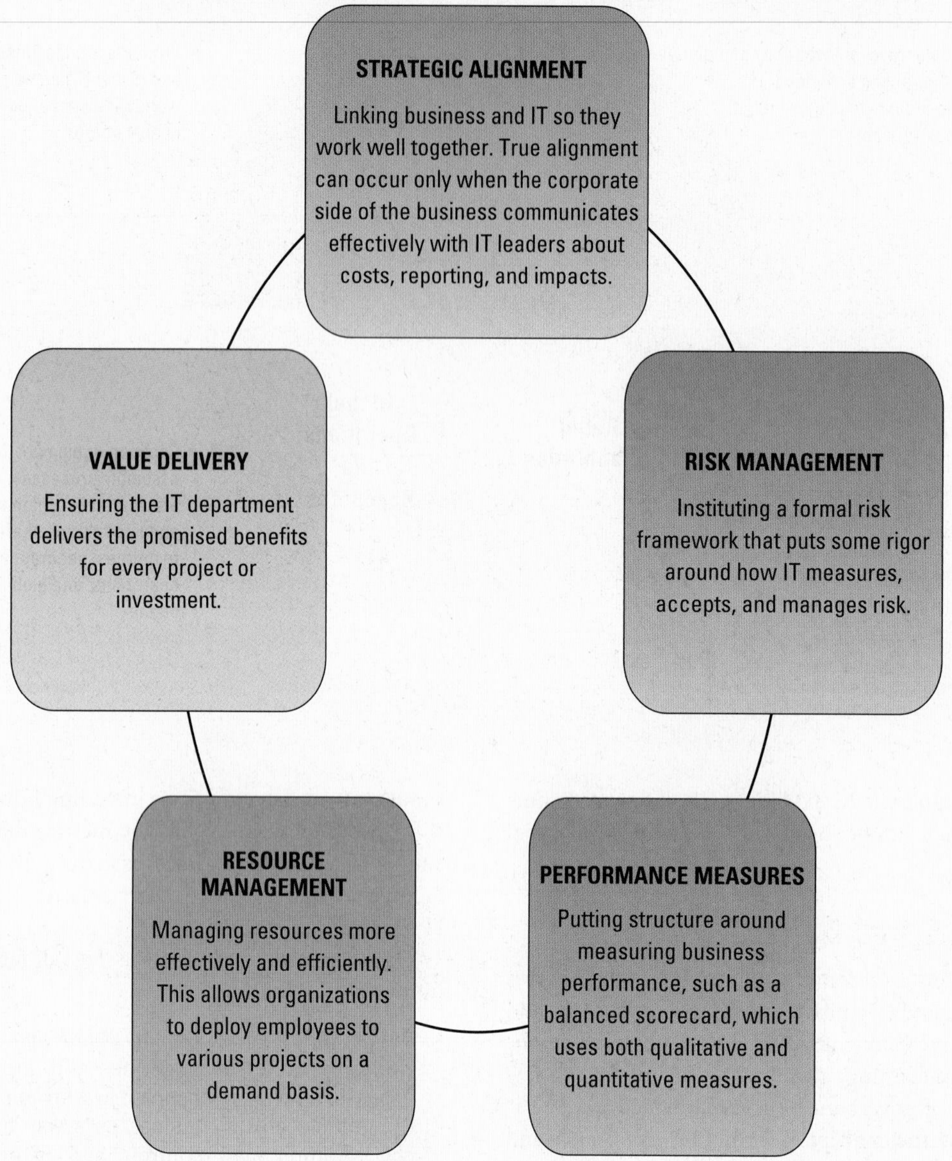

STRATEGIC ALIGNMENT

Linking business and IT so they work well together. True alignment can occur only when the corporate side of the business communicates effectively with IT leaders about costs, reporting, and impacts.

VALUE DELIVERY

Ensuring the IT department delivers the promised benefits for every project or investment.

RISK MANAGEMENT

Instituting a formal risk framework that puts some rigor around how IT measures, accepts, and manages risk.

RESOURCE MANAGEMENT

Managing resources more effectively and efficiently. This allows organizations to deploy employees to various projects on a demand basis.

PERFORMANCE MEASURES

Putting structure around measuring business performance, such as a balanced scorecard, which uses both qualitative and quantitative measures.

- **CMMI:** Created by a group from government, industry, and Carnegie Mellon's Software Engineering Institute, the **Capability Maturity Model Integration method (CMMI)** is a process improvement approach that contains 22 process areas. It is divided into appraisal, evaluation, and structure. CMMI is particularly well-suited to organizations that need help with application development, life cycle issues, and improving the delivery of products throughout the life cycle.[5]

●● LO12.4

Identify why an organization would need to understand global enterprise architectures when expanding operations abroad.

GLOBAL ENTERPRISE ARCHITECTURES

An **enterprise architecture** includes the plans for how an organization will build, deploy, use, and share its data, processes, and IT assets. An organization must manage its global enterprise architecture to support its global business operations. Management of a global enterprise architecture is not only technically complex, but also has major political and cultural implications. For example, hardware choices are difficult in some countries because of high prices, high tariffs, import restrictions, long lead times for government approvals, lack of local service or

> # MANAGING GLOBAL ENTERPRISE ARCHITECTURES, INCLUDING INTERNET, INTRANET, EXTRANET, AND OTHER TELECOMMUNICATION NETWORKS, IS A KEY GLOBAL IT CHALLENGE FOR THE 21ST CENTURY.

replacement parts, and lack of documentation tailored to local conditions. Software choices also present issues; for example, European data standards differ from American or Asian standards, even when purchased from the same vendor. Some software vendors also refuse to offer service and support in countries that disregard software licensing and copyright agreements.

The Internet and the World Wide Web are critical to international business. This interconnected matrix of computers, information, and networks that reaches tens of millions of users in hundreds of countries is a business environment free of traditional boundaries and limits. Linking to online global businesses offers companies unprecedented potential for expanding markets, reducing costs, and improving profit margins at a price that is typically a small percentage of the corporate communications budget. The Internet provides an interactive channel for direct communication and data exchange with customers, suppliers, distributors, manufacturers, product developers, financial backers, information providers—in fact, with all parties involved in an international organization.[6]

The Paris-based organization Reporters without Borders notes that 45 countries restrict their citizens' access to the Internet. "At its most fundamental, the struggle between Internet censorship and openness at the national level revolves around three main means: controlling the conduits, filtering the flows, and punishing the purveyors. In countries such as Burma, Libya, North Korea, Syria, and the countries of Central Asia and the Caucasus, Internet access is either banned or subject to tight limitations through government-controlled ISPs. These countries face a lose-lose struggle against the information age. By denying or limiting Internet access, they stymie a major engine of economic growth. But by easing access, they expose their citizenry to ideas potentially destabilizing to the status quo. Either way, many people will get access to the electronic information they want. In Syria, for example, people go to Lebanon for the weekend to retrieve their email," said Virgini Locussol, Reporters Without Borders desk officer for the Middle East and North Africa.[7]

Figure 12.5 displays the top 10 international telecommunication issues as reported by the IT executives at 300 Fortune 500 multinational companies. Political issues dominate the listing over technology issues, clearly emphasizing their importance in the management of global enterprise architectures.[8]

Estimating the operational expenses associated with international IT operations is another global challenge. Companies with global business operations usually establish or contract with systems integrators for additional IT facilities for their subsidiaries in other countries. These IT facilities must meet

FIGURE	12.5	Top 10 Telecommunication Issues

Network
- Improving the operational efficiency of networks
- Dealing with different networks
- Controlling data communication security

Regulatory Issues
- Dealing with transborder data flow restrictions
- Managing international telecommunication regulations
- Handling international politics

Technology and Country-Oriented Issues
- Managing network infrastructure across countries
- Managing international integration of technologies
- Reconciling national differences
- Dealing with international tariff structures

local and regional computing needs, and even help balance global computing workloads through communications satellite links. However, offshore IT facilities can pose major problems in headquarters' support, hardware and software acquisition, maintenance, and security. This is why many global companies

things onto corporate networks, we open up holes in the environment." Drugmaker Pfizer found this out the hard way. An employee's spouse loaded file-sharing software onto a Pfizer laptop at home, creating a security hole that appears to have compromised the names and Social Security numbers of 17,000

> ## It is now more important than ever for an organization to have well-rehearsed and frequently updated processes and procedures to insure against a variety of adverse scenarios.

prefer to outsource these facilities to application service providers or systems integrators such as IBM or Accenture to manage overseas operations. Managing global enterprise architectures, including Internet, intranet, extranet, and other telecommunication networks, is a key global IT challenge for the 21st century.

●● LO12.5

Explain the many different global information issues an organization might encounter as it conducts business abroad.

GLOBAL INFORMATION ISSUES

While many consumer gadgets and software applications can benefit a company—for instance, by helping employees get their jobs done more efficiently—the security implications are legion, said Ken Silva, chief security officer at VeriSign, which specializes in network security software. "When we bolt those

current and former Pfizer employees, according to a letter Pfizer sent to state attorneys general. Pfizer's investigation showed that 15,700 of those employees actually had their data accessed and copied.[9]

With war and terrorist attacks in many people's minds, security is a hot topic. For businesses, too, security concerns are widespread. Increasingly opening up their networks and applications to customers, partners, and suppliers using an ever more diverse set of computing devices and networks, businesses can benefit from deploying the latest advances in security technologies. These benefits include fewer disruptions to organizational systems, increased productivity of employees, and greater advances in administration, authorization, and authentication techniques.

Businesses must have the appropriate levels of authentication, access control, and encryption in place to ensure (1) that only authorized individuals can gain access to the network, (2) that they have access to only those applications for which they are entitled, and (3) that information cannot be understood or altered while in transit. Figure 12.6 displays a recent survey concerning both the level of physical security

| FIGURE | 12.6 | Physical Security Integration and Best Security Practices |

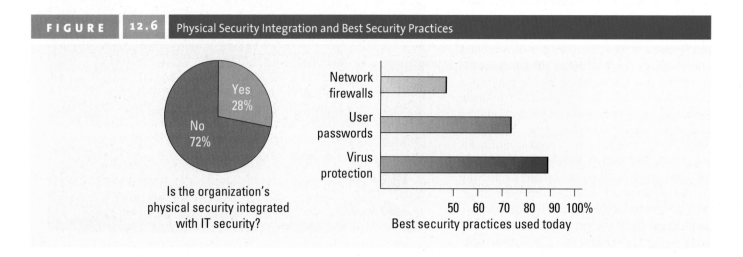

Is the organization's physical security integrated with IT security?

Best security practices used today

integration and the current security practices used by most organizations.[10]

Security breaches not only inconvenience business users and their customers and partners, but can also cost millions of dollars in lost revenues or lost market capitalization. The business cost of inadequate security does not stop at inconvenience and loss of revenues or market valuation. It can even force a business out of existence. For example, in early 2002 British Internet service provider Cloud-Nine Communications was the victim of a distributed denial-of-service (DDoS) attack that forced the company to close operations and to eventually transfer over 2,500 customers to a rival organization. While disruptive technologies can help a company to gain competitive advantage and market share (and avoid real business disruptions), lack of security can have the opposite effect, causing profitable companies to lose market share or even their entire business within hours or days of an attack.[11]

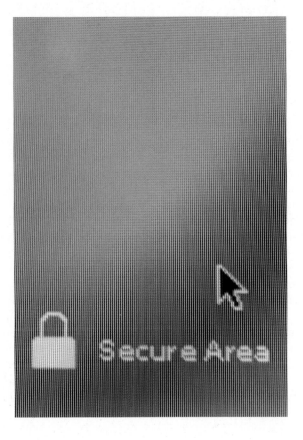

It is now more important than ever for an organization to have well-rehearsed and frequently updated processes and procedures to insure against a variety of adverse scenarios—Internet email and denial-of-service attacks from worms and viruses, loss of communications, loss of documents, password and information theft, fire, flood, physical attacks on property, and even terrorist attacks.

Rather than fight the trend, some companies are experimenting with giving employees more choice regarding the technology they use—so long as they accept more responsibility for it.

In 2005, BP began a pilot project that gives employees about $1,000 to spend on productivity-enhancing tools in addition to standard-issue equipment, according to a report from the Leading Edge Forum. But before they can participate, employees must pass a test of their computer literacy skills.[12]

The company takes other steps to give employees free rein while mitigating risk. BP cordons off its network by letting employees link to the Internet via consumer connections, from outside the firewall, in the case of its 18,000 laptops. At the same time it beefs up security on those machines. This lets employees safely experiment with software such as Amazon's on-demand computing and storage services.

Deperimeterization occurs when an organization moves employees outside its firewall, a growing movement to change the way corporations address technology security. In a business world where many employees are off-site or on the road, or where businesses increasingly must collaborate with partners and customers, some say it's not practical to rely on a hardened perimeter of firewalls. Instead, proponents of deperimeterization say companies should focus on beefing up security in end-user devices and an organization's critical information assets.[13]

Information Privacy

For many years, global data access issues have been the subject of political controversy and technology barriers in global business environments. These issues have become more prevalent

BUSTED Cyberprotest

Hackers attacked the United Nations official website, forcing some sections to be taken offline, including a section by Ban Ki-Moon, the UN Secretary General. Slogans accusing the United States and Israel of killing children appeared on the pages reserved for statements from Secretary General Ki-Moon.

The hackers' names are "kerem125," "Gsy," and "M0sted," and they describe their actions as "cyberprotest." In other attacks by hackers using the same names, they have claimed to be from Turkey. The UN was forced to take down the affected pages for repair but later managed to restore the secretary general's statements.

The electronically connected world is a playground for such hackers, and tracking them is next to impossible. What types of global information issues can you anticipate as you expand your systems? Why is information privacy such a hard issue to monitor globally?

> # INFORMATION PRIVACY CONCERNS THE LEGAL RIGHT OR GENERAL EXPECTATION OF INDIVIDUALS, GROUPS, OR INSTITUTIONS TO DETERMINE FOR THEMSELVES WHEN AND TO WHAT EXTENT INFORMATION ABOUT THEM IS COMMUNICATED TO OTHERS.

with the growth of the Internet and the expansion of ebusinesses. *Transborder data flows (TDF)* occur when business data flows across international boundaries over the telecommunications networks of global information systems. Many countries view TDF as violating their national sovereignty because transborder data flows avoid customs duties and regulations for the import or export of goods and services. Others view transborder data flows as violating their laws to protect the local IT industry from competition or their labor regulations from protecting local jobs. In many cases, the data flow issues that seem particularly politically sensitive are those that affect the movement out of a country of personal data in ebusiness and human resource applications.[14]

Many countries, especially those in the European Union (EU), may view transborder data flows as a violation of their privacy legislation since, in many cases, data about individuals are being moved out of the country without stringent privacy safeguards. Figure 12.7 highlights the key provisions of

a data privacy agreement between the United States and the European Union. The agreement exempts U.S. companies engaging in international ebusiness from EU data privacy sanctions if they join a self-regulatory program that provides EU consumers with basic information about, and control over, how their personal data are used. Thus, the agreement is said to provide a "safe harbor" for such companies from the requirements of the EU's Data Privacy Directive, which bans the transfer of personal information on EU citizens to countries that do not have adequate data privacy protection.[15]

Information privacy concerns the legal right or general expectation of individuals, groups, or institutions to determine for themselves when and to what extent information about them is communicated to others. In essence, information privacy is about how personal information is collected and shared. To facilitate information privacy, many countries have established legislation to protect the collection and sharing of personal information. However, this legislation varies greatly around the globe.

| FIGURE | 12.7 | U.S.–EU Data Privacy Requirements |

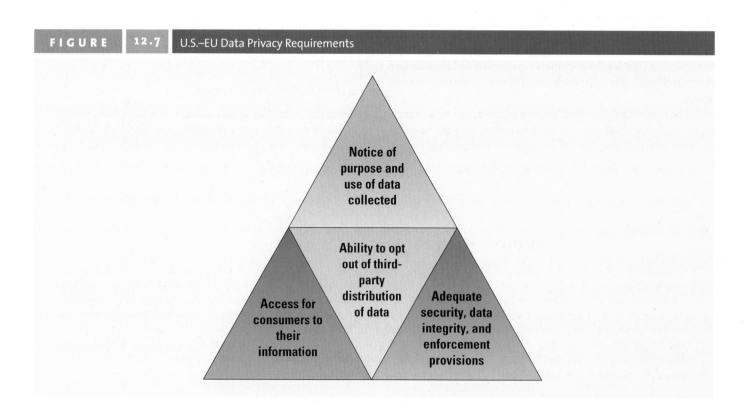

Europe

On one end of the spectrum lies European nations with their strong information privacy laws. Most notably, all member countries of the European Union adhere to a directive on the protection of personal data. A directive is a legislative act of the European Union that requires member states to achieve a particular result without dictating the means of how to achieve that result.

The directive on the protection of personal data grants European Union members the following rights:

- The right to know the source of personal data processing and the purposes of such processing.
- The right to access and/or rectify inaccuracies in one's own personal data.
- The right to disallow the use of personal data.

These rights are based on key principles pertaining to the collection or storage of personal data. The directive defines personal data to cover both facts and opinions about an individual. Any organization processing personal data of a person living in the European Union must comply with these key principles as outlined in the directive; these state that the data must be:

- Fairly and lawfully processed.
- Processed for limited purposes.
- Adequate, relevant, and not excessive.
- Accurate.
- Not kept longer than necessary.
- Processed in accordance with the data subject's rights.
- Not transferred to countries without adequate protection.

This last right restricts the flow of personal information outside the European Union by permitting its transfer to only countries that provide an "adequate" level of privacy protection—adequate in the sense that these other countries have to offer a level of privacy protection equivalent to that of the European Union. When first implemented, this part of the directive caused some concerns since countries outside the EU had much weaker privacy protection laws. Organizations in the United States were greatly concerned because they were at a legal risk if the personal data of EU citizens were transferred to computer servers in the United States—a likely scenario in today's global world of ebusiness. This led to extensive negotiations. The result was the establishment of a "safe harbor" program in the United States. This program provides a framework for U.S. organizations to show evidence of compliance with the EU directive. In this way, American companies can self-declare their compliance with the key principles of the directive and do business with EU nations without worrying about EU citizens suing them.

The United States

On the other end of the spectrum lies the United States. Information privacy is not highly legislated nor regulated. There is no all-encompassing law that regulates the use of personal data or information. In many cases, access to public information is considered culturally acceptable, such as obtaining credit reports for employment or housing purposes. The reason for this may be historical. In the United States, the first amendment protects free speech, and in many instances the protection of privacy might conflict with this amendment.

There are some exceptions. Though very few states recognize an individual's right to privacy, California's constitution protects an inalienable right to privacy. The California legislature has enacted several pieces of legislation aimed at protecting citizen information privacy. For example, California's Online Privacy Protection Act, established in 2003, requires commercial websites or online services that collect personal information of California residents to clearly post a privacy policy on the website or online service and to comply with this policy.

Other nationwide exceptions include the Children's Online Privacy Protection Act (COPPA) and the Health Insurance Portability and Accountability Act (HIPAA).[16]

COPPA is a federal law established in 1998 that applies to the collection of personal information from American children who are under 13 years of age. The act outlines what a website should include in its privacy policy, how to seek consent from a parent or guardian, and the responsibilities a website operator has to protect children's online safety and privacy. This law applies to any website that is perceived to be targeting American children. For example, if a toy company established in Canada wanted to sell toys in the United States, the company's website should have to comply with the collection and use of information as outlined in COPPA. To show compliance requires a substantial amount of paperwork. As a result, many websites disallow underage users to join online communities and websites. Not complying with COPPA can be costly. In September 2006, the website Xanga, an online community, was fined $1 million for violating COPPA legislation.

HIPAA was enacted by the U.S. Congress in 1996. Provisions in HIPPA establish national standards for the electronic data interchange of health care-related transactions between health care providers, insurance plans, and employers. Embedded in these standards are rules for the handling and protection of personal health care information.

Canada

Canada's privacy laws follow very closely to the European model. Canada as a nation is quite concerned about protecting the personal information of its citizens. Its primary privacy law is the Personal Information Protection and Electronic Document Act (PIPEDA). The purpose of PIPEDA is to provide Canadians with a right of privacy with respect to how their personal information is collected, used, or disclosed by an organization. This is most important today, especially in the private sector, when information technology increasingly facilitates the collection and free flow of information.

Its precursor was the Privacy Act established in 1983 that restricted the handling of personal information within federal government departments and agencies only. This information concerned such things as pension and employment insurance files, medical records, tax records, and military records.

PIPEDA took effect in January 2001 and, like the Privacy Act, applied only to federally regulated organizations. By January 2004, PIPEDA's reach extended beyond government borders and applied to all other types of organizations, including commercial businesses. By doing so, Canada's PIPEDA law brought Canada into compliance with the European Union's directive on the protection of personal data. Hence, since January 2004, Canada no longer needed to implement safe harbor provisions for organizations wishing to collect and store personal information on European Union citizens.

● ● ● **LO12.6**

Identify global system development issues organizations should understand before building a global system.

GLOBAL SYSTEMS DEVELOPMENT

It is extremely difficult to develop a domestic information system, but the added complexity of developing a global information system quadruples the effort. Global information systems must support a diverse base of customers, users, products, languages, currencies, laws, and so on. Developing efficient, effective, and responsive information systems for multiple countries, differing cultures, and global ebusinesses is an enormous challenge for any organization. Managers should expect conflicts over local versus global system requirements and difficulties agreeing on common system features. For the project to succeed, the development environment should promote involvement and ownership by all local system users.

One of the most important global information systems development issues is the global standardization of data definitions. Common data definitions are necessary for sharing information among the parts of an international business. Difference in language, culture, and technology platforms can make global data standardization quite difficult. For example, what Americans call a "sale" may be called "an order booked" in the United Kingdom, an "order scheduled" in Germany, and an "order produced" in France. These are all referring to the exact same business event, but could cause problems if global employees have different versions of the data definition. Businesses are moving ahead to standardize data definitions and business processes. Many organizations are implementing corporate wikis where all global employees can post and maintain common business definitions.

Organizations can use several strategies to solve some of the problems that arise in global information systems development. First is transforming and customizing an information system used by the home office into a global application. This ensures the system uses the established business processes and supports the primary needs of the end users. Second, is setting up a multinational development team with key people from several subsidiaries to ensure that the system design meets the needs of all local sites as well as corporate headquarters. Third, an organization could use centers of excellence where an entire system might be assigned for development to a particular subsidiary based on its expertise in the business or technical dimensions needed for successful development. A final approach that has rapidly become a major development option is to outsource the development work to global or offshore development countries that have the required skills and experience to build global information systems. All of these approaches require development team collaboration and managerial oversight to meet the global needs of the business.

Integrating Global Systems

Information technology has penetrated the heart of organizations and will stay there in the future. The IT industry is one of the most dynamic in the global economy. As an industry, it not only creates millions of high-level jobs, but also helps organizations to be more efficient and effective, which in turn stimulates innovation. The integration of business and technology has allowed organizations to increase their share of the global economy, transform the way they conduct business, and become more efficient and effective (see Figure 12.8).

The past few years have produced a confluence of events that has reshaped the global economy. Around the world, free-market competition has flourished and a new globally interdependent financial system has emerged. Reflecting these changes, core business relationships and models are dramatically changing, including shifts from:

- Product-centricity to customer-centricity.
- Mass production to mass customization.
- The value in material things to the value of knowledge and intelligence.

In concert with these trends, a new series of business success factors and challenges has emerged that is helping to determine marketplace winners and losers:

- Organization agility, often supported by a "plug and play" IT infrastructure (with a flexible and adaptable applications architecture).
- A focus on core competencies and processes.

- A redefinition of the value chain.
- Instantaneous business response.
- The ability to scale resources and infrastructure across geographic boundaries.

These developments add up to an environment that is vastly more complex than even five years ago. This in turn has resulted in organizations increasingly embracing new business models. The new environment requires organizations to focus externally on their business processes and integration architectures. The virtually integrated business model will cause a sharp increase in the number of business partners and the closeness of integration between them.

Never before have IT investments played such a critical role in business success. As business strategies continue to evolve, the distinction between "the business" and IT will virtually disappear.

●● SECTION 12.2 21st Century Organizational Trends

LEARNING OUTCOMES

LO12.7 Explain the six best practices of innovation.

LO12.8 Identify how energy consumption and recycling IT equipment can lead to greener IT.

LO12.9 Describe the three ways organizations can use social networking.

LO12.10 Explain virtual worlds and virtual workforces and their impact on business.

FIGURE 12.8 The Integration of Business and Technology

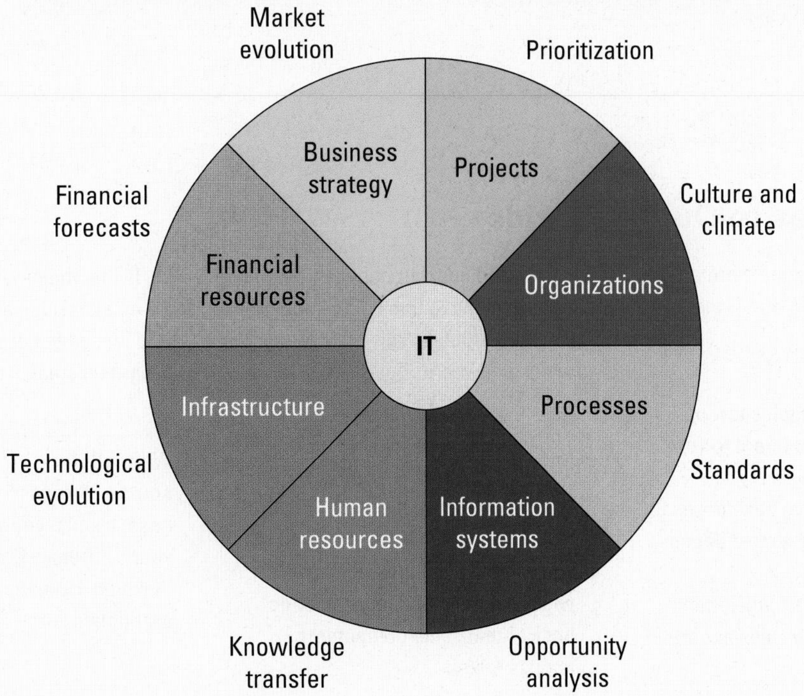

21ST CENTURY ORGANIZATION TRENDS

Many people have no idea how they would get any work done on business trips if they did not have a laptop. They simply cannot remember how they lived without their BlackBerry. Their cell phones might as well be surgically attached to their ear, it is so crucial to their job. It is hard to conceive of getting through the day without Google, or, if the person is under 40, text messaging or Facebook to stay in touch with an extended network of colleagues. In just a decade or less, technology has done a number on the way we work.

And in the next decade, the relentless march of computer power and Internet connection speeds will bring more profound changes to work than anything seen so far. Consider just a few of the breakthroughs technology visionaries think will occur in coming years. Picture Apple's slick iPhone shrunk to the size of a credit card. Then imagine it can connect not only to contacts on the latest social network, but also to billions of pea-sized wireless sensors attached to buildings, streets, retail products, and clothes—all simultaneously sending data over the Internet. This will allow tracking and managing more than static information; users will be able to track events in the physical world, from production on a factory floor to colleagues' whereabouts to how customers are using products. All that information will be much easier to view and analyze, using hand and arm gestures to control commands and viewing results with special glasses that make it seem as if the user is gazing at a life-size screen. Just imagine producing detailed prototypes of product or design ideas via a 3D printer that creates plastic models from computerized specs as easily as a paper printer spews out reports today.[17]

Organizations are facing technological changes and challenges more extensive and far reaching in their implications than anything since the modern industrial revolution occurred in the early 1900s. Organizations that want to survive in the 21st century must recognize these technological changes and challenges, carry out required organizational changes in the face of it, and learn to operate in an entirely different way. Today's organizations focus on defending and safeguarding their existing market positions in addition to targeting new market growth. The primary changes and challenges organizations are focusing on in the 21st century include:

- Innovation: finding new.
- Social entrepreneurship: going green.
- Social networks: who's who.
- Virtual worlds: it's a whole new world.

 **LO12.7**

Explain the six best practices of innovation.

INNOVATION: FINDING NEW

In the past, a company primarily focused on operational excellence, now innovation is driving the wheels of IT. *Innovation* is the introduction of new equipment or methods. The current impetus to innovate comes from the need to cut costs, while still creating a competitive advantage. Fundamental shifts in technology will make it possible for businesses to realize IT's promise of technology-enabled innovation, responsiveness, and speed.

omg lol

Things We'll Say to Our Grandkids

According to *Wired* magazine, here are the top 10 things we will say to our grandkids:

1. Back in my day, we only needed 140 characters.
2. There used to be so much snow up here, you could strap a board to your feet and slide all the way down.
3. Televised contests gave cash prizes to whoever could store the most data in their head.
4. Well, the screens were bigger, but they only showed the movies at certain times of day.

5. We all had one, but nobody actually used it. Come to think of it, I bet my LinkedIn profile is still out there on the web somewhere.
6. *英语曾经是统治语言。疯狂,哼?* Translation: "English used to be the dominant language. Crazy, huh?"
7. Our bodies were made of meat and supported by little sticks of calcium.
8. You used to keep files right on your computer, and you had to go back to that same computer to access them!

9. Is that the new iPhone 27G? Got multitasking yet?
10. I just can't get used to this darn vat-grown steak. Texture ain't right.

With all that you have learned in this course, forecast new industry and business trends you'll encounter throughout your career. Create three statements that you believe you'll be saying to your grandchildren.

Surfers from around the world converged on Maverick's at Pillar Point, just a few miles from San Francisco, to challenge each other on the big waves that have made this a legendary surfing destination. The sixth Mavericks Surf Contest had been announced only 48 hours earlier to ensure optimal wave conditions for the contestants. Surfers from as far away as Australia, Brazil, and South Africa scrambled to make their way to this invitation-only competition. It was magical to watch these athletes challenge 20-foot waves with an ease and grace that made it all seem so natural.

Beneath the surface, though, is a different story, one that contains important lessons for business executives. While all attention was on the athletes riding their surfboards, the technology and techniques used to master big-wave surfing have evolved over decades, driven by dedicated, perhaps even obsessed, groups of athletes and craftsmen. Executives can gain significant insight into the innovation process by looking at this sport and following the six best practices of innovation (see Figure 12.9).[18]

Find Your Relevant Edge

First, to push performance levels, organizations must find the relevant edge. In the case of big-wave surfers, there has been an ever-expanding search for the breaks that would produce bigger and rougher waves to test new board designs and surfing practices.

Following the lead of surfers, business executives need to find relevant edges that will test and push their current performance. For example, companies making diesel engines and power generators should be actively engaged in finding ways to more effectively serve lower-income customers in remote rural areas of emerging economies. These demanding customers could prompt significant innovation in both product design and distribution processes in an effort to deliver greater value at lower cost. The innovations resulting from these efforts on the edge could lead to significant improvements in product lines.

Assemble Innovation Hothouses

Second, attract motivated groups of people to these edges to work together around challenging performance issues. In the late 1950s, Waimea Bay, on the north shore of Oahu, became the test bed for athletes seeking to push the boundaries of big-wave surfing. In the isolation of the north shore, dedicated surfers spent 8 to 10 hours each day, every day, challenging themselves and each other on the big waves. The real advances in surfing technology and practices occurred at the breaks where surfers gathered and formed deep relationships over extended periods. They learned rapidly from each other and pushed each other to go to the next level.

Large companies have become very adept at establishing remote outposts in places like Beijing, Hyderabad, Haifa, and St. Petersburg to attract local talent and push forward challenging research and development projects. Often, though, these outposts either become disconnected from their parent companies or fail to establish deep links with other leading-edge participants in the area. The key challenge is to connect these company-owned facilities more effectively with their local environments as well as with each other through challenging and sustained innovation initiatives that build long-term, trust-based relationships. Performance improvement generally comes first in the form of tacit knowledge that is difficult

---

| FIGURE | 12.9 | Six Best Practices of Innovation |

Mix Practitioners and Developers

Celebrate Diversity

Look Around

Assemble Innovation Hothouses

Reward Risk Takers

Find Your Relevant Edge

INNOVATION

to express and communicate more broadly. People have to be there to gain access to this tacit knowledge.

Reward Risk Takers

Third, recognize that the people who are likely to be attracted to the edge are big risk takers. This is a key reason the edge becomes such a fertile ground for innovation. It attracts people who are not afraid to take risks and to learn from their experiences. They relentlessly seek new challenges. Executives need to be thoughtful about how to attract these people, provide them with environments to support risk taking, and reward them for both successes and failures.

Celebrate Diversity

Fourth, recognize that the edge fosters not just risk taking, but very different cultures that are also edgy. The advances in big-wave surfing did not come from the casual surfers but from those who developed an entire lifestyle and culture, fostered by intense and even obsessive concentration on pushing the envelope. Executives need to find ways to protect and honor these edgy cultures, whether they are inhabited by tattooed web designers or the next generation of employees who learned how to innovate as members of guilds in World of Warcraft.

Look Around

Fifth, find ways to appropriate insights from adjacent disciplines and even more remote areas of activity. Early advances in surfing technology came from the aerospace industry because some of the employees in this industry were also avid surfers. Some of surfer Laird Hamilton's greatest insights came from his experiences as an expert windsurfer and his colleagues' experiences with snowboarding. By attracting diverse backgrounds and experiences to the edge, executives can foster creative breakthroughs.

Mix Practitioners and Developers

Sixth, bring users and developers of technology close together. It is no accident that the most innovative surfers also tended to be expert shapers of surfboards. These folks not only designed surfboards but also shaped the materials into the finished product and then took them out to life-threatening breaks to test and refine them. They were relentless tinkerers, integrating experience, intuition, and craft to come up with creative new boards. Technology and practice are intimately linked. Very little performance improvement comes directly out of the technology itself. It is only when seasoned practitioners engage with the technology, especially in close-knit communities, and evolve their practices to better use it, that the real performance breakthroughs occur.

●● LO12.8

Identify how energy consumption and recycling IT equipment can lead to greener IT.

SOCIAL ENTREPRENEURSHIP: GOING GREEN

Social responsibility implies that an entity whether it is a government, corporation, organization, or individual has a responsibility to society. *Corporate policy* is a dimension of social responsibility that refers to the position a firm takes on social and political issues. *Corporate responsibility* is a dimension of social responsibility that includes everything from hiring minority workers to making safe products. *Sustainable, or "green," IT* describes the manufacture, management, use, and disposal of information technology in a way that minimizes damage to the environment, which is a critical part of a corporation's responsibility. As a result, the term has many different meanings, depending on whether you are a manufacturer, manager, or user of technology. This section covers energy consumption, recycling IT equipment, and greener IT.

Energy Consumption

As a threat to operations and the bottom line, corporate computing's fast-growing power consumption is forcing companies to adopt green energy practices. Engineers at Hewlett-Packard made a startling realization about the servers running the company's computing systems. Surging power consumption, along with rising energy costs, will soon make it more expensive to keep a server going for a year than to acquire one in the first place. Left unchecked, costs like these interfere with HP's goal of cutting energy consumption 15 percent by 2010.[19]

When HP began constructing a new 50,000-square-foot building to house high-powered computers, it sought advice from Pacific Gas & Electric. By following the California power company's recommendations, HP will save $1 million a year in power costs for that data center alone, PG&E says.

Like HP, companies across the globe are adding equipment to keep up with surging computing needs—and then are forced to make substantial changes to curtail the leap in costs associated with running the big buildings, or data centers, housing all that gear. "Data centers use 50 times the energy per square foot than an office [does]," said Mark Bramfitt, principal program manager at PG&E. Figure 12.10 displays the breakdown of power usage in the typical data center.[20]

Industry experts say the power consumption of data centers is doubling every five years or so, making them one of the fastest-growing drags on energy in the United States. Figure 12.11 displays data center energy bills.[21]

With demand for computer power exploding, energy consumption by data centers doubled between 2000 and 2006, and could double again by 2011. So the pressure is on tech companies, utilities, and builders to come up with new ways of cutting energy consumption. Here are some of the ways they are responding.

Sun Microsystems: Throughput Computing

A decade ago, the chip industry had a single focus: making the digital brains of computers process data ever faster. But Sun Microsystems chip architect Marc Tremblay saw a fatal flaw in that strategy. Faster chips would run hotter, and eventually they would burn out. So he designed what's known as a multicore chip, which has several processors on a single sliver of silicon, each of them running cooler and sucking less energy but collectively getting more work done. He also enabled each processor to perform more than one task at a time. The processors on Sun's Niagara server computers, based on Tremblay's designs, consumed just 70 watts of power, about one-third of a conventional microprocessor.[22]

Virtualization

It used to be possible to run only one application at a time on a given server. That meant if the application was not needed at any given time, the server just was not being used. Analysts estimate only 10 to 20 percent of the capability of a typical server is used. *Virtualization* is a framework

Sustainable, or "green," IT describes the manufacture, management, use, and disposal of information technology in a way that minimizes damage to the environment, which is a critical part of a corporation's responsibility.

| FIGURE | 12.10 | Breakdown of Power Usage in the Typical Data Center |

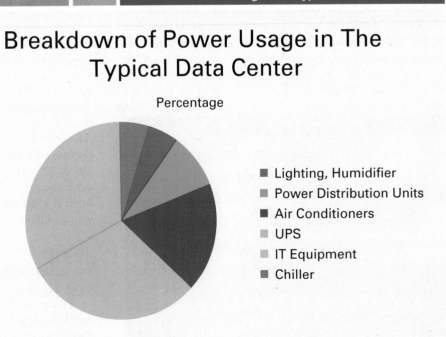

Breakdown of Power Usage in The Typical Data Center

Percentage

- Lighting, Humidifier
- Power Distribution Units
- Air Conditioners
- UPS
- IT Equipment
- Chiller

FIGURE 12.11 The Energy Bill

The Electric Bill

How Does A Company Track Data Center Usage?

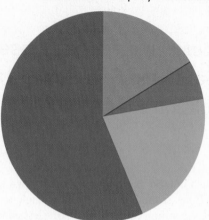

- IT pays bill
- Incentive to keep electric costs low
- IT does not manage bill
- Facilities pays IT bill; IT unaware

Smart Cooling

Hewlett-Packard Research Fellow Chandrakant Patel came up with a new approach to data center energy use: Think of the data center as one giant machine. Out of that came HP's Dynamic Smart Cooling technology. Thousands of heat sensors monitor temperatures, and software directs the air-conditioning system to put the big chill on the places that need it most. Projected energy savings: 20 to 45 percent.[25]

Alternative Energy Sources

Web search giant Google, which operates some of the largest data centers in the world, has committed to using cutting-edge technologies to power and cool its data centers, including wind and solar power. It's already using wind to power a data center in the Netherlands, and there's speculation it may tap wind for a major new facility in Council Bluffs, Iowa.[26]

of dividing the resources of a computer into multiple execution environments. Virtualization software allows IT managers to easily load multiple programs on a single machine and move programs from one computer to another on the fly to make maximum use of a cluster of servers. This significantly reduces energy use because fewer servers are needed. Virtualization software has been used for decades on mainframe computers, but it only became popular on PC servers recently.[23]

Energy Rebate Programs

Pacific Gas & Electric's Mark Bramfitt saw virtualization as a great way to reduce energy use in Northern California's data centers, so he designed an innovative data center energy-saving program. Companies get rebates for reducing the number of servers they use in their data centers. In just one year, Bramfitt received more than 47 applications from data center operators and paid out four rebates. He is also urging other utilities to adopt similar programs. So far, three others have followed suit.[24]

Biology Meets Chips

IBM researcher Bruno Michel and his team at IBM Zurich Research Laboratory are applying biological principles to deal with the heat problem in computing. Just as the human vascular system cools our bodies, Michel is designing devices that cool chips using liquid delivered through capillary-like circulation systems. Typically, the processors in server computers are air-cooled; chilled air is blown over metal caps on top of the chips, where tiny fins dissipate heat. One of Michel's inventions is a metal cap that fits over a processor and sprays jets of water out of 50,000 nozzles into microscopic channels etched in the metal. The channels behave like capillaries, circulating the liquid efficiently and cutting the energy required to pump the water.[27]

Government Involvement

The European Union has imposed limits on carbon emissions. Since 2005, the Emission Trading Scheme has required 12,000 iron, steel, glass, and power plants to buy CO_2 permits, which allows them to emit the gas into the atmosphere. If a company exceeds its limit, it can buy unused permits from other companies that have successfully cut their emissions. If they are unable to buy spare permits, however, they are fined for every excess ton of CO_2. Because IT contributes to the total carbon emissions in a company, carbon cap and trade or tax laws will impact how technology is managed. The EU and many U.S. states also have laws that require computer equipment, which contains many toxic substances, be recycled.[28]

Recycle IT Equipment

Sustainable IT disposal refers to the safe disposal of IT assets at the end of their life cycle. It ensures that **ewaste,** or old computer equipment, does not end up in a landfill, where the toxic substances it contains can leach into groundwater, among other problems. Many of the major hardware manufacturers offer take-back programs, so IT departments do not have to take responsibility for disposal. Some U.S. states and the European Union have laws requiring that ewaste be recycled. For example, Dell and Sony will take back any of their products for free and Toshiba will take back its laptops. Apple charges a fee, but will waive it if you are purchasing a new product. HP also will charge you, but will give you a credit toward future HP purchases. For a complete list of recycling programs in the United States, visit the Computer Take-Back Campaign website (www.computer takeback.com). According to the Computer TakeBack Campaign, Maine, California, Texas, Oregon, Maryland, Washington, and Minnesota have ewaste laws. Some of these laws apply only to equipment manufacturers; others apply to end users. In 2007, ewaste bills were introduced in 23 states. Companies that mind their energy consumption and dispose of used equipment responsibly now will be better off when regulations are imposed.

Complying with ewaste regulations should become easier for IT managers due to new manufacturing regulations. The EU Directive on the Restriction of the Use of Certain Hazardous Substances in Electrical and Electronic Equipment, which took effect July 1, 2006, restricts the use of six hazardous materials in the manufacture of certain electronics: lead, mercury, cadmium, hexavalent chromium, polybrominated biphenyls, and polybrominated diphenyl ether (the last two are flame retardants used in plastics). Such requirements reduce the toxicity of electronics, and thus, the ewaste they produce.[29]

In 2006, obsolete desktops, laptops, and servers accounted for 18 billion pounds of electronic trash worldwide, but the major companies involved in ewaste recovery (Dell, HP, and IBM) recovered only 356 million pounds—about 2 percent.

Only about one-third of all U.S. companies have an IT asset disposal policy. The rest are either doing nothing or dumping them into municipal landfills. According to National Geographic's *The Green Guide,* 50 to 80 percent of recycled electronics end up in developing nations, where they are disassembled by untrained workers without the proper equipment. This exposes them to toxic substances such as mercury, cadmium, and lead. If the equipment is left in landfills, those same toxins end up in water sources.

Greener IT

At Sun Microsystems, OpenWork, the company's telecommuting program, provides employees with shared office space, home equipment, and subsidies for DSL and electricity, according to Dave Douglas, vice president of eco responsibility at Sun. More than 56 percent of Sun's employees are currently in the program. "In the last five years we have cut our office space by one-sixth and have saved over $60 million a year on space and power," Douglas said. Sun also saves an estimated 29,000 tons of CO_2 per year due to reduced employee commuting. That is equivalent to taking 5,694 cars off the road for one year, according to the EPA's carbon calculator.[30]

Dow Chemical's process control automation system will shut a plant down if it is not compliant with air and water emissions requirements. Dow also uses a monitoring system to measure the air and water emissions at its plants and is deploying an environmental reporting system to manage reporting of this

Living the
DREAM

Smart Cities

Smart cities are being created around the globe with the use of advanced technology coupled with strong government. Smart cities use mobility, construction, energy, transportation, and the latest green technology in new and innovative ways to help the environment. A few examples include:

- San Francisco's California Academy of Sciences building sports a living roof and is one of the most sustainable structures in the world. Its 2.5-acre "living roof" features local plants and a glass canopy of photovoltaic cells that produces energy for the building.
- Stockholm uses sensors, software, and computer networks to monitor traffic during peak periods.
- Shanghai boasts the world's first low-pollution magnetic railway that transports passengers at more than 100 mph.
- Massachusetts plans to install 300 wind turbines in its towns and cities.

- San Francisco's smart trash provides incentives and a go-green attitude to induce San Franciscans to recycle 72 percent of their refuse. SF Recycling & Disposal sorts glass, plastic, and paper products at Pier 96 and presses the materials into compact cubes.

What types of programs are being deployed in your city to green the environment? What types of programs are being deployed around your school to help green the environment? Devise a new program using technology that your school could implement to help green the environment.

data to state and federal authorities, said CIO and Chief Sustainability Officer David Kepler.

IT systems can also help save energy by controlling heat and air-conditioning in office buildings. Wireless sensors can be used to measure airflow and room occupancy. If the occupancy sensors (which turn lights on and off when people enter or leave a room) are networked to airflow sensors, the amount of air-conditioning used when people are not in a room can be reduced, said David Kepler. "The basic idea is to collect data on how the facility is using energy and use that information to define patterns that can help change what you are doing and reduce operating costs."

To keep up with its explosive growth, Google is building data centers off the beaten path, in places like Lenoir, North Carolina; Mount Holly, South Carolina, and Council Bluffs, Iowa. A 30-acre facility in The Dalles, Oregon, is the most recent of them to be completed and put into operations. The Dalles, a town of about 12,000, provided the perfect location for Google, with its hydroelectric dam, affordable land, and a 15-year tax incentive. An industrial-strength power grid connects the dam to Google's complex, where massive cooling systems rise above two data center buildings. Google spends approximately $600 million to build a major data center, requiring a staff of 100 to 200 operate. Figure 12.12 displays the current ways companies are choosing to go green.[31]

⚫⚫ LO12.9

Describe the three ways organizations can use social networking.

SOCIAL NETWORKS: WHO'S WHO

Encover Chief Executive Officer Chip Overstreet was on the hunt for a new vice president for sales. He had homed in on a promising candidate and dispensed with the glowing but unsurprising remarks from references. Now it was time to dig for any dirt. So he logged on to LinkedIn, an online business network. "I did 11 back-door checks on this guy and found people he had worked with at five of his last six companies," said Overstreet, whose firm sells and manages service contracts for manufacturers. "It was incredibly powerful."

So powerful, in fact, that more than a dozen sites like LinkedIn have cropped up in recent years. They are responding to a growing impulse among web users to build ties, communities, and networks online, fueling the popularity of sites such as News Corp.'s MySpace. As of April, the 10 biggest social-networking sites, including MySpace, reached a combined unique audience of 68.8 million users, drawing in 45 percent of active web users, according to Nielsen/NetRatings.[32]

Corporations and smaller businesses have not embraced online business networks with nearly the same abandon as teens and college students who have flocked to social sites. Yet companies are steadily overcoming reservations and using the sites and related technology to craft potentially powerful business tools. Figure 12.13 displays the three types of social networking an organization can implement: passive search, boomerangs, and marketing networks.

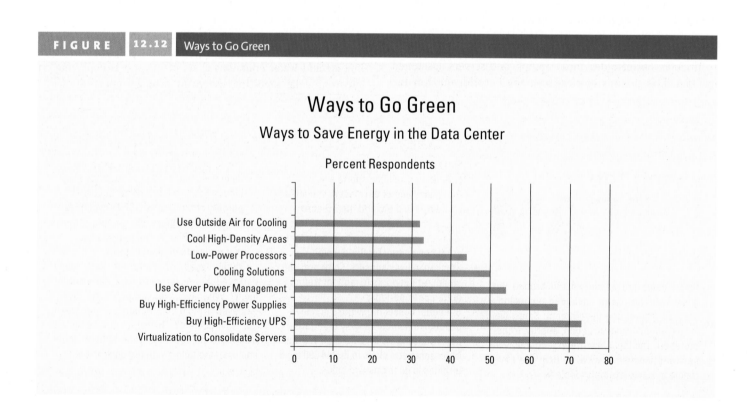

FIGURE 12.12 Ways to Go Green

Ways to Go Green
Ways to Save Energy in the Data Center

Percent Respondents

- Use Outside Air for Cooling
- Cool High-Density Areas
- Low-Power Processors
- Cooling Solutions
- Use Server Power Management
- Buy High-Efficiency Power Supplies
- Buy High-Efficiency UPS
- Virtualization to Consolidate Servers

0   10   20   30   40   50   60   70   80

> # COMPANIES CONSIDERING BUILDING ONLINE COMMUNITIES FOR ADVERTISING, BRANDING, OR MARKETING WILL NEED TO CEDE SOME DEGREE OF CONTROL OVER CONTENT.

Passive Search

Recruiters at Microsoft and Starbucks, for instance, troll online networks such as LinkedIn for potential job candidates. Goldman Sachs and Deloitte run their own online alumni networks for hiring back former workers and strengthening bonds with alumni-cum-possible clients. Boston Consulting Group and law firm Duane Morris deploy enterprise software that tracks employee communications to uncover useful connections in other companies. And companies such as Intuit and Mini USA have created customer networks to build brand loyalty.

Many companies are leery of online networks. Executives do not have time to field the possible influx of requests from acquaintances on business networks. Employees may be dismayed to learn their workplace uses email monitoring software to help sales associates' target pitches. Companies considering building online communities for advertising, branding, or marketing will need to cede some degree of control over content.

None of those concerns are holding back Carmen Hudson, manager of enterprise staffing at Starbucks, who said she swears by LinkedIn. "It's one of the best things for finding mid-level executives," she said.

The holy grail in recruiting is finding so-called passive candidates, people who are happy and productive working for other companies. LinkedIn, with its 6.7 million members, is a virtual Rolodex of these types. Hudson says she has hired three or four people this year as a result of connections through LinkedIn. "We've started asking our hiring managers to sign up on LinkedIn and help introduce us to their contacts," she says. "People have concerns about privacy, but once we explain how we use it and how careful we would be with their contacts, they're usually willing to do it."

Boomerangs

Headhunters and human resources departments are taking note. "LinkedIn is a tremendous tool for recruiters," said Bill Vick, the author of *LinkedIn for Recruiting*. So are sites such as Ryze, Spoke, OpenBc, and Ecademy. Many companies are turning to social networks and related technology to stay in touch with former employees. Consulting firm Deloitte strives to maintain ties with ex-workers and has had a formal alumni-relations program for years. It bolstered those efforts earlier this year, tapping business networking services provider SelectMinds to launch an online alumni network.

Ex-Deloitte employees can go to the site to browse 900 postings for jobs at a range of companies. They can also peruse open positions at Deloitte. The online network is an extension of an offline program that includes networking receptions and seminars.

Deloitte makes no bones about its aim to use the network to lure back some former employees, or so-called boomerangs. "Last year, 20 percent of our experienced hires were boomerangs," said Karen Palvisak, a national leader of alumni relations for Deloitte.

Boomerangs cost less to train than new hires and they tend to hit the ground running. As the labor market tightens, alumni become an increasingly attractive source of talent. Last year, 13 percent of employees who had previously been laid off were rehired by their former employers, according to a survey by Right Management Consultants of more than 14,000 displaced employees at 4,900 organizations.

Marketing Networks

Business-oriented networks help executives find employees, and they're increasingly useful in other areas, such as sales and marketing. When Campbell

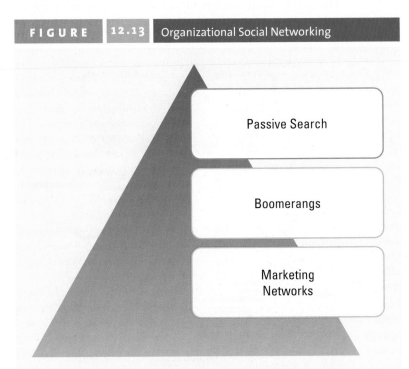

FIGURE **12.13** Organizational Social Networking

- Passive Search
- Boomerangs
- Marketing Networks

Soup Co. asked independent location booker Marilyn Jenett to select a castle in Europe for a promotion, she put a note on business networking site Ryze, offering a finder's fee to anyone who could suggest the right place.

Jenett got seven responses, including one pointing her to Eastnor Castle. She was so pleased with the location that she booked it again for another event. Jenett said Ryze also helped her develop another small business, a personal mentoring program called Feel Free to Prosper.

Social networks also help forge community with, and among, would-be customers. A group of Mini Cooper owners joined the company for its two-week cross-country car rally. Participants took part in company-sponsored events, such as the official wrap party overlooking the Hudson River and the Manhattan skyline in New Jersey.

But they also planned their own side events along the way with the help of the community forums on the Mini Owner's Lounge site, sponsored by Mini USA. Each month, about 1,500 to 2,000 new owners become active in the community. "Our very best salespeople are Mini owners, and they like to talk about their cars," said Martha Crowley, director of consulting for Beam Interactive, which provides various Internet marketing services for Mini USA.[33]

●● LO12.10

Explain virtual worlds and virtual workforces and their impact on business.

VIRTUAL WORLDS: IT'S A WHOLE NEW WORLD

Virtual is the theme of web 2.0. Two primary types of virtual must be considered when looking at the 21st century world. This includes virtual worlds and virtual workforces (see Figure 12.14).

Virtual Worlds

In the midst of the sprawling online virtual world Second Life, a new edifice recently surfaced, the digitized headquarters of *Wired* magazine on a one-acre lot. Garish neon-pink sliding doors lead to a conference room shaped like a Shuttle PC where as many as 50 people can sit on chairs that resemble circuit breakers and watch a screen that looks like a graphics card. *Wired,* meanwhile, unveiled its building in Second Life to kick off a package of stories on the game published October 17. The company expects to use its new virtual building to let writers chat with one another and to host three or four virtual Q&A events a month with real-world as well as Second Life notables, says Chris Baker, senior associate editor at *Wired* magazine. "It's kind of a toe in the water for us," he said, adding that *Wired* is also actively looking to set up in other virtual worlds as well. "We are still not sure how to make use of this space; this is the test case."

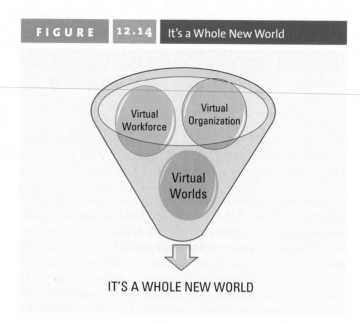

FIGURE 12.14 It's a Whole New World

IT'S A WHOLE NEW WORLD

Wired's virtual headquarters are right next to the offices of CNET Networks, which recently unveiled its own five-story office in Second Life. The building is an exact replica of the company's glass-and-brick headquarters in San Francisco, and it is set amid vast lawns overlooking Second Life's blue ocean.

Big media's land grab is well under way in Second Life, the online realm where real people, under the guise of avatars, mill and mingle and, in some cases, make a living. The game's audience, swiftly approaching 1 million, is growing at about 38 percent month over month, according to its creator, Linden Lab. The outfit added 200,000 to 250,000 new players—many of

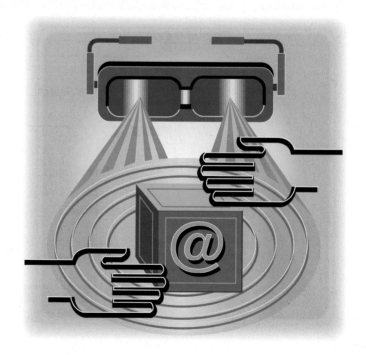

them the coveted younger early adopters—in one month alone. "Second Life is almost a phenomenon like YouTube, it's reached critical mass," said Baker.

Like so many other companies already setting up shop in Second Life, news organizations and other media outlets do not want to be left behind. As the virtual world grows up, it will get more attractive to companies that want to send a multimedia message. "Everyone's been searching for the killer broadband offering, and this is it," said Justin Bovington, CEO of Rivers Run Red, which helps companies like BBC Radio One create events and design buildings inside Second Life.

Companies as varied as Adidas, Sun Microsystems, and Toyota want to promote their products and ensure their brands are getting exposure amid the consumers, many of them young, who are spending increasingly long stretches not just on the Internet, but also immersed in virtual worlds. In-game advertising revenue in the United States was expected to rise from $186 million in 2005 to $875 million in 2009, according to Yankee Group.[34]

Media companies even face competition from virtual upstarts inside Second Life, including "New World Notes" and "SL Herald." Reuters commissioned its longtime tech reporter, Adam Pasick, to cover Second Life full-time and act as Reuters' Second Life bureau chief. Pasick's avatar sports a green shirt, a grim businesslike expression, and a press badge. One of his first stories reported on a U.S. congressional committee's investigation of online virtual economies like Second Life and Vivendi Universal's World of Warcraft and how virtual assets and income received in the games should be taxed.

Another Reuters story is an interview with the virtual president of Second Life's most popular bank, Ginko Financial. The Reuters site also offers a variety of market information, such as the exchange rate between the Linden dollar, a currency used in Second Life, and the U.S. dollar. Another table tracks the number of U.S. dollars ($404,063, at recent count) spent by players on Second Life in the past 24 hours. "Second Life is a really hot economy," said Pasick, who, in the game, goes under the name of Adam Reuters. "It was a natural for Reuters." "Second Life offers numerous features and options for businesses, and is a canvas that allows companies to do what they want to do in Second Life," said David Fleck, Linden's vice president of marketing. The following are a few examples of how businesses are using Second Life to compete in the global economy.[35]

Sun Microsystems

Sun Microsystems held a Second Life press conference with John Gage, chief scientist at Sun. The company created an area called Sun Pavilion, where a video blog of all of Sun's activities will be streamed. There were 60 avatars at the press conference—in Second Life terms, that's a full house.[36]

Warner Bros. Records

Warner Bros. promoted singer Regina Spektor's fourth album, *Begin to Hope,* by

building a chic Manhattan loft within Second Life. As Spektor's music played, the loft's lighting and décor changed to roughly illustrate the song lyrics—a new marketing experience that was part video game, part music video.[37]

American Apparel

American Apparel launched a virtual store in Second Life in July 2006. The hip T-shirt maker is debuting styles before they are launched in the physical world and is offering cross-promotions. Visitors to the virtual store receive 15 percent off real-world purchases.[38]

Lego

Lego regularly visits university and corporate campuses to host events where new types of robots are built using Lego's popular Mindstorm Robotics Inventions kits. Recently, Lego hosted one such Big Robot on Campus gathering in Second Life, drawing robot makers from different locales to meet in cyberspace.[39]

Adidas Adidas is working on selling virtual gym shoes in Second Life. The company hopes to test-market styles before rolling them out in the real world, tracking which color combos or designs prove popular among Second Lifers.[40]

Toyota Toyota's marketing plan for its hip, boxy Scion includes an art gallery in Los Angeles (Scion Space) and sponsored screenings of indie films (the Scion Independent Film Series). Now the pop-culture-aware carmaker is also a presence in Second Life, where it offers a virtual version of the Scion xB.[41]

Dartmouth College Educational institutions such as Dartmouth College are increasingly becoming a presence in the virtual world. In a Second Life version of Hanover, New Hampshire, where Dartmouth is located, the school's Institute for Security Technology Studies conducts emergency-response exercises in the virtual space.[42]

Major League Baseball Major League Baseball held a simulcast of its home-run derby within Second Life, with video streams of the event shown on screens within a digitized baseball stadium. Branching into Second Life made sense to MLB execs; MLB.com has a robust online community in its chat rooms.[43]

Virtual Hospital Palomar Pomerado Health opened a new state-of-the-art hospital—in Second Life. The opening of the virtual hospital followed the December 2007 groundbreaking for the health care provider's real-world $773 million, 600-bed Palomar Medical Center west in Escondido, California. With completion of the first phase of the hospital still three years away, PPH created the facility and all of its technology in the Second Life virtual world to show its 900,000 clients in Southern California what is to come. The Second Life hospital shows off operating rooms equipped with robotics technology and functional imaging systems that support medical procedures such as cardiovascular surgery. Using Second Life to receive user feedback is a cost-effective method—much better than just herding people into a room for a focus group.[44]

Virtual Workforce

Sunday morning and Tuesday afternoon are becoming completely the same, said KLM Chief Information Officer Boet Kreiken. At the same time, employees throughout organizations are becoming much more comfortable with a range of technologies.

In years past, employees might have had only a PC at home. Today they may juggle a network linking several PCs, printers, and backup devices connected to a high-speed Internet connection—in addition to a set-top box, gaming console, high-definition TV, and all manner of other web-based services such as YouTube and News Corp.'s MySpace. The benefits for businesses include lower costs and greater productivity, but figuring out how to communicate with off-site employees is crucial.

Traffic surrounding Microsoft headquarters in Redmond, Washington, has become so congested that Washington State Governor Chris Gregoire nearly missed a 9 a.m. speech at the company's main campus. Roads leading to the software maker simply were not designed to handle the 35,000 commuters who report for work there each day. The gridlock that greeted Gregoire was just the latest reminder that Microsoft needs to tackle its commuter crisis—and quickly.

Microsoft has embarked on a program aimed at getting more employees to work from home and other off-site locales, joining the growing ranks of companies to catch the virtual-workplace wave. About 17 percent of the U.S. workforce in 2009 was expected to get its job done at a home office more than two days per week, said Charlie Grantham, executive producer of consulting firm Work Design Collaborative. That is up from 11 percent in 2004.[45]

Letting employees work from outside the office keeps cars off the road, plus the practice can foster employee retention, boost worker productivity, and slash real estate costs. At IBM, about 42 percent of the company's 330,000 employees work on the road, from home, or at a client location, saving the computer company about $100 million in real estate-related expenses a year. VIPdesk, an employer of at-home customer-service reps, hangs onto 85 percent of its employees each year, compared with the 10 to 20 percent rate for traditional call centers, according to consulting firm IDC. And virtual workers are about 16 percent more productive than office workers, according to Grantham's research.

For all the benefits of freeing workers from the office, drawbacks abound. First, not everyone wants to leave. Some fear they will step off the corporate ladder, while others need a busy environment to stay productive. Some managers are reluctant to scatter direct reports because keeping tabs on a virtual workforce can be harder than managing those close at hand. Some virtual workers can feel lonely, isolated, or deprived of vital training and mentoring. And communication breakdowns can impede innovation, trust, job satisfaction, and performance.

Obstacles like these have prompted IBM, Sun Microsystems, and other companies to seek a host of creative solutions to the problems that virtual work presents. Some turn to a combination of mobile devices, email, instant messaging, and collaboration software to help colleagues stay in touch.

Tools for the Virtual Workforce

Mobility and wireless capabilities are the tools of the virtual workforce and include:

- **Mobile commerce (m-commerce),** the ability to purchase goods and services through a wireless Internet-enabled device.

- **Telematics,** the blending of computers and wireless telecommunications technologies with the goal of efficiently conveying information over vast networks to improve business operations. The most notable example of telematics may be the Internet itself, since it depends on a number of computer networks connected globally through telecommunication devices.

- **Electronic tagging,** a technique for identifying and tracking assets and individuals via technologies such as radio frequency identification and smart cards.

Other companies, including Microsoft, WebEx, and Citrix, also specialize in online conferencing and collaboration software that makes it easier for people in different locations to work together and conduct meetings. At Groove Networks, the company set a policy that if one person was operating virtually in a meeting, then everyone would sit in their offices and the entire meeting would be virtual. "Because there's a big sensory difference in that experience, it made sure that everyone was on a level playing field," she said. Another way to bridge the physical distance is to provide a worker with the tools needed to stay connected to colleagues.

For the virtual worker, a laptop, high-speed Internet access, and a personal digital assistant or mobile phone are required. But some companies go an extra mile to outfit virtual employees. IBM provides a universal messaging service that lets executives give a single phone number to clients and colleagues. The service then forwards calls to wherever that executive might be

located, at home, on a cell phone, or in a so-called emobility center, one of the temporary offices set up by IBM in locations around the world. Patrick Boyle, director of health care and life-sciences sales at IBM, spends about half his time traveling, working from taxis, airport lounges, planes, and coffee shops. He is also a frequent user of emobility centers and considers headsets an essential tool of the trade. ■

CHECK OUT www.mhhe.com/baltzanm

for additional study materials including quizzes and PowerPoint presentations.

If your students are looking for an introduction to MIS concepts and business concepts have them visit the Appendices that accompany this text. The following is an overview of the appendices and the associated topic areas. Appendices are located on this textbook's website at www.mhhe.com/baltzanm.

Appendix	Description
A. Business Basics	■ Types of Business ■ Internal Operations of a Corporation ■ Accounting ■ Finance ■ Human Resources ■ Sales ■ Marketing ■ Operations/Production ■ Management Information Systems
B. Hardware and Software	■ Hardware Basics ■ Computer Categories ■ Software Basics
C. Networks and Telecommunications	■ Network Basics ■ Architecture ■ Topology ■ Protocols ■ Media ■ Ebusiness Networks
D. Systems Development Life Cycle	■ Systems Development Life Cycle ■ Plan ■ Analysis ■ Design ■ Development ■ Test ■ Implement ■ Maintain ■ Software Problems Are Business Problems

A

acceptable use policy (AUP) A policy that a user must agree to follow in order to be provided access to a network or to the Internet.

accounting Analyzes the transactional information of the business so the owners and investors can make sound economic decisions.

accounting and finance ERP component Manages accounting data and financial processes within the enterprise with functions such as general ledger, accounts payable, accounts receivable, budgeting, and asset management.

accounting department Provides quantitative information about the finances of the business including recording, measuring, and describing financial information.

adware Software that generates ads that install themselves on a computer when a person downloads some other program from the Internet.

affinity grouping Determination of which things go together.

agile methodology Aims for customer satisfaction through early and continuous delivery of useful software components.

analysis latency The time from which data is made available to the time when analysis is complete.

analysis phase Analyzing end-user business requirements and refining project goals into defined functions and operations of the intended system.

analytical CRM Supports back-office operations and strategic analysis and includes all systems that do not deal directly with customers.

analytical information Encompasses all organizational information, and its primary purpose is to support the performing of managerial analysis tasks.

anti-spam policy States that email users will not send unsolicited emails (or spam).

application architecture Determines how applications integrate and relate to each other.

application programming interface (API) A set of routines, protocols, and tools for building software applications.

application service provider (ASP) A company that offers an organization access over the Internet to systems and related services that would otherwise have to be located in personal or organizational computers.

application software Used for specific information processing needs, including payroll, customer relationship management, project management, training, and many others.

arithmetic/logic unit (ALU) Performs all arithmetic operations (for example, addition and subtraction) and all logic operations (such as sorting and comparing numbers).

artificial intelligence (AI) Simulates human intelligence such as the ability to reason and learn.

As-Is process model Represents the current state of the operation that has been mapped, without any specific improvements or changes to existing processes.

asset Anything owned that has value or earning power.

associates program (affiliate program) Businesses can generate commissions or royalties from an Internet site.

association detection Reveals the degree to which variables are related and the nature and frequency of these relationships in the information.

attribute Characteristics or properties of an entity class.

authentication A method for confirming users' identities.

authorization The process of giving someone permission to do or have something.

automatic call distribution A phone switch routes inbound calls to available agents.

availability Addresses when systems can be accessed by users.

B

backdoor program Viruses that open a way into the network for future attacks.

backup An exact copy of a system's information.

backward integration Takes information entered into a given system and sends it automatically to all upstream systems and processes.

balance sheet Gives an accounting picture of property owned by a company and of claims against the property on a specific date.

balanced scorecard A management system (not only a measurement system) that enables organizations to clarify their vision and strategy and translate them into action.

bandwidth The difference between the highest and the lowest frequencies that can be transmitted on a single medium, and it is a measure of the medium's capacity.

banner ad Small ad on one website that advertises the products and services of another business, usually another dot-com business.

benchmark Baseline values the system seeks to attain.

benchmarking The process of continuously measuring system results, comparing those results to optimal system performance (benchmark values), and identifying steps and procedures to improve system performance.

binary digit (bit) The smallest unit of information that a computer can process.

biometric The identification of a user based on a physical characteristic, such as a fingerprint, iris, face, voice, or handwriting.

black-hat hacker Breaks into other people's computer systems and may just look around or steal and destroy information.

blog Website in which items are posted on a regular basis and displayed in reverse chronological order.

Bluetooth A telecommunications industry specification that describes how mobile phones, computers, and personal digital assistants (PDAs) can be easily interconnected using a short-range wireless connection.

bookkeeping The actual recording of the business's transactions, without any analysis of the information.

break-even point The point at which revenues equal costs.

brick-and-mortar business A business that operates in a physical store without an Internet presence.

broadband High-speed Internet connections transmitting data at speeds greater than 200 kilobytes per second (Kbps), compared to the 56 Kbps maximum speed offered by traditional dial-up connections.

bullwhip effect Occurs when distorted product demand information passes from one entity to the next throughout the supply chain.

business continuity planning (BCP) A plan for how an organization will recover and restore partially or completely interrupted critical function(s) within a predetermined time after a disaster or extended disruption.

business-critical integrity constraint Enforces business rules vital to an organization's success and often requires more insight and knowledge than relational integrity constraints.

business facing process Invisible to the external customer but essential to the effective management of the business and includes goal setting, day-to-day planning, performance feedback, rewards, and resource allocation.

business intelligence Refers to applications and technologies that are used to gather, provide access to, and analyze data and information to support decision-making efforts.

business process A standardized set of activities that accomplish a specific task, such as processing a customer's order.

business process improvement Attempts to understand and measure the current process and make performance improvements accordingly.

business process management (BPM) Integrates all of an organization's business processes to make individual processes more efficient.

business process model A graphic description of a process, showing the sequence of process tasks, which is developed for a specific purpose and from a selected viewpoint.

business process modeling (or mapping) The activity of creating a detailed flow chart or process map of a work process showing its inputs, tasks, and activities, in a structured sequence.

business process reengineering (BPR) The analysis and redesign of workflow within and between enterprises.

business requirement The detailed set of business requests that the system must meet in order to be successful.

business wiki Collaborative web pages that allow users to edit documents, share ideas, or monitor the status of a project.

business-to-business (B2B) Applies to businesses buying from and selling to each other over the Internet.

business-to-business (B2B) marketplace An Internet-based service that brings together many buyers and sellers.

business-to-consumer (B2C) Applies to any business that sells its products or services to consumers over the Internet.

buyer power High when buyers have many choices of whom to buy from and low when their choices are few.

byte Group of eight bits represents one natural language character.

C

cache memory A small unit of ultra-fast memory that is used to store recently accessed or frequently accessed data so that the CPU does not have to retrieve this data from slower memory circuits such as RAM.

call scripting system Accesses organizational databases that track similar issues or questions and automatically generates the details for the customer service representative who can then relay them to the customer.

campaign management system Guides users through marketing campaigns performing such tasks as campaign definition, planning, scheduling, segmentation, and success analysis.

capability maturity model integration method (CMMI) A process improvement approach that contains 22 process areas.

capacity planning Determines the future IT infrastructure requirements for new equipment and additional network capacity.

capital Represents money whose purpose is to make more money, for example, the money used to buy a rental property or a business.

central processing unit (CPU) (or microprocessor) The actual hardware that interprets and executes the program (software) instructions and coordinates how all the other hardware devices work together.

change control board (CCB) Responsible for approving or rejecting all change requests.

change management A set of techniques that aid in evolution, composition, and policy management of the design and implementation of a system.

change management system Includes a collection of procedures to document a change request and define the steps necessary to consider the change based on the expected impact of the change.

chief information officer (CIO) Responsible for (1) overseeing all uses of information technology and (2) ensuring the strategic alignment of IT with business goals and objectives.

chief knowledge officer (CKO) Responsible for collecting, maintaining, and distributing the organization's knowledge.

chief privacy officer (CPO) Responsible for ensuring the ethical and legal use of information within an organization.

chief security officer (CSO) Responsible for ensuring the security of IT systems and developing strategies and IT safeguards against attacks from hackers and viruses.

chief technology officer (CTO) Responsible for ensuring the throughput, speed, accuracy, availability, and reliability of an organization's information technology.

classification The assignment of records to one of a predefined set of classes.

click-and-mortar business A business that operates in a physical store and on the Internet.

clickstream Records information about a customer during a web surfing session such as what websites were visited, how long the visit was, what ads were viewed, and what was purchased.

clickstream data Exact pattern of a consumer's navigation through a site.

click-through A count of the number of people who visit one site and click on an advertisement that takes them to the site of the advertiser.

click-to-talk Buttons allow customers to click on a button and talk with a customer service representative via the Internet.

client Computer that is designed to request information from a server.

client/server network A model for applications in which the bulk of the back-end processing, such as performing a physical search of a database, takes place on a server, while the front-end processing, which involves communicating with the users, is handled by the clients.

cluster analysis A technique used to divide an information set into mutually exclusive groups such that the members of each group are as close together as possible to one another and the different groups are as far apart as possible.

clustering Segmentation of a heterogeneous population of records into a number of more homogeneous subgroups.

coaxial cable Cable that can carry a wide range of frequencies with low signal loss.

cold site A separate facility that does not have any computer equipment, but is a place where employees can move after a disaster.

collaboration system An IT-based set of tools that supports the work of teams by facilitating the sharing and flow of information.

collaborative demand planning Helps organizations reduce their investment in inventory, while improving customer satisfaction through product availability.

collaborative engineering Allows an organization to reduce the cost and time required during the design process of a product.

commercial off-the-shelf (COTS) A software package or solution that is purchased to support one or more business functions and information systems.

committee of sponsoring organizations (COSO) Evaluates internal controls such as human resources, logistics, information technology, risk, legal, marketing and sales, operations, financial functions, procurement, and reporting.

communication device Equipment used to send information and receive it from one location to another.

competitive advantage A product or service that an organization's customers place a greater value on than similar offerings from a competitor.

complex instruction set computer (CISC) chip Type of CPU that can recognize as many as 100 or more instructions, enough to carry out most computations directly.

compliance The act of conforming, acquiescing, or yielding.

computer Electronic device operating under the control of instructions stored in its own memory that can accept, manipulate, and store data.

computer-aided software engineering (CASE) Software suites that automate systems analysis, design, and development.

confidentiality The assurance that messages and information are available only to those who are authorized to view them.

consolidation Involves the aggregation of information and features simple roll-ups to complex groupings of interrelated information.

consumer-to-business (C2B) Applies to any consumer that sells a product or service to a business over the Internet.

consumer-to-consumer (C2C) Applies to sites primarily offering goods and services to assist consumers interacting with each other over the Internet.

contact center (call center) Customer service representatives (CSRs) answer customer inquiries and respond to problems through a number of different customer touchpoints.

contact management CRM system Maintains customer contact information and identifies prospective customers for future sales.

content filtering Occurs when organizations use software that filters content to prevent the transmission of unauthorized information.

content management system Provides tools to manage the creation, storage, editing, and publication of information in a collaborative environment.

control unit Interprets software instructions and literally tells the other hardware devices what to do, based on the software instructions.

cookie A small file deposited on a hard drive by a website containing information about customers and their web activities.

copyright The legal protection afforded an expression of an idea, such as a song, video game, and some types of proprietary documents.

core competency An organization's key strength or business function that it does better than any of its competitors.

core competency strategy When an organization chooses to focus specifically on what it does best (its core competency) and forms partnerships and alliances with other specialist organizations to handle nonstrategic business processes.

core ERP component Traditional components included in most ERP systems and they primarily focus on internal operations.

corporate policy A dimension of social responsibility that refers to the position a firm takes on social and political issues.

corporate responsibility A dimension of social responsibility that includes everything from hiring minority workers to making safe products.

corporation (also called, **organization, enterprise,** or **business**) An artificially created legal entity that exists separate and apart from those individuals who created it and carry on its operations.

counterfeit software Software that is manufactured to look like the real thing and sold as such.

cracker A hacker with criminal intent.

critical path A path from the start to the finish that passes through all the tasks that are critical to completing the project in the shortest amount of time.

critical success factor (CSF) A factor that is critical to an organization's success.

CRM analysis technologies Help organizations segment their customers into categories such as best and worst customers.

CRM predicting technologies Help organizations make predictions regarding customer behavior such as which customers are at risk of leaving.

CRM reporting technologies Help organizations identify their customers across other applications.

cross-selling Selling additional products or services to a customer.

cube The common term for the representation of multidimensional information.

customer facing process Results in a product or service that is received by an organization's external customer.

customer relationship management (CRM) Involves managing all aspects of a customer's relationship with an organization to increase customer loyalty and retention and an organization's profitability.

cyberterrorist Seeks to cause harm to people or to destroy critical systems or information and use the Internet as a weapon of mass destruction.

D

data Raw facts that describe the characteristics of an event.

database Maintains information about various types of objects (inventory), events (transactions), people (employees), and places (warehouses).

database management system (DBMS) Software through which users and application programs interact with a database.

database-based workflow system Stores documents in a central location and automatically asks the team members to access the document when it is their turn to edit the document.

data-driven website An interactive website kept constantly updated and relevant to the needs of its customers through the use of a database.

data flow diagram (DFD) Illustrates the movement of information between external entities and the processes and data stores within the system.

data latency The time duration to make data ready for analysis, i.e., the time for extracting, transforming, and cleansing the data, and loading it into the database.

data mart Contains a subset of data warehouse information.

data mining The process of analyzing data to extract information not offered by the raw data alone.

data-mining tool Uses a variety of techniques to find patterns and relationships in large volumes of information and infer rules from them that predict future behavior and guide decision making.

data model A formal way to express data relationships to a database management system (DBMS).

data warehouse A logical collection of information—gathered from many different operational databases—that supports business analysis activities and decision-making tasks.

decision latency The time it takes a human to comprehend the analytic result and determine an appropriate action.

decision support system (DSS) Models information to support managers and business professionals during the decision-making process.

demand planning system Generates demand forecasts using statistical tools and forecasting techniques.

denial-of-service attack (DoS) Floods a website with so many requests for service that it slows down or crashes the site.

dependency A logical relationship that exists between the project tasks, or between a project task and a milestone.

deperimeterization Occurs when an organization moves employees outside its firewall, a growing movement to change the way corporations address technology security.

design phase Involves describing the desired features and operations of the system including screen layouts, business rules, process diagrams, pseudo code, and other documentation.

development phase Involves taking all of the detailed design documents from the design phase and transforming them into the actual system.

digital asset management system (DAM) Though similar to document management, DAM generally works with binary rather than text files, such as multimedia file types.

digital Darwinism Organizations that cannot adapt to the new demands placed on them for surviving in the information age are doomed to extinction.

digital dashboard Integrates information from multiple components and tailors the information to individual preferences.

digital divide When those with access to technology have great advantages over those without access to technology.

digital wallet Both software and information—the software provides security for the transaction and the information includes payment and delivery information (for example, the credit card number and expiration date).

disaster recovery cost curve Charts (1) the cost to the organization of the unavailability of information and technology and (2) the cost to the organization of recovering from a disaster over time.

disaster recovery plan A detailed process for recovering information or an IT system in the event of a catastrophic disaster such as a fire or flood.

disruptive technology A new way of doing things that initially does not meet the needs of existing customers.

distributed denial-of-service attack (DDoS) Attacks from multiple computers that flood a website with so many requests for service that it slows down or crashes.

distribution management system Coordinates the process of transporting materials from a manufacturer to distribution centers to the final customer.

dividend A distribution of earnings to shareholders.

document management system (DMS) Supports the electronic capturing, storage, distribution, archival, and accessing of documents.

drill-down Enables users to get details, and details of details, of information.

E

ebusiness The conducting of business on the Internet, not only buying and selling, but also serving customers and collaborating with business partners.

ebusiness model An approach to conducting electronic business on the Internet.

ecommerce The buying and selling of goods and services over the Internet.

effectiveness IT metric Measures the impact IT has on business processes and activities including customer satisfaction, conversion rates, and sell-through increases.

efficiency IT metric Measures the performance of the IT system itself including throughput, speed, and availability.

egovernment Involves the use of strategies and technologies to transform government(s) by improving the delivery of services and enhancing the quality of interaction between the citizen-consumer within all branches of government.

elogistics Manages the transportation and storage of goods.

electronic bill presentment and payment (EBPP) System that sends bills over the Internet and provides an easy-to-use mechanism (such as clicking on a button) to pay the bill.

electronic catalog Presents customers with information about goods and services offered for sale, bid, or auction on the Internet.

electronic check Mechanism for sending a payment from a checking or savings account.

electronic data interchange (EDI) A standard format for exchanging business data.

electronic marketplace, or emarketplace Interactive business communities providing a central market space where multiple buyers and suppliers can engage in ebusiness activities.

electronic tagging A technique for identifying and tracking assets and individuals via technologies such as radio frequency identification and smart cards.

elevation of privilege Process by which a user misleads a system into granting unauthorized rights, usually for the purpose of compromising or destroying the system.

email privacy policy Details the extent to which email messages may be read by others.

emall Consists of a number of eshops; it serves as a gateway through which a visitor can access other eshops.

employee monitoring policy States how, when, and where the company monitors its employees.

employee relationship management (ERM) Provides employees with a subset of CRM applications available through a web browser.

encryption Scrambles information into an alternative form that requires a key or password to decrypt the information.

enterprise application integration (EAI) middleware Represents a new approach to middleware by packaging together commonly used functionality, such as providing prebuilt links to popular enterprise applications, which reduces the time necessary to develop solutions that integrate applications from multiple vendors.

enterprise architect (EA) Person grounded in technology, fluent in business, a patient diplomat, and provides the important bridge between IT and the business.

enterprise architecture Includes the plans for how an organization will build, deploy, use, and share its data, processes, and IT assets.

enterprise resource planning (ERP) Integrates all departments and functions throughout an organization into a single IT system (or integrated set of IT systems) so that employees can make decisions by viewing enterprisewide information on all business operations.

entity In the relational database model is a person, place, thing, transaction, or event about which information is stored.

entity-relationship diagram (ERD) A technique for documenting the relationships between entities in a database environment.

entry barrier A product or service feature that customers have come to expect from organizations in a particular industry and must be offered by an entering organization to compete and survive.

environmental scanning The acquisition and analysis of events and trends in the environment external to an organization.

epolicies Policies and procedures that address the ethical use of computers and Internet usage in the business environment.

eprocurement The B2B purchase and sale of supplies and services over the Internet.

estimation Determine values for an unknown continuous variable behavior or estimated future value.

eshop (estore or etailer) A version of a retail store where customers can shop at any hour of the day without leaving their home or office.

ethernet A physical and data layer technology for LAN networking.

ethical computer use policy Contains general principles to guide computer user behavior.

ethics Principles and standards that guide our behavior toward other people.

ewaste Old computer equipment where the toxic substances it contains can leach into groundwater, among other problems.

executive information system (EIS) A specialized DSS that supports senior-level executives within the organization.

executive sponsor The person or group who provides the financial resources for the project.

expense Refers to the costs incurred in operating and maintaining a business.

expert system Computerized advisory programs that imitate the reasoning processes of experts in solving difficult problems.

explicit knowledge Consists of anything that can be documented, archived, and codified, often with the help of IT.

extended ERP component The extra components that meet the organizational needs not covered by the core components and primarily focus on external operations.

extensible markup language (XML) A markup language for documents containing structured information.

extraction, transformation, and loading (ETL) A process that extracts information from internal and external databases, transforms the information using a common set of enterprise definitions, and loads the information into a data warehouse.

extranet An intranet that is available to strategic allies (such as customers, suppliers, and partners).

extreme programming (XP) methodology Breaks a project into tiny phases, and developers cannot continue on to the next phase until the first phase is complete.

F

failover A backup in which the functions of a computer component (such as a processor, server, network, or database) are assumed by secondary system components when the primary component becomes unavailable through either failure or scheduled downtime.

fair use doctrine In certain situations, it is legal to use copyrighted material.

fault tolerance A computer system designed that in the event a component fails, a backup component or procedure can immediately take its place with no loss of service.

feasibility study Determines if the proposed solution is feasible and achievable from a financial, technical, and organizational standpoint.

feature creep Occurs when developers add extra features that were not part of the initial requirements.

fiber optic (optical fiber) The technology associated with the transmission of information as light impulses along a glass wire or fiber.

finance Deals with the strategic financial issues associated with increasing the value of the business while observing applicable laws and social responsibilities.

financial accounting Involves preparing financial reports that provide information about the business's performance to external parties such as investors, creditors, and tax authorities.

financial cybermediary Internet-based company that facilitates payments over the Internet.

financial EDI (financial electronic data interchange) Standard electronic process for B2B market purchase payments.

financial quarter A three-month period (four quarters per year).

financial statement Written records of the financial status of the business that allow interested parties to evaluate the profitability and solvency of the business.

firewall Hardware and/or software that guards a private network by analyzing the information leaving and entering the network.

first-mover advantage An organization can significantly impact its market share by being first to market with a competitive advantage.

Five Forces model Helps determine the relative attractiveness of an industry.

flash memory A special type of rewriteable read-only memory (ROM) that is compact and portable.

for-profit corporations Primarily focus on making money and all profits and losses are shared by the business owners.

forecast Predictions made on the basis of time-series information.

foreign key A primary key of one table that appears as an attribute in another table and acts to provide a logical relationship between the two tables.

forward integration Takes information entered into a given system and sends it automatically to all downstream systems and processes.

fuzzy logic A mathematical method of handling imprecise or subjective information.

G

Gantt chart A simple bar chart that depicts project tasks against a calendar.

genetic algorithm An artificial intelligence system that mimics the evolutionary, survival-of-the-fittest process to generate increasingly better solutions to a problem.

geoeconomic The effects of geography on the economic realities of international business activities.

geographic information system (GIS) Designed to work with information that can be shown on a map.

gigabyte (GB) Roughly 1 billion bytes.

gigahertz (GHz) The number of billions of CPU cycles per second.

global inventory management system Provides the ability to locate, track, and predict the movement of every component or material anywhere upstream or downstream in the production process.

global positioning system (GPS) Is a constellation of 24 well-spaced satellites that orbit the Earth and make it possible for people with ground receivers to pinpoint their geographic location.

goal-seeking analysis Finds the inputs necessary to achieve a goal such as a desired level of output.

governance A method or system of government for management or control.

graphical user interface (GUI) The interface to an information system.

grid computing An aggregation of geographically dispersed computing, storage, and network resources, coordinated to deliver improved performance, higher quality of service, better utilization, and easier access to data.

groupware Software that supports team interaction and dynamics including calendaring, scheduling, and video-conferencing.

H

hacker People very knowledgeable about computers who use their knowledge to invade other people's computers.

hactivist Person with philosophical and political reasons for breaking into systems and will often deface the website as a protest.

hard drive Secondary storage medium that uses several rigid disks coated with a magnetically sensitive material and housed together with the recording heads in a hermetically sealed mechanism.

hardware Consists of the physical devices associated with a computer system.

hardware key logger A hardware device that captures keystrokes on their journey from the keyboard to the motherboard.

help desk A group of people who respond to internal system user questions.

hierarchical database model Information is organized into a treelike structure that allows repeating information using parent/child relationships, in such a way that it cannot have too many relationships.

high availability Refers to a system or component that is continuously operational for a desirably long length of time.

hoaxes Attack computer systems by transmitting a virus hoax, with a real virus attached.

hot site A separate and fully equipped facility where the company can move immediately after a disaster and resume business.

human resource ERP component Tracks employee information including payroll, benefits, compensation, and performance assessment, and assures compliance with the legal requirements of multiple jurisdictions and tax authorities.

human resources management (HRM) Includes the policies, plans, and procedures for the effective management of employees (human resources).

hypertext transfer protocol (HTTP) The Internet standard that supports the exchange of information on the WWW.

I

identity theft The forging of someone's identity for the purpose of fraud.

implementation phase Involves placing the system into production so users can begin to perform actual business operations with the system.

income statement (also referred to as **earnings report, operating statement,** and **profit-and-loss (P&L) statement**) Reports operating results (revenues minus expenses) for a given time period ending at a specified date.

information Data converted into a meaningful and useful context.

information accuracy Extent to which a system generates the correct results when executing the same transaction numerous times.

information architecture Identifies where and how important information, like customer records, is maintained and secured.

information cleansing or scrubbing A process that weeds out and fixes or discards inconsistent, incorrect, or incomplete information.

information ethics Concerns the ethical and moral issues arising from the development and use of information technologies, as well as the creation, collection, duplication, distribution, and processing of information itself (with or without the aid of computer technologies).

information granularity Refers to the extent of detail within the information (fine and detailed or "coarse" and abstract information).

information integrity A measure of the quality of information.

information partnership Occurs when two or more organizations cooperate by integrating their IT systems, thereby providing customers with the best of what each can offer.

information privacy Concerns the legal right or general expectation of individuals, groups, or institutions to determine for themselves, when, and to what extent, information about them is communicated to others.

information privacy policy Contains general principles regarding information privacy.

information reach Refers to the number of people a business can communicate with, on a global basis.

information richness Refers to the depth and breadth of information transferred between customers and businesses.

information security A broad term encompassing the protection of information from accidental or intentional misuse by persons inside or outside an organization.

information security plan Details how an organization will implement the information security policies.

information security policy Identifies the rules required to maintain information security.

information systems audit and control association (ISACA) A set of guidelines and supporting tool set for IT governance that is accepted worldwide.

information technology (IT) A field concerned with the use of technology in managing and processing information. Information technology can be an important enabler of business success and innovation.

information technology infrastructure library (ITIL) A framework provided by the government of the United Kingdom offering eight sets of management procedures.

information technology monitoring Tracking people's activities by such measures as number of keystrokes, error rate, and number of transactions processed.

infrastructure architecture Includes the hardware, software, and telecommunications equipment that, when combined, provide the underlying foundation to support the organization's goals.

innovation The introduction of new equipment or methods.

input device Equipment used to capture information and commands.

insider Legitimate users who purposely or accidentally misuse their access to the environment and cause some kind of business-affecting incident.

insourcing (in-house development) A common approach using the professional expertise within an organization to develop and maintain the organization's information technology systems.

instant messaging (IM or IMing) A type of communications service that enables someone to create a kind of private chat room with another individual in order to communicate in real-time over the Internet.

integration Allows separate systems to communicate directly with each other.

integrity constraint The rules that help ensure the quality of information.

intellectual property Intangible creative work that is embodied in physical form.

intelligent agent A special-purpose knowledge-based information system that accomplishes specific tasks on behalf of its users.

intelligent system Various commercial applications of artificial intelligence.

interactive voice response (IVR) Directs customers to use touch-tone phones or keywords to navigate or provide information.

interactivity Measures the visitor interactions with the target ad.

intermediary Agents, software, or businesses that bring buyers and sellers together that provide a trading infrastructure to enhance ebusiness.

international organization for standardization (ISO) A nongovernmental organization established in 1947 to promote the development of world standards to facilitate the international exchange of goods and services.

Internet A global public network of computer networks that pass information from one to another using common computer protocols.

Internet service provider (ISP) A company that provides individuals and other companies access to the Internet along with additional related services, such as website building.

Internet use policy Contains general principles to guide the proper use of the Internet.

interoperability Capability of two or more computer systems to share data and resources, even though they are made by different manufacturers.

intranet An internalized portion of the Internet, protected from outside access, that allows an organization to provide access to information and application software to only its employees.

intrusion detection software (IDS) Searches out patterns in information and network traffic to indicate attacks and quickly responds to prevent any harm.

inventory management and control system Provides control and visibility to the status of individual items maintained in inventory.

iterative development Consists of a series of tiny projects.

J

joint application development (JAD) A session where employees meet, sometimes for several days, to define or review the business requirements for the system.

K

key logger, or key trapper, software A program that, when installed on a computer, records every keystroke and mouse click.

key performance indicator (KPI) Measures that are tied to business drivers.

kill switch A trigger that enables a project manager to close the project prior to completion.

kiosk Publicly accessible computer system that has been set up to allow interactive information browsing.

knowledge management (KM) Involves capturing, classifying, evaluating, retrieving, and sharing information assets in a way that provides context for effective decisions and actions.

knowledge management system (KMS) Supports the capturing, organization, and dissemination of knowledge (i.e., know-how) throughout an organization.

L

liability An obligation to make financial payments.

limited liability Means that the shareholders are not personally liable for the losses incurred by the corporation.

limited liability corporation (LLC) A hybrid entity that has the legal protections of a corporation and the ability to be taxed (one time) as a partnership.

limited partnership Much like a general partnership except for one important fundamental difference; the law protects the limited partner from being responsible for all of the partnership's losses.

list generator   Compiles customer information from a variety of sources and segments the information for different marketing campaigns.

local area network (LAN)   Designed to connect a group of computers in close proximity to each other such as in an office building, a school, or a home.

location-based services (LBS)   Wireless mobile content services that provide location-specific information to mobile users moving from location to location.

logical view   Focuses on how users logically access information to meet their particular business needs.

logistics   The set of processes that plans for and controls the efficient and effective transportation and storage of supplies from suppliers to customers.

loose coupling   The capability of services to be joined together on demand to create composite services, or disassembled just as easily into their functional components.

loss   Occurs when businesses sell products or services for less than they cost to produce.

loyalty program   Rewards customers based on the amount of business they do with a particular organization.

M

magnetic medium   Secondary storage medium that uses magnetic techniques to store and retrieve data on disks or tapes coated with magnetically sensitive materials.

magnetic tape   Older secondary storage medium that uses a strip of thin plastic coated with a magnetically sensitive recording medium.

mail bomb   Sends a massive amount of email to a specific person or system resulting in filling up the recipient's disk space, which, in some cases, may be too much for the server to handle and may cause the server to stop functioning.

maintenance   The fixing or enhancing of an information system.

maintenance phase   Involves performing changes, corrections, additions, and upgrades to ensure the system continues to meet the business goals.

maintenance, repair, and operations (MRO) materials (also **called indirect materials**)   Materials necessary for running an organization but do not relate to the company's primary business activities.

malicious code   Includes a variety of threats such as viruses, worms, and Trojan horses.

management information system (MIS)   A general name for the business function and academic discipline covering the application of people, technologies, and procedures—collectively called information systems—to solve business problems

managerial accounting   Involves analyzing business operations for internal decision making and does not have to follow any rules issued by standard-setting bodies such as GAAP.

market basket analysis   Analyzes such items as websites and checkout scanner information to detect customers' buying behavior and predict future behavior by identifying affinities among customers' choices of products and services.

marketing   The process associated with promoting the sale of goods or services.

marketing communication   Seeks to build product or service awareness and to educate potential consumers on the product or service.

marketing mix   Includes the variables that marketing managers can control in order to best satisfy customers in the target market.

market segmentation   The division of a market into similar groups of customers.

market share   Calculated by dividing the firm's sales by the total market sales for the entire industry.

mashup editor   WYSIWYG (What You See Is What You Get) for mashups.

mass customization   Ability of an organization to give its customers the opportunity to tailor its products or services to the customers' specifications.

materials requirement planning (MRP) system   Uses sales forecasts to make sure that needed parts and materials are available at the right time and place in a specific company.

megabyte (MB or M or Meg)   Roughly 1 million bytes.

megahertz (MHz)   The number of millions of CPU cycles per second.

memory card   Contains high-capacity storage that holds data such as captured images, music, or text files.

memory stick   Provides nonvolatile memory for a range of portable devices including computers, digital cameras, MP3 players, and PDAs.

messaging-based work-flow system   Sends work assignments through an email system.

methodology   A set of policies, procedures, standards, processes, practices, tools, techniques, and tasks that people apply to technical and management challenges.

metropolitan area network (MAN)   A large computer network usually spanning a city.

microwave transmitter   Uses the atmosphere (or outer space) as the transmission medium to send the signal to a microwave receiver.

middleware   Different types of software that sit in the middle of and provide connectivity between two or more software applications.

mobile commerce, or **m-commerce**   The ability to purchase goods and services through a wireless Internet-enabled device.

model   A simplified representation or abstraction of reality.

modeling   The activity of drawing a graphical representation of a design.

multitasking   Allows more than one piece of software to be used at a time.

N

nearshore outsourcing   Contracting an outsourcing agreement with a company in a nearby country.

net income   The amount of money remaining after paying taxes.

network   A communications, data exchange, and resource-sharing system created by linking two or more computers and establishing standards, or protocols, so that they can work together.

network database model   A flexible way of representing objects and their relationships.

network operating system (NOS)   The operating system that runs a network, steering information between computers and managing security and users.

network topology Refers to the geometric arrangement of the actual physical organization of the computers (and other network devices) in a network.

network transmission media Various types of media used to carry the signal between computers.

neural network (an artificial neural network) A category of AI that attempts to emulate the way the human brain works.

nonrepudiation A contractual stipulation to ensure that ebusiness participants do not deny (repudiate) their online actions.

not-for-profit (or nonprofit) corporation Usually exists to accomplish some charitable, humanitarian, or educational purpose, and the profits and losses are not shared by the business owners.

O

offshore outsourcing Using organizations from developing countries to write code and develop systems.

online ad Box running across a web page that is often used to contain advertisements.

online analytical processing (OLAP) The manipulation of information to create business intelligence in support of strategic decision making.

online service provider (OSP) Offers an extensive array of unique services such as its own version of a web browser.

online training Runs over the Internet or off a CD-ROM.

online transaction processing (OLTP) The capturing of transaction and event information using technology to (1) process the information according to defined business rules, (2) store the information, and (3) update existing information to reflect the new information.

onshore outsourcing The process of engaging another company within the same country for services.

open source Any program whose source code is made available for use or modification as users or other developers see fit.

open system A broad, general term that describes nonproprietary IT hardware and software made available by the standards and procedures by which their products work, making it easier to integrate them.

operating system software Controls the application software and manages how the hardware devices work together.

operational CRM Supports traditional transactional processing for day-to-day front-office operations or systems that deal directly with the customers.

operational planning and control (OP&C) Deals with the day-to-day procedures for performing work, including scheduling, inventory, and process management.

operations management (OM) The management of systems or processes that convert or transform resources (including human resources) into goods and services.

opportunity management CRM system Targets sales opportunities by finding new customers or companies for future sales.

opt-in Implying that a company will contact only the people who have agreed to receive promotions and marketing material via email.

output device Equipment used to see, hear, or otherwise accept the results of information processing requests.

outsourcing An arrangement by which one organization provides a service or services for another organization that chooses not to perform them in-house.

owner's equity The portion of a company belonging to the owners.

P

packet-switching Occurs when the sending computer divides a message into a number of efficiently sized units called packets, each of which contains the address of the destination computer.

packet tampering Altering the contents of packets as they travel over the Internet or altering data on computer disks after penetrating a network.

partner relationship management (PRM) Focuses on keeping vendors satisfied by managing alliance partner and reseller relationships that provide customers with the optimal sales channel.

partnership Similar to sole proprietorships, except that this legal structure allows for more than one owner.

partnership agreement A legal agreement between two or more business partners that outlines core business issues.

peer-to-peer (P2P) network Any network without a central file server and in which all computers in the network have access to the public files located on all other workstations.

performance Measures how quickly a system performs a certain process or transaction (in terms of efficiency IT metrics of both speed and throughput).

personalization Occurs when a website can know enough about a person's likes and dislikes that it can fashion offers that are more likely to appeal to that person.

PERT (Program Evaluation and Review Technique) chart A graphical network model that depicts a project's tasks and the relationships between those tasks.

phishing Technique to gain personal information for the purpose of identity theft, usually by means of fraudulent email.

physical view The physical storage of information on a storage device such as a hard disk.

pirated software The unauthorized use, duplication, distribution, or sale of copyrighted software.

planning phase Involves establishing a high-level plan of the intended project and determining project goals.

podcasting Distribution of audio or video files, such as radio programs or music videos, over the Internet to play on mobile devices and personal computers.

polymorphic virus and worm Change their form as they propagate.

pop-under ad Form of a pop-up ad that users do not see until they close the current web browser screen.

pop-up ad Small web page containing an advertisement that appears on the web page outside of the current website loaded in the web browser.

portal A website that offers a broad array of resources and services, such as email, online discussion groups, search engines, and online shopping malls.

predictive dialing Automatically dials outbound calls and when someone answers, the call is forwarded to an available agent.

primary key A field (or group of fields) that uniquely identifies a given entity in a table.

primary storage Computer's main memory, which consists of the random access memory (RAM), cache memory, and the read-only memory (ROM) that is directly accessible to the CPU.

privacy The right to be left alone when you want to be, to have control over your own personal possessions, and not to be observed without your consent.

private exchange A B2B marketplace in which a single buyer posts its need and then opens the bidding to any supplier who would care to bid.

process modeling Involves graphically representing the processes that capture, manipulate, store, and distribute information between a system and its environment.

product life cycle Includes the four phases a product progresses through during its life cycle including introduction, growth, maturity, and decline.

production The creation of goods and services using the factors of production: land, labor, capital, entrepreneurship, and knowledge.

production and materials management ERP component Handles the various aspects of production planning and execution such as demand forecasting, production scheduling, job cost accounting, and quality control.

production management Describes all the activities mangers do to help companies create goods.

profit Occurs when businesses sell products or services for more than they cost to produce.

project A temporary endeavor undertaken to create a unique product, service, or result.

project assumption Factors that are considered to be true, real, or certain without proof or demonstration.

project charter A document issued by the project initiator or sponsor that formally authorizes the existence of a project and provides the project manager with the authority to apply organizational resources to project activities.

project constraint Specific factors that can limit options.

project deliverable Any measurable, tangible, verifiable outcome, result, or item that is produced to complete a project or part of a project.

project management The application of knowledge, skills, tools, and techniques to project activities to meet project requirements.

project management institute (PMI) Develops procedures and concepts necessary to support the profession of project management (www.pmi.org).

project management office (PMO) An internal department that oversees all organizational projects.

project manager An individual who is an expert in project planning and management, defines and develops the project plan, and tracks the plan to ensure all key project milestones are completed on time and on budget.

project milestone Represents key dates when a certain group of activities must be performed.

project objective Quantifiable criteria that must be met for the project to be considered a success.

project plan A formal, approved document that manages and controls project execution.

project scope Defines the work that must be completed to deliver a product with the specified features and functions.

project stakeholder Individuals and organizations actively involved in the project or whose interests might be affected as a result of project execution or project completion.

protocol A standard that specifies the format of data as well as the rules to be followed during transmission.

prototype A smaller-scale representation or working model of the user's requirements or a proposed design for an information system.

public key encryption (PKE) Encryption system that uses two keys: a public key that everyone can have and a private key for only the recipient.

pure-play (virtual) business A business that operates on the Internet only without a physical store.

R

radio frequency identification (RFID) Technologies using active or passive tags in the form of chips or smart labels that can store unique identifiers and relay this information to electronic readers.

random access memory (RAM) The computer's primary working memory, in which program instructions and data are stored so that they can be accessed directly by the CPU via the processor's high-speed external data bus.

rapid application development (RAD) (also called rapid prototyping) methodology Emphasizes extensive user involvement in the rapid and evolutionary construction of working prototypes of a system to accelerate the systems development process.

rational unified process (RUP) methodology Provides a framework for breaking down the development of software into four gates.

read-only memory (ROM) The portion of a computer's primary storage that does not lose its contents when one switches off the power.

real simple syndication (RSS) Family of web feed formats used for web syndication of programs and content.

real-time information Immediate, up-to-date information.

real-time system Provides real-time information in response to query requests.

recovery The ability to get a system up and running in the event of a system crash or failure and includes restoring the information backup.

reduced instruction set computer (RISC) chip Limits the number of instructions the CPU can execute to increase processing speed.

redundancy The duplication of information, or storing the same information in multiple places.

reintermediation Using the Internet to reassemble buyers, sellers, and other partners in a traditional supply chain in new ways.

relational database model A type of database that stores information in the form of logically related two-dimensional tables.

relational integrity constraint The rules that enforce basic and fundamental information-based constraints.

reliability Ensures all systems are functioning correctly and providing accurate information.

requirements definition document Contains the final set of business requirements, prioritized in order of business importance.

response time The time it takes to respond to user interactions such as a mouse click.

revenue Refers to the amount earned resulting from the delivery or manufacture of a product or from the rendering of a service.

reverse auction An auction format in which increasingly lower bids are solicited from organizations willing to supply the desired product or service at an increasingly lower price.

rivalry among existing competitors High when competition is fierce in a market and low when competition is more complacent.

router An intelligent connecting device that examines each packet of data it receives and then decides which way to send it onward toward its destination.

S

sales The function of selling a good or service and focuses on increasing customer sales, which increases company revenues.

sales force automation (SFA) A system that automatically tracks all of the steps in the sales process.

sales management CRM system Automates each phase of the sales process, helping individual sales representatives coordinate and organize all of their accounts.

satellite A big microwave repeater in the sky; it contains one or more transponders that listen to a particular portion of the electromagnetic spectrum, amplifying incoming signals, and retransmitting them back to Earth.

scalability Refers to how well a system can adapt to increased demands.

scope creep Occurs when the scope of the project increases.

script kiddies or script bunnies Find hacking code on the Internet and click-and-point their way into systems to cause damage or spread viruses.

scrum methodology Uses small teams to produce small pieces of deliverable software using sprints, or 30-day intervals, to achieve an appointed goal.

search engine optimization (SEO) Set of methods aimed at improving the ranking of a website in search engine listings.

secondary storage Consists of equipment designed to store large volumes of data for long-term storage.

secure electronic transaction (SET) Transmission security method that ensures transactions are secure and legitimate.

secure socket layer (SSL) (1) Creates a secure and private connection between a client and server computer, (2) encrypts the information, and (3) sends the information over the Internet.

selling chain management Applies technology to the activities in the order life cycle from inquiry to sale.

semantic web An evolving extension of the World Wide web in which web content can be expressed not only in natural language, but also in a format that can be read and used by software agents, thus permitting them to find, share, and integrate information more easily.

sensitivity analysis The study of the impact that changes in one (or more) parts of the model have on other parts of the model.

server Computer that is dedicated to providing information in response to external requests.

service A business task.

service level agreement (SLA) Defines the specific responsibilities of the service provider and sets the customer expectations.

service-oriented architecture (SOA) A business-driven IT architectural approach that supports integrating a business as linked, repeatable tasks or services.

shareholder Another term for business owners.

shopping bot Software that will search several retailer websites and provide a comparison of each retailer's offerings including price and availability.

sign-off The system users' actual signatures indicating they approve all of the business requirements.

slice-and-dice The ability to look at information from different perspectives.

smart card A device that is around the same size as a credit card, containing embedded technologies that can store information and small amounts of software to perform some limited processing.

smartphone Combines the functions of a cellular phone and a PDA in a single device.

sniffer A program or device that can monitor data traveling over a network.

social engineering Using one's social skills to trick people into revealing access credentials or other information valuable to the attacker.

social networking analysis (SNA) A process of mapping a group's contacts (whether personal or professional) to identify who knows whom and who works with whom.

social responsibility Implies that an entity, whether it is a government, corporation, organization, or individual, has a responsibility to society.

software The set of instructions that the hardware executes to carry out specific tasks.

sole proprietorship A business form in which a single person is the sole owner and is personally responsible for all the profits and losses of the business.

solvency Represents the ability of the business to pay its bills and service its debt.

source document Describes the basic transaction data such as its date, purpose, and amount and includes cash receipts, canceled checks, invoices, customer refunds, employee time sheets, etc.

spam Unsolicited email.

spamdexing Uses a variety of deceptive techniques in an attempt to manipulate search engine rankings, whereas legitimate search engine optimization focuses on building better sites and using honest methods of promotion.

spoofing The forging of the return address on an email so that the email message appears to come from someone other than the actual sender.

spyware Software that comes hidden in free downloadable software and tracks online movements, mines the information stored on a computer, or uses a computer's CPU and storage for some task the user knows nothing about.

statement of cash flow Summarizes sources and uses of cash, indicates whether enough cash is available to carry on routine operations, and offers an analysis of all business transactions, reporting where the firm obtained its cash and how it chose to allocate the cash.

statement of owner's equity (also called the statement of retained earnings or equity statement) Tracks and communicates changes in the shareholder's earnings.

statistical analysis Performs such functions as information correlations, distributions, calculations, and variance analysis.

strategic business units (SBUs) Consist of several stand-alone businesses.

strategic planning Focuses on long-range planning such as plant size, location, and type of process to be used.

structured collaboration (or process collaboration) Involves shared participation in business processes, such as work flow, in which knowledge is hard coded as rules.

supplier power High when buyers have few choices of whom to buy from and low when their choices are many.

supplier relationship management (SRM) Focuses on keeping suppliers satisfied by evaluating and categorizing suppliers for different projects, which optimizes supplier selection.

supply chain Consists of all parties involved, directly or indirectly, in the procurement of a product or raw material.

supply chain event management (SCEM)   Enables an organization to react more quickly to resolve supply chain issues.

supply chain execution (SCE) system   Automates the different steps and stages of the supply chain.

supply chain management (SCM)   Involves the management of information flows between and among stages in a supply chain to maximize total supply chain effectiveness and profitability.

supply chain planning (SCP) system   Uses advanced mathematical algorithms to improve the flow and efficiency of the supply chain while reducing inventory.

supply chain visibility   The ability to view all areas up and down the supply chain.

sustainable, or "green," IT   The manufacture, management, use, and disposal of information technology in a way that minimizes damage to the environment, which is a critical part of a corporation's responsibility.

sustainable IT disposal   The safe disposal of IT assets at the end of their life cycle.

sustaining technology   Produces an improved product customers are eager to buy, such as a faster car or larger hard drive.

switching cost   The costs that can make customers reluctant to switch to another product or service.

system availability   Number of hours a system is available for users.

systems development life cycle (SDLC)   The overall process for developing information systems from planning and analysis through implementation and maintenance.

system software   Controls how the various technology tools work together along with the application software.

system virtualization   The ability to present the resources of a single computer as if it is a collection of separate computers ("virtual machines"), each with its own virtual CPUs, network interfaces, storage, and operating system.

T

tacit knowledge   The knowledge contained in people's heads.

tactical planning   Focuses on producing goods and services as efficiently as possible within the strategic plan.

telecommunication system   Enables the transmission of data over public or private networks.

telematics   The blending of computers and wireless telecommunications technologies with the goal of efficiently conveying information over vast networks to improve business operations.

terabyte (TB)   Roughly 1 trillion bytes.

test condition   The detailed steps the system must perform along with the expected results of each step.

testing phase   Involves bringing all the project pieces together into a special testing environment to test for errors, bugs, and interoperability and verify that the system meets all of the business requirements defined in the analysis phase.

threat of new entrants   High when it is easy for new competitors to enter a market and low when there are significant entry barriers to entering a market.

threat of substitute products or services   High when there are many alternatives to a product or service and low when there are few alternatives from which to choose.

throughput   The amount of information that can travel through a system at any point in time.

time-series information   Time-stamped information collected at a particular frequency.

To-Be process model   Shows the results of applying change improvement opportunities to the current (As-Is) process model.

token   Small electronic devices that change user passwords automatically.

transaction   Exchange or transfer of goods, services, or funds involving two or more people.

transaction processing system   The basic business system that serves the operational level (analysts) in an organization.

transaction speed   Amount of time a system takes to perform a transaction.

transactional information   Encompasses all of the information contained within a single business process or unit of work, and its primary purpose is to support the performing of daily operational tasks.

transborder data flow (TDF)   Business data flows across international boundaries over the telecommunications networks of global information systems.

transformation process   Often referred to as the technical core especially in manufacturing organizations and is the actual conversion of inputs to outputs.

Transmission Control Protocol/Internet Protocol (TCP/IP)   Provides the technical foundation for the public Internet as well as for large numbers of private networks.

transportation planning system   Tracks and analyzes the movement of materials and products to ensure the delivery of materials and finished goods at the right time, the right place, and the lowest cost.

Trojan-horse virus   Hides inside other software, usually as an attachment or a downloadable file.

twisted-pair wiring   A type of cable composed of four (or more) copper wires twisted around each other within a plastic sheath.

U

unstructured collaboration (or information collaboration)   Includes document exchange, shared whiteboards, discussion forums, and email.

up-selling   Increasing the value of a sale.

user documentation   Highlights how to use the system.

utility software   Provides additional functionality to the operating system.

V

value-added   The term used to describe the difference between the cost of inputs and the value of price of outputs.

value-added network (VAN)   A private network, provided by a third party, for exchanging information through a high-capacity connection.

value chain   Views an organization as a series of processes, each of which adds value to the product or service for each customer.

videoconference   A set of interactive telecommunication technologies that allow two or more locations to interact via two-way video and audio transmissions simultaneously.

viral marketing   Technique that induces websites or users to pass on a marketing message to other websites or users, creating exponential growth in the message's visibility and effect.

virtualization A framework of dividing the resources of a computer into multiple execution environments.

virtual private network (VPN) A way to use the public telecommunication infrastructure (e.g., Internet) to provide secure access to an organization's network.

virus Software written with malicious intent to cause annoyance or damage.

voice over IP (VoIP) Uses TCP/IP technology to transmit voice calls over long-distance telephone lines.

volatility Refers to RAM's complete loss of stored information if power is interrupted.

W

waterfall methodology Activity-based process in which each phase in the SDLC is performed sequentially from planning through implementation and maintenance.

web 2.0 A set of economic, social, and technology trends that collectively form the basis for the next generation of the Internet—a more mature, distinctive medium characterized by user participation, openness, and network effects.

web-based self-service system Allows customers to use the web to find answers to their questions or solutions to their problems.

web conference Blends audio, video, and document-sharing technologies to create virtual meeting rooms where people "gather" at a password-protected website.

web content management system (WCM) Adds an additional layer to document and digital asset management that enables publishing content both to intranets and to public websites.

web log Consists of one line of information for every visitor to a website and is usually stored on a web server.

web mashup A website or web application that uses content from more than one source to create a completely new service.

web service Contains a repertoire of web-based data and procedural resources that use shared protocols and standards permitting different applications to share data and services.

web traffic Includes a host of benchmarks such as the number of page views, the number of unique visitors, and the average time spent viewing a web page.

what-if analysis Checks the impact of a change in an assumption on the proposed solution.

white-hat hacker Works at the request of the system owners to find system vulnerabilities and plug the holes.

wide area network (WAN) Spans a large geographic area, such as a state, province, or country.

wiki Web-based tools that make it easy for users to add, remove, and change online content.

WiMAX The Worldwide Interoperability for Microwave Access is a telecommunications technology aimed at providing wireless data over long distances in a variety of ways, from point-to-point links to full mobile cellular type access.

wireless fidelity (wi-fi) A means of linking computers using infrared or radio signals.

wireless Internet service provider (WISP) An ISP that allows subscribers to connect to a server at designated hotspots or access points using a wireless connection.

wireless media Natural parts of the Earth's environment that can be used as physical paths to carry electrical signals.

wire media Transmission material manufactured so that signals will be confined to a narrow path and will behave predictably.

workflow Defines all the steps or business rules, from beginning to end, required for a business process.

workflow management system Facilitates the automation and management of business processes and controls the movement of work through the business process.

workshop training Set in a classroom-type environment and led by an instructor.

World Wide Web (WWW) A global hypertext system that uses the Internet as its transport mechanism.

worm A type of virus that spreads itself, not only from file to file, but also from computer to computer.

NOTES

Chapter 1

1. Jon Surmacz, "By the Numbers," *CIO Magazine,* www.cio.com, accessed October 2004.

2. IT Centrix, "Optimizing the Business Value of Information Technology," www.unisys.com/products/mainframes/insights/insights_compendium, accessed December 10, 2004.

3. "IT Master of the Senate," *CIO Magazine,* www.cio.com, accessed May 1, 2004.

4. Glossary of Business Terms, www.powerhomebiz.com/Glossary/glossary-A.htm, accessed December 15, 2003; Financial Times, "Mastering Management," www.ft.com/pp/mfm, accessed December 15, 2003; "Glossary of Financial Terms," www.nytimes.com/library/financial/glossary/bfglosa.htm, accessed December 15, 2003; "Business Dictionary," www.glossarist.com/glossaries/business/, accessed December 15, 2003; and "Glossary of Business Terms," www.smallbiz.nsw.gov.au/smallbusiness/, accessed December 15, 2003.

5. Ibid.

6. "Integrating Information at Children's Hospital," *KMWorld,* www.kmworld.com/Articles/ReadArticle.aspx?ArticleID=10253, accessed June 1, 2005.

7. Dave Lindorff, "General Electric and Real Time," www.cioinsight.com/article2/0,3959,686147,00.asp, accessed March 1, 2004.

8. "IT Master of the Senate," *CIO Magazine,* www.cio.com, accessed May 1, 2004.

9. Cisco Press, www.ciscopress.com/index.asp?rl=1, accessed March 15, 2004.

10. "Integrating Information at Children's Hospital," *KMWorld.*

11. "Glossary of Business Terms," www.powerhomebiz.com/Glossary/glossary-A.htm, accessed December 15, 2003; Financial Times, "Mastering Management," www.ft.com/pp/mfm, accessed December 15, 2003; "Glossary of Financial Terms," www.nytimes.com/library/financial/glossary/bfglosa.htm, accessed December 15, 2003; "Business Dictionary," www.glossarist.com/glossaries/business/, accessed December 15, 2003; and "Glossary of Business Terms," www.smallbiz.nsw.gov.au/smallbusiness/, accessed December 15, 2003.

12. Ken Blanchard, "Effectiveness vs. Efficiency," Wachovia Small Business, www.wachovia.com, accessed October 14, 2003.

13. Lindorff, "General Electric and Real Time."

14. Cisco Press, www.ciscopress.com/index.asp?rl=1, accessed October 2003.

15. Ken Blanchard, "Effectiveness vs. Efficiency," Wachovia Small Business, www.wachovia.com, accessed October 14, 2003.

16. United Nations Division for Public Economics and Public Administration, www.un.com, accessed November 10, 2003.

17. Ibid.

18. EBay Financial News, "Earnings and Dividend Release," January 15, 2002.

19. "Sun and eBay Celebrate Record Uptime," www.sun.com/service/about/features/ebay.html, accessed January 14, 2004.

20. Michael E. Porter, *Competitive Strategy: Techniques for Analyzing Industries and Competitors.*

Chapter 2

1. "1,000 Executives Best Skillset," *The Wall Street Journal,* July 15, 2003.

2. "The Visionary Elite," *Business 2.0,* December 2003, pp. S1–S5.

3. "Boston Coach Aligns Service with Customer Demand in Real Time," www-1.ibm.com/services/us/index.wss, accessed November 4, 2003.

4. "Industry Facts and Statistics," Insurance Information Institute, www.iii.org, accessed December 2005.

5. Neil Raden, "Data, Data Everywhere," *DSSResources.com,* February 16, 2003.

6. Ibid.

7. Ibid.

8. Christopher Koch, "How Verizon Flies by Wire," *CIO Magazine,* November 1, 2004.

9. Neil McManus, "Robots at Your Service," *Wired,* January 2003, p. O59.

10. "Put Better, Faster Decision-Making in Your Sights," www.teradata.com, accessed July 7, 2003.

11. Ibid.

12. S. Begley, "Software au Natural," *Newsweek,* May 8, 2005.

13. Beth Bacheldor, "Steady Supply," *InformationWeek,* November 24, 2003, www.informationweek.com, accessed June 6, 2003.

14. McManus, "Robots at Your Service."

15. "Put Better, Faster Decision-Making in Your Sights," www.teradata.com; "Neural Network Examples and Definitions," ece-www.colorado.edu/~ecen4831/lectures/NNdemo.html, accessed June 24, 2007; Begley, "Software au Natural"; McManus, "Robots at Your Service"; Santa Fe Institute, www.dis.anl.gov/abms/, accessed June 24, 2007; and Michael A. Arbib, (ed. 1995), *The Handbook of Brain Theory and Neural Networks* L. Biacino and G. Gerla, "Fuzzy logic, continuity and effectiveness," *Archive for Mathematical Logic.*

16. Ibid.

17. www.columbiasportswear.com, accessed December 15, 2008.

18. "What Is BPR?" searchcio.techtarget.com/sDefinition/0,,sid182_gci536451,00.html, accessed October 10, 2005; BPR Online, www.prosci.com/mod1.htm, accessed October 10, 2005; Business Process Reengineering Six Sigma, www.isixsigma.com/me/bpr/, accessed October 10, 2005; and SmartDraw.com, www.smartdraw.com/, accessed October 11, 2005.

19. Ibid.

20. Ibid.

21. Ibid.

22. Michael Hammer, *Beyond Reengineering: How the Process-Centered Organization Is Changing Our Work and Our Lives* (New York: HarperCollins Publishers, 1996).

23. Richard Chang, "Process Reengineering in Action: A Practical Guide to Achieving Breakthrough Results (Quality Improvement Series)," 1996; H. James Harrington, *Business Process Improvement Workbook: Documentation, Analysis, Design, and Management of Business Process Improvement* (New York: McGraw-Hill, 1997); Hammer, *Beyond Reengineering;* Michael Hammer and James, Champy, "Reengineering the Corporation:

A Manifest for Business Revolution," 1993; "Government Business Process Reengineering (BPR) Readiness Assessment Guide, General Services Administration (GSA)," 1996; Richard Chang, "Process Reengineering in Action: A Practical Guide to Achieving Breakthrough Results (Quality Improvement Series)," 1996 and; Michael Hammer, "Beyond Reengineering: How the Process-Centered Organization is Changing Our Work and Our Lives," 1997.

24. Ibid.
25. Ibid.
26. Ibid.
27. Ibid.
28. Ibid.
29. H. James Harrington, *Business Process Improvement: The Breakthrough Strategy for Total Quality, Productivity, and Competitiveness* (New York: McGraw-Hill, 1991); and Hammer, "Beyond Reengineering.
30. Ibid.
31. Ibid.
32. Ibid.
33. Bjorn Andersen, *Business Process Improvement Toolbox* (Milwaukee, WI: ASQ Quality Press, 1999).
34. "What is BPR?" searchcio.techtarget.com/sDefinition/0,,sid182_gci536451,00.html; SmartDraw.com, www.smartdraw.com/; BPR Online, www.prosci.com/mod1.htm; and Business Process Reengineering Six Sigma, www.isixsigma.com/me/bpr/.
35. "What Is BPR?" searchcio.techtarget.com/sDefinition/0,,sid 182_gci536451,00.html, accessed October 10, 2005; BPR Online, www.prosci.com/mod1.htm, accessed October 10, 2005; Business Process Reengineering Six Sigma, www.isixsigma.com/me/bpr/, accessed October 10, 2005; and SmartDraw.com, www.smartdraw.com/, accessed October 11, 2005.

Chapter 3

1. Cisco Press, www.ciscopress.com/index.asp?rl=1, accessed March 1, 2005.
2. Adam Lashinsky, "Kodak's Developing Situation," *Fortune,* January 20, 2003, p. 176.
3. www.wired.com, accessed November 15, 2003.
4. Lashinsky, "Kodak's Developing Situation."
5. Clayton Christensen, *The Innovator's Dilemma* (Boston: Harvard Business School, 1997).
6. Internet World Statistics, www.internetworldstats.com, January 2007.
7. info.cern.ch, accessed March 1, 2005.
8. "Internet Pioneers," www.ibiblio.org/pioneers/andreesen.html, accessed March 1, 2005.
9. Gunjan Bagla, "Bringing IT to Rural India One Village at a Time," *CIO Magazine,* March 1, 2005.
10. Tim O'Reilly, "What Is Web 2.0: Design Patterns and Business Models for the Next Generation of Software," www.oreillynet.com/pub/a/oreilly/tim/news/2005/09/30/what-is-web-20.html, accessed June 25, 2007; and "Web 2.0 for CIOs," www.cio.com/article/16807, *CIO Magazine,* accessed June 24, 2007.
11. Ibid.
12. Ibid.
13. "The Complete Web 2.0 Directory," www.go2web20.net/, accessed June 24, 2007, and "Web 2.0 for CIOs," www.cio.com/article/16807.
14. Ibid.
15. Anne Zelenka, "The Hype Machine, Best Mashup of Mashup Camp 3," gigaom.com/2007/01/18/the-hype-machine-best-mashup-of-mashup-camp-3/, accessed June 14, 2007; and Webmashup.com, www.webmashup.com/Insert New 25, accessed June 14, 2007.
16. Ibid.
17. Ibid.
18. Ibid.
19. "Info on 3.9M Citigroup," *Money,* June 6, 2005.
20. Amy Johnson, "A New Supply Chain Forged," *Computerworld,* September 30, 2002.
21. "Pratt & Whitney," *BusinessWeek,* June 2004.
22. "Let's Remake a Deal," *Business 2.0,* March 2004.
23. Laura Rohde, "British Airways Takes Off with Cisco," *Network World,* May 11, 2005.
24. www.t-mobile.com, accessed June 2005.
25. www.idc.com, accessed June 2005.
26. "A Site Stickier Than a Barroom Floor," *Business 2.0,* June 2005, p. 74.
27. www.emarketer.com, accessed January 2006.
28. Heather Harreld, "Lemon Aid," *CIO Magazine,* July 1, 2000.
29. Rachel Metz, "Changing at the Push of a Button," *Wired,* September 27, 2004.
30. www.hotel-gatti.com, accessed June 2003.
31. Frank Quinn, "The Payoff Potential in Supply Chain Management," www.ascet.com, accessed June 15, 2003.
32. www.oecd.org, accessed June 2005.
33. www.vanguard.com, accessed June 2005.
34. "Watch Your Spending," *BusinessWeek,* May 23, 2004.
35. Jack Welch, "What's Right About Walmart," *CIO Magazine,* www.cio.com, accessed May 2005.
36. www.yankeegroup.com, accessed May 2005.
37. www.ingenio.com, accessed July 2005.
38. "E-Commerce Taxation," www.icsc.org/srch/government/ECommerce February2003.pdf, accessed June 8, 2004.

Chapter 4

1. Michael Schrage, "Build the Business Case," *CIO Magazine,* www.cio.com, accessed November 17, 2003.
2. Scott Berianato, "Take the Pledge," *CIO Magazine,* www.cio.com, accessed November 17, 2003.
3. Ibid.
4. Ibid.
5. AMA Research, "Workplace Monitoring and Surveillance," www.amanet.org, accessed March 1, 2004.
6. Ibid.
7. Ibid.
8. Andy McCue, "Bank Boss Quits after Porn Found on PC," www.businessweek.com, accessed June 2004.
9. AMA Research, "Workplace Monitoring and Surveillance," www.amanet.org, accessed March 1, 2004.

10. www.vault.com, accessed January 2006.

11. AMA Research, "Workplace Monitoring and Surveillance."

12. "Health Information Management," www.gartner.com, accessed November 16, 2003.

13. "2005 CSI/FBI Computer Crime and Security Survey," www.gocsi.com, accessed February 20, 2006.

14. Ibid.

15. www.ey.com, accessed November 25, 2003.

16. "The Security Revolution," *CIO Magazine,* www.cio.com, accessed June 6, 2003.

17. "Losses from Identity Theft to Total $221 Billion Worldwide," www.cio.com, accessed May 23, 2003.

18. "Sony Fights Intrusion with 'Crystal Ball,'" *CIO Magazine,* www.cio.com, accessed August 9, 2003.

19. Mark Leon, "Keys to the Kingdom," www.computerworld.com, accessed August 8, 2003.

20. "Spam Losses to Grow to $198 Billion," *CIO Magazine,* www.cio.com, accessed August 9, 2003.

21. "Teen Arrested in Internet 'Blaster' Attack," www.cnn.com, accessed August 29, 2003.

Chapter 5

1. Christine McGeever, "FBI Database Problem Halts Gun Checks," www.computerworld.com, accessed May 22, 2000.

2. www.cio.com, accessed November 2005.

3. "Distribution of Software Updates of Thousands of Franchise Locations Was Slow and Unpredictable," www.fountain.com, accessed October 10, 2003.

4. Christopher Koch, "A New Blueprint for the Enterprise," *CIO Magazine,* March 1, 2005.

5. "New Coalitions Increasing America's Crisis Preparedness," www.complianceexecutive.com, accessed November 29, 2007.

6. Ibid.

7. Bob Tedeschi, *"Protect Your Identity,"* pcworld.about.com/magazine/2212p107id118241.htm, accessed November 11, 2007.

8. "Password Management," www.fischerinternational.com, accessed December 1, 2007.

9. Martin Garvey, "Manage Passwords," *Information Week,* May 20, 2005.

10. Martin Garvey, "Security Action Plans," *Information Week,* May 30, 2005.

11. Ibid.

12. www.abercrombie.com, accessed November 29, 2008.

13. Erick Schonfeld, "Linux Takes Flight," *Business 2.0,* January 2003, pp. 103–105.

14. John Fontana, "Lydian Revs up with Web Services," *Network World,* March 10, 2004.

15. www.websidestory.com, accessed November 18, 2007.

16. Tim O'Reilly, "Open Source Paradigm Shift," tim.oreilly.com/articles/paradigmshift_0504.html, accessed January 11, 2008.

17. Julie Bort, "SOA Made Fast and Easy," *Network World,* October 22, 2007.

18. Dirk Slama, Robert Paluch, "Key Concepts of Service-Oriented Architecture," www.csc.com/cscworld/012006/web/web002.html, accessed on January 4, 2008.

19. Ibid.

20. "Achieving a Single Customer View," www.sun.com, accessed January 12, 2008.

21. "VMware—History of Virtualization," www.virtualizationworks.com/Virtualization-History.asp, accessed January 23, 2008.

22. "EPA Report to Congress on Server and Data Center Energy Efficiency," www.energystar.gov/ia/partners/prod_development/downloads/EPA_Report_Exec_Summary_Final.pdf, accessed January 23, 2008.

23. Paul Krill, "Impending Death of Moore's Law Calls for Software Development Changes," *InfoWorld,* May 24, 2005.

24. Ibid.

25. Geoffrey Thomas, "Seeing Is Believing," *Air Transport World,* June 2007, p. 54.

26. Julie Bort, "Subaru Takes a Virtual Drive," *Network World,* September 25, 2006.

27. "Google Groans Under Data Strain," www.byteandswitch.com/document.asp?doc_id=85804, accessed January 30, 2008.

28. Alan Joch, "Grid Gets Down to Business," *Network World,* December 27, 2004.

Chapter 6

1. "Google Reveals High-Profile Users of Data Search Machine," Reuters News Service, August 13, 2003, www.chron.com, accessed September 3, 2003.

2. Mitch Betts, "Unexpected Insights," *ComputerWorld,* April 14, 2003, www.computerworld.com, accessed September 4, 2003.

3. Ibid.

4. "Data Mining: What General Managers Need to Know," *Harvard Management Update,* October 1999.

5. Barbara DePompa Reimers, "Too Much of a Good Thing," *ComputerWorld,* www.computerworld.com, April 14, 2003.

6. Ibid.

7. "MSI Business Solutions Case Study: Westpac Financial Services," www.MSI.com, accessed August 4, 2003.

8. "Why Data Quality," www.trilliumsoft.com, accessed October 3, 2003.

9. Ibid.

10. Webopedia.com, www.webopedia.comTERM/d/database.html, accessed May 15, 2007; and Oracle Database, www.oracle.com/database/index.html, accessed May 17, 2007.

11. Ibid.

12. Ibid.

13. Chicago Police Department, gis.chicagopolice.org/, accessed June 23, 2004.

14. Ford's Vision, donate.pewclimate.org/docUploads/Ford.pdf, accessed June 18, 2003.

15. Webopedia.com, www.webopedia.comTERM/d/database.html; Oracle Database, www.oracle.com/database/index.html.

16. www.sitepoint.com/article/publishing-mysql-data-web, accessed May 16, 2007.

17. Ibid.

18. Oracle Success Stories, www.oracle.com/successstories/army, accessed May 15, 2003.

19. Kathleen Melymuka, "Premier 100: Turning the Tables at Applebee's," *ComputerWorld,* www.computerworld.com, accessed February 24, 2003.

20. Julia Kiling, "OLAP Gains Fans among Data-Hungry Firms," *ComputerWorld,* January 8, 2001, p. 54.

21. Tommy Perterson, "Data Cleansing," *ComputerWorld,* www.computerworld.com, accessed February 10, 2003.

22. "Dr Pepper/Seven Up, Inc.," www.cognos.com, accessed September 10, 2003.

Chapter 7

1. www.sabreairlinesolutions.com/about/history.htm, accessed January 22, 2008.

2. "Rip Curl Turns to Skype for Global Communications," www.voipinbusiness.co.uk/rip_curl_turns_to_skype_for_gl.asp July 07, 2006, accessed January 21, 2008.

3. "VoIP Business Solutions," www.vocalocity.com, accessed January 21, 2008.

4. www.skype.com, accessed February 15, 2008.

5. www.rei.com, accessed February 23, 2008.

6. Enrique De Argaez, "What You Should Know About Internet Broadband Access," www.internetworldstats.com/articles/art 096.htm, accessed January 29, 2008.

7. "Broadband Technology Overview," www.corning.com/docs/opticalfiber/wp6321.pdf, accessed February 1, 2008.

8. www.drpepper.com, accessed February 1, 2008.

9. "Navigating the Mobility Wave," www.busmanagement.com, accessed February 2, 2008.

10. www.mbia.com, accessed February 3, 2008.

11. Dan Nystedt, "Mobile Phones Grow Even More Popular," *PC World,* April 2006.

12. "How Do Cellular Devices Work," www.cell-phone101.info/devices.php, accessed February 9, 2008.

13. mobilementalism.com, accessed February 2, 2008.

14. V. C. Gungor, F. C. Lambert, "A Survey on Communication Networks for Electric System Automation, Computer Networks," *The International Journal of Computer and Telecommunications Networking,* May 15, 2006, pp. 877–897.

15. "CenterCup Releases PDA Caddy to Leverage Legalized Golf GPS," www.golfgearreview.com/article-display/1665.html, accessed February 3, 2008.

16. www.onstar.com, accessed February 10, 2008.

17. "Keeping Weeds in Check with Less Herbicide," www.ars.usda.gov/is/AR/archive/aug06/weeds0806.htm, accessed February 11, 2008.

18. www.gis.rgs.org/10.html, accessed February 7, 2008.

19. Coco Masters, "Bringing Wi-Fi to the Skies," www.time.com/time/specials/2007/article/0,28804,1665220_1665225,00.html, accessed February 20, 2008.

20. W. David Gardner, "McDonald's Targets Starbucks with Free Wi-Fi, Upscale Coffee Bars," *InformationWeek,* January 7, 2008.

21. "Security-Free Wireless Networks," www.wired.com, accessed February 11, 2008.

22. "Sprint Plans Launch of Commercial WiMAX Service in Q2 2008," www.intomobile.com, accessed February 10, 2008.

23. Deepak Pareek, "WiMAX: Taking Wireless to the MAX," CRC Press, 2006, pp. 150–51.

24. www.wimax.com, accessed February 9, 2008.

25. Mohsen Attaran, "RFID: an Enabler of Supply Chain Operations," *Supply Chain Management: An International Journal* 12 (2007), pp. 249–57.

26. Michael Dortch, "Winning RFID Strategies for 2008," *Benchmark Report,* December 31, 2007.

27. Ibid.

28. "RFID Privacy and You," www.theyaretrackingyou.com/rfid-privacy-and-you.html, accessed February 12, 2008.

29. "RFID Roundup," www.rfidgazette.org, accessed February 10, 2008.

30. Chris Silva, Benjamin Gray, "Key Wireless Trends That Will Shape Enterprise Mobility in 2008," www.forrester.com, accessed February 12, 2008.

Chapter 8

1. Norman E. Bowie, ed., *The Blackwell Guide to Business Ethics.* (Malden, MA: Blackwell, 2002).

2. Ibid.

3. Ibid.

4. Geoffrey Colvin, "Managing in the Info Era," *Fortune,* March 6, 2007, pp. F6–F9.

5. Christopher A. Bartlett and Sumantra Ghoshal, "Going Global: Lessons from Late Movers," *Harvard Business Review,* March–April 2000, pp. 132–34.

6. Stuart Crainer, *The Management Century* (New York: Jossey-Bass, 2000).

7. James Fitzsimmons and Mona Fitzsimmons, *Service Management,* 4th ed. (New York: McGraw-Hill Irwin, 2004).

8. Ibid.

9. William J. Hopp and Mark Spearman, *Factory Physics: Foundations of Manufacturing Management,* 2nd ed. (Burr Ridge, IL: Irwin, 2001).

10. Ibid.

11. Ibid.

12. Aaron Bernstein, "Backlash: Behind the Anxiety of Globalization," *BusinessWeek,* April 24, 2006, pp. 36–42. Terry Hill, *Manufacturing Strategy: Text and Cases* 3rd ed. (New York: McGraw-Hill, 2000).

13. Ibid.

14. Ibid.

15. Ibid.

16. Christopher A. Bartlett and Sumantra Ghoshal, "Going Global: Lessons from Late Movers," *Harvard Business Review,* March–April 2000, pp. 132–34.

17. Sharon Shinn, "What About the Widgets?" *BizEd,* November–December 2004, pp. 30–35.

18. Ibid.

19. James P. Womack, Daniel Jones, and Daniel Roos, *The Machine That Changed the World* (New York, Harper Perennial, 1991).

20. Ibid.

21. John Hagerty, "How Best to Measure Our Supply Chain," www.amrresearch.com, accessed March 3, 2005.

22. Andrew Binstock, "Virtual Enterprise Comes of Age," *InformationWeek,* November 6, 2004.

23. Mitch Betts, "Kinks in the Chain," *Computerworld,* December 17, 2005.

24. Walid Mougayar, "Old Dogs Learn New Tricks," *Business 2.0,* October 2000, www.Business2.com, accessed June 14, 2003.

25. "Creating a Value Network," *Wired,* September 2003, p. S13.

26. Fred Hapgood, "Smart Decisions," *CIO Magazine,* www.cio.com, accessed August 15, 2001.

27. "Creating a Value Network," *Wired.*

28. "Success Story," www.perdue.com, accessed September 2003.

29. "Creating a Value Network," *Wired.*

30. "The e-Biz Surprise," *BusinessWeek,* May 12, 2003, pp. 60–65.

31. Hagerty, "How Best to Measure Our Supply Chain."

32. Ibid.

33. Frank Quinn, "The Payoff Potential in Supply Chain Management," www.ascet.com, accessed June 15, 2003.

34. Mougayar, "Old Dogs Learn New Tricks."

35. Quinn, "The Payoff Potential," and William Copacino, "How to Become a Supply Chain Master," *Supply Chain Management Review,* September 1, 2001, www.manufacturing.net, accessed June 12, 2003.

36. Ibid.

Chapter 9

1. "Customer Success Stories," www.siebel.com, accessed November 12, 2003.

2. "Kaiser's Diabetic Initiative," www.businessweek.com, accessed November 15, 2003.

3. "Integrated Solutions—The ABCs of CRM," www.integratedsolutionsmag.com, accessed November 12, 2003.

4. Ibid.

5. "1800 flowers.com," *Business 2.0,* February 2004.

6. "The 'New' New York Times," *Business 2.0,* January 2004.

7. "New York Knicks—Success," www.jdedwards.com, accessed January 15, 2004.

8. "Barclays, Giving Voice to Customer-Centricity," crm.insightexec.com, accessed July 15, 2003.

9. "Customer Success—PNC Retail Bank," www.siebel.com, accessed May 5, 2003.

10. "California State Automobile Association Case Study," www.epiphany.com/customers/detail_csaa.html, accessed July 4, 2003.

11. www.salesforce.com, accessed June 2005.

12. "Vail Resorts Implements FrontRange HEAT," *CRM Today,* October 16, 2003, www.crm2day.com/news/crm/EpyykIIFyAq-EUbqOhW.php, accessed December 2, 2003.

13. "3M Accelerates Revenue Growth Using Siebel eBusiness Applications," www.siebel.com, July 30, 2002, accessed July 10, 2003.

14. www.enterprise.com, accessed June 15, 2004.

15. "Avnet Brings IM to Corporate America with Lotus Instant Messaging," www.websphereadvisor.com/doc/12196, accessed July 11, 2003.

16. Ibid.

17. Ibid.

18. www.nicesystems.com, accessed June 2005.

19. www.FedEx.com, accessed July 13, 2003.

20. "Documedics," www.siebel.com, accessed July 10, 2003.

21. Ibid.

22. Ibid.

23. "Customer Success—UPS," www.sap.com, accessed April 5, 2003.

24. Ibid.

25. "Customer Success—UPS."

26. "Supply Chain Planet," June 2003, http://newsweaver.co.uk/supplychainplanet/e_article000153342.cfm, accessed July 12, 2003.

27. "Customer Success—Cisco," www.sap.com, accessed April 5, 2003.

28. "Customer Success," www.costco.com, accessed June 2005.

29. "Customer Success," www.rackspace.com, accessed June 2005.

30. "Customer Success," www.siebel.com, accessed May 5, 2007.

31. "The Critical Shift to Flexible Business Intelligence," Used with Permission: Dr. Claudia Imhoff, Intelligent Solutions, Inc. "What Every Marketer Wants—And Needs—From Technology," Used with Permission: Dr. Claudia Imhoff, Intelligent Solutions, Inc. "Enterprise Business Intelligence," May 2006, Used with Permission: Dr. Claudia Imhoff, Intelligent Solutions, Inc. "The Business Case for Data Warehousing," Jill Dyche, 2005, (used with permission).

32. Ibid.

33. Ibid.

34. Ibid.

35. Ibid.

36. Ibid.

37. Ibid.

38. Ibid.

39. Ibid.

40. Ibid.

41. Ibid.

42. Ibid.

43. Ibid.

44. Ibid.

45. Ibid.

46. Ibid.

47. Ibid.

48. Ibid.

49. Ibid.

50. Ibid.

51. Ibid.

52. Ibid.

53. Ibid.

Chapter 10

1. "Customer Success Story—Turner Industries," www.jdedwards.com, accessed October 15, 2003.

2. "Success Stories," www.sap.com, accessed April 2005.

3. "Customer Success Story—Turner Industries," www.jdedwards.com, accessed October 15, 2003.

4. Michael Doane, "A Blueprint for ERP Implementation Readiness," www.metagroup.com, accessed October 17, 2003.

5. "Amazon Finds Profits in Outsourcing," *CIO Magazine,* October 15, 2002, www.cio.com/archive/101502/tl_ec.html, accessed November 14, 2003.

6. "D-FW Defense Contractors Show Mixed Fortunes since September 11," www.bizjournals.com/dallas/stories/2002/09/09/focus2.htm, accessed June 8, 2004.

7. Steve Konicki, "Collaboration Is Cornerstone of $19B Defense Contract," www.business2.com/content/magazine/indepth/2000/07/11/17966, accessed June 8, 2004.

8. "Knowledge Management Research Center," *CIO Magazine,* www.cio.com/research/knowledge, accessed December 2005.

9. "Harley-Davidson on the Path to Success," www.peoplesoft.com/media/success, accessed October 12, 2003.

10. "Customer Success Story—Grupo Farmanova Intermed," www.jdedwards.com, accessed October 15, 2003.

11. "Customer Success Stories," www.jdedwards.com, accessed October 15, 2003.

12. Michael Doane, "A Blueprint for ERP Implementation Readiness," www.metagroup.com, accessed October 17, 2003.

13. Megan Santosus, "In The Know," *CIO Magazine,* January 2006.

14. Ibid.

15. The Balanced Scorecard, www.balancedscorecard.org, accessed February 2008.

16. Ibid.

17. Ibid.

18. Ibid.

19. Ibid.

20. "Speeding Information to BMW Dealers," www.kmworld.com/resources/featurearticles/index.cfm?action=readfeature&Feature_ID=337, accessed June 8, 2004.

21. "Toyota's One-Stop Information Shop," www.istart.co.nz/index/HM20/PC0/PV21873/EX236/CS25653, accessed June 8, 2004.

22. Ibid.

23. "Amazon Finds Profits in Outsourcing," *CIO Magazine,* October 15, 2002, www.cio.com/archive/101502/tl_ec.html, accessed November 14, 2003.

24. "D-FW Defense Contractors Show Mixed Fortunes since September 11," www.bizjournals.com/dallas/stories/2002/09/09/focus2.htm, accessed June 8, 2004.

25. Steve Konicki, "Collaboration Is Cornerstone of $19B Defense Contract," www.business2.com/content/magazine/indepth/2000/07/11/17966, accessed June 8, 2004.

26. "Knowledge Management Research Center," *CIO Magazine,* www.cio.com/research/knowledge, accessed December 2005.

27. Megan Santosus, "In The Know," *CIO Magazine,* January 2006.

28. Ibid.

29. "Speeding Information to BMW Dealers," www.kmworld.com/resources/featurearticles/index.cfm?action=readfeature&Feature_ID=337, accessed June 8, 2004.

30. Megan Santosus, "In The Know," *CIO Magazine,* January 2006.

31. Ibid.

32. "Knowledge Management Research Center," *CIO Magazine,* www.cio.com/research/knowledge, accessed December 2005.

33. Ibid.

34. Ibid.

35. Ibid.

36. Ibid.

Chapter 11

1. www.businessweek.com, accessed November 1, 2005.

2. "Software Costs," *CIO Magazine,* www.cio.com, accessed December 5, 2003.

3. "Defective Software Costs," *National Institute of Standards and Technology (NIST),* June 2002.

4. Ibid.

5. *CIO Magazine,* June 1, 2006, p. 55; "The Project Manager in the IT Industry," www.si2.com, accessed December 15, 2003; www.standishgroup.com, accessed December 12, 2003; Jim Johnson, "My Life Is Failure," p. 46; and Gary McGraw, "Making Essential Software Work," *Software Quality Management,* April 2003, www.sqmmagazine.com, accessed November 14, 2003.

6. Ibid.

7. Ibid.

8. Ibid.

9. "Customer Success Story—PHH," www.informatica.com, accessed December 12, 2003.

10. *CIO Magazine,* June 1, 2006; "The Project Manager in the IT Industry"; www.standishgroup.com; Johnson, "My Life Is Failure"; and McGraw, "Making Essential Software Work."

11. Ibid.

12. Ibid.

13. Ibid.

14. "Building Events," www.microsoft.com, accessed November 15, 2003.

15. Agile Alliance Manifesto, www.agile.com, accessed November 1, 2003.

16. "Software Metrics," *CIO Magazine,* www.cio.com, accessed December 2, 2003.

17. "Building Software That Works," www.compaq.com, accessed November 14, 2003.

18. "Software Metrics," *CIO Magazine.*

19. www.agile.com, accessed November 10, 2003.

20. "Python Project Failure," www.systemsdev.com, accessed November 14, 2003.

21. *CIO Magazine,* June 1, 2006; "The Project Manager in the IT Industry"; www.standishgroup.com; Johnson, "My Life Is Failure"; and McGraw, "Making Essential Software Work."

22. Ibid.

23. McGraw, "Making Essential Software Work."

24. *CIO Magazine,* June 1, 2006; "The Project Manager in the IT Industry"; www.standishgroup.com; Johnson, "My Life Is Failure"; and McGraw, "Making Essential Software Work."

25. Ibid.

26. "Top Reasons Why IT Projects Fail," *InformationWeek,* www.infoweek.com, accessed November 5, 2003; www.calpine.com, accessed December 14, 2003; "The Project Manager in the IT Industry," www.si2.com, accessed December 15, 2003, www.standishgroup.com, accessed December 12, 2003; and www.snapon.com, accessed December 13, 2003.

27. Ibid.

28. Ibid.

29. Ibid.

30. Ibid.

31. Ibid.

32. www.standishgroup.com, accessed November 14, 2003.

33. Ibid.

34. www.microsoft.com, accessed November 16, 2003.

35. "REI Pegs Growth on Effective Multi-channel Strategy," *Internet Retailer,* www.internetretailer.com, accessed February 17, 2005; and Alison Overholt, "Smart Strategies: Putting Ideas to Work," *Fast Company,* April 2004, p. 63.

36. *CIO Magazine,* June 1, 2006; "The Project Manager in the IT Industry"; www.standishgroup.com; accessed December 12, 2003; Johnson, "My Life Is Failure"; and McGraw, "Making Essential Software Work."

37. Ibid.

Chapter 12

1. *BusinessWeek: Innovation,* http://www.businessweek.com/innovate/, accessed February 15, 2008.

2. −45. Ibid.

CREDITS

Chapter 1

Page 2, © Photodisc/Getty Images.

Page 4, © GRAFIKA/Miyano Takuya/Norihiro Uehara.

Page 6, © Digital Vision/Punchstock.

Figure 1.1, page 6, Paige Baltzan.

Page 9, Stockbyte/Punchstock Images.

Page 13, © BananaStock Ltd.

Figure 1.10, page 13, www.cio.com, accessed August 2005.

Figure 1.11. page 13. "What Concerns CIOs the Most?" www.cio.com. Accessed November 17, 2003.

Figure 1.12, page 14, www.cio.com, accessed August 2005.

Page 16, Ryan McVay/Getty Images.

Figure 1.13, page 17, United National Division for Public Economics and Public Administration, www.un.com, accessed November 10, 2003.

Page 17, Imagemore Co., Ltd./Getty Images.

Page 20, Ryan McVay/Getty Images.

Figure 1.17, page 20, Porter, Michael E., Competitive Strategy: Techniques for Analyzing Industries and Competitors, The Free Press, 1998.

Figure 1.18, page 21, Porter, Michael E., Competitive Strategy: Techniques for Analyzing Industries and Competitors, The Free Press, 1998.

Page 22, Jason Reed/Ryan McVay/Getty Images.

Figure 1.19, page 23, Porter, Michael E., Competitive Strategy: Techniques for Analyzing Industries and Competitors, The Free Press, 1998.

Figure 1.20 top left, page 24, Photo courtesy Hyundai Motor America.

Figure 1.20 top right, page 24, Photo courtesy Audi of America.

Figure 1.20 bottom left, page 24, Courtesy Kia Motors American, Inc.

Figure 1.20 bottom right, page 24, Courtesy General Motors.

Figure 1.21, page 24, Porter, Michael E., Competitive Strategy: Techniques for Analyzing Industries and Competitors, The Free Press, 1998.

Figure 1.22, page 25, Porter, Michael E., Competitive Strategy: Techniques for Analyzing Industries and Competitors, The Free Press, 1998.

Figure 1.23, page 26, Porter, Michael E., Competitive Strategy: Techniques for Analyzing Industries and Competitors, The Free Press, 1998.

Page 26, Digital Vision/Getty Images.

Chapter 2

Page 28, RF/Corbis.

Figure 2.3, page 32, Google Analytics, www.google.com/analytics, accessed July 13, 2007.

Figure 2.4, page 33, Google Analytics, www.google.com/analytics, accessed July 13, 2007.

Figure 2.9, page 38, www.visualmining.com, accessed June 24, 2005.

Figure 2.10, page 38, www.visualmining.com, accessed June 24, 2005.

Page 39, Alexander Heimann/AFP/Getty Images.

Page 40, AP/Wide World.

Page 41, Jeff Greenberg/Photoedit.

Page 43, Getty Images/Rubberball.

Page 45, Getty Images/Blend Images.

Figure 2.13, page 46, Michael Hammar and James Champy, Beyond Reengineering, How the Process-Centered Organization Is Changing Our Work and Our Lives, New York: HarperCollins, Publisher, 1996.

Figure 2.14, page 47, Michael Hammar and James Champy, Beyond Reengineering, How the Process-Centered Organization Is Changing Our Work and Our Lives, New York: HarperCollins, Publisher, 1996.

Figure 2.15, page 47, Michael Hammar and James Champy, Beyond Reengineering, How the Process-Centered Organization Is Changing Our Work and Our Lives, New York: HarperCollins, Publisher, 1996.

Figure 2.16, page 48, Michael Hammar and James Champy, Beyond Reengineering, How the Process-Centered Organization Is Changing Our Work and Our Lives, New York: HarperCollins, Publisher, 1996.

Figure 2.18, page 49, www.smartdraw.com, accessed June 24, 2004.

Figure 2.19, page 49, www.smartdraw.com, accessed June 24, 2004.

Figure 2.20, page 50, www.smartdraw.com, accessed June 24, 2004.

Figure 2.22, page 53, www.smartdraw.com, accessed June 24, 2004.

Figure 2.23, page 53, www.smartdraw.com, accessed June 24, 2004.

Figure 2.24, page 54, www.smartdraw.com, accessed June 24, 2004.

Figure 2.25, page 54, www.smartdraw.com, accessed June 24, 2004.

Chapter 3

Page 56, © Ingram Publishing/AGE Fotostock.

Figure 3.1, page 59, Adam Lashinsky, "The Disrupters," Fortune, August 11, 2003, pp. 62–65.

Figure 3.3, pages 60, www.internetworldstats.com/stats.htm, accessed January 2006.

Figure 3.4, pages 61, www.internetworldstats.com/stats.htm, accessed January 2006.

Page 61, Digital Vision/Getty Images.

Page 65, Stockbyte/Getty Images.

Page 67, Thinkstock/Getty Images.

Page 73, Jason Reed/Getty Images.

Page 78, fStop/PunchStock.

Page 83, © Comstock/PunchStock.

Figure 3.5, page 61, www.expedia.com, accessed October 13, 2003; www.apple.com, accessed October 13, 2003: www.dell.com, accessed October 13, 2003; www.lendingtree.com, accessed October 13, 2003: www.amazon.com, accessed October 13, 2003; www.ebay.com, accessed October 13, 2003; www.cisco.com, accessed October 13, 2003.

Figure 3.9, page 63, Tim O'Reilly, "What Is Web 2.0: Design Patterns and Business Models for the Next Generation of Software", 9/30/2005.

Figure 3.10, page 64, Tim O'Reilly, "What Is Web 2.0: Design Patterns and Business Models for the Next Generation of Software", 9/30/2005.

Figure 3.32, page 84, "E-Commerce Taxation," www.icsc.org/srch/government/ECommerce-February2003.pdf, accessed June 8, 2004.

Figure 3.35, page 85, "E-Commerce Taxation," www.icsc.org/srch/government/ECommerce-February2003.pdf, accessed June 8, 2004.

Chapter 4

Page 88, © Comstock/PunchStock.

Page 90, © Royalty-Free/CORBIS.

Page 92, Don Farrall/Getty Images.

Figure 4.2, page 93, Scott Berianato, "Take the Pledge," www.cio.com, accessed November 17, 2003.

Figure 4.13, page 101, AMA Research, "Workplace Monitoring and Surveillance," www.amanet.org, April 2003, accessed March 1, 2004.

Figure 4.14, page 101, AMA Research, "Workplace Monitoring and Surveillance," www.amanet.org, April 2003, accessed March 1, 2004.

Figure 4.15, page 102, AMA Research, "Workplace Monitoring and Surveillance," www.amanet.org, April 2003, accessed March 1, 2004.

Figure 4.18, page 105, "2004 CSI/FBI Computer Crime and Security Survey," www.usdoj.gov/criminal/cybercrime/FBI2005.pdf.

Figure 4.19, page 105, "2005 CSI/FBI Computer Crime and Security Survey," www.usdoj.gov/criminal/cybercrime/FBI2005.pdf.

Figure 4.21, page 108, "The Security Revolution," www.cio.com, accessed June 6, 2003.

Figure 4.22, page 108, "Losses from Identity Theft to Total $221 Billion Worldwide," www.cio.com, May 23, 2003.

Page 109, TRBfoto/Getty Images.

Figure 4.23, page 110, "Losses from Identity Theft to Total $221 Billion Worldwide," www.cio.com, May 23, 2003.

Figure 4.24, page 111, "Spam Losses to Grow to $198 Billion," www.cio.com, accessed August 9, 2003.

Page 111, Enamul Hoque/Rod Steele/Getty Images.

Page 112, Digital Vision/Getty Images.

Figure 4.27, page 114, "Spam Losses to Grow to $198 Billion," www.cio.com, accessed August 9, 2003.

Figure 4.28, page 115, "Spam Losses to Grow to $198 Billion," www.cio.com, accessed August 9, 2003.

Chapter 5

Page 116, © Royalty-Free/CORBIS.

Figure 5.1, page 119, BusinessWeek, January 10, 2005.

Figure 5.2, page 120, InformationWeek, August 9, 2004.

Page 122, © W.C. Mendenhall/U.S. Geological Survey.

Page 125, Keith Brofsky/Getty Images.

Page 127, © Royalty-Free/CORBIS.

Page 128, Nick Koudis/Getty Images.

Chapter 6

Page 140, Jason Reed/Ryan McVay/Getty Images.

Page 143, The McGraw-Hill Companies, Inc./John Flournoy, photographer.

Page 145, © Royalty-Free/CORBIS.

Page 146, Simon Fell/Getty Images.

Page 150, © Nova Development.

Page 151, © Royalty-Free/CORBIS.

Figure 6.8, page 154, Webopedia.com, www.webopedia.comTERM/d/database.html, accessed May 15, 2007; Oracle Database, www.oracle.com/database/index.html, accessed May 17, 2007; www.sitepoint.com/article/publishing-mysql-data-web, accessed May 16, 2007.

Page 155, Digital Vision/Getty Images.

Page 160, © Digital Vision/PunchStock.

Chapter 7

Page 164, RF Digital Vision Disk.

Page 166, Robin Jareaux/Getty Images.

Page 167, Jason Reed/Getty Images.

Page 173, Image 100/CORBIS.

Page 174, © Royalty-Free/CORBIS.

Page 176, © Royalty-Free/CORBIS.

Figure 7.13, page 179, AP/Wide World.

Page 181, C Squared Studios/Getty Images.

Page 183, © Royalty-Free/CORBIS.

Page 184, Getty Images.

Page 189, Getty Images.

Chapter 8

Page 194, Photodisc/Getty Images.

Page 196, Digital Vision/Getty Images.

Page 199, © Royalty-Free/CORBIS.

Page 199, © Charles Smith/CORBIS.

Page 201, Ryan McVay/Getty Images.

Page 202, Chad Baker/Ryan McVay/Getty Images.

Figure 8.11, page 210, William Copacino, "How to Become a Supply Chain Master," Supply Chain Management Review, September 1, 2001, www.manufacturing.net, accessed June 12, 2003.

Figure 8.12, page 210, William Copacino, "How to Become a Supply Chain Master," Supply Chain Management Review, September 1, 2001, www.manufacturing.net, accessed June 12, 2003.

Figure 8.15, page 212, William Copacino, "How to Become a Supply Chain Master," Supply Chain Management Review, September 1, 2001, www.manufacturing.net, accessed June 12, 2003.

Figure 8.16, page 213, William Copacino, "How to Become a Supply Chain Master," Supply Chain Management Review, September 1, 2001, www.manufacturing.net, accessed June 12, 2003.

Figure 8.17, page 213, William Copacino, "How to Become a Supply Chain Master," Supply Chain Management Review, September 1, 2001, www.manufacutirng.net,accessed June 12, 2003.

Chapter 9

Page 216, RF Digital Vision Disk.

Page 219, Rim Light/PhotoLink/Getty Images.

Page 224, The McGraw-Hill Companies, Inc./John Flournoy, photographer.

Page 228, Comstock/PictureQuest.

Figure 9.10, page 229, "Finding Value in the Real-Time Enterprise," *Business 2.0,* November 2003, pp. S1–S5.

Figure 9.11, page 230, "Finding Value in the Real-Time Enterprise," *Business 2.0,* November 2003, pp. S1–S5.

Page 232, Somos/Veer/Getty Images.

Figure 9.12, page 233, www.donotbuydodge.ca, accessed April 2007.

Page 234, © Jason Reed/Getty Images.

Figure 9.13, page 235, used with permission, Claudia Imhoff and Richard Hackathorn, April 2007.

Figure 9.16, page 237, used with permission, Claudia Imhoff and Richard Hackathorn, April 2007.

Chapter 10

Page 244, Eyewire/Getty Images.

Page 246, © Comstock/PunchStock.

Figure 10.1, page 246, "ERP Knowledge Base," www.cio.com, accessed July 2005.

Figures 10.4, page 248, Exact Software, "ERP-II: Making ERP Deliver On Its Promise to the Enterprise", jobfunctions.bnet.com/whitepaper.aspx?docid_144338, accessed July 25, 2007.

Figure 10.5, page 249, Exact Software, "ERP-II: Making ERP Deliver On Its Promise to the Enterprise", jobfunctions.bnet.com/whitepaper.aspx?docid_144338, accessed July 25, 2007.

Figure 10.6, page 249, Exact Software, "ERP-II: Making ERP Deliver On Its Promise to the Enterprise", jobfunctions.bnet.com/whitepaper.aspx?docid_144338, accessed July 25, 2007.

Figure 10.7, page 250, Exact Software, "ERP-II: Making ERP Deliver On Its Promise to the Enterprise", jobfunctions.bnet.com/whitepaper.aspx?docid_144338, accessed July 25, 2007.

Figure 10.8, page 250, Exact Software, "ERP-II: Making ERP Deliver On Its Promise to the Enterprise", jobfunctions.bnet.com/whitepaper.aspx?docid_144338, accessed July 25, 2007.

Figure 10.9, page 251, Michael Doane, "A Blueprint for ERP Implementation Readiness," www.metagroup.com, accessed October 17, 2003.

Figure 10.10, page 252, Kaplan, Robert, Norton, David, "The BSC: Translating Strategy into Action" (Vintage Books: 1998) The Balanced Scorecard Institute, www.balanced-scorecard.org/, accessed May 15, 2007.

Page 253, Digital Vision/Getty Images.

Page 254, Comstock Images/Alamy.

Figure 10.12, page 255, www.sap.com.

Figure 10.13, page 255, www.sap.com.

Page 257, Photo Courtesy of U.S. Army/U.S. Coast Guard photograph by Petty Officer 2nd Class Kyle Niemi.

Page 258, Getty Images.

Figure 10.16, page 259, Supply Chain Metrics.com, www.supplychainmetric.com/, accessed June 12, 2007.

Page 260, Ingram Publishing/SuperStock.

Page 262, Corbis/PictureQuest.

Chapter 11

Page 274, Digital Vision/Getty Images.

Page 276, © Royalty-Free/CORBIS.

Page 278, Ryan McVay/Getty Images.

Figure 11.1, page 279, "Software Costs," CIO Magazine, www.cio.com, accessed December 5, 2003.

Page 280, Ryan McVay/Getty Images.

Figure 11.7, page 284, Agile Alliance Manifesto, www.agile.com, accessed November 1, 2003.

Page 284, © Getty Images/Photodisc.

Page 286, © Stockbyte/PunchStock.

Page 290, Ryan McVay/Getty Images.

Figure 11.12, page 290, "Top Reasons Why IT Projects Fail," InformationWeek, www.infoweek .com, accessed November 5, 2003.

Page 294, © Beathan/CORBIS.

Figure 11.19, page 296, Deni Connor, "IT Outlook Declines Due to Outsourcing, Offshoring," www.nwfusion.com/careers/ 2004/

0531manside.html, accessed June 8, 2004.

Figure 11.22, page 298, Todd Datz, "Outsourcing World Tour," *CIO Magazine,* July 15, 2004, pp. 42–48.

Chapter 12

Page 300, © Royalty-Free/CORBIS.

Page 303, Noel Hendrickson/Getty Images.

Page 307, Getty Images.

Page 309, Bryan Mullennix/Getty Images.

Page 311, Chad Baker/Ryan McVay/Getty Images.

Page 312, Simon Fell/Getty Images.

Page 315, © Comstock/JupiterImages.

Page 318, Jack Star/PhotoLink/Getty Images.

Page 319, Bryan Mullennix/Getty Images.

Page 322, Shakirov/Getty Images.

Page 324, © Royalty-Free/CORBIS.

INDEX